Women and Information Technology

Women and Information Technology
Research on Underrepresentation

Edited by J. McGrath Cohoon and William Aspray

The MIT Press
Cambridge, Massachusetts
London, England

MIT Press books may be purchased at special quantity discounts for business or sales promotional use. For information, please e-mail ⟨special_sales@mitpress.mit.edu⟩ or write to Special Sales Department, The MIT Press, 55 Hayward Street, Cambridge, MA 02142.

This book was set in Sabon on 3B2 by Asco Typesetters, Hong Kong. Printed and bound in the United States of America.

Library of Congress Cataloging-in-Publication Data

Women and information technology : research on underrepresentation / edited by J. McGrath Cohoon and William Aspray.
    p.   cm.
Includes bibliographical references and index.
ISBN 0-262-03345-3 (hc : alk. paper)
1. Computers and women. 2. Sex differences in education. 3. Women computer scientists. I. Cohoon, J. McGrath. II. Aspray, William.
QA76.9.W65W66   2006
004′.082—dc22   2005052253

10 9 8 7 6 5 4 3 2 1

Contents

Acknowledgments

The editors wish to express our gratitude to those who helped make this book possible. We thank Robert Prior of The MIT Press for his interest in the project, Caroline Wardle of the National Science Foundation for her work on the Information Technology Workforce program that we mined so extensively for this book, the National Center for Women and Information Technology for its encouragement of our efforts to base interventions on high-quality research, and Indiana University for its support of William Aspray's work on this project. Most of the reviews for each chapter were done by other authors who contributed to this book, but we did get help from three outside reviewers: Dorothy Bennett of the Education Development Center, Elizabeth Gorman of the University of Virginia, and Gerhard Sonnert of Harvard University. We appreciate their generosity and thank them for improving the quality of this volume. Finally, Joanne Cohoon gives special thanks to her husband, Jim Cohoon, for his encouragement and help with everything she does.

Introduction

Despite general increases in women's representation in science, engineering, and mathematics, women's representation in computer science is not approaching parity with men's. A glance at the data in figure I.1, showing women's portion of computing degrees awarded in the United States between 1966 and 2003, makes it clear that many of the gains in women's formal computing education achieved by the mid-1980s were lost in subsequent years. Only at the graduate level is the trend toward parity, but the numbers at this level are small, and the percentage of women awarded doctorates has only recently reached 20 percent. Similar patterns of low female participation in computing are apparent in data for both youth and the workforce, making the overall picture one of a heavily male-dominated field.

Extensive effort has been put into promoting women's participation in computing for several reasons. These reasons range from ethical to economic, and they are discussed in both chapters 1 and 13. Nevertheless, we have to face the fact that twenty-five years of interventions have not worked.

There may be many reasons for the continued decline in women's participation in computing. We reject the idea that biological gender differences explain the situation, noting the variance over time as the most obvious counterexample. One possible explanation is that the causes are so numerous and deep-seated in our institutions that society is not willing to make the changes that would produce gender equity. Another possible explanation is that the issue is complex, making it difficult to know how to go about reaching gender balance in information technology (IT). It is this latter explanation that led us to write this book.

Well-intentioned interventions, based on the best intuition of pioneering activists, have not been able to reverse the downward trends, perhaps because more nuanced strategies based on the complexities of the situation were needed. Developing those strategies and documenting their success requires that we shine the hard, cold light

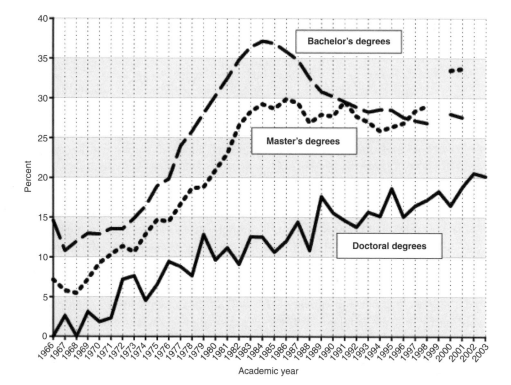

Figure I.1
Trends in women's representation in postsecondary computing in the United States
Notes and Sources: The figure and notes are from the Computing Research Association Web page, ⟨http://www.cra.org/info/education/us/women.html⟩. © 2005 Computing Research Association. All rights reserved. According to the National Science Foundation, data are missing for bachelor's and master's degrees granted in 1999 because "detailed national data were not released for the academic year ending 1999 by the National Center for Education Statistics." Degrees in a given July–June period are referred to by the year in which the period ended; e.g., 2000 means the twelve-month period ending June 2000. Data were obtained from the National Science Foundation, Division of Science Resources Statistics, science and engineering degrees: 1966–2001, NSF 04–311, project officers Susan T. Hill and Jean M. Johnson (Arlington, VA, 2004). National Science Foundation, Division of Science Resources Statistics, science and engineering degrees by race/ethnicity of recipients: 1992–2001, NSF 04–318, project officers Susan T. Hill and Jean M. Johnson (Arlington, VA, 2004). National Science Foundation, Division of Science Resources Statistics, science and engineering doctorate awards: 2003, NSF 05–300, project officer Joan S. Burrelli (Arlington, VA, 2004).

of scientific research on the situation. We have dedicated this book to efforts that do just that—engage in rigorous social science investigations of these complex phenomena. It is our intention only to admit research, not rhetoric, not hunches, not folk wisdom, and see what we learn based on this research.

There are at least two reasons why it is appropriate for a book on this topic at this time. First, the change in the computing landscape has made some of the earlier social science research obsolete. For example, there was a whole body of research in the 1980s and early 1990s predicated on unequal access to computing. Recent statistics, however, show that the gender gap in access has substantially narrowed, thus calling into question the applicability of these earlier studies. Fortunately there is a new generation of research coming along. Due to the wisdom and foresight of the National Science Foundation (NSF), there has been a surge in research into this area in the past five years. The first results of these programs are now ready for sharing, and we took advantage of that availability in putting together the examples of research that are collected in this volume. In particular, we invited a select group of early awardees who had funding from the Information Technology Workforce (ITWF) NSF program to submit papers of their own choosing to this book. We rounded out this collection of papers by seeking out an international perspective from researchers whose work we respect. We included a set of literature reviews for a picture of where the research enterprise now stands as well as an important tool for researchers in the field.

There are several different ways to think about the chapters in this volume. One of them is the research method employed. Social science research can be grouped into two categories: quantitative and qualitative. Qualitative research seeks deep understanding of an issue through comprehensive data that describe the richness of social life and emphasize the importance of context. These data are often collected through field research involving direct observation or interviews. Quantitative research seeks to measure the critical and countable elements of an issue. Quantitative data are often collected through surveys and experiments, and then analyzed using statistical methods. We include examples of both types in this volume.

Another way of thinking about the chapters is by their content. The chapters are organized into three sections, each beginning with a literature review: on girls (chapter 1), postsecondary education (chapter 5), and careers in IT (chapter 13). Each literature review introduces the basic factors thought to affect the gender composition of computing at a particular stage of life and the key literature covering this field.

The remainder of each section is devoted to individual research studies, starting with the most general and working toward the most specific reports.

Table I.1 gives an overview of the various topics and methods covered in each chapter. It lists the basic concepts and ideas, population, and methods discussed in each chapter. This guide to the chapters includes more details than the next few paragraphs, where we compare the various chapter contents and note themes.

The research chapters in part I all address points at which girls' interest in computing might diverge from boys'. Lecia J. Barker's study (chapter 4) talks about middle school girls, and the striking differences of sixth- and seventh-grade girls from eighth-grade girls. Jane Margolis's study (chapter 3) looks at high school students. And Oksana Malanchuk's study (chapter 2) looks at adolescents in eighth and eleventh grades as well as three years after high school. Another theme that runs through all three of these studies is the interaction between gender and ethnicity. The Barker study looks at Latina/Hispanic girls. The Malanchuk study looks at African Americans. And the Margolis study looks at Latinas, African Americans, and Asians. Each study compares these populations to white girls. A third theme that runs through all three studies in this section is the influence of psychological and institutional factors on girls' participation in computing. Chapter 2 discusses psychological issues such as one's self-concept of computer skills. Chapter 3 considers institutional factors such as the nature of guidance counseling. And chapter 4 looks at disconnects between the psychological and the institutional when it considers how teachers fail to understand which arguments in favor of IT would persuade girls.

There are also several themes running through the chapters in part II. Most studies of higher education focus on a single country. Maria Charles and Karen Bradley (chapter 6) are a rare exception in the research on gender and IT for their cross-national comparison of computing education. One issue they confront is the variety in disciplinary approaches to computing that is evident across countries. A number of the other studies in this section also address questions about computing disciplines. J. McGrath Cohoon's and Sandra Katz's chapters (7 and 12, respectively) consider issues related to the most prevalent computing discipline—namely, computer science. Cohoon focuses primarily on out-of-classroom factors and identifies those that contribute to gender-balanced retention. In contrast, the Katz chapter looks specifically at curricular content to identify how mastery leads to retention. Sylvia Beyer's and Jean C. Robinson's chapters (11 and 9, respectively) compare computer science with other computing disciplines with an eye toward which are

Table I.1
Chapter sketches

	Topics covered	Description
Chapter 1 Lecia J. Barker and William Aspray, "The State of Research on Girls and IT"	School policy; curriculum; course election; relationship with teachers; teacher training; relationships with family and local community; presence and use of computers; relationships with peers; popular culture; games; gender differences in attitude, confidence, interest, and experience; life aspirations	Review of the recent research literature specific to girls in IT in Western culture.
Chapter 2 Nicole Zarrett, Oksana Malanchuk, Pamela E. Davis-Kean, and Jacquelynne Eccles, "Examining the Gender Gap in IT by Race: Young Adults' Decisions to Pursue an IT Career"	Child aptitude; educational expectations; self-concept of computer skills; IT courses taken; encouragement from others; stereotypes about the computer field; ethnic differences among women seeking an IT career	Quantitative analysis of longitudinal data measuring 1,482 adolescents and their families in one eastern U.S. county. The study tracks youth from seventh grade until three years past high school to measure factors that influence their decision to pursue an IT career. Attention is focused on how the gender gap differs by race.
Chapter 3 Joanna Goode, Rachel Estrella, and Jane Margolis, "Lost in Translation: Gender and High School Computer Science"	School structures such as course offerings, teacher qualifications, tracking patterns, and school norms; psychological and sociological factors that influence students' choices to study computer science	Qualitative analysis of why so few women and minority students study computer science. At three Southern California public high schools, interviews were conducted with students, teachers, counselors, principals, and school district officials, and multiple direct observations of the classroom were made. An active research approach was used to investigate the role of CS teachers in constructing an alternative classroom culture and pedagogy.

Table I.1
(continued)

	Topics covered	Description
Chapter 4 Lecia Barker, Eric Snow, Kathy Garvin-Doxas, and Tim Weston, "Recruiting Middle School Girls into IT: Data on Girls' Perceptions and Experiences from a Mixed-Demographic Group"	Experiences with and perceptions of IT; new information gained about careers and high school courses in science and technology from attending a special event; what they want to do when they grow up	Qualitative analysis of the relationship between the assumptions underlying attempts to recruit girls into IT and the messages and methods employed. Survey data were collected from 717 mixed-demographic middle school girls attending a Girls Exploring Science, Engineering, and Technology event in the Denver metropolitan area.
Chapter 5 J. McGrath Cohoon and William Aspray, "A Critical Review of the Research on Women's Participation in Post-secondary Computing Education"	State of social science research on women in postsecondary computing; culture and image of computing; experience; entry barriers; curricula; role models; mentoring; student-faculty interactions; peer support; confidence and other personal characteristics; pedagogy; theory	Review of the research literature on women's participation in postsecondary computing in the United States.
Chapter 6 Maria Charles and Karen Bradley, "A Matter of Degrees: Female Under-Representation in Computer Science Programs Cross-Nationally"	Sex segregation of computer science programs and in comparison to engineering; cross-national variation in female representation in computer science; comparison of empirical patterns with theoretical accounts	Multinational study of the relationship between cultural beliefs and women's participation in computing. The study employs new data from OECD reports of first-degree recipients in twenty-one industrial countries, mostly Western democracies. Analyses test neo-institutionalist theory that cultural beliefs influence organizational forms as well as personal interests, aptitudes, and behaviors.

Table I.1
(continued)

	Topics covered	Description
Chapter 7 J. McGrath Cohoon, "Just Get Over It or Just Get on with It: Retaining Women in Undergraduate Computing"	Gender composition of students and faculty; student attrition rates; same-sex peer support; attracting women to CS; support from faculty, encouraging students to persist; support from faculty, mentoring for diversity; support from faculty, concern about insufficient faculty; faculty expectations, homework hours; faculty expectations, focus on academics	Nationwide study of factors that lead to gendered outcomes in 209 undergraduate computer science departments in the United States. Data are collected from interviews of faculty, focus groups with students, and surveys of faculty and department heads, and analyzed at the department level.
Chapter 8 Jolene Kay Jesse, "The Poverty of the Pipeline Metaphor: The AAAS/CPST Study of Nontraditional Pathways into IT/CS Education and the Workforce"	Characteristics of nontraditional students; student demographics; educational backgrounds; reasons for choosing IT/CS; reasons for choosing institutions; educational experiences; satisfaction with educational experience; finance; postgraduation educational plans and experiences; perceptions of field; perceptions about students; weed-out courses; recruitment efforts; faculty awareness of nontraditional students; needs of nontraditional students	Regional study of nontraditional students at twenty institutions. Data are collected from interviews with faculty, students, and employed graduates, and from a survey of alumni.
Chapter 9 Christine Ogan, Jean C. Robinson, Manju Ahuja, and Susan C. Herring, "Gender Differences among Students in Computer Science and Applied Information Technology Universities"	Demographics of undergraduate and graduate students in computer science and other computing-related disciplines; computing experiences; reasons for choosing IT; attitudes about computer work	Comparative analyses of undergraduate to graduate and computer science degree programs to other computing-related degree programs. Data were collected from a survey of students at five universities.

Table I.1
(continued)

	Topics covered	Description
Chapter 10 Roli Varma, Amit Prasad, and Deepak Kapur, "Confronting the 'Socialization' Barrier: Cross-Ethnic Differences in Undergraduate Women's Preference for IT Education"	Being a woman in the CS/CE program; confidence; CS/CE careers for women	Cross-ethnic differences in undergraduate women's preferences for IT education. Data were collected from interviews with 150 students in five ethnic/racial groups. Analysis is based on Bourdieu's theory of habitas.
Chapter 11 Sylvia Beyer and Michelle DeKeuster, "Women in Computer Science or Management Information Systems Courses: A Comparative Analysis"	Educational goals; computer experience and confidence; beliefs and stereotypes about their field; personality and stress; role models and mentors	Comparative analysis of women majoring in computer science and management information systems at one university. Data were collected from surveys of undergraduates in selected CS and MIS courses, and from institutional records of math ACT scores and course grades.
Chapter 12 Sandra Katz, John Aronis, Christine Wilson, David Allbritton, and Mary Lou Soffa, "Traversing the Undergraduate Curriculum in Computer Science: Where Do Students Stumble?"	Achievement and persistence; home access to computers; computing experience; confidence; encouragement; technical topics that are critical to students' subsequent academic performance	Quantitative analysis of undergraduate computer science students' academic performance at one institution. Survey data and exam scores are analyzed to identify critical topics that predict grades in subsequent computing courses and persistence in the major.

Table I.1
(continued)

	Topics covered	Description
Chapter 13 Kathryn M. Bartol and William Aspray, "The Transition of Women from the Academic World to the IT Workplace: A Review of Relevant Research"	Pipeline metaphor; degree programs; perceptions of careers in IT; confidence and self-efficacy; mentoring; role models; career advice; typical female IT positions; male-dominated culture; pay issues; satisfaction and commitment in IT; conflicts with family responsibilities; professional identification and commitment; why women's representation in IT is important	Review of the research literature on transitions to the IT workforce in the Western world.
Chapter 14 Kathryn M. Bartol, Ian O. Williamson, and Gosia A. Langa, "Gender and Professional Commitment among IT Professionals: The Special Case of Female Newcomers to Organizations"	Job satisfaction; organizational commitment; work-life balance; organizational fit; perceived organizational support; professional commitment; professional experience	Quantitative analysis of data from a set of surveys relating professional commitment to job satisfaction and perceived organizational support. Data were collected from 393 seniors at four universities, with a follow-up after employment, and from 634 veteran workers in IT.
Chapter 15 Karen Chapple, "Foot in the Door, Mouse in Hand: Low-Income Women, Short-Term Job Training Programs, and IT Careers"	Skills training; soft skills; IT training programs; technical skills; types of worker experiences; career ladders; advancement through education and training; technical careers	Qualitative analysis of the impact that job-training programs have on the entry and advancement of low-income women in IT. Interview data identified outcomes for ninety-two graduates from six nonprofit training programs in three U.S. metropolitan areas.
Conclusion		

attractive to women. Jolene Kay Jesse's study (chapter 8) considers nontraditional students, a high percentage of whom are women and minorities, and the for-profit institutions that cater to them. Roli Varma's study (chapter 10) also explores cross-ethnic differences in undergraduate women's preferences for IT education. Two other themes common to several chapters in this section are experience and confidence (see chapters 9, 10, 11, and 12).

Part III focuses on pathways into the IT workforce. Kathryn M. Bartol's chapter (14) considers the traditional path for female college graduates. Karen Chapple's chapter (15) looks at a nontraditional path—short-term job training programs, which are a common route for low-income women. Both of these chapters examine not only the path but how the women fare once they enter the IT workforce.

Our concluding chapter discusses what the research chapters collectively tell us about the status of research-based knowledge on women's participation in IT. The implications for theory and policy are considered.

I

Diverging Interests

1

The State of Research on Girls and IT

Lecia J. Barker and William Aspray

This chapter critically surveys the scholarly social science literature about girls' involvement with IT, and the ways in which this involvement impinges on pathways into IT education or careers. Topics include school policy, curriculum, and course election; relationships with teachers; teacher training; the presence and use of computers; differences in attitude, confidence, interest, and experience between boys and girls; relationships with families and the local community; relationships to peers; life aspirations; popular culture; and computer games.

In a useful earlier literature review, Dryburgh (2000) classified research conducted in the 1990s on the underrepresentation of girls and women in computer science. She carefully distinguished studies that produced generalizable findings from those that were based on exploratory, pilot, small, or qualitative studies, and therefore needed more research. The factors that Dryburgh considered conclusively related to underrepresentation for girls include mixed-sex instruction, the lack of role models (though she recommends research into the degree to which role models lead to participation), and the fact that the beliefs of male peers about "who does computing" are stronger than those of females. This chapter has a broader scope than did Dryburgh's, expanding the analysis to more than computer science per se as well as reviewing the extensive literature that has appeared since the late 1990s.

Scope

In preparing the literature review, we were challenged by the wide array of scholarly disciplines that address relevant issues. In order to keep this chapter manageable and focused on girls and IT, we have looked with differential depth at these various literatures. We have paid the most attention to articles focused directly on girls and IT, and because of that, certain journals are more heavily represented in our presentation, such as the *Journal of Educational Computing Research*. Nevertheless, we have searched more widely; some of the other literatures we have looked at include the educational use of technology, girls in science and mathematics, psychological gender differences in children, socioeconomic influences on education and career choice, the influences of popular culture on children, and ethnographic studies on general and school culture.

The writing of this chapter was motivated by two factors. First, the literature has expanded in the past five years, in part because of the funding provided through the National Science Foundation ITWF program, and none of the existing literature reviews have fully captured the emerging literature. Second, the rapid spread of computing access through the increased availability of personal computers and the emergence of the Internet requires that we rethink some of the prior questions about girls and IT. For example, much of the literature on this subject in the 1980s and early 1990s focused on the differential access of boys and girls to computing technology. That difference has largely faded. According to the National Telecommunications and Information Administration (NTIA) report, *A Nation Online* (2002), as of September 2001, 90 percent of all U.S. children were using computers, 75 percent of all fourteen to seventeen year olds and 65 percent of all ten to thirteen year olds were using the Internet, two million additional Americans were beginning to use the Internet each month, and the use of the Internet by males and females was almost identical: 53.9 percent of males and 53.8 percent of females. Therefore, access to computers by boys and girls is much less important as a research topic today. Access across race/ethnicity continues to be a problem, however. In 2001, the National Assessment of Educational Progress ("The Nation's Report Card") surveyed more than three thousand students about computer use in the home. While 90 percent of white students reported having a computer in their home, only 72 percent of black and 68 percent of Hispanic students had computers (National Center for Educational Statistics 2004). We recognize that gender and race/ethnicity are inextricably linked. In a literature review, Harrell (1998) points to how gender, affluence, and cultural background are interrelated factors in determining enthusiasm for and participation in computing, implying that a focus on gender alone is too narrow. Still, because relatively little research has been conducted on girls who are members of minority groups, or because the representation of minority girls in samples is too small to measure difference, we have chosen a broad focus on girls in this chapter.

Increased access has caused us to concentrate on more recent literature. Access began to be much more universal in the United States in the early 1990s. As a result, we have not considered here any literature that was published prior to 1994, and we eliminated from our analysis some of the literature published in the mid-1990s that we believe to be dated. Thus, even when there is a frequently cited journal article that introduced a relevant theme such as the gender biases in computer games (e.g., Kiesler, Sproull, and Eccles 1985), we have not discussed it here if the computer environment has changed sufficiently enough that there is a new generation of games whose gender bias creates concern.

With increased access comes new levels of familiarity with computers. A person considered a novice in 2000 might have been seen as an expert in 1990. A number of older studies used outdated scales to measure familiarity or confidence with IT by having outmoded tasks to test against as basic knowledge, such as the ability to turn on the computer and start up a program. Selwyn (1998) recognized this problem as early as 1997 and began to design new instruments for measuring attitudes toward computers. The problems of old measurement standards, as pointed to in Selwyn's study, is another reason why we limit our literature search to the past ten years.

We have limited the literature we consider to *research* publications. Many books and articles propound on the reasons for gender imbalance in IT. While there is value in these publications, we limit this review to only those based in empirical or scholarly theoretical work. Another body of literature discusses various implementations attempted as solutions to the imbalance. Those articles are considered here only when they include a scientifically sound evaluation of the implementation, so that the reader can learn about the underlying causes by examining the analysis of the empirical results.

The chapter is organized into sections corresponding to the topics listed above in the first paragraph. In addition to pointing to and describing briefly the publications that fit within a given theme, such as career aspirations, we also identify topics related to the theme that have not received adequate attention from the social science researchers. For example, the literature on career aspirations often gives statistics about the greater likelihood of boys than girls to be interested in pursuing a computer science degree in college and a career in computing, but the literature is surprisingly silent on the reasons for these aspirations.

The fact that we cite a particular article does not necessarily mean that we endorse its findings. It might be that there are methodological limitations to a particular study or the results might hold true in its domain but not more widely. We are relatively confident, however, that each article we cite meets the research standards we described above. We might have been more selective in which articles to cite—for example, by more closely scrutinizing the method used in the research or considering only studies with large sample sizes. Instead, because of the limited availability of peer-reviewed research publications specifically about girls and their paths and issues with respect to IT careers (as opposed to information literacy, for one); because of the many methodological challenges in doing this kind of research (e.g., parental consent; difficulties in obtaining large sample sizes or control groups in educational settings); and because small or ethnographic studies often bring more value than large quantitative ones in suggesting issues or providing deep understanding, we have been encompassing in our selection of research articles to cite.

Methodology

While the majority of the publications we cite are focused directly on girls and IT, we also include some other literature. This literature is intended to fill in gaps in the core girl-IT citations. For example, we did not find any literature specifically on how parents' educational level or socioeconomic standing affected the likelihood of a girl to pursue an IT education or career but we did find literature arguing that a higher educational level and higher socioeconomic standing of parents was strongly correlated with the child's decision to attend college and enter a professional career (Lankard 1995). This correlation seems to bear on a girl's likelihood of entering into a college degree program in IT and pursuing a professional career in IT. With the help of a professional librarian, we searched for a wide body of literature in the following ways, identifying through this search more than three thousand possible citations:

• We identified a number of education journals that consider computing issues and then scoured their tables of content back to 1994.

• We conducted searches using Google and the Digital Library of the Association for the Advancement of Computing in Education, using such terms in combination as gender, girl, computing, computer, curriculum, professional development for teachers, research, technology, popular culture, and so on.

• We hired a research librarian to examine the Social Science Citation Index, track down references we found in papers, and search various sources including Education Full-Text, PsychINFO, the IEEE Computer Society Digital Library, the ACM Digital Library, and Dissertation Abstracts.

• We used the resources of the U.S. Department of Education's Educational Resources Information Center (ERIC); in particular, we used their digests (miniliterature reviews on general topics such as the career aspirations of children) to understand the state of research in many related areas.

For each of the literatures described above, we employed selection criteria that enabled us to remain focused on our main topic. In this way, we reduced the number of articles for careful review to fewer than three hundred. We are unable to describe fully our selection criteria, which evolved as we searched through the literature and are based somewhat on subjective judgments, but the following selection decisions give a sense of what we both included and excluded:

• We have included research only from English-speaking and other Western European countries because we cannot be certain that other countries are sufficiently similar in culture, economic issues, and policy for us to draw inferences that might illuminate the U.S. situation.

• We were cautious in drawing inferences from studies about K–12 mathematics education because so much of the K–12 instruction on IT is carried out in a computer laboratory setting, unlike the setting for most mathematics instruction.

• We were more generally cautious about drawing inferences from the literature on girls' relation to mathematics and science because of the different patterns across fields in higher education. For example, mathematics undergraduate degrees have rough gender parity, whereas the percentage of women receiving computer science baccalaureates is persistently low. We do sometimes include literature on mathematics and science if it addresses how these disciplines are perceived by girls or teachers as belonging in the male domain.

• We have cited literature surveys in our chapter, not for their own intrinsic findings, but for the convenience of pointing the reader to other relevant literature. We have separately reviewed what appeared to us to be relevant publications cited in these literature surveys.

• We have excluded literature about undergraduate students because the K–12 and college environments are different; when undergraduates reported their earliest interactions with or interest in IT, however, we believe this to be relevant to K–12 students.

• We have not included articles on learning with computers (for instance, distance learning), even when they discuss gender differences.

• We have not included articles that examine gendered differences in interaction or communication styles online (when the sole basis for our consideration was that they employed IT).

• We have ignored a large body of literature on gendered differences of adults and technology because we are not sure of the applicability of these findings to children in their various developmental stages.

• We have not considered the gendered impacts of computer games that are unrelated to children's choices of IT education or career. (For example, we have not considered the claims that computer games make boys more violent or girls more communicative.)

• We have not considered stereotypical images of careers that just happen to be delivered through a computer medium, such as clip art. But we do consider what school Web pages say about gendered career patterns and the espoused beliefs of those who create them.

• We were not particularly interested in the literature on engendering computer or information literacy in children, although findings of differential use, experience, ownership, and related topics are reviewed.

With assistance from our graduate students, we reviewed each of these three hundred or so articles for objective, methodology, major results, study limitations, and citations to other literature. In this way, we selected from that set those articles and books actually cited in this chapter. Near the beginning of the project, based on our previous knowledge of the field, we identified a set of issue categories that we believed were relevant to understanding the involvement of girls with IT. We tested that categorization by seeing how well these three hundred articles fit within the categories, and ended up eliminating or merging some categories and creating several new ones. These categories are the topics of the main sections of this chapter.

Much of the research on girls and IT (and closely related topics as we have defined them here) is based in survey research, and implicitly assumes a male-female dichotomy and/or conflates sex with gender (see the next section for discussion). Our review includes this literature. Nevertheless, we feel that this literature presents a too narrow understanding of the issues. We have thus augmented our literature survey with theoretical writings on gender and culture. Yet it is probably fair to say that we have been more thorough in identifying and reviewing the empirical literature than in incorporating interpretive or critical literature.

The next section presents the theoretical underpinning of gender in our work as well as a brief discussion of the role of feminist theory in understanding gender issues in education. We then examine the reasons people seek to increase the participation of girls in IT. The review of research literature attempting to explain and understand girls' participation follows these sections.

Theoretical Underpinnings: Gender and Feminist Education Studies

Gender and the Male-Female Dichotomy

What it means to be male or female is culturally and situationally variable; it is neither genetically inherent in an individual nor defined or enacted in the same way across all social groups. In addition, being male in a social group is deeply related to being female in that group—each gender informing and defining the other through the roles one takes on (or does not take on) as well as the behaviors considered locally appropriate (or inappropriate) (Tracy 2002). Gender identity varies within particular contexts and forms, is reinforced within relationships and situations, and interacts with other types of identities in ways that influence beliefs about who takes on those identities. As Tracy writes,

In American society, for instance, the interactional identities of elementary school teacher, secretary, or nurse are expected to go with the master identity of being female whereas the interactional identities of surgeon, engineer, or manager are expected to go with the master identity of male. To the degree an interactional identity is strongly associated with some master identity, whether it be gender, race, or age, that interactional identity takes on some of the broader master identity features with which it is associated.

One's gender identity affects a group's expectations about the kinds of activities an individual will (or should) participate in. The tools and paraphernalia associated with those activities often take on meaning as male or female, accordingly (Christie 2004). For example, expecting parents find out the sex of their baby so that they can plan for clothing and nursery selections; the colors pink and purple are often associated with girls in the United States, and boys refuse to wear them. Certain types of discourse and behaviors are allowed and disallowed depending on one's identity, and these social expectations arise in a variety of situations, from interactions with one's own family, teachers, and religious leaders to interactions with peers and the media. Socialization begins the moment someone asks, "Is it a boy or a girl?" Infants are frequently dressed in gender-specific ways, indicating how one is supposed to interact with the infant: treat the baby like a boy or a girl (Paoletti 1997).

Gendered behaviors taken on by boys and girls (and shaping behavior through adulthood) are identifiable in many ways and evident to others. For instance, communication behaviors (e.g., the degree to which swearing is considered a norm violation; the amount of vocal pitch variation), ways of dressing, and ways of interacting with others can vary across gender.

We understand gender to be a set of social categories that shape not only tacit beliefs about how a girl or a boy believes that she or he her/himself should behave but also the way that others treat girls and boys as gendered beings, and the way others interact with boys and girls based on deeply ingrained expectations about how they *should* respond. We agree with Barnett and Rivers (2004), however, that males and females are not necessarily as different as they are often described in popular nonfiction. Barnett and Rivers point out that the research on which such writing bases claims about male-female differences (e.g., the value of interpersonal relationships, communication style, etc.) is often based on small, ethnographic studies with questionable capacity for generalization. Males and females may share many more similarities than research suggests, but authors frequently privilege statistical difference in reporting rather than not finding any variation.

When discussing how to gain wider and more diverse participation in IT, Brunner and Bennett (1998) and especially Bennett, Brunner, and Honey (1999) argue that one should not be trying to reinforce existing gender stereotypes or be looking for the gender-neutral solution but rather should seek ways to validate both masculine and feminine views of technology. Another important point that they make is to indicate clearly that not all men hold the so-called masculine view and not all women the feminine view. While these representations as masculine and feminine may be useful characterizations that reflect predominant stereotypes of males and females, any given individual may have both, neither, or either one of the stereotypical views. Some researchers have correlated their findings with categories from the Bem sex roles inventory (Bem 1974).

Although much of the literature that we review dichotomizes the male/female experience and identity, several other studies are consistent with the view of gender proposed above, including Thorne (1992, 1997 [cited in Stepulvage 2001]), Cassell and Jenkins (1998), Stepulvage (2001), Faulkner et al. (2004), and others. We also recognize the difficulty of studying gender as a set of social expectations, and the need to conflate gender and sex. In a later section on what we refer to as "difference" literature, we return to these issues of theory and gender. We review there empirical studies that examine differences between boys' and girls' confidence and attitudes toward computer technology, confidence with computers, interest in machines and people, and computer experience. We also discuss some of the limitations of this difference approach.

Feminist Approaches to Gender in Education Research

Philosopher of education Kenneth Howe (1997) has provided a theoretical discussion of two feminist approaches to gender and education, the humanist and relational approaches, which may prove useful in understanding girls and IT. Humanist feminism "defines women's oppression as the inhibition and distortion of women's potential by a society that allows the self-development of men" (Young 1990, 73; quoted in Howe 1997, 39). Under this view, women are limited by cultural norms and expectations, and are not given the same freedom to overcome these bonds as are men. Applying this view to education, one might simply remove obstacles that limit a woman's right to choose certain educational paths (e.g., the Title IX legislation), or go further and take compensatory action such as special scholarships for women, affirmative action to redress gender balance issues in public school administration, or establish programs encouraging teachers to pay greater attention to girls in the classroom. This approach seeks to modify existing institutions while also preserving their fundamental values and methods.

Howe discusses and largely agrees with the criticisms of humanist feminism as an approach for solving problems of gender equity in education. He argues that institutions long privileging a "male clientele" will have numerous and deeply ingrained characteristics that favor males, and these compensatory acts suggested by the humanist feminists may actually be counterproductive. That is, their veneer of fairness or equity may mask those deeply ingrained features that still favor males. Howe applies this contention to science and mathematics education, but in a way that could also readily apply to computer education:

Consider the admonition to educators to treat boys and girls equally and to provide girls with additional resources and help in math and science. It may do little good to give girls extra resources and help if these are devoted to preparing them for a curriculum and modes of interaction that are foreign or hostile to who they are. What good does it do to ask girls more questions and to engage them more actively in classroom work if they find the classroom and the curriculum to be out of touch with their experiences and interests and to even devalue them? Even if the practices themselves are changed to include cooperative rather than competitive methods of teaching in order to, say, accommodate girls' "learning styles," this is not likely to achieve the same desired results if the goals of education remain the same—goals rooted in competition and the traditional ideal of the educated person [which as argued earlier, means educated male]. (Howe 1997, 40 [footnotes and references excised from the quotation])

The second approach is relational (or gynocentric) feminism, which defines women's oppression as "the devaluation of women's experience by a masculine culture [and that] argues for the superiority of the values embodied in traditionally female experience" (Young 1990, 73–74; quoted in Howe 1997, 41). This approach has been adopted from Gilligan's (1982) theoretical psychological work on moral reasoning, in which she asserts that men and women have different beliefs about how one should interact with and value others, based on their own experiences, and neither is superior to the other. The approach has also been applied, more controversially, by Belensky and colleagues (1986) in educational theory to different patterns of learning and thinking in boys and girls. It is also the approach in Noddings's (1984) work in the philosophy of education. Howe writes of Noddings's philosophy:

She is critical of, among other things, the emphasis on competition and testing; the disciplinary knowledge that defines a liberal education; the same education for all in the name of equality of educational opportunity; and the evaluation of virtually every activity (even providing hungry children with food) in terms of how well it contributes to mastering the prescribed curriculum—characteristics that are presumably definitive of a male-oriented ethics of principles. (1997, 43–44)

Noddings is interested in a revolutionary reworking of public education. Her approach is in direct opposition to the Bush administration's more recent "No Child Left Behind" policy, which measures all students by a common metric and focuses on failures to meet those measures. Instead, Noddings wants to help each individual student develop to the maximum their own unique skills and interests. The emphasis in this philosophy is on sensitive and extensive mentoring, greater attention to discussion with and among students and less on didactic instruction of a canon of knowledge, and a complete remake attuned to a feminist perspective of the curriculum, the methods of instruction, and the structure of schools.

Neither Noddings nor Howe discuss how Noddings's philosophy might be applied to IT education, but we might draw some inferences. There would be less emphasis on classroom lecture on the principles of computing and more time devoted to letting students discover on their own in the computer laboratory, following their personal interests. Because effort would be taken to allow each student the time and facilities to discover things for themselves with the computer, teachers would have to take steps to ensure that no group of students monopolized access to the computer, the computer laboratory, or the teacher's time. More time would be devoted to discussion between teacher and student, and among students. Applications of computing introduced in the classroom would be broadened and customized to the particular set of students. The curriculum would not be designed specifically with the purpose of preparing students for college computer science courses. Interestingly, some of these ideas are aligned with known best practices for female retention in undergraduate computing study (see Cohoon and Aspray, this volume).

In the next several sections, we describe the reasons offered for increasing the participation of girls and women in IT, followed by educational policies that function to keep girls out of computing, at both the national and school levels.

Why Involve Girls in IT Careers?

There are at least four reasons why it is important to increase the representation of women in IT. First, increasing the number of women will increase the qualified labor pool that the United States depends on to drive the innovation and product development in IT that is so key to the U.S. economy. The United States had a critical shortage of IT workers during the dot-com boom—a shortage that could have been entirely met if women had been represented at the levels men were (Freeman and Aspray 1999). While there is not a critical shortage of IT workers in the United States today, the Bureau of Labor Statistics (2002) predicts that several IT occupations will be among the fastest growing over the decade 2002–2012.

Second, many IT jobs have favorable working conditions and pay at well above the national average. Many of these higher-skill, higher-pay jobs are filled by college graduates. Women make up more than half of college graduates, but they occupy less than one-third of these quality jobs. Making IT more gender inclusive will open new opportunities for financial well-being to a large sector of the U.S. population.

Third, many people have remarked on the value of a diverse workforce. For example, William Wulf (1999), president of the National Academy of Engineering, has written: "Since the products and processes we create are limited by the life experiences of the workforce, the best solution—the elegant solution—may never be considered because of that lack. . . . At a fundamental level, men, women, ethnic minorities, racial minorities, and people with handicaps, experience the world differently. Those differences in experience are the 'gene pool' from which creativity springs."

Similarly, chair and chief executive officer of Lockheed Martin Norm Augustine stated: "If in your employment practices you ignore 85 percent of the newly available talent in this country, how are you going to be a great company? How are you going to compete against companies that recruit from the country's entire pool of talent? And so, if for no other reason than self-interest, we ought to do more to maintain a diverse workforce" (quoted in Brainard n.d.).

A gender-balanced workforce is more likely to understand the needs and concerns of a wider segment of the customer base, and will design products accordingly (Wulf 1999). The automotive industry has recognized this fact. Ford organized a design team including an unprecedented number of women engineers for the Winstar mini-van a few years ago. The hope was that this team would design in features that meet the concern of the many women who regularly drive minivans. More recently, Volvo formed an all-women team to design the YCC [Your Concept Car] prototype "by women, for women." As discussed in another section of this chapter, most software, especially game software, has been designed for male users. There are only a few examples of designing software specifically for female users, notably Brenda Laurel's failed company Purple Moon. Software that is more engaging to women, whether targeted at women or gender neutral, might go a long way toward improving the software available to the entire population.

Fourth, applying computing as a tool for solving big problems is considered critical to the U.S. future and economy. The National Science Foundation, for example, has recommended investing a billion dollars per year into the Cyberinfrastructure Initiative (Atkins 2003; Harsha 2004). Yet computing remains something akin to a craft, as was writing and reading during the Middle Ages, when understanding or producing the written word could only be accomplished through access to a person who had acquired these skills. Today, while most Americans can use a computer, most look on it as a magical box, with little or no understanding of what makes it work, leaving it to a specialized few to develop hardware and software or repair it. Such a critical need should represent and include the voices of all those who it is intended to serve.

These four reasons for increasing gender balance in the IT workforce can be addressed through various kinds of policy initiatives—labor and workforce, immigration, and research funding policies, for example. Three educational policies affecting the IT gender balance are the subject of the next section.

Educational Policies Affecting Girls' Participation in IT Careers

In the 1980s and 1990s, policy was directed at access issues—at getting computers and, later, Internet connections into the classrooms. During the Clinton-Gore years, these included the Technology Opportunity Program of the National Telecommunications and Information Administration, the Community Technology Centers Program of the Department of Education, the universal service provisions of the Telecommunications Act of 1996 that provided public schools and libraries with computer technology at discount prices, and the Snowe-Rockefeller-Exon-Kerrey Amendment that required private suppliers to offer service to these public institutions at affordable rates. While the digital divide issues of unequal access between rich and poor, urban and rural, and white and minority communities persist, great strides have been made to bring computing technology into U.S. schools. Unfortunately, as this one goal nears attainment, educational policy has not moved on to the next critical steps—of incorporating this technology into an effective learning strategy with teachers who, in spite of the efforts of the U.S. Department of Education's Preparing Tomorrow's Teachers to Use Technology Program, have been trained and have the time to be effective.

A second educational policy concerns the goal of computer education. The focus has been on "information fluency" or "information literacy" (National Research Council 1999; Snyder 2003). These skills are useful for every citizen to thrive in an emerging digital society where people increasingly have to obtain government and other essential information through the mediation of computers, and where more and more jobs are enabled by computers. But this education is not enough to prepare one for IT jobs. It does not teach students the fundamentals of computing and computer science that are crucial for these IT jobs. In almost all public high schools in the United States, either computer science courses do not exist, are elective, or are part of extracurricular activities. In each of these situations, only a small number of students will gain this valuable computer science education. The recently formed Computer Science Teachers Association, organized by the ACM, has prepared a "model computer science curriculum" for integrating computer science into all levels of education. What this means is that when they do learn deeper-level computing concepts, young people often obtain their first experiences with computers and computing in informal ways. The lack of computing instruction in formal settings allows computing to remain a mystery for the majority.

A third educational policy that affects computer education for U.S. children is President Bush's No Child Left Behind policy. States and districts are narrowly focused on improving students' test scores on existing subjects, possibly in order to qualify for federal education funding now distributed through states. According to a Rand Corporation study, such a concentration on testing can cause administrators to focus resources on tested subjects at the expense of other subjects or distract their attention from other needs (e.g., the national need for a better-informed citizenry of information workers and developers) (Stecher 2002). The integration of computer science into all levels of education, as advocated by the Computer Science Teachers Association and supported by its model computer science curriculum (Tucker et al. 2003), is unlikely to happen, especially in this time of federal mandates for account-ability and high-stakes testing under the No Child Left Behind mandate. The current policy functions to exclude the integration of knowledge and skills considered criti-cal to the U.S. economy.

Formal and Informal Educational Settings

School Curriculum and Course Election

What is taught at school and what students are required to learn influence students' (and parents') beliefs about what knowledge is important and what is interesting. School curricula privilege certain subjects and ways of learning over others. For ex-ample, that reading and writing in middle school are required, but drawing is not, illustrates our societal beliefs about what kind of knowledge and means of expres-sion are important. Those who excel in privileged subjects and ways of learning are rewarded. In most school districts in the United States, students are required to learn keyboarding and usually basic computing applications, just as they must learn to use a pencil in primary grades. Current educational policy, however, does not re-quire that students study computer science or more advanced computer applica-tions, even for those students preparing for college.

Computing is frequently taught as part of extracurricular informal education pro-grams, such as Girl Scouts or summer camp. Its absence in the mainstream curricu-lum and presence in informal curricula give the implicit message that computer science is superfluous, something neither important nor required, but there to learn about if one has the inclination. In contrast, mathematics, biology, and chemistry are taught as part of the core curriculum, and these are on the college preparation list. As a result of these policies, students must learn something about these valued subjects since not only are students exposed to their content, but their parents, teachers, and counselors encourage them to do well in these subjects. By the time students get to the college level, they know what these subjects are about and have had some success in them.

There is variation across schools, particularly across secondary schools, in the degree to which students are exposed to computing applications other than basic ones (e.g., PowerPoint), communication tools, programming, and games. Some schools integrate the use of computing into subject areas, including familiarizing students with digital libraries (e.g., the Digital Library of Earth System Education) and designing Web pages. These curricula are better at showing the wide applicability of IT and the social uses to which it is put, thus potentially increasing girls' interest in this technology as well as their familiarity, experience, and comfort with IT. Even when students are required to study technology, though, their participation does not necessarily affect their interest, although it has been shown to improve their perceptions of the difficulty of studying and working with technology (Boser, Daugherty, and Palmer 1996). One Australian study suggests that if a technology curriculum is to be introduced for improving attitudes, it should emphasize a broad range of computing activities in preference to focusing on skill development within a single area since diversity of computing experience had a greater effect on changing attitudes for the better (Jones and Clark 1995).

The educational philosophy of course election provides a vehicle for gendered differences in preparation for college study of computing. Depending on a school's resources, middle school students can elect to take courses in the arts (e.g., drawing, music, and dance), technology (e.g., robotics, shop, and advanced computing), and foreign languages, among others. There are gendered differences in which courses are elected (American Association of University Women 1998). For example, boys take more classes in which computers are used than do their female peers (Colley et al. 1994; Shashaani 1994; all cited in Kirkpatrick and Cuban 1998, n. 11). In their 1996 study on gender differences in middle and high school technology classes (construction, woodworking, manufacturing, drafting, and communication) in four Connecticut school districts, Silverman and Pritchard (1993) found that girls and boys enjoyed technology classes for the same reasons; however, girls were much less likely than boys to enroll. The unfortunate effect of girls opting out of computing courses is that they may be less prepared not only for computer science but also for other subjects. For instance, enrollment in a computer course was a major success factor in applying spreadsheet problem-solving methods in a prealgebra course (Dugdale, DeKoven, and Ju 1998; this is the only recent study that we have found that shows the positive impact of formal computer education on K–12 course work).

Computer science, as taught at the college level, includes technical, mathematical, and scientific components. Many—but by no means all—of the college students who excel in computer science courses have strong backgrounds in math and science. Many also have formal or informal training in computing before arriving at college. The students with this prior experience seem to be more comfortable and confident in college computer science courses, and there may also be something in their earlier math, science, and computing training that provides a foundational knowledge useful for the college computer science courses (e.g., algorithmic thinking). Certainly the students who have experience in computing are more immediately successful in introductory programming courses in college. The Cohoon and Aspray chapter in this volume, in a section on experience, presents five studies, and discusses both the positive relationship between prior experience and success in the first college computer science course, and the gendered differences in the effect of experience.

A few studies have examined factors influencing IT course election. In a 1995–1996 survey of 2,842 students (52 percent female) in five high schools in a southwestern U.S. state, Moses, Howe, and Niesz (1999) consider patterns of course election for the science, technology, engineering, and mathematics (STEM) disciplines, including computer science. They found that girls had slightly higher educational aspirations than boys, that boys planned to take more pipeline courses than girls (though the actual difference was negligible), and that boys had taken or planned to take significantly more of the most advanced pipeline courses. (A pipeline course is one providing the academic preparation for college study. In this study, pipeline courses included trigonometry, calculus, chemistry, physics, and computer programming. Advanced pipeline courses were the three most advanced subjects in the pipeline list: computer programming, calculus, and physics.) Boys showed more positive attitudes toward the pipeline courses: more so than girls, they liked the courses, understood what was covered in these classes, expected to use the courses as adults, and perceived that doing well in these courses was important for their future. The authors concluded that despite strong educational aspirations, girls are more likely to view these pipeline courses as undesirable, thus opting out of courses that are valuable preparation for later educational and career possibilities.

The policy of election, combined with a gendered view of computing, results in high school computer science classrooms dominated by boys. When the majority of students in a class are boys, girls are less willing to enroll in the class. In one study, most girls expressed an unwillingness to take classes where they would be one of a few girls and did not picture themselves in careers that were in the masculine domain. Those who did enroll felt that they were "pathbreakers," faced with proving that girls could do what boys could do (Silverman and Pritchard 1996). Girls often make these curricular choices under the subtle influences of the adults around them. A 1990 ERIC educational digest reviewed research showing that school counselors work with teachers to channel students into certain educational paths, sometimes discouraging girls from taking advanced math or science because of disciplinary stereotypes (Dunham 1990). We have no evidence of whether that has changed; however, we know that girls continue to be more likely to pursue traditional areas of study for women, with the exception of biology and statistics, as evidenced by Advanced Placement test takers (shown in figure 1.1; see also College Board 2004).

Factors influencing this gendered difference in course election are many and their interaction is not well understood. It could be that girls have internalized messages from peers or society at large that math and science courses are not appropriate choices for girls and have decided for themselves not to elect these courses. It may be that other decision makers in the school system—girls' parents, teachers, and guidance counselors—are steering them away from these courses. In any event, it is

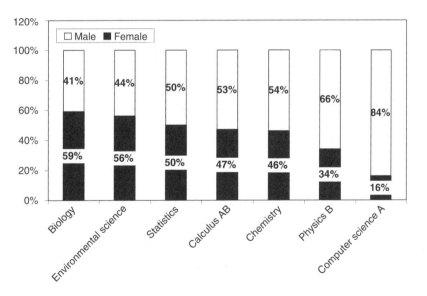

Figure 1.1
Gender composition of AP test takers, 2004
Source: College Board, 2004.

only because election is a standard part of the educational philosophy that college-bound girls can graduate from high school with a weaker background in math, science, and computing.

The causes for the gendered differences in election of high school courses in math, science, and computing need further examination. More specifically, are parents, teachers, and guidance counselors more likely to advise boys than girls to take these courses? Are there structural features in the school election system that contribute to the gender difference in course election noted here? For example, are electives courses that are thought by some to be more attractive to girls, such as literature and art courses, offered at the same time as the math and science electives so that the students have to make a choice between humanities and science courses? Are the course requirements of the school system sufficiently great that students have to choose between humanities and science courses because there is not enough room in their schedule for elective courses in both? Is the system so rigid in terms of both prerequisites and the grade levels at which these classes are offered that students who choose a humanities path (or a science one) of electives in middle school are locked into this path for the remainder of their K–12 education?

It would also be useful to look at the impact of K–12 course election on college behavior and performance. Are students who have more high school classes in math, science, and computing more likely to matriculate at technologically strong colleges and universities, enroll in computing courses or majors, achieve better grades in these introductory courses, or remain in the computing major? Do the students with this prior background in math, science, and computing feel more comfortable and confident in the lower-level undergraduate computing courses?

Relationships with Teachers

Teachers' beliefs and attitudes about appropriate behaviors and roles for boys and girls, combined with their attitudes and beliefs about technology, can subtly influence girls to not study computers. Students and teachers maintain a variety of relationships, including those in the formal classroom environment, extracurricular activities, and one-on-one personal contact. Teachers are generally perceived by their students as having legitimacy, authority, and expertise; they thereby influence the opinions and behaviors of their students, both in the short and long terms. Research shows that teachers' expectations of students significantly influence student learning and that these expectations are internalized by students (Bamburg 1994; Raffini 1993). Through their verbal and nonverbal interactions with students, teachers explicitly and implicitly communicate their tacit beliefs to students, who come to believe what teachers communicate. For example, studies have found that teachers smile more, make more frequent eye contact with, and move physically closer to students they perceive as having high abilities than they do with students they perceive as having low abilities.

Teachers express and act on their beliefs about appropriate and possible roles as well as behaviors for boys and girls, praising and scolding children accordingly (Fagot et al. 1985). For instance, teachers let girls give up more easily than they do boys, giving girls answers when they are having problems, while they are more likely to make boys figure out the answers for themselves (Sadker and Sadker 1995; Koch 1994). Further, teachers tend to overrate males' abilities, underrate females' abilities, and maintain more positive attitudes toward male students in mathematics classes (Li 1999).

In mathematics and science, subjects often considered to be in the male domain, teachers make more eye contact and interact more with boys than with girls; they also encourage boys more than they do girls (Li 1999; American Association of University Women 1998). This conveys an implicit message to girls that their input and learning is less important than that of boys in these subjects. In this way, many girls come to believe that they either cannot or should not solve problems on their own, which can undermine their confidence (American Association of University Women 1998).

Given the general belief about computing being in the male domain, we have no reason to believe that behavior in computing courses is different in the vast majority of U.S. schools from that reported here in the mathematics and science education research. In fact, the research supports this claim in mixed-gender high school computer science classes. In all-female classrooms, girls report significantly greater teacher support with technology use than females in mixed-gender classes (Crombie and Armstrong 1999; Crombie, Abarbanel, and Trinneer 2002). Teachers also perceive boys as having greater computer competence than girls. These perceptions are visible in teachers' discourse with students and others. In a small ethnographic Australian study of four elementary school classrooms, for example, Singh (1993) describes a primary classroom teacher who discusses his male students as being necessarily assertive, competitive, and competent with respect to the computer by virtue of the fact that they are boys. He believes one girl is also competent, but in fact, it turns out that she is not. Still, the teacher voices this erroneous opinion because he knows her mother and sisters, and believes that she comes from a "long line of competent women"; that is, he marks this girl as different from other girls (47). Given the strength of teachers' expectations in shaping students' behaviors and achievements (Bamburg 1994; Raffini 1993; Gonder 1991), it might be unexpected and unlikely for girls to be able to achieve competency with computers without intervening requirements, such as information literacy standards.

Teachers also influence students by being role models, subtly and nonsubtly demonstrating to students appropriate topics of educational interest, social norms, and gendered behaviors. They are among the most common role models for young people because of the large amount of time they spend together and the authority relationship the teacher has with the student. The teacher training process and ongoing in-service expectations make teachers explicitly aware that students will mimic teacher behaviors, and thus it is expected that teachers will act intentionally to serve as positive role models. Even beyond the teacher's conscious attempt to serve as a role model, the student may identify with the teacher's personality, beliefs, and ways of acting. (Lee [1998] argues that this is true except in the case of girls in non-Catholic private girls' schools, where students are unlikely to see their teachers as role models or "possible selves.") Not surprisingly, teachers' attitudes toward technology can influence how students perceive technology (Brosnan 1997). Students may also draw inferences about the gendered division of labor from the mere presence of male and female teachers teaching certain subjects and having certain competencies. Based on a study in thirty Canadian primary schools, Jenson and Brushwood Rose (2003) present case studies showing that women teachers, regardless of their computing expertise, are unlikely to be thought of as technical experts; they describe male teachers making hardware and software decisions, and acting as gatekeepers for accessing computer equipment. They contend that their findings are consistent with several other qualitative studies. Computing is masculinized by virtue of who can easily access it, who fixes it, and who makes purchasing decisions (Bryson and de Castell 1998). Teachers are influenced and perceived within the same kinds of sociocultural beliefs as their students, and even if they wish to contest these relationships in their classes, existing power relationships and cultural assumptions inside and outside the schools makes it difficult for them to do so (Clegg 2001).

Many teachers continue to be low users of technology in their classrooms, although this situation is slowly changing as a result of several notable situations, including the U.S. Department of Education's significant funding of the Preparing Tomorrow's Teachers to Use Technology (PT3) program, the vast investment of placing computers and Internet connections into schools, the fact that most students are coming into school with experience from home—leading to both students and their parents demanding computing resources and instruction at school—and the increasing ubiquity of computing in every aspect of our daily lives. Many teachers use computers only for the purpose of rewarding students or keeping students busy while others work, often leading to dominance of the computers by boys as they elbow out the girls (e.g., Kinnear 1995; Ertmer et al. 1999). When the computer is "just" a reward, the failure of some teachers to set rules about how long each child can use the computer also gives way to boys' assertion over girls (Singh 1993). This lack of action is an implicit consent and condoning of this behavior. Teacher training, both in terms of skill with computing and classroom management, lags behind the placement of computers in classrooms.

Teacher Training for General Computer Use

What teachers know regarding computers, and regarding teaching with and about computers, has an impact on children's use, attitudes, and computing-related behaviors. The majority of elementary school teachers are women, and many of them have low computing skills. The U.S. Department of Education has attempted to rectify this problem with the PT3 program. Most schools of education in the United States begrudgingly integrated computer use into preservice programs. This frequently took the form of learning specific software packages (e.g., Inspiration) for concept mapping or requiring a threaded discussion for classes. The latter were often resisted by undergraduate preservice teachers for taking up too much additional time.

Teachers need training to be able to use computers effectively in the classroom as well as time to implement their use. Further, teachers need training for introducing fundamental computing concepts. Unfortunately, in several studies teachers reported not having enough time to become knowledgeable about effective ways of teaching with computers in the classroom, how to use a computer, or how to judge software for quality or gender bias (Bhargava 2002; Bryson and de Castell 1998; Guha 2003). To the extent that girls model their behavior after female teachers who feel uncomfortable using computers or have little knowledge about them, then the girls might continue feeling less comfortable (at least at school) using computers and see computing as a male activity.

Several studies show that teachers who have familiarity with computers are more likely than other teachers to use computers in class and teach about computers. In a large study ($N = 516$) using data from 1994, Becker (2000) found a positive correlation between teachers' use of computers in the classroom and formal training with computers. In a Dutch study of 236 teachers, Van Braak (2001) found that teachers who were technical innovators, taught a technology-related subject, and had greater computer experience were more likely to use a computer in their teaching. In a survey of 149 elementary teachers, Guha (2001) found that computer knowledge, training, and comfort with computers were positively correlated with computer usage in the classroom, regardless of other demographic variables such as years teaching, age, or gender. Guha (2003) surveyed and conducted in-depth interviews with elementary teachers with respect to their use of computers for instruction. Teachers who had lower computer abilities felt less comfortable with computers and feared to use them since they might lose authority in the event that children, who tended to have computers at home, would have greater computing skill than they did. Evans-Andris (1995) found that teachers unfamiliar with software or computers did not guide students during computer time. Consistent with Guha's (2003) findings, Evans-Andris also discovered that teachers unfamiliar with computers were often intimidated by children's superior knowledge, and were more likely to use the computer as a surrogate teacher for children to use passively than as a tool that the children would use to actively solve problems or otherwise apply.

Training for K–12 Computer Science Teachers

Where computer science is taught in schools, it is a rarity to find a teacher who has both strong teaching credentials and strong technical training in computing (CSTA [Computer Science Teachers Association] Model Curriculum). Schools have reached out to people with IT-related degrees who often do not have a foundation in educational methodology. Although this is true of STEM teachers in general, it is especially problematic in IT because an IT professional can earn substantially higher wages in industry and because few preservice programs provide instruction in computer science education. In some states, the computer science major does not qualify for certification. Industry demand and state educational policies reduce the likelihood that public schools will attract computer science teachers who have a formal education in computer science. Thus, K–12 computer science teachers frequently are missing either educational or computing backgrounds. The consequence is that those teachers who have educational but not computing backgrounds deliver to their students what they have taught themselves; this tends to focus on learning a programming language or manipulating games more often than providing organized theoretical knowledge or applying that knowledge to real-world problems. Teachers who have computing but not educational backgrounds are ill prepared to communicate these ideas and concepts to students, or design powerful learning opportunities and assessments; these teachers are also less likely to call into question their gendered beliefs about what kinds of people do what kinds of tasks, but instead to act on a lifetime of socialization and experience. In contrast, most teacher preparation programs require that students at least familiarize themselves with research on gender and minorities in school systems.

The Association of Computing Machinery has recently initiated the Computer Science Teachers Association, one goal of which is to train high school computer science teachers both for improving pedagogy and the gender balance of classrooms. Training for gender equity in IT in schools is rare. Bhargava (2002) reports on tools that have been developed to guide teachers in the use of non-gender-biased software, though it is not clear how widely these are used nor whether this has become a mainstream part of the preservice teacher curriculum. Sanders (2002) was involved in the professional development of teachers who needed to learn C++ for the computer science Advanced Placement test. Teachers spent half of their time learning the programming language, and the other half learning about gender equity issues and strategies for increasing the number of girls in their classes. Although there was a marked increase in the number of teachers attempting to increase the number of girls as a result of the training, the number of girls enrolling in the computer science classes did not increase. We do not know the reasons. It may be the result of teachers self-reporting their activities, professional development not aligned with best practices (i.e., sustained overtime), poor training, using male-oriented assignments, resistant girls, or some other reason. Administrators should also be aware of the persuasive power of school-related images. Based on her research on Web site images, Maboudian (2000) has argued that school Web sites contain gender-biased or gender-shaping messages. For example, one Web site shows only boys in the computer lab and presents girls only in cheerleading costumes. Teachers should be thoughtful about the meaning behind such images. School policies and teachers can have a significant influence on children, but no influence is greater than that of family.

Use of Computers at School and Home

The availability of computers in the home, school, and other places influences children's experiences with computing, and shapes their perceptions of how they get used and who uses them. The presence and use of computers is one of the most studied topics of any covered in this chapter. From the 1980s through the mid-1990s, access to a computer and the Internet was a major policy issue in the United States—an issue known as the digital divide. Poor, rural, and minority families had much less access to these tools than did the nation as a whole. The most recent data from the National Telecommunications and Information Administration (NTIA) indicate that access to both computers and the Internet is spreading rapidly in the United States, and that the divide in access that separated black and white, rich and poor, urban and rural is shrinking. The NTIA (2002) data indicate that 54 percent of the U.S. population was using the Internet in September 2001 and 66 percent used computers. Ninety percent of U.S. children between the ages of five and seventeen used computers, while 75 percent of fourteen to seventeen year olds and 65 percent of ten to thirteen year olds used the Internet. The presence of computers at school substantially narrowed the gap in computer usage rates for children from high- and low-income families. Increases in use (although from a smaller base) were rising most rapidly among blacks, Hispanics, and rural households (between a 24 and 33 percent increase in the period from August 2000 to September 2001). This led the Bush administration to announce the end of the digital divide.

To some degree, the NTIA 2002 report emphasizes those points that support the politics of the Bush administration. The report also shows the persistence of a digital divide along certain lines. Black and Hispanic children were more than three times as likely to have access to computers only at school, not at home. Black and Hispanic children were twice as likely as white or Asian American children to not be using a computer at all. For a good analysis of this report and the political context in which it is set, see Jesse (2004).

Use of Computers at School

As we have mentioned above, the date when studies were conducted matters because of the rapid introduction of computers into the public schools in the United States throughout the 1990s. Several studies report on the relative use of computers at school by boys and girls. In a study of 500 middle school students in the Houston area, Miller, Chaika, and Groppe (1996) reported that 88 percent of girls and 90 percent of boys were using computers at school; this was not a statistically significant difference. Consistent with these findings, Miller, Schweingruber, and Brandenburg (2001) found no significant gender differences in knowledge of using a computer, how they learned to use a computer, use of the computer at school, use of computers with others, and Internet uses among 512 middle school students from

Houston. They concluded that the gender gap among children in access, use, and perceived expertise is narrowing considerably. As for what uses were made of computers by girls in school, Miller, Chaika, and Groppe report students using them to search the Internet, prepare documents with word processing, develop and present school projects, play games, do homework, view CD-ROM materials, check out library books, and view simulations.

An introduction to computers and keyboarding is now commonly taught in middle school in the United States. Children are not motivated to pursue further study of computing by these classes, however. For example, in an Australian study of thirty-three girls ranging from thirteen to seventeen years of age, Clarke and Teague (1996) reported that students were taught keyboarding, word processing, and other introductory applications. The students found these applications limited, boring, and menial—much more so than their home computer use. To the extent that this is the primary way children are introduced to computers and their use, the limited nature of the applications may be a real turnoff to both boys and girls.

Home and Other Extracurricular Uses of Computers
Like computer use at school, home use of computers has also increased in general in the United States. Most studies show that boys use computers more frequently than do girls at their own homes and the homes of friends, summer camps, and after-school clubs. In older studies, access was much more common at home for boys than for girls: in the United States (Kirkpatrick and Cuban 1998), New Zealand (Fletcher-Flinn and Suddendorf 1996), Scotland (Durndell and Thomson 1997), and Israel (Levine and Donitsa-Schmidt 1995). In a more recent study of 1,400 Canadian children in seventh and tenth grades (Lupart and Cannon 2002), the authors found that more boys than girls used computers at home, boys were younger than girls when they began using computers, boys used the Internet more than girls, and boys used their computers at home on average more hours per day than girls. This latter point was also noted by Kirkpatrick and Cuban (1998) as well as Durndell, Glissov, and Siann (1995). Two somewhat older studies, however, report no gender difference for time spent on the computer for those who had their own computer at home (Fletcher-Flinn and Suddendorf 1996; Dugdale, DeKoven, and Ju 1998). These differences may be due in part to the age groups sampled. The 2001 National Assessment of Educational Progress (NAEP; National Center for Education Statistics 2004) study shows a difference across age groups in terms of amount of computer use. In this large study ($N > 6,800$), fourth-grade boys and girls report about

the same usage of computers outside of school. Eighth-grade boys, though, report somewhat more usage outside of school than do girls.

Research on the purpose of computer use by girls and boys outside of school shows that boys and girls use computers for many of the same applications, but for different amounts of time. In a survey of 291 parents (Kafai and Sutton 1999), it was reported that boys use games, educational software, and the Internet more than do girls. Both Lupart and Cannon (2002) and Miller, Schweingruber, and Brandenburg (2001) identified e-mail and homework as the main use of computers by girls. The large NAEP study referenced above found that 90 percent of fourth-grade boys and girls report that they play games on the computer at home. By eighth grade, however, boys are significantly more likely to spend large amounts of time playing computer games than are females, while girls spend more time than boys communicating synchronously and asynchronously with others via the Internet (e.g., e-mail, instant messaging, chat) (National Center for Education Statistics 2004). Clearly, the routinizing of computer use in the home makes an impact on children's perceptions of computers.

The Impact of Experience

There is a positive correlation between experience with computers and girls' attitudes toward them. In a study of ninth-grade German students (Schaumburg 2001), girls who were provided with a laptop computer used computers more at both school and home, and they learned more about computer hardware, software, and the Internet as compared to a control group. A broader range of experiences may make a greater impact than experience with a limited number of applications. In a study of 231 girls fifteen years of age in single-sex and coeducational schools in Australia, Jones and Clark (1995) found a positive correlation between the diversity (but not the quantity) of computer experience to girls' positive attitudes about computing. The presence of a computer in a home also seems to be positively correlated with attitude, according to two relatively large studies in the United States (Levine and Donitsa-Schmidt 1995; Frantom, Green, and Hoffman 2002).

Influences beyond the Classroom

Research on Differences in Attitude, Confidence, Interest, and Experiences

One's attitudes toward, confidence with, and experience using a tool or set of tools are related to academic and career choices in which these are the predominant focus.

Therefore, a great deal of research has concentrated on the differences between boys and girls in terms of their attitudes toward, confidence using, and experience with computer technology. Generally speaking, these studies are not necessarily focused on developing IT but more often toward the use of computing technology in the service of some other goal (e.g., learning; communicating with friends via the Internet) or simply learning to use the computer itself (e.g., keyboarding; Web development). Such studies are extremely numerous. We thus present here a range of studies looking at different aspects of computing use, attitudes, and experience. Note that these studies are designed to look for differences and describe probabilities, not similarities nor generalities. A general criticism of research that looks for differences is that it fails to report on similarities that may be important (American Association of University Women 1998; Barnett and Rivers 2004).

One group of difference studies focuses on confidence and attitudes toward technology. These studies more frequently show that girls are less confident using computers than are boys. In their 1998 review article, Kirkpatrick and Cuban (1998) say that in early grades, the gap between males and females in achievement and attitude is minor, but the gap increases as they get older, as does the confidence gap. Levine and Donitsa-Schmidt (1998), however, found a positive correlation between computer experience, computer knowledge, and computer confidence. With the better access to computers in more recent years, one might speculate that the confidence gap will have decreased. Yet four studies show that the confidence gap persists (Fitzpatrick and Hardman 2000; Light et al. 2000; Schaumburg 2001; Frantom, Green, and Hoffman 2002). Yet Fitzpatrick and Hardman also found the gap widens as children grow older. They surveyed 120 seven- and nine-year-old boys and girls and discovered that the seven-year-old girls expressed more confidence working with computers than did nine-year-old girls. In addition, the younger girls were more motivated to work with computers than were their male peers.

The issue of girls' confidence is poorly understood and disputed in the literature. Reviewing research on adolescent girls from the 1980s to the 1990s, Eckert (1995) argues that adolescent girls experience a "crisis of confidence," in which girls have greater awareness and less satisfaction of their bodies, are more concerned about their popularity and being liked, and are more prone to depression and suicide. Barnett and Rivers (2004), though, call into question the research on which these confidence studies are based. They contend that Carol Gilligan's original study on which many others were based was a small, ethnographic study of upper-class white girls attending a private school and that an influential report by the American

Association of University Women was methodologically flawed (both cited in Barnett and Rivers 2004). They also present a meta-analysis of research including 150,000 subjects in which there was little difference between boys and girls in confidence (Kling, Hyde, Showers, and Buswell 1999; cited in Barnett and Rivers 2004).

Boys and girls hold different beliefs about who should study or be involved in computing. Durndell and Thomson (1997) administered three surveys to sixteen to eighteen year olds at three different times, the most recent being 1995. Female students were significantly more likely than males to believe they were not qualified to study computing. This may be explained by the fact that the data were collected ten years ago, since ten years ago boys were more likely to have and/or use a computer at home than were girls. In several studies, boys held more stereotypical beliefs about who should engage in computing than did girls (Fletcher-Flinn and Suddendorf 1996; Boser, Daugherty, and Palmer 1996; Whitley 1997). Nevertheless, such beliefs can change over time, as shown in a study where younger boys held more stereotypical views than did older children (Fletcher-Flinn and Suddendorf 1996). In contrast to findings that boys have stronger opinions on computing than girls, in a study of 574 students in ten rural school districts, Frantom, Green, and Hoffman (2002) report that boys were more likely than girls to agree that "girls can do technology as well as boys," but they had higher variance in their answers than did girls. Boys were also more likely than girls to agree that "technology is as difficult for girls as it is for boys."

Other difference studies concern interest in technology and assertiveness with technology. Durndell and Thomson (1997) reported that sixteen- to eighteen-year-old girls were more likely than their male peers to indicate greater interest in people than in objects. Similarly, in a study of 155 seventh graders, Boser, Daugherty, and Palmer (1996) found that girls expressed less interest in technology and perceived it as more difficult to learn than did males. In several studies, boys were observed dominating computer use at school, though not under all circumstances. Freeman and Somerindyke (2001) observed preschool children playing with two computer programs in a university laboratory school and noted boys dominating the computer. Likewise, Koch and Upitis (1996) observed a Canadian classroom of seventh and eighth graders for two years. They found that boys dominated computer use at school during free computer time, and girls were not likely to use the computer even if they did have free time, but especially if there were other students already sitting at the computer. In this case, a computer "in-group" was formed on the basis of frequency of use, further concentrating the gender disparity; students who had computers at home were more likely to be part of the in-group at school. In a study of 120 seven- and nine-year-old students in England comparing behavior of same-sex and mixed-sex pairs, the authors found that boys dominated the computer when collaboration with girls broke down (Fitzpatrick and Hardman 2000).

Girls' gender identity may influence assertiveness with computer use at school. Stepulvage (2001) discovered that girls are more likely to take on passive roles when working alongside boys on the computer. She argues that although girls do engage with computer technology and occupy positions that enable development of expertise in IT, this computing competence must mesh with the constitution of a heterosexual gender identity. Finally, based on her teaching and research experience in a midwestern elementary school (not a formal study), Hanor (1998) contends that boys physically and verbally discourage girls from using computers. In her observations from teaching (again, not a formal study), Hanor describes access barriers as teacher training issues. She claims that teachers need to manage several access barriers for girls in the classroom: the boys' computer use discouraging the girls' use, not knowing that use of the computer is a choice, conflicts in scheduling, competing work requirements, and teaching assistants more likely to select boys than girls.

The majority of difference studies, such as those reviewed above, equate sex with gender and use gender as a monolithic category across socioeconomic groups. There have been attempts to avoid equating gender and sex, using psychological gender theory. Under this theory, persons are considered to have high or low masculinity scores, and these are not opposites but independent constructs. For example, Brosnan (1998) found that high femininity correlated with a poorer attitude toward technology and that high masculinity correlated with a better attitude and higher scores on a computer-based track. Yet Charlton (1999) found that both higher masculinity or femininity correlated with greater comfort, but that greater masculinity was related to greater engagement and greater femininity was associated with lesser overuse. Such studies, while more illuminating than those that conflate gender and biological sex, do not generally provide a deeper understanding of how gender identity interacts with the attitude toward IT. Further, "difference" implies that the determining variable is masculinity and femininity, rather than providing understanding of technologies as embedded in a cultural setting, where meanings are created and assigned as part of ongoing interactions among children and adults. In contrast, like Huff (1996), Clegg (2001) argues that attitudes and experiences with technologies are embedded in the technology (hardware and software) and the social practices surrounding technologies. In other words, designers project themselves into the technologies they create.

Findings usually conclude that girls hold less positive attitudes toward and confidence with technology. To the extent that the underlying belief of these studies is that girls and boys both need to have positive values and high confidence with IT, conclusions generally point to a deficit among girls: they are lacking something boys have. Elkjær (1992) describes the issue differently, however, arguing that gender and gender differences are relative constructs, and that boys' behaviors (dominance; failure to admit lack of knowledge) create the problem for girls, who become passive in the presence of boys' dominance and believe that they know less simply because boys believe they know more. Studying actual skill and knowledge, rather than perceptions thereof, would furnish teachers and parents with concrete ideas about what girls and boys need to learn. Further, if the result of such assessments is insignificant difference, this message could be conveyed to girls to boost their confidence.

Influence of Families and Community

A girl's relationships with her parents and siblings are usually her strongest early relationships, and her first exposure to beliefs about possible and appropriate roles for girls and boys. (This is similarly true for boys.) Despite the image of the rebellious teen, these relationships between child and parent persist over time. Families form their own ways of behaving, enacting their belief systems. There is disagreement, but what is shared is often larger than what is not. As a child grows up, she or he will often look to parents and older siblings to be role models and opinion leaders. As with the teacher relationship, beliefs are communicated in many ways, both explicitly and implicitly. It is traditional from birth for parents to treat boys and girls in gendered ways, by virtue of their sex. This is also manifest in the way parents often encourage boys and girls to take different educational paths as well as prepare for different careers.

Parents' religious beliefs frequently shape their views about gender-appropriate lives for their children. Because of the strong force of religion, parents will generally try to instill their personal religious belief in their children, and they will employ religious organizations to attempt to do so. Some religions maintain belief systems that place girls and boys in more traditional gender roles than others. Likewise, parents who value education or who themselves are highly educated are more likely to have children who value and pursue education. Even if parents value education, there can be gender differences in the way they apply their desire for educating their children. They might not encourage their daughters, for example, to pursue science and engineering disciplines or believe that these are appropriate occupational goals—unless one or both of the parents are in these occupations (Rayman and Brett 1993).

In many U.S. communities, there is homogeneity across households in socioeconomic status, education level, and type (e.g., professional versus vocational) of occupations held. In cases where the parents are typical of other members of the community, the local community can reinforce the messages being delivered to students by their parents. For example, in a wealthy, well-educated community, it is expected that every child will go to college and form a professional family; this message is subtly communicated to children in every local contact they have.

Another influence of the community lies in the range of activities it offers to its youth. The availability and nature of activities is likely to vary by the demographics of the local community (rural versus urban or suburban, socioeconomic distribution, religious affiliation, etc). Opportunities for scouting, participation in clubs, sports, and service can enrich children's experiences and shape their beliefs. For instance, playing on a soccer team can be empowering (President's Council on Physical Fitness and Sports 1997; Zimmerman and Reavill 1999) and participation in Girl Scouts may provide girls with direct experience of computing.

Although hardly any literature explores the influence of parents and local community on children's attitude and behavior specifically toward computing, two studies offer small insights in passing. Margolis and Fisher's ethnographic study (2002) of undergraduate computer science majors at Carnegie Mellon University revealed that fathers often provided their sons with computers and spent time "tinkering" on the machine with them. Mothers were less likely to be involved in tinkering, and the males frequently described their mothers as either computer phobic or computer incompetent. Women much less frequently described similar bonding experiences on the computer with either parent. (Interestingly, in a study of single-sex schooling at Catholic and independent schools in the United States, Lee (1998) notes that in mixed-sex schools, schools with high levels of parental influence led to a greater gender gap in mathematics achievement, favoring boys.) Considering the growing ubiquity of computers, including school requirements that children be "technologically literate," we wonder to what degree parents continue to treat their sons and daughters differently with respect to computing. For example, are there gendered differences in their encouragement to use computers, what to use them for, spending time at the computer with the child, encouraging education training and careers in computing, and making opportunities for them to attend computer camp?

Relationships with Peers and the Impact of Single-Sex Schools

Peers are a powerful influence on children's beliefs and behavioral choices, and this influence is in force from the time that children begin having peers. Especially as children enter the teenage years, they have an amplified need to conform or to inhabit a persona that is acceptable to other children. For example, teenagers cast various kinds of persona as nerds, geeks, jocks, or the popular set. They are careful about which type they act like and form cliques with children of similar persona (Adler and Adler 1998).

Peers influence children's beliefs about the value of education, appropriate and possible gender performance, and academic choices. Eckert (1995) argues that childhood is a series of stages in which children are constantly looking toward the next step of being a child. That is, children are not making behavioral decisions based on what they think they will be as adults (who work and have careers) but instead toward the next stage forward, which may be eighth graders for sixth graders and high school students for eighth graders. Eckert writes, "Few kids in this life stage consider adulthood desirable, nor do they consider the behavior of adults to be particularly statusful [*sic*]." Rather, at this stage girls and boys work on more fully being heterosexual persons—not in the sense of sex or sexuality but in the sense of performing the interactive behaviors of persons who fit into appropriate roles for their sex.

Eckert's view has implications for girls' choice of course work. As discussed above in the section on course election, it is during early middle school when children begin to have choices about the courses they take. The choice of courses is based not solely on what they enjoy but on the type of person they hope to be and the type of person they hope their peers will believe they are. They are likely to choose courses that are locally considered more appropriate for one gender or the other. Those who make choices outside these norms may suffer from negative attention from their peers. Where math, science, or computing courses are considered "nerdy" or for boys, a powerful force is in play to quash girls' interest in these topics.

Single-sex schools and classes have been one approach taken to improve the engagement and achievement of girls, and several studies compare girls in single-sex classroom environments with those in coeducational ones. Jones and Clark (1995) found that girls from single-sex schools had more experience and more positive attitudes toward computers than did girls from coeducational settings. Nevertheless, experience with computers was the variable that best predicted attitude and not the fact that the class contained only girls. Crombie, Abarbanel, and Trinneer (2002) surveyed 250 students in an elective eleventh-grade science course across a three-year period. One of the classes was all-female. Girls in the same-sex class had higher computer confidence, but lower confidence than the males in the mixed-sex class. Girls in the same-sex class were also more vocal than coed girls, and perceived stronger support from and interacted more with teachers; this was similar to boys' perceptions of teacher support. Lee (1998) found that in Catholic all-girl schools, girls had higher educational aspirations and greater intention to participate in non-traditionally female careers. In fact, girls in Catholic same-sex schools had higher mathematics and science achievement than did girls in Catholic coeducational schools. It is unclear the degree to which this is a function of parental choice and influence or of peers.

Life Aspirations

A significant body of literature investigates career factors. Family situation, which includes socioeconomic status, educational level, and religion, are the single-greatest influence on a child's career development (see reviews in Naylor 1986; Lankard 1995; Whiston and Keller 2004). Lower levels of parent education are correlated with less likelihood of the child—boy or girl—going to college or entering a professional career (DeRidder 1990). Family income has a particular effect on girls' career development. Lower-income families may be more likely to take a strategy of devoting limited resources to their male children's career development or to being more likely to hold views that see homemaker roles for girls—for which less occupational preparation is needed (Lankard 1995). Children whose parents work in professional occupations perceive a wider range of career choices (Mullis, Mullis, and Gerwels 1998). To the extent that parents are aware of IT careers, girls will likely know more about and be more inclined to pursue them.

Girls and boys allow their (and their families') cultural beliefs about appropriate gender roles to guide their career explorations as opposed to their personal interests (Farmer 1995). In a longitudinal study of 208 children, Helwig (1998) explored children's perceptions of whether occupations were male or female. Occupations are considered to be male if at least 70 percent of the people holding those positions currently are male, to be female if at least 70 percent of the people holding them currently are female, and otherwise are characterized as gender-neutral occupations. Eighty-three percent of second-grade boys chose male occupations, and the percentage increased to 93 percent by sixth grade. Fifty-six percent of second-grade girls chose female occupations, but the number decreased to 30 percent by sixth grade. For both boys and girls, career expectations are related to their parents' expectations for them, especially their mother's. By sixth grade (as compared to second grade), the career that the child desires, the career that the child expects, and the career their parents expect for them all match more closely. Instead, as girls got older, they were more likely to select male occupations (19 percent in second grade, and 48 percent in sixth grade). Helwig suggests that both boys and girls recognize the social rewards and higher pay of male occupations by the time they are sixth graders, thus accounting for this increased interest in male occupations. Another explanation may be that sixth-grade girls are beginning to perceive that women's traditional roles tend to be subordinated to those of males (Eckert 1994). It also could be inferred that many high schools are doing a good job of preparing both boys and girls for a variety of careers.

One could conclude that the vast majority of the boys and almost half of the girls at the sixth-grade level might be open to a computing career since it is high paying and is probably seen as having the high social rewards of a male occupation. Still, another recent and large study (Lupart and Cannon 2002) of seventh and tenth graders in an urban community in Canada showed much less enthusiasm by girls for IT careers. Girls self-report a greater likelihood of expectation of finishing high school and completing more than one university degree than do boys. Yet while both boys and girls rated highly "earning a great deal of money" and "high status in society" as significantly important factors in a career choice, boys rated these two factors significantly more highly than did girls. Seventh-grade girls rated most highly the career of artist (which included designer, interior decorator, musician, and actor), with health professional second highest and IT professional dead last. Also low in the rankings for seventh-grade girls were the occupations of engineer, architect, and geologist. Seventh-grade boys, by contrast, had IT professional (which included computer engineer and computer scientist) as their first choice. Girls in single-sex classes may be more likely to pursue an IT career, however. Crombie, Abarbanel, and Trinneer (2002) conducted a similar study of 250 students in elective computer science classes in Ottawa, Canada, but had access to both all-female and mixed-sex classes. Boys reported the highest intentions to pursue college study of computing, followed by girls in the single-sex classes, followed by girls in the mixed-sex classes.

Most of the studies cited so far in this section do not describe what it is about an IT career that makes it much less attractive to girls than to boys. Two other studies provide some clues, although neither definitively answers this question. Clark and Teague (1996) studied thirty-three Australian girls, ages thirteen to seventeen, from diverse backgrounds. Most of the girls favored a career in a socially oriented or socially important field such as medicine, law, or business. Although it is not clear how they came up with these particular choices, they did report that they were most interested in jobs that provided job satisfaction as well as ones with social orientation such as communicating with and meeting new people. In school, these students had learned only mundane computing skills associated with keyboarding, word processing, and elementary applications. When asked about computing careers, they indicated that they saw computing as boring and menial. When asked, they could not provide the interviewers with examples of computing careers other than those directly associated with keyboarding and word processing. Interestingly, the girls were excited about their use of home computers, which they used for their own goals. The children in this study had a limited conception of the kinds of careers that fall under IT.

Many outreach programs are held each year to encourage girls to enter IT careers. Some extracurricular computing experiences, however, may reverse girls' decisions to pursue an IT career, despite the best efforts of teachers, counselors, and persons who arrange career experiences for students. Taylor (2003) evaluated the educational outcomes of an internship program for high-achieving high school students. Boys in the study were given highly technical jobs and integrated well into corporate life. In contrast, the girls involved were given jobs they considered boring (e.g., Web design) and felt unchallenged. Unlike many of the boys, none of the girls decided to pursue careers in IT. A conclusion to draw from this is that extracurricular computing experiences also involve a set of best practices, but these are out of the control of the teachers, counselors, and persons who arrange career experiences for students.

While the literature about career choice is abundant, much of it is not specific to careers in IT, and most of the studies that do consider IT careers address whether, rather than why, these careers are or are not ones made by girls. Research into ways girls can be recruited into IT study and careers is minimal (see the literature review in Barker, Snow, Garvin-Doxas, and Weston, this volume). For example, further study of the depth, extent, impact, and nuances of the widely held belief that boys are interested in computers as toys while girls are interested in them as agents of social change would help inform interventions.

Images in Popular Culture

An often-heard explanation for the underrepresentation of girls in computing is the media portrayal and a popular conception/stereotype of computer science or computer professionals (or even users) as so-called geeks or nerds, who are usually males. The images of males and females in mass media carry implicit and significant messages about idealized views of males and females in culture. For example, television commercials caricature women using vacuums (or showing men how to use these complicated machines) and men fascinated by an automobile's lock mechanism. Likewise, television programming and commercials, music, videos, movies, popular magazines, and books contain and transmit implicit as well as explicit messages about the values, expected behaviors, and communication styles of girls and boys at different ages. These messages often present boys and girls in terms of the traditional gender-role binary, as do games (arcade, computer, board, educational, etc.) and toys (e.g., lavender and pink bicycles for girls; racing flames for boys). The Internet presents a more diverse range of opportunities—some of which, like television, present gendered roles and others do not.

The degree to which explicitly and implicitly gendered messages from mass media, toys, music, and games influence children's behavior is unclear. In the early 1960s, scholars began studying the effects of television viewing, hypothesizing that long-term exposure to television cultivates attitudes and values in viewers, though they acknowledge that these attitudes and values are already present in a society (cf. Gerbner 1969). Goffman (1979) argued that magazine advertisements both reflect and influence our conceptions of appropriately masculine and feminine behavior. There is some evidence that adolescents are more influenced by the portrayals of appropriate sex roles in mass media than are adults (see the review in Chapin 2000).

Media images more frequently depict computer programmers and developers as males, and women as users. For example, in advertisements of technology products, women are often presented as passive and inexpert users to show how simple some device is to use, suggesting that "this computer is so easy to use, even a woman can use it" (Jenson and Brushwood Rose 2003, 172). Men, on the other hand, are characterized as deep thinkers concerned with the future (Dilevko and Harris 1997). For many years, home computer and computer game sellers almost exclusively targeted male users and "toys for boys" (Bryson and de Castell 1998).

The popular image of computer people as geeks may or may not be a barrier to girls' study of IT. A computer geek is someone obsessed with computers or computing, and who is also antisocial (Webster's 2003). A full-page advertisement in *USA Today*, a national newspaper dropped in front of hotel room doors across the United States, shows Best Buy Co., Inc.'s new subsidiary Geek Squad described as "an elite tactical unit trained to seek out and eradicate evil computer activity." Consistent with "geek culture" (Svitavsky 2001), the employees are presented as though they are engaged in a role-playing game, pretending to be police officers. Five "agents" are shown in the advertisement, each wearing a "special agent badge," short-sleeved white shirts, and narrow black ties. The males' high-water black pants proudly expose white socks against black shoes, a fashion faux pas. The lone female wears a black skirt and black tights, and naturally she also wears glasses and has very short (blond) hair. In their book about children's peer culture in schools, Adler and Adler (1998) describe the social stratification of children based on cliques and groups—a social system that is likely familiar to many who attended large high schools in the United States. The kind of boys (and sometimes girls) who fit into the admittedly extreme portrayal in the Geek Squad advertisement tend to be members of marginalized groups, not of the coveted "popular" group in school. Thus as role models, such representations may work against efforts to involve girls in computing study or careers.

Many groups whose members are passionate about or even obsessed with computers have appropriated the term geek, subverting it into "proud self-identification" (Svitavsky 2001). The term has also been appropriated by female groups such as GirlGeeks.org and ⟨www.GeekGirls.org⟩, and is intended to make it acceptable to like computers. The fact that these groups must explicitly take pride in their geek proclamation makes geekiness as unacceptable in larger culture. The statistics about girls' participation suggest that such labeling has not been an effective strategy. One might speculate that despite the rhetoric, girl geeks, like their male counterparts, continue to be alien others relative to their peers. Nevertheless, popular conceptions about what the term geek means might be changing. More research is needed to determine whether this strategy is working since younger people may now perceive geeks as "hipsters" who indulge in techie toys.

Little research has been conducted on children's perceptions of computer users. In a small qualitative study with high school students, Griffiths and Heath (1996) found that students did not have a clear conception of the physical attributes of technologists (e.g., male, bald). Two other small studies found that when asked to draw either a computer user or a "technologist," primary school girls drew pictures of males more often than boys drew females (Brosnan 1999; Levin and Barry 1997). Interestingly, in one study the boys who drew pictures of females as technologists attended a school with female computing teachers (Levin and Barry 1997), supporting the claim that role models in and of themselves influence perceptions of appropriate roles. In another study, boys drew males and girls drew females, with few exceptions (Sheehan 2003). Selwyn (1998) interviewed ninety-six twelfth- and thirteenth-grade Welsh students in focus groups, asking why students were not using computers in school and college. Student explanations included inability, inappropriateness, and perceived disdain for computers. About one-third of the students expressed a "global disdain" for IT, which was not focused on technology but on the users. This third of the students saw the students as either "hyperintelligent," sad and unapproachable, or lonely and socially isolated.

Computer Games

It has been argued that computer games, both for entertainment and education, are an important vehicle for becoming familiar and gaining confidence with computers (Cassell and Jenkins 1998). Computer games have typically been designed for, bought by, and overwhelmingly used by boys and young men to the virtual exclusion of girls and women (Huff 1996; Cassell and Jenkins 2000; Jenson and Brushwood Rose 2003).

Much research has looked at the content of games, finding them overloaded with violence and competition, and few, if any, females (Jenson and Brushwood Rose 2003). When there are females, they are often presented as hapless victims who need males to rescue them or "huge-breasted vixens with guns" (Lynn et al. 2003, 145). There was a concerted effort in the 1990s to build software that was more interesting to girls. These approaches included appealing to girls' "traditional feminine" interests (e.g., playing with dolls like Barbie), nontraditional masculine interests, and gender-neutral interests (Lynn et al. 2003). For example, the company Purple Moon and its founder Brenda Laurel received considerable attention in the 1990s for their efforts to build software for girls (Cassell and Jenkins 2000). Most of these efforts failed, however. Girls continue to purchase a fraction of the computer games that boys do, so demand for and therefore supply of "girls" games remains relatively small (Lynn et al. 2003).

In spite of the considerable literature on who buys computer games and what the content is, there is little, if any, good analysis of the impact of these computer games on attitudes, beliefs, and future behaviors. Much of the literature makes an interpretive leap that if it is being used, then it must be indirectly influencing children to enter IT study and careers. Yet we found no studies on effect on behavior (other than game playing itself) or attitudes toward computing. We also do not know the causality or directionality of the argument here; it might be that the people playing games were predisposed to certain attitudes and interests, and that they chose to play computer games on that account.

Summary

Scope and Limits of the Literature Review

In this chapter, we have surveyed the scholarly social science literature about girls' involvement with IT, and the ways in which this involvement impinges on future education or careers in IT. We have intentionally not considered the many books and articles that propound on the reasons for gender imbalance or proffer solutions, unless these publications are solidly grounded in research. Although the majority of articles that we have considered in this review are empirically based, we believe it is critically important also to consider publications grounded in theory. These theoretical works provide a framework for thinking about this intractable problem of underrepresentation and offer a way of examining assumptions (e.g., concerning the male-female dichotomy) that are implicit in many of the empirically grounded studies.

Boundaries for this review were determined on both practical and intellectual grounds. The body of social science literature on girls or children is vast, and even with the help of our graduate students and a research librarian, we could not consider the full range of potentially pertinent articles. Even the literature on girls in the STEM disciplines is so large as to make it problematic to survey. At least five reasons, however, make us cautious of including the STEM literature, based in the differences between the STEM and computing disciplines:

1. The patterns for participation of women vary across the STEM disciplines and are often strikingly different from those in computing (e.g., biology, chemistry, mathematics, and some engineering disciplines). The participation of women is dropping in computing.

2. Introductory STEM courses are a required part of the public school curriculum and thus are given the official imprimatur of importance. Computing beyond

information literacy is either not taught in the public schools or is only offered as an elective.

3. Computing is frequently seen as most like mathematics of all the STEM disciplines, but their methods of instruction are often quite different. Computing is taught in a laboratory setting, and mathematics is only occasionally taught this way.

4. The thrust of national educational policy is to move toward teaching all students the basics of information fluency that will enable them to function as citizens in the modern world. This education is not sufficient preparation for college-level courses in computer science. In contrast, most K–12 education in the STEM disciplines is oriented toward academic preparation, at least for those students in the academic tracks.

5. Whereas most STEM education is learned in the formal classroom, computers are introduced to children in informal ways, such as using a computer at home or at a friend's house, participating in a computer club, or using a computer in an unstructured environment at school.

Thus, we have included STEM literature in this review only where we had a specific reason to believe it was applicable. One other restriction in the range of literature we reviewed concerns its currency. One of the most striking changes in the computing landscape is the rapid growth in access to computers in the past decade. Social science researchers of the early 1990s often attributed the underrepresentation of girls in computing in part to the lack of access, which was low for boys, but much lower for girls. But access has become much greater for both boys and girls, and there are serious questions about the relevance of access as a cause of underrepresentation today. Similarly, technological advances such as the Internet, the World Wide Web, multimedia, and a vast array of packaged software have changed the ways that boys and girls interact with computers. For these reasons, we have restricted our review to publications since 1994, except in cases where there was a specific reason to include an earlier work (e.g., research on influences on career aspirations).

In considering such a large body of literature, one encounters studies of varying methodological quality. It is difficult to critique in just a few sentences the methodological quality of theoretical or qualitative studies, and we will not try to do so here. Nevertheless, the most common type of study considered in this review is the quantitative empirical one.

It is not uncommon, especially in the older literature, to find that essentialist dichotomies are drawn between girls and boys, and the way each thinks and acts. In contrast, we understand gender to be a set of social categories that shape how a girl or boy should behave, and also the way that others treat girls and boys as well as expect them to behave. These social categories, which are often locally contextualized, must be taken into consideration in order to understand how girls relate to IT; essentialist dichotomies have a limited explanatory value.

Reasons Explored for Underrepresentation of Girls in Computing

National and Educational Policies

Policy has been a tool used to redress the underrepresentation of women in IT. In particular, the national educational policy of the Clinton-Gore administration made computers and Internet access widely available, narrowing the access gap for girls and boys in the United States. Policy has not enabled teachers the time, training, or reward structure to incorporate this newfound access into effective learning strategies, however. Hence, the largely female teacher population (especially in primary grades) is unlikely to serve as role models who demonstrate competence with computing. A current policy that focuses on the goal of information literacy for the citizenry does not provide sufficient education for gaining IT employment. President Bush's No Child Left Behind policy redirects resources to testing (primarily mathematics and literacy) and away from other educational needs, including and especially the sciences.

The educational philosophy of course election provides a vehicle for gendered difference in preparation for college study of computing. Computing courses are an elective rather than required, and girls are less likely to enroll in these preparatory courses. As a result, the public school computing courses are dominated by boys, raising a further barrier for girls with an interest in preparing for a computing career. The literature does not make it clear, though, what are the direct causes for gendered difference in election of computer science courses nor how to change the minds of girls who avoid them. Instead, several indirect influences are explored; these factors likely work in combination.

Relationships with Teachers and Teacher Training

Relationships with teachers are a powerful shaping force on children, in both formal and informal settings. Given a widespread belief among teachers that computing is a male domain, their action inside and outside the classroom communicates that attitude to their students—boys and girls alike—through a variety of explicit and implicit mechanisms.

What teachers know regarding computers, and with regard to teaching with and about computers, has an impact on children's use, attitudes, and computing-related behaviors. The predominantly female, often computer-challenged population of elementary school teachers reinforces among students the idea that females are not good at computing. It is unusual to find a K–12 teacher with both strong teaching credentials and a strong mathematics-science-computing background. Little training is given to teachers to teach computing subject matter effectively or in a way that encourages girls as well as boys, and few tools are available to help. Perhaps because of the limitations in teacher training and science backgrounds, teachers are all too frequently not in a position to provide a learning experience that captures the interest of all students, offers the appropriate preparation for the college study of computer science, or shows that computing can be about more than games or hacking.

Use of Computers at School and Home
Patterns of use in computers have changed over time. With computers more widely available in schools today than there were a decade ago, some studies show little difference in the percentage of boys and girls using computers in school (at least in the United States). Yet despite the availability of computers, other studies have shown that boys dominate the actual use of computers at school and elect to take more courses that study computers. Other studies (not entirely consistent with one another) show that more boys use computers at home (and for more hours) than girls do, boys were younger when they first began using computers, and boys and girls primarily use computers for different purposes, particularly as they move toward adolescence. While use is a major area of study, little research explores the relationship between computer use and entry into IT careers.

Differences in Attitude, Confidence, Interest, and Experience
A large body of literature explores differences between boys and girls in attitude, confidence, interest, and experience. These studies generally show that girls have less positive attitudes, less confidence, less interest, and less experience with computers than do boys. While most readers will find this evidence compelling, a few recent studies have begun to question these results because of their concerns that this literature conflates issues of sex and gender while neglecting the socioeconomic context. Studying actual skills and knowledge, rather than perceptions of skill and

knowledge, as do most of these studies, would improve understanding of these issues.

Family and Community

Family and local community are a powerful influence on a girl's interests along with her educational and career aspirations. The literature on influence of home and local community on a girl's interest in and attitudes toward computing is sparse, but some evidence suggests that the home environment is more supportive of boys than girls being interested in computing.

Influence of Peers

Peers have a strong influence on children, especially in the teen years. Girls and boys are unlikely to choose elective courses in computing if they believe that these courses are inappropriate for their gender. Several studies show that children believe that computing is most appropriate for boys. Single-sex schools have been one approach for providing greater engagement and achievement for girls. The literature indicates that girls attending single-sex schools tend to have more positive attitudes toward computers than girls in coeducational settings and to be more open to nontraditional careers for their gender. Socioeconomic status is also a consideration: children in single-sex settings are more likely to have relatively affluent parents and therefore to enter professional careers of one type or another.

Life Aspirations

Another body of literature discusses life aspirations and how they affect a girl's interest in computing along with her decisions about whether to participate in computing inside and outside of school. A more general body of literature shows that socioeconomic variables of family affect aspirations for college education and professional career. Children's expectations about their lives are related to their parents' expectations. Although girls show higher expectations of graduating from high school and attending college, several studies indicate that girls are less likely to aspire to a degree or career in computing. Some of these general studies about career choice are old, however, and it is unclear whether they would still hold in this era when it is more acceptable for women to pursue a professional career. Much of the literature is not specific to IT. We do not know if, as several studies suggest, attitudes toward IT change as children move from elementary to middle school. We also do not have studies on whether the widespread belief is true that boys are interested in computers as toys while girls are interested in computers as agents of social change, or if true, how this difference might affect career aspirations.

Images in Popular Culture

It is widely believed that images in the media and popular culture more generally reinforce the message of computer professionals as geeks or nerds. Studies of television and magazine advertisements show how gender stereotypes are reinforced, and suggest that popular culture can be a powerful shaping force on gender identity development and maintenance for children. Still, little research is available on children's perception of computer users, although there is some evidence that both girls and boys perceive computer users as male. The image of geek may be changing, becoming more attractive for both boys and girls.

Computer Games

There is a widespread belief that computer games are one of the reasons why girls are less likely than boys to pursue computing. Computer games are widely regarded as a way for a child to become familiar and gain confidence with computers. There is clear evidence that most games are designed for and bought by boys and young men, and that the content is often violent and reinforces sexual stereotypes. The scholarly community, like other interested parties, altogether too often makes this interpretive leap from being used to having impact. Yet little research studies the impact of playing computer games on computer skills, knowledge, attitudes and beliefs, and future behavior with respect to career entry.

Acknowledgments

This material is based on work supported by the National Science Foundation under grant number EIA–0244604. Any opinions, findings, and conclusions or recommendations expressed in this material are those of the authors and do not necessarily reflect the views of the National Science Foundation.

   The authors would like to thank all of our collaborators for their contributions to this chapter. We thank Evan Hofmockel and Christopher Hovey for creating and managing our reference database. We are grateful to research librarian Melanie A. Groth for carefully searching dozens of databases for relevant research. Finally, we extend special thanks to our graduate students Alla Genkina, Troy Campbell, and Brett Maddex for evaluating and summarizing hundreds of articles.

References

Adler, P., and P. Adler. 1998. *Peer power: Preadolescent culture and identity.* New Brunswick, NJ: Rutgers University Press.

American Association of University Women. 1998. *Separated by sex: A critical look at single-sex education for girls.* Washington, DC: American Association of University Women Foundation.

Atkins, D. 2003. *Revolutionizing science and engineering through cyberinfrastructure: Report of the National Science Foundation blue-ribbon advisory panel on cyberinfrastructure.* Washington, DC: National Science Foundation.

Bamburg, J. 1994. *Raising expectations to improve student learning.* Oak Brook, IL: North Central Regional Educational Laboratory.

Barnett, R. C., and C. Rivers. 2004. *Same difference: How gender myths are hurting our relationships, our children, and our jobs.* New York: Basic Books.

Becker, H. J. 2000. How exemplary computer-using teachers differ from other teachers: Implications for realizing the potential of computers in schools. *Journal of Research on Computing in Education* 26, no. 3:291–321.

Belensky, M. F., B. M. Clinchy, N. R. Goldberger, J. M. Tarule. 1986. Women's Ways of Knowing: The Development of Self, Voice, and Mind. New York: Basic Books.

Bem, S. L. 1974. The measurement of psychological androgyny. *Journal of Consulting and Clinical Psychology* 42:155–162.

Bennett, D., C. Brunner, and M. Honey. 1999. Gender and technology: Designing for diversity. In *Report from the Center for Children and Technology.* New York: Education Development Center.

Bhargava, A. 2002. Gender bias in computer software programs: A checklist for teachers. *Information Technology in Childhood Education Annual,* no. 1:205–218.

Boser, R., M. Daugherty, and J. Palmer. 1996. *The effect of selected instructional approaches in technology education on students' attitude toward technology.* Reston, VA: Council on Technology Teacher Education.

Brainard, S. G. n.d. Globally diversifying the workforce in science and engineering. Concept paper, Global Alliance for Diversifying the Science and Engineering Workforce. ⟨http://globalalliancesmet.org/about_concept2.htm⟩.

Brosnan, M. J. 1997. The fourth "R": Are teachers hindering computer literacy in school children? *Educational Review* 21, no. 1:29–37.

Brosnan, M. J. 1998. The impact of psychological gender, gender-related perceptions, significant others, and the introducer of technology upon computer anxiety in students. *Journal of Educational Computing Research* 18, no. 1:63–78.

Brosnan, M. J. 1999. The "draw-a-computer-user" test: A new methodology, an old story? *European Journal of Psychology of Education* 3:375–385.

Brunner, C., and D. Bennett. 1998. Technology perceptions by gender. *Education Digest* 63, no. 6:56–58.

Bryson, M., and S. de Castell. 1996. Learning to make a difference: Gender, new technologies, and inequity. *Mind, Culture, and Activity* 3, no. 2:119–135.

Bryson, M., and S. de Castell. 1998. New technologies, gender, and the cultural ecology of primary schooling. *Educational Policy* 12, no. 5:542–567.

Bureau of Labor Statistics. 2002. *The ten fastest growing occupations, 2002–12.* ⟨http://www.bls.gov/news.release/ecopro.t04.htm⟩.

Cassell, J., and H. Jenkins, eds. 1998. *From Barbie to Mortal Kombat: Gender and computer games.* Cambridge, MA: MIT Press.

Cassell, J., and H. Jenkins. 2000. Chess for girls? Feminism and computer games. In *From Barbie to Mortal Kombat: Gender and computer games*, ed. J. Cassell and H. Jenkins. Cambridge: MIT Press.

Chapin, J. R. 2000. Adolescent sex and mass media: A developmental approach. *Adolescence* 35, no. 140:799–841.

Charlton, J. P. 1999. Biological sex, sex-role identity, and the spectrum of computing orientations: A reappraisal at the end of the 90s. *Journal of Educational Computing Research* 21, no. 4:393–412.

Christie, A. A. 2004. How adolescent boys and girls view today's computer culture. Paper presented at the National Educational Computing Conference, New Orleans.

Clarke, V., and J. Teague. 1996. Characterizations of computing careers: Students and professionals disagree. *Computer Education* 26, no. 4:241–246.

Clegg, S. 2001. Theorising the machine: Gender, education, and computing. *Gender and Education* 13:307–324.

College Board. 2004. *Advanced Placement national summary report.* Available at ⟨http://apcentral.collegeboard.com⟩.

Colley, A. M., M. T. Gale, and T. A. Harris. 1994. Effects of gender role identity and experience on computer attitude components. *Journal of Educational Computing Research* 10, no. 2:129–137.

Committee on Information Technology Literacy. 1999. *Being fluent with information technology.* Washington, DC: National Academy Press. Available at ⟨http://www.cra.org/govaffairs/blog/archives/000084.html⟩.

Crombie, G., T. Abarbanel, and A. Trinneer. 2002. All-female classes in high school computer science: Positive effects in three years of data. *Journal of Educational Computing Research* 27, no. 4:385–409.

Crombie, G., and P. I. Armstrong. 1999. Effects of classroom gender composition on adolescents' computer-related attitudes and future intentions. *Journal of Educational Computing Research* 20, no. 4:317–327.

DeRidder, L. 1990. *The Impact of Parents and Parenting on Career Development*. Knoxville, TN: Comprehensive Career Development Project.

Dilevko, J., and R. Harris. 1997. Information technology and social relations: Portrayals of gender roles in high tech product advertisements. *Journal of the American Society for Information Science* 48, no. 8:718–727.

Dryburgh, H. 2000. Underrepresentation of girls and women in computer science: Classification of 1990s' research. *Journal of Educational Computing Research* 23, no. 2:181–202.

Dugdale, S., E. DeKoven, and M. K. Ju. 1998. Computer course enrollment, home computer access, and gender: Relationships to high school students' success with computer spreadsheet use for problem solving in pre-algebra. *Journal of Educational Computing Research* 18, no. 1:49–62.

Dunham, P. H. 1990. *Procedures to increase the entry of women in mathematics-related careers*. Columbus, OH: ERIC Clearinghouse for Science Mathematics and Environmental Education.

Durndell, A., P. Glissov, and G. Siann. 1995. Gender and computing: Persisting differences. *Educational Research* 37, no. 3:219–227.

Durndell, A., and K. Thomson. 1997. Gender and computing: A decade of change? *Computers and Education* 28, no. 1:1–9.

Eckert, P. 1994. Entering the Heterosexual Marketplace: Identities of Subordination as a Developmental Imperative. Working Papers on Learning and Identity 2. Palo Alto, CA: Institute for Research on Learning.

Eckert, P. 1995. Adolescent trajectory and forms of institutional participation. In *Pathways through adolescence: Individual development in relation to social contexts*, ed. Lisa Crockett and Ann Crouter (pp. 175–196). Hillsdale, NJ: Lawrence Erlbaum.

Eckert, P. 1997. Gender, race, and class in the preadolescent marketplace of identities. Paper presented at the ninety-sixth annual meeting of the American Anthropological Association, Washington, DC.

Elkjær, B. 1992. Girls and information technology in Denmark: An account of a socially constructed problem. *Gender and Education* 1/2:25–40.

Ertmer, P. A., A. Addison, M. Lane, E. Ross, and D. Woods. 1999. Examining teachers' beliefs about the role of technology in the elementary classroom. *Journal of Research on Computing in Education* 32, no. 1:54–72.

Evans-Andris, M. 1995. An examination of computing styles among teachers in elementary schools. *Educational Technology Research and Development* 43, no. 2:15–31.

Fagot, B., R. Hagen, M. Leinback, and S. Kronsberg. 1985. Differential reactions to assertive and communicative acts of toddler boys and girls. *Child Development* 56:1499–1505.

Farmer, H. S. 1995. Gender differences in adolescent career exploration. *ERIC Clearinghouse on Counseling and Student Services*. Greensboro, NC: ERIC Digest.

Faulkner, W., K. Sorensen, H. Gansmo, E. Rommes, L. Pitt, V. Lagesen Berg, C. McKeogh, P. Preston, R. Williams, and J. Stewart. 2004. *Strategies of inclusion: Gender and the information society*. Edinburgh: SIGIS.

Fellows, M. R. 1993. Mathematicians and education reform, 1990–1991. *Conference board of the mathematical sciences: Issues in mathematics education* 3:143–163.

Fitzpatrick, H., and M. Hardman. 2000. Mediated activity in the primary classroom: Girls, boys, and computers. *Learning and Instruction* 10, no. 5:431–446.

Fletcher-Flinn, C. M., and T. Suddendorf. 1996. Computer attitudes, gender, and exploratory behavior: A developmental study. *Journal of Educational Computing Research* 15, no. 4:369–392.

Frantom, C. G., K. E. Green, and E. R. Hoffman. 2002. Measure development: The children's attitude towards technology scale (CATS). *Journal of Educational Computing Research* 26, no. 3:249–263.

Freeman, N. K., and J. Somerindyke. 2001. Social play at the computer: Preschoolers scaffold and support peers' computer competence. *Information Technology in Childhood Education Annual*: 203–213.

Freeman, P., and W. Aspray. 1999. *The supply of information technology workers in the United States*. Washington, DC: Computing Research Association.

Gerbner, G. 1969. The television world of violence. In *Mass media and violence*, ed. D. Lange, R. Baker, and S. Ball. Washington, DC: U.S. Government Printing Office.

Gilligan, C. 1982. *In a different voice*. Cambridge, MA: Harvard University Press.

Goffman, E. 1979. *Gender advertisements*. Cambridge, MA: Harvard University Press.

Gonder, P. O. 1991. *Caught in the middle: How to unleash the potential of average students*. Arlington, VA: American Association of School Administrators.

Griffiths, A. K., and N. P. Heath. 1996. High school students' views about technology. *Research in Science and Technological Education* 14, no. 2:153–162.

Guha, S. 2001. Integrating computers in elementary grade classroom instruction: Analysis of teachers' perceptions in present and preferred situations. *Journal of Educational Computing Research* 24, no. 3:275–303.

Guha, S. 2003. Are we all technically prepared? Teachers' perspective on the causes of comfort or discomfort in using computers at elementary grade teaching. *Information Technology in Childhood Education Annual* 24, no. 3:317–349.

Hanor, J. 1998. Concepts and strategies learned from girls' interactions with computers. *Theory into Practice* 37, no. 1:64–71.

Harrell, W. 1998. Gender and equity issues effecting educational computer use. *Equity and Excellence in Education* 31, no. 13:46–48.

Harsha, P. 2004. *NSF funding outlook grim but cyberinfrastructure's a priority, says NSF director*. ⟨http://www.cra.org/govaffairs/blog/archives/000084.html⟩.

Helwig, A. A. 1998. Gender-role stereotyping: Testing theory with a longitudinal sample. *Sex Roles: A Journal of Research* 42, no. 5–6:403–423.

Howe, K. 1993. Equality of educational opportunity and the criterion of equal educational worth. *Studies in Philosophy and Education* 11:329–337.

Howe, K. 1997. Gender. In *Understanding equal educational opportunity: Social justice, democracy, and schooling*. New York: Teachers College Press.

Huff, C. 1996. Unintentional power in the design of computer systems. *Computers and Society*: 6–9.

Huff, C., and J. Cooper. 1987. Sex bias in educational software: The effect of designers' stereotypes on the software they design. *Journal of Applied Social Psychology* 17, no. 6:512–532.

Jenson, J., and C. Brushwood Rose. 2003. Women@work: Listening to gendered relations of power in teachers' talk about new technologies. *Gender and Education* 15, no. 2:169–181.

Jesse, J. K. 2004. The digital divide: Political myth or political reality? In *Chasing Moore's law: Information technology policy in the United States*, ed. W. Aspray. Raleigh, NC: SciTech Publishing.

Jones, T., and V. A. Clark. 1995. Diversity as a determinant of attitudes: A possible explanation of the apparent advantage of single-sex settings. *Journal of Educational Computing Research* 12, no. 1:51–64.

Kafai, Y., and S. Sutton. 1999. Elementary school students' computer and Internet use at home: Current trends and issues. *Journal of Educational Computing Research* 21, no. 3:345–362.

Kiesler, S., L. Sproull, and J. S. Eccles. 1985. Pool halls, chips, and war games: Women in the culture of computing. *Psychology of Women Quarterly* 9, no. 4:451–462.

Kinnear, A. 1995. Introduction of microcomputers: A case study of patterns of use and children's perceptions. *Journal of Educational Computing Research* 13, no. 1:27–40.

Kirkpatrick, H., and L. Cuban. 1998. Should we be worried? What the research says about gender differences in access, use, attitudes, and achievement with computers. *Educational Technology* 38, no. 4:56–61.

Kling, K. C., J. S. Hyde, C. Showers, B. Buswell. 1999. Gender differences in self-esteem: A meta-analysis. *Psychological Bulletin* 125:470–500.

Koch, C., and R. Upitis. 1996. Is equal computer time fair for girls? Potential Internet inequities. In *Proceedings of the 6th Annual Conference of the Internet Society*. Reston, VA: The Internet Society.

Koch, M. 1994. No girls allowed! *Technos: Quarterly for Education and Technology* 3, no. 3:14–17.

Lankard, B. A. 1995. *Family role in career development. ERIC Digest*, no. 164. Columbus, OH: ERIC Clearinghouse on Adult Career and Vocational Education.

Lee, V. 1998. Is single-sex secondary schooling a solution to the problem of gender inequity? In *Separated by sex: A critical look at single-sex education for girls*, ed. American Association of University Women. Washington, DC: American Association of University Women Foundation.

Levin, B. B., and S. M. Barry. 1997. Children's views of technology: The role of age, gender, and school setting. *Journal of Computing in Childhood Education* 8, no. 4:267–290.

Levine, T., and S. Donitsa-Schmidt. 1995. Computer experience, gender, and classroom environment in computer-supported writing classes. *Journal of Educational Computing Research* 13, no. 4:337–357.

Levine, T., and S. Donitsa-Schmidt. 1998. Computer use, confidence, attitudes, and knowledge: A causal analysis. *Computers in Human Behavior* 14, no. 1:125–146.

Li, Q. 1999. Teachers' beliefs and gender differences in mathematics: A review. *Educational Research* 41, no. 1:63–76.

Light, P., K. Littleton, S. Bale, R. Joiner, and D. Messer. 2000. Gender and social comparison effects in computer-based problem solving. *Learning and Instruction* 10:483–496.

Lupart, J., and E. Cannon. 2002. Computers and career choices: Gender differences in grades seven and ten students. *Gender, Technology, and Development* 6, no. 2:233–248.

Lynn, K.-M., C. Raphael, K. Olefsky, and C. M. Bachen. 2003. Bridging the gender gap in computing: An integrative approach to content design for girls. *Journal of Educational Computing Research* 28, no. 2:143–162.

Maboudian, W. 2000. Gender representation in visuals on school Web pages: Course for in-service teachers. *Society for Information Technology and Teacher Education International Conference 2000*, no. 1:276–281. Available at ⟨http://dl.aace.org/489⟩.

Margolis, J., and A. Fisher. 2002. *Unlocking the clubhouse: Women in computing.* Cambridge, MA: MIT Press.

Miller, L., M. Chaika, and L. Groppe. 1996. Girls' preferences in software design: Insights from a focus group. *Interpersonal Computing and Technology: An Electronic Journal for the Twenty-first Century* 4, no. 2:27–37.

Miller, L. M., H. Schweingruber, and C. L. Brandenburg. 2001. Middle school students' technology practices and preferences: Reexamining gender differences. *Journal of Educational Multimedia and Hypermedia* 10, no. 2:125–140.

Mortimer, J., K. Lee, and C. Lee. 1992. *Influences on adolescents' vocational development.* Berkeley, CA: National Center for Research in Vocational Education.

Moses, M. S., K. R. Howe, and T. Niesz. 1999. The pipeline and student perceptions of schooling: Good news and bad news. *Educational Policy* 13, no. 4:573–591.

Muller, C. B. 2002. The underrepresentation of women in engineering and related sciences: Pursuing two complementary paths to parity. In *Pan-organizational summit on the U.S. science and engineering workforce*, ed. Marye Ann Fox (pp. 119–126). Washington, DC: National Academies Press.

Mullis, R. L., A. K. Mullis, and D. Gerwels. 1998. Stability of vocational interests among high school students. *Adolescence* 33:699–707.

National Center for Educational Statistics. 2003. National Assessment of Educational Progress. *Education Statistics Quarterly* 5, no. 4.

National Center for Educational Statistics. 2004. *NAEP data tool.* ⟨http://nces.ed.gov/nationsreportcard/naepdata/getdata.asp⟩.

National Research Council. 1999. *Being fluent with information technology.* Washington, DC: National Academy Press.

National Telecommunications and Information Administration, with the Economics and Statistics Administration. 2002. *A nation online: How Americans are expanding their use of the Internet.* Washington, DC: NTIA.

Naylor, M. 1986. Family influences on employment and education: Overview. *ERIC Digest*, no. 56. Columbus, OH: ERIC Clearinghouse on Adult Career and Vocational Education.

Noddings, N. 1984. *Caring, a feminine approach to ethics and moral education*. Berkeley: University of California Press.

Oberman, P. 2002. Academic help-seeking in the high school computer science classroom: Relationship to motivation, achievement, gender, and ethnicity. PhD diss., Emory University.

Paoletti, J. 1997. The gendering of infants' and toddlers' clothing in America. In *The material culture of gender/the gender of material culture*, ed. K. Martinez and K. Ames. Wilmington, DE: Henry Francis du Pont Winterthur Museum.

President's Council on Physical Fitness and Sports. 1997. *Physical activity and sport in the lives of girls: Physical and mental health dimensions from an interdisciplinary approach.* Washington, DC: U.S. Department of Health and Human Services.

Raffini, J. 1993. *Winners without losers: Structures and strategies for increasing student motivation to learn.* Needham Heights, MA: Allyn and Bacon.

Rayman, P., and B. Brett. 1993. *Pathways for women in the sciences.* Wellesley report, vol. 1. Wellesley College Center for the Study of Women, Wellesley, MA.

Sadker, M., and D. Sadker. 1995. *Failing at fairness: How our schools cheat girls.* New York: Touchstone.

Sanders, J. 2002. Snatching defeat from the jaws of victory: When good projects go bad; girls and computer science. Paper presented at the annual meeting of the American Educational Research Association, New Orleans.

Sax, L. J., M. Ceja, and R. T. Teranishi. 2001. Technological preparedness among entering freshmen: The role of race, class, and gender. *Journal of Educational Computing Research* 24, no. 4:363–383.

Schaumburg, H. 2001. Fostering girls' computer literacy through laptop learning: Can mobile computers help to level out the gender difference? Paper presented at the National Educational Computing Conference, Chicago.

Schott, G., and N. Selwyn. 2000. Examining the "male, antisocial" stereotype of high computer users. *Journal of Educational Computing Research* 23, no. 3:291–303.

Selwyn, N. 1998. What's in the box: Exploring learners' rejection of educational computing. *Educational Research and Evaluation* 4, no. 3:193–212.

Shashaani, L. 1994. Gender differences in computer experience and its influence on computer attitudes. *Journal of Educational Computing Research* 11, no. 4:347–367.

Sheehan, R. 2003. Children's perception of computer programming as an aid to designing programming environments. In *Interaction design and children: Proceeding of the 2003 conference on interaction design and children.* New York: ACM Press.

Silverman, S., and A. M. Pritchard. 1993. *Building their future: Girls in technology and education in Connecticut.* Hartford: Connecticut Women's Education and Legal Fund.

Singh, P. 1993. Institutional discourse: A case study of the social construction of technical competence in the primary classroom. *British Journal of Sociology of Education* 14, no. 1:39–58.

Snyder, L. 2003. *Fluency with information technology: Skills, concepts, capabilities.* Washington, DC: Addison-Wesley.

Stepulvage, L. 2001. Gender/technology relations: Complicating the gender binary. *Gender and Education* 13, no. 3:325–338.

Stepulvage, L., and S. Plumeridge. 1998. Women taking positions within computer science. *Gender and Education* 10, no. 3:313–326.

Stecher, B. M. 2002. Consequences of large-scale, high-stakes testing on school and classroom practice. In *Making sense of test-based accountability in education*, ed. L. S. Hamilton, B. M. Stecher, and S. P. Klein. Santa Monica, CA: Rand Corporation.

Svitavsky, W. 2001. Geek culture: An annotated interdisciplinary bibliography. *Bulletin of Bibliography* 58, no. 2:101–108.

Taylor, A. 2003. Finding the future that fits. Paper presented at the eighty-fourth annual meeting of the American Educational Research Association, Chicago.

Thorne, B. 1992. Girls and boys together ... but mostly apart: Gender arrangements in elementary schools. In *Education and gender equality*, ed. J. Wrigley. London: Falmer Press.

Tracy, K. 2002. *Everyday talk: Building and reflecting identities.* New York: Guilford Press.

Tucker, A. E., F. Deek, J. Jones, D. McCowan, C. Stephenson, and A. Verno. 2003. *K–12 task force.* ⟨http://www.acm.org/education/k12/⟩.

Van Braak, J. 2001. Individual characteristics influencing teachers' class use of computers. *Journal of Educational Computing Research* 25, no. 2:141–157.

Webster's. 2003. *New millennium dictionary of English.* Los Angeles: Lexico Publishing Group, LLC.

Whiston, S. C., and B. K. Keller. 2004. The influences of the family of origin on career development: A review and analysis. *The Counseling Psychologist* 32, no. 4:493–568.

Whitley, B. E., Jr. 1997. Gender differences in computer-related attitudes and behaviors: A meta-analysis. *Computers in Human Behavior* 13, no. 1:1–22.

Wigfield, A., and J. Eccles. 2000. Expectancy-value theory of achievement motivation. *Contemporary Educational Psychology, Special Issue: Motivation and the Educational Process* 25:68–81.

Wulf, W. A. 1999. Diversity in engineering. In *Moving beyond individual programs to systemic change.* West Lafayette, IN: Women in Engineering Programs and Advocates Network Member Services.

Wulf, W. A. 2001. *Testimony to the commission on the advancement of women and minorities in science, engineering, and technology development.*

Yelland, N., and M. Lloyd. 2001. Virtual kids of the 21st century: Understanding the children in schools today. *Information Technology in Childhood Education Annual*: 175–192.

Young, I. M. 1990. *Throwing like a girl and other essays in feminist political theory.* Bloomington: Indiana University Press.

Zimmerman, J., and G. Reavill. 1999. *Raising our athletic daughters.* New York: Main Street Books.

2

Examining the Gender Gap in IT by Race: Young Adults' Decisions to Pursue an IT Career

Nicole Zarrett, Oksana Malanchuk, Pamela E. Davis-Kean, and Jacquelynne Eccles

By the year 2010, it has been estimated that 25 percent of all new jobs created in the private and public sectors will be technologically oriented (American Association of University Women 2000). Yet access to IT is highly skewed by race, gender, and income, favoring males over females, whites over African Americans, and wealthier sectors in comparison to less privileged populations (Cooper and Weaver 2003). Although representing 46 percent of the total workforce, women account for less than 30 percent of the IT workforce (U.S. Department of Commerce 2003) and only 10 percent of executives in Fortune 500 computer companies (Xie and Shauman 2003). Despite the growing need for qualified applicants for IT positions, the number of women in advanced IT careers actually continues to decline (Information Technology Association of America 2003; Panteli, Stack, and Ramsay 2001). Likewise, blacks, who make up more than 12 percent of the U.S. population, only represent 5 percent of the IT field (U.S. Department of Commerce 2003); their proportion in IT to their presence in the national population is well below average. The purpose of the current investigation is to examine factors that might be influential in developing individuals' IT career aspirations, and how they may differ by race and gender, in order to gain a greater understanding of the gender and race gaps in the computer industry.

Inequality in the labor force results from a process of differentiation that begins and accumulates in the earlier stages of life decisions. Thus, decisions made regarding schooling and choices of course work may well determine whether or not you pursue a college education and the particular major you choose to complete. For example, families who provide early access to computers are more likely to have children, both boys and girls, who pursue math, science, and computer-related courses (Simpkins, Davis-Kean, and Eccles 2005). Research has begun to uncover factors that are necessary to increase equity in IT, such as providing youth greater access to computers (National Center for Education Statistics 2003; U.S. Department of Commerce 2003), creating computer programs that appeal to all children, and getting key socializers involved (parents, teachers, etc.) who can help change girls' and boys' attitudes toward computers and who encourage youth to perceive themselves as good at computer tasks (American Association of University Women 2004). But more work is needed in order to delineate the specifics of what works and for whom.

Although trends found for the underrepresentation of women and blacks in IT run parallel, research that has investigated these groups independently suggests that many of the underlying barriers that prevent women from entering IT are different from those that create disparities in IT by race (Garcia and Giles 2003). Little attention has been paid to the intersectionality of these group identities (interaction of race and gender) as they are related to pursuing a career in IT. In this chapter, we attempt to address these issues by examining factors that might be influential in developing individuals' IT career aspirations, and how they may differ by race and gender. Utilizing the Eccles model and theory on the development of expectations and values (Eccles et al. 1983), the current investigation examines adolescents' pursuit of IT as a dynamic process that includes the consideration of multiple social, psychological, and structural factors in adolescents' developmental trajectories that are influential to their educational and occupational choices.

The Expectancy-Value Model

According to the Eccles expectancy-value model, achievement motivation (performance, persistence, and task choice) is directly linked to two primary components: a person's expectations for success and the value that the individual attaches to various options. Expectancies and values have consistently been shown to predict both academic success (Eccles et al. 1983; Eccles, Adler, and Meece 1984; Meece, Wigfield, and Eccles 1990) and academic and occupational choices (Eccles, Barber, and Jozefowicz 1998). Previous research indicates that both expectancies and values may be key components of youths ultimately deciding to pursue a career in IT. That is, males and females have been found to differ on measures directly assessing expectations for success in computer-related tasks, and this might be a primary factor influencing women's choice to pursue an occupation other than one in the IT field. For example, among college students in Canada, Brosnan (1998) found that female students reported being less comfortable and confident with the computer than male students. They also felt more inhibited about pursuing IT careers because of the anxiety they experienced whenever they had to work with computers. This gender disparity was also found in Spain (Farina et al. 1991), Great Britain (Colley, Gale, and Harris 1994), Australia (Okebukola and Woda 1993), and the United States (Reinen and Plomp 1997).

In addition, males and females have been found to differ on the interest they have toward computers and the value they place on entering the IT field. The American Association of University Women (2000) captured this premise best when it stated in a report, "Girls are engaged with the world, while boys are engaged with computers." The association found that many girls insist on their computing abilities and skills, while simultaneously describing their disenchantment with the field, its careers, and its social context (ibid.). It is unclear, however, how perceptions of value and ability as well as its influence on individuals' IT pursuits may differ by the intersection of race and gender. Therefore, we believe that in order to understand youths' IT career decisions, it is important to not only consider the direct influence of early social psychological factors on adolescents' IT aspirations but also to examine how these early experiences indirectly influence youths' later career considerations through how they shape youths' expectancies and values regarding computer-related careers three years after high school (see appendix 2.1 for a modified Eccles expectancy-value model).

Determinants of Pursuing an IT Career

In addition to youths' socioeconomic status and academic achievement as measured in the eighth grade, early determinants thought to play a key role in adolescents' later IT-related career pursuits three years after high school included: access to a home computer, perceptions of ability and interest in math, concerns about race and gender discrimination, and academic expectations for IT's general influence on youths' later career decisions (Simpkins, Davis-Kean, and Eccles 2004; Vida and Eccles 2003). Moreover, both the positive and negative attitudes that youths held toward computers and the advice and encouragement they received from others about pursuing IT three years after high school were also considered.

Home Resources   Research suggests that having early and consistent access to a computer is at least one means of nurturing individuals' interest and feelings of competency in computer tasks in addition to advancing one's computer skills. Nelson and Cooper (1997) found that the more experience a child had with computers, the more competent they felt and the more positive their attitude was toward computer-related tasks. By age ten, boys had significantly more access to and experience with computers than did girls, and this seemed to translate into differential feelings of competence by the fifth grade. Access to a home computer has also been thought to play a major role in blacks' underrepresentation in IT (Papadakis 2000; National Center for Education Statistics 2003).

Although the gap between those who have access and those who do not has decreased in recent years, there still remains a major divide in computer and Internet use along demographic and socioeconomic lines in which blacks and Hispanics are still among those with the least amount of access (National Center for Education Statistics 2003; U.S. Department of Commerce 2004). According to the Department of Commerce Census Bureau Survey of September 2001, 60.2 percent of blacks were still not connected to the Internet (and 68.4 percent of all Hispanics) (posted November 2004). The U.S. Board of Education attributes much of the later racial/ethnic differences in computer skill and use to this difference found in home access. When only looking at the children who had access to a computer at home, few of the differences found between black and white youths remain (National Center for Education Statistics 2003). Access to home computers may also be an issue for children from lower socioeconomic backgrounds. The National Center for Education Statistics (2003) found that children with more highly educated parents as well as those living with higher family incomes have greater access to computers than those of less-educated and/or lower-income households.

Having a computer in the home has not only been found to be related to interest and feelings of competency toward computers but appears to be highly influential for keeping youths in the pipeline. Access has been found to relate to higher achievement in math and reading (Atwell and Battle 1999), the choice of math and science courses in high school (Simpkins, Davis-Kean, and Eccles under review), and achievement in college-level programming courses (Bunderson and Christensen 1995; Byrne and Lyons 2001). With this research in mind, we examined our sample of youths to determine if similar race differences existed in access to computers in the home.

Math Self-Concept and Values   Despite strides in girls' participation and performance in math and science courses in the past decade, gender gaps in adolescents' confidence and value/interest in mathematics and physical science remain (Margolis and Fisher 2002; Fennema 2000; Xie and Shauman 2003; Linver and Davis-Kean forthcoming). In studies of normative populations, Eccles and her colleagues have found consistent evidence of gender differences in expectations for success and confidence in one's abilities for math (especially among junior and senior high school students) (e.g., Eccles et al. 1993; Linver and Davis-Kean forthcoming). Consistent findings, detected as early as among first graders, suggest that boys are more confident and interested in math than are girls. Therefore, because computer science is commonly grouped with math and science (both informally and organizationally) (Margolis and Fisher 2002), a lack of confidence and interest in math early on may lead individuals to opt out of more advanced math-related courses like computer science.

Race and Gender Discrimination   Wilder, Mackie, and Cooper (1985) looked at a sample of women who attended Princeton University and not only had advanced mathematics preparation (80 percent of the sample studied calculus in high school) but also had as much experience and knowledge of programming languages as the male students examined. Despite the fact that the women's computer skills and knowledge were not objectively different from the males, the researchers discovered that the women perceived themselves as less capable of computer tasks than the males. Even more surprisingly, when Wilder, Mackie, and Cooper explored perceived computer competence by computer experience, they found that females who had computer experience in high school rated themselves as less comfortable or competent than did the males who had no high school computing experience. These findings were only to be replicated once again at Princeton seventeen years later (Cooper and Weaver 2003) and elsewhere (Beyer et al. 2003), suggesting that the digital divide results from more than just gender differences in experience or skill, and highlighting the persistence and cultural embeddedness of what defines the computer industry.

Some researchers (American Association of University Women 2000, 2004; Cooper and Weaver 2003) assert that the computer gender disparity and its persistence is primarily a result of the genderization of the IT profession. Girls and boys alike tend to view the computer world/professionals as male (Nelson and Cooper 1997; American Association of University Women 2000). For example, the American Association of University Women (2000) found that although its sample of middle school girls rarely reported overt discrimination (they were not told they were less competent than boys at computer-related tasks or discouraged from enrolling in computer-related courses), when asked to describe a person who "is really good with computers," they consistently described a man. Chappel (1996) and others (Cooper and Weaver 2003; American Association of University Women 2000,

2004; Kaiser Family Foundation 1999) explain that the idea of the "computer as male" likely emerges because computer programs and games favor male interests as well as male identification. Girls, in response, are likely to feel greater anxiety or reticence toward an activity that has been clearly delineated as one that is not for them.

The message relayed to women that they are "outsiders" in the IT profession is only further reinforced in the workplace by the sheer lack of women in the field. Not only are women underrepresented in the field but those women who persist in IT are often found in the lower-status and lower-paying IT jobs. In the United Kingdom (Panteli, Stack, and Ramsay 2001) as well as the United States and Europe (Tijdens 1997), women in the IT profession were found to be markedly underrepresented in the higher levels of IT (management, hardware, and systems and software design were almost exclusively male) and vastly overrepresented at the lower levels (customer service and support fields). These statistics lead us to ask if the underrepresentation of women and blacks in IT might be due, at least to some degree, to an awareness of overt forms of gender and race discrimination that are known to exist in the higher echelons of such (prestigious) professions as IT. Further research is necessary to decipher whether women's underrepresentation in the higher levels of IT is due to differences in course work or other preparation to enter the field or to the basic discrimination that occurs in the computer industry and its prerequisites. In the current investigation, we examined how adolescents' expectations concerning their experience with gender discrimination may influence their decisions to pursue an IT career and/or its impact on the expectancies and values they have toward the field. Youths' feeling of inefficacy to combat race discrimination was also assessed as another type of discrimination that may help explain the underrepresentation of blacks in IT-related careers.

Attitudes toward Computers   We also explored adolescents' attitudes toward the IT field as another way to determine whether women disidentify with "male" characteristics often attributed to the computer field (and its employees). For example, Eccles, Barber, and Jozefowicz (1998) found that female students were more likely to value people-oriented careers than male students, and that male students placed a higher value on wealth and competitive positions and were generally more interested in careers that involved the use of machinery, math, and/or computers. Likewise, Margolis and Fisher (2002) found that among college students' interested in computer science, undergraduate women were interested in computer science as a "tool" to solve real-world problems (e.g., in biomedical research), while the men tended to value computers and computing for their own sake. Although computing is an integral part of medical research, environmental science, art, music, famine control, and so on, the way in which computer science is portrayed in the classroom and by the wider society as a solitary field primarily focused on technical detail may be a major reason why women opt out of the IT field (Margolis and Fisher 2002; American Association of University Women 2000). In the current study, youths' attitudes toward the technology field was examined by asking them whether they agreed with some of the common positive and negative attitudes that exist toward computers.

Others' Encouragement and Advice   Previous research has shown that when children receive different feedback on their performance in various school subjects, different advice regarding the importance of certain subjects, different information about the occupational opportunities they should be considering, and different opportunities for developing various skills, then it is likely that they will develop different self-perceptions and expectations for success as well as different ideas for which domains they are best suited (Jacobs and Eccles 1992; Eccles, Barber, and Jozefowicz 1998). With continued reinforcement for traditional gender role behaviors and values by parents, teachers, peers, and other socializers, the likelihood that youths will acquire nontraditional skills and values or pursue such long-term goals is diminished. Therefore, we asked youths whether they received supportive advice and encouragement from others about pursuing an IT career to determine whether groups differed in the degree of support they received from others dependent on their gender and race as well as how this support might be influential on youths' IT-related occupational attitudes (expectancies, values, and aspirations).

Summary of Research Questions
Consistent with previous research concerned with keeping women (and minorities) in the math and science pipeline (Eccles 1994; Eccles, Barber, and Jozefowicz 1998; Margolis and Fisher 2002; Xie and Shauman 2003; Garcia and Giles 2003), the current investigation examines how earlier psychological and sociocultural factors, measured when participants' were in the eighth and eleventh grades as well as three years after high school, relate to adolescents' aspirations to pursue an IT career three years after high school both directly and indirectly, through their relation to youths' expectancies and values of computer occupations (see appendix 2.1 for

the research model). Our main focus is to understand the gender and race gap in the computer industry, so we pay close attention to how these early factors may differentially affect adolescents' occupational pursuits dependent on their race and gender.

Sample and Methods

Participants are from the Maryland Adolescent Development in Context Study (MADICS) (P. I. Jacquelynne Eccles and Arnold Sameroff), a community-based longitudinal study of adolescents and their families aimed at examining the influences of social context on the psychological determinants of behavioral choices and developmental trajectories during adolescence. The sample is a purposive subsample (based on the parents' willingness to participate and a stratified sampling procedure designed to get proportional representations of families from each of the twenty-three middle schools being studied) of the Comer and Cook school evaluation study, which included all enrolled seventh graders in the district in September 1991. Although the participants are not a random sample of their cohort, there is little systematic bias in the MADICS sample when compared to the larger Comer and Cook sample.

The sample of 1,482 adolescents (49 percent female) and their families is unique in that it includes a large proportion of African American families (61 percent African American and 35 percent Euro-American), with as broad a range of socioeconomic status as the Euro-American families (mean pretax family income in 1990: $42,500–52,500; range $5,000–75,000). The sample is drawn from an eastern U.S. county composed of rural and urban settings, and both low- and high-income neighborhoods.

Longitudinal data were collected at six time points. The first four waves of data were collected from multiple informants (parents, youths, and school record data) and included demographic information from the parents. Wave 1 was collected in fall 1991 (when the adolescents were in the seventh grade and the first year of middle school); wave 2 was collected in summer 1992; wave 3 was collected in summer/fall 1993 in conjunction with the transition into high school; wave 4 in 1996 when the youths were in the eleventh grade; wave 5 in 1998—one year after most of the youths had graduated from high school; and wave 6 in 2000—three years after high school. Waves 1, 3, and 4 involved in-home interviews and self-administered questionnaires. As often as possible, the interviewer's race was matched to that of the primary caregiver. Wave 2 was a telephone interview designed to get specific information on parents' family management strategies and goals for their children. Waves 5 and 6 were mailed questionnaires to the adolescents only.[1]

Using a combination of mailed surveys and telephone interviews (coupled with a variety of tracking strategies, including earlier parent contacts, the State Motor Vehicle Department records, social security numbers, and forwarding address information available from the post office), MADICS retained at both waves 3 and 4 over 70 percent of the original wave 1 sample. At wave 5, the retention rate for the target youths was still about 62 percent of the original wave 1 sample. At wave 6, it was about the same.

For the present investigation, we report on information collected at three time points: after adolescents completed the eighth grade (mean age = 14.2) (wave 3: spring 1994), when they were in the eleventh grade (mean age = 17.1 years) (wave 4: 1996), and when they were three years post high school (wave 6: 2000). The longitudinal sample (that participated at each of these waves *and* responded to all our measures) included 118 African American males, 147 African American females, 80 Euro-American males, and 98 Euro-American females. Other ethnic groups were not included in the analysis due to the small sample size (e.g., 25 youths self-identified as Asian American or a mixed ethnic group).

In order to determine how the indicators studied differed by groups, univariate analyses of variance were run separately for each indicator of IT pursuits examined. Including the whole sample to get the most power out of our analyses, we used post hoc contrasts for comparisons between groups. All reported findings of differences between groups were significant at the $p < .05$ level according to Bonferroni standards.[2] Second, bivariate correlation analyses were used to look at the direct relation between the social psychological indicators and the IT aspirations as well as their indirect relation to the IT aspirations through examining how they related to youths' IT expectancies and values.[3] These analyses included only the longitudinal sample.

IT Aspirations   In order to assess adolescents' potential to pursue an IT career three years after high school, we asked them, "Have you ever considered getting a job in IT? If so, which ones?" Jobs in IT fields were coded into two categories: "soft" and "hard" computer jobs. Soft computer jobs included such occupations as Internet journalism, research, telecommunications, help desk, resource guides, teaching, and "statistics." Some adolescents reported already being in the IT field, but needing training. They were mainly in audio/stereo sales or secretarial work, coded as soft IT occupations. Hard computer jobs included network/systems administrator, information systems/technology, programmer/computer engineer, and so forth. Responses were then coded as 1 = no consideration, 2 = considering pursuing a soft IT career, and 3 = considering pursuing a hard IT career. Adolescents' who reported pursuing a college major in the computer science field were coded as having the highest potential for considering and eventually establishing themselves in a computer-related occupation (coded as 4). A college major in IT included such fields as computer programming, computer science, and computer art.

IT Expectancies   Eccles and her colleagues (1983) define expectancies as individuals' beliefs about how well they will do on upcoming tasks (with a specific focus on personal efficacy expectations). Therefore, in the current study, expectations for success were measured by asking participants to consider "how good they thought they would be at an occupation that used computers for hard computer tasks" (hard computer jobs consisted of developing hardware, software, Web sites, graphic arts, media interface, or programming) as well as soft computer tasks (such jobs as communications, accounting, word processing, business related/inventory maintenance, etc.). (See appendix 2.2 for sample item, scale means, and alpha.)

IT Values   The value component of the model is defined by four components: attainment value, intrinsic value, utility value, and cost. In the current study, we will be focusing specifically on intrinsic value, or the enjoyment the individual gets from performing the activity and/or the subjective interest the individual has in the domain. Sample items, scale means, and alphas of these and other indicators used in our analyses are included in appendix 2.2.

Results

IT Expectancies, Values, and Career Aspirations

According to the Eccles expectancy-value model, adolescents' task-specific expectancies of success and interest are important predictors of their academic and occupational pursuits. Therefore, we first examined how IT expectancies and values, as measured three years after high school, related to youths' IT-related career considerations. In support of the Eccles model, the current investigation found that adolescents' expectancies of success and interest in the computer field three years after high school were strongly related to their IT career aspirations.

Expectancies of success (self-concept of ability) at hard computer tasks were related to IT aspirations for all groups examined (BM, $r = .28$; BF, $r = .33$; WM, $r = .31$; WF, $r = .39$) as were expectations of success at soft IT jobs for all groups except white males (BM, $r = .25$; BF, $r = .32$; WF, $r = .24$). That is, for the groups explored, the belief that they would be good at IT tasks resulted in the pursuit of an IT career. These findings support our premise that self-concept of computer ability is a primary factor that promotes the gender differentiation of those who consider pursuing IT from those who do not.

Although the valuing of hard computer tasks was *not* related to males' IT career, it seems to be a primary factor in women's decisions to pursue an IT career. The more that the females believed they would enjoy a computer-based job, the more likely they were to aspire for a career in IT (hard jobs: BF, $r = .21$; WF, $r = .21$; and soft jobs: BF, $r = .21$; WF, $r = .19$). These findings suggest that the development of adolescents' expectancies and values are as important to consider as youths' aspirations, if we are to gain further understanding of adolescents' occupational decisions/pathways into and out of IT.

Who Is Pursuing an IT Career?

Second, we looked at how these expectations, values, and career aspirations differed by race and gender. Gender by race differences in youths' aspirations to pursue an IT career and the level of advancement in the career (soft, hard, and computer science major) were examined using chi square analyses. A gender difference was found: black and white males were more likely to consider pursuing an IT career than white and black females ($\chi^2[3, N = 762] = 21.22$, $p = .00$). Black males were most likely to report that they are considering a career in advanced (hard) IT (adjusted standardized residual [asr] = 2.6). White males, however, were most likely to major in IT (asr = 2.3) and thus held the highest potential to pursue the field. White females were least likely to pursue an IT-related career, with 62.2 percent indicating no consideration of IT careers, and were least likely of any of the other groups to be majoring in IT (asr = -2.5). Black females, given their proportion in the sample, were most unlikely to pursue a career in hard IT (asr = -2.3) ($\chi^2[9, N = 700] = 26.03$, $p = .01$). Interestingly, for each group examined, those youths who reported considering an IT career were most likely to consider pursuit

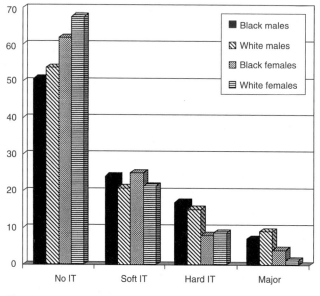

Figure 2.1
Comparison of IT career aspiration percentages between groups

of a soft IT profession. In fact, among soft IT careers, no differences between groups were found: Both black and white females were as likely to aspire to a soft IT career as were the males (see figure 2.1). These results suggest that although gender differences exist in considerations of pursuing an IT career in the higher echelons of the IT industry, females *do* consider pursuing careers in the IT field, but ultimately they aspire to pursue the less profitable, less prestigious soft computer professions.

IT Expectancies   Youths reported their perceived ability at using the computer as a tool (what we refer to as soft computer jobs) and their abilities at tasks that are considered more advanced, or hard, computer skills (such as programming, software development, etc.). When we looked at soft computer jobs (e.g., communications, accounting, word processing, etc.), no difference between groups was found ($F[3, 530] = .861$, $p = .461$). On the other hand, when asked to consider how good they would be at an occupation that used computers for hard computer jobs (e.g., developing hardware and/or software, programming, etc.), differences between the groups were apparent ($F[3, 784] = 12.37$, $p = .000$). By Bonferroni standards, black males rated themselves as more capable than both black and white females.

White males rated themselves as more capable than white females, but *not* black females. Rather, black females, perceiving themselves as good at hard computer jobs as white males, rated their ability at hard computer jobs significantly higher than did white females (see table 2.1 for means).

IT Values/Interest   When we looked at whether the groups differed in their interests in soft or hard IT careers, our findings suggest that there were no differences in their preferences for soft IT careers ($F[3, 525] = 1.37$, $p = .250$), but preferences for hard computer careers were somewhat differentiated by group ($F[3, 784] = 3.08$, $p = .027$). Black males reported they would enjoy hard computer jobs significantly more than white females. All other groups reported similar levels of enjoyment (see table 2.1 for means). Interestingly, however, when we split the sample into college and noncollege youths, we found that black females' higher computer interests were most represented by the noncollege sample.

What May Be Influencing the Pursuit of an IT Career?

Our findings above highlight the gender disparity in IT career goals among young adults three years after high school. Similar to previous research and national statistics, our findings suggest that the males held much greater potential and higher aspirations for pursuing an IT career than the females. Once we looked at differences by race, though, a different and possibly more nuanced story about women's IT career pursuits emerged. In consideration of these findings, we next examined factors thought to influence youths' IT career decisions to determine the impact they had on youths' IT career-related decisions, and how these factors and their influence differed by race and gender.

Among the indicators we studied there were similarities, but also major differences in what contributed to adolescents' IT career pursuits (their expectancies, values, and aspirations) dependent on their gender and race.

Black Females   Although white women reported feeling the least competent (expectancies) and least interested in computer tasks, and were not at all on track to pursue an IT career, the story for black females shows quite the opposite. Black females were as confident and interested in computer tasks as the males (see table 2.1 for means), and although not on track for hard computer careers, they were highly likely to consider a career in the soft computer sciences.

Table 2.1
Means and standard deviations of independent variables by race and gender

Independent variable	Race by sex group	Mean	SD	N
Parent education				
	Black males	14.17	2.44	470
	Black females	14.19	2.45	424
	White males	15.27	2.92	223
	White females	14.98	2.88	237
Parent occupation				
	Black males	67.58	21.25	292
	Black females	66.99	22.37	239
	White males	70.00	21.25	132
	White females	68.40	21.05	149
Family income				
	Black males	11.29	5.07	295
	Black females	11.02	5.37	253
	White males	12.92	4.87	151
	White females	12.62	4.62	173
Home resources				
	Black males	1.58	1.34	201
	Black females	1.63	1.38	282
	White males	2.17	1.28	126
	White females	2.24	1.34	177
Child achievement				
	Black males	−.53	.92	367
	Black females	.08	.92	363
	White males	.29	.93	165
	White females	.61	.85	182
Math self-concept				
	Black males	4.91	1.41	299
	Black females	4.61	1.59	299
	White males	4.91	1.58	152
	White females	4.81	1.66	164
Math value				
	Black males	3.02	1.00	252
	Black females	2.85	1.15	253
	White males	2.61	1.02	127
	White females	2.79	1.02	134
Education expectations				
	Black males	5.49	1.63	275
	Black females	6.28	1.59	275

Table 2.1
(continued)

Independent variable	Race by sex group	Mean	SD	N
	White males	5.58	1.61	153
	White females	6.17	1.50	162
Gender discrimination				
	Black males	1.95	.55	258
	Black females	2.36	.70	261
	White males	1.63	.38	143
	White females	2.06	.54	154
Race discrimination				
	Black males	2.36	.64	259
	Black females	2.25	.62	265
	White males	2.17	.73	146
	White females	2.24	.77	154
Computer self-concept hard				
	Black males	3.89	1.24	201
	Black females	3.48	1.45	280
	White males	3.78	1.17	126
	White females	3.11	1.29	177
Computer self-concept soft				
	Black males	4.53	1.50	109
	Black females	4.75	1.22	207
	White males	4.66	1.06	70
	White females	4.59	1.14	144
Enjoy computers hard				
	Black males	4.03	1.40	201
	Black females	3.74	1.57	281
	White males	3.78	1.26	126
	White females	3.59	1.49	176
Enjoy computers soft				
	Black males	3.95	1.75	109
	Black females	4.01	1.67	205
	White males	4.41	1.50	69
	White females	4.02	1.44	142
Positive computer attitude				
	Black males	3.42	.76	201
	Black females	3.26	.71	281
	White males	3.39	.69	125
	White females	3.40	.65	175

Table 2.1
(continued)

Independent variable	Race by sex group	Mean	SD	N
Negative computer attitude				
	Black males	4.16	.64	201
	Black females	4.17	.63	281
	White males	3.96	.71	126
	White females	3.92	.63	176
Others influence				
	Black males	1.78	.69	198
	Black females	1.81	.77	277
	White males	1.78	.72	125
	White females	1.73	.75	176

Similar to all other groups examined, black females' attitudes about computers (both positive, $r = .14$, and negative, $r = -.21$), and the encouragement and support of others ($r = .35$) three years after high school were found to be directly predictive of their aspirations to pursue an IT career during this time (see table 2.2). There were some early factors in black females' adolescent development, however, that were important for setting them on course to pursue a career in IT (or keep them out of IT) through the influence they had on the development of black females' IT-related expectancies and values (see tables 2.3 and 2.4 for relation indicators to values and expectancies, respectively). These factors included having access to a home computer during childhood (preschool through high school), high eighth-grade academic achievement, valuing math, and holding high educational expectations as measured during the eleventh grade.

Consistent with national trends, the black youth in our sample were also less likely to have had computer resources than the white adolescents ($F[3, 786] = 12.57$, $p = .000$), with black females being the least likely to have had computer resources in their home (from preschool through high school) than all other groups examined (see table 2.1 for means). Crucially, our data suggest that having access to a home computer during childhood was related to black females' expectation that they would perform well in soft IT careers (e.g., word processing, communication) ($r = .14$).

Although black females (similar to white females) expected to attain higher levels of education than did the males ($F[3, 865] = 14.80$, $p = .000$) (see table 2.1 for

Table 2.2
Correlations of independent variables with IT job potential

	IT job potential whole sample	IT job potential black males	IT job potential black females	IT job potential white males	IT job potential white females
Parent education	.048	.225**	−.085	.013	−.040
Parent occupation	.063	.132	.046	.113	.016
Family income	.038	.085	.039	−.037	.089
Race	−.05	—	—	—	—
Sex	.16***	—	—	—	—
Child aptitude	.067	.163*	.102	.056	.076
Math scores	.164**	.213*	.107	.142	.164
Math value	.103*	.074	.110	.264*	.101
Academic expectations	−.023	.034	−.085	.128	−.026
Race discrimination	.089*	.188*	.080	.111	.000
Sex discrimination	−.010	.195	.035	−.012	.009
Home resources	.045	.105	.056	−.091	.099
Computer self-concept	.283***	.340**	.257**	.298*	.267**
Computer hardware	.346***	.275***	.328***	.308**	.390***
Computer software	.232***	.252*	.322***	−.041	.236**
Positive computer	.161***	.191*	.141*	.204*	.019
Negative computer	−.212***	−.198**	.207**	.272**	.212**
Enjoy hard computer	.191***	.086	.205**	.133	.212**
Enjoy soft computer	.130**	.070	.211**	.086	.188*
Others' influence	.294***	.258**	.352***	.363***	.282***

Notes:
*$p < .05$
**$p < .01$
***$p < .001$

means), it was those who had lower educational aspirations who were most likely to enjoy a career in the hard computer sciences ($r = −.16$). These findings stand in contrast to our findings for all other groups where having high academic expectations at grade eleven was related to later having a high self-concept of ability in soft IT careers (BM, $r = .36$; WM, $r = .28$; WF, $r = .26$). In fact, the majority of the black women who reported considering soft IT were among the noncollege bound youths. Thus, the more education black females expected to attain when they were in the eleventh grade, the less interested they were in hard computer science careers three

Table 2.3
Correlations of independent variables with enjoyment in computers (value IT)

	Computer value black males		Computer value black females		Computer value white males		Computer value white females	
	Hard	Soft	Hard	Soft	Hard	Soft	Hard	Soft
Parent education	-.015	-.141	-.027	.011	.061	-.015	.046	.001
Parent occupation	-.058	.110	-.009	.098	.017	-.254+	-.032	.051
Family income	-.092	-.174	-.022	-.103	.008	-.104	.196*	.193*
Child aptitude	.112	.132	-.063	.134	.078	.015	.036	.051
Math scores	.042	.034	.035	.003	.114	-.001	-.035	.063
Math value	.019	.014	.180*	.141	.020	.027	-.029	-.048
Academic expectations	-.005	.080	-.157*	-.103	-.008	-.095	-.051	-.104
Race discrimination	-.021	-.059	.069	.067	.108	-.133	-.036	.039
Sex discrimination	-.040	-.020	-.074	.012	.053	-.091	-.115	-.179+
Home resources	.033	.044	.002	.007	.145	-.127	.014	.073
Positive computer	-.012	-.028	-.044	-.085	.011	-.118	.137	.070
Negative computer	-.056	-.101	-.108+	-.159*	-.051	.023	-.128+	-.222**
Hardware computer	.071	.065	.389***	.136	.311***	-.059	.297***	-.001
Software computer	.100	.098	.226**	.251***	.141	.293*	.219**	.366***
Others' influence	.042	.088	.079	-.006	.173+	.161	.230**	.020

Notes:
* $p < .05$
** $p < .01$
*** $p < .001$
+ $p < .10$

Table 2.4
Correlations of independent variables with perceived computer ability (IT Expectancies)

	Computer self-concept black males		Computer self-concept black females		Computer self-concept white males		Computer self-concept white females	
	Hard	Soft	Hard	Soft	Hard	Soft	Hard	Soft
Parent education	.124	.237*	-.007	.059	.097	.268*	.006	.077
Parent occupation	-.016	-.035	-.055	.005	.188+	.208	.139	.118
Family income	-.015	.047	.034	-.013	-.003	.216	.222**	.357***
Child aptitude	.002	.195	-.024	.244**	.001	.409**	.078	.145
Math scores	.074	.220*	.076	.231**	.178+	.273*	.187*	.328***
Math value	.144	.247*	.105	.099	.166	.087	.061	.104
Academic expectations	.072	.359**	.035	.146	.118	.282*	.058	.258**
Race discrimination	-.075	-.135	-.040	-.094	.002	-.174	-.049	-.071
Sex discrimination	-.081	-.018	.075	.132	-.120	-.105	.049	-.110
Home resources	.057	.064	.079	.144*	.080	.118	-.039	.066
Positive computer	.142*	.125	.049	.049	.209*	-.127	.181*	.164
Negative computer	-.315***	-.318***	-.136*	-.270***	-.158+	-.149	-.206**	-.399***
Enjoy hard computer	.071	-.100	.389***	.226**	.311***	.141	.297***	.219**
Enjoy soft computer	.065	-.098	.136	.251***	.059	.293*	.001	.366***
Others' influence	.215**	.225*	.174**	.184**	.123	.011	.370***	.219**

Notes:
* $p < .05$
** $p < .01$
*** $p < .001$
+ $p < .10$

years after high school. Although measures of socioeconomic status were not related to black women's feelings of competence around computers, their valuing of computers, or their career aspirations in IT, this finding suggests that pursuing a soft IT profession might be a viable career option for those black women who lack the resources to pursue further education or higher-prestige careers.

Black females' academic achievement was, however, important for ensuring that black females were at least on track for later considering the pursuit of an IT career. The higher the achievement in grade eight, the more black females expected to do well in a soft computer job three years after high school ($r = .24$). This is especially significant to note because black females' achievement was only higher than that of black males (see table 2.1 for means).

Additionally, we found that black females' perceptions of ability and valuing of math were indirectly influential on their IT aspirations through its relation to black females' later IT-related expectancies and values. Valuing math in eleventh grade may not have a major impact on white females' decisions to pursue an IT career but might be a prominent factor for black females' IT pursuits. Black youths were more likely to report math as interesting or important than the white youths examined ($F[3, 766] = 4.54$, $p = .004$) (see table 2.1 for means), and this valuing of math was predictive of black females' enjoyment and interest in hard computer jobs ($r = .18$). Similar to all other groups, black females perception of their math ability in eleventh grade was positively predictive of how good they thought they would be at soft computer jobs when asked three years after high school (.23). All groups held similar views of their ability at math as measured in the eleventh grade (math self-concept).

Therefore, black females who enjoyed and felt they would be good at hard or soft IT job components when asked three years after high school, were those who (likely) had access to a computer throughout their childhood, had high eighth-grade achievement, and valued and felt they were good at math, but had low academic expectations in eleventh grade. In turn, black females who enjoyed (valued) and believed in their computer competence (expectancy), as well as those who had been given advice to pursue this choice and held more positive and less negative attitudes about computers, ultimately aspired to pursue an IT-related occupation.

White Females   Whereas black females seem to be somewhat invested in the computer field, white females are clearly disenchanted by the computer industry. As reported earlier, white females expressed the least enjoyment (value) and confidence (expectancies) in computers in comparison to all other groups according to Bonferroni standards (see table 2.1). We found that there were some early determinants indirectly influential on white females' later IT aspirations through their relation to white females IT-related expectancies and values (see tables 2.3 and 2.4). Similar to the other groups examined, white females' math self-concept was a major positive predictor of their IT pursuits through its influence on their expectancies of success in the field (hard, $r = .19$; soft, $r = .36$), as was their family's socioeconomic status. Family income was positively related to whether white females enjoyed both hard and soft computer jobs ($r = .20$ and $r = .19$, respectively) and whether they thought they would be good at either ($r = .22$ and $r = .36$). Although Bonferroni post hoc contrasts indicated that white females had the highest eighth-grade achievement scores in comparison to all other groups, their high achievement was not at all related to their IT career considerations. Similar to the males, though, having high academic expectations at grade eleven was related to later having a high self-concept of ability in a soft IT career (WF, $r = .26$).

Distinctly unique to white females was the importance of expectations concerning gender discrimination as a deterrent from an IT profession, although according to Bonferroni standards, white females did not expect to experience as much gender discrimination as black females did ($F[3, 816] = 51.40$, $p = .000$). White females' expectations about gender discrimination are predictive of their aspirations to pursue an IT career indirectly through their influence on girls' interest/enjoyment in computers ($r = -.18$). Essentially, the more that white females expected to experience gender discrimination when asked in eleventh grade, the less they thought they would enjoy a soft computer job three years after high school. Such findings suggest that white females' expectations of facing gender discrimination in the pursuit of an IT career may be a primary reason why they opt out of persisting in that direction.

Similarly to black females, determinants measured three years after high school that were found to be directly influential on white females' IT aspiration included the positive and negative attitudes these females held about computers as well as the encouragement and/or advice they received from others about the IT field (see table 2.2). It should be noted that none of the groups differed in their endorsement of positive attitudes about computers (e.g., interesting people work with computers) ($F[3, 782] = 2.60$, $p = .051$) (see table 2.1 for means), and positive attitudes were related to having IT aspirations either directly (BM, $r = .19$; BF, $r = .14$; WM, $r = .20$) or indirectly through the youths' expectations of success at hard computer jobs (BM, $r = .14$; WM, $r = .21$; WF, $r = .18$) for all the groups. Groups did differ on their endorsement of negative attitudes about computers (e.g., computers are a waste of intelligence) $(F[3, 784] = 8.11$, $p = .000)$, and white females were the most likely to endorse these negative attitudes three years after high school (significantly different than black youths' attitudes by Bonferroni standards; see table 2.1 for means). This is especially important because the endorsement of negative computer attitudes was related to IT aspirations for all groups in the expected direction: adolescents who held negative attitudes toward computers were not aspiring to pursue an IT career (BM, $r = -.20$; BF, $r = -.21$; WM, $r = -.27$; WF, $r = -.21$). Additionally, the more that the youths endorsed negative attitudes about the IT profession, the less capable they felt they would be at any computer-related occupation (BM, $r = -.32$; BF, $r = -.14$; WM, $r = -.16$; WF, $r = -.21$), and among the females, those who held negative attitudes about IT were less likely to value soft IT careers (BF, $r = -.16$; WF, $r = -.22$).

As mentioned previously, our findings indicate that receiving encouragement and advice from significant others—like parents, teachers, and peers (socialization)—is an important factor in all youths' decisions to pursue an IT career. Receiving encouragement and advice from others was directly related to youths' considerations of pursuing an IT career for all groups examined (BM, $r = .26$; BF, $r = .35$; WM, $r = .36$; WF, $r = .28$). This socialization was also evident for adolescents' career aspirations through the influence it had on adolescents' perceptions of ability in both hard and soft computer jobs (range of correlations [r] from .17 to .37). These findings are especially noteworthy for white females who reported receiving the least amount of advice in comparison to all other groups (see table 2.1 for means).

Thus, while most white females shun IT as a career choice, those who aspire for an IT career three years after high school are those who have been influenced by their family and friends to go into the field, and held less negative preconceptions about the type of people who go into the field, in addition to valuing and feeling competent at hard as well as soft computer job aspects by the time of their college years. Furthermore, findings suggest that some early determinants are critical for decisions to pursue IT through their influence on the development of white females' positive IT-related expectancies and values. White females who during the eleventh grade perceived themselves as good at math, had high educational expectations, and had less of an expectation that they would experience gender discrimination in the future were more likely to aspire to an IT career because they enjoyed both hard and soft computer jobs, and believed that they would be good at them.

Black Males   Interesting findings concerning black males' IT career aspirations are also important to note here and should be considered in future programs for promoting blacks to pursue careers in IT. Black males were found to hold high regard for the computer field (positive attitudes), were confident about their computer abilities when asked three years after high school, and had equally high values for prerequisites of this field (math) as measured in the eleventh grade, yet they are still not present in the IT industry. Among black males, there were multiple early determinants found to be directly related to their later IT aspirations three years after high school, including family income, eighth-grade academic achievement, concerns about race and gender discrimination and math ability in the eleventh grade, as well as the more recent advice and encouragement that black males received about pursuing IT as measured three years after high school (see table 2.2). How much black males valued math and how far they planned to go in school (academic expectation) in the eleventh grade were also influential on their later IT aspirations through the impact these factors had on black males' perceived ability at soft IT jobs (see table 2.4).

Although black males may express similar levels of interest in pursuing an IT career as white males do, concerns about race and gender discrimination may be one reason black males eventually opt out of these occupational pursuits. Surprisingly, black males who had higher expectations of experiencing gender discrimination and greater feelings of inefficacy in combating race discrimination were more likely to aspire to an IT-related career ($r = .20$ and $r = .19$, respectively).[4] Black males' level of concern regarding their future experiences of discrimination may be dependent on their chosen career paths. Those who are pursuing more prestigious careers may be more vigilant (or simply more realistic) about the race and gender discrimination they may face as one of only a few black males to pursue employment in the field. Therefore, although black males may express similar levels of interest in pursuing an IT career as white males, concerns about or experiences of race discrimination may be one reason black males eventually opt out of these occupational pursuits.

It is also just as likely that the IT field is known to be less traditional, and thus less discriminatory, than other industries and therefore appears a promising career option to black males who are concerned about facing discrimination at work. In fact, black males in our sample held highly positive attitudes about computers and the IT field in general. According to Bonferroni standards, black males were least likely to endorse negative attitudes about computers and most likely to enjoy a computer career in comparison to all other groups examined (see table 2.1). Likewise, similar to the other groups, the advice and encouragement that black males received from others about pursuing an IT career was as predictive of later IT career decisions ($r = .26$) as for black females and white males, and they received as much of this support as did black females and white males. As previously mentioned, along with the influence of math self-concept in the eleventh grade on later IT pursuits found for all groups (BM, $r = .21$), black males' belief in the importance of math (math value) was related to black males' expectations of success at soft computer jobs ($r = .25$). This is promising because black males reported valuing math significantly more so than the white youths. Although the Eccles model and previous research findings would suggest that youths continue pursuit (and achieve) in tasks that they like and feel that they are good at (Jacobs et al. 2002), future research is needed to confirm how the math values of the black males in our sample map onto their chosen course work.

Although black males held high aspirations to pursue an IT career, their lower academic achievement in comparison to all other groups may be the primary reason black males are underrepresented in the IT industry (see table 2.1). In support of this assertion, we found that achievement was directly related to IT aspirations for black males ($r = .16$). Therefore, although black males may hold high regard for the computer field and its prerequisites, their performance in computer-related course work and exams may not be up to the standards required to successfully qualify for a job in the IT field (or continue successfully pursuing the field). In support of this premise, research by Katz et al. (2003) suggests that black males enter undergraduate computer science programs with lower math SAT scores than white and Asian males.

Other forces that may have kept our sample of black males out of IT is that they came from families with slightly lower education (in comparison to white males and females, but similar to that of black females) and held lower academic expectations themselves (lower in comparison to white females, but similar to that of white males). Black males who came from more educated families were more likely to consider pursuing a profession in IT ($r = .23$).[5] Similar to white males and white females, having high academic expectations at grade eleven related to black males later having a high self-concept of ability in a soft IT career ($r = .36$).

Hence, while it is unclear how race discrimination plays a part in black males' IT career-related pursuits, there are some factors that seem to put them on track for pursuing a career in the computer industry. They tend to hold highly positive attitudes about computers and the IT field, receive encouragement and advice from others to pursue IT, and enjoy and feel they are good at math. For these youths, it seems the major forces that work against their later IT pursuits are their lower academic achievement and academic expectations, along with, possibly, their lower socioeconomic status.

White Males   Many of the predictive factors of white males' IT pursuits were those that they reported having equal or greater access to in comparison to all other groups examined (see table 2.1): receiving encouragement and advice from others, and holding less negative attitudes about the computer field were directly related to white males' IT aspirations ($r = .36$ and $r = -.16$, respectively). In contrast, white males' value of math in eleventh grade, although significantly lower than that of black males, was directly related to their later aspiring to an IT-related career three years after high school ($r = .26$) (see table 2.2). Of the other early indicators measured when youths were in the eighth and eleventh grades, parent education ($r = .27$), academic achievement ($r = .41$), math self-concept ($r = .27$), and academic expectation ($r = .28$) were all indirectly influential on white males' IT aspirations through their positive relation to these youths' perceptions of their soft computer abilities three years after high school (see table 2.4).

Although white males, similar to black males, held lower academic expectations than the females did, having higher academic expectations at grade eleven was related to white males later having a high self-concept of ability in a soft IT field three years after high school ($r = .28$). Therefore, encouraging males to hold higher educational goals may help promote a growth in the number of males who pursue an IT career, although this intervention would likely not have much of an effect on getting more females to pursue IT.

Indeed, among white males most likely to aspire to an IT career are those who were influenced by their family and friends to do so; who held some positive, but also considerably more negative perceptions of IT workers than those who didn't go into the field; and who valued math in high school in addition to valuing and feeling competent in hard or soft IT job components. Additionally, white males who came from families that were more educated and had high academic achievement and expectations themselves early on (eighth and eleventh grades, respectively) as well as believed that they were good at math in the eleventh grade were likely to believe they were good at soft computer skills, and thus held a higher likelihood that they would ultimately aspire to an IT-related career.

Conclusions and Implications

The current findings suggest three major points concerning the differences found for IT occupational choices by gender and race: early psychological, social, and academic experiences help shape/guide youths' later career decisions; there appear to be some real-world limitations that keep some youths out of the IT pipeline; and stereotypes and discrimination, whether existent in either blatant or more subtle ways, operate to discourage underrepresented groups from pursuing an IT career.

First, our findings suggest that a strong relation exists between early psychological and sociocultural factors and the later aspirations youths have regarding the computer industry mainly through their influence on youths' development of expectancies and values regarding the field. For example, adolescents' interest in and feelings of competence toward math by the eleventh grade is important for their later enjoyment in and/or feeling of competency toward computer-oriented tasks. This finding has critical implications for future interventions. Whereas earlier experiences and attitudes may not be found by researchers to directly influence later occupational and academic behaviors/decisions (in this case, IT-related aspirations), they play a key role in shaping important precursors to youths' career decisions—namely, youths' interest/enjoyment and feelings of competency in computers. Thus, early interventions are more significant than perhaps youths have "let on" in previous research. It is also important to note that the influence and input of socializers such as parents, teachers, and peers were important factors for all the groups examined, and hence should be a focal point for promoting youths to pursue IT. Therefore, interventions focused on such issues as stressing the importance of early encouragement of children's interest and confidence in math and technical/physical sciences (because of their later influence on occupational choices), increasing computer provisions, and teaching parents to make computers a priority and value in the home are as essential as the interventions instilled in schools.

This leads to our second point: that there appear to be some real-world limitations that keep some youths from pursuing a computer science career. Socioeconomic status (parent education, occupation, and family income) was a key predictor of later IT career pursuits. These findings raise greater concern for black youths who come from families with slightly lower education and income. But it is also troublesome that we still found deficits in the amount of computer resources provided in the home for black youths in a normative sample. This racial differential between who has access to computer resources and socialization and who does not can only perpetuate the race disparities found in the IT industry. This gap between those who have access to technology and those who do not—as mentioned earlier, commonly referred to as the digital divide—only exacerbates existing social gaps in our society: those already excluded become further disadvantaged from higher positions in the U.S. economy (Latimer 2001).

Differences by race in adolescents' achievement are also an important limitation to youths' IT career pursuits, especially for black males. The black males in our sample appear to really want to establish themselves in the IT field, but many have not reached the academic achievement levels necessary to go to college and successfully pursue such a career. Computer companies, along with school counselors and parents, need to do more outreach that focuses on informing youths about what it takes to successfully pursue an IT career. For black females, future research and policy need to explore ways in which we can promote these youths to strive for the more prestigious and economically promising hard computer professions. We must encourage black females in the belief that they have a place in the upper echelons of the computer industry by providing them with greater provision of resources and more opportunities for an education after high school to realize their IT goals.

Lastly, our findings suggest the necessity for future research to address how race and gender discrimination contribute to the underrepresentation of women and blacks in the advanced computer sciences. A significant body of research documents how gender and race schemata along with stereotyped expectations are detrimental to the academic as well as career pursuits of both females (Heilman 2001; Jacobs and Eccles 1992; Wigfield et al. 2002) and some racial minorities (Powell and Butterfield 1997; Steele 1997). Overall, the current study, along with others (American Association of University Women 2000, 2004; Xie and Shauman 2003; Margolis and Fisher 2002; Cooper and Weaver 2003), strongly suggests the need to change the "face" of the computer world as to who is considered the "ideal" IT professional in order to appeal to and meet the needs of underrepresented groups. For white females especially, we need to begin by focusing on how to promote computer science as an attractive, enjoyable career option that serves multiple purposes, including those that contribute to the greater social good and the larger community.

Acknowledgments

This research is supported in part by the NSF grant #EIA–0089972 on women and minorities in IT awarded to Jacquelynne S. Eccles and Pamela Davis-Kean. The original data collection was supported by funding from the MacArthur Research Network on Successful Adolescent Development in High Risk Settings, chaired by Richard Jessor, and in part by The National Institute of Child Health and Human Development (NICHD) grant #R01-033437. We gratefully acknowledge the contributions of the following people to this project (listed alphabetically): Todd Bartko, Elaine Belansky, Celina Chatman, Diane Early, Kari Fraser, Katie Jodl, Ariel Kalil, Linda Kuhn, Karen McCarthy, Steve Peck, Rob Roeser, Arnold Sameroff, Sherri Steele, Cynthia Winston, and Carol Wong.

Appendixes

Appendix 2.1
Modified Expectancy-Value Model

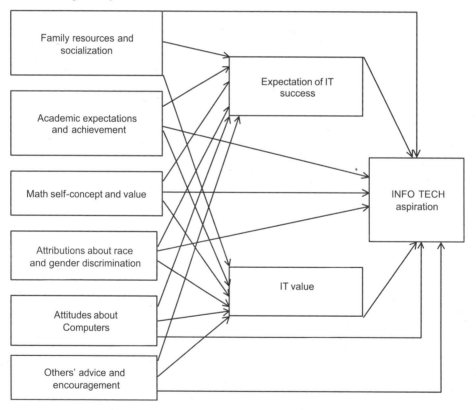

Appendix 2.2
Constructs and Measures

Scale	Reliability (Cronbach alpha)	Example item
I. Family and youth 8th grade		
Family income*	Single item	From all sources of income you mentioned, tell me your total family income before taxes in 1993.
Parents' occupational status*	Open ended	Status classified using the Nam and Powers (1983) scoring system.
Parents' education*	Single item	The highest level of education across mothers and fathers (in years).
Home resources	Single item	Did you have computers at home while you were: (asked in the pre-elementary, elementary, middle school, and high school years) (yes/no). Sum score of home resources was used.
Youth's academic achievement*	NA	A standardized score of the mean of youths' course grades and Maryland subject achievement tests.
II. Youth 11th grade		
Math self-concept	.89	How good are you at math? (1 = not at all; 7 = very good)
Value of math	.63	Do you learn things in math that help with your everyday life?
Academic expectation	Single item	How far do you think you will actually go in school? (1 = 11th grade or less, 6 = graduate from a 4-year college, 8 = earn a doctorate)
Expectations of gender discrimination	.67	Do you think it will be harder or easier for you to get ahead in life because you are a (boy/girl)? (1 = a lot easier; 5 = a lot harder)
Inefficacy to combat race discrimination	.83	There is little you can do to avoid racial discrimination at the job you will have in the future. (1 = strongly disagree; 5 = strongly agree)
III. Youth 3 years post–high school		
IT career aspirations	Single item	"Have you ever considered getting a job in information technology? If so, which ones?" (1 = none, 2 = soft IT, 3 = hard IT, 4 = IT as college major)

Appendix 2.2
(continued)

Scale	Reliability (Cronbach alpha)	Example item
Self concept of ability at hard computer jobs	.93	How good would you be at an occupation that used computers for "hard" IT jobs (e.g., developing hardware, developing software, programming, etc.)?
Self concept of ability at soft computer jobs	.80	How good would you be at an occupation that used computers for "soft" IT jobs (e.g., word processing, accounting, etc.)?
Enjoyment of hard computer tasks	.92	How much do you think you would enjoy a job that used computers for "hard" IT jobs (e.g., developing hardware, developing software, programming, etc.)?
Enjoyment of soft computer tasks	.84	How much do you think you would enjoy a job that used computers for "soft" IT jobs (e.g., word processing, accounting, communications, business-related, etc.)?
Positive computer attitude	.62	Computers can solve social problems. (1 = disagree; 5 = strongly agree)
Negative computer attitude	.78	Working on computers is isolating and deprives people of social interaction. (1 = strongly disagree; 5 = strongly agree)
Influence of others	Single item	Adolescents reported how much encouragement and/or advice they received. (1 = none, 2-advice *or* encouragement, 3 = advice and encouragement)

*Parents reported family income, parents' occupational status, and parents' educational attainment. Youths' academic achievement was obtained through school archival records. All other measures were based on youth reports.

Notes

1. For more information about the MADICS data, please refer to our Web site, ⟨http://www.rcgd.isr.umich.edu/garp/⟩.

2. Exact *p* values and further details of the Bonferroni contrasts are available by contacting the first author of this chapter, who can be reached at ⟨nzarrett@umich.edu⟩.

3. For the combined effect of key indicators used in the current chapter on IT career pursuits (hierarchical regression analyses), see Zarrett and Malanchuk (forthcoming).

4. Additional analyses using hierarchical regression indicate that black males' inefficacy in fighting race discrimination remains significant even once accounting for the shared variance of other indicators ($B = .14$, $p < .05$). Gender discrimination findings are explained once more promixal determinants (three years after high school) are entered into the model. For more details, see Zarrett and Malanchuk (forthcoming).

5. There is a significant zero-order correlation between parents' education and IT aspirations, but the effect disappears in a multiple regression when youths' academic achievement is entered into the equation. This suggests that black males who rise above their socioeconomic status and are high academic achievers themselves are those most persistent in the IT field. For more details, see Zarrett and Malanchuk (forthcoming).

References

American Association of University Women Educational Foundation. 2000. *Tech-savvy: Educating girls in the new computer age.* Executive report. Washington, DC: AAUW.

American Association of University Women Educational Foundation. 2004. *Under the microscope: A decade of gender equity projects in the sciences.* Executive summary. Washington, DC: AAUW.

Atwell, P., and J. Battle. 1999. Home computers and school performance. *Information Society* 15:1–10.

Beyer, S., K. Rynes, J. Perrault, K. Hay, and S. Haller. 2003. Gender differences in computer science students. In *Proceedings of the thirty-fourth SIGSCE technical symposium on computer science education*, 49–53. New York: ACM Press.

Brosnan, M. J. 1998. The role of psychological gender in the computer-related attitudes and attainments of primary school children (aged 6–11). *Computers and Education* 30, nos. 3–4:203–208.

Bunderson, E. D., and M. E. Christensen. 1995. An analysis of retention problems for female students in university computer science programs. *Journal of Research on Computing in Education* 28, no. 1:1–18.

Byrne, P., and G. Lyons. 2001. The effect of student attributes on success in programming. In *Proceedings of the sixth annual conference on innovation and technology in computer science*, 49–52. New York: ACM Press.

Chappel, K. K. 1996. Mathematics computer software characteristics with possible gender-specific impact: A content analysis. *Journal of Educational Computer Research* 15:25–35.

Colley, A., M. Gale, and T. Harris. 1994. Effects of gender role identity and experience on computer attitude components. *Journal of Educational Computing Research* 10, no. 2:129–137.

Cooper, J., and K. D. Weaver. 2003. *Gender and computers: Understanding the digital divide.* Mahwah, NJ: Lawrence Erlbaum Associates, Inc.

Eccles, J. S. 1994. Understanding women's educational and occupational choices: Applying the Eccles et al. model of achievement-related choices. *Psychology of Women Quarterly* 18:585–609.

Eccles [Parsons], J. S., T. F. Adler, R. Futterman, S. B. Goff, C. M. Kaczala, J. L. Meece, and C. Midgley. 1983. Expectations, values, and academic behaviors. In *Perspective on achievement and achievement motivation*, ed. J. T. Spence, 75–146. San Francisco: W. H. Freeman.

Eccles [Parsons], J. S., T. Adler, and J. L. Meece. 1984. Sex differences in achievement: A test of alternate theories. *Journal of Personality and Social Psychology* 46:26–43.

Eccles, J. S., B. Barber, and D. Jozefowicz. 1998. Linking gender to educational, occupational, and recreational choices: Applying the Eccles et al. model of achievement-related choices. In *Sexism and stereotypes in modern society: The gender science of Janet Taylor Spence*, ed. W. B. Swann, J. H. Langlois, and L. A. Gilbert, 153–192. Washington DC: APA Press.

Eccles, J. S., A. Wigfield, R. D. Harold, and P. Blumenfeld. 1993. Ontogeny of children's self-perceptions and subjective task values across activity domains during the early elementary school years. *Child Development* 64:830–847.

Farina, F., R. Arce, J. Sobral, and R. Carames. 1991. Predictors of anxiety towards computers. *Computers in Human Behavior* 7:263–267.

Fennema, E. 2000. Gender and mathematics: What do we know and what do we need to know? Paper presented at the National Institute for Science Education Forum, Detroit.

Garcia, O. N., and R. Giles. 2003. *Research foundations on successful participation of underrepresented minorities in information technology: Final report from a cyberconference.* ⟨http://www.cise.nsf.gov/new/div/eia/cwardle/it_mnor/itminorities_final_report.htm⟩.

Heilman, M. E. 2001. Description and prescription: How gender stereotypes prevent women's ascent up the organizational ladder. *Journal of Social Issues* 57:657–674.

Information Technology Association of America. 2003. *New ITAA data show decline in women, minorities in high tech workforce.* ⟨http://www.itaa.org/news/pr/PressRelease.cfm ?ReleaseID=398276642⟩.

Jacobs, J., and J. S. Eccles. 1992. The impact of mothers' gender stereotypic beliefs on mothers' and children's ability perceptions. *Journal of Personality and Social Psychology* 63:932–944.

Jacobs, J., S. Lanza, W. Osgood, J. S. Eccles, and A. Wigfield. 2002. Changes in children's self-competence and values: Gender and domain differences across grade one through twelve. *Child Development* 73:509–527.

Kaiser Family Foundation. 1999. *Kids and media @ the new millennium: A comprehensive national analysis of children's media use.* Menlo Park, CA: Kaiser Family Foundation.

Katz, S., J. Aronis, D. Allbritton, C. Wilson, and M. L. Soffa. 2003. Gender and race in predicting achievement in computer science. *IEEE Technology and Society Magazine: Special Issue on Women and Minorities in Information Technology* 22, no. 3:20–27.

Latimer, C. P. 2001. *The digital divide: Understanding and addressing the challenge.* New York: New York State Forum for Information Resource Management.

Linver, M. R., and P. E. Davis-Kean. Forthcoming. The slippery slope: Predicting trajectories of males' and females' mathematics grades, interest, and self-concept in Junior high and high school. In *New directions for child and adolescent development; Math and science courses, grades, and career goals: Longitudinal perspectives on the influence of gender and beliefs*, ed. J. Jacobs and S. Simpkins. San Francisco: Jossey-Bass.

Margolis, J., and A. Fisher. 2002. *Unlocking the clubhouse: Women in computing.* Cambridge, MA: MIT Press.

Meece, J. L., J. Wigfield, and J. S. Eccles. 1990. Predictors of math anxiety and its consequences for young adolescents' course enrollment intentions and performances in mathematics. *Journal of Educational Psychology* 82:60–70.

Nam, C. B., and M. G. Powers. 1983. *The socioeconomic approach to status measurement: With a guide to occupational and socioeconomic status scores.* Houston: Cap & Gown Press.

National Center for Education Statistics. 2003. *Computer and Internet use by children and adolescents in 2001.* ⟨http://nces.ed.gov/pubsearch/pubsinfo.asp?pubid=2004014⟩.

Nelson, L. J., and J. Cooper. 1997. Gender differences in children's reactions to success and failure with computers. *Computers in Human Behavior* 13:247–267.

Okebukola, P. A., and A. B. Woda. 1993. The gender factor in computer anxiety and interest among some Australian high school students. *Educational Research* 35:181–189.

Panteli, N., J. Stack, and H. Ramsay. 2001. Gendered patterns in computing work in the late 1990s. *New Technology, Work, and Employment* 16:3–17.

Papadakis, E. 2000. Environmental values and political action. *Journal of Sociology* 36:81–97.

Powell, G. N., and D. A. Butterfield. 1997. Effect of race on promotions to top management in a federal department. *Academy of Management Journal* 40:112–128.

Reinen, I. J., and T. Plomp. 1997. Information technology and gender equality: A contradiction in terminis? *Computer and Education* 28:65–78.

Simpkins, S. D., P. E. Davis-Kean, and J. S. Eccles. 2004. The intersection between self-concept and values: Links between beliefs and choices in high school. In *New directions for child and adolescent development; Math and science courses, grades, and career goals: Longitudinal perspectives on the influence of gender and beliefs*, ed. J. Jacobs and S. D. Simpkins. San Francisco: Jossey-Bass.

Simpkins, S. D., P. E. Davis-Kean, and J. S. Eccles. 2005. Parents' socializing behavior and children's participation in math, science, and computer out-of-school activities. *Applied Developmental Science* 9:1.

Simpkins, S. D., P. E. Davis-Kean, and J. S. Eccles. Under review. The role of activity participation and beliefs in high school math and science course selection. *Developmental Psychology*.

Steele, C. M. 1997. A threat in the air: How stereotypes shape intellectual identity and performance. *American Psychologist* 52:613–629.

Tijdens, K. G. 1997. Behind the screens: The foreseen and unforeseen impact of computerization on female office worker's jobs. *Gender, Work, and Organization* 6:47–57.

U.S. Department of Commerce. 2003. *America's new deficit: The shortage of information technology workers.* ⟨http://www.technology.gov/reports/itsw/itsw.pdf⟩.

U.S. Department of Commerce. 2004. *A nation online: How Americans are expanding their use of the Internet.* ⟨http://www.ntia.doc.gov/ntiahome/dn/html⟩.

Vida, M., and J. S. Eccles. 2003. Predicting mathematics-related educational and career choices. Paper presented at the biennial meeting of the Society for Research on Child Development, Tampa.

Wigfield, A., A. Battle, L. B. Keller, and J. S. Eccles. 2002. Sex differences in motivation, self-concept, career aspiration, and career choice: Implications for cognitive development. In *Biology, sociology, and behavior: The development of sex differences in cognition*, ed. A. V. McGillicuddy-De-Lisi and R. De-Lisi. Greenwich, CT: Ablex.

Wilder, G., D. Mackie, and J. Cooper. 1985. Gender and computers: Two surveys of computer-related attitudes. *Sex Roles* 13:215–228.

Xie, Y., and K. Shauman. 2003. *Women in science*. Cambridge, MA: Harvard University Press.

Zarrett, N., and O. Malanchuk. Forthcoming. Who's computing? Gender and race differences in young adults' decisions to pursue an IT career. In *New directions for child and adolescent development; Math and science courses, grades, and career goals: Longitudinal perspectives on the influence of gender and beliefs*, ed. J. Jacobs and S. Simpkins. San Francisco: Jossey-Bass.

3

Lost in Translation: Gender and High School Computer Science

Joanna Goode, Rachel Estrella, and Jane Margolis

Prologue

Carolina is one of six females taking the computer programming course at East River High School, a predominantly Latino/a high school located in a low-income neighborhood on the east side of Los Angeles. She is one of the top students in her honors geometry class and has a strong history of academic achievement, particularly in mathematics and science. Carolina was recruited, along with other similarly strong female mathematics students, by a well-meaning and committed mathematics teacher, who had been assigned to teach programming and was eager to increase female enrollment in what had been a predominantly male classroom. As the course evolved, the teacher, who was teaching himself programming while running the course, decided to take advantage of the more knowledgeable students by pairing "experts" with "novices." With two exceptions, these pairs included an older, more tech-savvy male—the "big brother"—and a younger, inexperienced female. Despite the girls' high standing in high-level mathematics classes, the students quickly fell into "traditional" roles, with girls taking on more "secretarial" tasks. Carolina, who found this arrangement to be frustrating, states: "We [the girls] called them 'big brothers.' . . . I would type and he [her partner] would, like, think about it—we would both think about it, but he would, like, be the one with the most ideas. . . . I was not always able to understand the ideas. Sometimes I just went along with it."

Meanwhile, across town in a school on the more affluent west side of Los Angeles, Grace, a Filipina senior at Canyon High School, is the only female in her Advanced Placement computer science course (APCS). Unlike the other female student who quit after the first semester, Grace decided to "stick it out" because, as she states, she is "not a quitter." Moreover, Grace is interested in technology and plans to major in computer engineering. She became hooked on computers because of her interest in cell phone technology. In the Philippines, there are many cottage industries focused on making the cell phone more fun, unique, and "hip," and this was fascinating to Grace, piquing her curiosity and prompting her to pursue computer science. In addition, Grace's father has experience working with computers, particularly in Web design, which Grace believes also influenced her technology interests. Grace lives in downtown Los Angeles, but travels a long distance to Canyon High because of its reputation as a good school with a full range of course offerings.

Grace had a difficult time being the only girl in the APCS, especially after her other female classmate dropped out after the first semester. Most of the males in the class were already quite knowledgeable about computing, having spent years of playtime at home and with friends at the computer. In class, they tended to dominate the discussions and often diverted the teacher's attention during class time on debates about material that extended beyond the scope of the class. Grace's confidence in her ability to shine in this subject was shaken by her experience in this class: "Oh, gender is, like, a big thing, it's also, like, if you're, like, a girl and if you go to a class that's mostly male dominant, you get, like, . . . you feel inferior because there's all these guys and you're the only girl in there, so it feels like . . . [like] they're gonna, like, be like better than you and sometimes you feel bad, like oh my gosh, all these guys, and what am I against them, you know? . . . So I don't know. Sometimes I feel like they have, like, a better start than me."

Introduction

For the last three years, we have been engaged in research that examines why so few African American, Latino/a, and female students are learning computer science at the high school level. While we emphasize that race is a salient factor for students in the context of schools, this chapter focuses on the issue of gender, specifically the dearth of females in high school computer science classes (Margolis et al. 2003). Considering how today's technological tools have become more mainstream, and women now rival their male counterparts in the use of communication technologies (Lenhart, Rainie, and Lewis 2001; Goode 2004), we were interested in understanding how and why the gender gap in who is learning how to invent and create new technologies stubbornly persists. In 2001–2002, at the nation's PhD-granting departments of computer science and engineering, just 7 percent of computer science bachelor's degrees—the standard credential for obtaining positions in software design—were awarded to African Americans and Latino/as of both sexes, and just 18 percent to women (Taulbee Report Survey 2002). The trend is reflected in high school as well, where only 17 percent of the APCS exam takers are women, and the combined percentage for African American and Hispanic students hovers around 6 percent (College Entrance Examination Board 2003).

While home is where many adolescent male students get introduced to computing, and where many hone their computing skills and knowledge through game playing, exploration and tinkering, school is an important site for being exposed to and learning computer science, especially for students who don't have the resources at home and/or peer and social networks outside of school that nurture along any budding interests. While multiple pathways into the world of computing certainly do exist (Jesse, this volume), enrollment in computer science programs and classes are a crucial indicator of how few women are learning and/or being engaged with this subject. Yet as the opening vignettes convey, computer science in the schools often reflects the culture and domain of a subset of boys who are already immersed in the activity and knowledge of computing when entering the class (Schofield 1995; American Association of University Women 2000; Margolis and Fisher 2002). For girls who enroll in computer classes beyond the introductory level, their experiences are too often (though not exclusively) discouraging ones.

In this chapter, we present four themes that suggest some reasons why and how high school female students are—or are not—drawn into the field of computer science through their high school experiences. These themes are derived from interviews with high school students and educators along with our observations of their school contexts. First, despite the national and local initiatives to "bring schools into the twenty-first century," we have discovered how *few* computer science learning opportunities actually exist at the high school level, especially in schools that serve communities of color. Even at schools that are "heavily wired," computer science is too often interpreted as "computer literacy" and only low-level user skills are taught. And despite the importance of computation across various disciplines and occupations, the integration of computer science with other subjects in high school is hard to find. Thus, we discovered that many women of color simply do not have the *opportunity* to study computer science.

Second, we found that notions of *relevance* play a key role in influencing females' choices to enroll or not enroll in computer science classes. A limited and narrow presentation of what computer science is as well as what computer scientists actually do impacts students' take on how computer science could further their academic and career endeavors.

Third, for the female students who do take computer science, we have witnessed an accumulation of negative experiences in classroom settings, as captured by the opening vignettes, where greater male technology experience/expertise and female social isolation and insecurity are part of the cultural landscape. We have found that most of the females in our study lack the kinds of technology-oriented peer social networks enjoyed by the tech-savvy ("techie") males we interviewed. Given that most of the male tech-savvy students reported that a majority of their computer science knowledge was acquired at home or with friends, the significance of play, experimentation, and social networks in computer science learning cannot be understated.

Fourth, all of these experiences are then compounded by the way that computer science is motivated and "interpreted" for the students. Despite the critical-thinking and problem-solving skills that are the foundation of computer science, we witnessed how the curriculum of most computer science classes at the high school level are missing a higher-order thinking focus. Unfortunately, educators routinely fail to provide a compelling context and motivation for learning computer science for students who may not be singularly interested in the computer. Moreover, they often neglect to create learning environments that make the connections between computer science and the academic interests and pathways of "nontraditional" students, especially females. Our chapter concludes with an account of an action-research component of this study that strives to build a cadre of teachers as they work on redefining computer science for their students by restructuring the content and pedagogy in their classrooms to attract as well as retain increased numbers of female and other underrepresented students.

Theoretical Framework and Data Collection Strategies

Our framework for investigating the computing gender gap at the high school level focuses on the complex interaction of factors that impact students' "decisions" to study (or not study) computer science. It is a model formulated by Oakes (1990) for examining the low numbers of women and non-Asian minorities in mathematics and science education. This model takes into account the interaction of structural aspects of schools, such as tracking, with relevant psychological and sociological influences, such as gender and racial identity, peer dynamics, and so on. We are guided by the theoretical proposition that there is an intricate interplay between students' interest in computer science in school and the structural and psychological constraints both at home and school, and within and between social groups. For instance, as Oakes's (1985) research shows, and our study affirms, student placement in classes often reflects the perceptions and biases of teachers and counselors, rather than the abilities or aspirations of the students. This is just one example why we must study both the structural as well as the psychological factors that promote the participation of girls in high school computer science classrooms.

We also consider what makes computer science "unique" and different from mathematics and science. The widespread representation of males as the computer science "doers" and experts is further exacerbated by the informal technology knowledge of boys and girls. For a substratum of boys, video games and hours of related tinkering and experimentation are the "hook" that gets them interested in computer science. These games, designed by males for boys, are not pulling girls in to the same extent. In addition, the field of computer science is distinguished from other mathematics and science courses by the fact that most educators themselves have little computer science experience, and tend to be unfamiliar with the field in general. As a result, many educators are often not in a position to acquaint girls with and encourage them to pursue a course of study in computer science.

The heart of our research data is collected from observations and interviews with students and educators in three public high schools located in the Los Angeles Unified School District, one of the nation's most racially diverse school districts: a predominantly Latino/a school (East River), a predominantly African American school (Windward), and a racially mixed high school (Canyon). We have conducted over two hundred interviews with students and teachers. Our primary data collection strategies included weekly classroom observations, formal interviews, and informal discussions with students, teachers, and administrators. We interviewed a minimum of sixty students from each school who were either engaged in a technology course or an advanced mathematics class. In addition, a total of four focus groups were held with students of color and female students at Canyon High School; the purpose of these groups centered on the question of underrepresentation of both race and gender in computer science. We interviewed teachers who currently or formerly taught technology or advanced mathematics courses as well as key administrators at each school. Finally, we held regular meetings (once every three months) with four to six teachers at each school who either taught a computing course or who taught mathematics and worked with students of color. The foci of these meetings were threefold: to receive feedback on our research, to engage them in discussion about the state of computer science at their school, and to better understand the how these teachers and administrators perceived their student body, and how this perception influenced prioritization (or lack thereof) of specific curricula.

Extensive field notes—taken during interviews, observations, focus groups, and discussions—were analyzed alongside the formal interviews. The interviews averaged about forty minutes each, and were transcribed and then coded and analyzed using Atlas.ti software. Our student interview protocol consisted of open-ended questions that covered the following domains:

• Academic background (educational history, academic interests, current class schedule, etc.)

• Computing history and affinity toward/current knowledge of computing (i.e., when/where did they first learn how to use computers, what do they currently know how to do on computers, what do they like to do on computers, and what don't they like about computers?)

• Experience in computer classes

• Mathematics background and interest

• Computing at home (i.e., what kinds of hardware/software access did they have, what did they use the computer for at home, did their families use the computer, and how knowledgeable were family members about computing?)

• Friends and computing (i.e., did they engage in computing activities with friends, did they have friends who had extensive knowledge about computers, what were their friends' attitudes about the computer or about people who are interested in computers?)

• Perceptions of computer science and computer scientists

This chapter pulls from data from two (East River and Canyon) of the three schools we researched because these were the two schools that offered computer courses beyond the introductory level, and this provided some semblance of a "computer science pipeline" at the time of our research.[1] It is important to note that we are not attempting to prove particular hypotheses, nor are we trying to empirically test a particular theory in order to arrive at a finding that can be generalizable to a particular populace. What we are trying to understand more in-depth are the dynamics in the schools we are studying so we can then generate theories that could help explain the gender gap in computer science at the high school level. We employ qualitative methods, using the words of our research subjects and our experience and insights as observers within their context, in order to create a more detailed picture of this phenomenon. It is our belief that by doing so, we will be better equipped to eventually devise interventions that honor the complexity of this issue.

School Settings

East River: Technology Rich but Curriculum Poor

East River High School is located in a predominantly working-class community east of Los Angeles, in an area surrounded by industrial warehouses.[2] Latinos/as, many of whom are first- and second-generation immigrants, make up 99 percent of the school population. Four out of five students qualify for the free/reduced school lunch program, and 30 percent of the students are English-language learners. To accommodate 4,700 students, East River operates on a year-round three-track calendar, so while two-thirds of the students are in school at any given time, one-third are on vacation (or "off track"). Ironically, while this school has been "red flagged" for low test scores, it also has a history of being "technology rich." A cadre of older, male teachers at this school have been the front-runners in the school district in bringing computers into the classroom and wiring the school onto a network. In fact, at East River, the school's 4.8–1 student-to-computer ratio is better than the state average of 5.3–1. Moreover, 104 classrooms are connected to the Internet (California Department of Education 2003). The girls at East River excel in mathematics courses and consistently outnumber their male peers in Advanced Placement mathematics courses (California Department of Education 2003).

Despite the physical presence of a large quantity of networked computers, East River has never offered APCS and only offered programming in one track for two semesters. The computing curriculum at the school is largely vocational and not used for advanced academic study. Students who enroll in introductory computer courses learn keyboarding and word processing, while students in the popular Internet publishing class follow a scripted curriculum to learn to make drawings and business cards as well as to duplicate advertisements from the yellow pages. Students must take the Internet publishing course for four semesters before they are permitted to create Web pages.

Rather than acquiring the knowledge that allows one to create and problem solve with technology, the computing to which these students are exposed teaches only basic user skills. As one student stated, "From what I've heard it's like they make them type, and then they copy, paste, copy, paste, copy, paste." Even though computers are equally distributed in each classroom, students do not report use of computers in their academic courses. Students interested in academic, challenging computing experiences at East River are denied an important learning opportunity. While many of the educators at East River view higher-level computing classes as inappropriate due to the low levels of English-language and basic skills, there are students who are interested in and would benefit from a rigorous computing curriculum. For example, as Gabriela, a self-identified techie, notes, "Well, there are a lot of people into computers, but they don't take the classes because they feel that it's beneath them. Well, it's pretty much true because half of the classes here are like basic typing and stuff; more than half of everyone knows how to do that anyway."

Several years ago, a programming class was offered on one of the school's tracks, but it was taken off the curriculum when the school was flagged for low test scores. Because of low enrollment, the principal felt he could not justify the class expense when the school had testing pressures to address. As we also noted over two years of observations, the content of the course itself consisted of mostly low-level syntax-oriented tasks, and the class was not a success for the few female participants, as reflected in the opening vignettes.

Canyon: A Segregated Pipeline

Unlike East River, which is surrounded by industrial warehouses, Canyon High School, located in the western part of the city, is encircled by multimillion-dollar mansions and has an unfenced, green, tree-filled campus. The breezy sea air is much gentler than the stuffy, smoggy air that East River students breathe. Despite its location in a white, wealthy section of Los Angeles, the school population is ethnically diverse. Canyon, a math-science magnet and charter school, currently takes students from over a hundred different zip codes. In the 2002–2003 school year, 43 percent of its students were white (this figure includes a large number of students of Eastern European descent), 24 percent African American, 24 percent Latino/a, and 8 percent Asian American/Pacific Islander. The school serves relatively few students who qualify for a free or reduced-price lunch: just 24 percent are eligible (compared to 62 percent countywide). Furthermore, only 6 percent of the students are not yet proficient in English. Of the three schools in our study, the parents of Canyon students have the highest number of years of formal education: 81 percent have some college education (versus 55 percent countywide) and 63 percent have a college degree (compared with just 34 percent countywide).

Reflecting the community in which it is situated, Canyon is one of the more well-resourced schools in the district. There are several computer labs on campus and every non-technology-oriented classroom has at least four computers in it. Unlike East River, Canyon offers a complete computer science pipeline, including data processing (which has a programming component to it), programming, and APCS. The instructor for all three of these courses does not yet hold a teaching credential but has worked in the technology industry as a programmer and an IT manager. The curriculum for the APCS course covers data structures, algorithms, and the management of complex, large-scale programs. This college-level course incorporates a larger problem-solving orientation and is more aligned with the computer science field than any other class we observed. While the presence of more authentic computer science content seems to be in place here, the class enrollment reveals a very segregated pipeline.

Despite Canyon High's racial and ethnic diversity, African American, Latino/a, and female students are seriously underrepresented in the upper-level computer science class. While data processing and programming classes, which satisfy a school technology requirement, have a fairly diverse population of students, the numbers of African American, Latino/a, and female students dramatically drop away at the Advanced Placement level. In the 2001–2002 school year, out of fifteen students, there were only two females (one Filipina and one Persian, but the latter dropped out halfway through the year), one African American male, two Latino males, and the remaining students were white males (several of whom were Russian immigrants). In the 2002–2003 school year, there were again fifteen students, but only three were female (two Asians and one white). That year, there were no African Americans and only two Latinos enrolled in the course.

Reduced Access to Computer Science

The disparities between East River and Canyon illustrate how computer science course offerings in this school district fall along racial and socioeconomic lines. APCS (the benchmark course for higher-level computer science) is far more likely to be offered in schools serving more affluent white and Asian students (such as Canyon) than in those serving large numbers of low-income students of color—schools that rarely offer courses beyond low-level vocational ones (such as East River) (Goode 2004). We have found that a vocational, rather than an academic, model of computing dominates the computer science curriculum in schools serving predominantly low-income students of color. This vocational model of computer science too often reflects the low expectations a school has for its students. Yet despite the views of many educators at schools such as East River that higher-level computing classes would be inappropriate for their students due to the low levels of English-language and basic skills, we encountered students who would be quite capable to enroll in and learn about computing beyond the introductory level.

When we began our research in 2001, all of the three high schools in our study offered computer programming and two of the three offered APCS. Yet by the 2002–2003 school year, the second year of our study, two of the three schools eliminated their computer science classes above the introductory basic skills level. The reasons offered for these course reductions are many: testing and the accountability movement that has relegated computer science to being an "extra," low expectations for students, the lack of available teachers and training, and a systemwide misunderstanding of the interdisciplinary and academic worth of computer science. Indeed, in the midst of a national and local educational campaign to bring the schools "into the twenty-first century," computer science offerings in this district are being cut and reduced. We have also found that while the amount of technology in a school is often presented as an indicator of the quality of education, the presence of computers in the schools can be deceiving. Schools can be simultaneously technology rich and curriculum poor. These access and curriculum issues then impact students' opportunities to learn computer science, especially female students and students of color in general.

Though Canyon High and East River High differ drastically in terms of student demographics and educational resources, both schools consistently have a disproportionately low number of female students in computer science courses. In the following sections, we present several themes that address the interplay between school structure and psychological dynamics that we have found to impact female students' engagement with computer science.

Perceptions of Computer Scientists and the Field

When asked to describe their image of a computer scientist, interviewees at all three schools came up with inconsistent and uninformed portrayals, having never encountered a computer scientist and being unsure of what one does. Several students cited Bill Gates as their primary image of a computer scientist. Others guessed that computer scientists "walk around in a white lab coat," merging their images of biological or chemical laboratory scientists with computer scientists. Almost every interviewee pictured in their mind a white or Asian male, some adding that they were "geeks."

For most of these students who have not experienced adults or other students doing interesting things with technology, their images of who works in computer science comes largely from popular culture. When asked how these images came to their minds, most students, male and female alike, cited the media as their primary source. As Nicole, a Filipina programming student at Canyon, states: "I think that more guys are, like, into computers than are there girls 'cause in a lot of pictures that I see about, like, computers and stuff, mostly the users are guys that I can see in pictures. There's not really as much women as there.... [In] magazines, newspapers, books, it's basically all guys."

Print media are not the only arenas wherein the white or Asian male is portrayed as the quintessential prototype for a computer scientist. Students referred to the same stereotyped image in movies and on television as well. It is, as one student called it, the "Hollywood description." While this Hollywood depiction may not be entirely accurate, for students living in a media-saturated society who have no access to people in the field, the Hollywood image translates into a perceived reality. Moreover, the underportrayal of women in computing is reaffirmed within educational settings. Though 72 percent of California's teaching force are women, only a quarter of the APCS teachers are women (Goode 2004).

Breaking the Image of the "Lone" Programmer

For our female interviewees, what is perhaps more unappealing than the stereotyped or Hollywood image of a computer scientist is the notion that computer scientists are antisocial, and that the nature of their work is solitary and isolating. Though practicing computer scientists work in groups to plan and implement solutions, many female students, when describing their image of computer science, speak of a "lone" programmer, staring at a computer. Grace, an APCS student who expressed a great deal of interest in technology, was turned off to programming because of this particular vision of computer science, remarking: "I think I prefer the hardware side more because programming is just not my style because I don't like to sit at a computer all day and just stare at a screen."

This image of computer science as solitary work, of men sitting in front of a computer, "working on it 24-7," as one female student stated, is not only a turn off, it is also misleading. Computer scientists at the university level and those working in the field indicate that a large portion of their job involves working as part of a team to achieve their given solutions. Yet the image of the solitary, geeky, overworked male computer scientist persists, not only because of what students see in the media, but because this image of computer science work is often affirmed through high school computer science curriculum. For instance, at Canyon all programming assignments are individually based projects. There are no group assignments. We have observed a learning atmosphere that perpetuates the image of lone programmers working on a formal process of writing a program. Despite the rich collaboration of designers across disciplines in the academic domain of computer science, not once did we see teachers encourage group work as a valued component of the design process. Nor were creative solutions or alternative approaches encouraged—a critical trait in the work of professional computer scientists. In other words, these classrooms furthered an implicit message that this is a solitary business.

Hollywood, print media, and the classroom all perpetuate erroneous images of computer science and computer scientists. For students with no access to people working in the field or who are technology enthusiasts, these arenas form the foundation of their understanding of what it may be like to work in this field, thereby helping to shape their decisions to study or not study computer science. Social networks, therefore, play a key role in providing a better understanding of the realm of possibility afforded by computer science, and in piquing the interest of students who might not otherwise picture themselves working in this field or succeeding in a computer science class.

Importance of Social Networks

Family backgrounds and peer networks are critical to consider when one examines who does or does not enroll in computer science. At Canyon, all of the most tech-savvy males we interviewed in the APCS class had prior programming experience that they received from home. Most of these students became interested in programming because of their love of video games and their desire not only to understand how these games were created but also to attempt to create games of their own. These students reported learning programming by tinkering with the computer, reading books on their own, and learning through friends and/or relatives who either worked in the field or had extensive programming knowledge. Not only did these techie students have social networks that helped them to further their knowledge but they also had the financial resources to purchase all the latest software and hardware, a fast Internet connection, and so on. Several of the Canyon techie males owned more than one computer, and being able to build a computer from scratch seemed almost common knowledge. Two of the students we interviewed even set up a kind of business for themselves where they assembled or troubleshot computers for different clients. These male students' prior knowledge was so extensive that they claimed their primary motivation for taking the APCS class was to "have fun," as they felt the curriculum was too easy for them. In fact, they made no secret about the fact that they were unchallenged by the curriculum. On more than one occasion, these students were observed rolling their eyes during class discussions or making snide remarks about what they construed to be their female teacher's lack of knowledge. These actions not only reflected a disrespectful attitude but they also created an intimidating environment for the female students who were not as experienced as their male techie counterparts.

At East River, networks for the most tech-savvy males also existed, though overall, students had far less access to technology at home compared to Canyon students. Still, like at Canyon, the males in programming at East River arrived at class with more gaming knowledge and other computing experiences at home as compared to the female students. This expertise impacted both the composition of the programming course and, consequently, the classroom culture. Fernando, a twelfth grader who had enrolled in the course for two consecutive years, was considered by all of his classmates and his teacher to be the most knowledgeable programming student. He had been turned on to programming a few years earlier by a male friend, who encouraged him to build and host Web sites for extra money—an endeavor that served as a part-time job for him throughout high school. Fernando's own pursuit of more computing knowledge at East River inspired three of his closest friends to enroll during Fernando's second year in the programming course. And while we witnessed Fernando frequently and patiently aiding his posse of friends as well as many of his neighboring male classmates with code, he persistently resisted helping the remaining students in class, particularly the four females, with their assignments. When asked about his least favorite aspect of the course, he confirmed that he found having to assist other students in class frustrating. Leo, Fernando's most tech-savvy friend, furthered this sense of animosity, asserting, "My least favorite [part of the class] is that there are people that ask a lot of dumb stuff, stuff they should know." This hostility did not escape the attention of the girls, as will be described later in this chapter.

It is important to note that familial networks played an extremely significant role in piquing girls' interest in computer programming. With the exception of one student, all of the females we interviewed at Canyon who actively chose to enroll in the programming or APCS course because of interest in the subject matter had a family member who either shared the interest or worked in the computer field.[3] Two interviewees had fathers who worked in Web design and these students took the course, at least in part, to understand their fathers a little better. One of these interviewees stated that she was curious about the kind of work her father did because she always saw him in front of the computer, occasionally yelling at it when he couldn't get something to work. Another interviewee worked part-time for her father, who has a garage Web business, and she wanted to learn more about what she could do with computers. Another female interviewee, whose father is an electrical engineer and whose brothers are also studying electrical engineering in college, took the APCS class because she was annoyed at being left out of technology-centered conversations with her father and male siblings.

While knowing someone close to them who was an expert in the computing field did not ensure that the females in our study pursued a sustained course of study in computer science, of importance is the fact that it helped pique their interest in the subject. Moreover, it appeared to make them more comfortable in acting on these interests by enrolling in a computer science course. But the nature of the social networks for females and males was qualitatively different. The female students in our study were not part of a socially based computing community, as were the boys who were gamers or enthusiasts who regularly attended computer shows. Nor did the females have the same range of technology knowledge as did the APCS males. Likewise, most of the East River students came from families that did not have parents at home with computing knowledge to impart to their children, and their computing resources at home were much more limited than in the Canyon homes. A question that emerges, then, is what should the schools be doing to compensate for these types of social networks and communities that are available for some students and not for others, yet appear to be so critical to students' jump-start into computing?

Students without technology-oriented familial or social networks find themselves at a grave disadvantage when it comes to succeeding in a computer science class, for they are without the critical resource and reference point enjoyed by more privileged, tech-savvy students. Not only does the absence of these networks affect their ability to succeed in the computer science classroom but it also serves as an obstacle to truly understanding the possibilities inherent within the field of computer science.

Furthermore, it renders it difficult for students to see the connections between computer science and other courses of study and/or career paths.

Connection (or Lack Thereof) to Career Choices

At East River, many of the Latina students we interviewed were college-bound honors students from advanced mathematics classes. Among them were students who planned on being doctors, lawyers, architects, engineers, and teachers.[4] They were active and committed learners, and spent time between academic terms at special mathematics intersessions because of the scheduling interruptions of their year-round school. Despite being the most academically elite students in the school, these female students had little understanding of how computer science could support their academic and career plans. Teri, for example, strives to be an architect, but has never heard of computer-aided drafting. Kara aims to pursue criminology as a career, but cannot imagine how computing might assist her profession. Most of these students argue that their core academic subjects are their priorities for getting into college and pursuing their career. They value "creativity" and purpose, but unfortunately do not associate these qualities with what turns out to be their limited understanding of computer science.

The story is similar for the female students at Canyon. Examples of some of the career choices of our female interviewees include doctor, lawyer, teacher, public relations professional, and writer. As with the female students at East River, most of the female students we interviewed at Canyon did not make a connection between computer science and their career choices. Nevertheless, there were several female students who reported finding programming interesting, were intrigued by its creative aspects, and felt an intense sense of accomplishment when solving a difficult programming task. Yet these positive attributes proved not to be strong enough to persuade the majority of the female students we interviewed to continue to pursue computer science in high school. Of the nineteen Canyon female interviewees, only two who took a lower-level course in the computer science pipeline said that they would pursue further study. These two students mentioned their love of problem solving and logical reasoning as a key impetus for continuing to pursue computer science, describing it as "challenging" and "fun."

We were intrigued, then, as to why so few female students who expressed interest in computer science continued with the course of study at Canyon, a school with the resources that would allow for the continuance of this computer science learning opportunity. Indeed, even at East River, despite the existing computer science vacuum, there were several female interviewees who also found programming interesting, but expressed no desire to pursue the subject. For interested female students at both schools, the primary reason articulated for not pursuing computer science as a course of study was that it wasn't worth taking more advanced classes because they didn't "buy" them enough academically. In other words, the decision not to pursue computer science was a strategic one on the part of these students—a decision that they felt would preserve their competitive standing in the academic marketplace.

Competitiveness for College (Academic Relevance)

In today's increasingly competitive market for college acceptance, it seems almost naive to assume that students choose their high school courses primarily because of interest in a particular subject of study. For students "in the know"—that is, high-achieving students who are planning to apply at elite colleges and understand how to work through the proper academic pathways—courses are treated as commerce. For instance, with the average-weighted grade point average (GPA) of students accepted into the University of California at Los Angeles or Berkeley resting at 4.24, college-bound students are faced with intense pressure to take courses that will push their GPA higher in order to make them more competitive in terms of their college applications. Indeed, many of the female students we interviewed were high achievers, focused on succeeding academically and getting accepted into a good college. These students have tight schedules, filled with classes that their counselors tell them will look favorable in the eyes of college admissions counselors. Neither programming nor APCS are marketed as one of those classes. The high-achieving, college-bound females we interviewed claimed that they simply do not have the time in their schedules to pursue computing. In fact, programming at East River satisfies the same requirement as completing another technical art course, including floristry. At Canyon, not only is programming *not* seen as a class that would pique the interest of college admission counselors but it is also on an equal level with data processing in terms of fulfilling a high school graduation requirement. Thus, students who are wary of risking their GPAs often take the easier of the two courses.

University admissions guidelines play a confusing role here too, and it is in this arena where the structure of high school clashes with state policy. While California state policy emphasizes the importance of technology in improving education, and millions of dollars have been spent creating digital high schools and stressing computers as central to education reform, little has been done at the university level to affirm the significance of computing to education.[5] For example, the University of California has established a list of courses that students are required to take to meet its minimum college eligibility requirements (also known as the A-G requirements). Yet despite the increasing importance placed on technology by the state of California, the only computing course that satisfies any of the A-G requirements is APCS—a course not offered to students at East River.

Many elite students at East River, especially girls, express that they feel knowing computers beyond typing buys them little in terms of the immediate goal of being college eligible. And in a sense, they are right. At Canyon, where there is an abundance of Advanced Placement (AP) classes from which to choose, students are taught by counselors that while all AP courses increase your GPA, not all AP courses are considered equal. According to teachers and administrators we interviewed, students are told by their guidance counselors that there are prime AP courses that they should target, such as AP European history, AP English, and AP government. Again, the notion of courses as commerce is helpful here. While taking an AP class will inevitably buy you something (in this case, an extra point for your GPA), each course is treated as a commodity with differential value. This value, however symbolic (and erroneous), holds weight in the eyes of students in pursuit of higher education and influences decisions not to take courses that will in any way place their GPA at risk. In this sense, many girls' decisions to not enroll in computer science reflect a strategic choice to protect their college-going course schedule.

Yet while it may not buy them enough in terms of college credits, the fact remains that females, however few, did take APCS at Canyon and programming courses at both schools (when it was offered). Our data reveal that their experiences within this classroom environment tended to have a negative impact on not only their affinity to computer science but also their understanding of it as a subject of study.

Climate in Computer Science Classrooms

The following is a summary of our observation field notes for a Canyon APCS class:

On this particular day, when the teacher wrote a problem on the board for the class to work through, three to four of the most tech-savvy male students shouted out possible methods for solving the problem, argued with each other, then got up from their seats and stood in front of the board to discuss the problem, blocking the view from the rest of the class.[6] This classroom discussion then turned into a long private debate among these male students. The teacher, who appeared pleased that the problem engendered so much interest and debate, did not do anything to include the other students. These silent students sat at their desks, listening to these techies argue while looking at their backs. While the blocking of the whiteboard was not necessarily a common occurrence, the reduction of classroom discussion into a private debate among the class techies has been a common event in our observations. Also common was the teacher's lack of acknowledgment of this problem. Again, this appeared to stem not from a purposefully gendered agenda but rather from the teacher's excitement that her students were engaging in debate—an excitement that kept her seeing and changing the dynamics of this debate in terms of who was participating and who was silent.

Several of the Canyon female interviewees commented on this particular dynamic, telling us that they felt intimidated by the large disparity in experience between themselves and the males in their computer classroom. Jennifer, an APCS student, noted how asking for help became difficult for her: "What I don't like? Well, I do think that it's a bit intimidating to be in the class when everybody else really thinks they have a strong handle on it and, yeah, I don't know. It's all these other guys, they seem to know exactly what they're doing, and it's sometimes been difficult even asking for help."

Elizabeth, another APCS student, described the male behavior as "showing off," adding that it seemed to take up a great deal of class time: "Yeah, I saw some showing off. And yeah, it was like mostly, like, three or four people doing the talking. And like, they go off on other stuff about technology that we don't really know about, or that I don't even know about, like more advanced code or, like, I don't know, like electronics and stuff."

Grace described to us her difficult time being "the only girl in there," especially after her other female classmate dropped out after the first semester. Our observations, coupled with our interviews with her, reveal that her feeling of conspicuousness and inferiority is not just an internal psychological response at being different but is, at least in part, triggered by the beliefs and behavior of the males in the APCS classroom. One male techie scoffed at the difficulties experienced by not only the one female in the class but the Latinos as well. Privately, in an interview, this student ridiculed Grace's and the Latinos' lack of programming knowledge, calling their class work "a joke." Moreover, this student stated that he and some of the other techie males in the class often made fun of these students, expressing irritation at what they felt was a curriculum that was watered down to accommodate those with less experience.

We also witnessed more subtle yet disturbing gender dynamics in the second round of observations in an East River programming class. This programming class included a cohort of twelve older, more knowledgeable boys, and four younger, less knowledgeable girls. Unlike the previous year, however, the four females in this course were not honors students and did not know each other, but all had expressed interest in wanting to learn about computers. They also began the academic year in the course along with their male classmates. Still, their stories reveal a more hostile programming environment than the previous year. The boys, mostly seniors with prior computing knowledge obtained at home, flaunted their knowledge, upsetting and agitating the girls. Alicia told us: "The seniors make us feel bad ... 'cause they think they're good. They are good. They'll be talking down to us." And Cara said, "I don't like [the boys in the class] because they think they're all that 'cause they're seniors and they think we're the dumb freshmen."

This group of girls huddled around a couple of computers and worked together as a group, while the boys worked independently around them. The girls depended much more on the teacher for assistance, while the boys would ask a male neighbor for aid first, relying on the teacher as a last resort. Closer observation of the boys, though, showed that many of them "shared code" with each other in order to complete assignments. Often a male would allow a peer to copy his code, and then another, and so on. The girls were largely kept out of this "in the know" circle, and as a result, completed their assignments long after their male classmates, perpetuating their standing as the least knowledgeable students in the class.

Our observations of this class also exposed disturbing trends in the ways that the teacher treated the male and female students. For instance, the teacher would select one of the girls each day to return the attendance sheets to the office, a five-minute trip, but in dozens of our observations, never once sent a male student. When a few computers were broken, it was the girls who were relieved of the assignment and allowed to work on homework from other courses in the classroom space of the lab.

Though the dynamics of this programming class were different from the "big brothers" class described in the opening vignette and the Canyon APCS class, the outcomes were largely the same with males occupying the more knowledgeable position and females always being in the less knowledgeable position.

Engagement in the Computer Science Classroom

The situation we observed in Canyon, the one school with advanced-level computer science, is that the students' who enrolled in this class were predominantly the tech-savvy males and the "converted." While APCS is formally designed as a first course introduction to the science of computer science, and the College Entrance Examination Board (2002) suggests only intermediate algebra as a prerequisite, students who succeed in computer science often enter the course with a great deal of knowledge and experience in computing, having learned most of their computing from home and with peers.

Unfortunately, in neither school did we find a curriculum that successfully incorporated the interests of a broader segment of the student population, including women students, to the study of computer science. For instance, assignments in the East River programming class rarely played to the academic strengths or interests of the girls, and generally failed to even capture the girls' interests. It is important to remember that the girls enrolled in the class were honors mathematics students and top achievers in the school. One assignment, for example, required students to write a program that when given the dimensions of a several rectangular rooms in a house, would compute the cost of carpeting the home—a problem that at best uses middle school mathematics skills. This problem could easily be solved using simple multiplication and addition with a calculator, and failed to capitalize on the high-level processing power that the field of CS draws on. Other assignments hovered at the same low-level implementation of programming and focused on basic trivia games, including a hangman game, a state capital trivia game, a tic-tac-toe game, and a program that provides a test for students studying the area of basic geometric figures. Despite the fact that many of the females in the class excelled in their honors mathematics courses, their problem-solving and creative skills were rarely utilized in the programming class. In fact, none of the assignments legitimately represented the types of complex, real-life problems that would otherwise be difficult or lengthy to tackle without the field of computer science. Instead, students only encountered simple programs that focused on basic input and output processes. Students were never encouraged to define their own problems or specify the parameters—an important component of programming. Nor were connections to other academic subjects (besides low-level mathematics) tapped into through the curriculum of this class.

At Canyon, the curriculum in the programming class is vastly different from that of the APCS class. In the APCS class, much of the curriculum is geared toward honing problem-solving skills in order to best prepare students for the AP test at the year's end. A typical lesson plan involves the teacher putting a sample AP question on the board, which the class is expected to discuss and try to solve together, after which time the teacher hands out a set of questions that the students are expected to answer individually. There are multiple avenues through which students can arrive at the answer. Their objective is to use their problem-solving and logical-reasoning skills as well as their knowledge of Java or C++ to come up with a solution. In contrast, the curriculum for the introduction to programming course is textbook based. Students read assigned portions of the textbook and then try to re-create the project discussed in the given chapter. Sample projects include writing a program that calculates the timing for a traffic signal, a program where you can create movie tickets, and a program that calculates GPAs. The textbook gives step-by-step guidelines on how to create a program for the given project, even offering the exact code needed. Unlike in the APCS class, students in the programming course simply follow directions as dictated in the textbook, using Visual Basic as their programming language. All programming students therefore follow a similar course in order to achieve the same solution for the presented problem. Thus, the course is closer to a cut-and-paste format than one that engages in problem solving and logical reasoning. This format is not only less challenging and creative for students but it also keeps them from truly understanding the programming language itself and the multiple ways in which it can be used to solve a problem. This has been a critique given about the class by both male and female students alike.

And again, all assignments in the programming course are individually based, with no group work or whole-class discussions. Students without knowledge of how computer science is used in the real world are therefore left with the impression that computer science is solitary in nature. This proved to be a turnoff for the females in our study who conceptualized computer scientists as antisocial and isolated. The programming course at Canyon, in short, reinforced negative stereotypes about computer science and computer scientists. In fact, like East River's programming course, Canyon's did not provide students with a concrete idea of how computer science is applied in the real world, nor what the field of computer science currently looks like, rendering it difficult for someone with no prior knowledge of the field to find it appealing. Unfortunately, the introduction to programming course often failed to engage the interests of students and therefore served more as a turnoff than a stepping-stone to APCS.

What we found was that computer science is too often decontextualized and robbed of connections to subjects and arenas that interest the women in our study. This is similar to the American Association of University Women findings that "computer science instruction that emphasizes the 'web' of associations between programming, design, and other areas of the curriculum would help to attract a more diverse group of learners, and would advance computer fluency for all students" (2000, 43).

Needed: Computer Science Teachers to Revision an Alternative Classroom Culture and Pedagogy

In our research, we have encountered countless well-intentioned educators who do not have access to the knowledge and resources required to present a more accurate and relevant computer science curriculum to students. We place our observations within the context of the immense challenges presented to computer science teachers: teacher education programs do not offer methods classes for computer science teachers, creating no clear pathway for becoming a computer science teacher. In fact, the computer science teachers we have encountered came from a variety of disciplines, including mathematics, English, social studies, music, art history, and business. As a result, few of these teachers themselves have a familiarity with the modern field of computer science. And unlike other teachers, computer science teachers rarely have a home department, resulting in limited (if any) opportunities to collaborate with colleagues to develop curriculum and support their teaching endeavors. These teachers also have technical requirements they must work around, taking on an additional role as troubleshooter for the computers in the classroom. Moreover, the constantly changing field of computer science presents barriers to teachers who strive to keep up with the field. The programming language for APCS, for example, has changed from Pascal to C++ to Java, all within the last six years. Keeping up-to-date with these changes, without any professional development support, seems to be an insurmountable challenge. With such bare essential needs not addressed, it is not surprising that few teachers have the time or the will to think about alternative pedagogy and curriculum that can be meaningful for females as well as a more diverse pool of male students. And yet, teachers are one of the critical gatekeepers assuring the existence and success of a diverse classroom, and this must be their challenge.

With a better understanding of the challenges encountered by high school computer science teachers, we felt compelled to utilize our resources and connections to work with a group of urban educators as part of an ongoing action-research relationship. This type of alliance combines theory and practice, places researchers alongside practitioners, and aims to create a reflective and iterative cycle where practice and theory inform each other to make change rooted in praxis (Avison et al. 1999). To this end, we have formed an educational partnership, the Computer Science Equity Collaborative, consisting of the University of California at Los Angeles (UCLA) Graduate School of Education and Information Studies, the UCLA School of Engineering and Applied Science, and officials from the Los Angeles Unified School District. The first endeavor of the collaborative was a 2004 summer institute with twenty-five local high school APCS teachers involved in a week of activities at UCLA, including discussions around issues of equity in computer science, computer science instruction, showcases of interdisciplinary computer science applications around campus, and the modeling of an engaging, active pedagogy aimed at dispelling the image of computer science as an individualist field about computers. Highlighting the multidisciplinary problem-solving nature of computer science, we have challenged these teachers to take more active roles in the recruitment and retention of females and students of color in their classes. Moreover, we have garnered the commitment of district officials and school principals to support these teachers. Our hope is to keep this community of educators connected together to support each other, and we intend to learn what works in their classrooms and what doesn't. Rather than sitting back and passively researching classroom dynamics, we will engage in a partnership with these educators, trying to support their efforts to recruit and retain more females and other underrepresented students into their classes. Since our institute, the number of APCS classes has doubled in the district, and female enrollment in APCS courses in the district has increased 75 percent.

Summary

The challenge before educators is not just to recruit females and other underrepresented students into computer science and APCS courses but to engage them and provide them with support. Without meaningful assignments that immerse students in higher-order thinking tasks and interdisciplinary contexts, many students will fail to see the relevance of computing in their own interests. As in a literature class, pedagogy for computer science class should not be reduced to a study of grammar and syntax. Often missing from advanced computer science classes is the creation of a context that would capture the interests of a broader range of students, beyond (but not excluding) the technology-focused students. This requires consciously aware and committed educators who reset the tone, hold a larger understanding of the computer science field, and challenge old notions of who is capable, able, and potentially interested in learning this subject. Taking into account students' motivation for learning—and what is meaningful for different groups of students—is critical. An important task will be to dispel the prevalent myths about computer science: that it is only about the love of the computer, that it is solitary, that it is focused on tinkering and gaming rather than being relevant to real-world issues, and that only antisocial people engage in it.

We have witnessed female high school students who want to be more deeply involved with technology, who know it is part of their future, and who dream big, but who have no understanding of what deeper involvement entails or what preparation is required. This is a reflection of unequal home resources and a lack of learning opportunities in the schools as well as a "better start" for male students. The most pressing problem in schools serving the lowest-income students is one of access—the courses simply aren't there. There are also the issues of teacher training and pedagogy, however—the need for teachers to be properly prepared and proactive in recruiting females and underrepresented students into their classes, and to alter their pedagogy to engage what has become the nontraditional student. We found that the scientific heart of computer science is "lost in translation" at the high school level, and as a result, the field continues to lose the participation and interest of a broad layer of students, especially females.

Notes

1. In the context of our research of the educational opportunities at the high school level, we define the computer science pipeline as the curriculum and opportunities available to students to learn computer science within their schools.

2. The names of all schools, students, and educators have been changed to protect confidentiality.

3. As opposed to taking the course because of a graduation requirement or because it was the only class that fit into their schedules.

4. The career choices that these top-achieving female students identify with present an interesting topic for further exploration. We refer readers to the research of Linn and Hyde (1989) that concluded that a major sex difference in interests in mathematics and science is their perceived usefulness, and the research of Eccles that found that "women select the occupations that best fit their hierarchy of occupationally relevant values," and that helping others and doing something worthwhile for society is high in that hierarchy (1994, 600). Further

discussions on women's values and career interests are found in Margolis and Fisher (2002, 55).

5. Digital high schools were authorized by the 1997 California State Assembly bill for the Digital High School Education Technology Grant Program. The legislation specifies that "it is the intent of the Legislature that all high schools in the state become 'digital high schools' by the end of the first year of the twenty-first century and that these schools fully integrate computers, networks, training, and software to achieve computer literacy in all pupils and faculty and to improve academic achievement." Among the program objectives are "to provide all high school pupils with basic computer skills, improve pupil achievement in all academic subjects, and increase collaboration among high schools, postsecondary institutions, industry and community organizations."

6. The APCS classroom setup is such that six computing tables are put together to form a hexagon, with six of these hexagonal formations spread out in the room. The techies sit together, covering the two hexagons closest to the teacher.

References

American Association of University Women. 2000. *Tech-savvy: Educating girls in the new computer age.* Washington, DC: American Association of University Women.

Avison, D., F. Lau, M. Myers, and P. Nielson. 1999. Action research. *Communications of the ACM* 42, no. 1:94–97.

California Department of Education. 2003. California Basic Educational Data System. Retrieved August 2004. ⟨http://www.cde.ca.gov/ds/sd/cb/cbedshome.asp⟩.

College Entrance Examination Board. 2002. *Computer science course description.* New York: College Board.

College Entrance Examination Board. 2003. *Advanced Placement program: California and national summary reports.* New York: College Board.

Eccles, J. S. 1994. Understanding women's educational and occupational choices. *Psychology of Women Quarterly* 18:585–609.

Goode, J. 2004. Mind the gap: The digital dimension of college access. PhD diss., University of California, Los Angeles.

Lenhart, A., L. Rainie, and O. Lewis. 2001. *Teenage life online: The rise of instant-message generation, and the Internet's impact on friendships and family relationships.* Washington, DC: Pew Internet and American Life Project.

Linn, M. D., and J. S. Hyde. 1989. Gender, mathematics, and science. *Educational Researcher* 18, no. 8:17–27.

Margolis, J., and A. Fisher. 2002. *Unlocking the clubhouse: Women in computing.* Cambridge, MA: MIT Press.

Margolis, J., J. J. Holme, R. Estrella, J. Goode, K. Nao, and S. Stumme. 2003. The computer science pipeline in urban schools: Access to what? For whom? *IEEE Technology and Society* 22, no. 3:12–19.

Oakes, J. 1985. *Keeping track: How schools structure inequality.* New Haven, CT: Yale University Press.

Oakes, J. 1990. Opportunities, achievement, and choice: Women and minority students in science and mathematics. *Review of Research in Education* 16:153–222.

Schofield, J. W. 1995. *Computers and classroom culture.* Cambridge: Cambridge University Press.

Taulbee Report Survey. 2002. *2001–2002 Computing Research Association Taulbee Survey.* ⟨http://www.cra.org/statistics/home.html⟩.

4

Recruiting Middle School Girls into IT: Data on Girls' Perceptions and Experiences from a Mixed-Demographic Group

Lecia J. Barker, Eric Snow, Kathy Garvin-Doxas, and Tim Weston

Girls use computers as frequently as do boys, but are significantly less likely than boys to participate in study leading to IT development and design careers (National Center for Education Statistics 2004). The low participation of women in IT professions has potential harm for women's economic well-being, the overall economy, and the IT industry. For these and other reasons, much energy is committed to recruiting girls into IT academic and extracurricular programs. Convincing girls to participate in academic programs is especially important since girls either enter related undergraduate programs with less experience than their male counterparts or do not enter them at all (Cohoon and Aspray, this volume). What is more, when they enter IT academic programs with less experience, they often lose confidence and subsequently leave programs at higher rates than do more experienced students (usually men) (Cohoon 2001).

Quite frequently, recruiters ask high school counselors and teachers for the names of girls with demonstrated ability in math or science to populate their outreach programs for increasing participation in IT. Such girls may have an existing interest in mathematics, science, engineering, or technology, or very likely have a parent who is employed in a related field. These girls are more likely to enter STEM preparatory programs. Thus recruiting can sometimes be characterized as "saving the saved." In contrast, little is known about how to recruit the average girl, who is required to take mathematics and science classes, but who perhaps gets more excited about other types of classes or activities. What is more, an often-heard criticism of research on girls (or any other monolithic category) is that the category ignores socioeconomic differences across subgroups. What motivates a Hispanic/Latina girl might well be different from what motivates an African American one, for example. Hence, recruiters must use their best guesses in terms of the kinds of recruiting messages that would work to persuade non-predisposed girls to participate in their programs. Informing the recruiting process has been the goal of an ongoing research project conducted by the authors.

This chapter presents the results of a survey administered to a large and mixed-demographic group of middle school girls in an attempt to better understand what interests them with respect to STEM in general and IT in particular. Seven hundred and seventeen girls attending a STEM recruiting event completed the survey. Some, but certainly not all, of these girls were likely to pursue mathematics or science study or careers. In addition to questions about the girls' perceptions of the event itself, we asked the girls about their experiences with and perceptions of computing, whether they used a computer at home, and an open-ended question about what they wanted to do when they grow up. In this chapter, we will report the results of the survey, including the findings that were and were not significantly different across demographic and age groups. We begin with a review of the relevant literature on girls, recruiting for academic programs, and career aspirations. Then, we describe the event, research methods, and results of the study. We conclude by discussing the results, and offering implications for recruiters and researchers.

Literature Review

The Difficulty of Recruiting Middle School Girls

A combination of powerful forces works against the recruiter aspiring to increase middle school girls' participation in IT activities and programs of study. As described in more detail in Barker and Aspray (this volume), middle school is a critical juncture during which girls begin to construct their identities as sexual beings, which most often means feminine and heterosexual (Stepulvage 2001; Eckert 1995). In building and being cast into a heterosexual identity, girls choose and are guided toward activities that are appropriately feminine given their local setting. Similarly, girls are more likely to choose to participate in social contexts in which their appearance and communication style do not mark them as nonstandard (i.e., situations in which being a male is "normal" and being a female is unusual). Thus, participating in computing activities or study (beyond IT literacy) can be unattractive to girls since it is perceived to be something for boys to do—to belong in the "masculine domain" (Cockburn 1985; Wajcman 1991; Lie 1995; all cited in Stepulvage 2001). In addition, unlike mathematics and certain sciences (e.g., biology and chemistry), most college-bound secondary school children in the United States are not required to study computing beyond the fundamental skills of information literacy. Given girls' perception that the study of computers is in the male domain and the possibility of choosing certain aspects of their curriculum, girls tend to self-select out of the study of computers or advanced applications (e.g., Flash and Photoshop). The reasonableness of their choice is reinforced in three ways: computing classrooms comprise mostly boys, the female "pathbreakers" who do take those classes often suffer negative attention from their peers (Silverman and Pritchard 1993), and the composition of classrooms that are traditionally appropriate for females (e.g., non-computer art and music) is mostly girls.

Research on Recruiting

Student recruiting is a routine activity of every college and university; not surprisingly, the majority of research and the descriptions of student recruiting are based on the challenges of higher education. Typical messages include information about the recruiting institution that might appeal to potential recruits based on their demographic, academic, geographic, and attitudinal characteristics; these messages are delivered by means of personalized letters, flashy Web pages, telephone solicitations, site visits, or previews, or through informing important, influential adults expected to relay the information to high school girls (e.g., parents, teachers, and counselors) (Hossler 1999; Anderson 1994; Strauss 1998).

Research on higher education recruiting shows that the opinions of parents and peers along with the social and educational climate of an institution hold greater weight for women than they do for men (Golotti and Mark 1994). It may be safe to draw an analogy to the influence of social climate where girls have similar choices for high school (e.g., districts with open enrollment). Yet it is generally the case that the students who are successfully recruited are predisposed to becoming recruits. That is, they intend to go to college; they are just not sure which college.

Many universities, schools, and organizations across the nation recruit high school girls into STEM outreach programs and events. Little is known about the effectiveness of their strategies, however. In a recent report published by the American Association of University Women (2004), Kafai and her colleagues examined 416 projects intended to increase girls' interest in pursuing STEM study and careers. They point out that few of these projects listed their recruiting procedures, so it is difficult to track which procedures are effective either for getting girls into the particular event or tracing longer-lasting persuasive effects of events.

A few programs mention their methods in reports and on their Web sites. For example, Smith College's successful Summer Science and Engineering Program brings "academically talented" high school girls to campus for a month. The kind of personal interest and attention organizers show girls in this and similar projects make these programs especially attractive (though also of questionable sustainability). Recruiting methods generally include personal contact and invitations, peer pressure (having girls recruit other girls or recruiting in groups), and contact with role models. Another program, Sport Science at Temple University, recruits by means of interesting girls in sporting events. Programs often make recommendations for recruiting messages, which almost always promise female-friendly pedagogy and curriculum or emphasize talk about careers (Anderson 1993; Flowers 1998; Institute for Women in Trades, Technology, and Science n.d.; Thom 2002). Career, however, is an abstract concept that makes assumptions with which girls in many sociocultural groups may not identify or which is part of a distant future that receives little thoughtful consideration by a middle school girl (Whiston and Keller 2004; Eckert 1995).

A small body of research has examined recruiting of middle school children into magnet school programs, though this research generally describes methods rather than exploring efficacy. Magnet schools offer specialty programs (e.g., mathematics or performance arts) and were originally introduced to desegregate public school districts (Klauke 1988). Most magnet schools give tours with presentations to visitors and ask current magnet students to make presentations at feeder schools; other methods include using parents to make presentations or phone calls to other parents and direct mail (American Institutes of Research 1998; Miller, LaVois, and Thomson 1991). In one study of two science magnet schools, African American middle school girls were recruited by means of developing partnerships with minority math, science, and engineering clubs at nearby universities and involving minority undergraduates as role models in recruiting (Adenika-Morrow 1996). Students surveyed in a technology magnet high school stated three main reasons for choosing their school: abundant computers, special courses in multimedia design, and the low enrollment of the school; these results suggest that the majority of the students were already predisposed toward technology (this school was also disproportionately male) (Van Buren 2000).

At the high school level, recruiting girls into IT has largely focused on getting them into AP computer science courses since these classes are among the few comprehensive IT experiences available to students. The percentage of girls taking the

AP computer science test has held steady at only 16 to 17 percent since 1999 (College Board 2003). Carnegie Mellon University's recruiting of females into high school AP computer science classes addressed the issue of social climate mentioned above. In professional development workshops on C++ instruction, high school teachers also were taught some methods for recruiting girls, including talking to each girl personally, asking girls to recruit their friends, holding all-girl computing events, and educating counselors, teachers, and parents (Margolis and Fisher 2002). It is clear that additional research is needed to identify effective means of attracting girls into IT study at all levels.

Research on Career Aspirations

During adolescence, many children begin gathering occupational information for informing their selection of possible careers. As students explore their vocational identities, their occupation aspirations and expectations evolve, with choices in the adolescent years being preliminary (O'Brien and Fassinger 1993; Helwig 1998; Whiston and Keller 2004). Helwig found that children choose fantasy careers (e.g., ballerina or hockey star) more often when they were very young than when they were in middle school. Over the few years between second and sixth grade, family and parents become an increasingly powerful influence, affecting the nature of information available to children and to which children are likely to pay attention. Although possibly surprising to the parents of adolescents, parents have greater influence than peers in career aspirations (Paa and McWhirter 2000).

Family influence is not necessarily the intentional guidance of children but refers more generally to the family's situation. Factors include geographic location, genetic inheritance, wealth and education level, family composition, parenting style, and parents' attitudes toward work and appropriate work for men and women (Naylor 1986). The family's socioeconomic status strongly influences adolescents' career goals (Whiston and Keller 2004). Adolescents whose parents work in professional and skilled occupations have broader career interests than do adolescents with parents in unskilled jobs (Mullis, Mullis, and Gerwels 1998).

While the expectations of the same-sex parent have a stronger influence on boys and girls (Paa and McWhirter 2000), the family's socioeconomic status may affect boys and girls differently. An Australian study of adolescents showed that girls' educational goals, but not career goals, were influenced by parents' expectations for them; the same was true for boys, but only for boys from working-class families

(Marjoribanks 1984). Adolescent boys and girls also perceive their opportunities differently depending on the social support for their choices. Consistent with Golotti and Mark's (1994) study about the social climate of colleges (see above), girls' career aspirations are influenced by knowing that they are supported by their peers, family, and teachers, while boys' career aspirations can be predicted by their family support alone (i.e., the support of peers and teachers had no predictive value on the career aspirations of boys) (Covell, MacIntyre, and Wall 1999). Thus, it is clear that many girls will not be exposed to certain types of careers except through school and outreach programs. In the next section, we present the results of a survey of 717 mixed-demographic girls intended to identify messages and methods that can overcome the influences of family, culture, and peers that keep girls out of IT study and careers.

Research Method

Description of the Recruiting Event

The survey was conducted at the 2004 STEM Event, a recruiting event held annually by a professional women's society. The organizers had the resources to support the attendance of 800 girls along with 130 teachers and chaperones. At 8:30 a.m. on the day of the event, the girls arrived at a four-star downtown hotel where they met in a large group setting for breakfast, while listening to a brief welcome speech and a preview of the day's activities. They were each given a T-shirt and a bagful of information and giveaways. They then visited exhibits presented by a variety of local and national groups, and attended three workshops demonstrating some real-world aspects of science, engineering, and technology. Following the workshops, the girls attended lunch, where they were asked to complete a survey. The event ended at 1:00 p.m., and the girls and their chaperones returned to their schools.

Based on girls' feedback from the prior year, workshop presenters were asked to provide interactive, hands-on experiences with special emphasis on the importance of studying science and mathematics during high school. The presenters were men and women from a wide variety of professional STEM occupations in industry, public service, and academe. Prior to the day of the event, the students indicated which workshops they wanted to attend, but in order to ensure that room capacity and hands-on opportunities could accommodate the number of attendees, assigning sessions to the girls was necessary. The result was that some girls attended their workshops of choice, while others were randomly assigned by their faculty sponsors to workshops other than those for which they signed up. Workshop examples include:

· A presentation by a forensics unit of the local police department in which two women discussed the college degrees that led them into forensics, followed by a fingerprinting workshop where girls searched for fingerprints and made imprints for further study

· A discussion on the use of technology for registering pets and other animals by two men from the Humane Society

· An overview of the Lego robots experience at the local high school computer magnet school, including hands-on operation of the robots

· A bingo game covering copyright law

In spite of the hands-on requirement, some workshops were engaging and others were not, according to both survey and observation data.

Subjects

Girls were recruited from middle schools in several public districts and private schools in the Denver metropolitan area. Approximately 800 girls registered for the event; 717 returned the survey. We do not know how the girls were recruited, although the organizers specifically asked the teachers and other chaperones to focus on members of minority groups. (Demographic data is presented in the findings section below.) In addition to the survey, four members of our research team experienced in ethnographic methods observed several of the workshops and exhibits. These observations and the open-ended survey data suggest that the group ranged from girls who are very likely to enter STEM programs of study to those who are highly unlikely to do so. We have no reason to believe that the recruiting was limited to a selection of girls who already exhibited high achievement in mathematics and science. The likelihood of some girls completing the survey more than other girls was minimized by an attractive incentive: in order to receive a raffle ticket to win two round-trip tickets on Frontier Airlines, in addition to other donated prizes, each girl had to turn in her survey. We cannot speak to selection bias in subgroups (e.g., whether seventh graders were recruited from science classes) but do believe that as a whole, the sample includes a range of girls and has minimal bias.

Survey Content and Analytic Method

In general, the survey's purpose was to understand the girls' experiences with and perceptions of computers, what they thought they had learned during the day about careers and high school courses in science and technology, and what they wanted to do when they grow up. In addition, the survey elicited direction for the next year's event, including whether girls enjoyed themselves, what they liked most and least, and suggestions for future events.

Demographic questions permitted analysis across grade levels and racial/ethnic groups. Data were entered into a Statistical Package for the Social Sciences database by record. Open-ended items were examined for patterns; categories emerging from this analysis became the codes for new variables. These codes were added to the database by record. We examined the means and frequencies of the girls' responses to select survey questions, and then compared the results across grade levels and major racial/ethnic groups for statistical significance, as possible given the data.[1] We conducted a series of ANOVA analyses and post hoc Tukey multiple comparisons to determine the self-reported impact of the event as well as whether the girls differed in their career choices across grade levels and racial/ethnic groups.

Findings

Diverse Range of Participants

Girls were asked to "check all that apply" for the race/ethnicity item. As shown in table 4.1, the event served a diverse group of girls: 55 percent white ($n = 373$), 23 percent Hispanic/Latina/Hispanic ($n = 152$), 8 percent African American/black ($n = 57$), 2 percent American Indian ($n = 12$), 3 percent Asian ($n = 18$), and 9 percent mixed ($n = 59$; includes girls who indicated more than one race/ethnicity).

Table 4.1
Reported race/ethnicity of girls surveyed

Race/ethnicity	N	%
White	373	55%
Latina/Hispanic	152	23%
African American/black	57	8%
Asian	18	3%
American Indian	12	2%
Mixed	59	9%
Valid responses	671	100%
Not reported*	46	—

Note: *These percentages reflect valid responses only ($n = 671$). Two percent ($n = 13$) of the survey respondents listed something other than a race/ethnicity and 5 percent ($n = 33$) did not respond to this question.

Girls ranged in age from ten to fifteen, but the majority were eleven to fourteen. Not surprisingly, age was highly correlated with grade level. At 39 percent, eighth graders made up a greater percentage of the total than sixth (30 percent) or seventh graders (31 percent). A larger proportion of eighth-grade Hispanic/Latina girls attended than did sixth- or seventh-grade Hispanic/Latinas (with statistical significance at $p < .003$). There were no other significant differences, however, in the proportions of girls of each racial/ethnic category across grade levels.

Perceptions of the Event and Beliefs about and the Home Use of Computers

Table 4.2 presents aggregate descriptive statistics for Likert-scale items assessing girls' perceptions of the events as well as beliefs about and the home use of

Table 4.2
Descriptive statistics of survey items

Survey questions/statements	Valid N	Mean	Std. dev.	Std. error mean	Item scale
The STEM event was fun	709	4.24	0.92	0.03	5-point: 1 = Not at all! 5 = A lot!
Today I learned about careers in science, engineering, and technology	714	4.24	0.87	0.03	5-point: 1 = Not at all! 5 = A lot!
Today I learned what high school classes I should take to enter the fields of science, engineering, and technology	712	3.41	1.29	0.05	5-point: 1 = Disagree! 5 = Agree!
Because of being here today, I am interested in having a career in science, engineering, or technology	709	3.73	1.21	0.05	5-point: 1 = Not interested! 5 = Very interested!
I like to use computers	712	4.36	1.08	0.04	5-point: 1 = Disagree! 5 = Agree!
When I grow up, everyone will need to know how to use a computer	711	4.26	1.02	0.04	5-point: 1 = Disagree! 5 = Agree!
Do you use a computer at home?	715	.92	0.275	0.01	0 = No, 1 = Yes

computers. Standard errors varied across question type. For the Likert–scale items reported on below, mean responses ranged from 3.41 to 4.36 with respective standard errors ranging from .05 to .03. For the yes/no question reported, the mean response was .92 with a standard error of .01.

Approximately 81 percent of the girls thought the event was somewhat fun or a lot of fun. Only 6 percent of the girls rated the event below a neutral point on the survey. Eighty-one percent of the girls reported having learned about science, engineering, and technology careers. The girls' mean responses to these two questions were not different across racial/ethnic groups. Nevertheless, there were significant differences between different grade levels on whether the girls had fun ($F = 16.164$, $df = 2$, $p = .0001$) and whether they learned about science, engineering, and technology careers ($F = 8.295$, $df = 2$, $p = .0001$). Post hoc tests showed that eighth-grade girls rated the event as significantly less fun than sixth- (mean difference = $-.470$, $p = .0001$) or seventh-grade girls (mean difference = $-.242$, $p = .009$). In addition, post hoc tests showed that eighth-grade girls reported learning significantly less about science, engineering, and technology careers than sixth- (mean difference = $-.319$, $p = .0001$) or seventh-grade girls (mean difference = $-.222$, $p = .017$).

Sixty-two percent of the girls reported that they were interested in a career in science, technology, or engineering as a result of participating in the event. There were significant differences between different grade levels on this question ($F = 5.145$, $df = 2$, $p = .006$). Post hoc tests showed that eighth-grade girls were significantly less interested in a career in science, technology, or engineering as a result of participating in the event than sixth- (mean difference = $-.320$, $p = .014$) or seventh-grade girls (mean difference = $-.293$, $p = .025$). These results suggest that the perceived impact of the event on eighth-graders was less than it was for the lower grades. Girls in general also reported learning less about the courses they need to take in high school than they learned about careers.

The majority of girls attending the STEM event reported liking computers (84 percent), even more than the number of girls reporting they had fun. Further, 81 percent of the girls believed that everyone will need to know how to use computers when they grow up. There were no differences in girls' beliefs on these items across grade levels or race/ethnicity. There were statistically significant differences, however, in whether different racial/ethnic groups of girls used computers at home ($F = 44.271$, $df = 2$, $p = .0001$). As shown in table 4.3, while 92 percent of the girls surveyed answered that they use a computer at home, Hispanic/Latina girls

Table 4.3
Computer use at home: Hispanic/Latina girls report less

Racial/ethnic category	Yes	No
White	99%	1%
Latina/Hispanic	76%*	24%
African American/black	93%	7%

Note: *Statistically significant difference from white, African American/black

were significantly less likely to use computers at home than white girls (mean difference = $-.230$, $p = .0001$) and black/African American girls (mean difference = $-.173$, $p = .0001$).

Career Choice

Among several other open-ended items, we asked, "What do you want to do when you grow up?" We received a wide variety of responses, which we coded into twenty categories; these are shown in table 4.4. The most commonly mentioned career fields were medicine and veterinarian. Although we specifically asked "What do you want to do?" rather than "What do you want to be?" most girls did not write in occupations or activities focused on personal gain, such as business or finance.

We recoded the original categories into three broad career possibilities for women; examples of the original categories and their recoding are shown in table 4.5. Recoding permitted us to look across groups for differences as well as to consider correlations between these and other survey items (e.g., responses to learning about science, engineering, and technology careers). The original categories were recoded as "science, technology, and engineering" (i.e., aligned with the event's recruiting goal); "traditional for women" (e.g., hairdresser, massage therapist, or nurse); and "professional emergent," which we considered careers in which women's presence is becoming commonplace, such as law and medicine. This latter category is somewhat less refined since it includes careers where women have traditionally been underrepresented, but where numbers are steadily rising (e.g., police officer) along with careers that women have traditionally held in a professional capacity (e.g., writer).

Table 4.6 shows the percentage of girls in each category. Forty-eight percent of them indicated a professional emergent career field, 17 percent indicated a traditional career field, and 13 percent indicated a science, technology, or engineering

Table 4.4
Career categories girls wrote in

Career code	N	Percent
Medicine	104	15.6%
Don't know	94	14.1%
Misc. (e.g., have fun)	78	11.7%
Veterinarian	60	9.0%
Law	47	7.0%
Arts (singer, painter, etc.)	45	6.7%
Science (e.g., chemist, forensic)	43	6.4%
Engineer	31	4.6%
Sports	27	4.0%
Law enforcement	27	4.0%
Teacher	23	3.4%
Architect	15	2.2%
Work with technology	14	2.1%
Writer/author/editor	14	2.1%
Clothes designer	8	1.2%
Pilot	8	1.2%
Cosmetology	7	1.0%
Restaurant (e.g., chef, waitress)	6	0.9%
Interior designer	5	0.7%
Psychology (including therapist)	4	0.6%
Armed forces	3	0.4%
Broadcasting	3	0.4%
Model	1	0.1%
Secretary	1	0.1%
Total	668	100.0%

field. Thirteen percent of respondents indicated that they did not know what they wanted to do when they grew up (the remaining were not valid responses).

Second, there were statistically significant differences between girls across different grade levels on whether they indicated "don't know" ($F = 6.821$, $df = 2$, $p = .001$). More than a quarter of sixth-grade girls wrote in that they did not know what they wanted to do when they grow up, with lower percentages of "don't know" by seventh and eighth graders. In fact, seventh-grade girls were significantly less likely to indicate "don't know" than either sixth- (mean difference = $-.100$, $p = .011$) or eighth-grade girls (mean difference = $-.111$, $p = .002$), as shown in table 4.8.

Table 4.5
Codes and recoding for "What do you want to do when you grow up?"

Recoded category	Original categories
Professional emergent	Medicine (excluding nurse), law, psychology (including therapist), vet, writer/author/editor, law enforcement, architect, armed forces, sports
Science, technology, and engineering	Work with technology, engineer, science (chemist, biologist, physicist, forensics)
Traditional for women	Cosmetology, secretary, massage therapy, clothes designer, teacher, the arts (singer, painter, etc.), interior designer, broadcasting, model, nurse
Don't know	Don't know
Miscellaneous	For example, "I want to have fun"

Table 4.6
Percentages of girls in recoded career categories

Recoded category	Valid N	% girls
Professional emergent	332	48%
Traditional for women	120	17%
Don't know	94	13%
Science, technology, and engineering	88	13%
Miscellaneous	65	9%
Total	699	100%

Table 4.7
One significant difference in career categories across race/ethnicity

Recoded category	White	Latina/ Hispanic	Black/African American
Professional emergent	44%*	54%	63%
Science, technology, and engineering	15%	7%	9%
Traditional for women	15%	8%	9%
Don't know	22%	15%	11%

Note: *Statistically significant difference

Table 4.8
Differences in career choice across grade levels

Recoded category	Sixth grade	Seventh grade	Eighth grade
Professional emergent	45%	58%	46%
Science, technology, and engineering	12%	11%	16%
Traditional for women	16%	21%	17%
Don't know	26%	10%*	21%

Note: *Statistically significant difference

Table 4.9
What girls liked best

What did you like best about today?	Valid N	Percent
Workshops/activities/exhibits	388	60%
Perks (e.g., food, giveaways)	109	17%
Learning about something (science, technology, career)	41	6%
Miscellaneous	110	17%
Total	648	100%

Most interestingly, there was only one statistically significant difference across racial/ethnic groups on whether girls indicated a professional emergent career field for women, as shown in table 4.7 ($F = 4.429$, $df = 2$, $p = .012$). For this analysis, we used the proportion of girls selecting each career choice as the three dependent variables, and race/ethnicity and grade as the factors. Post hoc tests show that white girls were significantly less likely than African American ones to indicate an emergent career field (mean difference $= -.188$, $p = .026$).

Girls' Preferences and Desires for the Event

We asked the girls four open-ended questions to find out what they liked and didn't like about the event in general and the workshops in particular. Table 4.9 shows that girls especially liked the workshops. Table 4.10 illustrates that the girls liked the workshops mainly because they allowed them to do something interactive, or because they appreciated the content or message (e.g., "I liked the assistive technology because you can see that even people with disabilities can do stuff that we thought was impossible"). Fifteen percent of the girls wrote in something about the opportunity to learn something they did not already know. When responding to

Table 4.10
What girls liked about the workshops

Reason liked workshop	N	Percent
Hands-on/active/engaging	208	42%
Like workshop content/message	186	38%
Relevant to career interests	18	4%
Learned about/used technology	17	3%

Table 4.11
What girls liked the least about the event

Category	Valid N	Percent
Workshops (no interest in topic, no choice, etc.)	118	32%
Not with friends	59	17%
Food related	57	16%
Too much talk, not enough action	98	28%
Miscellaneous	24	7%
Total	356	100%

what they liked least, the most frequent answer girls gave was about noninteractive events or events where there was "too much talk."

When girls wrote in something that they did not like about the event, about one-third described a dislike of a particular workshop topic or not getting to choose the topic. Although a few topics were indicated as least interesting, girls showed a great deal of variation in terms of what they liked best and least for workshops. Table 4.11 depicts the categories of comments girls wrote about what they liked the least, although 14 percent of the girls who wrote a response to this item indicated there was nothing they didn't like. Twenty-eight percent of the girls were unhappy about having to sit and listen to lecture or speakers, which is not surprising for middle school children. Importantly, 17 percent indicated disliking not being able to be with their friends for the workshops.

Discussion and Implications

Few Differences across Socioeconomic Groups

We found fewer differences across demographic groups of girls than one might expect. That is, except for one difference, girls in different racial/ethnic groups were equally likely to answer both Likert-scale and open-ended items similarly. White girls were less likely than were African American/black or Hispanic/Latina girls to indicate a professional emergent career field. Although the difference in percentage appears to show up in the science, technology, and engineering category, this is not a statistically significant difference. This may be due to inadequate sample size and statistical power, once the groups are broken down. An equally valid explanation is that when a parent works in a STEM discipline, their children are more likely to also choose a STEM discipline (Mullis, Mullis, and Gerwels 1998). White girls' parents are more likely to work in science, technology, and engineering disciplines than are the parents of African American/black or Hispanic/Latina girls. Yet on no other survey item did we find a similar difference. This is interesting since although we would also argue that more research is needed to understand qualitative differences, recruiters may not need to craft different messages within the medium of school-related events for influencing girls from different socioeconomic groups. More important would be to spend more time informing girls about which courses they should take to be competitive with boys in IT majors at college; the survey data show that girls were less likely to agree that they had learned which classes to take in high school than to agree that they had learned about science, technology, and engineering careers.

Implications for Targeting Age Groups

Eighth-grade girls rated the event as significantly less fun than did sixth- or seventh-grade girls, and they also reported learning significantly less about science, engineering, and technology careers than their younger peers. One interpretation of these findings is that eighth graders' attitudes toward what constitutes fun may have solidified in ways that exclude learning about science, technology, or engineering careers. It could also be that they have already had some of these experiences, including being presented with similar career-oriented information, so that the experience was less novel. Still, more eighth graders thought that the event was more fun and interesting than not fun or interesting, and they appreciated learning something new. Nevertheless, the vast majority of girls wrote in careers that were at odds with the organizers' goals. This suggests that a strategy beyond making the event interesting and fun must be used, such as teaching girls ways in which computing study can provide an avenue for making a difference in the lives of other people.

While their likelihood of choosing a STEM career was not different from their older peers, it appears that sixth graders were more likely to have indicated they did not know what they want to do when they grow up. It may be the case, then, that sixth-grade girls may be more impressionable than eighth-grade girls, and that targeting sixth graders may be more fruitful for recruiting efforts. Showing girls computing careers that are consistent with their beliefs about what it means to be a woman, female, or feminine may be a persuasive mechanism for increasing participation. Their beliefs about being these are not entirely clear, however, nor are how they differ across the three middle school grades. That is, generally speaking, the field makes a claim that young women want to go into computing and STEM fields in order to use their knowledge to accomplish some good for others (e.g., medicine), but these claims are based on research of college-aged women. Assuming that, as Eckert (1995) argues, sixth-grade girls are more focused on becoming eighth- or ninth-grade girls than they are on becoming adults with careers, and given the immediate need of ensuring that college-bound girls complete high school course work that will reduce the experience gap they face as first-year college students, more research is needed on discovering approaches that will work to convince girls that taking those courses is an appropriately feminine pursuit.

Impact of the Event on Career Choice and Opportunity

In the open-ended item "What do you want to do when you grow up?" the most commonly indicated careers were in medicine and veterinary, both of which could be characterized as altruistic careers. Only 13 percent of the girls indicated a science, technology, or engineering field. Although we might wonder whether a single-day event has the power to change attitudes, these results are somewhat surprising considering the girls' all-day presence at an event intended to interest them in STEM. On the Likert-scale item asking whether girls became interested in a career in science, technology, or engineering as a result of participating in the event, 62 percent of the girls reported that they had become interested. These results reveal a contradiction. It is not clear whether the high percentage of girls indicating increased interest responded because it was a socially correct answer or whether their open-ended responses reflected their authentic thoughts, perhaps from prior to the event. That is, for example, many of the girls wrote "thank you!" or other positive comments on the survey, and 14 percent of the girls responding to the item asking what they liked least about the event indicated that there was nothing they didn't like. Thus, it is hard to know the degree to which the event had a genuine effect on career choice.

In addition, sixth-grade girls were more uncertain about what they want to do when they grow up than were seventh- or eighth-grade girls. This difference may suggest an opportunity for making a greater impression, especially in light of the greater impression sixth- and seventh-grade girls reported on whether they learned about STEM careers as a result of attending the event.

Use of Computers at Home

Hispanic/Latina girls were less likely than white or African American/black girls to use computers at home. We have asked educators for their opinion of whether this is because Hispanic/Latinas are less likely to have a computer in the home or are just less likely to use a computer in the home, even if one is available. Educators have suggested the former: that it is an economic and not a cultural issue. Hispanics/Latinos are the fastest-growing minority group in the United States and the least represented in computing.[2] We believe this may be of concern, because research shows that experience and use are related to attitude toward computers (see the discussion in chapter 1 [Barker and Aspray], this volume); such research has been conducted under the premise that a student's attitude toward computers is a factor in predicting whether she will study computing. In addition, Margolis and Fisher (2002) reported that the males in their study were more likely than the females to have "tinkered" with computers at home. Tinkering, especially in collaboration with a parent, was considered to be an important introduction into the study of computing. Special attention may be needed to provide informal learning opportunities to Hispanic/Latina girls (and boys perhaps) given the lower likelihood of females both tinkering with the computer and having a computer in the home.

The Importance of Friends

In the open-ended item eliciting what they liked least about the event, 17 percent of the girls wrote that they disliked not being able to be with their friends in the workshops. In the Carnegie Mellon recruiting intervention, secondary computer science teachers were encouraged to recruit girls in groups. The data collected and analyzed here cannot tell us whether being with friends would increase the likelihood of taking the courses needed for entering college prepared competitively with male peers. Still, we agree with the organizers of the Carnegie Mellon teacher professional development workshops that girls might be more inclined to take such courses if their friends were with them and if they knew what these courses were. High school preparation is a more pressing and immediate need at this age level; girls in our study reported that they learned less about what courses to take in high school than about careers. Teaching girls the same strategies taught to teachers for taking classes dominated by boys (e.g., finding a friend or small group of friends) has the potential to make a difference in enrollment in both the near and long terms for girls and women.

Conclusion

Women continue to enter college with less computing experience than men, especially in terms of advanced applications and programming, and to leave undergraduate and graduate programs with fewer computer and information science degrees than men. Recruiting is an important, but understudied aspect of increasing the participation of women in IT disciplines. The function of recruiting is persuasion, or communication intended to influence, reinforce, or change another's beliefs, values, attitudes, or actions. Aristotle defined the art of persuasion in *On Rhetoric* (Roberts 1924), where he argued that for persuasion to occur, one must understand the good reasons, the emotional appeals, and the characteristics of speakers and others with influence that work together to convince a specific audience to think or act in a particular manner. Recruiting should be centrally concerned with persuasion, and in so doing, appeal to the motivations and interests of girls, rather than simply try to alter them. We offer the following recommendations to recruiters based on our study:

• Ensure that the content of events goes beyond "interesting and fun" to showing girls that IT career choices can help them make a difference in the lives of others. The majority of written-in responses to "What do you want to do when you grow up?" were aligned with jobs that help others (e.g., doctor).

• Make girls aware of the high school courses they need to take to minimize the experience gap in college IT programs; this should be part of the event message, not just career possibilities. That is, show girls the path to their career, starting in the immediate future.

• Give girls strategies for taking male-dominated classes, especially that of recruiting their friends into classes with them.

We believe that continuing research should test recruiting efforts in which workshops or activities align girls' existing interests with science, technology, and engineering. First, however, we need a better understanding of girls' views at different age levels of whether girls' interests are nurturing (e.g., medicine) or whether careers must appear to fit a feminine or female persona. Recruiting messages and methods need to be aligned with girls' age-relevant interests in these technical disciplines. Finally, research is needed to explore the degree to which one-day and other extra-curricular events have a lasting impact on girls' course election and career choices. Studies tracking students over several years are difficult to accomplish, but might be possible, and surveys of first-year college students that ask how many and perhaps the nature of recruiting events they attended since middle school might shed light on recruiting events' impact on choices. Only through additional research can we help to define interventions that work.

Notes

1. We cannot make any claims of statistical significance for American Indian, Asian, and mixed racial/ethnic groups; too few girls in each group participated in the survey.

2. According to Garcia and Giles, "The Hispanic population constitutes 10.40 percent of the U.S. population and contributes 5.84 percent of BS, 3.07 percent of MS, and 0.97 percent of PhD degrees in [computer science]." This participation is even lower than that of American Indians and Alaskan natives relative to the population: "0.7 percent of the U.S. population and contribute 0.49 percent of BS, 0.25 percent of MS, and 0.00 percent of PhD degrees in [computer science]" (2000, 65).

References

Adenika-Morrow, T. J. 1996. A lifeline to science careers for African American females. *Educational Leadership* 53, no. 8:80–83.

American Association of University Women. 2004. *Under the microscope: A decade of gender equity projects in the sciences.* Washington, DC: American Association of University Women Educational Foundation. Available at ⟨http://www.aauw.org/research/underthemicroscope.pdf⟩.

American Institutes of Research. 1998. *Evaluation of the magnet schools assistance program, grantees: Year 1 interim report.* ⟨http://www.ed.gov/offices/OUS/PES/esed/mag_eval⟩.

Anderson, B. T. 1993. How can middle schools get minority females in the math/science pipeline? *Education Digest* 59:39–42.

Anderson, C. 1994. Dear prospective student: An analysis of admissions materials from four universities. *College and University* 70, no. 1:26–28.

Cockburn, C. 1985. *Machinery of dominance: Women, men, and technical know-how.* London: Pluto Press.

Cohoon, J. M. 2001. Toward improving female retention in the computer science major. *Communications of the ACM* 44, no. 5:108–114.

College Board. 2003. *College-bound seniors 2003.* ⟨http://www.collegeboard.com/about/news_info/cbsenior/yr2003/html/2003reports.html⟩.

Covell, Katherine, Peter D. MacIntyre, and Julie Wall. 1999. Implications of Social Supports for Adolescents' Education and Career Aspirations. *Canadian Journal of Behavioural Science* 31, no. 2:63–71.

Eckert, P. 1995. Constructing meaning, constructing selves: Snapshots of language, gender, and class from Belten High. In *Gender articulated: Language and the socially constructed self,* ed. K. Hall and M. Bucholtz, 469–507. New York: Routledge.

Flowers, J. 1998. Improving female enrollment in tech ed. *Technology Teacher* 58, no. 2:21–25.

Garcia, O. N., and R. Giles. 2000. *Research foundations on successful participation on underrepresented minorities in information technology: Final report from a cyberconference.* ⟨http://www.cise.nsf.gov/itminorities/itminorities_final_report.pdf⟩.

Golotti, K. M., and M. C. Mark. 1994. How do high school students structure an important life decision? A short-term longitudinal study of the college decision-making process. *Research in Higher Education* 35, no. 5:589–607.

Helwig, A. 1998. Occupational aspirations of a longitudinal sample for second to sixth grade. *Journal of Career Development* 24, no. 4:247–265.

Hossler, D. 1999. Effective admissions recruitment. *New Directions for Higher Education* 108:15–30.

Institute for Women in Trades, Technology, and Science. n.d. *A trainer's workshop guide.* Alameda, CA: National iWITTS.

Klauke, A. 1988. *Magnet schools.* ERIC digest series no. EA 26, ED293225. Eugene, OR: ERIC Clearinghouse on Educational Management. Available at ⟨http://www.ericdigests.org/pre–928/magnet.htm⟩.

Lie, M. 1995. Technology and masculinity: The case of the computer. *The European Journal of Women's Studies* 2:379–394.

Margolis, J., and A. Fisher. 2002. *Unlocking the clubhouse: Women in computing.* Cambridge, MA: MIT Press.

Marjoribanks, K. 1984. Ethnicity, family environment, and adolescents' aspirations: A follow-up study. *Journal of Educational Research* 77:166–171.

Miller, L., C. LaVois, and W. Thomson. 1991. Middle school and medical school collaboration: A magnet school experience. *School Science and Mathematics* 91, no. 2:47–50.

Mullis, R. L., A. K. Mullis, and D. Gerwels. 1998. Stability of vocational interests among high school students. *Adolescence* 33:699–707.

National Center for Education Statistics. 2004. NAEP Data Tool. Retrieved October 15, 2004. ⟨http://nces.ed.gov/nationsreportcard/naepdata/getdata.asp⟩.

Naylor, M. 1986. *Family influences on employment and education: Overview.* ERIC digest no. 56, ED272702. Columbus, OH: ERIC Clearinghouse on Adult Career and Vocational Education. Available at ⟨http://www.ericdigests.org/pre–924/family.htm⟩.

O'Brien, K. M., and R. E. Fassinger. 1993. A causal model of the career orientation and career choice of adolescent women. *Journal of Counseling Psychology* 40:456–469.

Paa, H. K., and E. H. McWhirter. 2000. Perceived influences on high school students' current career expectations. *Career Development Quarterly* 49:29–44.

Roberts, W. R., trans. 1924. *On Rhetoric*. Oxford: Clarendon Press.

Silverman, S., and A. M. Pritchard. 1993. *Building their future: Girls in technology and education in Connecticut*. Hartford: Connecticut Women's Education and Legal Fund.

Stepulvage, L. 2001. Gender/technology relations: Complicating the gender binary. *Gender and Education* 13, no. 3:325–338.

Strauss, D. 1998. The use of the World Wide Web as a source of information during the college search process. Unpublished diss., Ohio State University.

Thom, M. 2002. Girls in science and technology: What's new, what's next? *Education Digest* 67, no. 5:17–24.

Van Buren, C. 2000. Multimedia learning at "the school that business built": Students' perceptions of education at New Technology High School. *Journal of Curriculum and Supervision* 15, no. 3:236–254.

Wajcman, J. 1991. *Feminism confronts technology*. University Park, PA: Pennsylvania State University Press.

Whiston, S., and B. Keller. 2004. The influences of the family of origin on career development: A review and analysis. *Counseling Psychologist* 32, no. 4:493–495.

5

A Critical Review of the Research on Women's Participation in Postsecondary Computing Education

J. McGrath Cohoon and William Aspray

Women's participation in postsecondary computing education is low at every degree level. In the last decade for which data are available, women's representation among those earning computer science diplomas declined from 51 to 40 percent of associate degrees, fluctuated between 29 and 27 percent of bachelor's degrees, rose from 26 to 34 percent of master's degrees, and fluctuated between 15 and 19 percent of doctoral degrees (IPEDS data for 1992–2002 academic years) (National Science Foundation 1999–2002). This extensive underrepresentation is documented in various data sets and has long been a recognized concern. Nevertheless, almost thirty years of efforts have failed to produce a sustained increase in women's participation in computing. Women remain seriously underrepresented, and the intentions of college-bound students (College Board 2002) indicate that the situation is not likely to improve any time soon.

Our review of the literature on women in postsecondary computer science leads us to the conclusion that two conditions contribute to the persistence of women's underrepresentation. The first condition is an inadequate understanding of the underlying and immediate causes. Much of what has been published is based on personal experience or observation of a single case, rather than being grounded in empirical evidence that can be generalized. The second condition is inadequate intervention efforts. Our focus for this chapter is on evidence-based social science research into the factors leading to women's underrepresentation.

The State of the Social Science Research

After four years of grants awarded by the NSF's Information Technology Workforce (ITWF) and Information Technology Research (ITR) programs, some observers believe that women's low participation in computing has been adequately studied. We disagree. In fact, the following paragraphs show that many factors have not yet received careful empirical examination. A similar finding was reached in a review of the 1990s' research (Dryburgh 2000) that located only one generalizable study in the literature and found only a few points of consensus among smaller studies. Our updated and broader review does not find the situation sufficiently improved—although funding from the ITWF program will significantly augment the research literature.

The shortage of reliable evidence specifically about women's participation in computing is one reason scholars frequently turn to the much larger body of research on women's participation in STEM disciplines. We must be cautious when making this leap, however, because computer science and computer engineering (CSE) differs from these other disciplines in meaningful ways. For example, when student course-taking patterns and grades are taken into account in other STEM disciplines, gender is no longer a factor in the choice of a major; but that is not the case in computer science (Strenta et al. 1994). Men and women with the same course-taking patterns and the same grades have different likelihoods of majoring in computer science (Strenta et al. 1994). Another obvious difference between CSE and other STEM disciplines is evident in degree trends. Only in CSE is the trend not toward gender parity. Thus, although the STEM literature can be instructive, it remains an open question as to when extrapolation to CSE is warranted. For the time being, we must cautiously infer from the STEM literature when there are no relevant results from CSE. In the long run, however, we should either develop criteria that enable us to determine when it is appropriate to use the STEM literature or evaluate the key STEM findings specifically for CSE.

Potential influences on the gender composition of computing are seldom discussed in relation to any theoretical perspective. Yet there are implicit theories underlying both the selection of factors to investigate and the explanations of why these factors might influence participation in computing. Underlying much of the work on the *culture of computing* is a theoretical perspective that ties computing to the masculine culture dominating modern society. From this vantage point, women are not present in computing either because they feel out of place or unwelcome in that culture, or because women outright reject the culture. A second, related, and perhaps most common approach in the literature is to link women's underrepresentation to early or ongoing *social* influences that maintain our gender-segregated society, steering women away from computing and men toward it. This process might occur through socialization, stereotypes, social networks, or discrimination. From this perspective, women's representation could still be a product of cultural beliefs about gender and technology, but the emphasis is on the social structures that sort men and women into or out of computing. A third underpinning theory is based on the view that men and women differ innately, and that women's "*natural*" values exclude technology such as computers. A fourth, but seldom seriously applied theoretical perspective views the gender composition of computing as a consequence of *rational choice*. This perspective gives rise to hypotheses that the requirements for continual updating of skills make computing a poor occupation for women who are likely to exit and reenter the workforce due to childbearing. These theoretical underpinnings are seldom articulated, and none of the studies we located were designed to test a particular theory. Still, movement toward more explicit consideration of theory might help advance empirical investigation of this issue.

It is appropriate to consider the kinds of evidence that social science research offers. Even well-crafted research projects vary in the strength of the evidence they provide. In quantitative studies, results vary in the strength of correlations between dependent and independent variables. Data collected over time or across different settings provide stronger results than cross-sectional or single case studies. Self-reported survey results are strengthened by confirmation through focus groups, interviews, or observation, and vice versa. We expected to find—and have found—evidence of widely different strengths in the studies we reviewed. Yet practical considerations of time, cost, and the patience of our study population make it unlikely we will ever carry out enough research projects to gain strong evidence of every aspect of this field of study. Therefore, we accept findings both when they contribute to a consensus of results from limited studies, and when they are definitive results from well-designed and implemented research.

Our Review Methodology

We consider ten factors that have received attention as potential explanations for the underrepresentation of women: the culture of computing, experience, barriers to entry, role models, mentoring, student-faculty interaction, peer support, curricula, pedagogy, and student characteristics such as academic fitness, values, confidence, and response to competition. For each of these topics, we offer a definition, explain why it is a potential factor in women's underrepresentation, discuss a few selected studies that produced noteworthy or enlightening results, and identify some important questions that remain open.

We organize our analysis around three aspects of participation: achieving women's presence in postsecondary computing programs, maintaining women's presence, and advancing women along a computing career path. In addition, we classify studies according to their focus on individual students, academic departments, and the discipline or profession in the United States or internationally.

We point out assumptions about deficiency or agency that are embedded but rarely discussed in the literature. These assumptions focus attention on students, departments, the discipline, or society as the source of impediments to women's participation and as viable points of intervention. For example, individual-level analyses typically assume that students not in CSE lack some necessary experience or personal characteristic such as ability, attitude, or interest that relates to participation in computing. These studies do not actually consider women deficient, but they do portray women's characteristics as different from men's characteristics in a way that inhibits women's ability to participate in computing as it is currently constructed. From this point of view, the absence of some essential ingredient leads women to bypass computing. To remedy the situation, interventions try to develop women's skill, improve women's attitude, or spark women's interest in computing.

Among studies that employ an institutional or department level of analysis, the typical assumption is that departments can be deficient in support, pedagogy, resource, or some other way that is necessary for women's participation, and that *departments* recruit, retain, and advance female students, or not. Institution- or department-level studies begin with hypotheses about how environmental differences in institutions and departments are related to women's participation. They might examine how CSE programs or departments differ from each other and the outcomes (e.g., departmental gender composition, the gender gap in attrition rates, or the gender gap in graduation rates) associated with these differences. Proposed interventions try to modify environmental characteristics to make them more conducive to women's participation.

Profession- or discipline-level analyses also make assumptions about deficiency or agency. They assume a deficit in the discipline, and that *disciplines* attract, include, and promote women, or not. Discipline-level studies begin with hypotheses about how gender segregation into certain disciplines is related to societal or disciplinary beliefs and structures. They might examine the relationship between gender composition and educational alternatives or beliefs about women's roles. Discipline-level studies might also ask about the nature of the discipline, and whether it is what it ought to be or how it has changed over time. From this point of view, women's representation is inextricably tied to the nature of the discipline, and cannot be changed without either changing women (perhaps through a societal redefinition of their role) or changing the discipline. Proposed interventions might try to redefine the discipline or societal beliefs about its nature and women's roles within it.

As we reviewed the literature, our analysis grid called attention to how infrequently the progression aspect of women's participation is addressed. Few studies consider how one level of postsecondary education affects whether men and women progress or advance to the next level of postsecondary education. This question may warrant attention because women's representation generally declines disproportionately between levels of education (the exception is from bachelor's to master's degrees), and between education and occupation.

An initial look at the education-to-occupation data shows that although career faithfulness is strong in computer science (Freeman and Aspray 1999), women's career faithfulness appears to be weaker than men's. Calculations using SESTAT data from the NSF (available online at ⟨http://www.srsstats.sbe.nsf.gov⟩) show that there is a seven-point gender gap in the percent of graduates with computer and mathematical sciences baccalaureate degrees who are employed in occupations closely related to their discipline. A smaller proportion of women than men put their bachelor's degrees to work in computing. To put computing's progression gap in perspective, we compared it with the gender gap in progression within science and engineering in general. The comparison showed that the computing gender gap in progression is larger than the four-point average gap between men and women with bachelor's degrees in science or engineering disciplines. (Specifically, in 1999, 49 percent of women with computer or mathematical sciences baccalaureates were employed in a closely related principal job, but 56 percent of men with similar degrees were. For scientists or engineers in general, 41 percent of women versus 45 percent of men were employed in a job closely related to their degree.) Thus, both in computing and in science and engineering, women were less likely than men to work in the occupation for which they studied, but the difference was slightly greater in computing. As a consequence, the step from bachelor's degree to computing professional is one more place where women's participation falls behind men's, and this falling-behind process is worse in computing than it is in science and engineering disciplines overall. This observation suggests that it could be productive to study factors that influence career faithfulness. (See, for example, the literature review in this book by Bartol and Aspray.)

Up to this point, we have been cavalier about our use of the terms CSE, computing, IT, and so on. Yet it is clear that more than semantic differences distinguish among these various names for our academic area of interest. For instance, there are a greater percentage of women in IT than in computer science programs, and a greater focus on applications and context. Some literature suggests that the latter differences are the reason for the former because women find applications and context more appealing than they find the arcane craft of programming. The validity of this hypothesis is being tested by research currently underway. (See, for example, the Robinson et al. study in this book.) When these findings become available, we will have a better idea about which distinctions are necessary or whether further study is needed. In the meantime, given the sparse literature, we will consider findings from all the computing disciplines to be relevant. These include computer science, computer engineering, (management) information systems, (library and) information science, and informatics.

Just as we have been cavalier about discipline names, we have also glossed over the issue of differences among women. For example, we know that minority women's representation in computing differs from white women's. Likewise, students who interrupt their formal education for work or family reasons (usually called nontraditional), often follow different career paths than those women who continue straight through all their schooling before entering the workforce. There may also be significant differences among women depending on their level of education, type of occupation, or employment setting planned. Until there is empirical evidence, we will assume that relevant factors apply to all women unless there are obvious distinctions, as in the case of child care.

A final caveat about our approach to the literature is that the research we are surveying is almost exclusively conducted in the United States. Although there is some excellent research produced in other countries, multinational studies are rare and it is difficult to know which results apply to other societies. Furthermore, comparisons using international data are fraught with difficulties stemming from differences in educational systems, record keeping, and culture. The caution needed when considering international results is balanced against the value that cross-cultural comparisons can provide. A good example of an enlightening study is Charles and Bradley's (2002), which shows that women's representation in nontraditional disciplines varies by both cultural beliefs about appropriate female roles and the structure of a nation's educational system. This finding may help explain why U.S. women are well represented in computing programs at community colleges and in certificate programs, but less well represented in computing programs at doctoral institutions.

Each of the ten factors we describe below has received attention for its contribution to women's representation in computing. Although it is possible that all of these factors play a role in the overall representation of women in computing, it is important to emphasize that any or all of the factors might not be relevant in a particular institution or for a particular student. Even factors with high-quality evidence showing the significant part they play in the gender composition of computing might not be relevant to a particular institution. Generalized results are just that: what is generally true. In a specific case, these factors allow us to make a reasoned guess as to why underrepresentation is present, but without further study, we cannot say with certainty that any or all of these factors apply in particular circumstances.

Theory

Theories help us sort through data to recognize what is relevant and fit discrete bits into an overall coherent explanation. Together with standards of practice for collecting and analyzing data, theories help us evaluate information and transform it into knowledge. Without theory, it is difficult to identify productive research questions, know when variation is substantively significant, and advance toward an understanding of reality from which we can make reasonable predictions about the outcomes of actions.

Several theories from social psychology, sociology, and women's studies have been used, most often implicitly, to pattern and explain the facts of women's underrepresentation in CSE. Examples include Eccles's expectancy-value model and Steele's stereotype threat social-psychological theories; Smith-Lovin and McPherson's network and Kanter's tokenism sociological theories; and Wajcman's feminist theories about gender and technology. Efforts are underway to develop a theory specifically explaining women's underrepresentation in IT. Trauth (2004) argues that the gender composition of computing is a product of the relationship between individual characteristics and the requirements and characteristics of the discipline.

The explicit use of an established theory is evident in the social psychology research that applies expectancy-value theory to account for the gender balance of computing. This theory explains course-taking and other achievement-related behaviors (Wigfield and Eccles 2000), proposing that gender stereotypes and inborn characteristics are exogenous variables that ultimately influence students' expectations of success with particular tasks as well as the value that students place on particular activities and outcomes. In turn, the value of an activity and the expectation of succeeding at the activity directly influence the choice to engage in that activity. The research on computer self-efficacy, experience, and stereotype threat relates to aspects of this model.

There are few other instances of the explicit use of theory in investigations of computing's gender composition. The chapters in this volume offer some examples, but they are rare in the literature on gender and IT.

Without theory, the research produces a collection of valuable observations that lack the context of a causal chain linking them to each other as well as to a meaningful outcome such as women's representation, retention, or progression to the next level. For example, the literature offers many reports of mentoring interventions, but there is no comprehensive theory of why or how mentoring works in academic settings. Theory building is underway for mentoring in organizational settings (McManus and Russell 1997), and that effort might be applied to academia, but until it is, we have only a fragmentary understanding of what conditions promote mentoring and positive mentoring outcomes.

Even when theory is invoked as a foundation for empirical research, study outcomes may not be tested against theoretical predictions, or the test can be less than convincing. Too much of the research into the gender composition of computing includes only formative evaluations (participant satisfaction with aspects of the program) rather than summative evaluations that measure whether predicted outcomes and impact were achieved. When summative evaluation is attempted, it must still meet several criteria if it is to be credible. The criteria considered most important by an NSF evaluation of research on programs for women and girls in STEM were:

• a cogent means of measuring outcomes;

• data from a sample larger than ten;

• appropriate measures of outcomes;

• a study design employing pre- and postassessments, a control group, or comparison;

• one or more data collection points;

• analytic techniques and inferences suitable for the nature and subject of study;

• overall scientific integrity. (Urban Institute Education Policy Center 2000)

We found few examples of published research on computing's gender composition that was tied to theory and met these criteria.

The Research

The Culture and Image of Computing

Culture includes everything we learn from each other as members of a human society. It is the language, custom, and conventions, beliefs, values, and artifacts that differentiate our "group" from other groups. It is created, maintained, and changed by the people who participate in it.

Like most professions, computing has a culture of its own. Some elements of computing's culture include:

• the jargon used to name hardware and software, techniques, and events (e.g., surfing, WYSIWYG, booting, and crashing);

• common practices such as gaming, using e-mail or instant messaging as the preferred communication mode, using an object-oriented approach to problem solving, or focus to the point of obsession;

• valuing speed, conciseness, and power;

• the physical artifacts of computing—the laptops, tablets, desktops, mainframes, peripherals, software, robots, books, and so on.

Many researchers in this field believe that there is a strong overlap between the attributes of computing culture and those of masculine culture. This hypothesis was put forward in the pioneering work of Kiesler, Sproull, and Eccles (1985), and is similar to the claims made by Wajcman (1991) for the relationship between technology and masculinity more generally. Their hypotheses are plausible. Evidence can be found in the themes of aggression, hierarchy, and dominance that are prevalent in both masculine and computing cultures. For example, the language of computing incorporates many violent terms such as hacking, blue screen of death, brute force, killer app, and number crunching. Likewise, computer games commonly feature competition, destruction, and carnage; and computer programmers revel in the feeling of power they experience from having the machine perform according to their will. These types of language and interest have been noted as distinctions between masculine and feminine behavior in Western culture (Tannen 1991). For instance, according to the Bem sex role inventory, male characteristics include aggression, ambition, competitiveness, dominance, and forcefulness.

A number of researchers in this field are interested in the image of computing. The image of computing is its public face, the way it is represented to and perceived by those outside the field. It consists of the stereotypes that serve as shorthand for the type of people who are in computing and the type of jobs that comprise the practice of computing. The image is selectively based on computing's culture—it may be accurate or distorted, but it is recognizable. For example, a familiar icon is the pale, socially awkward geek who has ill-defined boundaries between work and play, both of which involve intense engagement with a computer. Likewise, many people would recognize computing if described as a constantly changing, demanding, equipment-focused occupation involving massive amounts of technical minutia codified in unreadable or unread manuals.

Culture, stereotypes, and image are of interest to scholars because they are seen as both discipline- and society-level factors that might relate to women's representation in computing. It is an open question as to whether these factors are a consequence or a cause of women's scarcity. Recent evidence from interviews with graduating seniors at Carnegie Mellon University suggests that culture is a consequence of gender composition. As the gender composition of the computing program became more balanced, the culture changed (Blum and Frieze 2004). When women's representation rose to more than one-third of the undergraduates, gender differences in the value placed on computing diminished to the point that there was greater variation within gender than between men and women. Blum and Frieze conclude that attempts to reshape the culture of computing might be unnecessary or counterproductive. Their interesting finding must be replicated to ensure that the observed similarity of men and women in this single program is not actually due to recruiting procedures or some other idiosyncrasy of the program, rather than being generally due to computing culture in a gender-balanced environment.

While Blum and Frieze argue that computing culture is a consequence of its gender composition, most scholars contend that the causality goes in the opposite direction. Culture and image contribute to underrepresentation when women reject computing as an unappealing or inappropriate activity, when women conform to the stereotype that computing is male behavior, or when computing offers few opportunities for people with women's inherent or learned characteristics. Although we do not know of U.S. studies that show these results, we know of at least one European study that shows that the perception of computing as a masculine domain is related to the active rejection by women who could succeed (Wilson 2003).

These discipline- and society-level factors can also apply at the department and individual levels. At the department level, the degree to which the local culture matches the culture of the discipline and the degree to which the local culture communicates the same message of inclusion or exclusion that the discipline communicates will influence whether a department attracts or repels, retains or loses, and promotes or squanders those who do not fit the culture or image. At the individual level, people who are uncomfortable or feel unwelcome in "foreign" cultures will avoid those cultures if possible or leave them if they do not get acclimated; women who conform to gender stereotypes will be less likely to enter, persist, and progress in computing than will those who individuate from women as a group.

There is recent evidence from social psychology research that offers insight into the process by which individual behavior conforms or does not conform to stereotypes. According to experiments, the average person conforms to stereotypes unless they individuate or think of themselves as different from other members of the group to which they belong. Cultural beliefs about gender differences in ability affect self-assessments, which in turn affect aspirations (Correll 2004). The negative effects of stereotypes are overcome by calling attention to a person's unique qualities (Ambady et al. 2004). These general results suggest that the male stereotype of computing will lead women to underestimate their computing abilities and decrease the chances they will aspire to computing occupations. Those women who do engage in computing enter the field because they consider themselves to be different from women in general. This individuation may make it less likely that successful female computer scientists will bond with each other and work to promote greater participation of other women in the field. These hypotheses are considered in the chapter by Varma, Prasad, and Kapur (this volume).

The classic works on the culture of computing are descriptive. They include those by Turkle (1984) and Kiesler, Sproull, and Eccles (1985). These reports have become part of the mythology of the field. Turkle's ethnographic study of hacker culture at the Massachusetts Institute of Technology led her to describe it as "peculiarly male." The more general, but fragmentary studies and observations of Kiesler, Sproull, and Eccles led them to argue that computing is a culture created and transmitted by men. The shouting and swearing in arcades, war and sports games, focus on speed, images of men on software packaging, and utilitarian computer labs were all characteristics of the computer culture that fit masculine stereotypes.

Student selection of education and careers within the computing disciplines also provides evidence of the shaping role of culture. Researchers have noted that women appear to be better represented in certain IT specialties such as information science, technology and media studies, and systems engineering. These specialties seem to project a less masculine image than computer science does; and they appear to have a different culture. Using ethnographic research methods for the direct observation and comparison of educational environments, researchers examined the differences in customs and conventions that might affect women's participation (Barker and Garvin-Doxas 2004). The extensive observation, interviewing, and evaluation of artifacts led to the conclusion that the mainstream CSE program at the study institution typically exhibited much more abstract, impersonal, and hierarchical practices than did the technology, arts, and media program. Customs such as explaining the relevance of a new topic when it was introduced, using students' names, and cooperative learning differentiated the technology, arts, and media program culture from traditional CSE culture. The researchers hypothesized, but did not demonstrate, a causal link between the nature of the subcultures and women's representation in these IT specialties. They focus specifically on gender differences in communication or learning styles, but one could interpret their findings more generally as a matter of culture.

Many open questions remain about the relationship of culture and image to the gender composition of computing. For example, we would expect that differences in the culture of computing over time or across departments should be reflected in differences in levels of women's participation. This expectation implies that there is a computing culture that is national or international, but that assumption is open to question. If there is a national or international computing culture, to what extent can a department create its own subculture of computing? Questions also arise about the influence that computing culture has on individuals. We would expect that all else being equal, variation in individuals' perception of computing culture or their affinity for the culture they perceive would be associated with their participation in computing. Evidence of such a relationship would show that women computer scientists have more characteristics that fit the masculine stereotype or are more comfortable with masculine culture than the average woman. The social psychology findings on how individuation makes it more likely that a person's behavior will not conform to stereotypes should be tested for their applicability to computing. Furthermore, there is the question as to whether the masculine-oriented culture of computing makes departmental practices more important for retaining women than these practices would be in fields where the culture is not masculine stereotyped (as argued by Fox [2001] and Margolis and Fisher [2002b]). Finally, there is the question of how women's participation relates to changes in discipline boundaries as defined by academia and the professional organizations.

Experience

Precollege experience with computing includes informal experience with computer games and applications as well as formal experience with computing classes and other supervised school use. These initial encounters introduce people to the culture of computing; they shape impressions, and provide information about what is involved with studying and using computers. When one sex has earlier or greater exposure than the other, that experience builds their credentials, knowledge, and perhaps the confidence that they could succeed in a computing career.

When the personal computer first made private access possible, there were reports that boys reached college with more computing experience than girls (Kersteen et al. 1988). This disparity was probably a consequence of the many opportunities for first computing experiences that were designed with male users in mind (Cassell and Jenkins 1998). By attracting a largely male audience, these first computing experiences, such as games and camps, led to reports of gender differences in experience further down the line when students reached college (Shashaani 1997).

More recently, there are reports indicating that most forms of computing experience have equalized for boys and girls, so that college entrants now have similar amounts of game play, Internet, and e-mail use (DeBell and Chapman 2003). Other data show that among college-bound SAT takers in 2003, men and women had comparable computing experience in computer literacy, word processing, Internet activity, and creating spreadsheets and databases (College Board 2003). For the past eight years, however, women taking the SAT comprised an increasing majority of college-bound students with no computing work or experience, and women had less and less programming and computer graphics experience relative to their male colleagues. It is unclear if these inequalities are relevant to the gender balance in computing, but it seems quite likely that the equalized forms of experience are not relevant because computer literacy, word processing, Internet activity, e-mail, and spreadsheets and database creation did not coincide with an increase in women's entry and persistence in postsecondary computing.

Experience has been studied primarily because of its hypothesized associations with both student confidence and success in introductory courses—two factors that may affect participation in computing. Experience is not generally expected to have a direct association with participation. Instead, the link between computing experience and confidence is a step along the path to participation, as is probably the link between computing experience and academic success.

Research indicates that experience increases confidence, although the nature of the experience might affect the degree of increase (see Dickhauser and Stiensmeier-Pelster 2002; Lips and Temple 1990; Potosky 2002; Chua, Chen, and Wong 1999; Emurian 2004). In turn, confidence is believed to increase participation, as will be discussed in a later section of this chapter. The possible link between computing experience and academic success is explored here.

Research shows that prior computing experience is positively associated with academic success (Taylor and Mounfield 1994). For example, Sacrowitz and Parelius (1996) found that the 86 women in introductory courses at Princeton and Rutgers generally had less computing experience than their 194 male classmates. Among these mathematically able students who intended a technical major in spring 1995, those with little prior computing experience did not earn top grades in their introductory computer science classes. The average grades for men and women were similar, but women were not among the highest achievers. Similar grade consequences of experience and gender differences in experience were reported from various other single-institution studies (Bunderson and Christensen 1995; Margolis and Fisher 2002a; Brown et al. 1997). Thus, there appears to be a consensus that precollege computing experience contributes to success in a student's first college computing class.

Research also shows that students who get low grades in the introductory course are less likely to persist in the CSE major; however, low grades cannot adequately explain why women leave CSE at higher rates than men. Women with high grades also leave. Evidence for this assertion comes both from reports that women's grades in CSE are comparable to men's, and from research on choosing and leaving STEM disciplines. For example, a large study of first-year students at four highly selective institutions found that differences in introductory course grades did not adequately explain the effect of gender on persistence in computer science (Strenta et al. 1994). Other researchers proposed that the reason for the continuing gender difference in persistence is that women and men respond differently to grades—women have higher expectations than men, and women feel personally responsible if they fail to meet those expectations while men blame others.

A large single-institution study found support for the hypothesis that gender differences in responses to grades in computing courses help explain the gender gap in persistence. Jagacinski, LeBold, and Salvendy (1988) followed more than one thousand newly declared computer science majors to the end of their sophomore year in 1983. They determined that grades were important for men's and women's persistence. Yet women also left the major when their grades were not as high as the grades they received in high school. For women, the effect of grades was not a simple matter of how high they were, but how high they were relative to their high school grades. This finding, together with the finding about experience, suggests that women might leave at disproportionate rates when their grades are depressed by inexperience—grades that may be satisfactory to a male classmate, but fail to meet a woman's personal standards.

An alternative explanation for the way computing experience could affect academic success of CSE students is when instructors assume that students have more experience than formally required by their course (Bunderson and Christensen 1995). Instructor assumptions about prior knowledge are difficult to avoid when many students in a class are familiar with the concepts being presented, but the consequence is a fast-paced course where truly inexperienced students can flounder. Imagine having no computing experience when classmates have academic credit for six CSE courses—a situation identified by University of Virginia instructors who teach the introductory courses James P. Cohoon (personal communication). Designing and teaching courses that introduce computing to the uninitiated might reduce or eliminate the part experience plays in academic success.

Even as certain aspects of prior experience reach gender parity, there are still several unanswered questions regarding the effect of experience on the gender composition of postsecondary computing. These questions include whether particular gender differences in prior experience have an impact on each of the three stages of participation: achieving women's presence, retaining women, or advancing women in the discipline. Can curriculum and pedagogy intervene in these relationships? Information is also needed about whether there is a gender difference in the amount or nature of experience gained while a student is at the postsecondary level. Is it possible, say, that men and women have unequal access to research opportunities so that the experience gap grows during formal education? In particular, the structure of graduate school funding might give men more research experience and women more teaching experience. There is no research we are aware of that addresses this issue.

Entry Barriers
When Etzkowitz et al. (1994) discussed barriers to women in science and engineering, they considered factors that could differentially affect persistence at the PhD

level and progression into the academic workforce. We employ a narrower definition, focusing only on structural barriers that operate primarily at points of either entry to computing or progression in the discipline. Thus for our purposes, entry barriers include the selection criteria, application processes, articulation problems between two- and four-year colleges, tightly structured curricula that delay graduation for students who enter after their first year, difficult access due to high demand, and lack of transition programs for students who want to enter graduate study in computing but do not have an undergraduate computing major. These factors could act as barriers when they produce differential outcomes for men and women who want to switch into CSE from other majors, enter baccalaureate programs from community college, enter graduate programs from the workforce or a noncomputing undergraduate major, or enter the computing workforce after completing their studies.

Entry barriers of these types could have differential effects on men and women if the sexes tend to differ by admission qualifications, response to application procedures, need for efficient transfer or transition programs, or time of life when their computing interest develops. If barriers impede applicants without extensive programming experience, women would be disproportionately affected because they still arrive at college with less programming experience than their male classmates. Likewise, where introductory courses fail to take levels of student experience into account or if they expect particular types of computing experience, women's entry might be disproportionately impeded. Those who develop an interest in computing as they mature—a common occurrence for women—could be impeded by the tightly structured curricula typical of computing. Another way that entry barriers could have gendered consequences is if less assertive students are disadvantaged in their access to courses in overenrolled programs. Finally, varying degrees of entry barriers might be a reason why community colleges, four-year colleges, and graduate programs attract men and women in varying proportions.

Powerful evidence of the impact that removing entry barriers can have comes from Carnegie Mellon University. Students there are admitted directly into the School of Computer Science, and the school's selection had originally favored experienced students. In conjunction with other research-based interventions, admission officers began placing greater emphasis on applicants' "demonstrated independence, energy, creativity, and community involvement," and the "economic, ethnic, and gender diversity" of the incoming class (Margolis and Fisher 2002b, 136). The outcome reported was a dramatic increase in women's representation, with no loss of quality. Unfortunately, it is not possible to disaggregate this change from their other interventions, such as a national feeder group of guidance counselors and high school teachers who have a special knowledge of Carnegie Mellon.

A necessary accessory to the change in admission criteria was a change in the curriculum that established alternate pathways into the computing program, depending on each student's prior experience. Offering introductory courses tailored to different experience levels resulted in "increased levels of satisfaction among both more and less experienced students of both genders" (Margolis and Fisher 2002b, 130). It is unlikely that the admissions changes could have succeeded without this curricular accommodation, but it is unclear whether simply removing the experience barrier from introductory courses is sufficient to increase the gender balance in the program.

Because Carnegie Mellon reported such impressive results from removing experience-based entry barriers, it is surprising that we found no other reports of raising women's participation by removing entry barriers. Neither were there any studies that offered generalizable results since the Carnegie Mellon example is still only one institution. Thus, there is much research to be done on this potential contributor to women's underrepresentation. For instance, curricula that accommodate late entry to the field, bridging courses that facilitate migration from other disciplines, and programs or practices that facilitate progression from high school, community college, college, or graduate school all warrant investigation as potential methods of promoting women's entry and progression in CSE. Research is also needed to determine whether entry barriers can explain variation in the gender balance of fields in which women are less likely than men to participate. We also need to know more about the relationship between entry or progression and student assertiveness in the presence of barriers such as insufficient course offerings.

Curricula

We already discussed curricular issues that are related to entry barriers. Our focus in this section is on the issue of what computer science is or ought to be.

Efforts to achieve gender balance in computing are influenced by beliefs about whether the technical nature of the discipline inherently excludes women. Depending on one's belief, questions can arise about curricular content. Should computer science consider inclusiveness as it continually reconfigures itself, or is it possible to identify and mitigate its exclusiveness without changing the nature of the discipline?

Those who favor reconfiguring the discipline consider the relationship between gender and technology to be relatively fixed, but consider the nature of computer science to be continually evolving in response to new knowledge, technologies, applications, and student and employer interests. Proponents of this view consider it more pragmatic to alter CSE for appeal to women than it is to attempt fundamental changes in gender-related values and stereotypes. They observe that independent of familiarity and ability, women seem less likely than men to value and seek technical knowledge (Wigfield and Eccles 2000), and conclude that incorporation of nontechnical knowledge would improve computing's gender balance.

In comparison, those who favor mitigating technological gender differences consider the relationship between gender and technology to be socially defined and malleable; and they resist changing the discipline to suit values and stereotypes that may fit the current definition of feminine yet not be inherent characteristics of women. Proponents of this view are inclined to work toward changing stereotypes and other social forces that discourage women's participation in computing. Rather than creating a less technical track for women a la the corporate world's "mommy track," this perspective favors the development of techie women who succeed in a field that offers them as much opportunity as it offers men.

These different points of view influence the questions raised about curricular effects on women's participation. Those who consider the gender-technology relationship to be fixed focus on curricular content, and ask whether gender equity requires that computing consist of more than singularly technical skills and knowledge. They also ask what the proper skills and knowledge are for an inclusive computing discipline. Those who believe that the gender-technology relationship can be mitigated are less interested in content than they are in the other curricular features that favor men over women. Both viewpoints offer promising insights into opportunities for promoting gender balance in CSE.

Some disciplinary changes in computing are already taking place as new specialties combine IT with other areas of expertise, but evidence of their effect on gender composition is not yet available. For example, informatics emphasizes the context and application of IT. At Indiana University at Bloomington, the informatics program includes bioinformatics, chemical informatics, human-computer interaction design, new media, and health care informatics. Overall, the university's undergraduate enrollment is about 14 percent female. Another innovative program is offered by the University of Colorado at Boulder. It has six-course certificate programs in technology arts, and media—emphasizing multimedia design—and multidisciplinary applied technologies—stressing foundational computing skills for nonmajors. The technology, arts, and media program is approximately 52 percent female. The multidisciplinary applied technologies program was 38 percent female in its first year. The variance in gender composition of these three programs suggests that curricular characteristics might correlate with gender composition. Still, there are no systematic reports of the relationship between gender balance and curricula yet.

In addition to creating new specialties, some CSE departments have changed their curricula in an attempt to improve their gender balance. These changes include opportunities to apply computing expertise for social good. For example, the EPICS program at Purdue University awards academic credit to students working on technical problems for community service and education organizations. Over the first five years, 33 percent of the electrical and computer engineering students in the program were women compared with 12 percent women in the Purdue undergraduate electrical and computer engineering program as a whole (Jamieson 1991). The apparent attractiveness that computing for public service had for women fits with expectations based on the values research done by Eccles (Wigfield and Eccles 2000) and the findings from Carnegie Mellon (Margolis and Fisher 2002a). The evidence from Purdue's program, however, does not demonstrate that it actually draws women to computing, given the low percentage of women that Purdue's electrical and computer engineering program enrolled—12 versus 14 percent for computer engineering programs in doctoral institutions, or 16 percent for computer science programs in comparably ranked doctoral institutions—during the time when EPICS was offered. It seems that benefiting society is more appealing to the women than the men who are in computer science, and providing this opportunity could have a positive effect. Nevertheless, service-oriented computing does not appear to have been a sufficient motivation to draw women into Purdue's CSE program, nor is it clear that service-oriented computing improved women's retention.

The research that has been conducted thus far leaves many unanswered questions about the role that curricula might play in women's representation. From a department-level perspective, we would like to know if tailoring curriculum and course content to accommodate women's demonstrated interests and values results in more gender-balanced enrollment and retention. For example, if women's portion of enrollment increased after Purdue introduced its EPICS program, it would suggest that the curricular change helped to attract more women. At the discipline level, it would be useful to know which characteristics of the new specialty areas are associated with gender-balanced enrollments. Does less technical mean more female friendly? At the individual level, useful investigations include those that explore any differences between technically and nontechnically oriented women and their selection of and success in different types of computing curricula, and whether early filter courses, with their combination of heavy workloads and low grades, deter women more than men.

Role Models

A role model is a person who serves as an example of the values, attitudes, and behaviors associated with a role. Seeing someone socially similar to oneself in a role makes it more likely you could see yourself in that kind of a role. Socially similar to oneself here means either the same gender, race, or socioeconomic class.

Although lack of women role models has frequently been cited as an important reason there are few women in computing (Teague 2002; Townsend 1996), the concept of a role model is often conflated with that of a mentor. The distinction is that role models need not interact with students to be effective, whereas mentoring is an active process of sponsoring. Mentors are likely to be role models, but role models can be completely unaware of the part they play in demonstrating how to be a computer scientist. Role models can be found in the history of computing (Gurer 1998), in biographies of currently successful women in computer science or the computer industry, and even among the female faculty and upper-level students within one's own department. Their visibility is what makes them potential role models.

Same-sex role models are pertinent to women's representation because the small numbers of available women role models could inhibit women's recruitment, retention, and progression if same-sex role models are essential to participation in a discipline. We would expect that programs with a larger number of available role models would attract, retain, and advance higher proportions of women. Individual women who report having role models should be the ones more likely to enter, persist, and progress in computing.

In spite of the general endorsement of role modeling as a means to attract and retain women, the practice is not without question. Canes and Rosen (1995) found no support for the value of faculty role models in attracting women to a major. Their panel data from three institutions produced no evidence that increasing the number of female faculty generally translated into more female majors. Although their study did not focus on CSE, their finding offers no encouragement for the argument that women's choice of a CSE major may be influenced by the presence of faculty role models.

Whether or not faculty role models attract women into CSE, it is still possible that role models influence women's retention. When first-year female students are taught mathematics and science by women faculty, their course retention is higher (Robst, Keil, and Russo 1998). The impact of faculty gender is greatest in classes where there are few women students, as is often the case in CSE. Thus, there appears to be good potential for retaining initially interested women by offering them faculty role models.

Student role models might also help retain women. The University of Wisconsin at Parkside has a program in which female students who successfully completed the introductory CSE course comprise half of the computer laboratory staff. These lab assistants provide instructional aid and system maintenance, development, and administration (Haller and Fossum 1998). They might or might not form the kind of personal relationships that typify mentoring relationships, but they are certainly present and visible as potential role models who demonstrate that women can advance through the CSE major. Research from other disciplines suggests that the presence of women teaching assistants is a factor in improved course completion by women students, but the University of Wisconsin at Parkside study does not report on this issue (Butler and Christensen 2003).

The manner in which someone embodies a role could also affect whether he or she is an effective role model. For example, women who work incessantly and have no time for a personal life may not be acceptable role models for most women. Approximately fifty interviews with faculty and graduate students at one research university showed that physics, chemistry, electrical engineering, and computer science lost women in part because "there are no role models to show you how to get there" (Etzkowitz et al. 1994). In particular, female graduate students felt the need for female faculty to emulate. They rejected women who had made it by following a "male model" of being aggressive, competitive, and unconditionally devoted to work. Instead, they preferred to model themselves after the more scarce women who balanced their work with nonwork roles. Thus, being female may not be a sufficient qualification for an effective role model. There might be behavioral qualifications required of role models before they are effective for improving the retention of women.

There are many unanswered questions regarding the effect role models have on the entry, presence, and progression of women in CSE. Evidence from other disciplines suggests that individual student decisions to enter are not likely to be influenced by faculty role models, but that persistence might be influenced by both student and faculty role models. We do not know yet if these findings hold in CSE. We also do not know if departments with many women faculty, at least some of whom balance work life with personal life, retain more women than departments with a single female role model. Discipline-wide role modeling through professional society leadership or speaker programs should also be investigated to determine if these widely visible role models are associated with women's increased participation in CSE.

Mentoring

Mentoring is an active process of sponsorship by experienced members toward less experienced entrants or trainees. Mentoring can help professionalize the protégé. It provides an advocate as well as useful information about how to operate in a particular environment; and mentoring can offer social and emotional support.

This issue is pertinent to women's participation if mentoring interacts with gender to affect choice, persistence, and progress in computing, or if one sex is more likely than the other to make use of mentors. Students may have unequal access to mentors, or mentoring might be more necessary or effective under certain circumstances.

Studies in other disciplines found a variety of positive outcomes associated with mentoring (see, for example, Campbell and Campbell 1997; Tenenbaum, Crosby, and Gliner 2001; Ulku-Steiner, Kurtz-Costes, and Kinlaw 2000). For the most part, this research was conducted at single institutions; it targeted graduate students and included several disciplines. The consensus of results indicated that certain mentoring activities were related to positive student outcomes, ranging from increased satisfaction, productivity, or retention in the institution or program. Some studies dispute the importance of matching mentor and protégé by sex, but it appears that the dispute arises from the outcomes that were measured: students were more satisfied with same-sex mentors, but they benefited regardless of their mentor's sex (Campbell and Campbell 1997).

An example of the general benefits of mentoring can be seen in one graduate-level, single-university study that compared results for men and women, including those in male-dominated disciplines. Survey data obtained from more than three hundred students at two points in time show that faculty mentoring increased the protégé's academic self-confidence and career commitment (Ulku-Steiner, Kurtz-Costes, and Kinlaw 2000). Mentor support was measured as a combination of both affective support (such as sensitivity to students' nonacademic commitments) and instrumental support (such as finding financial aid). This comprehensive mentoring was positively associated with career commitment for both men and women, including women in male-dominated disciplines. In addition to its direct effect on career commitment, and regardless of the mentor's sex, mentoring was also positively associated with academic self-confidence, which in turn increased career commitment. This association was strongest for women in disciplines where the majority of faculty members were men—these women had the lowest level of self-confidence. Independent of other factors, mentoring explained a moderate amount of the variance in career commitment for both men and women (slightly more for men). This finding is contrary to the hypothesis that women have a particular need for mentoring.

Academic success associated with faculty mentoring has also been demonstrated at the undergraduate level. Mentored students in one university's three-year study earned a 0.3 of a point higher cumulative GPA than nonmentored students who entered the study institution at the same time with the same sex, ethnicity, and high school GPA (protégé mean = 2.45, control mean = 2.29, difference significant at the .01 level) (Campbell and Campbell 1997). Mentored students were also less likely than the comparison group to drop out of school.

Student-to-student mentoring can make a difference too. The Women in Engineering Program at Purdue University, for example, matched first-year female engineering students with upper-class women for formal and informal activities. This program contributed to an overall improvement in student retention and the eradication of any significant gender differences in the retention of engineering undergraduates (Matyas and Dix 1990).

A study of peer mentoring outcomes in computing was conducted at Victoria University of Technology in Australia. Its peer-mentoring program offered tangible and intangible support to students working toward a business computing degree. The university provided time, space, and equipment for participating students to meet with their assigned upper-level student mentor. The outcome of this interaction and assistance from students who had recently been through similar experiences was that participating women were retained at rates twice as high as nonparticipants (Craig 1998). This dramatic difference is surely due at least in part to students' self-selection into the program, but the 90 percent retention rate seems high enough to suggest that mentoring did help retain computing students.

A nationwide survey of faculty in 117 computer science departments in doctoral institutions showed that when mentoring is common, departments send more of their seniors to graduate programs, and to top-tier graduate programs, as compared to departments where mentoring is rare (Cohoon, Gonsoulin, and Layman 2004). The particular outcome depended on the type of mentoring activities practiced—whether they focused on research or on providing instrumental support for students.

Furthermore, in cases where mentoring was motivated by the desire for diversity, women were retained at rates comparable to men. The association between mentoring and gender-balanced retention in the average computer science department is reported elsewhere in this book (chapter 7), and it echoes the findings for doctoral institutions. Together, these studies offer strong evidence that faculty mentoring is an effective way to promote gender-balanced retention in CSE.

Even as we acquire evidence of mentoring's positive effects for CSE students, the research raises other questions. Are there conditions in which departments are more likely to have many faculty mentor women students? What role do rewards and incentives play in the prevalence of diversity mentoring? How important to mentoring is a formal departmental commitment to create gender diversity? Do men and women have equal access to and make equal use of mentoring? Is mentoring equally practical and effective at different stages of education and a professional career?

Student-Faculty Interactions

Student-faculty interaction comprises the nature of contact between students and CSE faculty—whether it is cordial, welcoming, supportive, impersonal, or so on. This interaction is influenced by faculty attitudes about students and the teaching enterprise, and by whether faculty see themselves primarily as gatekeepers or coaches. Student-faculty interaction is more common but less personal and ongoing than mentoring; it is more interactive than role modeling. The two components of student-faculty interaction that we consider are:

• Faculty *attitudes* such as valuing teaching and students, a willingness to engage students as individuals and go beyond the subject matter, an openness to questions, cognitive stereotypes of the ideal student, and a preference for students similar to themselves;

• Faculty *behaviors* such as reacting positively to questions both in and out of class, making time for students out of class, encouraging students as learners, and encouraging students to persist in the discipline. Each of these behaviors may represent a cluster of several specific behaviors. For example, encouraging students to persist in the discipline involves describing the field as well as its practice and practitioners. It also involves the manner in which faculty members respond when students are having difficulty but want to persist in the major, and how they respond when students express a desire to leave the field.

Student-faculty interaction is pertinent to women's participation in computing for a variety of reasons. Faculty members act as gatekeepers and important sources of information about how to succeed in the discipline. When faculty members hold stereotypes of the ideal student based on typically male behavior, there are likely to be consequences for women's participation. There is also the possibility that change or strained resources would lead faculty members to adopt exclusive practices that disadvantage women, as happens in work organizations (Reskin and Roos 1990). If students perceive that faculty members think they do not belong in the field, such students might be less likely to persist. In contrast, support from faculty can influence STEM students to persist despite a crisis of confidence (Seymour and Hewitt 1997). These scenarios describe plausible connections between the nature of student-faculty interactions and the gender composition of computing.

Strong evidence about student-faculty interaction comes from Fox's (2001) national study of doctoral programs in science. A large mail survey of students in chemistry, computer science, electrical engineering, and physics was conducted in 1994. The response rate of 61 percent makes it likely that the results accurately represent student experiences in these fields. Fox found that on the whole, women were less likely than men in these disciplines to report positive student-faculty interactions. "Women, compared with men, are less likely to report being taken seriously and respected by faculty," and are less likely than men to consider their relationship with an adviser to be collegial or a mentoring relationship (Fox 2001, 659). Furthermore, women in doctoral programs that graduate high (or improved) proportions of women reported being helped by their advisers "in learning to design research, to write grant proposals, to coauthor publications, and to organize people" to a greater extent than women in programs that graduated low proportions of women (Fox 2001, 659). Perhaps these supportive interactions with faculty would qualify as mentoring because of the established adviser-advisee relationship. Whatever we name them, these interactions were associated with a greater presence of women, and the women in departments where these interactions were more common both published more papers and had higher expectations of graduating than did women in departments where faculty seldom provided this kind of help.

There are no reports of studies similar to Fox's but limited only to CSE graduate programs. A Computing Research Association study funded by the NSF, however, should offer results soon. Preliminary findings from this national study, called the Recruitment and Retention of Female Graduate Students in CSE, indicate similar gender differences in student experiences to those reported by Fox.

Certain types of student-faculty interaction have also been shown to affect the gender balance of program retention in computer science. As reported elsewhere in this book (chapter 7), undergraduate computer science programs were likely to retain men and women at equal rates when faculty encouraged the students in their classes to persist in the major. This result fits with findings that in the average discipline, men were much more likely than women to choose college majors in departments with high-status rewards but unsupportive faculty (Hearn and Olzak 1981). Women were more likely to choose programs where the faculty were supportive despite the low-status careers for which they would be prepared.

The findings about the importance of student-faculty interaction in computer science show that women's relations with instructors and advisers can have a measurable impact on women's retention. Evidence from studies including other disciplines suggests that the nature of student-faculty interaction can also affect women's entry. Still, we do not know if positive student-faculty interactions help promote women to the next level of computing. Nor do we have reliable information about whether women who personally have positive interactions with faculty are more likely to choose, persist, and advance in computing, although there are focus group data suggesting that prospective graduate students are likely to reject CSE departments after meeting faculty they consider "weird" or "elitist" (Cohoon and Baylor 2003). Other useful studies could explore whether interactions with faculty from different cultures are any more or less likely to communicate negative gender stereotypes. It might also be interesting to examine whether there are different outcomes related to student-faculty interaction in traditional versus remote education.

Peer Support

Peer support is the student analog of interaction with faculty. It involves both the attitudes and behaviors of other students, although it also includes the support that comes from the mere presence of socially similar people. These people are generally members of a single age or ethnic group, although other characteristics can come into play. When defining "peer" in computer science, gender is a salient characteristic because people tend to interact with others who share age, beliefs, race, occupation, and gender (McPherson, Smith-Lovin, and Cook 2001), and at least at the undergraduate level, CSE is lacking in peers for anyone who is not white and male.

A lack of access to those similar to ourselves helps explain why work organizations, including academic departments, retain women at lower proportions when women are in a numerical minority (Reskin, McBrier, and Kmec 1999). It may be the case that similar processes are at work in CSE.

An alternative view of peer support comes from the literature on social networks. This approach to explaining the interaction of gender and occupation focuses on social connections—who men and women interact with and how. These connections, or social networks, affect what information is available and what behavior is deemed acceptable. Because people are more likely to have connections with others who are socially similar to themselves, women's social networks are less likely than men's to include someone in computing. This gender difference in networks would advantage men and disadvantage women with respect to information about computer science education and occupations as well as accessing job opportunities made available through networks of those already employed in computing occupations. In this way, social networks could have an impact particularly on women's entry into computing and may explain the findings from numerous small studies in different countries that suggest young women have inaccurate information about the nature of computing (Teague 2000).

We know that students are more likely to choose and persist in a science major when they have socially similar peers. For example, Astin and Astin's (1992) nationwide quantitative study from the later half of the 1980s found that peers had a measurable impact on whether the 27,065 college and university students they studied eventually majored in science, mathematics, or engineering. The effects they observed differed by discipline. In biology, the presence of socially similar peers had an impact on persistence; in physical sciences, peers affected recruitment; in engineering, peers affected both persistence and recruitment. Astin and Astin's study shows that peer support can be an important element, and it reinforces the need to conduct discipline-specific investigations. Qualitative findings from another study add a gender dimension by showing that personal recommendations swayed women more than men in their choice of a science major (Seymour and Hewitt 1997).

There is also new research reported elsewhere in this book (chapter 7) showing that peer support improves women's retention in computer science. It found that mid- to large-sized departments retained men and women at comparable rates as their enrollment approached gender balance. Both men and women reported that their persistence in computer science depended on having classmates they were comfortable asking for help. For women, the luxury of approaching someone of the same sex was less available than it was for the men in their classes. The measurable impact of this expressed need for same-sex peer support was demonstrated by the correlation between the proportion of women entering a program and their retention at rates comparable to the men in their program.

There is no evidence yet whether peer support affects progression in computing. Neither is it clear whether personal interactions with peers are required, or if the simple presence of socially similar peers is sufficient to influence choice, persistence, and progression in computing. Other potential studies could explore how race, age, and citizenship might interact with peer support; whether peer support can be programmed successfully; and how peer support comes into play in distance education.

Confidence and Other Personal Characteristics

Common gender differences in personal characteristics are frequently suspected of causing the gender disparity in entry, presence, and progression in computing. These differences include academic fitness, confidence in one's ability to succeed at computing, the interest or value attached to computing, and response to competition. In each case, according to this explanation, women's characteristics—either inherently or through socialization—differ from men's in regard to some ingredient necessary for participation in CSE as it is currently constructed. These supply-side explanations for women's underrepresentation concentrate on early divergent choices and preferences that build different skill sets for men and women.

Academic fitness, whether due to inadequate preparation or lesser native ability, could affect women's participation in computing if there is a gender difference in having the necessary foundation for success in computing. Research based on this perspective investigates whether gender differences in preparation are the probable reason fewer women than men choose, persist, and advance in CSE. Evidence in support of this view is available for science majors (Webb, Lubinski, and Benbow 2002; Strenta et al. 1994), but not for computer science (Strenta et al. 1994). And even with respect to the other STEM disciplines, gender differences in SAT scores "account for less than half of the total gender gap" in the choice of an academic major (Turner and Bowen 1999). Furthermore, this argument is weakened by trends toward gender parity in high school mathematics and science course taking and grades during the years when women's participation in computing was declining, and by the high proportion of baccalaureate degrees awarded to women—more than 45 percent for the past twenty years.

Confidence in one's own ability to succeed is a crucial determinant of academic course and career choices (Eccles 1994). Students who expect to succeed at a particular task are more likely to engage and succeed than are those who anticipate failure, particularly a public failure (Huff 2002). The expectation of success is based on a variety of factors including experience and the gender appropriateness of the task. According to this theory, gender stereotypes influence confidence, which in turn causes men and women to have different patterns of course taking and occupations. Support for this chain of reasoning was mentioned in the section on the culture and image of computing, where we reported experimental results demonstrating the relationship between gender stereotypes and aspirations.

It is well documented that women exhibit lower self-confidence than men when it comes to computing (Lips 2004; Lips and Temple 1990; Volet and Lund 1994; MIT 1995). The influence that gender stereotypes explanations have on self-perceptions and interpretations of experiences help to explain the lack of confidence (Beyer 1990, 1998). Although men and women are equally accurate in their self-perceived ability to answer questions on feminine and neutral topics, women were markedly less confident than men about their answers on masculine topics. Furthermore, evaluations of their own performance after completing a task showed that women biased their evaluations in the direction of their earlier expectations. In other words, a woman who expected to do poorly on a programming assignment would rate her work at a lower grade than she actually earned. Even in the face of experience, women continued to think of themselves as less competent than they were at tasks they considered masculine (Beyer 1990).

In spite of the negative consequences from low confidence, some women succeed in computing (Fisher, Margolis, and Miller 1997). These women report less confidence in their computing abilities than men report. For example, Beyer and her colleagues (2003) surveyed fifty-six students at a small midwestern university. The twenty-four women and thirty-two men were all enrolled in CSE courses during the 2001 academic year. Analyses found no significant difference in confidence between the majors (including intended majors) and the nonmajors; however, there was a notable difference in confidence between men and women. Nonmajor men were more confident than computer science major women, even controlling for mathematics ACT scores. This finding from a single-institution study, together with findings from studies at other institutions, lends weight to the assertion that even those women who choose, persist, and advance in computing do so under different conditions from their male colleagues. Because the study participants were computer science majors, this study calls into question whether confidence is strongly tied to the choice of a computing major. The report is silent about this question.

Theoretically linked to confidence in a causal explanation for women's under-representation is the value that men and women place on computing. Psychological and social psychology research has identified certain values that are both involved in career choice and vary by gender (Wigfield and Eccles 2000; Bandura 1977). For example, numerous studies have shown that decisions about course taking and careers weigh the enjoyment of a task, the amount of effort it takes, its usefulness, and the sacrifices it would require (Wigfield and Eccles 2000). Although they apply the same criteria, males and females evaluate particular tasks, such as those related to mathematics and computing, differently. For instance, boys are more likely than girls to consider mathematics useful (Wigfield and Eccles 2000), and male college students report being more comfortable using computers than women report (Mitra et al. 2000). Values related to work also differ by sex (Marini et al. 1996). Male and female high school seniors in 1991 shared more views on the importance of job attributes than they had in previous years, but they still differed in ways that could be crucial to the choice of a computing career (Marini et al. 1996). Marini and her colleagues found that men more than women valued leisure time, and women more than men valued work that offers intrinsic, altruistic, and social rewards. According to these findings, women would value computing careers less if they thought computing offered more leisure time and less rewards such as interesting work that allows you to be yourself, use skills, see results, be helpful to others and society, and have contact with people and opportunities to make friends (Marini et al. 1996). As a consequence, women would be less likely to enter computing.

An investigation of gender differences relevant to IT work-related values was conducted at a large midwestern university by Bair and her colleagues (2003). A total of 772 undergraduates, 47 percent of them women, participated in an online survey about their future careers and perceptions of programming as a career. The participants were not randomly selected, but the primary results still echoed those found in the Marini study. Interest was the top priority in career selection for both sexes, followed by money for men but not for women. In the Bair study, women valued challenging work second; but that attribute was far from important for either men or women in the Marini study, which investigated many more attributes than Bair did. Bair goes on to investigate perceptions of programming as a career using credibility ratings of descriptive statements. She found that non-IT women students were less likely than the professionals and students in IT to believe that "programming solves human problems and makes customers' and coworkers' lives easier and more enjoyable" (2003). This observed difference suggests that women, who value altruistic rewards much more than men do, might be less likely to enter CSE because they do not believe it offers the career features they value. Without more information, and a study design that includes a random sample and tests of significance for ratings by sex and major, it is not possible to know whether the observed difference in perception is a meaningful distinction between women in and out of computing, or whether it exists in the larger population.

Another personal characteristic that might help explain the gender composition of computing is the response to competition. Seymour and Hewitt (1997), in their book on student attrition from science, mathematics, and engineering, argue that men and women are deterred by the same conditions, but that women's socialization leaves them less equipped than men in terms of dealing with these conditions. In particular, they note that women are not prepared for the weed-out system that challenges students and encourages competition. Their assertion that women do not perform as well as men in competitive environments is supported by experimental evidence (Gneezy, Niederle, and Rustichini 2003), but it has not been tested in computer science. When the role of competition is tested in computer science, the additional links between performance and entry, persistence, and progression should be considered. Furthermore, while on the face of it the confidence factor appears to be relevant to women's participation, women's high representation in other competitive fields such as premed or prelaw suggests that competition alone cannot explain women's underrepresentation in computing.

There is much work to be done investigating the role that personal characteristics such as values, expectations of success, and response to competition play in computing's gender balance. We have yet to demonstrate whether there are differences among women who never choose computing, those who enter and leave, and those who advance beyond the baccalaureate level. We need to clarify whether local environments influence confidence regarding stereotypical masculine tasks. Do programs or faculty action in support of less confident students result in these students' retention and progression despite their self-doubt? Do departments that encourage cooperation have more gender-balanced retention? The most obvious questions are how values and confidence could explain changes in women's participation over time, and whether women's confidence and the gender gap in confidence vary with women's representation in a field. Likewise, was computing less competitive during the years when women's participation was high than when it was low?

Pedagogy

Pedagogy is the methods and practice of teaching. It includes instructional practices such as lectures, hands-on labs, homework, grading practices, cooperative learning, and any other method of bringing about student mastery of course material.

Pedagogical practices have been implicated in women's underrepresentation primarily because of the possibility that practices common in CSE education are better suited for men's learning styles than for women's. This explanation for women's underrepresentation makes sense if men and women learn, or prefer to learn, in different ways, and if academic success is linked to both pedagogy and participation in computing—assumptions that are not well supported yet.

Evidence of a relationship between gender and learning style continues to be contested, and none has been reported specifically for computer science. (An example of new research on this issue is presented in chapter 12, this volume.) There have been numerous studies finding that high school girls differ from boys in motivation, persistence, independence, risk taking, and the ways they learn new material (Ridley and Novak 1983; Dewck 1986). There are also studies that do not support these results, however (Meece and Jones 1996).

As the debate over gender and learning style continues (Pirolli and Recker 1995; Severiens and Tendam 1994; Fritz 1992; Philbin et al. 1995), influential reports have been published about the student exodus from college-level STEM disciplines as a consequence of poor teaching (Seymour and Hewitt 1997) and the positive effects of female-friendly pedagogy (Tobias 1990; Fencl 1997). The low quality of instructional practices associated with the loss of students from STEM led to hypotheses that women were especially vulnerable to the effects of inadequate pedagogy.

In CSE, research into this pedagogy hypothesis focuses on the influence of structured labs, collaborative methods such as pair programming, the style of knowledge sharing and assessment, and the use of particular programming methods. For each of these instructional methods, the hope is that women will be retained by improved student learning, performance, satisfaction, or attitudes toward computing.

Structured labs teach computer use through supervised hands-on experience. There is evidence from a single-institution study that this form of instruction influences computing behaviors and attitudes (Arch and Cummins 1989); however, it is not clear that reducing these gender differences contributes to women's participation in computing. The concrete instruction offered by a structured introduction to computing eliminated the initial gender differences that existed in computer use and appeal among 362 first-year college students (Arch and Cummins 1989). In contrast, the students whose introduction to computing was unstructured showed an increase in these gender differences at the end of the term. Thus, instructional methods influenced whether students had the type of attitudes and behaviors that might precede entry into a CSE major.

Whether computer use and appeal were actually related to majoring in CSE was not measured in the structured introduction study, although this relationship is a necessary link in the causal chain between structured hands-on instruction and the gender composition of computing. Numerous studies report the nuances of gender differences in attitudes toward computing (Shashaani 1997; Houle 1996), and they generally indicate that men have slightly more favorable attitudes toward computers than women have (Whitley 1997). In the same way that the relationship between confidence and participation in computing seems likely but is still not adequately understood, the relationship between attitudes toward computing and participation remains unclear.

Paired programming is another pedagogical innovation investigated for its potential to increase women's participation in computing. It is the formal practice of collaborative programming where two participants take turns writing code and monitoring what is written. Together, students brainstorm and work, using an interactive process to create a program. Because women are believed to prefer a collaborative approach to learning, and reports from courses that employ collaborative learning methods claim improved female persistence (Jagacinski, LeBold, and Salvendy 1988; Chase and Okie 2000), paired programming has been investigated as a way to improve women's participation in CSE. A single-institution study of 555 students, 25 percent of whom were women, compared outcomes for sections of an introductory programming course (McDowell et al. 2003). They found that paired students were retained at higher rates with no difference in performance by pairers versus nonpairers. Women's confidence in their solutions increased greatly with pairing, but remained lower than paired men's; and paired students, both male and female, were significantly more likely than unpaired students to declare a CSE major. The positive effects reported by this study indicate that paired programming should increase students' entry and retention in CSE, but would not shrink the gender gap in retention because there was no special improvement for women.

Knowledge-sharing and assessment techniques distinguish computer science instruction from instruction in the more gender-balanced technology, arts, and media program at the University of Colorado (Barker and Garvin-Doxas 2004). Extensive ethnographic research into pedagogical practices in these two programs identified very different instructional environments. Computer science was hierarchical, and it had an impersonal and defensive learning environment where communication was used for evaluation rather than mutual understanding. In contrast, the technology, arts, and media program employed student-centered, interactive, collaborative, hands-on learning. The authors hypothesize, but do not demonstrate, a link between these differences and women's retention.

The programming style required by instructors is another pedagogical issue that could affect women's participation if men and women have different styles. Turkle and Papert (1990) argue that men have a planned, logical, and abstract style, where-as women have an intuitive, creative, and concrete style. These differences leave women at a disadvantage because computing instruction typically requires the approach more common among men, and does not recognize or value women's ways of programming. Yet McKenna (2000) contends that there is no evidence of an innate difference in programming styles and that women are disadvantaged by the belief that only men have the ability to program in a manner suited to large, complex projects.

How to teach computing so that men and women master the material and acquire the skills is the subject of much debate and inquiry. Instructional methods that provide guided hands-on experience and peer interaction, and that value different styles of programming, have all been promoted as important for women's inclusion in computing. Nevertheless, their impact rests on the assumption that women and men have different learning needs or preferences, and the research on their value for increasing women's presence is far from conclusive. In the particular case of paired programming, it appears that we cannot expect to reduce the gender gap by employing this approach. Whether paired programming would have an indirect effect on women's representation is unexplored. We have also yet to discern whether pedagogical practices make a program or discipline more or less attractive to women, and whether they affect the likelihood that women will advance to the next educational or professional level in the field.

Conclusions and Recommendations

Our review demonstrates that we are closer to the beginning than to the end of research into the gender imbalance in postsecondary computing education. The most

Table 5.1
Things we "know"

---

1. Computing culture is masculine. Whether it has to be masculine, and whether the culture is a cause or a consequence of its gender composition, are different questions.
2. IT specialties have different cultures and gender compositions.
3. Women generally reach college with less programming experience than men.
4. Computing experience has a positive effect on both CSE grades and confidence.
5. When faculty mentor for diversity, this action equalizes the retention of undergraduate men and women.
6. Encouragement from faculty helps to equalize undergraduate retention.
7. Same-sex peers help to equalize undergraduate retention.
8. Women generally have less confidence than men in their ability to do CSE.
9. Differences in academic fitness are at most weak contributors to women's under-representation.
10. Paired programming improves overall student retention.

---

convincing evidence we have found comes from analytic social science research specifically on women in postsecondary computing. But that literature is small, amounting to fewer than fifty articles.

Most extensively written about so far in the scholarly literature are experience, confidence, mentoring, and student-faculty interaction. Least extensively covered are entry barriers, role models, and culture. Somewhere in between are curriculum, peer support, and pedagogy. Regardless of the coverage, each of our ten categories includes important questions that still need investigation.

The extent of coverage for a topic does not necessarily indicate the quality or adequacy of evidence. The quality or adequacy rests more on whether the study demonstrates a reliable link between women's participation and some preceding conditions—a link that is likely to exist in postsecondary computing in general. Using these criteria, we created the following tables of what the research tells us about the gender composition of computing (table 5.1) and what we suspect is true based on the limited results (table 5.2).

More high-quality evidence is becoming available as reports from research funded by the ITWF and ITR programs are published. Many of the initial projects funded by these initiatives are represented in this book, and more publications are expected as projects are concluded. Their results promise to substantially increase the published findings from research that is tied to theory and conforms to methodological standards.

Table 5.2
Things we believe and expect to establish

	Required for promotion to the list of known facts
1. Because they are conforming to gender stereotypes, most women do not engage in computing.	The existence of stereotypes and their influence over behavior is well demonstrated. The link between the stereotypes and engagement in computing has yet to be established.
2. Confidence, grades, and perceptions of grades all affect women's participation.	Confidence and perceptions of CSE grades vary by gender. The link between them and women's participation is not yet established. The distribution of CSE grades also varies by gender according to one study. This finding must be replicated and linked to women's retention and progression.
3. Structural barriers in the academy hinder women's entry into CSE.	One study reported increased entry by women when structural barriers were removed and a number of other steps were taken. The effect of removing structural barriers must be disaggregated from other intervention efforts and the findings must be replicated at other institutions.
4. Departments with computing curricula that emphasize real-world applications to topics and cover issues of recognized interest to women have more balanced gender composition.	There are well-known examples of computing curricula that are more gender balanced than typical computing programs. A careful analysis identifying their characteristics and demonstrating the link with women's representation is yet to be done.
5. Female role models have a positive influence on women's retention in computing.	Evidence in support of this hypothesis comes from mathematics and science. Credible research is still needed in CSE.
6. Peer mentoring improves women's retention.	One study from a computing program outside the United States and one from an engineering program within the United States show marked increases in retention from peer mentoring. Similar research is needed for CSE in the United States.
7. Instrumental support from faculty helps retain women in graduate computing programs.	Findings from research in STEM disciplines support this hypothesis. Research in CSE is needed to demonstrate that the findings also apply there.
8. Same-sex peers help increase women's entry and progression in CSE.	The influence of same-sex peers on *retention* in CSE is demonstrated, and findings from other disciplines indicate that same-sex peers influence entry and progression. The influence on entry and progression are yet to be shown for CSE.

Table 5.2
(continued)

	Required for promotion to the list of known facts
9. Self-confidence in computing ability affects the choice of computing major and career.	Research from social psychology has shown that self-confidence influences course taking and career choice in general, but empirical verification is needed for computing.
10. Women's entry into the discipline is affected by their perception that the occupation will provide opportunities to help people.	Women's preference for helping occupations is established, but no correlation has been established between this preference and women's entry into computing.
11. Supervised hands-on instruction improves attitudes toward computing, which in turn increases women's participation.	The link has yet to be shown between particular forms of instruction and women's entry, persistence, or progression in CSE.
12. Student-centered pedagogy increases women's entry into and persistence in computing.	Although research shows the benefits of student-centered pedagogy, evidence has not yet demonstrated a differential gender effect in CSE.

Of the seventeen postsecondary-level ITWF projects funded prior to 2003, most investigate several factors in one study, and several consider how the factors relate to more than one aspect of participation (achieving presence, maintaining presence, or advancing to the next level). As you can see in table 5.3, the majority of these studies measure individual-level factors (twelve studies, or 71 percent). Four of the postsecondary studies (24 percent) compare conditions and outcomes for different environments, either the department or different computing disciplines. One of the environment studies focuses on recruitment and retention, and compares graduate programs. Two of the environment studies investigate retention for undergraduates, one focusing on Latinos. Only one environment study compares computing disciplines, and the four projects that consider how women can be promoted to the next level of participation in computing all measure only individual-level factors.

Despite the significant contribution expected from the published results of the ITWF and ITR research, there are still important but overlooked issues. Little attention has been paid to the role of community colleges, the influence that educational environments have over students' advancement to the next educational or professional level, or the relationship between labor market opportunities and degree production. Broadening the scope of research to include these topics will help to clarify

Table 5.3
Postsecondary ITWF Projects

Lead PIs	Individual	Department	Discipline or society
Achieve presence	D. Martin M. Vouk C. Weinberger P. C. Thomson R. Varma S. Gregerman S. Beyer K. Spahn	J. M. Cohoon	R. Schnabel
Maintain presence	P. C. Thomson S. Gregerman B. Gutek S. Katz S. Beyer K. Spahn L. Werner	J. M. Cohoon J. M. Cohoon (a) L. Tornatzky	R. Schnabel
Advance to next level	P. C. Thomson S. Gregerman B. Gutek D. Llewellyn		

Notes:
(a) Second project led by same Principal Investigator (PI)
*One project was not categorized because its goal is descriptive only.

the general process of gender segregation in computing, and identify promising intervention points and methods.

The end of the twentieth century witnessed a worldwide trend toward the greater participation of women in science and engineering, and in higher education overall (Ramirez and Wotipka 2001). The only major discipline that bucked this global trend was computing. Understanding why and how computing achieved this dubious distinction will require the attention of historians and social scientists who can inform productive efforts for creating and maintaining gender equity in computing.

Acknowledgments

This chapter is based on work supported by the National Science Foundation under grant number #EIA–0244604. Any opinions, findings, and conclusions or recommendations expressed here are those of the authors, and do not necessarily reflect the views of the National Science Foundation.

References

Ambady, N., S. K. Paik, J. Steele, A. Owen-Smith, and J. P. Mitchell. 2004. Deflecting negative self-relevant stereotype activation: The effects of individualization. *Journal of Experimental Social Psychology* 40, no. 3:401–408.

Arch, E. C., and D. E. Cummins. 1989. Structured and unstructured exposure to computers: Sex differences in attitude and use among college students. *Sex Roles* 20, nos. 5–6:245–254.

Astin, A. W., and H. S. Astin. 1992. *Undergraduate science education: The impact of different college environments on the educational pipeline in the sciences, final report.* No. ED362404. Los Angeles: Graduate School of Education, UCLA.

Bair, B. A., P. Bhatt, M. Marcus, and M. Valli. 2003. *Gendered perceptions of programming as a career.* ⟨http://www.cse.ohio-state.edu/~bbair/WIC⟩.

Bandura, A. 1977. Self-efficacy: Toward a unifying theory of behavioral change. *Psychological Review* 84, no. 2:191–215.

Barker, L. J., and K. Garvin-Doxas. 2004. Making visible the behaviors that influence learning environment: A qualitative exploration of computer science classrooms. *Computer Science Education* 14, no. 2:119–145.

Beyer, S. 1990. Gender differences in the accuracy of self-evaluations of performance. *Journal of Personality and Social Psychology* 59, no. 5:960–970.

Beyer, S. 1998. Gender differences in self-perception and negative recall biases. *Sex Roles: A Journal of Research* 38, nos. 1–2:103–133.

Beyer, S., K. Rynes, J. Perrault, K. Hay, and S. Haller. 2003. Gender differences in computer science students. Paper presented at the ACM SIGCSE, Reno.

Blum, L., and C. Frieze. 2004. *As the culture of computing evolves, similarity can be the difference.* ⟨http://www-2.cs.cmu.edu/~lblum/PAPERS/TheEvolvingCSCulture.pdf⟩.

Brown, J., P. Andreae, R. Biddle, and E. Tempero. 1997. Women in introductory computer science: Experience at Victoria University of Wellington. Paper presented at ACM SIGCSE, 1997.

Bunderson, E. D., and M. E. Christensen. 1995. An analysis of retention problems for female students in university computer science programs. *Journal of Research in Computing in Education* 28, no. 1:1–18.

Butler, D. M., and R. Christensen. 2003. Mixing and matching: The effect on student performance of teaching assistants of the same gender. *Political Science and Politics* 36, no. 4:781–786.

Campbell, T. A., and D. E. Campbell. 1997. Faculty/student mentor program: Effects on academic performance and retention. *Research in Higher Education* 38, no. 6:727–742.

Canes, B., and H. Rosen. 1995. Following in her footsteps? Faculty gender composition and women's choices of college majors. *Industrial and Labor Relations Review* 48, no. 3:486–504.

Cassell, J., and H. Jenkins, eds. 1998. *From Barbie to Mortal Kombat: Gender and computer games*. Cambridge, MA: MIT Press.

Charles, M., and K. Bradley. 2002. Equal but separate? A cross-national study of sex segregation in higher education. *American Sociological Review* 67, no. 4:573–599.

Chase, J. D., and E. G. Okie. 2000. Combining cooperative learning and peer instruction in introductory computer science. In *Proceedings of the Thirty-First SIGCSE Technical Symposium on Computer Science Education, Austin, Texas*, 372–376. New York: ACM.

Chua, S. L., D.-T. Chen, and A. F. L. Wong. 1999. Computer anxiety and its correlates: A meta-analysis. *Computers in Human Behavior* 15, no. 5:609–623.

Cohoon, J. M., and K. M. Baylor. 2003. Female graduate students and program quality. *IEEE Technology and Society* 22, no. 3:28–35.

Cohoon, J. M., M. Gonsoulin, and J. Layman. 2004. Mentoring computer science undergraduates. In *Human perspectives in the Internet society: Culture, psychology, and gender*, ed. K. Morgan, J. Sanchez, C. A. Brebbia, and A. Voiskounsky, 31:199–208. Cadiz, Spain: WIT Press.

College Board, SAT Summary Reporting Service. 2002. *College-bound seniors: A profile of SAT program test takers*. Princeton, NJ: College Board.

College Board, SAT Summary Reporting Service. 2003. *College-bound seniors 2003*. ⟨http://www.collegeboard.com/about/news_info/cbsenior/yr2003/html/2003reports.html⟩.

Correll, S. J. 2004. Constraints into preferences: Gender, status, and emerging career aspirations. *American Sociological Review* 69 (February): 93–113.

Craig, A. 1998. Peer mentoring female computing students: Does it make a difference? In *ACM International Conference Proceeding Series Proceedings of the Third Australasian Conference on Computer Science Education*, 41–47. New York: ACM.

DeBell, M., and C. Chapman. 2003. Computer and Internet use by children and adolescents in 2001. *Education Statistics Quarterly* 5, no. 4:7–11.

Dewck, C. S. 1986. Motivational processes affecting learning. *American Psychologist* 41:1040–1048.

Dickhauser, O., and J. Stiensmeier-Pelster. 2002. Gender differences in computer work: Evidence for the model of achievement-related choices. *Contemporary Educational Psychology* 27:486–496.

Dryburgh, H. 2000. Underrepresentation of girls and women in computer science: Classification of 1990s' research. *Journal of Educational Computing Research* 23, no. 2:181–202.

Eccles, J. S. 1994. Understand women's educational and occupational choices: Apply the Eccles et al. model of achievement-related choices. *Psychology of Women Quarterly* 18:585–609.

Emurian, H. H. 2004. A programmed instruction tutoring system for Java: Consideration of learning performance and software self-efficacy. *Computers in Human Behavior* 20, no. 3:423–459.

Etzkowitz, H., C. Kemelgor, M. Neuschatz, and B. Uzzi. 1994. Barriers to women's participation in academic science and engineering. In *Who will do science? Educating the next generation*, ed. W. Pearson Jr. and A. Fechter, 43–67. Baltimore, MD: Johns Hopkins University.

Fencl, H. S. 1997. *Gender conscious content and pedagogy: Reforms throughout the UW system*. ⟨http://www.cic.uiuc.edu/groups/WISEPanel/archive/BestPractice/Best1Guidebook/gender_conscious.htm⟩.

Fisher, A., J. Margolis, and F. Miller. 1997. Undergraduate women in computer science: Experience, motivation, and culture. *SIGCSE Conference, 1997*, 106–110. New York: ACM.

Fox, M. F. 2001. Women, science, and academia: Graduate education and careers. *Gender and Society* 15, no. 5:654–666.

Freeman, P., and W. Aspray. 1999. *The supply of information technology workers in the United States*. No. ED459346. Washington, DC: Computing Research Association.

Fritz, R. L. 1992. *A study of gender differences in cognitive style and conative volition*. No. ED354379. Columbus, OH: Educational Research Information Clearinghouse.

Gneezy, U., M. Niederle, and A. Rustichini. 2003. Performance in competitive environments: Gender differences. *Quarterly Journal of Economics* (August): 1049–1074.

Gurer, D. 1998. Women role models in computer science history. *Computing Research News* 10, no. 4:2.

Haller, S. M., and T. V. Fossum. 1998. Retaining women in CS with accessible role models. In *Proceedings of the 29th SIGCSE Technical Symposium on Computer Science Education, Atlanta*, 73–76. New York: ACM.

Hearn, J., and S. Olzak. 1981. The role of college major departments in the reproduction of sexual inequality. *Sociology of Education* 54:195–205.

Houle, P. A. 1996. Toward understanding student differences in a computer skills course. *Journal of Educational Computing Research* 14, no. 1:25–48.

Huff, C. 2002. Gender, software design, and occupational equity. *SIGCSE Bulletin* 34, no. 2:112–115.

Jagacinski, C. M., W. K. LeBold, and G. Salvendy. 1988. Gender differences in persistence in computer-related fields. *Journal of Educational Computing Research* 4, no. 2:185–202.

Jamieson, L. 1991. Women, engineering, and community. *Computing Research News* 13, no. 3:2, 16.

Kersteen, Z., M. Linn, M. Clancy, and C. Hardyck. 1988. Previous experience and the learning of computer programming: The computer helps those who help themselves. *Journal of Educational Computing Research* 4, no. 3:321–333.

Kiesler, S., L. Sproull, and J. S. Eccles. 1985. Pool halls, chips, and war games: Women in the culture of computing. *Psychology of Women Quarterly* 9, no. 4:451–462.

Lips, H. M. 2004. The gender gap in possible selves: Divergence of academic self-views among high school and university students. *Sex Roles* 40 (March): 357–371.

Lips, H. M., and L. Temple. 1990. Majoring in computer science: Causal models for women and men. *Research in Higher Education* 31, no. 1:99–113.

Margolis, J., and A. Fisher. 2002a. Geek mythology and attracting undergraduate women to computer science. In *Impacting Change Through Collaboration, Proceedings of the Joint Nation Conference of the Women in Engineering Advocates Network and the National Association of Minority Programs Administrators, March 1997.* Available at ⟨http://www.cs.cmu .edu/~gendergap/papers⟩.

Margolis, J., and A. Fisher. 2002b. *Unlocking the clubhouse: Women in computing.* Cambridge, MA: MIT Press.

Marini, M. M., P.-L. Fan, E. Finley, and A. M. Beutel. 1996. Gender and job values. *Sociology of Education* 69, no. 1:49–65.

Matyas, M. L. E., and L. S. E. Dix, eds. 1990. *Science and engineering programs: On target for women?* Washington, DC: National Academies Press.

McDowell, C., L. Werner, H. E. Bullock, and J. Fernald. 2003. The impact of pair programming on student performance, perception, and persistence. Paper presented at the International Conference on Software Engineering, Portland, Oregon.

McKenna, P. 2000. Transparent and opaque boxes: Do women and men have different computer programming psychologies and styles? *Computers and Education* 35:37–49.

McManus, S. E., and J. E. A. Russell. 1997. New directions for mentoring research: An examination of related constructs. *Journal of Vocational Behavior* 51:145–161.

McPherson, M., L. Smith-Lovin, and J. M. Cook. 2001. Birds of a feather: Homophily in social networks. *Annual Review of Sociology* 27:415–444.

Meece, J. L., and G. M. Jones. 1996. Gender differences in motivation and strategy use in science: Are girls rote learners? *Journal of Research in Science Teaching* 33, no. 4:393–406.

MIT, EECS Ad Hoc committee. 1995. *Women undergraduate enrollment in electrical engineering and CS at MIT.* Cambridge, MA: MIT.

Mitra, A., S. Lenzmeier, R. Avon, N. Qu, and M. Hazen. 2000. Gender and computer use in an academic institution: report from a longitudinal study. *Journal of Educational Computing Research* 23, no. 1:67–84.

National Science Foundation. 1999–2002. *WebCASPAR: Integrated science and engineering resources data system.* ⟨http://webcaspar.nsf.gov⟩.

Philbin, M., E. Meier, S. Huffman, and P. Boverie. 1995. A survey of gender and learning styles. *Sex Roles* 32, nos. 7–8:485–494.

Pirolli, P. L., and M. Recker. 1995. Modeling individual differences in students' learning strategies. *Journal of Learning Sciences* 4, no. 1:1–38.

Potosky, D. 2002. A field study of computer efficacy beliefs as an outcome of training: The role of computer playfulness, computer knowledge, and performance during training. *Computers in Human Behavior* 18, no. 3:241–255.

Ramirez, F. O., and C. M. Wotipka. 2001. Slowly but surely? The global expansion of women's participation in science and engineering fields of study, 1972–92. *Sociology of Education* 74 (July): 231–251.

Reskin, B. F., D. B. McBrier, and J. A. Kmec. 1999. The determinants and consequences of workplace sex and race composition. *Annual Review of Sociology* 25:335–361.

Reskin, B. F., and P. A. Roos. 1990. *Job queues, gender queues: Explaining women's inroads into male occupations.* Philadelphia: Temple University Press.

Ridley, D. R., and J. D. Novak. 1983. Six related differences in high school science and mathematics enrollments: Do they give males a critical headstart toward science and math-related careers? *Alberta Journal of Educational Research* 29, no. 4:308–318.

Robst, J., J. Keil, and D. Russo. 1998. The effect of gender composition of faculty on student retention. *Economics of Education Review* 17, no. 4:429–439.

Sacrowitz, M. G., and A. P. Parelius. 1996. An unlevel playing field: Women in the introductory computer science courses. Paper presented at the proceedings of the twenty-seventh SIGCSE technical symposium on computer science education, Philadelphia.

Severiens, S. E., and G. T. M. Tendam. 1994. Gender differences in learning styles: A narrative review and quantitative meta-analysis. *Higher Education* 27, no. 4:487–501.

Seymour, E., and N. Hewitt. 1997. *Talking about leaving: Why undergraduates leave the sciences.* Boulder, CO: Westview Press.

Shashaani, L. 1997. Gender differences in computer attitudes and use among college students. *Journal of Educational Computing Research* 16, no. 1:37–51.

Strenta, A. C., R. Elliott, R. Adair, M. Matier, and J. Scott. 1994. Choosing and leaving science in highly selective institutions. *Research in Higher Education* 35, no. 5:513–547.

Tannen, D. 1991. *You just don't understand.* (Rev. ed.) New York: Ballantine Books.

Taylor, H. G., and L. C. Mounfield. 1994. Exploration of the relationship between prior computing experience and gender on success in college computer science. *Journal of Educational Computing Research* 11, no. 4:291–306.

Teague, J. 2002. Women in computing: What brings them to it, what keeps them in it? *Inroads SIGCSE Bulletin* 34, no. 2:147–158.

Tenenbaum, H. R., F. J. Crosby, and M. D. Gliner. 2001. Mentoring relationships in graduate school. *Journal of Vocational Behavior* 59:326–341.

Tobias, S. 1990. *They're not dumb, they're different: Stalking the second tier.* No. ED331702. Tucson, AZ: Research Corporation.

Townsend, G. C. 1996. Viewing video-taped role models improves female attitudes toward computer science. Paper presented at the proceedings of the twenty-seventh SIGCSE Technical Symposium on Computer Science Education, Philadelphia.

Trauth, E. M. 2004. Gender issues in IT organizations: Understanding the underrepresentation of women in IT; Toward a theory of individual differences. Paper presented at the proceedings of the 2004 SIGMIS Careers, Culture, and Ethics in a Networked Environment, Conference, Tucson.

Turkle, S. 1984. *The second self: Computers and the human spirit.* New York: Simon and Schuster.

Turkle, S., and S. Papert. 1990. Epistemological pluralism: Styles and voices within the computer culture. *Signs* 16, no. 1:128–157.

Turner, S. E., and W. G. Bowen. 1999. Choice of major: The changing (unchanging) gender gap. *Industrial and Labor Relations Review* 52, no. 2:289–313.

Ulku-Steiner, B., B. Kurtz-Costes, and C. R. Kinlaw. 2000. Doctoral student experiences in gender-balanced and male-dominated graduate programs. *Journal of Educational Psychology* 42:296–307.

Urban Institute Education Policy Center. 2000. *Summary report on the impact study of the National Science Foundation's program for women and girls.* Washington, DC: Urban Institute Education Policy Center.

Volet, S. E., and C. P. Lund. 1994. Metacognitive instruction in introductory computer programming: A better explanatory construct for performance than traditional factors. *Journal of Educational Computing Research* 10, no. 4:297–328.

Wajcman, J. 1991. *Feminism confronts technology.* University Park: Pennsylvania State University Press.

Webb, R. M., D. Lubinski, and C. P. Benbow. 2002. Mathematically facile adolescents with math-science aspirations: New perspectives on their educational and vocational development. *Journal of Educational Psychology* 94, no. 4:785–794.

Whitley, B. E. 1997. Gender differences in computer-related attitudes and behavior: A meta-analysis. *Computers in Human Behavior* 13, no. 1:1–22.

Wigfield, A., and J. Eccles. 2000. Expectancy-value theory of achievement motivation. *Contemporary Educational Psychology Special Issue: Motivation and the Educational Process* 25:68–81.

Wilson, F. 2003. Can compute, won't compute: Women's participation in the culture of computing. *New Technology, Work, and Employment* 18, no. 2:127–142.

II
Postsecondary Education

6

A Matter of Degrees: Female Underrepresentation in Computer Science Programs Cross-Nationally

Maria Charles and Karen Bradley

Thirty years of research, including contributions to the present volume, leaves little doubt that women are strongly underrepresented in computer-related degree programs and occupations in the United States. In this chapter, we contribute an international comparative perspective to this body of scholarship by presenting data on the gender composition of computer science programs of study in twenty-one industrial countries. Since most high-status jobs in the IT industry require an advanced degree in the field, computer science credentials represent key gateways for access to lucrative careers. The extent to which women's representation in these academic programs varies cross-nationally is therefore of significant social and policy interest.

Our analytic approach has been influenced by neoinstitutionalist theory, which emphasizes the importance of cultural ideas and belief systems in motivating the development of specific organizational forms as well as shaping people's interests, aptitudes, and behaviors (Jepperson 1991; Meyer 2001). Applied to the question of gender inequality, neoinstitutionalist research has pointed to the equalizing forces of globally diffusing norms of universalism and moral individualism (Ramirez, Soysal, and Shanahan 1997; Berkovitch 1999). These ideals have been codified in citizenship rights that were initially accorded only to white property-holding men, but were increasingly extended to lower-status groups, including women and nonwhites. The rise and diffusion of liberal-egalitarian principles during the second half of the twentieth century thus contributed to the gradual cultural redefinition of women as equal individuals and citizens.

Moreover, the meaning of citizenship was itself gradually expanded to include not just suffrage but also rights to education and equal opportunity in paid employment (Thomas et al. 1987; Ramirez and Cha 1990). With the establishment of such international organizations as the International Labor Organization and the United Nations Educational, Scientific, and Cultural Organization (UNESCO), the rights of women and girls to education and paid employment were formally codified at the global level. The same liberal-individualist principles led many national governments to adopt legislation mandating equal educational and labor market opportunities.[1] According to some neoinstitutionalist accounts, increased female access to higher education and the labor market should generate "spillover effects"—for instance, by undermining the male dominance of traditionally male-dominated occupations and fields of study (Ramirez 1987; Baker and Jones 1993; Hanson, Schaub, and Baker 1996; Ramirez and Wotipka 2001).

This understanding of the historical development of stratification systems is reminiscent of evolutionary arguments made by early structural-functional theorists (Goode 1963; Parsons 1970; Davis 1984). But rather than emphasizing the economic inefficiencies of discrimination, neoinstitutionalists treat globally diffusing norms as the driving forces behind declining gender discrimination in industrial societies.

We share the neoinstitutionalist view of cultural belief systems as consequential sociological driving forces, but seek to reconcile existing neoinstitutionalist accounts of gender stratification with the mounting evidence that many technical and scientific fields remain extremely and persistently sex segregated (Burton 1990; Seymour and Hewitt 1997; Xie and Shauman 2003). We argue that a "different but equal" form of egalitarianism shapes the development of modern gender-stratification systems, causing some forms of gender inequality to erode while others continue to thrive (Charles and Bradley 2002; Charles and Grusky 2004). As we show, sex segregation of the computer science field is one form of inequality that is alive and well in contemporary industrial societies.

"Women's Status," Cultural Beliefs, and Computer Science

The historical record provides much evidence of improvement in women's social and economic status in industrial countries. The last half century has indeed witnessed the extension of formal political and civil rights to women, the closing of the long-standing gender gap in college attendance and labor force participation, and the increasing prevalence of egalitarian attitudes concerning women's legal and social rights. There are some striking exceptions to these equalizing trends, however. One of the most notable is the persistence of extreme sex segregation within educational systems and labor markets—even in societies exhibiting a strong commitment to gender-egalitarian policies and practices (Bradley 2000; Jacobs 2003; Charles and Grusky 2004).

The unevenness of gender equalization and the relatively weak covariation among different indicators of "women's status" can be better understood if we distinguish between two ideological tenets that have historically supported systems of gender inequality. The first tenet, "gender essentialism," is the widely shared assumption that men and women are naturally and fundamentally different, with women better suited to nurturance and human interaction, and men better suited to technical tasks and abstract calculation or analysis. The second ideological tenet is "male primacy," which holds that men are generally more competent than women, and that men's traits and activities are more status worthy.

Our argument, in brief, is that the universalistic cultural values cited by neoinstitutionalist scholars work to erode one, but not both, of the cultural tenets undergirding gender inequality (Charles and Bradley 2002; Charles and Grusky 2004). While liberal-egalitarian ideals are increasingly viewed as inconsistent with cultural principles of male primacy, they do little to undermine standard essentialist visions of masculinity and femininity along with the gender-typed preferences and stereotypes that emerge from these visions. Because individuals continue to understand their competencies and those of others in gender-essentialist terms, sex segregation by field of study is likely to persist even in societies where legal barriers to women's participation in public sphere institutions (such as universities) have been fully eliminated.

What do these contentions imply about cross-national variability in the gender composition of computer science programs? Most obviously, essentialist definitions of masculine and feminine traits should contribute to the gender labeling of IT-related occupations and educational programs throughout the industrial world. With their strong emphasis on abstract logic, mathematical reasoning, and interaction with machines, the stereotypically masculine task profiles associated with computer science programs and IT jobs exhibit marked similarities to those for engineering, a strongly male-dominated field worldwide (Anker 1998; Charles and Bradley 2002). Despite the growing influence of liberal-egalitarian principles, hegemonic beliefs about gender difference lead girls to develop preferences and aspirations for nontechnical careers, underestimate their competence at mathematical tasks, and expect negative sanctions for gender-atypical choices (Bourdieu 2001; Correll 2001; Fenstermaker and West 2002; Ridgeway and Correll 2004).[2]

The influence of gender-essentialist norms on the gender composition of computer science programs may be moderated, however, by the relative newness of the IT field. Computer science programs and IT occupations underwent their most significant expansion during the last two or three decades of the twentieth century in most industrialized countries. Norms of "equal opportunity" were by that time officially mandated (if not necessarily rigorously enforced) in modern educational institutions, and women had by then achieved a strong numerical presence in most systems of higher education and postindustrial labor forces. This social and ideological context stands in contrast to that prevailing during the period in which engineering and other similarly technical fields were undergoing their expansion. The absence of a long legacy of sex segregation in the field, and the elimination of many blatantly discriminatory practices in the labor market and higher education, may increase the likelihood that women aspire to an IT career despite its prototypically male task profile. If so, we might expect stronger female representation in computer science occupations and degree programs than in older technical disciplines such as engineering.[3]

In this chapter, we utilize new data on gender distributions across fields of study in twenty-one industrial countries to address the following questions:

1. How sex segregated are computer science programs in these countries?

2. How does female representation in computer science programs compare to that in engineering, a more established degree program with a similar male-typed task profile?

3. How much does female representation in computer science vary cross-nationally?

4. To what extent do patterns of cross-national variability square with existing theoretical accounts of sex segregation?

We do not aim to provide definitive answers to these questions but hope that our exploratory analyses will yield insights useful to designing future research projects and data collection efforts in this field.

Data and Methods

Cross-national research on the gender composition of university-level computer science programs has been slowed by a paucity of internationally comparable data. UNESCO, the source of the most widely used international educational statistics, publishes information on graduates from a combined "computer science and mathematics" degree category. Comparisons of female representation in computer science across a large number of countries has therefore not been possible based on those data.

We draw on a new data set that provides a breakdown of "first-degree recipients" in 2001 by sex, country, and thirty-one academic subfields, including a disaggregated "computer science" category (Organisation for Economic Cooperation and Development 2004).[4] We restrict our discussion to *graduates* from these fields since dropout rates vary considerably among countries.[5] For countries with data available through both organizations, we found little difference between the Organisation for Economic Cooperation and Development and the UNESCO statistics on the gender composition of graduates from comparable fields (e.g., physical and biological science categories).[6] To facilitate cross-national comparison and eliminate empty cells, we aggregated subfields to arrive at the seven-field classification shown in table 6.1. The computer science category, which is of principal interest here, remains disaggregated. The twenty-one countries for which the requisite data are available are all industrialized, although they differ in their levels of economic development, social histories, and cultural traditions. Our country sample is heavily skewed toward affluent Western democracies. It includes three formerly Soviet states (the Czech

Table 6.1
Fields of study

Computing
System design, computer programming, data processing, networks, and operating systems—software development only (hardware development is classified with the engineering fields)

Education
Teacher training and education science

Engineering, manufacturing, and construction
Engineering and engineering trades, manufacturing and processing, and architecture and building

Health and life sciences
Medicine, medical services, nursing, dental services, and life sciences

Humanities and social sciences
Humanities and arts, social and behavioral sciences, journalism and information, business and administration, law, and social services

Math and physical sciences
Mathematics and statistics, and physical sciences

Other
Agriculture, forestry and fishery, veterinary, personal services, transport services, environmental protection, and security services

---

Note: For classificatory details, see United Nations Educational, Scientific and Cultural Organization (UNESCO) (1997, 35–39)

Republic, Hungary, and the Slovak Republic), and only one Asian country (South Korea). Unless otherwise indicated in the text, conclusions drawn from our correlation analyses do not differ when non-Western countries are omitted from the analyses.

Female representation in the seven fields of study was assessed using the field-specific segregation parameters (A_j) developed by Charles and Grusky (1995). These parameters contrast the (female-to-male) ratio in the respective field of study to that in the "average" field. They can be written as:

$$A_j = \ln(F_j/M_j) - \left[1/J \times \sum \ln(F_j/M_j)\right],$$

where F_j and M_j are the numbers of women and men graduates, respectively, in program j, and J is the number of programmatic categories.[7] Negative values indicate female underrepresentation, and positive values indicate female overrepresentation (relative to the other programmatic categories). The exponents of these segregation terms gives the factor by which men or women are overrepresented in the respective field.[8]

An important virtue of these segregation parameters is that they are not influenced by cross-national differences in the gender composition of higher education. Such compositional invariance is crucial in the present context since spillover arguments treat the overall female enrollment rate as a significant causal variable in the generation of sex segregation (on the advantages of using odds ratios for cross-national studies of sex segregation, see Charles and Grusky [2004]).

Using simple correlation analysis, we briefly consider associations between female representation in computer science degree programs and a variety of theoretically relevant macrolevel indicators. Data for these analyses are taken from several international sources, including the United Nations, the World Values Survey (WVS 1995), and the Third International Math and Science Survey (TIMSS 1995, 1999). Due to missing country values on some key covariates and the relatively small sample size, these correlation results should be regarded as provisional. More formal analysis, including multivariate modeling, will be required to adjudicate among competing interpretations of our bivariate results.

Findings

Table 6.2 presents country-specific segregation terms for seven programmatic categories: computing, education, engineering, health/life sciences, humanities and social

Table 6.2
Sex segregation parameters: Female representation in tertiary fields of study, 2001

Country	Computer science	Education	Engineering	Health/life	Humanities and social sciences	Math and physical sciences	Other
Australia	−1.05	1.33	−1.21	.90	.44	−.52	.12
Austria	−1.68	1.59	−1.45	.99	.52	−.32	.36
Belgium	−1.72	1.16	−1.32	1.23	.69	−.21	.16
Czech Republic	−1.86	1.19	−.87	1.23	.58	−.27	.00
Denmark	−1.70	1.00	−.95	2.21	.73	−.46	−.83
Finland	−.83	1.20	−1.83	1.51	.57	−.55	−.07
France	−1.52	1.50	−1.47	.83	.83	−.31	.14
Germany	−1.72	1.54	−1.35	1.21	.53	−.25	.05
Hungary	−1.54	1.21	−.93	1.04	.83	−.29	−.32
Ireland	−.61	1.58	−1.73	.84	.49	−.11	−.46
Korea, Republic	−.65	1.49	−1.05	.47	.24	−.26	−.24
Netherlands	−1.48	1.56	−1.62	1.39	.59	−.69	.24
New Zealand	−1.07	1.58	−.91	.60	.42	−.70	.07
Norway	−1.01	1.31	−1.20	1.65	.42	−1.01	−.16
Slovak Republic	−1.85	1.23	−.64	1.56	.53	−.19	−.63
Spain	−1.30	1.21	−1.24	.94	.41	−.01	−.02
Sweden	−.67	.94	−1.28	1.11	.24	−.39	.04
Switzerland	−1.54	1.52	−1.74	1.17	.71	−.53	.42
Turkey	−.58	.14	−.77	.82	.29	.18	−.08
United Kingdom	−1.13	1.02	−1.61	1.27	.43	−.36	.39
United States	−.74	1.19	−1.55	1.25	.42	−.26	−.31

Notes: Data are for first-degree recipients in tertiary educational systems (Organization for Economic Cooperation and Development 2004). Sex-segregation parameters (A_j) can be calculated as follows: $\ln(F_j/M_j) - [1/J * \Sigma \ln(F_j/M_j)]$, where F_j gives the number of women in field j, and M_j gives the number of men in field j.

Table 6.3
Male "overrepresentation factor": Computer science programs, 2001

Australia	2.86
Austria	5.37
Belgium	5.58
Czech Republic	6.42
Denmark	5.47
Finland	2.29
France	4.57
Germany	5.58
Hungary	4.66
Ireland	1.84
Korea, Republic	1.92
Netherlands	4.39
New Zealand	2.92
Norway	2.75
Slovak Republic	6.36
Spain	3.67
Sweden	1.95
Switzerland	4.66
Turkey	1.79
United Kingdom	3.10
United States	2.10

Notes: Values give the factor by which men are overrepresented in computer science programs in the respective country. They are calculated by taking inverse values of the "computer science" parameters shown in table 6.2 and converting the resultant positive values into exponential form.

sciences, math and physical sciences, and other. Again, negative values indicate female underrepresentation; positive values indicate female overrepresentation. Table 6.3 presents the "male overrepresentation" parameters for the computer science category. These are calculated by taking the inverse values of the parameters shown in the first column of table 6.2 and converting these positive values into exponential form (i.e., taking antilogarithms).

In the following paragraphs, the results are summarized with reference to the four questions enumerated above.

How sex-segregated are computer science programs in these countries? The uniformly negative coefficients in the first column of table 6.2 indicate that women are underrepresented in computer science programs in all twenty-one countries considered here. The degree of male overrepresentation ranges from a factor of 1.79 in Turkey (exponent of 0.58) to a factor of 6.42 in the Czech Republic (exponent of 1.86). We explore patterns of cross-national variability further on.

How does female representation in computer science programs compare to that in engineering?   We begin by considering whether the relatively recent rise of computer science programs and occupations might moderate tendencies for sex segregation. Our results provide little evidence that this is the case. The computer science field is no less extremely male dominated than is engineering, an older, more established technical field that underwent its initial period of expansion within a much less gender-egalitarian social and cultural context. Any integrating effect associated with the institutionalization of liberal-egalitarian policies and principles appears to be negligible in comparison to the power of essentialist gender stereotypes to affect the tastes, aspirations, and expectations of men and women.

One interesting finding is that three formally Soviet states (the Czech Republic, Hungary, and the Slovak Republic) show substantially stronger female representation in engineering than in computer science programs.[9] Women's relatively strong presence in engineering in these countries may be a remnant of Soviet educational policy, which called for sorting of students among educational programs based strictly on academic performance (rather than individual preferences), and Soviet efforts to expand the number of trained engineers as a vehicle for national advancement. These policies likely reduced the influence of essentialist preferences and stereotypes in the educational sorting process (Bialecki and Heyns 1993; Bradley and Charles 2003).[10] With the dissolution of the Soviet bloc, however, democratic principles emphasizing individual choice grew in influence, encouraging greater intrusion of gender-specific preferences and stereotypes into this process (Gerber and Schaefer 2004). New fields, such as computer science, may have been more susceptible to such "essentialist intrusion" than more established ones. Rather than working to *moderate* tendencies for sex segregation as suggested above, the newness of computer science may have in this context constituted a segregating force.

The segregation terms for the remaining five fields of study yield no big surprises and are consistent with findings from our previous cross-national research (Bradley 2000; Charles and Bradley 2002; Bradley and Charles 2003). Women are everywhere overrepresented in education, health and life sciences, and humanities and social sciences programs, and men are overrepresented in the mathematical and physical science category (except in Turkey). The catchall "other" category varies in its gender identification, most likely reflecting the cross-national heterogeneity of its programmatic makeup (on the diverse fields comprising this category, see table 6.1).

We turn next to questions pertaining to cross-national variability in the sex segregation of computer science.

How much does female representation in computer science vary cross-nationally?

Although men dominate computer science programs in all countries considered here, the degree of their overrepresentation does differ considerably. The most sex-segregated computer science program is found in the Czech Republic, where male overrepresentation is more than three times stronger than in Turkey, the country with the most gender-integrated program (6.42/1.79 = 3.59). In the following paragraphs, we briefly consider the empirical plausibility of various theoretical frameworks that can be applied to explain observed patterns of cross-national variation. As noted above, the bivariate correlations that we present should be treated as roughly indicative, not definitive, measures.

To what extent do patterns of cross-national variability square with existing theoretical accounts of sex segregation?

Structural-functional theories of modernization predict the decreasing importance of ascriptive characteristics such as gender within public sphere domains as economic development advances (Kerr et al. 1960; Parsons 1970; Jackson 1998). This general evolutionary principle would seem to suggest a stronger female presence in IT-related programs in more economically developed societies (at least to the extent that male domination of this field reflects ascriptive discrimination). We do not find a relationship between the level of economic development and women's representation in computer science programs that would support such a view ($r = -.041$), however.[11]

We also find no evidence of spillover effects whereby the large-scale incorporation of women into the labor market and higher education motivates or empowers women to pursue new or historically male-dominated fields (Berryman 1983; Ramirez 1987; McIlwee and Robinson 1992; Ramirez and Wotipka 2001). We examined zero-order correlations of women's representation in computer science programs with several conventional measures of public sphere incorporation, including women's share of the labor force, women's share of professional occupations, and women's share of tertiary students.[12] None were consistent with neoinstitutionalist spillover arguments ($r = -.27$, .05, and $-.02$, respectively).[13]

Available evidence does support an emphasis on cultural processes, however. Female representation in university-level computer science programs is significantly stronger ($r = .61$, $p = .004$) in countries where eighth-grade girls express greater interest, relative to their male counterparts, in pursuing a mathematically related career ("Would you like to work in a job that involved math?").[14] A higher score on this "aspirations" measure indicates greater female interest in "masculine" technical and mathematical pursuits, and perhaps a weaker influence of gender stereotypes at this pivotal phase of the educational career. The positive correlation that we find is consistent with our arguments regarding the central role of gender-essentialist cultural values in deterring women's entry into university-level computer science programs.[15]

The effect of the eighth-grade aspirations on programmatic distributions cannot be attributed to gender differences in mathematical ability (see also Xie and Shauman 2003). Based on data from the same international survey, we find that the correlation between girls' relative mathematical achievement and aspirations is negligible ($-.05$), as is the correlation between female math achievement and female representation in computing ($-.04$).[16] Although female underrepresentation in computer science is often attributed to inherent and therefore universal differences between the sexes in math ability and career preferences, it bears noting that country scores vary widely on both the achievement and aspirations variables.[17]

Here and elsewhere, we have linked the ubiquitousness and persistence of sex segregation across fields of study to deeply rooted cultural assumptions about gender difference, which have proven to coexist quite comfortably alongside liberal-egalitarian principles. Unfortunately, cross-nationally comparable indicators of liberal-egalitarian attitudes are hard to come by. One excellent indicator, which is available for only nine of our sample countries, is the percentage of the national population disagreeing with the statement that "a university education is more important for a boy than for a girl."[18] The small sample size notwithstanding, it is worth noting that these data provide no evidence that female representation in computer science is stronger where liberal-egalitarian attitudes are more prevalent. A bivariate scatter plot shows, if anything, an inverse association between these two variables ($r = -.47$). This can be attributed to women's strong representation in computer science in Korea and Turkey, two countries that score low on the liberal-egalitarian measure.[19] In any case, the findings are consistent with the claim that those forms of ("horizontal") sex segregation that are undergirded by gender-essentialist cultural values are relatively unaffected by the rise of liberal-egalitarian principles (Charles 2003; Charles and Grusky 2004).

Discussion and Conclusion

The data presented in table 6.2 reveal striking cross-national uniformity in the sex typing of computer science programs. Despite the relative newness of the IT field, women are no better represented in computer science than in the older and more established technical field of engineering. We attribute this pervasive sex segregation to the stereotypically male task profile associated with computer work, and the persistent power of gender-essentialist values and expectations to affect career choices, even in the most culturally "modern" societies.

Although computer science programs are male dominated in all twenty-one countries considered here, we do find considerable cross-national variability in the *degree* of male overrepresentation. The pattern of this variability is, however, inconsistent with standard evolutionary accounts, which link economic and cultural modernization to across-the-board improvement in the status of women. Our results provide little evidence that women's representation in computer science programs is stronger in the most economically developed countries, or that it is stronger in countries where women participate at higher rates in the labor market, higher education, or high-status professional occupations. Indeed, the three countries where women are best represented in computer science are Turkey, Ireland, and Korea, none of which are well-known for their gender-egalitarian practices or cultures.[20] This finding is consistent with previous research results, which have shown that some forms of sex segregation are most extreme in precisely those societies exhibiting the strongest commitment to gender-egalitarian policies and practices (Charles 1992; Bradley and Charles 2003; Charles and Grusky 2004).

To understand observed patterns of cross-national variability in the gender composition of computer science programs we must consider how structural features of modern polities, economies, and labor markets interact with deeply institutionalized ideologies of gender difference. Two sorts of structural processes are particularly relevant in this regard: the postwar expansion and diversification of higher education, and the postindustrial restructuring of economies and labor markets.

During the second half of the twentieth century, enrollment in tertiary educational institutions increased dramatically throughout the world. One important rationale for this "massification" of higher education was the rising popular understanding of education as a universal right of all citizens (Thomas et al. 1987; Ramirez and Cha 1990). Tertiary expansion and democratization occurred in large part through the proliferation of nonuniversity and vocational programs, many of which were developed explicitly to accommodate the perceived interests and preferences of growing numbers of tertiary-eligible women (e.g., in health care, early childhood education, tourism-hospitality, and domestic science). By supporting increased options for women to pursue female-typed programs of study, structural diversification has helped enact "separate but equal" cultural principles within systems of higher education (Fjelde 1991; Brinton and Lee 2001; Bradley and Charles 2003).

A second segregative structural feature of modern societies is their increasingly service-dominated economies. The consolidation of female "occupational ghettos" in the service sectors of postindustrial societies is a well-known phenomenon (Charles and Grusky 2004). It is also well-known that many service occupations have acquired deeply institutionalized gender labels. New tertiary programs have been developed to meet real or perceived female demand for credentials in growing, traditionally female-typed service fields, such as health care and early childhood education (Jones and Castle 1986; Bradley and Charles 2003). Although new occupations have emerged in IT-related fields as well, women's employment in this sector has typically been in relatively low-level service occupations that do not require a degree in computer science (on the growth of female employment in offshore telecommunications offices, see Breathnach [2002]).

The results in table 6.2 also reflect more directly cultural processes. Modern economies and tertiary systems support the development of gender-specific career aspirations, and they facilitate the realization of these aspirations. The consolidation of female niches within the academy and the economy reinforces cultural stereotypes that label abstract math, natural science, and engineering pursuits as masculine, and more expressive, human-centered fields as feminine. Such gender labels in turn shape preferences and self-evaluations of individual students, and serve to undermine female interest in historically male academic pursuits (Bourdieu 2001; Correll 2001; Ridgeway and Correll 2004). Girls may be less prone to "like" math or regard themselves as competent in math when a wide array of more "gender-appropriate" options present themselves.[21] Moreover, the relative material security enjoyed by citizens of advanced industrial countries supports the diffusion of what Inglehart (1997) termed "postmaterialist" value systems, which emphasize self-expressive (as opposed to instrumental) career goals. The proliferation of choices in modern educational systems in turn provides more options for accommodating gender-specific preferences. For women in affluent societies, freedom of choice thus implies both the right to be free from overt discrimination (should they elect to pursue a traditionally male-dominated field of study) and the right to choose poorly paid female-labeled career paths, if they so desire.

Given the strong influence of gender stereotypes on individual programmatic choices, it is perhaps not surprising that we find some of the highest levels of female representation in computer science programs in countries where the national government exerts strong control over curricular trajectories. In South Korea, for example, math is required through grade twelve and science through grade eleven. For Irish students, math and science course work is mandatory through the end of secondary schooling. State-mandated examinations then strongly influence access to tertiary institutions and academic majors. The process is even more bureaucratized in Turkey, where specific scores on secondary exams are required for admission to elite universities and technical programs. Restrictive government practices that minimize choice and prioritize merit may actually result in more gender-neutral distribution across fields of study. This may occur in two ways: by limiting the opportunity for the intrusion of the gender-essentialist labeling of programs, and by minimizing the impact of gendered student identities and preferences as students exercise academic choice.

National societies and institutions are today structured with reference to a set of globally diffusing cultural rules that distinguish between licit and illicit forms of inequality. These rules hold that inequalities among individuals can be justified only if they are based on differential contributions to the common good (i.e., functional "achievement"), or if they reflect differences in individual preferences or tastes (Thomas et al. 1987; Meyer 2001). Such cultural principles contribute to the gradual equalization of men's and women's formal rights and obligations, and they facilitate female access to higher education, the labor market, and other public-sphere institutions. But to understand women's extreme underrepresentation in computer science and other technical fields today we must avoid equating the rise of liberal egalitarianism with the erosion of gender essentialism. Liberal-egalitarian ideals have helped delegitimize norms of male primacy and the many forms of gender discrimination that these norms have sustained historically. Prevailing forms of egalitarianism do not delegitimate essentialist processes, however.

Scholars and policymakers often describe the paucity of women in IT-related occupations as detrimental to economic development and women's economic advancement.[22] In keeping with liberal-egalitarian principles, policy efforts aimed at redressing this underrepresentation focus on rooting discriminatory practices out of "the science pipeline," and devising policies to ensure that men and women have equal opportunities to pursue scientific careers, if they so desire.[23] In this policy environment, as in modern societies more generally, individual preferences are treated as sacrosanct, and there is little attention paid to the role of socialization, social exchange, and power differentials in generating gender-specific tastes and career aspirations.

Results of our analyses suggest that gender integration of IT-related academic programs and occupations would require a "second revolution" in gender equality —one that establishes a new definition of egalitarianism that goes beyond equality of opportunity, and is based on a broader public appreciation of the social and cultural processes by which gender-specific identities, expectations, and preferences are generated.

Acknowledgments

This research is supported by grants from the National Science Foundation (NSF HRD–0332852 and NSF SBR–9808038), the Spencer Foundation, and the American Educational Research Association.

Notes

1. The road to universalism has not been smooth. Initiatives to extend rights to women as individuals at times clashed with the paternalist initiatives of the state, as occurred with the spread of maternity legislation (Berkovitch 1999). Much debate also ensued around the turn of the twentieth century concerning the need to extend special protections to women (and children) in the form of protective labor legislation.

2. The mechanisms by which gender essentialism influences career outcomes are discussed in Charles and Grusky (2004, chapter 1).

3. This argument builds on Stinchcombe's (1965) notion of "cultural imprinting," whereby organizational characteristics are influenced by the cultural norms that are prevalent at the time of their founding. In a similar vein, Tolley (2003) asserts that shifting cultural ideas concerning gender and the nature of science affected female representation in specific scientific educational programs in the United States historically. Once a field is labeled male or female, its gender label becomes widely taken for granted and self-perpetuating.

4. The data, assembled by the Organisation for Economic Cooperation and Development, are available at ⟨http://www1.oecd.org/scripts/cde/members/EDU_UOEAuthenticate.asp⟩. Tertiary first-degree recipients include graduates under "Tertiary A, First Degree, All" and

"Tertiary B, First Degree, All." The duration of study required to earn such degrees ranges from three to six years, reflecting cross-national variation in the structural configuration of higher education systems.

5. Throughout the world, tertiary dropout rates are high. Levels of attrition are especially high among women in scientific fields (Seymour and Hewitt 1997; Herzig 2004).

6. Definitions that allowed for translation from one data set to another were derived from *Classifying Educational Programmes: Manual for ISCED–97 Implementation in OECD Countries, 1999 Edition.* UNESCO data were taken from table 6 in *Global Education Digest,* available at ⟨http://stats.uis.unesco.org/eng/ReportFolders/Rfview/explorerp.asp⟩.

7. These parameters are the field-specific terms comprising the *A* index, which measures overall levels of sex segregation (see Charles and Grusky 1995, 2004). They can also be derived from the sex-by-occupation interaction terms from a set of saturated log-linear models (one for each country).

8. The exponent is the value obtained if the base of the natural log ($e = 2.71828$) is raised to a power equal to the segregation parameter in question. For example, the exponent of the parameter 1.05 (taken from the first row of table 6.2) is equal to 2.86 because $2.71828^{1.05} = 2.86$. This means that men are overrepresented by a factor of nearly three (2.86) in computer science in Australia.

9. One non-Soviet state, Belgium, also follows this pattern.

10. Soviet countries indeed exhibited greater gender integration in technical fields and they were among the first to reach gender parity in tertiary educational enrollments (Bialecki and Heyns 1993). Nevertheless, women's public sphere incorporation was not the result of feminist "equal rights" activism but rather an outgrowth of Soviet policy efforts to raise the level of economic development by mobilizing all capable workers (Einhorn 1993; Bialecki and Heyns 1993).

11. Women's representation in computer science is measured using the segregation parameters in the first column of table 6.2. Data on per capita gross national product (GNP) in 2001 were taken from the United Nations' *Human Development Report* (2003). GNP values were logged.

12. Female representation in higher education is measured as women's share of tertiary students in the 1994–95 academic year (United Nations Educational, Scientific, and Cultural Organization 1997b, 1999). Data on women's share of the labor force and professional occupations are for the year 1990, and are taken from the United Nations's (1999) WISTAT database.

13. Some evidence of a possible spillover effect is found among advanced industrial societies, though. Omitting the five least developed countries (the Czech Republic, Hungary, Korea, the Slovak Republic, and Turkey), we find a positive relationship between the overall female enrollment rates and women's representation in computer science programs ($r = .49$, $p = .05$). One interpretation of these findings, should they hold up under multivariate analysis, is that segregative forces dominate as long as tertiary systems are undergoing structural diversification (i.e., expansion of programs intended to appeal to women), but that "empowerment" effects of the sort described by Ramirez and collaborators dominate once some ceiling of diversification is reached. Distinguishing the interactive relationships among economic develop-

ment, female tertiary enrollment rates, and sex segregation by field of study requires formal multivariate analysis as well as a larger sample of industrializing countries. In research funded by the National Science Foundation, we are carrying out such analyses based on data drawn from forty-four industrial, industrializing, and transitional societies (NSF HRD–0332852).

14. For the sixteen most advanced industrial countries, the correlation was yet stronger (.73). Data were taken from the 1995 and 1999 waves of the Third International Math and Science Survey (TIMSS) and were aggregated to the national level for boys and girls separately. We used data on students enrolled in the equivalent of the U.S. eighth grade since previous studies suggest that gender divergence in attitudes toward math and science occurs at around the eighth-grade level (Catsambis 1994; Hanson 1996).

15. This positive correlation is also consistent with the individual-level interpretation, supported by a great deal of microlevel survey research, that girls with more gender-essentialist attitudes are less likely to enroll in mathematically related programs of study (Shu and Marini 1998; Xie and Shauman 2003). Without microlevel data, we are unable to distinguish the effects of individual preferences from those of diffuse cultural ideologies (which influence decisions of even those individuals who do not themselves consciously subscribe to gender-essentialist beliefs).

16. The gender gap in mathematical achievement is measured as the difference in the mean standardized-test scores of eighth-grade girls and eighth-grade boys in the respective country.

17. For these twenty-one countries, scores on the math achievement variable range from -17 to $+5$, with a mean of -5.86 and a standard deviation of 5.95. Country scores on the math aspirations variable range from $-.23$ to $+.02$, with a mean of $-.10$ and a standard deviation of .05. In both cases, negative values indicate higher male than female scores, on average; positive values indicate higher female than male scores.

18. Data are taken from the 1995 World Values Survey. The same survey includes a variable indexing the percentage of the adult population agreeing with the statement that "both husband and wife should contribute to household income." Since this survey item alludes to the sexual division of labor in the family (arguably the quintessential manifestation of gender-essentialist ideology), it likely taps into an antiessentialist as well as a liberal-egalitarian sentiment. It therefore represents a less pure indicator of liberal egalitarianism. For the twenty-one countries with available data, the correlation of this variable with female representation in computer science is .27 ($p = .25$) (see also Charles and Bradley 2002).

19. Omitting these two countries, the correlation was $-.06$.

20. For example, all three countries score below average on the measure of gender egalitarianism referenced in note 18 (above scores for Korea, Turkey, and Ireland were 28, 44, and 59, respectively, compared to a mean score of 60 for the countries in our sample).

21. Our data do in fact suggest that attitudes toward math and mathematical careers are more strongly gender differentiated in more industrialized countries.

22. These concerns are not unfounded, given that professional IT jobs pay considerably better than most female-dominated occupations (Anker 1998; OECD 1998; Bureau of Labor Statistics 2004) and given the central role in national development that has been ascribed to IT (Drori et al. 2003).

23. On efforts by the Swedish government, see Wistedt (1998). On the United States, see Congressional Commission (2000). On Japan, see National Institute of Science and Technology Policy (1996). On international initiatives, see United Nations Development Fund for Women/United Nations Development Program (2004).

References

Anker, R. 1998. *Gender and jobs: Sex segregation of occupations in the world.* Geneva: ILO.

Baker, D. P., and D. P. Jones. 1993. Creating gender equality: Cross-national gender stratification and mathematical performance. *Sociology of Education* 66:91–103.

Berkovitch, N. 1999. *From motherhood to citizenship: Women's rights and international organizations.* Baltimore, MD: Johns Hopkins University Press.

Berryman, S. E. 1983. *Who will do science?* New York: Rockefeller Foundation.

Bialecki, I., and B. Heyns. 1993. Educational attainment, the status of women, and the private school movement in Poland. In *Democratic reform and the position of women in transitional economies*, ed. V. M. Moghadam, 110–134. Oxford: Clarendon Press.

Bourdieu, P. 2001. *Masculine domination.* Cambridge, MA: Polity Press.

Bradley, K. 2000. The incorporation of women into higher education: Paradoxical outcomes? *Sociology of Education* 73:1–18.

Bradley, K., and M. Charles. 2003. Uneven inroads: Understanding women's status in higher education. *Research in Sociology of Education* 14:247–274.

Breathnach, P. 2002. Information technology, gender segmentation, and the relocation of back office employment. *Information, Communication, and Society* 5:320–335.

Brinton, M. C., and S. Lee. 2001. Women's education and the labor market in Japan and South Korea. In *Women's working lives in East Asia*, ed. M. C. Brinton, 125–150. Palo Alto, CA: Stanford University Press.

Bureau of Labor Statistics, U.S. Department of Labor. 2004. *Occupational outlook handbook, 2004–05 edition.* 〈http://www.bls.gov/oco/ocos267.htm〉.

Burton, L., ed. 1990. *Gender and mathematics: An international perspective.* Exeter: Cassell Educational Limited.

Catsambis, S. 1994. The path to math: Gender and racial-ethnic differences in mathematics preparation from middle school to high school. *Sociology of Education* 67:199–215.

Charles, M. 1992. Cross-national variation in occupational sex segregation. *American Sociological Review* 57:483–502.

Charles, M. 2003. Deciphering sex segregation: Vertical and horizontal inequalities in ten countries. *Acta Sociologica* 46:267–287.

Charles, M., and K. Bradley. 2002. Equal but separate? A cross-national study of sex segregation in higher education. *American Sociological Review* 67:573–599.

Charles, M., and D. B. Grusky. 1995. Models for describing the underlying structure of sex segregation. *American Journal of Sociology* 100:931–971.

Charles, M., and D. B. Grusky. 2004. *Occupational ghettos: The worldwide segregation of women and men.* Palo Alto, CA: Stanford University Press.

Congressional Commission on the Advancement of Women and Minorities in Science, Engineering, and Technology Development. 2000. *Land of plenty: Diversity as America's competitive edge in science, engineering, and technology.* Washington, DC: CAWMSET.

Correll, S. J. 2001. Gender and the career choice process: The role of biased self-assessments. *American Journal of Sociology* 106:1691–1730.

Davis, K. 1984. Wives and work: The sex role revolution and its consequences. *Population and Development Review* 10:397–417.

Drori, G. S., J. W. Meyer, F. O. Ramirez, and E. Schofer. 2003. *Science in the modern world polity.* Palo Alto, CA: Stanford University Press.

Einhorn, B. 1993. *Cinderella goes to market.* London: Verso Press.

Fenstermaker, S., and C. West, eds. 2002. *Doing gender, doing difference: Inequality, power, and institutional change.* New York: Routledge.

Fjelde, H. V. 1991. Public-private tendencies within higher education in Norway from a women's perspective. In *Women's higher education in comparative perspective*, ed. G. P. Kelly and S. Slaughter, 117–130. Amsterdam: Kluwer Academic Publishers.

Gerber, T., and D. Schaefer. 2004. Horizontal stratification of higher education in Russia: Trends, gender differences, and labor market outcomes. *Sociology of Education* 77:32–59.

Goode, W. J. 1963. *World revolution and family patterns.* New York: Free Press.

Hanson, S. L. 1996. *Lost talent: Women in the sciences.* Philadelphia: Temple University Press.

Hanson, S. L., M. Schaub, and D. P. Baker. 1996. Gender stratification in the science pipeline: A comparative analysis of seven countries. *Gender and Society* 10:271–290.

Herzig, A. H. 2004. Becoming mathematicians: Women and students of color choosing and leaving doctoral mathematics. *Review of Educational Research* 74:171–214.

Inglehart, R. 1997. *Modernization and postmodernization.* Princeton, NJ: Princeton University Press.

Jackson, R. M. 1998. *Destined for equality: The inevitable rise of women's status.* Cambridge, MA: Harvard University Press.

Jacobs, J. 2003. Detours on the road to equality: Women, work, and higher education. *Contexts* 2:32–41.

Jepperson, R. L. 1991. Institutions, institutional effects, and institutionalism. In *The new institutionalism in organizational analysis*, ed. W. W. Powell and P. J. DiMaggio, 143–163. Chicago: University of Chicago Press.

Jones, J., and J. Castle. 1986. Women in U.K. universities, 1920–1980. *Studies in Higher Education* 11:289–297.

Kerr, C., J. T. Dunlop, F. H. Harbison, and C. A. Myers. 1960. *Industrialism and industrial man.* Cambridge, MA: Harvard University Press.

McIlwee, J. S., and J. G. Robinson. 1992. *Women in engineering: Gender, power, and workplace culture*. Albany: State University of New York.

Meyer, J. W. 2001. The evolution of modern stratification systems. In *Social stratification: Class, race, and gender in sociological perspective*, ed. D. B. Grusky, 881–890. 2nd ed. Boulder, CO: Westview Press.

National Institute of Science and Technology Policy. 1996. *The barriers against women majoring in science and engineering*. Tokyo: Science and Technology Agency.

Organisation for Economic Cooperation and Development. 1998. *The future of female-dominated occupations*. Paris: OECD.

Organisation for Economic Cooperation and Development. 2004. *Online education database*. ⟨http://www1.oecd.org/scripts/cde/members/EDU_UOEAuthenticate.asp⟩.

Parsons, T. 1970. Equality and inequality in modern society, or social stratification revisited. In *Social stratification: Research and theory for the 1970s*, ed. E. O. Laumann, 14–72. Indianapolis: Bobbs-Merrill.

Ramirez, F. O. 1987. Global changes, world myths, and the demise of cultural gender: Implications for the United States. In *America's changing role in the world system*, ed. T. Boswell and A. Bergesen, 257–273. New York: Praeger.

Ramirez, F. O., and Y.-K. Cha. 1990. Citizenship and gender: Western educational development in comparative perspective. *Research in Sociology of Education and Socialization* 9:153–173.

Ramirez, F. O., Y. Soysal, and S. Shanahan. 1997. The changing logic of political citizenship: Cross-national acquisition of women's suffrage rights, 1890 to 1990. *American Sociological Review* 62:735–745.

Ramirez, F. O., and C. M. Wotipka. 2001. Slowly but surely? The global expansion of women's participation in science and engineering fields of study, 1972–92. *Sociology of Education* 74:231–251.

Ridgeway, C. L., and S. J. Correll. 2004. Unpacking the gender system: A theoretical perspective on gender beliefs and social relations. *Gender and Society* 18:510–531.

Seymour, E., and N. M. Hewitt. 1997. *Talking about leaving: Why undergraduates leave the sciences*. Boulder, CO: Westview Press.

Shu, X., and M. M. Marini. 1998. Gender-related change in occupational aspirations. *Sociology of Education* 71:44–68.

Stinchcombe, A. L. 1965. Social structure and organizations. In *Handbook of organizations*, ed. J. G. March, 110–134. Chicago: Rand McNally.

Third International Mathematics and Science Study at the Eighth Grade (TIMSS). 1995. Boston: Boston College, International Association for the Evaluation of Educational Achievement.

Third International Mathematics and Science Study at the Eighth Grade (TIMSS). 1999. Boston: Boston College, International Association for the Evaluation of Educational Achievement.

Thomas, G. M., J. W. Meyer, F. O. Ramirez, and J. Boli, eds. 1987. *Institutional structure: Constituting state, society, and the individual.* Newbury Park, CA: Sage.

Tolley, K. 2003. *The science education of American girls.* London: RoutledgeFalmer.

United Nations. 1999. *Women's indicators and statistics database (WISTAT).* New York: United Nations.

United Nations Development Program. 2003. *Human Development Report.* New York: UNDP.

United Nations Educational, Scientific, and Cultural Organization. 1997. *Classifying educational programmes: Manual for ISCED–97 implementation in OECD countries, 1999 edition.* Paris: UNESCO.

United Nations Educational, Scientific, and Cultural Organization. Various years. *Statistical yearbook.* Paris: UNESCO.

United Nations Development Fund for Women/United Nations Development Program. 2004. *Bridging the gender digital divide.* New York: UNIFEM.

Wistedt, I. 1998. *Recruiting female students to higher education in mathematics, physics, and technology.* Stockholm, Sweden: National Agency for Higher Education.

World Values Survey (WVS). 1995. Distributed by JDSystems, Madrid.

Xie, Y., and K. A. Shauman. 2003. *Women in science: Career processes and outcomes.* Cambridge, MA: Harvard University Press.

7

Just Get Over It or Just Get On with It: Retaining Women in Undergraduate Computing

J. McGrath Cohoon

At a major computing industry conference in 2004, a panel of highly accomplished professional women advised an audience of about a thousand people that women are unlikely to succeed in IT careers if they are conscious of their minority status. The panelists thought it was a mistake to pay attention to gender. Their advice was to "just get over it." Unfortunately, this pragmatic individual response to women's underrepresentation (Ambady et al. 2004) will not result in a more inclusive field. Ignoring gender differences means disregarding the ethical issues of equal access to rewarding careers as well as workforce concerns about the supply of qualified professionals. It also means that society will forfeit the contribution women could make toward shaping our future through the creation of IT.

In this chapter, I summarize the findings of the first nationwide study of factors that lead to gendered outcomes in undergraduate computer science departments. This study produced a wealth of data about the process that allocates students to different fields of study. The evidence shows that environmental conditions in computer science programs are related to the balance of men and women enrolled, and whether the often small numbers of women who declare a computer science major are retained at rates comparable to their male classmates.

Data collected from interviews, focus groups, and surveys confirm the male-dominated gender composition of enrollment in computer science, and establish the extent of women's disproportionate attrition from the undergraduate major. The data show that in the United States, women generally comprised only 24 percent of undergraduates enrolled in computer science programs between 1994 and 2000. This representation is about what one would expect based on published reports of degrees awarded (Camp 1997; Computing Research Association 2002). More surprising is the contrast between women's 24 percent portion of enrollment and their attrition—women comprise 32 percent of those who switch to a different major.

Not only are women underrepresented in the computer science major but they are overrepresented in the 16 percent of computer science students who depart for another major each year.

Data also show that women's disproportionate attrition is not inevitable. Computer science departments can retain women at comparable rates to men. Even small changes in faculty attitudes and practices can make significant contributions to gender equity in retention. Equality of student outcomes vary with the following conditions: faculty concern over whether faculty staffing is adequate, and the extent to which faculty members encourage students to persist, mentor for diversity, and expect student success to result from homework and academic focus. Independent of these faculty behaviors, departments generally approach gender balanced retention when their enrollment is gender balanced so that women have the same access to same-sex peer support that men have.

Women's representation in postsecondary computing is more than just part of the gender imbalance on the path to a computing career. It is an instance of gender segregation in modern society and contributes to women's exclusion from the professional creation of technology. Higher education plays a role in maintaining this segregation. Men and women commonly study different disciplines, as evidenced by the gender makeup of the nursing, teaching, engineering, and computing fields. This educational separation is a consequence of numerous factors that operate at individual and cultural levels. The role of higher education becomes apparent when comparing students' pre- and postcollege career intentions. Examined over time, one can see trends in whether men and women leave college on more or less divergent occupational paths than they intended when entering college (Jacobs 1995). On the whole, these trends reflect larger cultural trends, but the decline and leveling off in gender segregation that occurred in the latter part of the twentieth century demonstrate that gender segregation is more than a product of early socialization—it is an ongoing process (Jacobs 1995).

Various theories attempt to explain the gender segregation process. Much of the research either implicitly or explicitly adopts a social-psychological view such as that articulated by Wigfield and Eccles (2000). They argue that individual choices are influenced by a variety of factors stemming from inborn traits and social stereotypes. These traits and stereotypes ultimately shape both the value and expectation of success that people associate with their performance of an activity. In turn, the value and expectation of success determine how likely it is that an individual will engage in a particular activity, such as majoring in computer science. Research conducted with this theoretical perspective examines microlevel factors such as students' confidence in and attitudes toward computing (Beyer et al. 2003), or it measures the effectiveness of efforts to make students feel that computing is enjoyable and masterable (McDowell et al. 2003).

Alternative theoretical perspectives are more common in sociology, where gender segregation is typically viewed from a macrolevel. This perspective emphasizes how the environment channels men and women into different fields. To explain this "horizontal gender segregation" (the clustering of men and women in different occupations, in contrast to clustering at different hierarchical levels), work based on macrolevel theory focuses on large-scale social patterns such as historical or international variation in the gender composition of computing. For example, Jacobs (1995) shows that gender segregation in academic specialties declined from the 1960s into the 1980s in the United States. He argues that higher education can maintain or undermine students' sex-typed choice of fields, and that "broad patterns in education and society" determine the nature of that influence (Jacobs 1996). Similarly, Charles and Bradley (2002) show that gender segregation in academic specialties varies by nation. They identify cultural beliefs about gender equality and the structure of a nation's educational system as two significant factors that influence women's representation in different fields of study.

The particular exclusion of women from fields leading to technology-creating professions has also been noted by feminist scholars. They explain this phenomenon in ways ranging from ecofeminist arguments that men and women have different, essentially inherent skills and interests (Belenky et al. 1996; Turkle and Papert 1990), to assertions that technology is an expression of the dominant male culture and is therefore rejected by women (Wajcman 1991; Wilson 2003), to contentions that women's underrepresentation among creators of technology is a product of stereotypes and malleable social structures that create as well as reinforce women's exclusion and men's inclusion (Sørensen 2002).

Between these micro and macro explanations fall the localized instances of men's and women's distribution across particular programs. Just as investigations of sex segregation in the workplace reveal that there is more to the story than can be seen from either an individual- or high-level view (Bielby and Baron 1986), examining differences in gender composition across postsecondary computer science programs shows that important variations exist within the broad patterns of gender segregation in higher education. This view of gender segregation in higher education has not been applied to postsecondary computing in prior studies, although gender distribution across disciplines has been considered as a factor in the relationship be-tween institutional characteristics and women's representation (Jacobs 1999).

The current study explicitly tests the extent to which the local environment influ-ences the gender composition of postsecondary computing. I analyze data collected directly from students and faculty, and employ a department-level view to learn how the equality of outcomes is shaped by the immediate and contemporary so-cial conditions. The result is a set of departmental features known to distinguish between environments with gender-neutral outcomes and those with gendered outcomes.

Study Methods

We employed multiple methods and studied a large number of institutions to obtain results that apply to undergraduate computer science programs in the United States in general. Data collection began in 2001 with interviews and focus groups at the eighteen undergraduate computer science departments that agreed to participate in this phase of the study, and it continued in 2002 with a survey of faculty and chairs at 209 study departments. We defined computer science as general computer and information sciences, computer programming, data-processing technology, informa-tion science and systems, computer systems analysis, and other information sciences following the definition used in the U.S. government's classification of academic pro-grams (Morgan and Hunt 2002).

The eighteen departments visited in the initial qualitative phase of our data collec-tion represented a mix of seventeen institutions varying in geographic location, insti-tutional type, highest degree granted, reputation for institutional quality, and gender composition. The geographic location included ten urban and seven nonurban insti-tutions (one institution had two departments participate in the study). The institu-tions were located across the United States, with clusters in the Northeast, the Southeast, and the Midwest as well as on West Coast. Eleven of the institutions were public and six were private. At twelve of the interview sites, the highest degree granted was a Ph.D. At three institutions, a Master of Science was the highest degree granted, and at two institutions a bachelor's was the highest degree granted. All had undergraduate degree programs. Finally, the study institutions were of varying pres-tige according to their 1993 NRC rankings with the median-ranked department rated at 3 on a 5-point scale of faculty quality. The lowest National Research Coun-cil (NRC) rating in our sample was 1.52 and the highest was 3.6.

A team of trained interviewers and focus group leaders traveled to each of the eighteen initial study departments, and conducted interviews with a total of 143 faculty members and chairpersons. They also conducted thirty-one focus groups (sex segregated in every case but one, where scheduling made separate groups impossible) with 182 undergraduate computer science students in sixteen departments. (Two of the sites were unable to recruit student participants.) The average number of participants in a focus group was six, but ranged from one (in which case a semi-structured interview was conducted) to eighteen. In every case, the moderator followed a scripted set of questions to ensure that all discussions covered the same set of issues, but moderator discretion determined the extent of probing and follow-up on any particular comment. The transcribed data from the interviews were coded and analyzed for dominant themes.

Focus group participants were recruited by an on-site contact person, and hence cannot be considered a random sample. Overall, 43 percent of the participants in the focus groups were women—a percentage that was much higher than women's representation in their departments. In the visited departments, the ratio of enrolled female to male majors averaged 24 percent, although it ranged from 7 to 45 percent. The average participant was twenty-three years old and a junior in college; the average participating woman was one year older. The youngest participant was eighteen, and the oldest was fifty. The students with whom we spoke were doing well academically—their mean GPA was 3.3 overall and 3.5 in their major. The women had a slightly higher overall GPA (3.4) than the men (3.3) and a slightly lower major GPA (3.4) than the men (3.5). Asian, black, and white students participated in the focus groups, with white students in the majority.

Data from the focus groups were used in the construction of the survey that followed. The survey went to faculty and chairs in the 209 largest (35 or more graduated in a single year) or most highly ranked computer science departments in the contiguous United States. We made every effort to obtain high response rates, including sending invited participants a two dollar bill as an advance token of appreciation and incentive to respond. An online questionnaire was used with great success and cost savings. Nonrespondents were then asked to complete the questionnaire via mail or telephone—a strategy that obtained responses from a final 10 percent of those who had not complied with e-mail reminders to complete the questionnaire. When data collection was closed, response rates were 76 percent of the eligible chairpersons (159 chairs) and 68 percent of the eligible faculty (1,716 faculty).

We used the survey data to construct independent variables that measure conditions and practices in our study departments. Faculty responses were aggregated to the mean departmental response on a particular item. For items that turned out to be significantly related to our dependent variable, we confirmed the relationship with alternative measures based on the percent of responding faculty who answered with a 4 or 5 on a 5-point response scale.

Official enrollment and disposition data were also collected from 75 of the 209 departments in the study. Not all institutions had records that made it possible to track students from one declared major to another, and not all of those institutions with the data were able or willing to provide it for this study. The 75 programs that did provide this data comprised the subset of our study institutions for which complete analysis was possible.

We used the official data to calculate overall attrition rates as well as rates of male and female attrition from the major. Our intention was to create a stable continuous measure of departmental outcomes by minimizing annual fluctuations and the influence of individual students. To accomplish this goal, we employed a method similar to demographic calculations of death rates with data covering a six-year period and allowing for entry of new students each year. For each sex, we measured attrition as the six-year average of the number of students who had declared a computer science major but subsequently switched to another major at their institution, divided by the total of these switchers plus the students who had remained in the computer science major. We calculated each department's gender gap in attrition rates by subtracting the female attrition rate from the male attrition rate to obtain a single measure of a variable we call the gendered attrition rate. Other measures of attrition were considered, but none offered the independent and consistent measure of the difference between outcomes for the men and women in a department.

It may help the reader to keep in mind that when the gendered attrition rate is positive, women are retained at higher rates than men. When it is negative, women are retained at lower rates than men. This means that variables positively correlated with gendered attrition have higher values when women are retained at higher rates, and they have lower values when women are retained at lower rates relative to the men in their department.

We attempted to explain the variation in two outcome measures—overall attrition from programs and the gendered attrition rate using data from the seventy-four study departments that provided both survey responses and official data for outcome measures. This report focuses on the gender balance in computing, so we discuss only findings relevant to the gender gap in attrition rates and mention overall attrition only briefly. The gender composition of enrollment was also investigated, but it is discussed here only as it contributes to retention.

Overall attrition rates varied independently of the gender gap in attrition rates, although the same conditions almost always prompted both men and women to stay or leave their computer science programs. We know that women generally left at high rates from the same departments that men left at high rates because the male and female rates were strongly correlated ($r = .89$, significant at .000). Both sexes tended to leave when the local job market was weak. Other conditions that prompted male and female departure from computing remain unidentified. We considered that overall attrition could be a consequence of numerous conditions such as program size and resources, faculty quality and preference for research over teaching, student workload, and the availability of support programs. Only the strength of the local job market had a robust connection to overall attrition from undergraduate computer science. Still, the local job market was not associated with gendered attrition rates in our national study. (An earlier statewide study had found evidence relating the two [Cohoon 2001], but the nationwide data did not corroborate this finding.) According to our national study, none of the factors that are related to gendered attrition have a measurable association with overall attrition. Women's attrition rates differ from men's to varying degrees, and this gender difference is not attributable to the same factors that prompt all students to find a different major.

In our analyses of the quantitative data, we investigated many hypotheses about the size of the gender gap in attrition rates. In addition to the hypotheses listed in appendix 7.1, we considered whether women's representation was influenced by factors such as program size, type of institutional control, highest degree offered, geographic location, and a variety of other propositions suggested by the faculty and students who spoke with us. Multivariate regression analyses yielded findings about six factors that are significantly related to the equal retention of men and women. It is important to remember that a lack of evidence for unsupported hypotheses is not equivalent to disproof. Our results allow for a confident assertion that the identified relationships are generally true; the remaining hypotheses may or may not be true. Only the hypotheses supported by multivariate analyses of the data are discussed in this chapter.

Description of the Average Computer Science Department

Descriptive information about the nature of undergraduate computing programs is informative and useful as benchmarks against which programs can assess

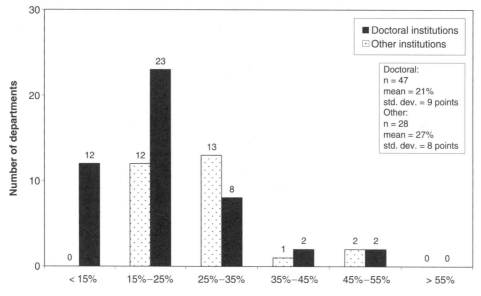

Figure 7.1
Variation in women's portion of undergraduate computer science majors

themselves. Data about gender composition and attrition in undergraduate computer science departments are provided here. Measures of significant faculty practices, expectations, and concerns are described along with findings.

Gender Composition of Students and Faculty

The variation in the gender composition of departments indicates that programs have different levels of success in recruiting women. As figures 7.1 and 7.2 show, women are better represented at the nondoctoral institutions, but their representation is low at most institutions. Despite the general underrepresentation, seven programs had student enrollments that were at least 35 percent female, and six programs employed women as at least 34 percent of their faculty.

Student Attrition from the Computer Science Major

In our study departments, the average annual attrition rates were 16 percent overall, 21 percent of enrolled women, and 15 percent of enrolled men. Overall attrition was similar in doctoral and nondoctoral institutions during our study period. As figure 7.3 shows, students switched to other majors at slightly higher rates in the doc-

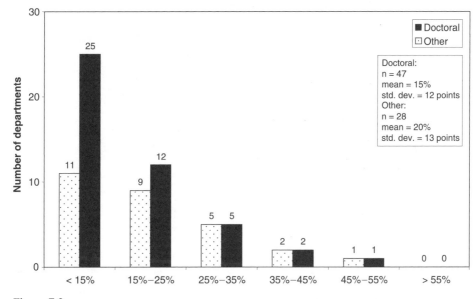

Figure 7.2
Variation in female portion of faculty

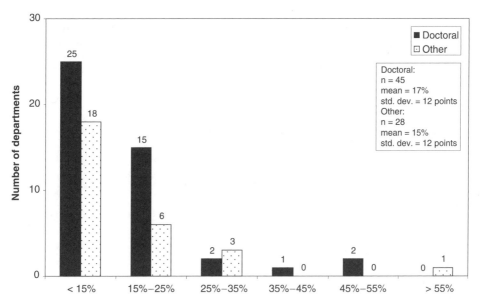

Figure 7.3
Variation in annual attrition from the computer science major

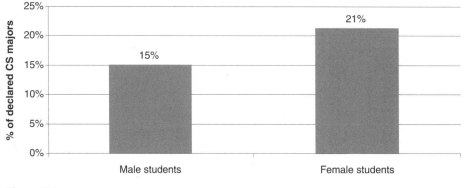

Figure 7.4
Average annual undergraduate attrition, 1994–95 to 1999–2000

toral institutions, but most of the departments in both institutional types lost less than 15 percent of their declared majors each year.

Figure 7.4 illustrates the typical gender gap in attrition rates; on average, women's attrition rate was six points higher than was men's in the same department. This difference existed despite the fact that rates for men and women were strongly correlated ($r = .89$, significant at .001 level). The size of this gap varied across departments—there were twelve departments where women were retained at equal or slightly greater rates than men—and this variation was not correlated with whether an institution granted PhDs.[1] The conditions associated with how women's retention compared with men's are what we investigated.

Findings

Our focus group data provided both insights into features of computing that attracted women to the major and illustrations of what retained women in undergraduate computer science. Our survey data provided measures of the relationship between various factors and women's enrollment and retention. I summarize and briefly discuss our findings in these subsections.

The variance in relative retention shown in figure 7.5 indicates that any pertinent inherent gender differences that may or may not exist can be overcome under certain conditions. Whether or not the sexes differ in ways that contribute to partic.ipation in computing, they are retained at the same rates in some departments. The

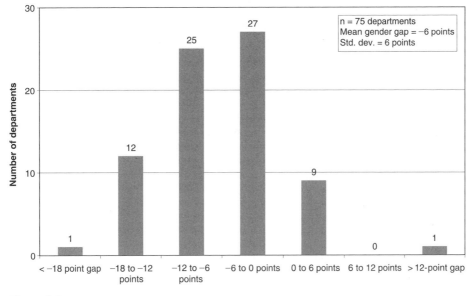

Figure 7.5
Variation in gendered attrition rates

major result of this project was to identify a small number of conditions that predict how similar attrition rates are for the men and women in a computer science department. These six factors, four of which involve faculty behaviors and attitudes, have a strong relationship with similar retention, explaining 46 percent of the variation in departments' gendered attrition rates. The same variables are relevant to programs in both doctoral and nondoctoral institutions, although their significance and the strength of the relationship varies somewhat between the two types of environments.

Multiple regression analysis identified the significant factors that predict gendered attrition rates. They are same-sex peer support, faculty emphasis on both homework and academic focus, support from faculty in the form of encouragement to persist as well as mentoring for diversity, and whether faculty members are concerned that their department has sufficient faculty. These findings are shown in table 7.1, and they indicate that although the average department loses women at a rate six points higher than the male attrition rate, the gender-balanced retention of students is a feasible goal for undergraduate computer science programs.

Table 7.1
Multiple regression of departmental factors on gendered attrition rates

	Beta
Female portion of enrollment	.37**
Faculty encourage student persistence	.33**
Faculty mentor for diversity	.30**
Faculty concern about insufficient faculty	−.26*
Expected homework hours	.29*
Believe good students limit extracurricular	.27*
Adjusted R square	.46**

Notes:
*$p < .01$
**$p < .001$

Same-Sex Peer Support (Beta = .37, Significant at .001)

Our data lend support to the hypothesis that gendered attrition rates are small in departments where the gender balance of enrolled majors approaches parity. Of all the factors we considered, available same-sex peer support, measured as the female portion of enrollment, had the strongest relationship with gendered attrition rates of any factors identified in this study.

Looking individually at retention rates for men and women, we see that as women's portion of enrollment increased, their attrition rates decreased ($r = −.34$, significant at .01); men's attrition rates might also be low in departments with gender-balanced enrollments, but the relationship failed to reach a statistically significant level ($r = −.19$, significant at .06). The finding about women's retention corroborates both single-institution observations of improved female retention rates following the successful recruitment of women (Blum and Frieze 2005; Margolis and Fisher 2002) and the finding of the statewide pilot study for this project (Cohoon 2001).

Although other researchers have described similar effects of numerical minority status (Kanter 1977), we relate it to same-sex peer support based on findings from our focus groups. According to both the men and the women who spoke with us, having a classmate to call on for help is one of the most effective ways of coping with the demands of a computer science major. Over and over we were told, "If I didn't have people here that I could come to and say, 'What does this mean?' I don't think I would have stayed at all." Students consistently reported that relying on peers was essential for persisting in a computer science program. Yet this coping strategy is less available to women than it is to men.

The average study department was only 24 percent female, so women had less opportunity than men to find a same-sex classmate to go to for help. In many classes, women had only two or three female classmates; in other courses, they had none. This scarcity required women to turn to their male classmates for help, so it is unsurprising that most of those with whom we spoke were quite comfortable relying on men. For example, one woman voiced a common experience when she told us that her closest friends were male. "I've always, ever since I was tiny, had guys for friends." Some women had no female friends at all. Preference for socially dissimilar friends is not the norm in our society, however, and even in computer science, there were many women who were unwilling to go to a male classmate for help. These women insisted that women were easier than the men in their classes to approach, that women were less likely than men to misinterpret the request for help, and that women were less likely than men to think that a question indicated inferiority. For these reasons, many women in our focus groups preferred to get assistance from their female classmates.

When enrollments are gender balanced, women have the option of same-sex peer support. When enrollments are not gender balanced, only men have that option, and women must approach the men in their class for the help they consider vital for making it through the program. This inequality in the conditions experienced by male and female computer science undergraduates explains why women leave departments where few women are enrolled, and it points to the importance of attracting women to a program.

Attracting Women to Computer Science

Perception and objective measures provided complimentary information about how women come to enroll in computer science. From the students' point of view, their attraction stemmed from self-assessment, past experience, and future expectations. More objective measures identified two environmental conditions that generally and consistently predicted women's representation in computer science. They were women undergraduate's representation at an institution and the degree to which a computer science program adapted to the job market.

Student Perceptions of What Attracted Them   A more detailed description of what students perceived as attractions to computing is provided in another report (Tillberg and Cohoon 2005). I summarize those findings in this section.

For the most part, the male and female students with whom we spoke felt initially attracted to computing for the same reasons. The similarities we observed suggest that the computer science major, as it is currently constructed, attracts primarily students who:

- reach college with positive computing experience from home, school, or work;
- were encouraged by parents or teachers to pursue this major;
- believe that they are skilled in mathematics or logic;
- enjoy programming;
- focus on rewarding careers that offer opportunity and flexibility.

These common characteristics imply that computer science has a core of experiences and characteristics that may be valuable for entry to the field, and that students of either sex may enter under the same set of conditions.

The gender differences we observed may point toward conditions that particularly attract women to computing. We found that women who do not like hardware, do play computer games, or want a lucrative career may still enter computing. These women entered when they recognized computing as a form of communication, a means of creative self-expression, or a path to a helping occupation. Women also entered when friends recruited them into the field or when they wished to defy stereotypes.

Building on what is particularly attractive to women could be a productive first step toward bringing more women to the discipline in its current form. However, one must also be cautious about the manner in which these enticements are utilized. In particular, playing on the defiance of stereotypes could be counterproductive if it reinforces the stereotypes instead of minimizing them.

Environmental Conditions Associated with Women's Enrollment   In addition to focus groups with students, the quantitative data we collected allowed some analysis of conditions associated with women's presence in a department. Although many variables were significantly correlated with women's portion of enrollment, only two relationships persisted when controlling for other factors. Multiple regression analyses of institutional gender composition and program ties to the job market

Table 7.2
Multiple regression of institutional and departmental factors on women's portion of enrollment in computer science

	Beta
Program adapts to changes in job market	0.27*
Female percent of institutional enrollment	0.51**
Adjusted R square	0.41**

Notes:
*$p < .01$
**$p < .001$

measured the combined linear effect as 41 percent of the variance in women's enrollment, as shown in table 7.2.

To measure the relationship between women's portion of enrollment and other characteristics of our study departments, we examined numerous departmental conditions. Many conditions were initially correlated with the average female percent of undergraduate enrollment during our six-year study period. They included: institutional gender composition (+, discussed below); size (−), measured by average class size; student quality (−), measured by median institutional SAT score for incoming first-year students; whether a program was located in a doctoral institution (−); and how closely the program was tied to the job market (+), as measured by chairperson responses on a 5-point scale from "not at all accurate" to "extremely accurate" to the question "Please indicate how accurately ['adapts to changes in the job market'] describes your undergraduate program in the past six years." Nevertheless, of all the initially correlated factors, only two remained significantly associated with women's representation when we conducted multiple regression analyses—institutional gender composition and department chair indications about the degree to which their program is tied to the job market.

Computer science departments located in institutions with high proportions of women had program enrollments that reflected this fact. This first finding helps explain previously published observations that women's representation in computer science was particularly low in programs located in engineering schools (Camp 1997), where women are typically scarce.

The second finding—that women's representation varied with program ties to the job market—echoes reports of strong female participation in nontraditional programs tailored to workforce entry and advancement such as those by DeVry and

Strayer (Malcom 2004), and helps explain why women's representation is higher among associate and master's degree recipients than among recipients of other degrees in computer science. Our interpretation of this finding is also corroborated by substituting a correlated variable ($r = .27$, significant at .001) that measures the average faculty member's opinion about whether the local job market promoted student persistence in the computer science major. (Faculty responded to the question "To what extent has the *local* job market hindered or promoted student persistence in your undergraduate program?" on a 5-point scale where 1 indicated "strongly hindered persistence," 3 indicated "neither hindered nor promoted persistence," and 5 indicated "strongly promoted persistence.") Both measures of ties to the job market are associated with greater representation of women, although the effect of the faculty measure dissipates when controlling for the chair's description of the program.

The lack of evidence that other factors contributed to gender-balanced enrollments does not imply that they play no role. Instead, the absence of support for other factors could be due to measurement error or the scarcity of effective intervention efforts. In any case, we can be confident that regardless of the particular circumstances, women's availability as potential majors in an institution and a program's clear preparation for employment are two factors that are reliably associated with women's equitable representation in undergraduate computer science programs.

Recruiting more women into postsecondary computing is essential to creating gender balance for at least two reasons: it increases women's representation in undergraduate programs and it helps retain the women who enter. Yet recruiting alone is not sufficient for creating gender balance in computing. Women must be retained at rates comparable to their male classmates or the effort to attract them will be squandered.

Support from Faculty: Encouraging Students to Persist (Beta = .33, Significant at .001)

Our evidence indicates that support from faculty is an effective way to balance retention rates. This support could come in a variety of forms, but we were only able to measure the effectiveness of two types: encouraging students to persist and mentoring for diversity.

The more influential form of faculty support for women is encouragement of student persistence in the major. Those departments where the average faculty member encourages students in their classes to persist generally retained women at rates comparable to men.

Less than half the faculty in the average department reported that they encouraged persistence. On a 5-point scale, faculty in the average department rated 3.4 as their level of agreement with the statement "I especially encouraged female students [in the largest undergraduate course I teach] to persist in this major." Interestingly, there was a strong correlation between this response and the response to the next question about especially encouraging male students ($r = .59$, significant at .01). This correlation, and the fact that both variables were associated with lower female attrition (although only encouraging females was statistically significant), led us to create a single measure of encouraging *students* to persist in the major. We did so by adding the responses for encouraging female students to the responses for encouraging male students, resulting in an average rating of 6.2 on a 10-point scale. Using the encouraging students variable, we found that in departments where attrition of men is high, the average faculty member was more likely to encourage persistence ($r = .23$, significant at .05). Women's attrition rates, however, were not measurably associated with faculty encouragement, as they had been with the encouraging female students variable; only the gender gap remained significantly correlated with encouragement. Regardless of which measure was used, our findings about gendered attrition remained the same: faculty encouragement to persist was associated with a smaller gender gap in attrition.

In contrast to encouraging persistence, the typical faculty member seemed to side with the professor who wrote, "We are overflowing with majors. If you figure out what makes students leave, please let me know!" She would prefer fewer students in her overcrowded program, so encouraging persistence would be counterproductive from her viewpoint. Likewise, a student reported, "I have a class now where the teacher keeps telling us to drop out and [he says] it's going to be a hard class. . . . He offered one dollar to each student that left the class." The class was not particularly challenging for this student, but if it had been, she had the instructor's blessing to leave.

Our survey data offered weak but statistically significant evidence for this interpretation of crowded programs leading instructors to discourage persistence—faculty members who encouraged students to persist taught slightly smaller courses than those who encouraged students to leave ($r = -.14$, significant at .05). Nevertheless, the size of enrollment has no significant relationship with the gendered attrition rates. None of the department characteristics that are associated with encouraging students to persist inform the relationship between gendered attrition and encouraging persistence. Other unmeasured factors, such as change in size or faculty perception of size, might be relevant, but they could not be measured with the available data.

Support from Faculty: Mentoring for Diversity (Beta = .30, Significant at .001)

Mentoring is associated with positive outcomes for computer science students, and mentoring motivated by the desire for diversity was associated with gender-balanced retention. Departments where the average faculty member mentored for diversity had significantly lower attrition of women than did departments where this activity was uncommon ($r = -.20$, significant at .05). No significant effect was observed for undergraduate men.

We defined mentoring as a set of activities that include:

- Involving individual students in professional activities
- Offering personalized advice to individual students
- Encouraging individual students
- Helping individual students establish careers

We also considered activities that were not specifically listed in our definition but that we categorize as mentoring. These activities fall into two groups. The first group is comprised of activities that focus on supporting students by helping them navigate rules, encouraging shy but competent students, or providing positive feedback. The second group of mentoring activities focuses on developing professional research skills by involving students in research, publishing with student coauthors, informing students of research opportunities, or supervising non-course-related work.

We found that the two types of mentoring are associated with different outcomes for undergraduate computer science students. As reported in Cohoon, Gonsoulin, and Layman (2004), support mentoring of computer science undergraduates in doctoral institutions positively correlates with students directly progressing to graduate school, and research mentoring positively correlates with the quality of the graduate program that students attend. Although women faculty members were more likely than men to engage in support-mentoring activities, initiate a mentoring relationship with an undergraduate student, and mentor women students, the results of mentoring activities were the same regardless of the sex of the faculty member.

Diversity mentoring is not defined by any type of mentoring activity. Instead, diversity mentoring is any mentoring activity that is motivated by the desire to overcome underrepresentation. The survey question asked faculty to indicate on a 5-point scale, where 1 is "not at all" and 5 is "completely," "the extent to which your mentoring efforts were motivated by … [the] desire to overcome under-representation." Our analyses of their responses found that only this motivation for mentoring was relevant to the equitable retention of women. In departments where more of the faculty members make a special effort to mentor particular students because they want to overcome under-representation, retention is equalized. In their own words, these faculty members wrote on the survey that their reason for mentoring was "I feel strongly that women should be encouraged in the fields of math and science. I grew up in a generation where this was not encouraged, and a couple of math teachers in high school and college encouraged me to pursue a math education." This was a select group, though. Less than 30 percent of the responding faculty members were even slightly motivated to mentor by the desire for diversity. Many more were instead motivated by talented students, like the "self-starters" who attracted the faculty member who wrote, "I require mentees to write a successful proposal before working with them." Women who lack confidence in their abilities are less likely to meet his criterion.

Some focus group discussions included examples of the positive effect that being mentored could have on students' confidence in their computing ability—a trait that women in computer science seem to have in small quantities (Beyer et al. 2003). For example, one woman described her slow start and her doubts about whether she could succeed in the computer science major. Her experience of working closely with faculty members who believed that she could master computer science was "probably the biggest encouragement to stay here." When she experienced self-doubt, this student's mentors expressed their confidence in her and worked to retain her instead of metaphorically holding the door open for her to leave.

There were also women who reported having faculty mentors who explicitly expressed their commitment to increasing the numbers of women in computing. Many of the focus group participants were uncomfortable with and laughed at this approach, but the student who experienced it said that she "felt better" when told, "Just keep at it. You can do it. We need more women in the field." This example suggests that actually voicing the diversity motivation might not be the best strategy, yet it illustrates how mentoring that was explicitly motivated by the desire to improve women's representation had the intended outcome, as our statistical results predict.

Women faculty members were more likely than men to put special effort into mentoring particular students in order to overcome underrepresentation (Cohoon et al. 2004). The sex of the faculty member, however, was not relevant to the outcome of diversity mentoring. Regardless of the faculty gender composition, departments where the average faculty member mentored undergraduates in order to overcome underrepresentation retained men and women at comparable rates. Again, this effect was independent of the type of mentoring activities; the motivation was the important element.

Support from Faculty: Concern about Insufficient Faculty Staffing (Beta = −.26, Significant at .01)

"Insufficient faculty" was a serious concern in the average computer science department during the study period. With declining enrollments in the post dot-com boom era, this issue may no longer be a common concern. But when our survey asked, "To what extent were the following conditions concerns that you had about your department in the past six years?" faculty members in the average department rated "insufficient faculty" as 4 on a 5-point scale. It was ahead of concerns about support staffing, physical resources, student quality, support from the dean, and the gender climate. In departments where this concern was the greatest, women left the undergraduate major at disproportionately high rates.

Faculty concern about having sufficient colleagues seems related to previous findings about resources and gendered attrition rates (Cohoon 2001). Concern about insufficient faculty was higher in departments where faculty turnover was high ($r = .26$, significant at .05), concern about lack of support from the dean was high ($r = .54$, significant at .001), and faculty thought about leaving because of dissatisfaction with the institutional support for their department ($r = .46$, significant at .001); all these factors were related to gendered attrition rates in a statewide study (Cohoon 2001).

The current study also shows that concern over sufficient faculty is more prevalent at public institutions ($r = .32$, significant at .001) and less prevalent at institutions where the median incoming student SAT score is high ($r = −.28$, significant at .001). Of these related factors, however, only being a public institution had a significant direct relationship with gendered attrition when controlling for other influences. There were only eight private institutions in the full analysis, so we cannot have much confidence in this observation until additional data are available. Another factor we considered—the ratio of faculty to students—also failed to explain gendered attrition rates. Measurement errors might account for the lack of corroborating statistical evidence about the meaning of insufficient faculty, but together with prior results, this association with gendered attrition suggests that faculty dissatisfaction has a particularly negative influence on their women students.

This finding emphasizes the central role that faculty play in the equality of retention. It fits with sociological theories that predict distressed environments will be particularly unfavorable to members of minority groups (Reskin and Roos 1990), but it raises more questions than it answers. Faculty members seem to be a key resource for equal retention, and when faculty members *feel* that there are too few of them, they might not support women students.

Faculty Expectations: Homework Hours (Beta = .29, Significant at .01)

The last two factors identified as significantly related to gendered attrition also raised many questions. These were unanticipated findings that contradicted hypotheses about the effects of a heavy workload and a narrow focus. Based on reports of students leaving STEM majors because they required too much work or too narrow of a focus (Seymour and Hewitt 1997), we had expected women to be disadvantaged in departments where faculty both expected many hours of homework per week and believed that student success required limiting extracurricular activities. Neither of these expectations were met; instead, women were retained at relatively higher rates in these departments. There may be a limit to this effect—an examination of the scatter plot for gendered attrition and homework hours in figure 7.6 suggests that there could be a leveling off of relative female retention when the faculty expect more than nine hours per week.

Women's attrition rates were slightly, but not significantly, lower in departments where faculty expected higher numbers in response to the question, "How many hours per week did you expect the average student to devote to homework assignments for [the largest undergraduate course you taught in the past six years]?" ($r = -.16$, significant at .10). Men's attrition rates were not related at all to the expected homework hours. On average, faculty expected that students spend seven hours per week on homework for one course, although this figure was eight hours at doctoral institutions. In the eight private institutions we studied, the mean

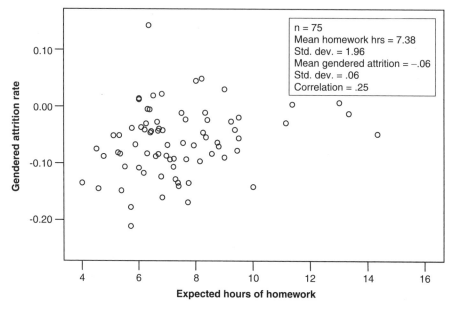

Figure 7.6
Expected homework hours and gendered attrition rates

expectation was nine hours per week. Homework expectations might have a different relationship with attrition at private versus public institutions, but more than eight cases will be needed to determine whether this is the case. Homework expectations were related to the gender gap in attrition rates regardless of student quality (median incoming SAT) or whether the institution was PhD granting.

Unpublished data from an introductory computer science course at one university lend support to this finding by documenting how valuable the computer science students in this course considered homework. Three hundred and sixty course evaluations asked how important assignments were for helping students understand the course content and succeed in the class. Male and female students rated homework as the most valuable component in the course.

These findings about the positive effect of homework on relative retention are difficult to explain given the many complaints we heard about the student workload in computer science. We found no support for an ad hoc hypothesis that emphasis on homework is related to faculty members' belief that computing is a learnable skill rather than an inborn talent. Instead, it might be that for students, homework is a route to improved confidence through intensive practice or that it defines performance expectations that might otherwise be vague. In a similar vein, homework might be less subject to the lowered performance that a stereotype threat can produce (Steele and Aronson 1995). The latter hypothesis fits with evidence that stereotypes affect public computing performance, but not computing done in private (Huff 2002).

Faculty Expectations: Focus on Academics (Beta = .27, Significant at .01)

Speculation on the reasons few women participate in fields like computing often focuses on women's breadth of interests and talents. Computing is said to require, or at least reward, narrow attention to technical minutia. This focus on computing to the exclusion of other interests is believed to be unappealing to women (Margolis and Fisher 2002). Therefore, we expected that women would leave in disproportionately high rates from departments where many faculty members believed that "good students limited their extracurricular involvements." Our analyses failed to support this hypothesis and instead indicated that the contrary was generally true.

It was uncommon for many faculty members to endorse the opinion that student success is enhanced by focusing on academics. In the average department, less than half the faculty agreed with the statement about limiting extracurricular involvement. Endorsement was more common in departments where women's representation was high ($r = .36$, significant at .01). Yet despite its unpopularity, when more faculty held this opinion, undergraduate women were retained at relatively high rates.

A possible explanation for this unexpected finding is that the women who have chosen a computer science major do so with the expectation of devoting most of their time to it. For example, women with whom we spoke described limiting other activities. One explained, "I have friends over for the gaming and stuff every Thursday, and half the time they're playing, I'm on my computer doing homework or working or whatever. It's like, you just don't do things." Similarly, another woman said, "I was in a sorority, but I quit that because it was too much time commitment.... I'm really trying to focus on school." Faculty recognition of this willingness to sacrifice other interests in order to succeed was associated with significantly reduced attrition rates for neither men nor women overall. Instead, it only distinguished attrition rates for men and women in the same departments.

Discussion

We focus on explaining equal retention to reveal how undergraduate programs contribute to the gender composition of women in computing. By taking a mid-level view, we take the spotlight off characteristics of female students and shine it on gendered attrition. From this perspective, we can see both characteristics of the average computer science program and the departmental variation that is not apparent from a discipline-level view. By examining the characteristics associated with this variation, we identify how local environments can counter prevailing cultural stereotypes and promote gender diversity in postsecondary computing. These local environments are the organizations responsible for producing an educated workforce and are the intervention points where measurable change can be attained by institutions willing to address this issue. By concentrating on retention, the element of computing's gender imbalance that is most under the control of postsecondary education, we isolate the influence of computing programs to demonstrate which specific local conditions can override the segregating effects of cultural context. Our approach made it possible to establish that departments with the identified characteristics are likely to support women's initial interest through attainment of the bachelor's degree. Women accomplish this uncommon feat despite any essential gender differences and a societal context where participation in postsecondary computing is unusual for women.

Our data show that the average department has a six-point gender gap in attrition/retention rates. This difference in outcomes means that some of the few women who are attracted to computing are squandered. But given only a six-point gap, one might wonder, how much attention does unequal retention warrant? The answer depends somewhat on whether you are interested only in action that will quickly and substantially change the gender balance of computing, or if you are also interested in understanding and influencing the processes that create and maintain the current imbalance.

The numbers alone are not terribly impressive when one considers a single year and a single department. For example, enrollment in the average study department was 24 percent female, and the annual female attrition rate was 21 percent. These rates signify that a hypothetical department with 400 majors would have 96 women, but lose 20 of them by the next year. If women in this department were retained instead at the average male rate of 16 percent, 15 women instead of 20 would leave before the next year. A difference of 5 women per year per department is far from staggering, but it does add up to the kind of waste caused by a slow leak during a drought. Looking at women's actual total attrition in all our study departments and comparing it to their hypothetical attrition at male rates, our departments annually lost 365 more women than they would have if women were retained at the same rates as men during our study period. Projecting to the nation, this is a yearly unnecessary loss of over 1,000 women who could have become computing professionals. As we scale up, it becomes clearer that in the same way conservation at every site is critical during a drought, conserving women in every department is critical to a nation's gender balance in computing.

The results reported here point to specific ways that the average department could retain women as well as men. Departments can recruit more women to increase the availability of same-sex peer support, and faculty can offer support to compensate for cultural stereotypes that women do not belong in computing. According to our analyses, no single one of the six actions promoting retention is sufficient, but together, they account for almost half of the difference between departments with equal and unequal retention rates.

As a single action, recruiting more women both contributes to retention and overcomes the scarcity of women. It has the strongest effect on retention of the factors considered here and adds to the total number of women who graduate. If all else was held constant, the gender gap in a department's retention rates would be one point smaller if four or five more women were recruited, and the outcome in our hypothetical department would be thirteen instead of nine women graduating per year. If retention is equivalent to conservation, recruitment locates and develops more resources; both are essential for increasing women's participation.

Departments recruit more women when their home institution enrolls more women and their program adapts to changes in the job market. The first factor may be a matter of exposing more women to the opportunity to study computing; more research is needed to determine whether this is the case. Without knowing more about the mechanism underlying the positive influence of women's representation at an institution, this factor provides little chance for action by a computing department since departments have little influence over their institution's gender composition. The second recruitment factor is largely under departmental control, however. Responsiveness to the job market is a feature that most programs could adopt.

Other ways that departments might attract more women are suggested by the characteristics particular to the women in our focus groups. In addition to the characteristics they shared with male classmates, the women we spoke with were more likely than men to be recruited by a friend, and to think of computing as a form of communication and creative self-expression, a path to a helping occupation, or a chance to defy gender stereotypes. It is a matter for further empirical investigation whether departments that capitalize on these factors actually enroll more women than those that recruit using other strategies.

In addition to providing women students with peers, departments can equalize retention by attending to faculty attitudes and behaviors. Student comments about faculty reinforce this interpretation of the statistical findings about the key role faculty play in student persistence. When asked to identify the most important factor in their ability to succeed, most computer science students said other students, but some argued that they had very positive experiences with helpful faculty: "Professors tend to be different in their office hours. They're much nicer than in the class, and they really talk to you about anything you want to talk about. I think because they are restricted in the class to the class time—but in their office hours they can be different people, usually nicer." When students had positive interactions with faculty, they considered these experiences to be most helpful for overcoming the challenges of a computing major.

A statewide study of attrition/retention (Cohoon 2001) showed some similar as well as different results compared with those reported here. In both cases, same-sex peer support had a clear positive effect on equal retention, and faculty behaviors in support of female students were also influential. Nevertheless, only the statewide study indicated that gendered attrition rates were influenced by faculty turnover, attitudes toward female students, and the approach to teaching, in addition to the presence of female faculty, institutional support, and the local job market. The statewide results about faculty turnover and institutional resources could be related to our nationwide result regarding sufficient faculty. When entered into a multiple regression with the other variables reported here, institutional support and faculty turnover show the same type of relationship evident in the statewide study (positive for support and negative for turnover), but the effects were weak and not statistically significant at the .05 level. Likewise, statewide findings about the positive influence of female faculty are only faintly echoed in the national study. Women faculty members are more likely than men to engage in the behaviors that promote equal retention, but according to the current study, the behaviors are crucial, not the sex of those who engage in them. Thus, the differences in results between the two studies suggest a more nuanced relationship between some departmental conditions and gendered attrition.

The differences in findings could be explained in several ways. Certain factors might interact with conditions in one state, yet not be generally important for gendered attrition from computer science in the nation as a whole. Alternatively, it might be the case that conditions changed somewhat in the different study time frames (1992 to 1997 for the statewide study, and 1994 to 2000 for the nationwide study), but this explanation seems less likely due to the considerable overlap in time frames. Another possible explanation for the different results is that the inclusion of smaller departments in the statewide study led to results that reflected some differences between small departments and the mid- to large-sized ones studied nationwide. What remains consistent across the two studies is that same-sex peer support and supportive faculty help retain women at comparable rates to men. More generally, both studies show that locally supportive environments can overcome the general lack of support in our culture for women's participation in postsecondary computing. The nature of local support may vary slightly, but the bottom line remains the same.

The results of this nationwide study also displayed many similarities with findings from research into women's representation in STEM fields. For example, like Astin and Astin (1992), we see that students are retained when they have socially similar peers. Like Fox (2001), Seymour and Hewitt (1997), and Hearn and Olzak (1981), we note that supportive interactions with faculty benefit female students in disciplines where women are a minority. Like Seymour and Hewitt (1997, 92–93, 232–233), we find that women are less likely than men to leave due to workload issues, although Seymour and Hewitt argue that workload does contribute to student attrition. Our findings also overlap with many of those reported by the Building Engineering and Science Talent (2004) blue ribbon panel on higher education: that programs contribute to STEM diversity when faculty members are committed to developing student talents, and when faculty mentor students, peer support is available, and students are actively recruited. Although we know that computer science differs from STEM in general (Strenta et al. 1994), corroborating these studies adds weight to the contention that there is a core set of conditions that are essential for moving toward gender diversity.

Our findings also add depth to Jacobs's (1995, 1996) reports on the role of higher education in the gender segregation process. We show that although higher education may act in concert with the prevailing cultural trends toward gender integration or segregation in particular fields, departmental subcultures influence this process. This observation about variation across institutions lends support to Jacobs's argument that gender segregation is re-created at the postsecondary level. At least in computer science, outcomes depend in large part on the actions and attitudes of faculty.

In addition to the sociological issues of higher education and gender segregation, our findings are relevant to feminist discussions of gender and technology. Variability across computer science departments reduces the credibility of gender essentialist assertions that women do not participate in computing because it offers a poor match with inherent female characteristics. Gender essentialist *beliefs* may still have significant influence on the distribution of men and women in computing, but variability across departments suggests that any innate differences are small and can be overcome (or amplified) by local conditions. We can say little about the argument that computing is an expression of male power and is actively rejected by women because our study investigates outcomes for students who, at least initially, embraced computing. Finally, we found no evidence that stereotypes about gender and computing distinguish supportive faculty, but we are investigating this question further with more discerning analytic tools.

Many more factors than those reported here were investigated, but they showed no persistent significant relationship with gendered attrition rates. Yet the absence of statistically significant correlations should not be taken to mean that these factors are not related to equal retention. Measurement error and the limitations of statistical analysis by multiple regression are only two of several reasons that could explain why an influential factor failed to meet the somewhat arbitrary cutoff for being confident that a relationship exists beyond the study sample. For example, survey research might be too clumsy a tool for measuring instructional practices or other more subtle influences. An insufficient self-awareness of one's behavior, unwillingness to report unpopular opinions, or inadequate common understanding of terms offered as response categories could all reduce the chances of accurately measuring certain behaviors and attitudes. Therefore, despite our failure to find supporting evidence, it could still be the case that women are generally retained as well as men in programs where hands-on instruction is common or women's organizations are active. Likewise, the provocative observations of interactions with public/private status raise more questions than we could answer with these data. This study only tells us with a fair degree of certainty that same-sex peers and supportive faculty are reliable indicators of a computer science department where men and women undergraduates have comparable retention rates. Multiple regression with seventy-four cases is likely to find factors that have strong effects, but miss the more subtle ones that might also be present. The model is far from fully specified; evidence in support of other factors that are broadly effective remains to be shown.

Finally, there is an important group that remains silent in this study: women who did not declare a computing major. Not having spoken with or surveyed them means that we cannot know if the women who are in computer science are atypical. It could be that practices effective for recruiting and retaining the women who declared a computer science major might not work for those women who never took computer science or considered a computing major. Thus, implementing interventions based on our findings might lead to success with a narrow range of women, yet fail to reach out to a broader audience. Further study is needed to give voice to this constituency and compare matched groups with women who attempt a computing degree.

Summary and Conclusion

This chapter summarizes the findings of the first nationwide study of factors that lead to gendered outcomes in undergraduate computer science departments. The study employed multiple methods, measures, and cases in order to describe conditions in the average undergraduate computer science program and quantify the extent to which these factors influence whether women are retained at rates comparable to their male classmates. The overall conclusion is that conditions in computer science programs have measurable consequences for the equitable retention of the relatively few women who declare a computer science major.

The leading result of this study is that faculty, as well as same-sex peers, play a key role in the retention of women in postsecondary computing. In departments where faculty members encourage students and mentor undergraduates because they want to eliminate underrepresentation, and where faculty emphasize homework and focus as the route to academic success in computing, outcomes for women approach those of men. The central role of faculty is further stressed by the fact that when average faculty members feel that their department suffers from an inadequate number of faculty, women students leave at higher rates than men.

The results of this study illustrate the process that allocates men and women into different fields during higher education. The results also speak to postsecondary computing education about ways to influence this process. They suggest an alternative to the "just get over it" slogan recommended for women. Instead of advising women to ignore the gender composition of their field, these results prompt advising academia to "just get on with it." Retaining women as well as men is demonstrably achievable, even in the context of a discipline that attracts many more students of one sex.

Acknowledgments

This chapter is based on work supported by the National Science Foundation under grant number EIA–0089959. Any opinions, findings, and conclusions or recommendations expressed in this material are those of the authors, and do not necessarily reflect the views of the National Science Foundation.

Appendix 7.1

Additional Study Hypotheses about Gendered Attrition

1. There are diminishing returns to mentoring female students out of proportion to their enrollment.

2. Faculty evaluations of student quality are positively associated with equitable retention of women.

3. Instructional methods affect equitable retention of women.

4. Cordial relations among faculty and students help retain women.

5. Gendered attrition rates (the difference between male and female attrition rates) are low in departments in which the gender balance of enrolled majors is close to parity.

6. Gendered attrition rates are low in departments in which faculty enjoy teaching undergraduates.

7. Gendered attrition rates are low in departments in which faculty believe they share responsibility for student success.

8. Gendered attrition rates are low in departments in which there are women faculty.

9. Gendered attrition rates are low in departments in which faculty turnover rates are low.

10. Gendered attrition rates are low in departments in which faculty members have a high opinion of female students in general.

11. Gendered attrition rates are low in the departments in which faculty members devote more time to mentoring students.

12. Gendered attrition rates for lower-level students are low in departments in which many female students are mentored by faculty.

13. Gendered attrition rates are low in departments in which the department has strong institutional support.

14. Gendered attrition rates are low in departments located where the local job market for graduates is strong.

15. Gendered attrition rates are low in departments that have programs designed to improve retention (e.g., peer mentoring, tutoring).

16. Gendered attrition rates are low in departments in which female students' mathematics SAT scores are equivalent to male students' scores.

17. Gendered attrition rates are low in departments in which instructors use pedagogical techniques appropriate for dependent learners (i.e., all the information students are required to master is explained and demonstrated by instructors or required readings).

Note

1. Gendered attrition was significantly correlated with whether an institution was public or private (when 1 = public and 0 = private, the correlation between gendered attrition and institutional type was $r = -.39$, significant at .001). Women's retention in computer science was closer to men's at private institutions than at public institutions. There were only eight private institutions in the final analysis, however, and the explanatory model for gendered attrition and results for other variables remained substantially the same when controlling for public/private status. For these reasons, I limit discussion of this distinction, but consider it an important avenue for further investigation.

References

Ambady, N., S. K. Paik, J. Steele, A. Owen-Smith, and J. P. Mitchell. 2004. Deflecting negative self-relevant stereotype activation: The effects of individualization. *Journal of Experimental Social Psychology* 40, no. 3:401–408.

Astin, A. W., and H. S. Astin. 1992. *Undergraduate science education: The impact of different college environments on the educational pipeline in the sciences, final report.* No. ED362404. Los Angeles: University of California Press.

Belenky, M. F., J. M. Tarule, N. R. Goldberger, and B. M. Clinchy. 1996. *Women's ways of knowing: The development of self, voice, and mind, tenth anniversary edition.* New York: Basic Books, Inc.

Beyer, S., K. Rynes, J. Perrault, K. Hay, and S. Haller. 2003. Gender differences in computer science students. Paper presented at the ACM SIGCSE, Reno.

Bielby, W., and J. Baron. 1986. Men and women at work: Sex segregation and statistical discrimination. *American Journal of Sociology* 91, no. 4:759–799.

Blum, L., and C. Frieze. 2005. As the culture of computing evolves, similarity can be the difference. *Frontiers: A Journal of Women Studies; Special Gender and IT Issue* 26, no. 1:110–125.

Building Engineering and Science Talent. 2004. *A bridge for all: Higher education design principles to broaden participation in science, technology, engineering, and mathematics.* San Diego: BEST.

Camp, T. 1997. The incredible shrinking pipeline. *Communications of the ACM* 40, no. 10:103–110.

Charles, M., and K. Bradley. 2002. Equal but separate? A cross-national study of sex segregation in higher education. *American Sociological Review* 67, no. 4:573–599.

Cohoon, J. M. 2001. Toward improving female retention in the computer science major. *Communications of the ACM* 44, no. 5:108–114.

Cohoon, J. M., M. Gonsoulin, and J. Layman. 2004. Mentoring computer science undergraduates. In *Human perspectives in the Internet society: Culture, psychology, and gender*, vol. 31, ed. K. Morgan, J. Sanchez, C. A. Brebbia, and A. Voiskounsky, 199–208. Cadiz, Spain: WIT Press.

Computing Research Association. 2002. *CRA Taulbee trends: Women students and faculty.* ⟨http://www.cra.org/info/taulbee/women.html⟩.

Fox, M. F. 2001. Women, science, and academia: Graduate education and careers. *Gender and Society* 15, no. 5:654–666.

Hearn, J., and S. Olzak. 1981. The role of college major departments in the reproduction of sexual inequality. *Sociology of Education* 54:195–205.

Huff, C. 2002. Gender, software design, and occupational equity. *SIGCSE Bulletin* 34, no. 2:112–115.

Jacobs, J. A. 1995. Gender and academic specialties: Trends among recipients of college degrees in the 1980s. *Sociology of Education* 68, no. 2:81–98.

Jacobs, J. A. 1996. Gender inequality and higher education. *Annual Review of Sociology* 22:153–185.

Jacobs, J. A. 1999. Gender and the stratification of colleges. *Journal of Higher Education* 70, no. 2:161–187.

Kanter, R. M. 1977. Some effects of proportions on group life: Skewed sex ratios and responses to token women. *American Journal of Sociology* 82, no. 5:965–990.

Malcom, S. 2004. If you're not there you can't do it: Advancing arguments for diversity in education. Keynote speech at the Grace Hopper Celebration of Women in Computing, Chicago, October 7.

Margolis, J., and A. Fisher. 2002. *Unlocking the clubhouse: Women in computing.* Cambridge, MA: MIT Press.

McDowell, C., L. Werner, H. E. Bullock, and J. Fernald. 2003. The impact of pair programming on student performance, perception, and persistence. Paper presented at the twenty-fifth International Conference on Software Engineering, Portland, Oregon.

Morgan, R. L., and E. S. Hunt. 2002. *Classification of instructional programs: 2000 edition.* Washington, DC: U.S. Government Printing Office.

Reskin, B. F., and P. A. Roos. 1990. *Job queues, gender queues: Explaining women's inroads into male occupations.* Philadelphia: Temple University Press.

Seymour, E., and N. Hewitt. 1997. *Talking about leaving: Why Undergraduates leave the sciences.* Boulder, CO: Westview Press.

Sørensen, K. H. 2002. *Love, duty, and the s-curve: An overview of some current literature on gender and ICT.* ⟨http://www.rcss.ed.ac.uk/sigis/public/documents/SIGIS_D02_Part1.pdf⟩.

Steele, C. M., and J. Aronson. 1995. Stereotype threat and the intellectual test performance of African Americans. *Journal of Personality and Social Psychology* 69, no. 5:797–811.

Strenta, C., R. Elliott, R. Adair, M. Matier, and J. Scott. 1994. Choosing and leaving science in highly selective institutions. *Research in higher education* 35, no. 5:513–547.

Tillberg, H., and J. M. Cohoon. 2005. Attracting women to the CS major. *Frontiers: A Journal of Women Studies; Special Gender and IT Issue* 26, no. 1:126–140.

Turkle, S., and S. Papert. 1990. Epistemological pluralism: Styles and voices within the computer culture. *Signs* 16, no. 1:128–157.

Wajcman, J. 1991. *Feminism confronts technology.* University Park: Pennsylvania State University Press.

Wigfield, A., and J. Eccles. 2000. Expectancy-value theory of achievement motivation. *Contemporary Educational Psychology, Special Issue: Motivation and the Educational Process* 25:68–81.

Wilson, F. 2003. Can compute, won't compute: Women's participation in the culture of computing. *New Technology Work and Employment* 18, no. 2:127–142.

8

The Poverty of the Pipeline Metaphor: The AAAS/CPST Study of Nontraditional Pathways into IT/CS Education and the Workforce

Jolene Kay Jesse

Nearly seven years ago at the time of this writing, William Bowen and Derek Bok wrote their seminal work *The Shape of the River*, which offered one of the first data-driven and cogently argued defenses of the use of affirmative action in college admissions.[1] In the preface to that edition, they explain why their book was not named *The Shape of the Pipeline*.

We often hear of the importance of keeping young people moving through the pipeline from elementary school to high school to college, on through graduate and professional schools, and into jobs, family responsibilities, and civic life. But this image is misleading, with its connotation of a smooth, well-defined, and well-understood passage. It is more helpful to think of the nurturing of talent as a process akin to moving down a winding river, with rock-strewn rapids and slow channels, muddy at times and clear at others. Particularly when race is involved, there is nothing simple, smooth, or highly predictable about the education of young people (Bowen and Bok 1998).

In other words, life doesn't happen in pipelines. It happens as people make choices and decisions based on the opportunities as well as constraints placed in front of them at different times in their lives. For some, they may proceed through life as through a pipeline, smoothly transitioning from one stage to the next. For many, however, there are more rocks and rapids that impede a smooth passage. In the field of information technology and computer science (IT/CS), those facing the most hard-to-navigate rapids seem to be disproportionately women and minorities.

There is a deeper problem with the pipeline metaphor, though, that is more troubling, especially in IT/CS. Using the language of economics, the pipeline is a supply-side metaphor—the problem lies with a lack of supply rather than a problem of creating demand. For academia, this leads to the mentality that we aren't doing anything wrong; rather, we simply aren't getting good enough students coming out of our high schools, middle schools, and elementary schools. That's where the problems are. If only they could get their acts together, we'd have enough students to fill our programs. This mentality leads to blinders, both in the way in which to approach the lack of diversity in the academy as well as in where to look for qualified students to fill college classrooms.

To move away from this, colleges and universities, and especially IT/CS departments and programs, will need to abandon the linear, supply-side thinking of the pipeline, and choose instead to focus on both building demand and looking for alternative supply lines, especially if diversifying the field is a goal. This will necessarily require some self-examination. What is it that we're doing that doesn't seem to create demand for our program among certain populations or is having a negative impact on some students' choices? What do we need to do to change that? How can we influence student choice? What "decision points" do we need to pay attention to in order to attract more diverse students to our program? In addition, what is needed is a broader examination of when students make the choice to pursue an IT/CS degree—especially when women and minorities are doing so. Diverse students may not be where one would traditionally go to look for them or be ready to pursue a degree at the "usual time" (e.g., right out of high school).

The Nontraditional Student in IT/CS

At a recent meeting of computer and social scientists who are actively conducting research into IT/CS education and workforce issues, a senior female computer science professor asked the question, "Where are all the older women students?" In the late 1970s when this professor had begun to teach introductory courses in computer science, she recalled always having older women students in her classes. When she went back to teaching introductory computer science courses more recently, she found there were no older women students in her classes. So where have they gone?

A quick look at the data may give us some idea. Table 8.1 shows the top ten producers of bachelor's degrees awarded in IT/CS in 2001. The number one producer is not the Massachusetts Institute of Technology, Carnegie Mellon, or a major research university but Strayer University, a for-profit university with various campuses in the Washington, DC, metropolitan area. Strayer was not only the number one producer overall but also awarded the most bachelor's degrees in IT/CS earned by women and African Americans. Strayer's major marketing emphasis is on "nontraditional students"—older, working adults who choose to study part-time while

Table 8.1
Top producers of IT/CS bachelor's degrees, 2001

Academic institution	Number of 2001 bachelor's degrees awarded
1. Strayer University	840
2. DeVry Institute of Technology (Addison, IL)	477
3. CUNY Bernard Baruch College	465
4. University of Maryland, Baltimore County	463
5. DeVry Institute of Technology (Phoenix, AZ)	440
6. DeVry Institute of Technology (City of Industry, CA)	349
7. Rutgers, the State University of New Jersey	336
8. DeVry Institute of Technology (Kansas City, MO)	316
9. DeVry Institute of Technology (Long Beach, CA)	301
10. James Madison University	393

working full-time. Strayer's dominance is not a fluke, either. Among the top ten institutions are also five campuses of the DeVry Institute of Technology, a for-profit university similar to Strayer with a nationwide distribution of campuses. Among the nonprofit universities listed, only one (Rutgers) has a highly ranked department in IT/CS, and some, such as the City University of New York and the University of Maryland, Baltimore County, service largely metropolitan and minority communities. This pattern is unique to IT/CS, and is markedly different from the other science and engineering disciplines and even business schools.[2]

Is this a problem? What does the dominance of for-profit universities in IT/CS education mean for the field and for the students who choose to get their degrees from them? Comparing the educational programs of for-profit and nonprofit universities is a difficult game at best, although there is some evidence that for-profit institutions are offering more occupational training than "foundational education" (Aspray 2004). Educational equivalency has always been hard to determine between institutions, and accreditation is not necessarily a good measure to judge equivalency. All colleges and universities, including for-profits, are accredited, and Strayer, DeVry, and Phoenix are no exception. Strayer is accredited by the Middle States Commission on Higher Education, the same accreditation agency for all of the participating study schools in Maryland and the District of Columbia. Strayer is not accredited by the Accreditation Board for Engineering and Technology, Inc., which grants accreditation to specific IT/CS programs. Not all of the study departments, however, are accredited by the Accreditation Board for Engineering and Technology either, including Johns Hopkins, the University of Virginia, and the University of Maryland.

There are some measures that can be used, however subjective, to ascertain the differences between for-profit and nonprofit colleges and universities. Examining what happens to their graduates after they finish their degrees is one way. For example, at least one study suggests that graduates from for-profit institutions are likely to have a high debt load, but are not always able to get the most desirable jobs in the labor market. This means that their return on their educational investment is often considerably less than those who attend more traditional universities (Thomas 2003).[3]

Simply paying attention to the language used to portray their activities is another good indication where for-profit and nonprofit universities diverge. Traditional non-profit universities are described by their tuition rates and endowments, academic reputations, educational programs, and the competition for admission to a limited number of available seats. The focus is on providing a broad and comprehensive education to a selective group of students. Descriptions of for-profit universities, on the other hand, are replete with analyses of rates of revenue growth, stock prices, expanding operating margins, and growing enrollments rather than selective admissions. In other words, the drive is to attract more students to programs while minimizing the costs of the actual educational experience. And for-profit institutions have recorded phenomenal gains in enrollments, especially in online ventures that have lower overhead costs, thus maximizing profits (Farrell 2004).

As mentioned earlier, many claim that for-profit institutions offer more technical training than broad-based education. Most hire professors on a course-by-course adjunct basis, usually providing no office space, and issuing curriculum guidelines and textbooks that instructors must follow. Few for-profit universities offer tenure or the kind of freedom to design research and courses that faculty on traditional campuses take for granted. For-profits are focused on growing enrollments, and they do this through highly visible advertising, unlike traditional institutions that focus on college fairs and name recognition. Their concentration is on growth in revenues, with the academic experience as a secondary consideration, and they seem to forgo altogether the academic mission to produce research that creates new knowledge. In short, it is as if for-profit colleges and universities and traditional colleges and universities inhabit different universes entirely.

Many of these differences can be explained by the fact that for-profits and non-profits may be tapping into very different markets. A recent *New York Times* article (Schwartz 2004) describes what nontraditional students want as quick-and-to-the-point course work, customer service, small classes, convenience, and an education that leads to employment. What they don't care about are "fancy campuses, dormitories, athletic complexes, tenured faculty, and the pond that shows up in every brochure" (28)—in other words, they don't want those things that increase the costs at traditional institutions or that they simply see as unnecessary for their academic experience. Indeed, more and more nontraditional students are willing to forgo the campus altogether and opt for an education done completely online. Online education is a major part of the growth in for-profit education enrollments, expanding beyond even the expectations of education market analysts. In 2003, for example, the University of Phoenix's online division posted a revenue growth of 61 percent, which was down from 2002's 70 percent and 2001's 81 percent growth rates, but still substantial (Farrell 2004).

While traditional colleges and universities have tried to tap into the lucrative and growing nontraditional market, they have not always met with great success. In the late 1990s and early 2000s, many major universities attempted to build for-profit online subsidiaries, only to have them fail utterly—notably New York and Columbia Universities. Some succeeded, however, such as the University of Maryland University Campus, which built on an existing distance-learning program. But even those successful online programs at traditional universities are often looked down on as second-rate or inferior education by those teaching in the more traditional programs at the same universities. At the root of this disregard seems to be a clash of cultures between traditional programs that emphasize a broad education based in part on theory and the production of knowledge, and nontraditional programs that focus on skills, employability, and maximizing profits.

Since the failure of many of their online ventures, most traditional colleges and universities have relinquished the nontraditional student market to the for-profits and to some state and private schools that have built programs specifically for nontraditional students. As one faculty member at an elite state university told us in an interview, "That's not our mission [to teach nontraditional students]." In addition, movements by many state governments and the federal government to hold universities more accountable for outcomes, including tracking graduation rates and time-to-degree statistics, has had the effect of forcing many state-funded colleges and universities that had educated a substantial number of nontraditional students, to focus on more traditional student populations that will graduate in four years and bolster their success rates.

Skill building has usually been considered the purview of community colleges, and traditionally adult education has centered on these institutions. But nontraditional students are finding more and more competition from traditional students for increasingly limited community college slots. Traditional-age students have been progressively using community colleges as cheaper alternatives for the first two years of their education before jumping to a four-year institution or are forgoing four-year institutions altogether for community college degrees. The median age of community college students dropped from 26.5 in 1991 to 23.5 in 1999. As competition for admission to traditional institutions increases and finances become increasingly tight at state universities, more and more traditional-age students are likely to pursue community college attendance (Adelman 2003). But traditional-age students are also feeling the pinch of budget cuts that have left fewer and fewer seats in community college classes available.

Nontraditional students may soon find their classes filled with more traditional-age students at for-profit institutions as well. In the drive to keep enrollments growing and revenue streams increasing, for-profits are searching for new markets and eyeing the traditional-age college student (Blumenstyk 2004). For-profits are also beginning to increase their class sizes and encourage students to take more of their classes online in order to keep costs down.

But if increasing numbers of students—both traditional and nontraditional—choose convenience, skill building, and fast programs over a theoretical, broad-based, academic education, are their degrees the same? If they are significantly different, should everyone be awarded a "bachelor's degree" regardless of the emphasis of their educational institution? Should we encourage more nontraditional students to attend traditional colleges and universities? Or is it all right to direct nontraditional students away from the traditional education market, where available slots are dwindling, and funnel them into institutions that are designed to give them what they seem to want? Are the degrees treated the same by employers? Finally, if traditional-age students also prefer skill building and convenience to the traditional university experience, will it affect our ability to finance programs at traditional universities that include as part of their mission the creation of new knowledge through research?

The AAAS/CPST Study of Nontraditional Pathways into the IT/CS Workforce

Our study began with these questions swirling in our heads. We set out to discover exactly what is a "nontraditional pathway," and who chooses it and why. We settled on a definition that focuses on student choices (Institute for Higher Education

Policy 2002) about when to start their education and decisions made to prolong the period of time it takes to earn their degree.[4] We opted for this formulation to focus on the students and not on particular institutions.

Our definition of a nontraditional student includes someone who:

- delays enrollment at least three years after graduating from high school or earning a GED;
- attends college mostly part-time;
- takes longer than six years to complete a degree;
- is employed full-time during most of their studies;
- has dependents while attending college.

Any students having one or more of these characteristics is considered a nontraditional student for the purposes of our study.[5]

Once we had opted for a student-centered definition of a nontraditional pathway, our first task was to recruit as many area colleges and universities that were major producers of IT/CS bachelor's degrees as possible to participate in a survey of alumni as well as interviews with current students and faculty. We were hoping that Strayer University would be in the pool of institutions, but despite an initial agreement, and after lengthy negotiations, it declined to participate. This left us with a gaping hole in our knowledge of who chooses to study at for-profit universities and what happens to them after they graduate. Nevertheless, we were able to recruit sixteen mid-Atlantic colleges to participate in our IT/CS bachelor's degree alumni survey, and twenty that allowed us to come onto their campuses and interview their faculty and students. Of these, four are major research universities (the University of Maryland at College Park, the University of Virginia, Virginia Tech, and Johns Hopkins), five are Historically Black Colleges and Universities (HBCU) (Hampton, Howard, Morgan State, Norfolk State, and the University of the District of Columbia), and two are liberal arts colleges affiliated with religious denominations that are retooling themselves to take advantage of the adult education market (the College of Notre Dame of Maryland and Columbia Union College) as well as other types of institutions (see table 8.2). In addition, we also recruited seventy-four businesses, nonprofit organizations, educational institutions, and government agencies in the Maryland, Virginia, and Washington, DC, area to participate in on-site interviews with employees and human resource and managerial staff.

In all, we interviewed 72 IT/CS faculty and 139 IT/CS students at the twenty institutions. All students and faculty were self-selected or chosen by their departments to

Table 8.2
Top producers of computer science bachelor's degrees in the Washington, DC, Virginia, and Maryland area, 1996, with rank and degrees awarded in 2001

Academic institution (national rank 1996) (national rank 2001)[1]	Number of 1996 bachelor's degrees awarded	Number of 2001 bachelor's degrees awarded
1. Strayer University* (1) (1)	396	840
2. University of Maryland, Baltimore County* (2) (4)	257	463
3. University of Maryland at College Park** (9) (14)	152	273
4. James Madison University** (25) (10)	117	293
5. George Mason University** (32) (54)	104	153
6. Villa Julie College* (46) (56)	84	148
7. Virginia Commonwealth University** (80) (40)	67	180
8. Virginia Polytechnic Institute and State University** (88) (63)	64	138
9. University of the District of Columbia** (96) (210)	60	56
10. Morgan State University** (130) (143)	49	77
11. Howard University** (189) (138)	40	79
12. Hampton University** (195) (314)	39	37
13. University of Virginia, main campus** (204) (165)	37	68
14. Towson State University** (214) (100)	35	101
15. George Washington University** (235) (178)	32	66
16. American University** (258) (429)	28	26
17. Old Dominion University** (275) (351)	27	33
18. Christopher Newport University** (299) (182)	25	65
19. College of William and Mary** (381) (220)	19	55
20. College of Notre Dame of Maryland** (402) (470)	18	24
21. Bowie State University* (417) (630)	17	15
22. Salisbury State University* (447) (208)	16	57
23. Norfolk State University** (474) (323)	15	36
24. Johns Hopkins University** (495) (268)	14	46
25. Gallaudet University* (552) (645)	12	15
26. Columbia Union College** (937) (395)	3	29

Notes: 1. Numbers in parentheses indicate the relative rank of the college or university in the production of bachelors degrees in the IT/CS field. The first parenthesis is the rank of that institution in 1996. The second parenthesis is the rank of the institution in 2001.
*Was asked to participate in the study
**Agreed to participate in the study

participate, so they do not represent a random sample. In addition to students and faculty 185 alumni from sixteen area colleges and universities filled out an online survey or returned a survey form by mail. A total of 115 employees with bachelor's degrees were interviewed, with deliberate oversample of women, underrepresented minorities, and those with nontraditional educational backgrounds. All, again, were self-selected from the businesses that agreed to participate in the study.

Student Demographics

The demographics of the student interviewees at the twenty area universities and colleges along with the alumni who answered our survey from the sixteen participating universities and colleges were remarkably similar. Given that we tried to intentionally oversample women, minorities, and nontraditional students in our interviews, we feel we came remarkably close to the actual population sample.

Of the 139 students interviewed, 33 percent (45) had one or more characteristic that qualified them as nontraditional, leaving 67 percent traditional students in our interviewee population. In our alumni survey, nearly 30 percent of the respondents had one or more nontraditional characteristic when they were a student, similar to our interviewee demographics. The demographics of our employee interviewees were somewhat different from our other two student populations. Unlike our student interviewees and alumni survey respondents, employees were asked if they were nontraditional students. Nearly 40 percent of our employee interviewees designated themselves as having been nontraditional students during the time they attended a university or college in pursuit of their IT/CS degree. We were also able to calculate whether employees had been nontraditional students using the criteria listed above. Using our measures, almost 50 percent of the employee interviewees had been nontraditional. Men were much more likely than women to have been nontraditional students with 80 percent of the male employee interviewees having at least one nontraditional characteristic versus just 31 percent of the females.

Our total student interview population was split almost fifty-fifty male to female. Of the nontraditional students, however, 36 percent were female and 64 percent were male. In the alumni survey, 60 percent of all the students were male and 40 percent were female—the exact same percentages found for those who had been nontraditional students—again, remarkably similar to our student interviewee demographics.

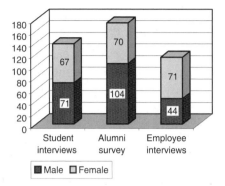

Figure 8.1
Gender breakout of survey and interview participants

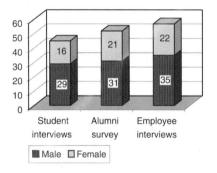

Figure 8.2
Gender breakout of nontraditional survey and interview participants

The demographics of our employee interviewees were somewhat different from our other two student populations. Of the 115 employees interviewed, women were greatly oversampled—62 percent were female and 38 percent were male, as shown in figure 8.1. Although there is a bias in our sample toward women, women and men were equally likely to have been nontraditional students (approximately 50 percent of each gender). Yet if we look at figure 8.2, which shows only at the nontraditional students, the percentages are nearly reversed, with 61 percent being male and 39 percent female.

In terms of ethnic makeup, in our nontraditional student interview set, 42 percent of those who indicated a race were African American. This fact is less remarkable given that five (25 percent) of our schools were HBCUs. What it might mean, how-

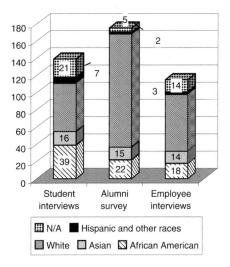

Figure 8.3
Race/ethnicity of survey participants

ever, is that the HBCUs are educating a significant number of nontraditional students. Of the remaining nontraditional students, 27 percent were white, 15 percent were Asian, and the rest did not identify a race. This compares to the 139 students in the overall population of our interview sample, which was 28 percent African American, 12 percent Asian, 40 percent white, and 5 percent other races. Nearly 20 percent of our sample did not indicate a race or ethnicity.

We had a much smaller population of African Americans in our alumni survey respondent pool. Only 13 percent of the overall respondents were African American, 75 percent were white, and the rest were largely Asian. Of those who had been nontraditional students, though, 17 percent indicated their race/ethnicity as African American (around 41 percent of all African American respondents), 10 percent were Asian (approximately 33 percent of all Asian American respondents), and the rest were white (about 26 percent of all white American respondents). Eight percent of the total sample did not indicate race/ethnicity.

Among the 115 employee interviews, the racial/ethnic makeup of the population was 57 percent white, 16 percent African American, 12 percent Asian, and 3 percent Hispanic or mixed race, as shown in figure 8.3. Twelve percent of the interviewees did not indicate their race/ethnicity. Figure 8.4 illustrates the race/ethnicity of nontraditional students. Whites clearly were more likely to have been nontraditional

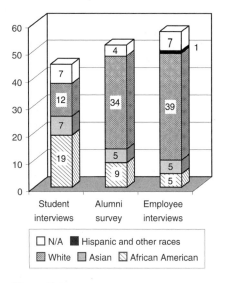

Figure 8.4
Race/ethnicity of nontraditional student survey participants

students—59 percent of all whites were nontraditional students, which was 68 percent of all nontraditional student employees. African Americans in our employee interviewee sample were less likely to have been nontraditional students than in either our student interviewee or alumni survey respondent pool—only 9 percent of nontraditional student employees were African American, which was 28 percent of all African American employee interviewees. The rest of the population of nontraditional student employees was Asian or did not respond to the race/ethnicity question.

Simply by looking at the demographics of our interviewees and survey respondents, one of our major findings is that nontraditional students at traditional nonprofit colleges and universities tend to be white males, although the HBCUs seem to also be educating a large number of African American nontraditional students. These two findings have major implications for any policies targeting nontraditional women and minorities in IT/CS education. The dominance of Strayer University and other for-profit institutions in the production of IT/CS bachelor's degrees awarded to women and minorities seems to have filled a market niche for these populations that the traditional universities have not taken advantage of. Indeed, if one pays close attention to their advertising, the for-profits seem to intentionally target women and minorities as their major customer populations, playing on the notion

Table 8.3
Have you previously attended another institution?

	Yes	No
Student interviewees		
Nontraditional	73% (33)	27% (12)
Traditional	22% (20)	78% (72)
All students	39% (53)	61% (84)
Alumni survey respondents		
Nontraditional	69% (36)	31% (16)
Traditional	15% (18)	85% (105)
All students	31% (54)	69% (121)
Employee interviewees		
Nontraditional	96% (55)	4% (2)
Traditional	88% (51)	12% (7)
All students	92% (106)	8% (9)

that programs are designed for them and that courses are populated with others like them.

Educational Backgrounds

Another important finding from our study is that nontraditional students especially, but IT/CS students in particular, are more likely to have attended multiple institutions before the one where they get their degree, and are likely to continue their education either by going to graduate school or taking training courses after they get their degree (see the discussion of future plans below). Therefore, IT/CS students are embracing lifelong learning, presumably in light of the need to keep current in the IT/CS field.

A significant population of both our student interviewees and alumni student respondents had attended other institutions before the one they were either currently attending or the one from which they had earned their IT/CS degree, as shown in table 8.3. Of the student interviewees, nearly 40 percent had attended another institution, but of the nontraditional students 73 percent had, compared to only 22 percent of traditional students.

Among the alumni survey respondents, 31 percent indicated that they had attended another institution before the one from which they received their IT/CS

Table 8.4
Type of institution attended prior to receipt of IT/CS degree

	Nontraditional	Traditional	All students
Student interviewees			
Community college	46% (15)	40% (8)	43% (23)
PhD granting	18% (6)	20% (4)	19% (10)
Foreign institution	12% (4)	15% (3)	13% (7)
HBCU	18% (6)	5% (1)	13% (7)
Liberal arts college	6% (2)	10% (2)	8% (4)
Women's college	0%	10% (2)	4% (2)
Alumni respondents			
Community college	59% (19)	39% (7)	52% (26)
Doctoral research	16% (5)	44% (8)	26% (13)
Master's colleges/universities	6% (2)	11% (2)	8% (4)
Baccalaureate colleges	9% (3)	6% (1)	8% (4)
International institutions	6% (2)	0%	4% (2)
HBCU	3% (1)	0%	2% (1)

degree. Similar to the student interviewees, nearly 70 percent of the alumni survey respondents who were nontraditional students indicated that they had attended another institution, contrasted to only 15 percent of alumni who had been traditional students.

For our 115 employee interview sample, more than 9 out of 10 (92 percent) had attended another institution prior to getting their IT/CS degree. For the employee interviewees who were nontraditional students, nearly all (96 percent) had attended another institution prior to getting their IT/CS degree. This is much higher than for the other two survey populations of nontraditional students.

Of the 53 student interviewees who indicated that they had attended another institution prior to receipt of the IT/CS degree, the largest percentage (43 percent) had attended a community college, followed by those attending a doctorate-granting institution, as illustrated in table 8.4. This ranking was true regardless of whether the students were traditional or nontraditional, although traditional students were more evenly distributed among a number of different types of institutions. Among the alumni survey respondents, 31 percent (or 54) indicated that they had attended another institution before the one from which they received their IT/CS degree. Similar to the student interviewees, nearly 70 percent of the alumni survey respondents who were nontraditional students indicated that they had attended another institution,

Table 8.5
Type of institution from which employees obtained their IT/CS degree

Type of institution	Nontraditional	Traditional	All students
Doctoral/research universities	40% (232)	62% (36)	51% (59)
Master's colleges/universities	42% (24)	14% (8)	28% (32)
Baccalaureate colleges	2% (1)	9% (5)	5% (6)
HBCU	2% (1)	9% (5)	5% (6)
International institutions	4% (2)	5% (3)	4% (5)
Associate's colleges	7% (4)	2% (1)	4% (5)
Specialized institutions	4% (2)	0%	2% (2)

contrasted to only 15 percent of the alumni who had been traditional students. The majority of alumni who were nontraditional students and attended another institution had attended a community college—nearly 60 percent had, compared to 39 percent of alumni who were traditional students.

For the employee interview sample, it is possible to classify the institutions from which the employees obtained their IT/CS degrees. Table 8.5 shows that of those employees who had indicated that they were nontraditional students, most had attended master's colleges and universities—42 percent, compared to just 14 percent of traditional student employees. Slightly more than 40 percent of nontraditional student employees had attended a doctoral research university, compared to 62 percent of traditional student employees. Traditional student employees were more likely than their nontraditional peers to have attended a doctoral/research university, a baccalaureate college, or a HBCU.

Employee interviewees were also asked if they had a degree from an institution other than the one from which they received their IT/CS degree. An astounding 37 percent (43) of the total 115 respondents indicated that they have a second degree from another institution. Of the employee interviewees who were nontraditional students, 53 percent (30) had another degree compared to the 13 or 22 percent of traditional students. Moreover, second degrees for most employee interviewees, both traditional and nontraditional students, were in fields outside of IT/CS, as shown in table 8.6.

Reasons for Choosing IT/CS

Both nontraditional and traditional IT/CS students like math and choose IT/CS because they are interested in the field. While their primary reason for going into the

Table 8.6
Field of degree for those IT/CS employees who had a second degree

Field of degree	Nontraditional	Traditional	All employees
Non-IT	68% (19)	46% (6)	61% (25)
Computer information systems	18% (5)	23% (3)	20% (8)
Computer science/computer engineering	7% (2)	15% (2)	10% (4)
Other IT	7% (2)	15% (2)	10% (4)

field may be an interest in IT/CS, secondary reasons do often hinge on employment-related outcomes such as higher salaries and opportunities for promotion. This is the same for both nontraditional and traditional students.

An interest in computing was the overwhelming response to inquiries about why students chose to study IT/CS as a major—over 60 percent of both traditional and nontraditional student interviewees cited an interest in computing. For nontraditional student interviewees, the next major influences on their decision to pursue a degree in IT/CS were work experience in the field (27 percent), job opportunities (24 percent), and earning potential (13 percent). For traditional students, after interest in the field, they mentioned most often a K–12 classroom experience (22 percent), job opportunities (19 percent), and that IT/CS was just a "natural fit" for them (13 percent). Moreover, only traditional students expressed an interest in the field based on parental or family influence (11 percent), or their interest in computer games or animation (7 percent). This contrasts somewhat with professors' opinions of students' motivations for entering the field. Many professors believe that students choose IT/CS solely because they think they can make a lot of money or have better job prospects rather than any true interest in the field. This rather negative perspective may lead professors to have a more jaded perception of students, especially those students less likely to choose the field in the first place, such as women and minorities.

Similar results were found in the survey responses to a list of possible influences on alumni's decisions to choose a career/degree in IT/CS. The alumni were asked to choose the most important influence on their choice from a list that included opportunities for promotion/advancement, salary potential, personal interest, family/parental influence, friend/peer influence, or other factors. Sixty-four percent of the respondents who had been traditional students and 57 percent of those who had been nontraditional ones selected personal interest in the field as the most important reason for choosing IT/CS as illustrated in figure 8.5. For nontraditional students,

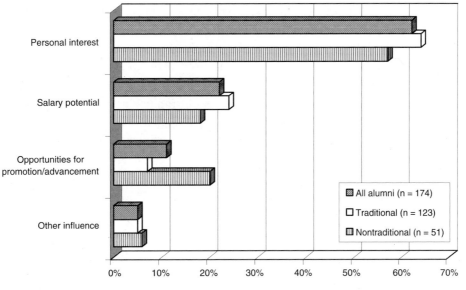

Figure 8.5
Why alumni chose to pursue an IT/CS degree

the next top reason was opportunities for promotion/advancement (20 percent) and then salary potential (18 percent). For traditional students, salary potential was the next most frequently chosen reason for choosing IT/CS (24 percent).

Reasons for Choosing Institutions

Students, both nontraditional and traditional, generally choose a college or university based on location, cost, reputation, and program specifics. Institutions wishing to attract more nontraditional students will be most successful if they can build on one or more of these variables, and if they can offer some kind of flexible scheduling of courses.

Student interviewees, both traditional and nontraditional, overwhelmingly choose their institutions based on location. Yet location can mean many things. For traditional students, it means getting away from parents or staying close to family, and choosing an urban environment or leaving a city. In other words, traditional students were more likely to see location as a choice. For nontraditional students, on the other hand, having a campus close to work or home was essential, and location was often combined with convenience as a reason for choosing an institution, making location more of a constraint than a choice.

The next most important concern for student interviewees in choosing an institution was cost, but for nontraditional students this was on an equal footing with the reputation of the institution. An institution's reputation was much more critical to nontraditional student interviewees than it was for traditional students. Traditional students, however, were more interested in program characteristics than nontraditional students.

After these four concerns—location, cost, program characteristics, and an institution's reputation—other influences on traditional and nontraditional students' selection of their institutions reflect a divide noted earlier. Traditional students were significantly more interested in campus life/atmosphere (27 percent mentioned this versus only 8 percent of nontraditional students), while only nontraditional students indicated that having weekend or night classes was a concern in their choice. Nontraditional students were also more likely to mention a small faculty-to-student ratio, and only nontraditional students indicated that they wanted to complete their degree quickly.

We probed students more directly about the importance of campus culture. Sixty-six percent of traditional students said that campus culture was indeed important to them compared to only 27 percent of nontraditional students. Traditional students mentioned most often the size of the school, along with a comfortable atmosphere, diversity of student population, and personal attention from faculty and staff. A few nontraditional students directly indicated that a physical campus was not important to them at all, while 8 percent of traditional students specifically stated that a physical campus was essential. Nontraditional students were also more likely to seek students who were similar to themselves in the institution; 9 percent of nontraditional students said that the presence of older students was an important part of campus culture.

In the alumni survey, the respondents were asked to indicate the importance of ten variables on their choice of academic institution based on a five-point scale ranging from "extremely important" to "not at all important." Alumni who had been nontraditional students ranked the geographic location of the campus as the most important reason for choosing the institution where they earned their IT/CS degree, followed by the convenience of the commute, the flexibility of course offerings, the cost, and the reputation of the institution/program/professors. This was markedly different from traditional students, whose most important concern was the reputation of the institution/program/professors followed by the geographic location, the cost, the flexibility of course offerings, the size and/or culture of the institution, and finally, the convenience of the commute.

More than one in three nontraditional alumni indicated that their employer's tuition reimbursement program had been a critical factor in their decision. Nontraditional alumni were also more likely to indicate that online courses were at least somewhat important, but online courses were not a major factor for any of the alumni, with nearly 57 percent of all alumni saying they were not very or not at all important and nearly 30 percent seeing them as not even applicable to their situation. The presence of women and minorities on a campus as well as having a relative or friend attend a particular institution were secondary concerns or not at all important for most alumni.

Among the employee interviewees, location was again the top influence on their choice of institution, but it was much more important for employees who had been nontraditional students than for those who had been traditional ones (61 versus 43 percent). Employees who had been traditional students were no more likely to mention the strong reputation of a program or an institution over location. Finally, traditional student employees were much more likely to have had a family member or a friend connected with an educational institution, and to mention the educational environment/atmosphere as being important factors in their choice of an institution.

Our results show that nontraditional and traditional students are making different calculations in selecting an academic institution. Nontraditional students value convenience and flexibility more than their traditional counterparts. Traditional students, on the other hand, seem more attracted to campus culture and program characteristics. They are not as far apart as some make them seem, however. While our data show a different ranking of importance on certain variables, both types of students put a premium on location, cost, and reputation, and while they might mention or rank other variables as important, these are generally secondary factors in their choice.

Educational Experiences

Most of our students, both nontraditional and traditional, in our interview population majored in computer science. This was not true of our alumni survey respondents, though. The majority of the alumni, both traditional and nontraditional students, had majored in computer information systems, business information

Table 8.7
Declared majors of student interviewees and alumni survey respondents

Student interview data	Nontraditional (n = 45)	Traditional (n = 93)	All students (n = 138)
Computer science	71% (32)	61% (57)	64% (89)
CIS/BIS/Other tech	24% (11)	37% (34)	33% (45)
Computer engineering	2% (1)	1% (1)	1% (2)
Other	2% (1)	1% (1)	1% (2)

Alumni survey responses	Nontraditional (n = 52)	Traditional (n = 123)	All alumni (n = 175)
Computer science	40% (21)	45% (55)	43% (76)
CIS/BIS/Other tech	56% (29)	54% (66)	54% (95)
Computer engineering	4% (2)	2% (2)	2% (4)

systems, and other technology-related majors (CIS/BIS/Other tech). The number of computer science majors in our interviewee pool is reflective simply of the number of computer science departments that agreed to participate in this study. Table 8.7 shows the breakdown of majors for the student interviewees and the alumni survey respondents.

Within our student interviewee population, traditional and nontraditional students were equally as likely to have a double major (although few students did) or a minor. The most popular double majors were math and business, and the minors most often chosen were math, computer science, information science, and computer and information sciences in some form depending on their major, as some computer science majors, for example, had a minor in computer and information sciences.

Among our student interviewees, both nontraditional and traditional students were equally as likely to have switched into IT/CS from another major; about 20 percent had, which is a considerable amount and underscores the importance of recruiting efforts within introductory computer science courses (see table 8.8). Almost 10 percent of both traditional and nontraditional students indicated that they chose their IT/CS major because of an experience they had in a college course.

When asked if they had contemplated switching out of their IT/CS major, traditional students were more likely to say that they had (20 versus 11 percent). By gender, however, women were significantly more likely to say that they had contemplated switching out of their IT/CS major (25 versus 11 percent). This indicates

Table 8.8
Switching majors

Have you changed majors into IT/CS from another major?
Student interview data

	Nontraditional (n = 45)	Traditional (n = 93)	All students (n = 138)
Yes	20% (9)	22% (20)	21% (29)
No	80% (36)	79% (73)	79% (109)

Have you contemplated changing your IT/CS major?
Student interview data

	Nontraditional (n = 45)	Traditional (n = 93)	All students (n = 138)
Yes	11% (5)	20% (19)	17% (24)
No	89% (40)	80% (74)	83% (114)

	Female (n = 34)	Male (n = 71)	All students (n = 112)
Yes	25% (17)	11% (8)	17% (24)
No	76% (17)	89% (63)	83% (114)

that retention efforts are still necessary for female IT/CS majors, though the largely male nontraditional students might not need special targeting.

The majority of both nontraditional and traditional students felt adequately prepared to begin a degree in IT/CS, although nontraditional students felt somewhat less prepared than their traditional counterparts (table 8.9). Only 52 percent of nontraditional students felt adequately prepared while 66 percent of traditional students felt that way. When asked to compare themselves to others in their program, nontraditional students were significantly more likely to say that their preparation was worse, while traditional students were much more likely to see their preparation as being the same or better than their peers.

By gender, although more than 50 percent of women said they were adequately prepared to begin their programs, women were significantly more likely to say they had not been adequately prepared compared to the men (table 8.10). Men were more likely to see themselves as better prepared than their classmates, although more men than women said that they were prepared worse as well. Women generally thought they were equally prepared as other students in their program.

Table 8.9
Preparation for degree by traditional/nontraditional students

Did you feel you were adequately prepared before beginning your current degree program?
Student interview data

	Nontraditional (n = 44)	Traditional (n = 89)	All students (n = 133)
Yes	52% (23)	66% (59)	62% (82)
No	48% (21)	34% (30)	38% (51)

How prepared were you compared to other students in the program?
Student interview data

	Nontraditional (n = 36)	Traditional (n = 76)	All students (n = 112)
Worse	44% (16)	21% (16)	29% (32)
Same	22% (8)	36% (27)	31% (35)
Better	33% (12)	43% (33)	40% (45)

Table 8.10
Preparation for degree by sex

Did you feel you were adequately prepared before beginning your current degree program?
Student interview data

	Female (n = 66)	Male (n = 68)	All students (n = 134)
Yes	55% (36)	68% (46)	62% (82)
No	46% (30)	32% (22)	39% (52)

How prepared were you compared to other students in the program?
Student interview data

	Female (n = 54)	Male (n = 59)	All students (n = 113)
Worse	24% (13)	32% (19)	28% (32)
Same	46% (25)	19% (11)	32% (36)
Better	30% (16)	49% (29)	40% (45)

When asked what other preparation they would have wanted, students, both traditional and nontraditional, were most likely to mention math and computer programming classes. Interestingly, nontraditional students were almost twice as likely to mention needing more math than were traditional students (27 versus 16 percent).

We also asked students if their conceptions of the IT/CS field and computer scientists or computer professionals had changed since they began their programs. Regarding the field, about 25 percent of both traditional and nontraditional students said that they had the same conception now as when they started. An equal number of nontraditional and traditional students said that they had a broader conception now than before they started. Nontraditional students were more likely to say that they had only had a vague conception of the field at first, and that they had thought it would be easier than it is. More traditional students indicated that they now see the field as more than just programming and that it is more detail oriented.

When we asked students about computer professionals, our expectations had been that most students would talk about the "nerd" stereotype. Few actually did, and most students talked more about the field or the actual work of computer scientists than about stereotypes. While much of the literature points to the nerd stereotype as a problem for women in particular, our data suggest that this is less of a problem than getting the word out about what computer scientists actually do.

When asked about courses they found particularly difficult, nontraditional students were about twice as likely as traditional ones to say that they had not encountered any difficult classes. Of those who found some courses to be extraordinarily difficult, most mentioned programming and math. Traditional students were more likely to indicate that operating systems and software design were difficult. Of those who found some courses to be difficult, traditional students were more likely than nontraditional ones to identify "weed-out" courses—in other words, courses that were intentionally made difficult to get some students to drop out of the program. Most students, however, did not cite these courses as a cause for dropping the program.

In comparing their abilities to do the course work, almost half of all nontraditional students and 42 percent of traditional students saw themselves as the same as other students or average (table 8.11). More traditional students said that they were better than their colleagues, and nontraditional students were slightly more likely to say that they were much worse, although few students saw themselves as

Table 8.11
Self-perceived ability to do course work

How would you describe your abilities to do your course work in comparison to the other students in your program?

Student interview data	Nontraditional (n = 45)	Traditional (n = 93)	All students (n = 138)
Much worse	4% (2)	1% (1)	2% (3)
Somewhat worse	2% (1)	3% (3)	3% (4)
Same/average	47% (21)	42% (39)	43% (60)
Somewhat better	24% (11)	32% (30)	30% (41)
Much better	11% (5)	9% (8)	9% (13)
Don't/unable to compare	7% (3)	2% (2)	4% (5)
Depends on class	0%	6% (6)	4% (6)
NA	4% (2)	4% (4)	4% (6)

Student interview data	Female (n = 68)	Male (n = 71)	All students (n = 139)
Much worse	0% (0)	4% (3)	2% (3)
Somewhat worse	4% (3)	1% (1)	3% (4)
Same/average	54% (37)	32% (23)	43% (60)
Somewhat better	22% (15)	38% (27)	30% (42)
Much better	6% (4)	13% (9)	9% (13)
Don't/unable to compare	4% (3)	3% (2)	4% (5)
Depends on class	4% (3)	4% (3)	4% (6)
NA	4% (3)	4% (3)	4% (6)

doing worse than their fellow students. By gender, women were much more likely to say that their abilities to do the course work in the program are the same or average, while the men saw themselves as doing somewhat or much better.

Almost all the students we interviewed were comfortable or very comfortable in their program or department. Only traditional students indicated some level of discomfort. A majority of students felt that all students are treated the same in the department, although among those asked a follow-up question, traditional students were much more likely to answer that they feel part of a group than were nontraditional students.

The vast majority of students felt that they had the same access to campus resources as the other students in their degree program, although nontraditional students were more likely to see a discrepancy in resource distribution. When asked to elaborate on the resources they were lacking, nontraditional students listed lab and computer access and financial aid as most problematic. Few traditional students saw lab or computer access as a problem. When queried about whether they had any difficulties in getting the classes they needed to complete their degrees, nontraditional students were almost twice as likely to say that they have had difficulties compared to traditional students. Difficulties were primarily scheduling, especially when key courses were offered at the same time. Both nontraditional and traditional students also complained that courses were not offered enough, that they were often full, or that they were not offered at convenient times. Only 4 percent of nontraditional students and no traditional students found it hard to transfer credits from other institutions.

Nontraditional students in our interview population were much more likely to have attended night or weekend classes, or to have taken an online course, although 39 percent of traditional students had also taken a night course. When asked about their experiences in these "alternative" classes, most students pointed to older/mature students in the class as a positive aspect. Alumni survey respondents who had been nontraditional students were almost twice as likely to have attended a night class and almost five times more likely to have taken a weekend course than their traditional student alumni counterparts. Interestingly, alumni that had been traditional students were more likely to have taken an online course than nontraditional alumni.

Traditional students were much more likely to have had a research experience with faculty or other students outside the classroom. It was also more probable that traditional students were planning on doing or already have done an internship or co-op job before they graduate. Most nontraditional students who were not planning on doing an internship indicated that they would like to do so.

Finally, both nontraditional and traditional students were equally likely to say that they had contemplated leaving college in the past year, although only 24 percent of all students said that they had contemplated doing so (table 8.12). Nontraditional students most often indicated that they had personal or family reasons for possibly leaving their education followed by the fact that there was too long a time commitment involved in getting a bachelor's degree. Traditional students were more likely to say they contemplated leaving for financial reasons or because they had gotten a job offer.

Table 8.12
Thoughts of leaving

In the past year, have you contemplated leaving college for any reason?			
Student interview data	Nontraditional (n = 45)	Traditional (n = 93)	All students (n = 138)
Yes	27% (12)	23% (21)	24% (33)
No	73% (33)	77% (72)	76% (105)

What were your reasons specifically?			
Student interview data	Nontraditional (n = 13)	Traditional (n = 20)	All students (n = 33)
Personal/family reasons	62% (8)	20% (4)	36% (12)
Economic/money reasons	15% (2)	30% (6)	24% (8)
Job offers/opportunities	15% (2)	25% (5)	21% (7)
Too long a time commitment	23% (3)	5% (1)	12% (4)
Program/department limitations	0%	15% (3)	9% (3)
Health reasons	15% (2)	5% (1)	9% (3)
Travel	8% (1)	5% (1)	6% (2)
Problems with faculty	0%	5% (1)	3% (1)
Job commitments	0%	5% (1)	3% (1)

Satisfaction

Most student interviewees indicated that they were satisfied with their choice of major and their institution. When asked to reassess their college decisions, however, 13 percent of the students indicated they would not have chosen the same major and 27 percent would not have chosen the same institution. There were not many patterns discernible between traditional and nontraditional students. One exception was traditional students' satisfaction with their institution. Eighty-four percent of traditional students indicated that they were satisfied with their institution, but only 44 percent said that they would choose it again; 10 percent said that they might choose it again. When asked if they would recommend the institution to a friend, 69 percent said yes, 11 percent said maybe, and only 3 percent said no. Similar patterns were found among nontraditional students to these questions, but the differences were not quite so stark.

We asked a series of questions in our alumni survey exploring satisfaction with one's IT/CS bachelor's degree program on a number of different variables. The respondents were asked to rate how satisfied they were on a five-point scale ranging from extremely satisfied to very dissatisfied. There were few differences between nontraditional and traditional alumni in terms of satisfaction with their IT/CS bachelor's program. Most alumni were very to extremely satisfied on most variables and the dissatisfaction was minimal. There are a few exceptions, however. Nontraditional alumni were less satisfied with career mentoring than their traditional counterparts, although 21 percent of nontraditional alumni did not see career mentoring as even applicable to their situation (compared to only 2 percent of traditional students). Interestingly, nontraditional alumni were more likely to be extremely to very satisfied with their working relationships with their professors than were traditional alumni, 16 percent of whom were somewhat to very dissatisfied (compared to only 6 percent of nontraditional alumni).

Mirroring the question above that dealt with internships, nontraditional alumni were much less satisfied with opportunities to participate in co-op and internship programs than were their traditional colleagues. This indicates that nontraditional students are not averse to doing co-ops or internships and do value them as part of their educational experience.

Financing

Within our student interview population, 73 percent of nontraditional students reported that they received financial aid, while 62 percent of traditional students did so. Among those who did receive financial aid, approximately half said that the aid has been adequate or somewhat adequate, with little difference between traditional and nontraditional students. Nevertheless, nontraditional students were over twice as likely as traditional students to say that they would not have attended college without financial aid.

The kind of financial aid that traditional and nontraditional students received differed markedly. While both relied on Stafford and PLUS loans, nontraditional students within our sample were almost twice as likely to be receiving a Pell Grant. Nontraditional students were also significantly more likely to be on the Montgomery GI Bill or to receive employer tuition assistance or reimbursement. Traditional students, on the other hand, relied more on family assistance and scholarships to pay for college.

Table 8.13
Source of financing

What was your main source of financing for your IT/CS degree? (please choose only one)

Alumni survey responses	Nontraditional (n = 50)	Traditional (n = 123)	All students (n = 173)
Financial support from parents/partners/other relatives not to be repaid	6% (3)	51% (63)	38% (66)
Loans from the school you attended, banks, federal/state government	38% (19)	34% (42)	35% (61)
Loans from parents or other relatives that must be repaid	2% (1)	3% (4)	3% (5)
Financial assistance or reimbursement from your employer	24% (12)	1% (1)	8% (13)
Tuition waivers, fellowships, grants, scholarships	6% (3)	6% (7)	6% (10)
Earnings from employment	18% (9)	2% (3)	7% (12)
Savings	4% (2)	1% (1)	2% (3)
Other	2% (1)	2% (2)	2% (3)

These findings are mirrored in our alumni survey (table 8.13). For traditional students, financial support from their families was number one (51 percent), followed by loans from banks, schools, or the government (34 percent), and finally tuition waivers, grants, and scholarships were a distant third (6 percent). Nontraditional students relied on a number of different kinds of financing: loans from banks, schools, or the government (38 percent), financial assistance/reimbursement from employers (24 percent), and earnings from employment (18 percent).

Clearly, nontraditional students rely on a combination of different sources to finance their education, piecing together packages that might have more or less flexibility. They are, therefore, more susceptible to changes in financial aid award packages and the declining purchasing power of the Pell Grant, which has not kept pace with inflation or rising tuition cost. Traditional students, on the other hand, largely rely on family and loans to see them through college, and are thus less vulnerable than their nontraditional counterparts.

Postgraduation Educational Plans and Experiences

Both nontraditional and traditional students had remarkably similar plans when asked if they wanted to continue their education after completing their bachelor's

Table 8.14
Plans for further education

Since completing your IT/CS bachelor's degree, are you pursuing any additional formal education?

Alumni survey responses	Nontraditional	Traditional	All students
Certificate program in IT/CS	21% (10) (n = 47)	19% (22) (n = 118)	19% (32) (n = 165)
Additional training courses in IT/CS	44% (21) (n = 48)	41% (49) (n = 120)	42% (70) (n = 168)
Graduate degree in an IT/CS field	24% (11) (n = 46)	18% (21) (n = 119)	24% (40) (n = 165)
Graduate degree in a non-IT/CS field	11% (5) (n = 45)	12% (14) (n = 119)	12% (19) (n = 164)
Other	10% (4) (n = 40)	8% (8) (n = 99)	9% (12) (n = 139)

degree. An astounding 77 percent of both nontraditional and traditional students said that they would continue their education either right away or in the future. About half of both populations sought at least a master's degree in an IT/CS field, while 18 percent indicated that they might want a business master's.

Among our alumni survey respondents, traditional and nontraditional alumni showed comparable similarities (table 8.14). Around one-quarter of both populations was pursuing a graduate degree in IT/CS, and over 40 percent were taking additional training courses. Among the employees that we interviewed, 74 percent indicated that they had plans to go back to school. This reinforces our earlier observation about the penchant for lifelong learning among students in the IT/CS field, where the perception is that the half-life of skills is getting shorter and shorter. These students, no matter what their circumstances, seem up to the challenge.

Teaching the Nontraditional Student

We interviewed seventy-two faculty at twenty area colleges and universities. About a third of our interviewees were women, and almost all were U.S. citizens or permanent residents. By race, 61 percent were white, 18 percent were African American, and the rest were largely Asian. Nearly 60 percent were either tenured or on the tenure track, while 33 percent were nontenure track and 8 percent indicated that the tenure system was not used at their institution. Approximately 20 percent of our interviewees were either department heads or deans. In our interviews, we asked many questions aimed at ascertaining both what professors wanted students to learn as well as their attitudes and experiences with different groups of students. We compare their answers below with the student responses wherever possible.

Perceptions of the Field

We began each interview by asking what each interviewee considered to be the defining characteristic of an IT/CS education. Nearly 30 percent cited "problem solving" as their primary view of what IT/CS entailed. Twenty-five percent saw their mission as preparing students for a career in the field, and another 24 percent wanted students to understand the fundamentals of computing. When asked about the core courses that should be included in an IT/CS program, answers ranged from just a few courses to whole IT/CS curricula. A few basic core courses could be teased from the answers: 90 percent mentioned a series of programming courses, followed by data structures (46 percent), systems analysis/design/software engineering (44 percent), and a database course (39 percent).

We then asked each professor if s/he felt that students had the same concept of IT/CS as they had (table 8.15). Two out of three said that students did not see IT/CS the same way. When queried about students' perceptions, professors complained that students saw IT/CS as just a way to a good job, as only programming, or that they didn't see the big picture. Fifty-seven percent of professors saw this difference in perception as problematic. This contrasts with 25 percent of all students and 29 percent of nontraditional students who indicated that their perceptions of the field had not changed since beginning their IT/CS degree. An additional 32 percent indicated that they had either only a vague view at first or now had a broader conception. This indicates that the majority of students may have either already "got it" or were getting it as they progressed through the program. Professors' perceptions of problems with students not seeing IT/CS the same way as they do might be unfounded or at least not as problematic as they might think.

When asked about important prerequisites, two-thirds of professors indicated that they would like to see students with precalculus math courses, as shown in figure 8.6. This seems to correspond with students' own idea that they wished they had more math in preparation for their degree program. While 18 percent of professors would like to see students with at least some introduction to computers, they

Table 8.15
Faculty interview regarding student conceptions

Do incoming undergraduates generally see IT/CS in the same terms as your concept?	
	Percentage (n = 72)
Yes	19% (14)
No	67% (48)
Unsure/don't know	10% (7)
NA	4% (3)

How do their perceptions differ?	
	Percentage (n = 53)
Way to a good job	23% (12)
Programming only	23% (12)
Don't see the big picture	21% (11)
Related to computer games/entertainment	15% (8)
Way to make money	13% (7)
Not much math involved	13% (7)
Related to computers only	9% (5)
Internet/Web sights	9% (5)
Tools only	4% (2)
Don't need to learn programming	2% (1)

Is that a problem?	
	Percentage (n = 54)
Yes	57% (31)
No	43% (23)

were also likely to list non-computer/math-based prerequisites as well, including discipline or work ethic, logic or critical thinking skills, an inquisitive nature and an open mind, and English or communication skills.

We also inquired about the skills that professors hoped to impart to their students (see figure 8.7 below). Again, problem solving was number one, with almost 40 percent mentioning it. The second most popular answer was the ability to learn or readiness for lifelong learning. As evidenced above by the students' and alumni's ambitions for further education, this notion of lifelong learning is being passed along. While 31 percent of professors wanted their students to gain at least a measure of technological literacy, professors were as likely to mention nontechnical skills among those they hoped to impart to their students, including creative thinking,

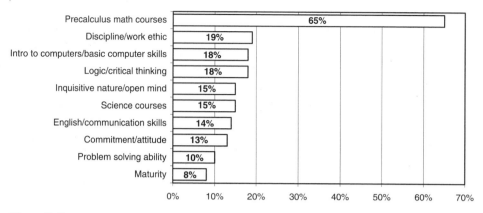

Figure 8.6
Top ten prerequisites for students to begin IT course work according to faculty
Note: Faculty could indicate more than one answer, so total > 100%.

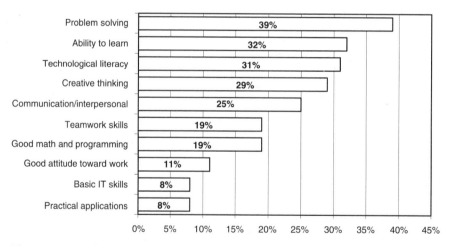

Figure 8.7
Top ten necessary skills faculty hope to impart to their students
Note: Faculty could indicate more than one answer, so total > 100%.

communication and interpersonal skills, teamwork, discipline, and a good attitude toward work.

Perceptions about Students

Professors were asked directly if they perceived any differences between nontraditional and traditional students. The differences most often cited in describing nontraditional students were overwhelmingly positive, including more mature, confident, serious, committed, and enthusiastic. In addition, nontraditional students were viewed as having more experience, more preparation, and better skills. In other words, nontraditional students were perceived to have most of the necessary prerequisites that professors' identified as being essential for success in an IT/CS program. The few negative responses to this question focused on nontraditional students having more outside commitments and being somewhat less confident in the beginning. About 8 percent of professors said they saw no differences between traditional and nontraditional students, and 6 percent said they had no or only limited experience with nontraditional students.

In contrast, we also asked professors if they perceived any differences between their male and female students. Forty-two percent said that they saw no differences at all between them. Some listed positive differences, including that women were more disciplined and focused, smarter, more serious, more mature, and overall just better. But we also had a number of more negative responses in which women were perceived as being less confident than their male counterparts, more likely to drop out, less adventurous, and less likely to enjoy programming or computer science.

When asked about underrepresented minorities, more professors were unwilling to answer this question, and about 13 percent said that they simply did not have any or enough experience with these students. Another 26 percent said that they saw no differences. Those willing to list differences had only negative observations of underrepresented minority students, including being less prepared, being more likely to struggle, having problems fitting in, and lacking communication skills.

We were generally heartened by the positive ratings that nontraditional students received from those who teach them. Important to keep in mind, however, is the preponderance of white males among nontraditional students at these institutions. The mixed perceptions of women and the mostly negative perceptions of underrepresented minorities are troubling, and also problematic from the standpoint of recruiting and retaining more of these students. These need to be addressed at a fundamental level before real diversity in the field might be achieved.

Weed-Out Courses

The concept of weed-out courses—courses specifically designed to cull weaker students out of a program—is problematic. Oftentimes, those weeded out are disproportionately members of underrepresented groups, including women and minorities, but also nontraditional students. The questions elucidated above showed that nontraditional students and women were more likely to see themselves as average or worse than their classmates. Combine this with a culture that condones weeding out, and the potential exists for more women and nontraditional students to drop out of IT/CS. Almost 40 percent of professors said that their program has weed-out courses. Another 33 percent said that they had courses that function as weed-outs, although they are not specifically designed as such. When asked a follow-up question about students that consistently do worse in these courses, 14 percent of professors did not perceive a pattern among students, while 11 percent identified nontraditional and weekend students as having difficulties with these courses.

Nearly half of the professors queried thought that students do perceive these courses as weed-outs. When asked if they thought that this perception affected students' ability to complete the course work, however, most said that it did not or that it made them work harder. This is corroborated somewhat by students' responses. Fifteen percent of professors said that students either drop out of these courses or try to avoid them altogether, and another 15 percent said that it does affect students' abilities to complete the course work. Only 11 percent of professors said that they try to help students get through difficult courses or offer tutoring.

Recruitment Efforts

Colleges and universities need to pay more attention to recruiting and retention, and to targeting their efforts at recruitment to various groups. Most professors do not engage in recruiting activities, and some programs indicate that they do no recruiting at all because they have more students than they have places. Yet achieving diversity requires special recruitment and retention efforts, regardless of the number of students already in the program. Those colleges and universities that are interested in enrolling more nontraditional students will need to evaluate carefully the messages they send out as well as the impact that might have on how welcome nontraditional students feel on their campuses.

Much of the literature on increasing the numbers of women and minorities in particular into IT/CS fields discusses the importance of recruitment efforts, especially for broadening the pool for student recruitment (Cuny and Aspray 2001). Most professors, though, indicated that undergraduate recruitment activities were concentrated at the university level, with no recruiting done by their specific departments. About 10 percent said that no recruitment was necessary, mostly because they already had too many students in the program. When asked specifically about the recruitment of nontraditional students, about 25 percent of the respondents said that there is no recruitment of nontraditional students at their institution, 15 percent thought there were no differences in recruiting nontraditional and traditional students, and 11 percent indicated that nontraditional students were targeted with special literature.

A little over half of the professors we spoke with did engage in some recruiting activities. Most had participated in open houses, career fairs, or campus tours. The second most mentioned recruiting activity involved visiting local high schools. Still, only 6 percent said that they recruited at community colleges, a prime locale for recruiting nontraditional students. Additionally, only 3 percent indicated that they did recruiting in their introductory courses, even though a positive experience in an introductory course influenced students' decisions to pursue an IT/CS degree. Finally, only 3 percent of professors had participated in special summer programs to attract minority students.

Awareness of Nontraditional Students

We wanted to ascertain professors' awareness of nontraditional students at their institutions and the problems these students might face. When asked about the attractiveness of their institution to nontraditional students, 25 percent of professors said that they offered night and weekend courses. Almost 20 percent correctly identified their location as being a prime reason for nontraditional students to choose their institution, 14 percent mentioned cost, another 13 percent specified the name recognition of the school, and 8 percent acknowledged the importance of degree flexibility. But about 18 percent said that there was nothing at all about their institution that would be attractive to nontraditional students, while 7 percent indicated that nontraditional students would be put off from going there.

In order to assess professors' awareness of the differences between nontraditional and traditional students in terms of actual schedules, we asked professors how they saw schedules differing for both categories of students on a daily basis as well as throughout the course of study. About 20 percent said that there were no differences between traditional and nontraditional students and no special treatment of nontraditional students at their institution, completely ignoring the likelihood that nontraditional students might take fewer courses, be on campus fewer hours, or take longer to finish their degrees. One-quarter of professors said that nontraditional students took night and weekend courses. Only 20 percent recognized that nontraditional students take fewer classes and that they were more likely to have outside commitments than their more traditional counterparts. Seventeen percent saw scheduling as a problem for nontraditional students, and 11 percent identified a longer time to earn degree as a result.

Most professors (61 percent) did not perceive any friction between nontraditional and traditional students, and only 10 percent saw some friction over campus resources. We found little evidence from our student and faculty interviews that nontraditional and traditional students might have conflicts. To the contrary, both students and faculty often saw benefits to having a mix of traditional and nontraditional students in the classroom.

In terms of day and evening classes, 22 percent of professors said that there were no differences at all between them. About 17 percent mentioned that labs were difficult either to schedule or hold during the evening hours, and 15 percent indicated that mostly adjuncts teach the night courses. Only 11 percent of professors thought that less work was given in the evening classes, but otherwise there were few negative opinions about the quality of instruction in evening classes when they are run as regular university courses and not part of a special nontraditional program.

Characteristics and Needs of Nontraditional Students

We asked professors to reflect on our definition of nontraditional students—beginning college at or after the age of twenty-one, and/or taking longer than six years to finish their degree—and identify other characteristics that describe nontraditional students (see figure 8.8 below). Most answers mirrored those categories added by the U.S. Department of Education report, including having children (26 percent), working full-time (15 percent), and attending school part-time (4 percent). Other responses were variations on these additions, such as having outside commit-

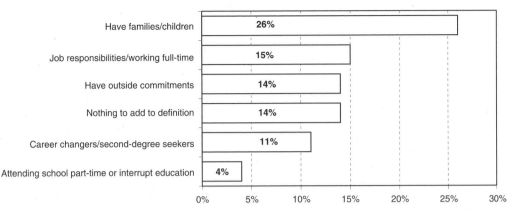

Figure 8.8
Additional characteristics faculty say describe nontraditional students
Note: Faculty could indicate more than one characteristic.

ments (14 percent). Around 14 percent of the professors we interviewed said they had nothing to add to the definition.

Professors were also asked about the most pressing needs of nontraditional students (see figure 8.9 below). Almost 30 percent listed more time or more time management as a necessity. More resources or financial support was mentioned by 18 percent of the respondents. Fourteen percent said that nontraditional students need course flexibility, 10 percent said they needed more support systems, and another 10 percent recognized the need for bridging programs or more tutoring to bring non-traditional students "up to speed" with their traditional counterparts.

Four percent identified a "sense of belonging" as important, and this might be the crux of the matter. While nontraditional students might certainly benefit from more time and resources, feeling that they belong at a university or college, and that the professors and academic staff understand their challenges and needs as well as their strengths, would go a long way to attracting nontraditional students of both genders and all ethnicities to a program.

Nontraditional students may not be that different from their more traditional counterparts. If they are choosing convenience over more traditional programs, it may just be because the more convenient programs also welcome and appreciate students. But nontraditional students are concerned about the reputation of the institution from which they get their degree, and have many of the same desires and concerns as traditional students.

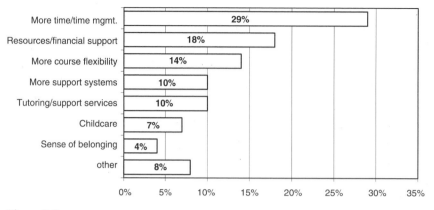

Figure 8.9
Most pressing needs of nontraditional students according to faculty

Conclusions

In general, we found that nontraditional students who find their way into more traditional academic institutions are largely invisible to both faculty and other students. There are few concessions made for them, either in course flexibility and/or programs to help them fill in gaps in their education or adjust to being back in school. Faculty have some positive opinions about nontraditional students, but they are not very informed about these students' needs or circumstances. Nontraditional students who choose this path (instead of going to institutions such as Strayer that may be more likely to cater to their needs) are more likely to be male and have considerable experience with higher education, through a community college or having already earned a degree. In short, the same variables that keep women and underrepresented minorities from choosing IT/CS education are compounded for nontraditional students who want to attend traditional universities. Moreover, the trend among traditional universities is to focus more on the traditional student, making it more difficult for nontraditional students to feel like they belong.

One might ask why we should be concerned about where nontraditional students get their degrees. One answer to that question might involve a discussion of the value to students of a degree from a for-profit versus a nonprofit institution in terms of potential income and debt load. Even more important than a degree's value, however, is the ability of degree holders to participate in knowledge creation rather than just acquiring technical skill proficiency. If women and minorities, as well as some white males, are overwhelming choosing for-profit institutions for their IT/CS education, their ability to participate in research and development of new IT/CS applications may be cut short if their degree is purely skill oriented and not imparting a more generalized theoretical background. In other words, these students, the IT/CS field, the IT workforce, and the nation as a whole will likely miss out on the creative talent these students could bring to the IT/CS enterprise.

Notes

1. This chapter is largely excerpted from the forthcoming report *Preparing Women and Minorities for the IT Workforce: The Role of Nontraditional Educational Pathways* being published by the American Association for the Advancement of Science (AAAS). The report includes data from a study conducted jointly by the AAAS and the Commission on Professionals in Science and Technology (CPST) with generous grant support from the National Science Foundation. Report authors include Shirley Malcom, Al Teich, Jolene Jesse, Eleanor Babco, and Lara Campbell. Nathan Bell of the CPST and Kathryn Grogan of the AAAS produced the charts and tables used in this chapter. Kathryn Grogan was instrumental in data preparation and analysis. The editing of the content and added analysis are purely my own.

2. While the number one producer of bachelor's degrees in business and management is the University of Phoenix (another for-profit university with multiple campuses), the rest of the top ten are dominated by major research-extensive universities including Texas A&M, Pennsylvania State, and the University of Florida. All data are provided by the CPST from the NSF WebCASPAR and the Department of Education NCES databases.

3. More information on the labor market experience of nontraditional and traditional students is elaborated in the full AAAS report.

4. We recognize that choices are made within a particular societal context and are not made without constraints. Our emphasis on choice, therefore, does not imply a denial of the importance of context and constraints but an examination of the choices students make within those contexts and constraints that constitute a pathway into a career.

5. In devising this definition we also relied on the U.S. Department of Education special report on nontraditional students, *The Condition of Education, 2002.*

References

Adelman, C. 2003. A growing plurality: The "traditional age community college dominant" student. *Community College Journal* (April/May): 27–32.

Aspray, W. 2004. Information technology workforce. In *Chasing Moore's law: Information technology policy in the United States*, ed. W. Aspray, 273–297. Raleigh, NC: Scitech Publishing, Inc.

Blumenstyk, G. 2004. U. of Phoenix to stoke booming growth in competing for traditional-age college students. *Chronicle of Higher Education* (June 25). Available at ⟨http://chronicle.com/prm/daily/2004/06/2004062504n.htm⟩.

Bowen, W. G., and D. Bok. 1998. *The shape of the river: Long-term consequences of considering race in college and university admissions.* Princeton, NJ: Princeton University Press.

Cuny, J., and W. Aspray. 2001. *Recruitment and retention of women graduate students in computer science and engineering.* Report of a workshop held June 20–21, 2000, organized by the Computing Research Association's Committee on the Status of Women in Computing Research. Washington, DC: Computing Research Association.

Farrell, E. F. 2004. Deeper pockets, different tactics: For-profit colleges thrive, but fears of a slowdown lead them to try new strategies. *Chronicle of Higher Education* 50, no. 23 (February 13): A26.

Institute for Higher Education Policy. 2002. *The policy of choice: Expanding student options in higher education.* Washington, DC: Institute for Higher Education Policy.

Schwartz, J. 2004. A different course. *New York Times*, April 25.

Thomas, S. L. 2003. Longer-term economic effects of college selectivity and control. *Research in Higher Education* 44:263–299.

9

Gender Differences among Students in Computer Science and Applied Information Technology

Christine Ogan, Jean C. Robinson, Manju Ahuja, and Susan C. Herring

A number of studies have addressed the problem of women's shrinking representation in computer science programs at the undergraduate and graduate levels (Cohoon 2001; Creamer, Burger, and Meszaros 2004; Margolis and Fisher 2002; Moorman and Johnson 2003). These studies and others document the problems and try to address the causes. Some studies propose and implement solutions (Margolis and Fisher 2002; Lee 2003; Natale 2002; Beyer et al. 2003; Beyer, Chavez, and Rynes 2002). All of this research focuses predominantly on educational programs or employment in the field of computer science specifically, rather than examining the trends in IT defined more broadly.

We report on a study comparing the demographics, attitudes, and computing-related behaviors of undergraduate and graduate students majoring in computer science with those majoring in other IT disciplines.

As Berghel and Sallach's (2004) research illustrates, the trend in those universities where computing is being taught is toward mergers with other departments or schools in which applied forms of IT are being taught. Those units include (but are not limited to) information systems (traditionally found in business schools), instructional technology (traditionally found in schools of education), information science (traditionally combined with library science), and the newest discipline, informatics (generally thought of as a set of disciplines at the intersection of people, technology, and information). Berghel and Sallach go so far as to call this a paradigm shift in the reorganization of academic instruction in computing and IT on campuses across the country. Further, they say that the "breadth and diversity of subject areas [in the new schools and colleges] suggests that the process of computer information technology program evolution has yet to slow down or stabilize" (84).

This trend is potentially important to expanding the educational involvement of women as they are more likely to have parity or near parity with men in certain disciplines, such as library and information science and education (Quint 1999; Wolverton 1999). These units traditionally have histories of recruiting and retaining larger numbers of women. Though programs targeted at women in computer science, like the one at Carnegie Mellon (Margolis and Fisher 2002), have illustrated that attention to problems within the discipline can result in increased recruitment and retention of women, lessons might also be learned by examining the differences between the characteristics of the students, the nature of the programs, and the institutional climate in the related IT disciplines. As we have previously pointed out (Ahuja et al. 2004), students in these applied fields are grounded in the contexts of real-world problems, study in a more gender-balanced environment, and may experience a more woman-friendly culture.

Among the findings that emerge repeatedly from previous research is that girls and women are less likely to choose computing as a career in the first place, for reasons that have been traced variously to a lack of aptitude, interest, or experience regarding computers, on the one hand (Badagliacco 1990; Kramer and Lehman 1990; Young 2000), and cultural stereotypes and perceptions that computing is a mostly masculine activity, on the other (Kiesler, Sproull, and Eccles 1985; Turkle 1988). If few women opt to study IT, efforts to make IT education more women-friendly can have a limited effect, at best. The question arises, therefore, whether applied IT careers attract more women, and more generally, what kind of students enroll in applied IT programs, as compared to computer science programs. Answering this question is an important first step in understanding the potential of new, interdisciplinary, applied IT disciplines to foster more equitable outcomes for women in computing technology fields.

The research question for this part of a larger study of educational experiences and the institutional culture of IT education is as follows: Are there significant differences in the demographics, computing experiences and behaviors, and attitudes toward computing between undergraduate and graduate students studying computer science and students studying IT in some other applied discipline in the university? Because the IT disciplines being studied involve elements of computer science, it is possible that the male-dominated culture will be represented in these units. This study was designed to determine whether that has happened.

Method

As part of a larger study of departments and schools where IT is taught—including computer science, management information systems, informatics, instructional systems technology, and information science/studies—at five U.S. institutions, we conducted a Web-based survey of all male and female undergraduate and graduate students in those units. The universities included Indiana University–Bloomington, the University at Buffalo (formerly SUNY-Buffalo), the University of Illinois at Urbana/Champaign, the University of Michigan at Ann Arbor and Dearborn, and the University of Washington. These publicly funded institutions were selected based on the minimum requirement of having a computer science unit and at least two other IT-related units. We also gave preference to institutions with programs in instructional technology and/or informatics because these are relatively less common.

The survey was conducted in March and April 2004 by the Center for Survey Research at Indiana University. We selected a Web-based format for the survey because IT students would be most comfortable with it. Response rates have been found to be roughly equal for Web and mail surveys (Truell, Barlett, and Alexander 2002). The majority of students were contacted directly through their university e-mail accounts. For reasons of student privacy, students in three units were contacted through an administrator in their unit via e-mail. Students answered a hundred questions related to their attitudes and behaviors regarding the use of computers, demographic information, and information about mentoring, stress, and burnout. Questions were adapted from a variety of other studies. Some published scales were used for questions related to mentoring, stress, and work-life balance, but those are not reported in this chapter. Only part of the data from the survey will be addressed here. It was not possible to determine the total response rate because we were not informed of the number of students in the units where the administrator made first contact with the students. The response rates for the rest of the students ranged from 32 to 85 percent by academic unit.[1] Though the total number of respondents was 1,768, the number we will use to report the results for this chapter is 1,516. The remainder of the surveys did not respond to the question asking for their gender. The results were analyzed using statistical software, SPSS 11.

Analysis

To assess the differences in gender by the type of program, we split the sample, placing all computer science students in one group and the rest of the students from applied IT disciplines in another. In the computer science group, a total of 508 males and 115 females completed the survey, while in the applied IT group, a total of 414 males and 479 females did so.[2] The proportions of responses by gender are in keeping with what we expected: more women in the applied IT units. In three of the units where library and information science is the focus of study, about twice as many women responded to the survey as did men (96 men and 215 women). The primary analysis tools were cross-tabulations of the data by the type of program (computer science or applied IT) with the variables in question (discussed below), with differences measured primarily through the Cramer's V (or phi) statistic. We also used factor analysis to determine which variables could be used together because they tap similar dimensions. Simple frequencies are also reported in the analysis. When those are used, we have not applied any statistical comparisons.

Demographics

The sample was skewed more toward undergraduate students in the computer science part of the sample (57 versus 23 percent of the applied IT sample). Master's students made up 12.8 percent of computer science students and 65.2 percent of the applied IT students. Doctoral students comprised 30.2 percent of the computer science students and 11.8 percent of the applied IT students. When the year in school was broken down by gender, interesting patterns emerged, as shown by the counts of males and females given in table 9.1. Calculations with the data in this table show that disregarding gender, computer science students are predominantly

Table 9.1
Year in school by gender for computer science and applied IT units
($N = 1,456$)

	Males	Percentage males*	Females	Percentage females*
Computer science				
Undergraduates	275	57.1%	64	56.1%
Master's students	63	13.1%	13	11.4%
PhD students	144	29.9%	37	32.5%
Applied IT				
Undergraduates	141	35.2%	56	12.2%
Master's students	206	51.4%	357	77.8%
PhD students	54	13.5%	46	10.0%

Notes: One hundred and nineteen computer science students (18.3% of total) and 193 applied IT students (16.6% of total) did not identify their year in school in any of these categories
*Percent within gender in computer science or applied IT

undergraduates (56.9 percent), but the next largest category is doctoral students. The applied IT units tend to have the most students in the master's category (65.5 percent), with undergraduates coming in second (22.9 percent). There are several reasons why the distributions differ. In computer science, students who come to graduate school are primarily seeking a doctorate and may acquire a master's degree along the way, but the master's degree is not the main goal of most graduate computer science students. The goal of these students is more frequently a career in academia, where the doctorate is the minimum requirement. In the applied IT fields, the professional master's degree is highly valued for students who seek jobs in industry. Some schools where library and information science is taught do not even offer undergraduate degrees (two in our sample).

The distribution of males and females in the applied IT units also varies, with many more women enrolled in the master's degree programs than men (77.8 versus 51.4 percent). Most of this difference is accounted for by the large enrollments of women in units where library and information science is taught, and especially in courses of study related to library science. Seventy-nine percent of library science students and 82 percent of librarians are female, according to a 2002 report (Maata 2003). There are fewer numbers of women in the doctoral programs at the PhD level (13.5 versus 10 percent). At the undergraduate level in the applied IT units, men are almost three times as prevalent as women (35.2 versus 12.2 percent). These differences show up primarily in units where informatics or information systems is the focus.

In terms of age, the computer science students fit a more traditional age pattern, while the applied IT students tend to be older (see table 9.2). Almost all of the computer science students, including those in the doctoral program, are under the age of thirty-five. In the applied IT schools, however, 27.5 percent of the total number of people responding to the question asking when they were born were age thirty-five and over, and 11.1 percent of those students were age forty-five or more. The high numbers of students of nontraditional age obviously impacts the results of this study, particularly in those students' attitudes and experiences related to computing.

Other demographic patterns are consistent with the age and year-in-school data. Of those who said they live with a spouse or domestic partner, 75 percent were students in applied IT programs. In computer science, 95 men and 24 women reported living with a spouse or domestic partner, while 203 women and 155 men in the applied IT group reported doing so. In the computer science group of students, only 25 men and 3 women said they had any children living in their households.

Table 9.2
Age by gender for computer science and applied IT units
(N = 1,496)

	Males	Percentage male	Females	Percentage female
Computer science				
18–24	329	65.3%*	70	62.0%
25–34	160	31.7%	39	34.5%
35–44	14	2.8%	1	.9%
45–54	1	.2%	3	2.7%
55–65	0	.0%	0	.0%
Applied IT				
18–24	156	38.1%	95	20.2%
25–34	166	40.6%	220	46.8%
35–44	62	15.2%	82	17.4%
45–54	18	4.4%	61	13.0%
55–65	7	1.7%	12	2.6%

Notes: Two hundred and fifty-two students did not identify their age, and a few other responses could not be interpreted
*Percent within gender in computer science or applied IT

Again, in the applied IT group, many more of the men (65) and women (85) said they had children in their homes.

We also asked whether respondents were currently employed. Since the survey was administered during the school year, answering that question in the affirmative would mean that they were employed while studying. In the computer science group, 277 (54.5 percent) men and 66 (57.4 percent) women said they were employed, while 321 (77.5 percent) men and 398 (83.1 percent) women in the applied IT group reported current employment. The high percentages of both men and women reporting employment in the applied IT group is also an indicator of their nontraditional student status. But it impacts the time available to be spent on their studies and pursuing extracurricular activities related to their majors.

Some other studies have found a relationship between parents' careers and socio-economic status and the field of study chosen by their children (Tilleczek and Lewko 2001; Shashaani 1994). In our survey, whether or not the father was employed in an IT field was not significantly different for men and women in either the computer science or applied IT groups. More women in the computer science group (4.5 percent of men versus 13.2 percent of women), however, reported having mothers who worked in an IT field than did men in computer science (phi = .14, $p < .002$). An equal percentage of men and women in the applied IT group (4.6 percent) reported having a mother who worked in IT (4.6 percent).

We asked questions about whether respondents' fathers and mothers held traditional views about the roles men and women should adopt—for example, that men should be the primary wage earners and women should be the primary child care providers in the home. Though the responses to these questions do not qualify as demographic information, it is important to provide the results based on those questions here as they may be related to the age and year-in-school distribution. For both the computer science and applied IT groups, we found gender differences for the fathers' views. Men tended to have fathers with more traditional views than did women (phi = .09, $p < .01$ for applied IT, and phi = .10, $p < .03$ for computer science). Yet the difference was only significant for computer science students when it came to reporting on their mothers' views, with a higher percentage of men in the computer science group reporting their mothers had traditional views (phi = .11, $p < .01$).[3] Stated differently, more women in computer science reported that their mothers did not hold traditional views than the men in those units did. This finding is consistent with Shashaani's (1994) finding that children's attitudes related to computers often follow from the gendered views of their parents regarding appropriate sex roles in the field of computing.

Computer Experiences

Though earlier studies found that men used computers at younger ages than did women (Badagliacco 1990), more recent studies have found no age differences (Beyer, Chavez, and Rynes 2002; Beyer et al. 2002; Colley and Comber 2003). This is to be expected as personal computer household penetration rates have been steadily increasing from the time of the personal computer's inception in the early 1980s, particularly among higher socioeconomic status households (U.S. Department of Commerce 2000; U.S. Census Bureau 2001). In this study, however, men in both the computer science and applied IT groups tended to begin using computers earlier than women did (see table 9.3). Yet when we compared men and women across units, we found that men in applied IT were much more likely to learn earlier and on their own while women learned later and through school or other organized instruction (Kendall's tau-c = .21, $p < .000$). The difference was also significant for

Table 9.3
When and where respondent learned to program a computer by gender for computer science and applied IT units
(N = 1,250)

	Males	Percentage male*	Females	Percentage female*
Computer science (N = 602)				
On their own as a child	108	22.1%	6	5.3%
On their own as a teenager	135	27.6%	11	9.7%
Classes in summer or at camp	35	7.2%	8	7.1%
Classes in middle/high school	116	23.7%	47	41.6%
Classes at a university	95	19.4%	41	36.3%
Applied IT (N = 648)				
On their own as a child	29	8.5%	14	4.6%
On their own as a teenager	78	22.7%	18	5.9%
Classes in summer or at camp	13	3.8%	16	5.2%
Classes in middle/high school	78	22.7%	70	23.0%
Classes at a university	145	42.3%	187	61.3%

Notes: Cramer's V = .28, p = .000 (for differences between men and women in computer science), and Cramer's V = .29, p = .000 (for differences between men and women in applied IT)
*Percent within gender in computer science or applied IT

the computer science group, though (Kendall's tau-c $<=$ .08, $p < .04$). The surprise in this finding is that a difference persists in the computer science group where men and women in this traditional age group have had the opportunity to work with computers most of their lives. The high percentage of older students in the applied IT group would partially explain the difference in age of exposure and opportunity.

When we asked about game-playing activity when the respondents were children, much higher frequencies were reported by computer science majors than by the applied IT group majors. Moreover, also consistent with previous research (Fromme 2003; Oosterwegel, Littleton, and Light 2004), the males in both groups reported more computer game playing than the females (Kendall's tau-c = .36, $p < .00$ for computer science, and Kendall's tau-c = .18, $p < .000$ for applied IT). From ages twelve to seventeen, the main activity reported by men in the computer science group was games (48.2 versus 38.8 percent of the men in the applied IT group). For women in computer science, the most popular activity was communicating with friends (32.7 versus 14.4 percent of women in the applied IT group). Perhaps more important than the variety of activities each group mentioned was the finding that men and women in both groups chose different activities (Cramer's $V = .28$, $p < .000$ for the computer science group, and Cramer's $V = .28$, $p < .000$ for the applied IT group). The largest percentage of women in the applied IT group chose the "other" category (45.2 percent). We asked the respondents to specify what they meant by "other." Because so many of this group were born and grew up in the time before the personal computer was available, a majority of the respondents who cited "other" said they didn't have a computer and had no exposure to a computer in the ages between twelve and seventeen.

A similar kind of response came from the applied IT group when we asked when they learned to program a computer; 15.2 percent of these respondents said they didn't know how to program. We were not surprised by that because many students in applied IT programs may work only with computer applications. The older students in these programs who did not know how to program likely also hadn't learned programming skills in their current course of study. No computer science student declared a lack of programming knowledge. Of the respondents who answered with one of the fixed choices, men in both groups tended to learn at younger ages and more on their own than in structured environments (see table 9.3). The differences between the place and the time that men and women learned to program was significant for both groups (Cramer's $V = .29$, $p < .000$ for applied IT, and Cramer's $V = .28$, $p < .000$ for computer science).

Reasons for Choosing IT

People choose their careers in a variety of ways. Often the choice is attributed to some person who served as an inspiration. We asked the respondents to identify individuals—parents, teachers, employers, friends, spouses, and so on—by gender as the primary individual who encouraged them to study IT. Of those who identified someone, men were identified more often by males and females were more often identified by women for both groups. The differences were greater for the applied IT group than for the computer science group, however (Cramer's $V = .33$, $p < .000$ for applied IT, and Cramer's $V = .19$, $p < .000$ for computer science) (see table 9.4). A few other variations between groups are interesting to note. Students' fathers seemed to be much stronger influences for both male and female computer science students (21 percent for men and 27.2 percent for women) than they were for the applied IT group (12.1 percent for men and 7.1 percent for women).

Table 9.4
Gender of person identified as individual who most encouraged respondent to study IT by gender of respondent for computer science and applied IT units
($N = 671^*$)

	Male	Percentage male**	Female	Percentage female**
Computer science				
Person identified was male	169	75.4%	41	56.2%
Person identified was female	48	21.4%	26	35.6%
Person identified was spouse	7	3.1%	6	8.2%
Applied IT				
Person identified was male	117	69.2%	74	36.1%
Person identified was female	39	23.1%	92	44.9%
Person identified was spouse	13	7.7%	39	19.0%

Notes: Cramer's V = .19, $p = .05$ (for differences between men and women in computer science), and Cramer's V = .33, $p = .05$ (for differences between men and women in applied IT)
*N is particularly low as the rest of the respondents either identified "nobody" or "other" as the answer
**Percent within gender in computer science or applied IT

This finding is consistent with that from a survey of members in the online community Systers (Turner, Bernt, and Pecora 2002) in which women working in IT careers who majored in computer science or information systems as undergraduates said their parents, and particularly their fathers, were influential in making the decision. Shashaani (1994) also found that parental encouragement positively affected children's attitudes related to computing. About half of all the students in the applied IT group and half of the men in the computer science group said that nobody had encouraged them to study IT. Yet only one-fourth of the women in computer science said that nobody encouraged them.

We also explored reasons why the students had chosen their particular IT field of study to determine if there were gender differences and differences between students in computer science or applied IT fields. Questions about various aspects of the nature of IT work were placed on a four-point scale as to their level of importance from not at all important to very important. In today's job market, finding well-paid employment is one of the central issues in choosing a career. The students in this study were no exception. Of the applied IT group, 82 percent of the respondents said that finding well-paid employment was either a somewhat or very important factor. There were no differences between men and women in their responses. Computer science students also counted salary as important, but in this case the men placed slightly more emphasis on this as a factor in choosing IT than did women (Kendall's tau-c = .07, $p < .03$). Other factors that men and women in both the applied IT and computer science groups found equally important were having a flexible work schedule and the challenge inherent in the subject matter.

Having a personal interest in the subject matter was given high priority by both groups, with 78.9 percent of the men in the computer science group rating it as very important. There were no differences between men and women in the applied IT group on this factor, but women in the computer science group rated this factor significantly lower than men did (Kendall's tau-c = $-.11$, $p < .001$). This may be an area for further exploration if these women decide not to persist to graduation in computer science.

Men and women are known to have different levels of interest in helping others as part of their life's work (Creamer, Burger, and Meszaros 2004), but when we asked this question of the computer science group, there were no gender differences. Only 12.7 percent of men and 15.8 percent of women said that helping others was a very important factor in majoring in an IT field. This is not particularly surprising as helping others is not generally thought of as a characteristic of work in computer science (Bentson 2000). But differences did show up in the applied IT group (Kendall's tau-c = .14, $p < .000$), with women expressing significantly more interest in this factor. Because the applied IT group includes a fairly wide range of potential career paths, it is possible that several of those might include jobs where helping others is part of the description.

Role models often inspire people to adopt a particular course of study. Technology-adoption research has found that women are more likely than men to start using a new technology because people they like and respect are doing so (Venkatesh and Morris 2000). In our study, about four out of ten men and women students in the computer science group responded that they were studying IT because the people they admired and respected are studying or working in this field. Men said this factor was either somewhat or very important a little less often than did women in computer science (38.5 versus 43.9 percent), but this difference was not significant. Still, the difference on this factor for men and women in the applied IT group was significant (Kendall's tau-c = .11, $p < .003$). Women in the applied IT group were more likely to say they were drawn to the field because of the people they admired and respected than did men in this group.

We expected that a person's perceived skill in a discipline would be a very important factor for selecting a major. There were significant differences between men and women in both the computer science and applied IT groups on this factor. One question asked how important the statement "I've always been good with computers" was in making the decision to major in IT. Men were much more likely to say that this was somewhat or very important than were women (84.7 percent of men and 66 percent of women in computer science, and 72.9 percent of men and 53 percent of women in applied IT fields) (Kendall's tau-c = −.18, $p < .000$ for computer science, and Kendall's tau-c = −.28, $p < .000$ for applied IT). We emphasize that this variable measures the student's perception of their skill with computers, not the actual skill. Previous research (McCoy and Heafner 2004; Young 2000; Herring 1993), however, has found that women tend to rate their computer skills lower than do men. And the question relates to the relative importance this factor had in deciding on a major. Nevertheless, since the question did not ask them directly about their perceived computer skill, it may be that women believe their skills are just as good as those of the men, but that the skill level was not so important in attracting them to IT. Yet that conclusion is found not to be valid in the analysis of the variables in the computer attitudes section below.

The series of questions about choice of major was followed by a question about the respondents' relative satisfaction with the decision to major in an IT field. Overall, both groups were quite satisfied with their majors. Only forty-one of the applied IT group and fifty-five in the computer science group said they were somewhat or very dissatisfied with their decision. Further, men and women in both groups were equally satisfied with the choice they had made. Women in the computer science group were a little less satisfied than men in that group, but the difference was only close to being significant ($p < .06$). When we asked the respondents how confident they were that they would complete their current degree program, however, differences between groups (and not between gender within a group) appeared. Overall, students in the applied IT group expressed higher confidence that they would complete their degrees (Kendall's tau-c = .12, $p < .000$). In the applied IT group, about 87 percent of the men and 91 percent of the women were very confident of degree completion, while in the computer science group 77 percent of men and 76 percent of women expressed that level of confidence.

Attitudes about Computer Work

We asked a battery of questions used in previous surveys regarding individuals' skills, efficacy, comfort, and use of computers. Previous studies have found that women are likely to have less confidence and lower comfort levels than men (Compeau, Higgins, and Huff 1999; Durndell and Haag 2002; Lee 2003). But Oosterwegel, Littleton, and Light found that both boys and girls who had images of themselves as skilled with computers were less likely to express doubts about their computer efficacy:

The results indicated no overall sex difference in "actual vs. ideal" self-perception in relation to computer games or tasks. Nor were there overall sex differences in children's aspirations to be good with computers. However, the boys saw themselves as better with computer games than with school-type ICT [Information and Computer Technology] tasks, whereas the reverse was true for girls. Individual boy respondents saw themselves as very different from girls (more so than individual girls saw themselves as different from boys) whether in general or in relation to computer games and tasks. Boys and girls were considered to be more different from one another with regard to computer games than either on ICT tasks or in general. (2004, 225)

In our survey, we should not have observed much distance between the respondents' personal evaluation of how good they are with computers and their levels of confidence and comfort with computers because both men and women in this survey had chosen majors that required working with computers. Yet that was not the case.

Comfort levels with computers were much higher for men than for women. That was true of both the computer science and the applied IT groups (Kendall's tau-c = .22, $p < .000$ for applied IT, and Kendall's tau-c = .19, $p < .000$ for computer science). In both groups, about half of the women said they were very comfortable using computers, but 86 percent of the men in computer science and 77.3 percent of the men in the applied IT group expressed that level of comfort. A related question asked how comfortable the respondent felt when trying new things on a computer. Gender differences emerged again for both groups, though the difference was larger for the applied IT group (Kendall's tau-c = .20, $p < .000$ for applied IT, and Kendall's tau-c = .11, $p = .000$ for computer science). It was surprising that even in the computer science group, 5.2 percent of women said they were not too comfortable trying new things on the computer while none of the men in the computer science group expressed that view.

Self-confidence levels with computers, a related concept to comfort with computers, were also lower for women than for men in both groups. In the computer science group, 13.1 percent of the women versus 2.6 percent of the men said they were not very or not at all confident when working with computers. In the applied IT group the confidence gap was also large, with 3.1 percent of the men and 11.3 percent of the women responding in those categories. The differences in both groups were significant (Kendall's tau-c = .31, $p < .000$ for applied IT, and Kendall's tau-c = .25, $p < .000$ for computer science).

Given the gender gap in comfort and confidence, we expected that when the students were asked to rate their computer skills and grades in programming classes compared to those of their classmates, the women would rate themselves lower than the men. The men in computer science rated their skills at the highest levels, as better or much better than others in their major (67.1 percent of computer science and 43.2 percent of the men in the applied IT group), while the women in the applied IT group rated their skills the lowest (24 percent rated their skills as better or much better compared to 33 percent of the women in computer science). The same level of gender difference emerged for both groups, however (Kendall's tau-c = .24, $p < .000$ for computer science and applied IT). Of course, we have no way of knowing what grades either group actually received. It is entirely possible that women only think their grades are lower than those of their classmates.

Differences between men and women also appeared in their reported ease at learning new programming languages. Of those respondents who have learned programming, men in both the computer science and applied IT groups reported they learn new computer languages more easily than women said they learned those languages (Kendall's tau-c = .15, $p < .04$ for the applied IT group, and Kendall's tau-c = .11, $p < .03$ for the computer science group). Similarly, more men reported getting high grades in programming classes, but the difference was significant only in the computer science group (Kendall's tau-c = .10, $p < .01$).

Finally, we looked at students' perceived interest and engagement in addressing problems they encounter in the course of their computer work. We first asked about the degree of appeal the challenge of solving problems with computers had for them. Men in both the computer science and applied IT groups expressed a higher attraction to this challenge (Kendall's tau-c = .19, $p < .000$ for the applied IT group, and Kendall's tau-c = .08, $p < .01$ for the computer science group). The difference was smaller for the computer science group, however, with 4 percent of the men and 2.6 percent of the women saying the challenge was not at all appealing. Overall, men in the applied IT group said they liked to spend more of their free time on the computer than women said they did (Kendall's tau-c = .11, $p < .002$), but men and women in the computer science group said they liked to spend about the same amount of their free time with computers (in gaming or other activities). But when it came to interest in black box issues, men were more likely in both groups to say that they were interested in understanding how computers work (Kendall's tau-c $= .22$, $p < .000$ for the applied IT group, and Kendall's tau-c $= .10$, $p < .002$ for the computer science group).

The persistence issue was approached through a question that asked how likely it was that the respondent would stick with a problem with a computer program that could not be immediately solved. In both groups, men expressed a greater willingness to stick with the problem (Kendall's tau-c $= .19$, $p < .000$ for the applied IT group, and Kendall's tau-c $= .10$, $p < .003$ for the computer science group). Persistence was also measured through a question that asked how hard it is for the respondent to stop once they start work using computers. On this question, no differences were found for either group. Similarly, no differences emerged for either group on the responses to a question that asked how likely a person would be to continue to think about a problem that was left unsolved in a computer class.

The variables listed above (along with a few others) related to attitudes about computer work were factor analyzed. Following varimax rotation, a three-factor solution emerged. Three of the questions related to ease of learning computer languages, self-rating of programming skills, and self-assessment of the grades the respondent received in programming classes loaded on the first factor, which we labeled "skill." The second factor included the questions about comfort with computers, comfort with trying new things on the computer, and self-confidence when working with computers. We called this scale "comfort." The third factor included questions related to enjoyment and persistence; that is, how much the respondent enjoyed talking with others about computers, how interested the respondent was in understanding how computers work, and how hard it is for the respondent to stop work once they start working on a computer. This scale also included questions related to thinking about an unsolved problem after computer class and the relative appeal the challenge of solving computer problems had to the respondent. Our label for this scale was "engagement." Cronbach's alpha measure of reliability was calculated to be .71 for the three-factor solution. The variables for each of the three factors were formed into additive scales and correlated with gender for the computer science and applied IT groups.

The three new variables—skill, comfort, and engagement—significantly correlated with gender for both groups. Though the Pearson's r was higher for the

Table 9.5
Relationship between gender and attitudes toward computer work for computer science and applied IT units

	Correlation	Significance
Computer science		
Skill*	r = .19	p = .01
Comfort**	r = .28	p = .01
Engagement***	r = .13	p = .01
Applied IT		
Skill	r = .29	p = .01
Comfort	r = .34	p = .01
Engagement	r = .21	p = .01

Notes:
*Composite of three variables measuring respondents' assessment of grades in programming classes, ease of learning computer languages, and rating of personal skill in programming
**Composite of three variables measuring respondents' assessment of comfort with computers, comfort in learning new things on computers, and self-confidence when using computers
***Composite of five variables measuring respondents' interest in understanding how computers work, degree of difficulty leaving work on a computer once they have started, persistence in thinking about unsolved problems from computer class, degree of appeal for the challenge of solving computer problems, and enjoyment received from discussing computers with others

applied IT group than for the computer science group in all cases (see table 9.5), significant gender differences were found. In other words, men in both groups expressed feeling more skill and comfort, and said they were also more persistent in dealing with computer issues.

Patterns in the Groups

We began this study by suggesting that the nature of the structure of the programs in IT education that were more applied would be more woman-friendly and would therefore result in larger numbers of women in these programs who would persist to graduation. We noted that the problem of declining numbers of women in computer science programs might be addressed by examining the environment for women in the applied programs. This first part of our study of five institutions where computer science and other IT disciplines are taught surveyed the undergraduate and graduate students to determine if there were differences in the demographic characteristics, the uses of and attitudes toward computers, and the reasons for selecting a particular IT discipline for a major. Though the results for specific variables have been reported above, it is good to look at the overall picture of the men and women students in these two kinds of IT educational programs.

The similarities between the women in these groups may be as interesting as the differences. We were somewhat surprised to find that women still don't feel as good about their abilities related to computers and computer programming as men do—whether that be in computer science or the applied units. It may be that the lack of confidence in their skills leads women to be less comfortable. The lack of confidence might stem from a lack of encouragement from teachers, friends, and family since half of women in the applied IT group and one-quarter of women in the computer science group said nobody had encouraged them to go into an IT field. Even though men in both groups also said nobody encouraged them, men have other ways of building up confidence in their skills. Overall, men in both groups began using computers and learning to program them at younger ages and on their own. Mastering computer skills has its own way of reinforcing a perception of higher ability, and women either didn't have that opportunity or chose not to take it at the early age that men did. The result is that women end up in these college-level programs feeling a great deal of uncertainty about their skills. When other people have provided encouragement for these students, that has usually followed gender lines, with men being more encouraged by other men and women by other women. The group of women in computer science was an exception in that they said that their fathers were most important in making the decision to major in computer science. That was not so true of the women who had chosen an applied IT field.

The biggest differences between men and women in the two groups are demographic; men and women in the applied IT units tend to be older, and men and women in computer science tend to fall into traditional age groups for undergraduate and graduate students. This is not surprising given the number of older students in professional programs of all kinds in the university. Often in early to midcareer, people decide to return to school to improve their chances of moving up a career ladder. And computer science is not generally considered to be a strictly professional program. This means that reasons for entering the particular IT discipline may vary more widely between these groups than by gender within a group. The challenge of the subject matter and the flexible work schedule, however, were reasons equally chosen by men and women in both groups. And men in both groups were more likely than women to say that being good with computers was a reason for entering

the field. Consistent with other studies, women in the applied IT area said that helping others was a reason for choosing an IT major. Perhaps the link between helping
others and majoring in computer science needs to be made to attract more women
to that major.

Though we believe that women in the applied IT fields may see some advantages
to studying IT outside a traditional computer science environment, in fact women in
the applied majors suffer from some of the same problems related to their self-
esteem regarding computer efficacy. The discomfort and self-confidence issues for
women in both groups played out in their assessment of the grades they get in
programming classes when they compare themselves to their classmates. Women in
both computer science and applied IT disciplines began working and playing on
computers later than their male counterparts. Women in both groups tended to
have been encouraged more frequently by other women than by men.

Most of the findings in this part of our study support earlier findings of several
other studies that look at women's attitudes and performance related to technology.
While this study hoped to find that women in applied IT disciplines would have superior levels of self-confidence and perceived degree of skill in the use of computing
technology, that was not the case. We are concerned that the gender differences
found in studies over the last fifteen to twenty years persist today, even among populations of students who choose to major in computer science and in applied IT
fields. We would support the conclusions of Clegg (2001) that call for policies to
change the discourse related to women and computing. Her charge is that the disciplinary boundaries of computer science must be challenged so that the skills
required to succeed in this field are not "culturally overlaid with the aura of masculinity" (320). That happens, Clegg notes, because technology frequently drives the
curriculum in schools rather than using technology when it "advances real educational capacities" (320). We agree with Clegg that the "questions concerning who
has the power to shape the production and reproduction of gendered meanings
in technology, and how transformations can be achieved, remain central in both
theory and practice" (321). Though Clegg's criticisms were directed at mainstream
computer science, it appears from this study that they could be applied to applied
technology fields as well. Our continued study of these institutions should reveal
what other factors are responsible for the outcome of this survey.

This study has only addressed part of this issue: how men and women undergraduate and graduate students in computer science and applied IT disciplines use computers, perceive their personal levels of skills and confidence, and choose to enter

and remain in their fields of study. Future work in our larger study will try to determine whether policies that continue the gendering of IT work exist at the same levels in applied disciplines as they have historically existed in computer science.

Acknowledgments

This study was funded by a National Science Foundation ITWF grant (no. 0305859), "Toward Gender Equitable Outcomes in Higher Education: Beyond Computer Science."

Notes

1. Though these response rates are lower than we would have liked, they are not unusual for Web-based surveys. Because we did not conduct a random sample survey, however, we make no claims as to the representativeness of this study. We present the results of the survey for what it is: responses from students in IT programs at five research universities in the United States. Yet we believe that these responses are not atypical for most students in IT programs in the United States.

2. For this analysis, we combined undergraduate and graduate students in each type of unit. While future analyses may focus on specific educational levels, a preliminary analysis of student attitudes by educational level did not reveal significant age- or educational-level-dependent differences. Also, splitting the sample by the type of unit, gender, and level would have made statistical differences difficult to determine. Further, the library and information science programs tend not to include an undergraduate component.

3. Because this study is not based on a random sample of students in the selected academic units, we cannot report the sampling error when percentages are given. Nevertheless, we do report statistical significance levels as a way of understanding the importance and the degree of difference between groups and between males and females for the variables in this research.

References

Ahuja, M., J. Robinson, S. C. Herring, and C. Ogan. 2004. Exploring antecedents of gender equitable outcomes in IT higher education. Paper presented at SIGMIS, Tucson.

Badagliacco, J. 1990. Gender and race differences in computing attitudes and experience. *Social Science Computer Review* 8:42–63.

Bentson, C. 2000. Why women hate IT. *CIO Magazine.* ⟨http://www.cio.com/archive/090100_women.html⟩.

Berghel, H., and D. L. Sallach. 2004. A paradigm shift in computing and IT education. *Communications of the ACM* 47:83–88.

Beyer, S., M. Chavez, and K. Rynes. 2002. Gender differences in attitudes toward and confidence in computer science. Paper presented at the annual meeting of the Midwestern Psychological Association, Chicago.

Beyer, S., K. Rynes, M. Chavez, K. Hay, and J. Perrault. 2002. Why are so few women in computer science? Paper presented at the annual meeting of the American Psychological Association, New Orleans.

Beyer, S., K. Rynes, J. Perrault, K. Hay, and S. Haller. 2003. Gender differences in computer science students. Paper presented at SIGCSE, Reno.

Clegg, S. 2001. Theorising the machine: Gender, education, and computing. *Gender and Education* 13:307–324.

Cohoon, J. M. 2001. Toward improving female retention in the computer science major. *Communications of the ACM* 44:108–114.

Colley, A., and C. Comber. 2003. Age and gender differences in computer use and attitudes among secondary school students: What has changed? *Educational Research* 45, no. 2:155–165.

Compeau, D., C. A. Higgins, and S. Huff. 1999. Social cognitive theory and individual reactions to computing technology: A longitudinal study. *MIS Quarterly* 23:145–158.

Creamer, E. G., C. J. Burger, and P. S. Meszaros. 2004. Characteristics of high school and college women interested in information technology. *Journal of Women and Minorities in Science and Engineering* 10:67–78.

Durndell, A., and Z. Haag. 2002. Computer self-efficacy, computer anxiety, attitudes towards the Internet, and reported experience with the Internet, by gender, in an East European sample. *Computers in Human Behavior* 18:521–535.

Fromme, J. 2003. Computer games as a part of children's culture. *Game Studies* 3, no. 1. ⟨http://www.gamestudies.org/0301/fromme/⟩.

Herring, S. C. 1993. Gender and democracy in computer-mediated communication. *Electronic Journal of Communication* 3, no. 2. ⟨http://hanbat.chungnam.ac.kr/~leejh/txt/Herring .txt⟩.

Kiesler, S., L. Sproull, and J. Eccles. 1985. Pool halls, chips, and war games: Women in the culture of computing. *Psychology of Women Quarterly* 9:451–462.

Kramer, P., and S. Lehman. 1990. Mismeasuring women: A critique of research on computer avoidance. *Signs* 16, no. 1:158–172.

Lee, A. C. K. 2003. Undergraduate students' gender differences in IT skills and attitudes. *Journal of Computer-Assisted Learning* 19:488–500.

Maata, S. 2003. Salaries stalled, jobs tight. *Library Journal* (October 15). ⟨http://www .libraryjournal.com/article/CA325077⟩.

Margolis, J., and A. Fisher. 2002. *Unlocking the clubhouse: Women in computing.* Cambridge, MA: MIT Press.

McCoy, L. P., and T. L. Heafner. 2004. Effect of gender on computer use and attitudes of college seniors. *Journal of Women and Minorities in Science and Engineering* 10:55–66.

Moorman, P., and E. Johnson. 2003. Still a stranger here: Attitudes among secondary school students towards computer science. Paper presented at the meeting of ITiCSE, Thessaloniki, Greece.

Natale, M. J. 2002. The effect of a male-oriented computer gaming culture on careers in the computer industry. *Computers and Society* 32, no. 2 (June): 24–31.

Oosterwegel, A., K. Littleton, and P. Light. 2004. Understanding computer-related attitudes through an idiographic analysis of gender- and self-representations. *Learning and Instruction* 14:215–233.

Quint, B. 1999. Gender equity in salaries achieved for some information professionals, but not for others. *Information Today* 16, no. 11:60–61.

Shashaani, L. 1994. Socioeconomic status, parents' sex-role stereotypes, and the gender gap in computing. *Journal of Research on Computing in Education* 26:433–451.

Tilleczek, K. C., and J. H. Lewko. 2001. Factors influencing the pursuit of health and science careers for Canadian adolescents in transition from school to work. *Journal of Youth Studies* 4:415–429.

Truell, A. D., J. E. Barlett, II, and M. A. Alexander. 2002. Response rate, speed, and completeness: A comparison of Internet-based and mail surveys. *Behavior Research Methods, Instruments, and Computers* 34, no. 1:46–49.

Turkle, S. 1988. Computational reticence: Why women fear the intimate machine. In *Technology and women's voices*, ed. C. Kramarae, 41–61. New York: Routledge.

Turner, S. V., P. W. Bernt, and N. Pecora. 2002. Why women choose information technology careers: Educational, social, and familial influences. Paper presented to the annual meeting of the American Educational Research Association, New Orleans.

U.S. Census Bureau. 2001. *Computer use and ownership* ⟨http://www.census.gov/population/www/socdemo/computer.html⟩.

U.S. Department of Commerce. 2000. *Falling through the Net: Toward digital inclusion; A report on Americans' access to technology tools.* ⟨http://www.ntia.doc.gov/reportsarchive2000_2003.html⟩.

Venkatesh, V., and M. Morris. 2000. Why don't men ever stop to ask for directions? Gender, social influence, and their role in technology acceptance and usage behavior. *MIS Quarterly* 24, no. 1:115–139.

Wolverton, M. 1999. The school superintendency: Male bastion or equal opportunity? *Advancing Women.* ⟨http://www.advancingwomen.com/awl/spring99/Wolverton/wolver.html⟩.

Young, B. J. 2000. Gender differences in student attitudes toward computers. *Journal of Research on Computing in Education* 33:204–216.

10

Confronting the "Socialization" Barrier: Cross-Ethnic Differences in Undergraduate Women's Preference for IT Education

Roli Varma, Amit Prasad, and Deepak Kapur

I would say that they're unique, you see them as ... you look at [a] girl ... she'd walk in as a fresher taking classes, and me and my friends always say that we'll give her three weeks. I mean maybe I'm being inconsiderate, maybe I'm basing it on appearance, and how she looks at a computer and the way she reacts to the computer versus somebody who comes and sits on the computer and knows, and is very, like,... knows all the windows tricks and knows all the commands.... So based on the lack of feel for the computer [I or other males view females in the way described].

—a male student

And ... men seem to have, at least some of the men that I've met in there,... seem to have more of a different attitude. Like, you know, I'm worried about whether I know everything. And there're a lot of guys that I've met in the program who may not know as much as me, but they've got the attitude that they know a lot ... so I'm wondering ... if they are going to have no problem getting a job after graduation, just because they have that attitude on, yeah, I know this, or I am so experienced. You know, that sort of a thing. Whereas the women tend to not act like that.... It's like sometimes I feel I have more knowledge, but they're more open about or they're more confident about what they think they know.

—a female student

The fact that there are fewer female students in computer science and computer engineering (CS/CE) courses, as compared to males, has been a serious concern for academics and policymakers (American Association of University Women 2000; Carver 2000; Camp 2002; Varma 2003). Scholars have not only analyzed different facets of gender disparity in CS/CE but have also attempted to provide policy guidelines in order to change the existing situation. A number of factors have been identified as affecting the enrollment and retention of female students in CS/CE programs such as: computer games being seldom designed with girls' interests in mind (Cassell and Jenkins 1998); the masculinity of computers, a lack of confidence, and gender socialization (Margolis and Fisher 2002); motivational differences (McClelland 2001); differences in learning strategies (Stepulevage and Plumeridge 1998); behaviors and negative attitudes toward women (Seymour and Hewitt 1997; Crombie, Abarbanel, and Anderson 2000); and the crises of nontraditional students, a lack of debugging skills, and poor time-management skills (Varma 2002).

This chapter, which is based on in-depth interviews with 150 male and female students belonging to five different ethnic/racial groups, is an attempt to contribute to this debate. We analyze the perceptions of male and female CS/CE undergraduate students with regard to gender-related issues and show how they are articulated. We shed light on the processual nature of the articulation of gendered perceptions by:

• showing how they occur through a dynamic and dialectical interplay of several factors such as gendered socialization, the attitudes of male students and instructors, the perception of females of their position in the program, curriculum, and so on;

• highlighting how the social backgrounds of racial/ethnic groups as well as males and females critically impact their perceptions.

We utilize Pierre Bourdieu's concept of "habitus" to explain how a set of experiences—in the school and through socialization at home or outside—constitute the "dispositions" of male and females students, which continually reproduce gendered and gendering differences, even though, as we found in our study, a majority of both male and female students feel that there is no gender difference. The two quotes at the beginning of this chapter—definitely not exceptions—exemplify that social environment in CS/CE programs is evidently gendered. The relevant thing to note about these quotes is that because gender differentiation constitutes the habitus of the students, even simple everyday actions are articulated through a gendered lens, which contributes to the further gendering of social interactions within the CS/CE field.

Before we move further, we would like to clarify how we are using the concept of habitus. According to Bourdieu, "the structures constitutive of a particular type of environment (e.g., the material condition of existence characteristic of class condition) produce *habitus*, systems of durable, transposable *dispositions*, structured structures predisposed to function as structuring structures" (1977, 72). Three aspects of Bourdieu's theory of practice, which are embodied in his concept of habitus, are relevant for the argument presented here:

• Any social action is articulated through the dialectic of past and present experiences. Past experiences, such as early childhood socialization, play a role by constituting the dispositions of the actors, but they acquire significance only in relation to the present social context within which the actor is performing his or her action.

• Social interaction between two individual actors always bears the imprint of the broader social context, which is embodied in one's habitus. The habitus is stable, but continually transforming through the dialectic of past and present experiences and individual actions in relation to the broader social context.

• Social actions are not simply a result of the objective evaluation of the conditions (e.g., instructor's gender bias) but always concatenated with one's subjective evaluations of the event, which is done through the dispositions that constitute one's habitus.

Through the concept of habitus, we argue that there are several social practices or experiences that explain and cause gender disparity in CS/CE programs. When students interpret particular social actions (such as the presence of fewer females or the instructor's behavior), all these practices are concatenated because they are expressed through the habitus and not simply as a response to the particular and immediate event. Males and females, however, interpret particular social interactions and the existing conditions within the CS/CE programs differently. We found that there are differences also along racial and ethnic lines. We contend that this happens because the set of dispositions that constitute the habitus of males and females, and also different racial/ethnic groups, are somewhat different, which makes them give different meanings to the same actions, or give a gendered connotation to a common and everyday social behavior.

Method

The focus of the study was undergraduate women in different ethnic groups. Interviews were conducted with women who had decided to major in the computer science or computer engineering fields so that they could identify the reasons for their attachment to a CS/CE education and career despite various barriers. In addition, the views of male students in each ethnic group for a comparative analysis were sought. The study was carried out at four-year colleges and universities that granted undergraduate degrees in one or more CS/CE programs, and were designated as a minority-serving institution such as a Hispanic-serving institution, a historically black college, or a tribal university.

Primary data were acquired through in-depth interviews in 2002–2003. The sessions involved using interview guides, asking open-ended questions, recording the answers, and following up with additional relevant questions or probes. The technique of in-depth interviews was considered useful mostly because there is little information on the barriers women in different ethnic groups face in pursuing CS/CE.[1] Interviews also seemed the most appropriate way to track down the factors relevant to a preference for CS/CE education. Interactive probing through interviews permitted access to the unconscious and inaccessible aspects that had a bearing on the tangible and intangible barriers women face in pursuing a CS/CE education.

Interviews were conducted with 150 subjects, including 15 male and 15 female students at seven institutions majoring in computer science or computer engineering, and belonging to each of the following five racial/ethnic groups—namely, white, black, Hispanic, Asian, and American Indian.[2] Random sampling was used to select subjects on sites with sufficient numbers of women and men. Nevertheless, purposive sampling was used on sites where the numbers of some minority groups (e.g., American Indians and Asians) and women majoring in either discipline were small.

In this chapter, we have analyzed the responses of our interviewees on eight out of a total of sixty-one questions that we had asked them: In your opinion, what is it like to be a woman in your CS/CE program? Do any incidents come to mind that are related to being a woman in the program? Do you consider yourself as strong or stronger in CS/CE as the other women and men in your program? Why do you think there are so few women in your CS/CE program? Do women encounter obstacles that men do not? In your experience, how do the men you know in CS/CE view the women in their program? In your opinion, are careers with a CS/CE degree attractive to women? And if you could change some things about your current CS/CE program to make it more attractive to women, what would they be and why? These eight questions were chosen because they reveal the perceptions of female and male students with regard to gender-related issues.

Being a Woman in the CS/CE Programs

Just that sometimes, like, I'm scared to speak or ask questions because, you know, I mean, guys might think, you know, because I'm a woman. You know, 'cause I'm a lady.
—a female American Indian student

When the students were asked whether any incident comes to mind that is related to being a woman in the CS/CE program, 58 percent of them said none (see table 10.1). More females replied in the negative (62.7 percent) than males (53.4 percent). Yet what we found is that even when students negated any experience of gendered

Table 10.1
Memory of incidents related to being a woman in the program

Categories	White (%)		Black (%)		Hispanic (%)		American Indian (%)		Asian (%)		Total* (%)
	F	M	F	M	F	M	F	M	F	M	
None	47	53	60	60	73	40	73	60	60	53	58 (87)
Prejudice	13	13	20	7	7	13		7	13	7	9 (13)
Instructor-related issues	13	13		20		7		7			6 (9)
Socialization	7					7	7	7	13	7	5 (7)
Privileged		13	7			13	7	7			4 (6)
Fewer females	7	13	7	7							2 (3)
Other	13	7	7	7	20		7	13	7	20	10 (15)
No response			7	7		20	7		7	13	6 (9)
Total	100%	99%	101%	101%	100%	100%	101%	101%	100%	100%	101% (150)

Note: *Totals in the right-hand column are in percentages (rounded off to the nearest whole number) with the actual numbers in parentheses.

interactions in the program, they would often still express that there were some essential gender differences between males and females. For example, one female student said, "No.... Mainly, they [males] adapt more easily so." Another female student added after replying in the negative, "I guess we're more stubborn."

The consciousness of being a female (and different from males) in CS/CE is reinforced for a variety of reasons, most of all due to the fact that there are fewer females in these programs. When the students were asked, "What is it like to be a woman in your CS/CE program?" a large number of them (27 percent) mentioned the presence of fewer females (see table 10.2). When students were asked about incidents that related to being a woman in the program, the response of only 2 percent was that there are fewer females.

Bourdieu (1977, 1990, 2001; see also Moi 1991; Krais 1993; Swartz 1997) argues that "symbolic violence" is an important strategy of the dominant group to control and maintain its privileges and practices. Symbolic violence, according to Bourdieu, does not entail any overt acts of violence; rather, it is a method of censoring voices, beliefs, and practices by designating them unorthodox (or "heterodox," as Bourdieu would put it) or anomalous in relation to the already existing practices and beliefs (which are favorable to the members of the dominant group). The first instance of symbolic violence, however, as our study shows, occurs not in censoring certain behaviors and practices but in defining the presence of a group in a particular domain such as a specific career or program in college (in our case, females in CS/CE programs) as an anomaly. Hence, the very fact that there are fewer females in CS/CE programs becomes an anomaly that needs to be explained and made sense of. To clarify at the outset, we are not trying to assert that there are no gender or racial/ethnic differences, or that such differences are constructed with no real basis. Instead, what we are attempting to show is how the presence of fewer females necessitates that both males and females make sense of it through essential gender differences—and this is done in relation to an individual's past experiences.

Both the males and the females in our study utilized their habitus (i.e., their past social experiences embodied in their consciousness) to make sense of the anomaly of fewer females in CS/CE through the gendered categorization of behaviors and abilities. Males (29 percent) were more conscious of the anomaly of the presence of fewer females in CS/CE than females were (24 percent). One of the male students said, "I think, the only thing I can think of is in some of the classes I've been, there might be like two girls, maybe two or three girls. And they sort of sit together, and *it's almost them against us*, or something like that" (emphasis added). The presence of fewer females, therefore, constitutes the first instance of the gendering of the CS/

Table 10.2
What is it like to be a woman in your CS/CE program?

Categories*	White (%)		Black (%)		Hispanic (%)		American Indian (%)		Asian (%)		Total* (%)
	F	M	F	M	F	M	F	M	F	M	
Fewer females	33	47	7	13	33	40	20	7	27	40	27 (40)
No gender difference	33	13	27	27	27	13	20	33	40	7	23 (34)
Prejudices	7	13	20	7	13	33		7	7	13	10 (15)
Privileged		7		7			7	7		20	8 (12)
Equalizer	7		13	13	7		7		13	7	7 (10)
Racial minority			13	7	13		7	13			5 (8)
Male preoccupation			7	7			7	7			3 (4)
Discrimination	13	13	13	20			7				3 (4)
Other	7	7	13		7	7	20	20	7	13	12 (18)
No response						7	13	7	7		3 (5)
Total	100%	100%	100%	101%	100%	100%	101%	101%	101%	101%	101% (150)

Note: *Totals in the right-hand column are in percentages (rounded off to the nearest whole number) with the actual numbers in parentheses.

CE programs.[3] Moreover, since the present context (the presence of fewer females) is framed in relation to the already existing habitus in the student's mind, the relationship becomes gendered and females are marked out. Hence, even though a majority of students say that they cannot think of instances that remind them of being a woman in the CS/CE programs, we have to be careful because very often simple, everyday actions that may not seem gendered, exemplify gender differentiations.

Among the males, more whites (47 percent), Hispanics (40 percent), and Asians (40 percent) noticed that there were fewer females than blacks (13 percent) and American Indians (7 percent). Interestingly, whites (13 percent), Asians (7 percent), and Hispanics (0 percent) were also the least likely to respond that there was no gender difference. Males belonging to these three ethnic/racial groups were also much more unsympathetic in their responses toward the existing gender disparity in CS/CE programs. An Asian male said, "To be a woman in computer science? It is greater [better] if you just change your major into something else. [Why do you say that?] Because, like, just stories I've heard and its inside scene from different professors. I don't think that they expect a woman to be in the computer science field. Nope."

Similarly, a white male responded, "I think that there is a lot of bias that comes in and it's also a part of the mentality of the woman coming in. She thinks that there's going to be a bias so she can find it where she needs to. I think that in general, this department has been very, very good about accepting female students and female faculty, and being very warm and accepting of, or rather impartial toward, either men or women. However, there're of course those issues everywhere, so." Black (27 percent) and American Indian (33 percent) males more often responded that there was no gender difference, and they were also more sympathetic when they talked about prejudice toward females. This could be because blacks (10 percent) and American Indians (10 percent), apart from Hispanic females (13 percent), were the only ones to express that their racial status further erodes their numbers in the class. A greater consciousness of racial discrimination perhaps makes the students belonging to these racial/ethnic groups more sensitive to gender discrimination.

As for the females, the consciousness of their anomalous position sometimes makes them respond negatively to what is regarded as feminine. A black female student reflected such a concern vividly when she said, "Like, there's this one girl that's in the program. And . . . I guess, to a guy, she wouldn't appear to look smart, I mean because, like, she, you know, tries to dress up every day. You know, be all pretty or whatever, like wear heels, . . . she wears dresses really feminine. . . . And I guess *guys kind of tend to see her as, like, a girl rather than a, like, a smart person*" (emphasis added).

Very often females, like their male counterparts, made sense of the presence of fewer females in the CS/CE programs through gender differences. For example, a white female student said, "I don't think it is any different from being a man. It just so happens that men have more logical minds. You know what I mean? Women are good at English, [and] men are more good at math. That's, like, always been the kind of norm. But for some odd reason, I'm better at math. But there is generally a lot fewer women in computer science than there are men."

The response of the female student exemplifies the processual and dialectical character of gendered perception, and illustrates the importance of our framework in analyzing gender-related issues in CS/CE programs. The student begins with a negation of gender differences; thereafter, she expresses the stereotype of an intrinsic male-female difference and then attempts to explain her own ability (of being good at math) by pointing out that she may be an exception because there are so few women in the program. Moreover, as the quote at the beginning of this section shows, a particular reaction of being a female is intimately connected to a female's perception of how a male thinks about females. Such a perception, however, is not a figment of females' imagination; it has to be seen in the broader gendered context of the CS/CE program.

Being a woman in the CS/CE programs at present, therefore, means to be constantly aware that they are perceived as an anomaly. Males are more conscious of this, and their day-to-day actions, which are interpreted through a gendered lens, continuously reinforce a gendered interpretation of women's actions and even their presence in the program. There are racial/ethnic differences among the responses of the males, as we have described, but it seems the consciousness of being a woman far overwhelms the responses of females and hence shows insignificant ethnic/racial differences. Nevertheless, females—not unlike the males—very often interpret the presence of fewer females through essential gender differences.

I Am As Good If Not Better

Actually, I think I'm definitely as good as them. . . . I don't want to say I'm better, but I work harder.
—a white female student

Students were in general guarded in their response to the question of whether they consider themselves as good as or better than other female and males students in the

CS/CE program. Nevertheless, the responses of the students show some fascinating gender and racial/ethnic differences (see table 10.3).

A significant percentage of male students (27 percent) chose not to respond to this question. In terms of race and ethnicity, a majority of the white (67 percent) and black (53 percent) males did not respond. We cannot ascertain the exact reasons for these nonresponses, yet it is evident from the people who did respond, particularly the females, that they responded because they felt the need to expressly prove their worth. Thus, the racial and ethnic differences in the no response category could be a reflection of who feels the need to overtly state their worth. Students were aware that even though the presence and success of males is considered a norm in the CS/CE field, it is the white male who forms the role model in this regard. A black student, while responding to what it was like being a woman in a CS/CE program, said, "As far as being a woman, I don't think they expect too many women to be in that area; as far as black woman, they don't expect you to be there at all. They all expect [it to be a] male issue, a white male issue." What we are trying to indicate is that students are aware that CS/CE programs are not only seen as male domains but usually the white male is seen as the role model, and that impacts students' responses, particularly those of blacks and whites, perhaps because race in the United States is so often seen through the dualist lens of white and black.

Irrespective of their race or ethnicity, a majority of females said that they were as good as, if not better than, other students, including the males. If we add to this category of females, other females who thought they were better in some areas and not in others (i.e., who responded yes and no), we find that almost 80 percent of women felt confident that they were as good in CS/CE as anybody else in the class, at least in some areas. In terms of racial/ethnic differences among the females, the Asian students' responses stand out. All the Asian females felt that they were as good as, if not better than, their classmates. A significant percentage of Asian women (67 percent) also felt that females do not encounter any obstacle that is unique to being a woman in the program. As one Asian female remarked, "Like, the whole gender thing doesn't really intimidate me at all. I'm just another person in the same program as they are."

Female and male students cited several reasons why they felt they were as good as, if not better than, their female and male classmates (see table 10.4). A large percentage of students (42 percent) felt that they were as good as anybody else (i.e., their response was "same"). One student responded, "I'll say about the same. There are some qualities that some people have that other people don't, so like it kind of

Table 10.3
Are you as strong or stronger than other female and male students?

Categories	White (%) F	White (%) M	Black (%) F	Black (%) M	Hispanic (%) F	Hispanic (%) M	American Indian (%) F	American Indian (%) M	Asian (%) F	Asian (%) M	Total*
Yes	73	27	87	20	60	53	80	60	100	53	61 (92)
Yes and no	13			13	13			7		13	6 (9)
Don't know				7						7	1 (2)
No	13	7	13	7	20	7	13	7			9 (13)
No response		67		53	7	40	7	27		27	23 (34)
Total	99%	101%	100%	100%	100%	100%	100%	101%	100%	100%	100% (150)

Note: *Totals in the right-hand column are in percentages (rounded off to the nearest whole number) with the actual numbers in parentheses.

Table 10.4
Reasons why a student thinks s/he is as strong or stronger as compared to other students

Categories	White (%)		Black (%)		Hispanic (%)		American Indian (%)		Asian (%)		Total* (%)
	F	M	F	M	F	M	F	M	F	M	
Same	15	25	38	20	36	75	58	70	33	50	42 (42)
Drive	8	25	15		9		8				7 (7)
Attitude	8			40					13		6 (6)
Hard work	8					13	8			10	4 (4)
Grades	8								20		4 (4)
Grasping ability	8								13		3 (3)
Experience	15									10	3 (3)
Knowledge		25						10			1 (1)
Variable	8		15	20	18	13		10		20	10 (10)
Other	8			20	9		16	10	20	10	10 (10)
No reason given	15	25	31		27		8				11 (11)
Total	99%	100%	99%	100%	99%	101%	98%	100%	99%	100%	101% (101)
	(13)	(4)	(13)	(5)	(11)	(8)	(12)	(10)	(15)	(10)	(101)

Note: *Totals are in percentages (rounded off to nearest whole number) with the actual numbers in parentheses.

all averages out in the end." Some students felt that they were as good as others because of their attitude or drive. One Asian female student, who thought she was as good as, if not better than, others because of her attitude, commented, "I may be better than many students because of [my] strong background in math and sciences back in India. I think you have to be smart to be successful." But then she added, "A lot of smartness does come from learning, so at the beginning nobody knows anything." Among the students who thought they were not as good as others (i.e., responded no), drive (39 percent) was cited as an important reason.

It has been generally argued that females in CS/CE programs suffer because of a lack of confidence. Males also feel the need to bolster their confidence every once in a while, however. An Asian male said, "Yes, [I am as good as others,] as I get to know more people, I feel more confident because some of the people that I consider to be really smart, I actually find that I am on the same level as some, not all of them, but more than I thought." The crucial thing to note here is that even though this male student expresses some insecurity with regard to his confidence, it is not given a gendered spin. This again exemplifies our claim that the marking out of the females, which occurs in the context of the presence of fewer females, leads to a gendering of only female behaviors and practices.

Often, males as well as females referred to their grades, ability to work hard, or job experience to argue why they were as good as, if not better than, other students. Several male students belonging to different racial and ethnic groups said that they found many of their female friends as smart as, if not smarter than, themselves. A belief in one's ability, as is evident from the answers to the question "Do you feel you are as good as, if not better than, others?" does exist among the females, and often males also thought that their female colleagues were as good as them. But such a belief is frequently challenged by the belief in and experience of males' chauvinistic behavior toward females in CS/CE programs. We have to keep in mind that males need not directly express chauvinistic behavior toward females in the classroom or otherwise. But because social interaction in the CS/CE programs take place through and within a set of dispositions (that constitute the habitus of these students) that is gendered, such evaluations are not unusual, and even one action that reflects such chauvinism enforces such a belief. That is to say, male-female interactions in CS/CE programs, even if they are between particular people and about particular issues, often have a broader connotation and have to be analyzed as such.

When the students were asked how the males in CS/CE view their female classmates, most of the students (56 percent of the females and 60 percent of the males) replied that males treat females as equal and as peers. Yet 20 percent of the females and 13 percent of the males thought that men were chauvinistic—in the sense that there is a belief that men think that they are smarter or more capable than women. A white female said, "I'm sure they think that we aren't anywhere as good as they are. They're all extremely egotistical." When she was asked how the women viewed the men, she replied, "They're all nerds. They have absolutely no lives. Yeah . . . and nothing else." A Hispanic female observed that "they think that you are not as smart as they, but you know it's normal." Such beliefs and experiences, even though they are not that of the majority, continue to affect the interactions in CS/CE programs because they start constituting the dispositions of students, leading to, for example, a lack of confidence or fear among females about presenting their ideas. Habitus as a theory of practice, therefore, provides a useful framework to understand how social interactions in the CS/CE programs have a gendered impact because they are articulated through the dialectic of past and present experiences, and concatenated with other social actions that constitute the broader context that is gendered.

Males, when they talked about male chauvinism, said that they thought or had heard other men refer to females in the class as "little sisters." It is relevant to note that the same students who talked about females being referred to as little sisters because the females, according to them, needed help, did not use a similar phrase for the males needing help. Again, with regard to male chauvinism too, particular social experiences have an impact on how people think. As a black male told us, "A few have issues with them [females]. Like, they feel that a woman is inferior, period. And since I grew up in an intercity black family with a woman as the head of my household, so I view women totally differently." What we find is that because of the differing habitus of different racial/ethnic groups, and among males and females, the reactions are different.

There were several students who cited instances of gender prejudice in the CS/CE programs (see table 10.1). Among the responses of students, three categories stand out: prejudice (9 percent), instructor-related issues (6 percent), and socialization (5 percent). Another category, privileged (4 percent), also bears on students' responses. The relevant thing to note about these responses, however, is that even though they can be classified in different categories, it is evident that most often they reflect a person's wider set of dispositions that constitute his or her habitus. Hence, a black male student replied, "There is a fellow classmate of mine, whenever she produces work, it's questioned because, you know, they might say, 'Oh, where did you get it from? I know you didn't do it. Who did you copy it from?'" When we asked the student why that is the case, he responded, "Because, no offense, but most of them do that, they use the fact that they are female to get things done. I've seen personally even teachers are submissive to females rather than males, and, like, once that happens to a few girls, it's kind of, like, everyone's questioning all females and, like, that's [a] problem."

As we can see from this quote, even though the student expresses a genuine concern over the way his female friend is questioned, his explanation eventually takes a gendered form. Male students, even when they mentioned cases of prejudice against females, explained the existence of such prejudice as a result of the females' dependency, which arises out of their being privileged. Female students are well aware of the existence of such a conception among males and its implication toward discrediting their work. A female student informed us that "some classmates, like one or two, they say, like, if I get an interview or whatever, they say it's because, like, I'm pretty.... And that's not true, [I get interview calls] because I've [got] a good GPA and I have a nice résumé."

Several male students, irrespective of their race or ethnicity, expressed that females receive privileged treatment. They are often aware that their female colleagues perceive the treatment meted out to them differently. Nonetheless, they continue to believe that females are more privileged. A white male student put it thus: "The only thing that comes to my mind is, there is a special treatment, for instance by Professor S.... From what I remember, the few girls in this class, essentially what happens is, he makes it easier for them to pass, at the same time what I heard from them, he makes it more difficult for the girls to pass." It seems confounding how males and females belonging to the same class view the behavior of the instructor so differently. The problem is that because of socialization at home as well as in school, and the fact that CS/CE programs reflect gendered constructions in different ways, the males' dispositions are tuned to see females as an anomaly within the CS/CE programs, and so they continue to visualize different actions and behavior along gendered lines, which in turn leads to the further gendering of social interactions.

A larger percentage of female students (15 percent) stated that there was no gender difference as compared to male students (8 percent), and almost an equal number of females from different racial/ethnic groups thought there was no gender difference. Irrespective of their racial or ethnic status, though, an almost similar number of females and males felt that there were prejudices against women in CS/CE programs. Sometimes, such prejudices were interpreted through the lens of intrinsic male/female difference, but women in general expressed confidence that they are competent enough to cope with it. Several women, irrespective of their racial or ethnic status, also thought that the fact that females are beginning to join CS/CE programs, and hence going against the stereotype, is acting as an equalizer. Again, this was at times expressed in light of the particular social background of a student. For example, a black female student said, "As far as, like, being a minority woman, not everybody is a minority it seems like. But being a minority woman, it is kind of neat just because you know, like, it's saying you know, like, you are being masochistic, you know what I mean. I don't know, it is just kind of neat."

CS/CE Careers for Women

Some [CS careers] are [good for women] and some aren't. A lot of women don't want to be away from home or away from the family. I'm a really family-oriented person, and a lot of my friends are.... I don't think there are a lot of positions where you could say, "I'm a woman. I want to do this." ... You know, you might have kids. You know, it's still all that maternity leave thing. You know, even with all the laws and everything. But still, I think it's a hindrance for a lot of women.
—a black female student

A majority of students (62 percent) said that a CS/CE career was favorable to women. A larger percentage of females (68 percent) thought this to be the case than males did (56 percent). Students cited a variety of reasons to explain why a CS/CE career was favorable to females.

The responses of the women who said that a CS/CE career is attractive reflect a combination of the advantage of being fewer in number, and hence in greater demand, and the advantages they have over males. A black female said, "Yes. Because I believe that companies are going to look for a token." An Asian woman explained, "Personally, I feel like that gives us an advantage to be a woman just because they don't have so many, and they'd wanna kind of change things, as an advantage. I just applied for an internship and there were some group activities, and at the group activities the guys were, like, more pouncing on each other, trying to take step, and the girls were kinda more relaxed, and we got the problem solved."

Some women thought that a CS/CE career is attractive to females because they can work from home (5 percent). The fact that a CS/CE career nowadays allows for the possibility of working from home was a big relief for several women because, as the quote at the beginning of this section shows, being at home and with their family is a big concern for females. In our sample, at least some males and females belonging to all five racial/ethnic categories had children (while none of the males had more than two children, some of the females did). Yet it was only the females who mentioned that taking care of children and home took up a lot of their time. Females also stated they would like to combine having a home with children and their work; no male expressed such a desire, even though several of them had children too. Several females thought that a CS/CE career was attractive for females because it was challenging and satisfying. A white female said, "To me it is. Because that's what I want to do. And it's satisfaction. It's hard, but it's fun. It's challenging. I get a sense of accomplishment. But, yeah, ... you could get that somewhere else, but for me, it's been the only field where I've actually been challenged." One encouraging aspect of the females' responses was that some of them cited their own case as evidence that women should find a CS/CE career more attractive.

Among the people who said that a CS/CE career was not attractive for women, the most frequent reason cited was that it is unfeminine (33 percent). Males far outnumbered the females in saying that a CS/CE career may not be attractive for females because it is unfeminine. Forty-one percent of the males who thought that a CS/CE career was not attractive to females, said it was because the career was unfeminine. More white (27 percent), Hispanic (19 percent), and Asian males (13 percent) gave this reason than blacks (6 percent) and American Indians (7 percent). These cases again illustrate how the responses of males and females as well as those of different ethnic/racial groups are guided by their habitus.

We were also interested in finding out what suggestions students themselves had for making CS/CE programs attractive to women. We found that a large percentage of the respondents (25 percent) were unsure of what changes could be made for this purpose. Some of them (8 percent) said that no change was required in the system.

Nearly 10 percent of the respondents felt that hiring more women faculty in CS/CE programs would make them more attractive to females. A white female noted, "I think more female faculty would help. Especially undergrad. To have somebody to go to and talk [to]. Because female, women, talk differently than men." The males who suggested that having more female faculty would make CS/CE programs more attractive to females, thought that it would provide females with more role models. "I suppose it would help to have more role models for women," one white male commented. A black male responded, "Maybe have more minority women faculty. We can't change the way people think, and especially older people, you know they're like, this is the way I've got here and this is the way it's going to be."

More male respondents recommended changes such as providing more women faculty, offering more scholarships, influencing females in high school, and advertising than did female respondents. On the other hand, more females than males recommended changes such as influencing girl students in elementary schools through mentorship program and support groups as well as making curriculum more sensitive to female needs. The concern of females, therefore, is not so much directed at having more support as having a more *understanding support*, either through faculty, mentors, or support groups that can understand their interests better, or a curriculum that is more sensitive to their needs.

The suggestions of the students also showed certain racial/ethnic differences. Whites (15 percent) and blacks (19 percent) said hiring more women faculty would help make CS/CE programs more attractive to women, while none of the Asians thought so. Asians suggested that changes should be implemented more in terms of the material conditions, such as offering monetary help (10 percent) or supplementary and introductory courses (20 percent). For Hispanic students, the most important concerns were providing support groups (10 percent), doing better advertisement to attract more females (10 percent), and making changes in the curriculum (10 percent).

The responses of Hispanic students, as for students belonging to other racial/ethnic groups, have to be seen in light of their social background—Hispanic students (10 percent) were the only ones (apart from one American Indian) to say that their social background was an obstacle to pursuing a CS/CE career. A Hispanic male student explained that "for Hispanics, I'd say it's mostly just cultural. It's tough to say because, you know, I've worked with people out at [X] outreach programs and everything like that. And I mean, I remember it's like 40 percent Hispanic kids don't even graduate high school, much less even go on to college, much less even pursue a technical degree."

The social background that Hispanics saw as an obstacle was articulated as something particular to them. A Hispanic female said, "As a Hispanic, I would say that the way the race is, that family comes first, so there're times when I'm trying to study for a test or something and I get a call from my parents.... I have to, like, go home. See, that is one thing that is challenging; if you're a Hispanic, your parents teach you that your family comes first, regardless [of] whatever happens, you know, you have to be there." Similarly, an American Indian male said, "As far as, like, putting a computer language into use back home, like, say, if I'm from [X] I say the woman does not have the chance to put her knowledge to use in the [existing

American Indian] cultural context, so the value of knowing how to program is not there." What we again find, therefore, is that the habitus of students varies with regard to gender or race and ethnicity, and it affects their responses toward CS/CE education.

Conclusion and Implications

In this chapter, we have attempted to refine the debate over gender disparity and issues in CS/CE programs by showing how different social behaviors and experiences act dialectically in constituting a gendered environment in the programs, thereby affecting the perceptions of students and impacting their responses. The analytic framework of habitus that we have used here allows us to understand some key aspects of gender-related issues in CS/CE education. For example, the role of early socialization has been emphasized by many scholars; but the question arises, Why did the number of females who earned bachelor's degrees in computer science increase until 1985 and then decline?[4] Does this mean that gendered socialization during childhood and school did not have a significant impact until 1985? Our study shows that the impact of socialization is not redundant but instead becomes visible in the context of the present gendered environment in CS/CE, which in turn emerges in the first instance because the presence of females in these programs is seen as an anomaly.

It is also striking, as we have described in this chapter, that most students, males and females included, believe that there is no gender difference or that they do not remember any instances that remind them of being a woman in CS/CE programs, and yet their responses often have gendered connotations. Further, it seems intriguing that even though so many studies have emphasized that females suffer from a lack of confidence, which we found in our study too, an overwhelming majority of them told us that they thought they were as good as, if not better than, other male and females students.

An important implication of the theoretical framework that we have used here is that it allows us to understand the processual nature of the articulation of gendered perceptions in CS/CE programs. Past experiences, such as early gendered socialization, do have an impact, but they take prominence when they are articulated through and within the dialectic of the present gendered environment in CS/CE programs. Moreover, social actions do not take place independently of each other but are concatenated with each other, and the responses of students are based on their dispositions, which constitute their habitus. Hence, even though females feel confident, the belief and experience of male chauvinistic behavior challenges their confidence, making them conscious of their being an anomaly within CS/CE programs.

Similarly, males most often said that they find that they are as good as other female and male students, and frequently praised the abilities of their female colleagues, but as we have shown in this chapter, they still often gave a gendered spin to the simple, everyday actions of females. The other important implication of our theoretical framework is that it makes it evident that the gendered and gendering issues within CS/CE programs cannot be seen or tackled as female problems because they are equally (or more) male problems. In fact, females' perceptions of themselves are intimately connected to what males think of females, which itself is concatenated with, and arises out of, several other factors that constitute the gendered environment of CS/CE programs and the habitus of the students.

As we have shown, there are several objective conditions, either in school (i.e., in CS/CE programs) or outside it, that critically impact the existing gender disparity in CS/CE programs. Through the concept of habitus, however, we have illustrated that more often than not, it is the subjective evaluation of these objective conditions that gives even simple, everyday actions or behaviors a gendered flavor, thereby further gendering social interactions within programs. The set of dispositions that constitute the habitus of students changes over time. But even as special measures are undertaken to recruit and retain more females in CS/CE programs, gendered perceptions and interactions may continue to exist. Hence, along with changes in objective conditions such as curriculum, advertisement, hiring more female mentors or faculty, and so on, there is a need to discuss these issues not only among academics and policymakers but also with students.

Our aim here has not been to offer new policy guidelines but to show how the policy guidelines can be refined and made more effective. This chapter shows that even though on the surface the responses of males and females as well as students belonging to different racial/ethnic groups may reveal some similarities, we have to be careful and analyze them in light of their habitus. For example, for a Hispanic, an Asian, a black, a white, or an American Indian student, social background constitutes different elements, and in order for the policies to be effective we have to be sensitive to these differences. To put it succinctly, in Dean John White's words, "If we want a different outcome, we're going to do things differently. We're making too little progress doing more of the same thing" (quoted in Cuny and Aspray, 2002, 168).

Acknowledgments

This research was supported by a grant from the National Science Foundation (EIA–0305898). We would like to thank all the interviewees, who gave us their valuable time, and Bhavana Upadhyaya, for assisting in the data analysis.

Notes

1. Existing studies have not made a distinction among different fields in science and engineering when assessing the underrepresentation of women. Margolis and Fisher (2002) have done an empirical study specific to computer science at the Carnegie Mellon University on this issue. Their study, however, does not have a diverse representation of women, especially minority women.

2. This racial/ethnic classification is similar to that used by the National Science Foundation.

3. There has been a particular line of study in the social sciences that following Georg Simmel (1950), has attempted to analyze the significance of numbers in social life and show how "numerical modifications effect quantitative transformations in group interaction" (Kanter 1977, 965).

4. The number of females earning bachelor's degrees in computer science increased from 2,463 to 14,431 between 1979 and 1985, and then steadily declined to 7,063 in 1995. From 1995 on, the number of females earning bachelor's degrees in computer science steadily increased, but by 2000 it was still below the 1985 mark (National Science Board 2004, 2–23).

References

American Association of University Women. 2000. *Tech-savvy: Educating girls in the new computer age.* Washington, DC: AAUW.

Bourdieu, P. 1977. *Outline of a theory of practice.* Trans. R. Nice. New York: Cambridge University Press.

Bourdieu, P. 1990. *The logic of practice.* Trans. R. Nice. Stanford, CA: Stanford University Press.

Bourdieu, P. 2001. *Masculine domination.* Trans. R. Nice. Stanford, CA: Stanford University Press.

Camp, T., ed. 2002. *Special Issue on Women and Computing, SIGCSE Bulletin* 34, no. 2:1–208.

Carver, D. L. 2000. *Research foundation for improving the representation of women in the information technology workforce: Virtual workshop report.* Arlington, VA: National Science Foundation.

Cassell, J., and H. Jenkins, eds. 1998. *From Barbie to Mortal Kombat: Gender and computer games.* Cambridge, MA: MIT Press.

Crombie, G., T. Abarbanel, and C. Anderson. 2000. Getting girls into tech classrooms. *National Association of Secondary School Principals Bulletin* 84:64–73.

Cuny, J., and W. Aspray. 2002. Recruitment and retention of women graduate students in computer science and engineering: Results of a workshop organized by the Computing Research Association, San Francisco, June 21–22, 2000. *SIGCSE Bulletin: Special Issue on Women and Computing* 34:168–174.

Kanter, R. M. 1977. Some effects of proportions on group life: Skewed sex ratios and responses to token women. *American Journal of Sociology* 82, no. 5:965–990.

Krais, B. 1993. Gender and symbolic violence: Female oppression in the light of Pierre Bourdieu's theory of social practice. In *Bourdieu: Critical perspectives*, ed. C. Calhoun, E. LiPuma, and M. Postone, 156–177. Chicago: University of Chicago Press.

Margolis, J., and A. Fisher. 2002. *Unlocking the clubhouse: Women in computing*. Cambridge, MA: MIT Press.

McClelland, M. 2001. Closing the IT gap for race and gender. *Educational Computing Research* 25:5–15.

Moi, T. 1991. Appropriating Bourdieu: Feminist theory and Pierre Bourdieu's sociology of culture. *New Literary History* 22, no. 4:1017–1049.

National Science Board. 2004. *Science and engineering indicators*. NSB 04–1A. Arlington, VA: National Science Foundation.

Seymour, E., and N. M. Hewitt. 1997. *Talking about leaving: Why undergraduates leave the sciences*. Boulder, CO: Westview Press.

Simmel, G. 1950. *The sociology of Georg Simmel*. Trans. and ed. K. H. Wolff. Glencoe, IL: Free Press.

Stepulevage, L., and S. Plumeridge. 1998. Women taking positions within computer science. *Gender and Education* 10:313–327.

Swartz, D. 1997. *Culture and power: The sociology of Pierre Bourdieu*. Chicago: University of Chicago Press.

Varma, R. 2002. Women in information technology: A case study of undergraduate students in a minority-serving institution. *Bulletin of Science, Technology, and Society* 22:274–282.

Varma, R., ed. 2003. *Special Issue on Women and Minorities in Information Technology, IEEE Technology and Society* 22, no. 3:1–48.

11

Women in Computer Science or Management Information Systems Courses: A Comparative Analysis

Sylvia Beyer and Michelle DeKeuster

This chapter discusses our research on three issues related to women's representation in undergraduate IT majors. First, we present our findings regarding gender differences in computer science and management information systems (MIS) students. Second, we explore the predictors of female and male students' academic success in computer science and MIS. Third, we compare our findings for computer science and MIS students.

Both computer science and MIS fall within the broad area called IT. Computer science is more technical, and requires the ability to design, implement, and manage complex information systems. MIS is less technical, but requires more business expertise, and rests on the ability to collect, process, and distribute data for use in decision making in businesses. Much of the previous research on women in IT implicitly assumed that results would generalize from one IT area to other fields within IT. In contrast, we hypothesize that results from one area of IT do not necessarily generalize to another, using computer science and MIS as our test cases. Given the inherent differences between these two fields, coupled with the different atmospheres likely encountered in highly technical versus business-oriented fields, we expected different challenges for women majoring in computer science versus MIS.

Prior to discussing our results, we present a literature review of variables that relate to women's entry, persistence, and academic success in computer-related fields. Our previous research found that women have inaccurately low self-efficacy in domains traditionally considered masculine, including mathematics and chemistry (Beyer 1990, 1998, 1999b, 2002; Beyer and Bowden 1997). Low self-efficacy has also been found for computer science (e.g., Beyer et al. 2003; Dickhäuser and Stiensmeier-Pelster 2003; Lips 2004). Although women extensively use computers as tools, they typically have little experience in programming (Beyer, DeKeuster, Rynes, and DeHeer 2004; Beyer, Rynes, and Haller 2004; Margolis and Fisher 2002).

Computer science is stereotyped as even more male dominated than the traditional male bastions of chemistry and mathematics (Beyer 1999a). Both men and women *incorrectly* believe that male computer science majors have higher GPAs than female ones (Beyer 1999a). In addition, the stereotypes about individuals in computer-related fields are unflattering: computer science majors are perceived as intelligent, but interpersonally deficient and asocial (American Association of University Women 2000; Beyer, Rynes, and Haller 2004). This has been termed the "computer nerd syndrome," "geek mythology," or "hacker mentality" (Jepson and Perl 2002; Margolis and Fisher 2002; Rasmussen and Hapnes 1991). Computer science is incorrectly perceived as involving only programming and no creativity (Craig et al. 1998; Rasmussen and Hapnes 1991; Schinzel 1997). The stereotypes of computer science majors as nerds, their perceived obsession with machines and lack of interest in people, and associations of technology with masculinity conflict more with the gender roles of women than with those of men (Cross and Madson 1997; Markus and Kitayama 1991). Women's desire to have a more "balanced" life with multiple roles and goals (Eccles 1994; Eccles, Barber, and Jozefowicz 1999) possibly deters women from majoring in computer science. Unfortunately, women are not aware that computer-related work can be people oriented (Teague and Clarke 1991). At this point, we know very little about the stereotypes about MIS students. The present research aims to fill this gap.

We have at least a rudimentary understanding of what deters women from taking computer science classes (see also Lagesen 2002; Margolis and Fisher 2002). Departmental and classroom climates in computer science also affect the academic success of students (Margolis and Fisher 2002). Unfortunately, computer science courses are "bastions of poor pedagogy" (American Association of University Women 2000, 41), with instructors who are more aloof and unsupportive than those in other disciplines (Barker, Garvin-Doxas, and Jackson 2002). Social support and faculty encouragement are even more important to women's than men's decisions to enroll in or leave computer science (Cuny et al. 2003; Margolis and Fisher 2002). Indeed, "female students in technical disciplines, perhaps partly because of their 'outsider-ness,' are especially vulnerable to poor teaching, inhospitable teaching environments (such as large classes), and unhelpful faculty" (Margolis and Fisher 2002, 83). Again, we know much less about MIS students because presently most research on gender issues in MIS has focused on the workforce. While such research represents a laudable effort, we believe that an examination of gender issues in MIS undergraduate education is imperative because it represents a bottleneck in the supply of women qualified to enter the MIS workforce. For this reason, we will examine gender issues in MIS students.

In addition, we know little about whether variables such as computer self-efficacy, stereotypes about computer science or MIS, gender roles, stress, and role models affect students' success in computer science or MIS courses. A unique goal of our research was to identify a profile of students in general, with a special interest in women, who do well in these classes. Understanding what contributes to success in computer science or MIS can aid in our efforts to recruit and retain computer science or MIS majors.

Method

Participants

All participants were enrolled at the University of Wisconsin–Parkside, a small, public university. We note that this might limit the generalizability of our findings to similar institutions.

For our computer science sample, 180 students (62 females and 118 males) enrolled in a computer science course in 2001 or 2002 filled out our survey. Ninety-one students were computer science majors (21 females and 70 males) enrolled in a variety of the computer science courses required for the major. Eighty-nine students were non-CS majors (41 females and 48 males) enrolled in one of several computer literacy courses offered by the computer science department. These computer literacy courses (e.g., computer productivity tools) do not carry credit toward the major. Our sample consisted of 67.8 percent Caucasian, 8.9 percent Asian, 7.2 percent Hispanic, and 6.1 percent African American students. The remaining participants chose not to identify their race. We note that computer science nonmajors were younger (at an average age of 22.7 years) than computer science majors (25.1 years).

For our MIS sample, 98 business majors (47 females and 51 males) enrolled in an MIS course during the 2001 and 2002 academic years filled out our survey. Fifty-four students (18 females and 36 males) had MIS as their concentration within the business major (referred to as MIS majors). Forty-four students (29 females and 15 males) had a business concentration outside of MIS (referred to as non-MIS majors), but were taking an MIS course designed for nonmajors. Our sample consisted of 74.5 percent Caucasian, 5.1 percent Hispanic, 3.1 percent Asian, and 2 percent African American students. The remaining participants chose not to identify their race.

MIS majors (at an average age of 25.1 years) and nonmajors (24.4 years) did not differ much in age.

To encourage participants to complete the survey, a nominal reward of two dollars was included with the survey. Both samples received identical surveys except that questions referred to computer science or MIS, respectively. We assessed students' computer experience and self-efficacy, beliefs and stereotypes about computer science or MIS, gender roles and stress, and role models. We used a combination of existing instruments and items created specifically for our research. Most survey questions used either five- or seven-point Likert rating scales. Furthermore, we had students' permission to obtain their ACT scores and college grades.

Materials

Mathematical Preparation, Computer Experience, and Self-Efficacy   To assess participants' mathematics preparation, we obtained their mathematics ACT scores. To assess the frequency of computer use and computer experience, we asked students how many hours per week they used a computer and what kinds of computer experiences they had (e.g., programming), respectively. We assessed how comfortable students are with computers by asking if they had ever opened up a computer to install hardware. To gauge participants' self-efficacy regarding computer skills, we asked how difficult eight specific computer tasks would be for them. Factor analysis yielded two separate factors: one measured self-efficacy for relatively easy computer tasks that do not require programming, and the other measured self-efficacy for more complex computing tasks involving programming.

Beliefs and Stereotypes about Computer Science and MIS   We assessed whether students felt that females have as much computer ability as males. We constructed scales to assess stereotypes about both majors by having participants rate the personality characteristics of computer science or MIS majors. A factor analysis of the eleven items yielded three factors: "nerd," popular, and good student characteristics (e.g., hardworking, intelligent). We asked students to estimate how many hours per week a computer scientist or an MIS professional works. We used seven items from the Role Conflict Scale (Lips 1992) to assess participants' opinions of the compatibility of work and family for women in both majors, and the sociability of computer scientists or MIS professionals. Also, we constructed a twelve-item scale measuring students' beliefs regarding what a computer science or an MIS degree would enable them to do (e.g., help people). We constructed a gender-discrimination scale that included four items: "female students aren't taken seriously by male faculty," "ability of female computer science or MIS students is often underrated by others," "faculty often question female computer science or MIS students' commitment to their studies," and "I believe there is gender discrimination in the computer science or MIS program." We formed a composite gender-discrimination score of the sum of these four items.

Gender Roles and Stress   Participants completed the Bem Sex Role Inventory (Bem 1974), which consists of forty traits that are rated with respect to the self (e.g., nurturing, aggressive). Their gender roles were classified according to norms provided by Bem. Participants also filled out a fourteen-item stress scale (Cohen, Karmarck, and Mermelstein 1983).

Role Models   We asked students to rate the knowledge of their high school computer teachers and asked them to indicate the sex of these teachers. In addition, we inquired whether they knew someone with a computer science or an MIS degree prior to taking their first computer science or MIS course.

Results

We will present the results in two sections. Part 1 examines gender differences in between computer science and MIS students. In Part 2, our goal is to predict students' computer science or MIS GPAs after the spring 2003 semester—that is, one to three semesters after they had filled out the initial survey. In both parts, we will compare the findings for computer science and MIS students.

One limitation of the present research is the relatively small sample of female computer science majors. We are currently gathering additional data to increase our sample size, so we remind the reader that the present findings for female computer science students should be considered somewhat preliminary.

Part 1: Gender Differences in Computer Science versus MIS Students

To analyze gender differences, we performed separate 2 (participant gender) × 2 (major versus nonmajor status) analyses of variance for computer science and MIS students. Analyses on dichotomous data used χ^2 statistics. Table 11.1 presents the means. Because the issue of interest is gender differences, we will not report on the significant main effects of students' major status. Significant interactions between

Table 11.1
Means for computer science and MIS students

Dependent variables	Computer science students				MIS students			
	Majors		Nonmajors		Majors		Nonmajors	
	Women	Men	Women	Men	Women	Men	Women	Men
Mathematics ACT scores	24.4	24.6	21.7	22.2	20.6	21.5	22.1	20.6
GPA in CS/MIS classes	2.8	2.8	2.5	2.6	3.1	3.1	3.4	3.1
Hours/week computer used for enjoyment	5.9	11.3	8.0	10.5	4.3	11.0	3.8	4.5
Programming experience	95.2	97.1	53.7	72.9	88.9	97.2	17.2	40.0
Installed RAM	42.9	81.4	40.0	58.3	38.9	72.2	3.4	46.7
Computer self-efficacy***	4.1	5.5	3.8	4.1	4.9	5.8	4.1	3.9
Females have as much computer ability as males***	6.3	6.6	6.6	6.3	6.8	6.3	6.6	7.0
Stereotype that CS/MIS majors are good students***	6.1	6.0	6.2	6.1	5.9	5.6	5.3	5.3
Stereotype that CS/MIS students are nerdy***	4.5	4.9	4.9	5.0	4.2	4.2	4.2	4.7
Stereotype that CS/MIS students are popular***	4.1	4.0	3.6	3.9	4.4	4.7	4.5	4.1
Belief that women computer scientists/MIS professionals can't combine family and a career***	2.6	2.5	2.4	2.6	1.9	2.3	2.5	2.6
Estimated hours/week worked by a CS/MIS professional	46.9	45.3	47.9	44.6	46.3	49.2	47.7	47.8
Perception that computer scientists/MIS professionals are loners***	2.4	3.2	3.0	3.5	2.3	2.6	2.9	3.0
Belief that CS/MIS degree enables one to help others**	3.3	3.2	3.4	3.2	3.9	3.3	3.7	3.6
Gender discrimination***	2.6	1.9	3.1	3.1	2.5	1.8	2.6	2.3
Masculinity***	4.9	5.1	4.9	5.3	5.0	5.6	5.0	5.5
Stress*	1.9	1.7	1.9	1.7	1.8	1.5	1.8	1.2
Knowledge of computer teachers in high school***	4.6	4.3	4.8	4.5	5.2	4.6	5.3	4.3
Sex of computer teachers in high school***	3.6	3.9	4.0	4.0	5.5	3.1	4.3	4.1
Knew someone in CS/MIS	61.9	48.6	41.5	52.1	38.9	45.7	44.8	33.3

Notes:
* 1–4 scale
** 1–5 scale
*** 1–7 scale

gender and major status will of course be mentioned. Please note that when we refer to "students" in the results, we include both majors and nonmajors. If the results apply only to majors or nonmajors, we explicitly state that. Differences in number (N) are due to either missing values, or the addition or deletion of a few questions in surveys distributed in different semesters.

Mathematical Preparation, Computer Experience, and Self-Efficacy   There were no significant gender differences in ACT mathematics scores for computer science, $F(1, 89) < 1$, or MIS students $F(1, 52) < 1$. Male computer science students spent more time using a computer for enjoyment than did female ones, $F(1, 171) = 8.04$, $p = .01$. For MIS students, a significant interaction between gender and major status indicates that while male MIS majors spent more time than female MIS majors using a computer for enjoyment, there was no gender difference in the amount of time that nonmajors spent on the computer, $F(1, 91) = 5.71$, $p = .02$.

In the computer science sample, more men than women had experience using computers for programming, $\chi^2(1, N = 180) = 9.91$, $p < .002$, or had installed hardware such as RAM in a computer, $\chi^2(1, N = 179) = 16.37$, $p < .0001$. Similarly, in the MIS sample, more men than women had programming experience, $\chi^2(1, N = 98) = 13.42$, $p < .0001$, or had installed RAM in a computer, $\chi^2(1, N = 98) = 22.86$, $p < .0001$.

To determine whether there was a gender difference in computer self-efficacy when controlling for mathematical ability, we regressed participants' self-efficacy on gender, major status, mathematics ACT score, and their interactions. Lower Ns for these analyses are due to the fact that ACT scores were unavailable for some participants. For computer science students, the interaction between mathematics ACT scores and gender, $F(1, 85) = 4.01$, $p = .05$, and that interaction between gender and major, $F(1, 85) = 5.16$, $p = .03$, predicted students' computer self-efficacy. As can be seen in figure 11.1, male computer science students' computer self-efficacy did not depend on their math ACT score, whereas female computer science students' computer self-efficacy did. Women with low math ACT scores had lower computer self-efficacy than women with high math ACT scores. Furthermore, female computer science majors had less computer self-efficacy than male majors regardless of their ACT scores, although the confidence gap was smallest for female and male computer science majors with high math ACT scores. Thus, female computer science students' computer self-efficacy was lower than males', even when we statistically controlled quantitative ability. For the MIS sample, men and women were equally confident regarding their computer abilities, $F(1, 49) < 1$.

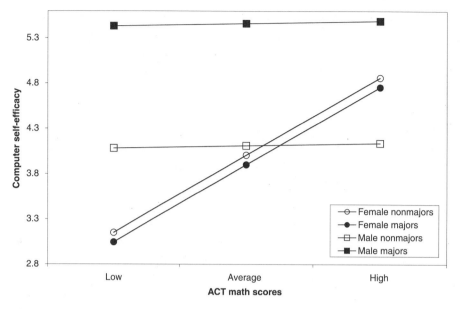

Figure 11.1
Computer science students' computer self-efficacy

Beliefs and Stereotypes about Computer Science and MIS   In the computer science sample, there was a borderline significant gender by major status interaction for students' opinion that females have as much computer ability as males, $F(1, 119) = 3.64$, $p = .06$. Male majors and female nonmajors were more likely than female majors and male nonmajors to believe that women's computer ability equals men's. In contrast, female and male MIS students did not differ in their opinion that women's computer ability equals men's, $F(1, 38) < 1$. The fact that female computer science majors were less convinced than male majors of women's computer ability is troubling in light of the finding that this variable is important in predicting course success (see part 2).

There were no gender differences in the stereotypes that computer science students are good students, $F(1, 176) < 1$, nerds, $F(1, 147) < 1$, or popular, $F(1, 176) < 1$. Similarly, there were no gender differences in the stereotypes that MIS students are good students, $F(1, 67) = 1.04$, $p = .31$, nerds, $F(1, 69) < 1$, or popular, $F(1, 65) < 1$. Thus, computer science students, and to a somewhat lesser degree MIS students, were perceived to be good students, but somewhat nerdy and not very popular. Male computer science students felt that computer scientists are loners more than female computer science students did, $F(1,169) = 10.38$, $p = .002$. Yet there was no gender difference in the stereotype that MIS professionals are loners, $F(1,94) < 1$.

There was no gender difference in the perception that women can combine family and career in computer science, $F(1,175) < 1$, or MIS, $F(1,93) = 1.32$, $p = .25$. Female computer science students, however, believed that computer scientists work more hours per week than male computer science students did, $F(1,168) = 5.70$, $p = .02$. There was no gender difference for the estimated number of hours an MIS professional works each week, $F(1,93) < 1$.

Students were asked to rate what either degree would allow them to do. The only item for which we found a gender difference was "helping people." For the computer science sample, there was no gender difference, $F(1,176) < 1$, but female MIS students were more likely to believe that an MIS degree enables one to help people than males did, $F(1,88) = 4.94$, $p = .03$.

Finally, there was no gender difference in perceived gender discrimination in the computer science program, $F(1,167) < 1$. Nevertheless, female MIS students reported greater gender discrimination in the MIS program than did male MIS students, $F(1,95) = 4.40$, $p = .04$.

Gender Roles and Stress   Not surprisingly, male computer science and MIS students' gender roles were more masculine than were female computer science and MIS students', $F(1,171) = 6.85$, $p = .01$, and $F(1,95) = 8.17$, $p = .005$, respectively. For example, men were more likely to describe themselves as independent, assertive, and forceful than women. As part 2 will show, these gender roles have implications for success in computer science and MIS courses. Women reported greater feelings of stress than men in the computer science, $F(1,145) = 4.81$, $p = .03$, and MIS samples, $F(1,68) = 9.60$, $p = .003$. Part 2 will reveal the negative consequences of this for academic success.

Role Models   Participants rated how knowledgeable their computer teachers had been in high school. Lower Ns than for other analyses indicate that some students did not have a computer teacher in high school. No gender differences emerged for how knowledgeable CS participants rated their high school computer teachers, $F(1,160) < 1$. In contrast, female MIS students rated their high school computer teachers as more knowledgeable than their male MIS counterparts did, $F(1,89) = 6.54$, $p = .01$. Female and male computer science students did not differ in the sex of their computer teachers in high school, $F(1, 166) < 1$. For MIS students, however, there was a highly significant interaction between participant gender and major status, $F(1, 89) = 8.67$, $p = .004$. While there was no gender difference for nonmajors, female majors indicated that they had had more female computer teachers in high school than male majors indicated.

Forty-nine percent of computer science participants knew someone with a computer science degree prior to taking their first computer class. This did not differ significantly by gender, $\chi^2(1, N = 180) = .042$, $p < .84$. Forty-two percent of participants knew someone with an MIS degree prior to taking an MIS class. This also did not differ significantly by gender, $\chi^2(1, N = 97) = .003$, $p = .96$.

Part 2: Predictors of Student Success in Computer Science and MIS Courses

A second goal of this study was to determine if the variables we assessed could predict computer science or MIS GPAs. We are presenting the results of multiple regression analyses where gender, major status (major versus nonmajor), students' responses on their initial surveys, and their interactions were used to predict students' GPAs after spring 2003, one to three semesters after they had filled out the initial surveys, as mentioned above.

Computer Experience and Self-Efficacy   It seems reasonable to expect that computer experience variables such as prior programming experience or having installed RAM would predict computer science or MIS GPAs, giving male students an edge in their class performance. Yet none of the computer experience variables in this study predicted these GPAs one to three semesters later.

The effect of computer self-efficacy indicates that those computer science students with the highest computer self-efficacy also had the highest computer science GPAs one to three semesters later, $F(1, 167) = 4.99$, $p = .03$. The finding from part 1 that female computer science students have lower computer self-efficacy thus implies a negative effect on their computer science GPA. Computer confidence did not predict MIS GPAs, $F(1, 90) < 1$.

Beliefs and Stereotypes about Computer Science and MIS   The borderline interaction between gender and students' belief that women have as much computer ability as men indicates that the more female computer science students thought that women's computer ability equals men's, the higher their computer science

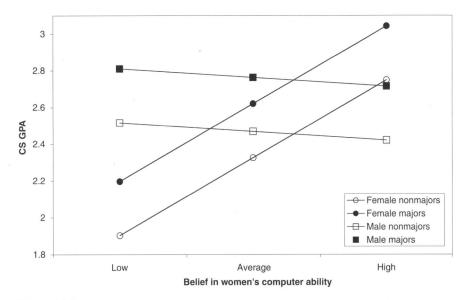

Figure 11.2
Computer science students' belief that women have as much computer ability as men predicts computer science GPA

GPAs, $F(1, 113) = 3.70$, $p = .06$. This is of concern because as part 1 pointed out, female computer science majors were less likely than male CS majors to believe that women have as much computer ability as men. As can be seen in figure 11.2, male computer science students' beliefs about female students' competence did not predict their computer science GPAs. Gender differences in MIS students' opinion that women have as much computer ability as men did not predict MIS GPAs, $F(1, 134) < 1$.

Computer science students who believed that computer scientists enjoy being around and working with people had higher computer science GPAs one to three semesters later than did students who thought that computer scientists are less social, $F(1, 166) = 6.57$, $p = .01$. Figure 11.3 illustrates the significant triple interaction between gender, major status, and the belief that computer scientists work with people, $F(1, 166) = 5.64$, $p = .02$. Female computer science majors who believed that computer scientists enjoy being around and working with people had higher computer science GPAs than did female computer science majors who did not believe that computer scientists work with people. This relation was somewhat

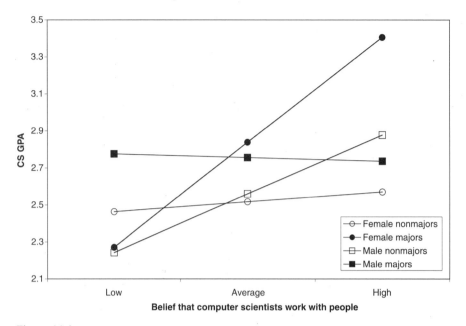

CS GPA

Belief that computer scientists work with people

- ─○─ Female nonmajors
- ─●─ Female majors
- ─□─ Male nonmajors
- ─■─ Male majors

Figure 11.3
Belief that computer scientists work with people as predictor of computer science GPA

attenuated for male nonmajors, and nonexistent for male majors and female nonmajors.

The interaction between major status and the perception that MIS professionals work with and enjoy being around people predicted MIS GPAs, $F(1, 87) = 6.26$, $p = .01$. No gender effects emerged for MIS students. Contrary to computer science students, MIS majors who thought that MIS professionals enjoy being around and working with other people had *lower* MIS GPAs. This relation did not hold for nonmajors.

Computer science students who believed that there was gender discrimination in their program had lower computer science GPAs one to three semesters later, $F(1, 165) = 4.57$, $p = .03$. There was also a borderline interaction between gender and perceived gender discrimination, $F(1, 165) = 3.55$, $p = .06$. Figure 11.4 reveals that perceived gender discrimination related negatively to female students' computer science GPAs, but did not predict male students' computer science GPAs. For MIS students, the belief that there was gender discrimination in the MIS program predicted lower MIS GPAs for male and female students alike, to a borderline signifi-

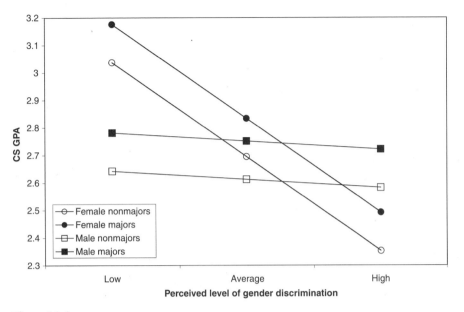

Figure 11.4
Gender discrimination in the computer science program as predictor of computer science GPA

cant degree, $F(1, 90) = 3.15$, $p = .08$. In part 1, we reported that female students perceived more gender discrimination in the MIS department than male students did. This should depress female MIS majors' MIS GPA.

Gender Roles and Stress There was a borderline interaction between gender and students' masculinity as measured by the Bem Sex Role Inventory (i.e., those who described themselves as assertive, independent, forceful, competitive, etc.), $F(1, 165) = 3.66$, $p = .06$, indicating that female computer science students with a masculine gender role had lower computer science GPAs than female students who were less masculine. Figure 11.5 shows that for male students, masculinity was unrelated to computer science GPAs. In contrast, MIS students who were high in masculinity had *higher* MIS GPAs than those who scored lower in masculinity, $F(1, 88) = 4.29$, $p = .04$ (see figure 11.6). As we pointed out in part 1, males are more masculine than females. Thus, male MIS students' MIS GPAs might benefit from their masculine gender role.

Stress predicted lower GPAs for both computer science, $F(1, 139) = 4.71$, $p = .03$, and MIS, $F(1, 63) = 6.14$, $p = .02$. Although stress affected the GPAs of

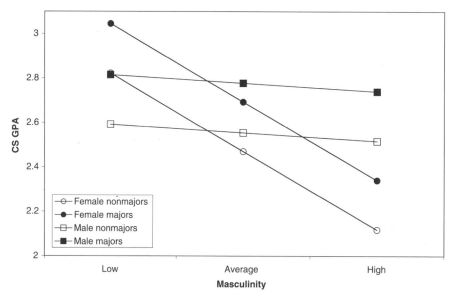

Figure 11.5
Masculinity as predictor of computer science students' GPA

male and female students equally, women's higher levels of stress (see part 1) should have a negative effect on their computer science and MIS GPAs.

Role Models   Students who knew a computer scientist prior to taking their first computer science class had higher computer science GPAs than did students who did not know one, $F(1, 170) = 5.38$, $p = .02$. As can be seen in figure 11.7, there was a borderline interaction between gender and knowing a computer scientist, $F(1, 170) = 2.96$, $p = .09$, indicating that this relation was stronger for female than male students. For the MIS sample, knowing someone with an MIS degree prior to taking an MIS class did not predict MIS GPAs, $F(1, 89) < 1$.

Discussion

This research examined a large number of variables that could adversely affect women's entry, retention, and academic success in computer science or MIS. Below we compare our findings for computer science and MIS in tabular form. We subsequently discuss our findings regarding gender differences and predictors of academic

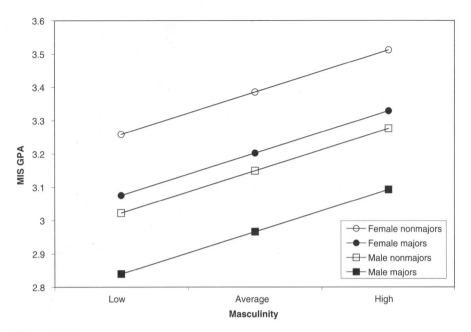

Figure 11.6
Masculinity as a predictor of MIS students' GPA

success. Furthermore, we outline the implications of our results for women's entry, persistence, and academic success in computer science and MIS.

Comparison of Computer Science and MIS Findings

Table 11.2 summarizes our major findings regarding gender differences in computer science and MIS students. Table 11.3 lists predictors of computer science and MIS GPAs. Both tables emphasize the similarities and differences in our results for computer science and MIS students.

Tables 11.2 and 11.3 clearly illustrate that only a few of our results regarding significant gender differences and predictors of academic success held for both computer science and MIS. We note that most of the findings that held for both computer science and MIS students are those that have also been mentioned in the research literature of fields outside of IT. For example, gender differences in computer use for enjoyment, programming experience, and masculinity have been found for undeclared first-year students (Beyer, Rynes, and Haller 2004); women generally report higher levels of stress than men (Ptacek, Smith, and Zanas 1992);

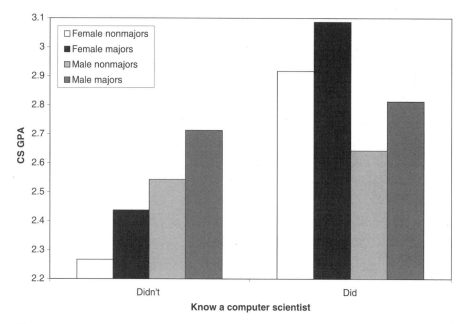

Figure 11.7
Knowing a computer scientist as predictor of computer science GPA

and stress has been shown to negatively affect academic performance in the natural sciences (Hackett et al. 1992). Thus, the fact that our findings for these variables converged for computer science and MIS merely demonstrates general gender differences or effects, rather than the generalization of findings from one area in IT to another.

We highlight one finding that is specific to computer science: male computer science students had higher computing self-efficacy than did female computer science students, whereas there was no gender difference for MIS. This is particularly interesting because male MIS students had more programming experience than female MIS students. Apparently for MIS students, this difference in programming experience did not translate into lower computer self-efficacy for women. We may speculate whether the greater prominence of the male "hacker" culture in computer science contributes to female computer science students' lower computer self-efficacy. It is striking that female computer science majors' computer self-efficacy was actually lower than the computer self-efficacy of female MIS majors (see table 11.1).

Table 11.2
Significant gender differences by IT discipline

Dependent variable	Direction of result	Discipline specificity
Computer use for enjoyment	CS: Males greater than females; MIS: Male majors greater than female majors	CS and MIS
Programming experience	Males greater than females	CS and MIS
Masculinity	Males greater than females	CS and MIS
Stress	Females greater than males	CS and MIS
Computing self-efficacy	Males greater than females	CS only
Belief that women's computing ability equals men's	Male majors greater than female majors; female nonmajors greater than male nonmajors	CS only
Estimated work hours of CS/MIS professionals	Females greater than males	CS only
Belief that CS/MIS professionals are loners	Males greater than females	CS only
CS/MIS major allows graduates to help others	Females greater than males	MIS only
Gender discrimination in department	Females greater than males	MIS only
Knowledge of computer teachers in high school	Females greater than males	MIS only
More female computer teachers in high school	Female majors greater than male majors	MIS only

Table 11.3
Predictors of computer science and MIS GPAs for computer science and MIS

Predictor of CS/MIS GPA	Direction of result	Discipline specificity
Gender discrimination in department	Females in CS, and males and females in MIS: Lower GPA	CS and MIS
Stress	Lower GPA	CS and MIS
Computing self-efficacy	Higher GPA	CS only
Belief that women's computing ability equals men's	Higher GPA	CS only
Knowing someone in CS/MIS	Higher GPA	CS only
Masculinity	Females in CS: Lower GPA MIS: Higher GPA	Opposite results for CS and MIS
Belief that CS/MIS professionals enjoy working with people	Female CS majors: Higher GPA MIS students: Lower GPA	Different results for CS and MIS

We also note that gender differences in stereotypes and perceptions about computer science and MIS are particularly field specific. Thus, we caution researchers to be careful in generalizing findings pertaining to stereotypes and perceptions of one IT field to another.

This low level of generalizability of findings across two IT fields cannot simply be dismissed as an artifact of different levels of statistical power for the two samples. Although our sample size for computer science was almost double that for MIS, several findings held only for MIS. The differences in our results for computer science and MIS do suggest that researchers should not assume the generalizability of results across IT disciplines.

Gender Differences and Predictors of Academic Success

Although we found no gender differences in mathematical preparation, female computer science, but not MIS, students' computing self-efficacy was lower than that of their male counterparts. Other researchers have also found lower computing self-efficacy in women (e.g., Lips 2004). In fact, girls have lower computer self-efficacy than boys as early as fifth grade (Dickhäuser and Stiensmeier-Pelster 2003). One cause of women's low self-efficacy may be their less playful and relaxed attitude toward computers (Rasmussen and Hapnes 1991). They see computers as tools rather than toys (Berg et al. 2002; Margolis and Fisher 2002). We know that self-efficacy is affected by the amount of previous experience with computers (Zubrow 1987). Indeed, women reported less programming experience than men. It is likely that a lack of programming experience coupled with less hands-on technical experience, such as installing internal components, adversely affects women's computer self-efficacy. Still, other factors probably contribute to female computer science students' lower self-efficacy. Despite female MIS students' lesser programming experience, they did not have significantly lower computer self-efficacy than male MIS students.

Eccles's (1994; Eccles, Barber, and Jozefowicz 1999; Jacobs et al. 2002) and Bandura's (1997) research has shown that self-efficacy affects aspirations, educational choices, intrinsic motivation, and persistence (for a review, see Beyer 1995). This suggests that female computer science students' lower computer self-efficacy decreases the likelihood that they will major in computer science and increases the likelihood that female computer science majors will change their major. Lips and Temple (1990), using structural equation modeling to predict entry into computer science, also suggested that efforts to increase women's computing and mathematical self-efficacy would positively affect the number of women majoring in computer science. Computer self-efficacy predicts future involvement with computers (Compeau, Higgins, and Huff 1999).

Instructors may play a positive role in bolstering female students' self-efficacy. Instructors who encourage their female students and steer them to activities that increase their practical skills such as internships or teaching or lab assistantships may not only increase female computer science students' practical skills but their computer self-efficacy as well. Such actions may be of lesser importance for female MIS students, whose computer self-efficacy was not different from their male counterparts'. So far, few interventions aimed at increasing the representation of women in computer science have emphasized skill development (American Association of University Women 2004). Beyer and Langenfeld (2000) found that women's self-perceptions are more influenced by evaluative feedback than men's, especially when the feedback is negative. Men often discount negative feedback (Roberts and Nolen-Hoeksema 1989, 1994). This suggests that the same negative comment from an instructor is more likely to lead to performance decrements for females than males. Female computer science students' lower computer self-efficacy is of concern because self-efficacy predicts computer science GPAs. Both female and male computer science students with low computer self-efficacy had lower computer science GPAs than their more self-efficacious counterparts.

Interestingly, computer experience did *not* predict either computer science or MIS GPAs. We note that other researchers did find a relation between computer experience and grades (Bunderson and Christensen 1995; Byrne and Lyons 2001; Margolis and Fisher 2002; Sackrowitz and Parelius 1996). Our finding may be attributable to either or both of the following reasons: possibly women quickly make up any initial deficit in computer experience, or alternatively, previous computer experience is not absolutely essential for success in computer science or MIS courses, as long as the student possesses the appropriate quantitative preparation. As we mentioned in part 1, there were no gender differences in the math ACT scores of male and female students, suggesting that male and female students had equivalent levels of math preparation.

It is important to note that despite the fact that female computer science students had less experience with computers and lower computer self-efficacy, they did not have more negative attitudes toward computer science, MIS, or computers per se than did male students. We also emphasize that there were few gender differences regarding stereotypes about computer science or MIS. The few gender differences that emerged actually suggest more positive attitudes on the part of females. For example, female MIS students were more likely than male MIS students to believe that an MIS degree would enable them to help people, and female computer science students had less negative perceptions of computer scientists than did male computer science students. Female and male students alike perceived computer science majors—and to a somewhat lesser degree, MIS majors—to be intelligent but somewhat nerdy and unpopular. Computer scientists and MIS professionals were seen as loners. Although male and female students subscribed equally to the stereotypes of computer science and MIS majors, these stereotypes conflict more with women's rather than men's gender roles (Cross and Madson 1997; Markus and Kitayama 1991). For instance, women more so than men value careers that allow them to help others, work with people, and provide the opportunity to combine career and family (Creamer, Burger, and Meszaros 2004; Eccles 1994; Margolis and Fisher 2002; Sax 1994). Even though few students believed that women in computer science or MIS cannot combine raising a family and having a career, female computer science students thought that computer scientists work more hours than male computer science students thought, which should raise doubts about the compatibility of career and family life. The belief that computer scientists enjoy working with people positively predicted computer science GPAs more strongly for female than male computer science students. This suggests that for female computer science majors, the ability to be around and work with people is an important concern that motivates them to do well (cf. Margolis and Fisher 2002). This disconnect between women's goals and their perceptions of computer science and MIS might deter female nonmajors from majoring in computer science or MIS, and might increase the attrition rate of female computer science and MIS majors. Because the stereotypes of MIS majors were less "nerdlike," female students are probably less deterred from majoring or remaining in MIS than computer science. This might explain, in part, why MIS is less male dominated than computer science.

We found that gender stereotypes play an important role. For example, female computer science majors were less likely than either male computer science majors or female nonmajors to espouse the belief that women are as good at computers as men. This may negatively impact their GPAs in computer science courses because the belief that women's computer ability equals men's positively predicted the computer science GPAs of female computer science students. This suggests that the less female computer science students buy into the cultural stereotype about women and computers, the better their performance in computer science courses. Another study found that female majors in math-intensive fields who had a feminine gender identity had more negative implicit (i.e., unaware) attitudes toward math than did their male counterparts (Nosek, Banaji, and Greenwald 2002). Female computer science or MIS majors do not have to "endorse gender stereotypes consciously for these stereotypes to have a mental existence and to influence behavior" (Nosek, Banaji, and Greenwald 2002, 57).

We assessed computer science and MIS students' gender roles because previous research suggested that women who pursue male-dominated majors often have nontraditional gender roles (Casserly and Rock 1985; Lent, Lopez, and Bieschke 1991). We found that masculinity negatively predicted computer science GPAs for female computer science students. In stark contrast, masculinity positively predicted MIS GPAs. Maybe the advice to "act like a man" to succeed in male-dominated domains is counterproductive for women in computer science, but may work for female MIS majors to some degree.

Interestingly, women perceived more gender discrimination in the MIS program at our institution than did men, whereas no gender difference emerged for computer science. These results are of course specific to our institution. In another computer science department, however, 18 percent of women reported feeling that they were treated differently from men (Bunderson and Christensen 1995). We did find that perceived gender discrimination was a negative predictor of female and male students' MIS GPAs and female students' computer science GPAs. Thus, perceived gender discrimination is a critical variable that negatively relates to the academic performance of female and even some male students. This chilling effect on performance is likely to deter female nonmajors from taking further computer science or MIS courses, and may lead female computer science or MIS majors to change their major.

One of the most interesting findings of this study was the importance of high school computer teachers. Female MIS majors had more female computer teachers in high school than men had—a difference not found for MIS nonmajors or computer science students. In addition, female MIS students rated their former computer teachers as more knowledgeable than male students did. The retrospective nature of these accounts makes it impossible to disentangle whether this difference in experiences with female computer teachers is real. Conceivably, competent female computer teachers in high school serve as an inspiration for women. On the other hand, female MIS students may incorrectly remember how many female computer teachers they had. Yet a study of female engineering students in Germany also found that secondary school teachers encouraged these talented young women (Blättel-Mink 2002). Furthermore, a case study of female informatics (computer science) students in Germany found that positive experiences with computer teachers in secondary school cemented their interest in computer science (Huber et al. 2001). Over 39 percent of female engineering students had fathers who were engineers, again pointing to the importance of role models (Blättel-Mink 2002). Indeed, Norwegian research found that role model days for students at the secondary school level can increase female participation in computer science courses (Lagesen 2002; MacKeogh 2002).

In our sample of computer science students, females were not significantly more likely to rate their former computer teachers as knowledgeable or to indicate that their teachers had been female. But another question relating to role models turned out to be important for them. Having known a computer scientist prior to taking computer science classes positively predicted computer science GPAs more strongly for female compared to male computer science students. This suggests that exposure to computer scientists relates positively to performance in computer science courses. Thus, exposure to role models, be it computer teachers in high school or computer scientists, might be a crucial predictor of eventual interest and success in a computer-related major. We point out again that although role models play an important role for computer science and MIS students, different role models seem to affect computer science versus MIS students.

Conclusions

Our findings suggest possible avenues for increasing the representation of women in computer science and MIS. It appears that role models are critical in getting women interested in computer-related fields. To increase retention, departments need to carefully avoid creating any perception of gender discrimination, which was found to be a negative predictor of GPAs in computer science and MIS. At the same time, our results indicate that computer science departments that communicate to their students that women have as much computer ability as men and that computer scientists work with people rather than just machines, may have a positive impact on their female students' course success.

Computer science is notorious for its demanding course work and programming assignments that keep students up until the morning hours. We found that computer science and MIS students who experience high levels of stress have lower CS and MIS GPAs than students who experience less stress. Hackett, Betz, Casas, and Rocha-Singh (1992) also found that stress is inversely related to academic success and persistence, especially for women in male-dominated fields. Importantly, female computer science and MIS students experienced higher levels of stress than did male students. Computer science and MIS courses may thus weed out otherwise highly capable students, especially women, who turn to majors that are less stressful.

We also point out again that computer experience did *not* predict either computer science or MIS GPAs in our sample of male and female students with approximately equivalent levels of math preparation. Computer science and MIS departments that have stringent entry requirements focusing on computer or programming experience should take note of this. Computer experience may be important in other ways, however. For example, one potential explanation of women's lower computer self-efficacy is a lack of experience in programming and hands-on technical expertise such as installing RAM. We found no gender differences in experience with e-mail, word processing, or data analysis. Indeed, researchers using national data found the same (College Board 2003; DeBell and Chapman 2003). Thus, experience in these areas cannot explain the gender difference in computer self-efficacy. To increase the number of women in computer-related fields, we have to realize that exposing them to computers is not enough. Programming experience and the comfort level with computers that comes from opening up a machine, putting it back together, and having it work, might be crucial experiences for all students interested in computer-related fields, but might be particularly important for women's computer self-efficacy.

Beyond the specific findings of this research, a key contribution of this study to the literature on women in IT is the fact that it points out that generalizations from research on women in one IT area, such as computer science, to a different area in IT, like MIS, are inappropriate. The factors that attract and keep women in IT as well as predict their academic success differ by IT discipline. Women majoring in computer science are different in their aptitude, interest, and a host of psychological variables, and face different challenges in their academic departments than women majoring in MIS. Research on increasing the representation of women in IT needs to carefully take these facts into account.

Acknowledgments

This research was supported by a grant from the National Science Foundation (EIA–0089957).

References

American Association of University Women. 2000. *Tech-savvy: Educating girls in the new computer age*. Washington, DC: AAUW.

American Association of University Women. 2004. *Under the microscope: A decade of gender equity projects in the sciences*. Washington, DC: AAUW.

Bandura, A. 1997. *Self-efficacy: The exercise of control*. New York: Freeman.

Barker, L. J., K. Garvin-Doxas, and M. Jackson. 2002. Defensive climate in the computer science classroom. In *Proceedings of the thirty-third technical symposium on computer science education*. New York: ACM Press.

Bem, S. 1974. The measurement of psychological androgyny. *Journal of Counseling and Clinical Psychology* 42:155–162.

Berg, V. A. L., H. J. Gansmo, K. Hestflatt, M. Lie, H. Nordli, and K. H. Sorenson. 2002. Gender and ICT in Norway: An overview of Norwegian research and some relevant statistical information. *SIGIS*, IST–2000–26329.

Beyer, S. 1990. Gender differences in the accuracy of self-evaluations of performance. *Journal of Personality and Social Psychology* 59:960–970.

Beyer, S. 1995. Maternal employment and children's academic achievement: Parenting style as mediating variable. *Developmental Review* 15:212–253.

Beyer S. 1998. Gender differences in self-perception and negative recall biases. *Sex Roles* 38:103–133.

Beyer, S. 1999a. The accuracy of academic gender stereotypes. *Sex Roles* 40:787–813.

Beyer, S. 1999b. Gender differences in the accuracy of grade expectancies and evaluations. *Sex Roles* 41:279–296.

Beyer, S. 2002. The effects of gender, dysphoria, and performance feedback on the accuracy of self-evaluations. *Sex Roles* 47:453–464.

Beyer, S., and E. M. Bowden. 1997. Gender differences in self-perceptions: Convergent evidence from three measures of accuracy and bias. *Personality and Social Psychology Bulletin* 23:157–172.

Beyer, S., M. DeKeuster, K. Rynes, and J. DeHeer. 2004. The temporal stability of gender differences in MIS students. In *Proceedings of the tenth annual meeting of the Americas conference on information systems*, 1197–1204. New York: AMCIS.

Beyer, S., and K. Langenfeld. 2000. Gender differences in the recall of performance feedback. Paper presented at the annual meeting of the Midwestern Psychological Association, Chicago.

Beyer, S., K. Rynes, and S. Haller. 2004. What deters women from taking computer science courses? *IEEE Technology and Society* 23:21–28.

Beyer, S., K. Rynes, J. Perrault, K. Hay, and S. Haller. 2003. Gender differences in computer science students. In *Proceedings of the thirty-fourth SIGCSE technical symposium on computer science education*, 49–53. New York: ACM Press.

Blättel-Mink, B. 2002. Studium und Geschlecht: Faktoren einer geschlechterdifferenten Studienwahl in Baden-Württemberg (University study and gender: What affects gender-congruent choices of a university major in Baden-Württemberg). *Arbeitsbericht* (July).

Bunderson, E. D., and M. E. Christensen. 1995. An analysis of retention problems for female students in university computer science programs. *Journal of Research on Computing in Education* 28:1–15.

Byrne, P., and G. Lyons. 2001. The effect of student attributes on success in programming. In *Proceedings of ITiCSE*, 49–52. New York: ACM Press.

Casserly, P. L., and D. Rock. 1985. Factors relating to young women's persistence and achievement in advanced placement mathematics. In *Women and mathematics: Balancing the equation*, ed. S. F. Chipman, L. R. Brush, and D. M. Wilson, 225–247. Hillsdale, NJ: Lawrence Erlbaum.

Cohen, S., T. Karmarck, and R. Mermelstein. 1983. A global measure of perceived stress. *Journal of Health and Social Behavior* 24:385–396.

College Board. 2003. *College-bound seniors, 2003.* ⟨http://www.collegeboard.com/about/newsinfo/cbsenior/yr2003/html/2003reports.html⟩.

Compeau, D., C. A. Higgins, and S. Huff. 1999. Social cognitive theory and individual reactions to computing technology: A longitudinal study. *MIS Quarterly* 23:145–158.

Craig, A., J. Fisher, A. Scollary, and M. Singh. 1998. Closing the gap: Women education and information technology courses in Australia. *Journal of Systems and Software* 40:7–15.

Creamer, E. G., C. J. Burger, and P. S. Meszaros. 2004. Characteristics of high school and college women interested in information technology. *Journal of Women and Minorities in Science and Engineering* 10:67–78.

Cross, S. E., and L. Madson. 1997. Elaboration of models of the self: Reply to Baumeister and Sommer (1997) and Martin and Ruble (1997). *Psychological Bulletin* 122:51–55.

Cuny, J., W. Aspray, J. Cohoon, and J. Jesse. 2003. Factors concerning recruitment and retention of women graduate students in computer science and engineering. In *Proceedings of the National Science Foundation's ITWF and ITR/EWF principal investigator conference*, ed. R. Varma, 86–90. Albuquerque: University of New Mexico.

DeBell, M., and C. Chapman. 2003. Computer and Internet use by children and adolescents in 2001. *Education Statistics Quarterly* 5:7–11.

Dickhäuser, O., and J. Stiensmeier-Pelster. 2003. Gender differences in the choice of computer courses: Applying an expectancy-value model. *Social Psychology of Education* 6:173–189.

Eccles, J. S. 1994. Understanding women's educational and occupational choices: Applying the Eccles et al. model of achievement-related choices. *Psychology of Women Quarterly* 18:585–609.

Eccles, J. S., B. Barber, and D. Jozefowicz. 1999. Linking gender to educational, occupational, and recreational choices: Applying the Eccles et al. model of achievement-related choices. In *Sexism and stereotypes in modern society: The gender science of Janet Taylor Spence*, ed. W. B. Swann Jr. and J. H. Langlois, 153–192. Washington, DC: American Psychological Association.

Hackett, G., N. E. Betz, J. M. Casas, and I. A. Rocha-Singh. 1992. Gender, ethnicity, and social cognitive factors predicting the academic achievement of students in engineering. *Journal of Counseling Psychology* 39:527–538.

Huber, B., I. Reiff, E. R. Ben, and B. Schinzel. 2001. Frauen in IT- und ausgewählten technischen Ausbildungen und Berufen in Baden-Württemberg [Women in IT and selected technical educational and professional settings in Baden-Württemberg]. *Arbeitsbericht* 213.

Jacobs, J., S. Lanza, D. W. Osgood, J. S. Eccles, and A. Wigfield. 2002. Changes in children's self-competence and values: Gender and domain differences across grades one through twelve. *Child Development* 73, no. 2:509–527.

Jepson, A., and T. Perl. 2002. Priming the pipeline. *SIGCSE Bulletin* 36, no. 2:36–39.

Lagesen, V. A. 2002. Squares and circles: Getting women into computer science. *SIGIS*, IST–2000–26329, 1–28.

Lent, R. W., F. G. Lopez, and K. J. Bieschke. 1991. Mathematics self-efficacy: Sources and relation to science-based career choice. *Journal of Counseling Psychology* 38:424–430.

Lips, H. M. 1992. Gender- and science-related attitudes as predictors of college students' academic choices. *Journal of Vocational Behavior* 40:62–81.

Lips, H. M. 2004. The gender gap in possible selves: Divergence of academic self-views among high school and university students. *Sex Roles* 40:357–371.

Lips, H. M., and L. Temple. 1990. Majoring in computer science: Causal models for women and men. *Research in Higher Education* 31:99–113.

MacKeogh, C. 2002. Women in technology and science role model project. *SIGIS*, IST–2000–26329, 1–19.

Margolis, J., and A. Fisher. 2002. *Unlocking the clubhouse: Women in computing*. Cambridge, MA: MIT Press.

Markus, H. R., and S. Kitayama. 1991. Culture and the self: Implications for cognition, emotion, and motivation. *Psychological Review* 98:224–253.

Nosek, B. A., M. R. Banaji, and A. G. Greenwald. 2002. Math = male, me = female, therefore math ≠ me. *Journal of Personality and Social Psychology* 83, no. 1:44–59.

Ptacek, J. T., R. E. Smith, and J. Zanas. 1992. Gender, appraisal, and coping: A longitudinal analysis. *Journal of Personality* 60:747–770.

Rasmussen, B., and T. Hapnes. 1991. Excluding women from the technologies of the future? A case study of the culture of computer science. *Futures* 23:1107–1119.

Roberts, T.-A., and S. Nolen-Hoeksema. 1989. Sex differences in reactions to evaluative feedback. *Sex Roles* 21:725–747.

Roberts, T.-A., and S. Nolen-Hoeksema. 1994. Gender comparisons in responsiveness to others' evaluations in achievement settings. *Psychology of Women Quarterly* 18:221–240.

Sackrowitz, M. G., and A. P. Parelius. 1996. An unlevel playing field: Women in the introductory computer science courses. In *The proceedings of the SIGCSE technical symposium on computer science education*, 37–41. New York: ACM Press.

Sax, L. J. 1994. Retaining tomorrow's scientists: Exploring the factors that keep male and female college students interested in science careers. *Journal of Women and Minorities in Science and Engineering* 1:45–61.

Schinzel, B. 1997. Why has female participation in German informatics decreased? Women, work, and computerization: Spinning a web from past to future. In *Proceedings of the sixth international IFIP conference*, ed. A. Lehto and J. Eriksson, 365–378. Bonn, Germany.

Teague, J., and V. Clarke. 1991. Fiction and fact: Students' and professionals' perceptions of women in computer science. In *Proceedings of the conference on women, work, and computerization*, 377–390. Helsinki: Ministry of Social Affairs and Health.

Zubrow, D. 1987. How computing attitudes change during the freshman year. In *Computing and change on campus*, ed. S. Kiesler and L. Sproull, 195–211. New York: Cambridge University Press.

12

Traversing the Undergraduate Curriculum in Computer Science: Where Do Students Stumble?

Sandra Katz, John Aronis, Christine Wilson, David Allbritton, and Mary Lou Soffa

As Camp (1997, 2000) stated in her widely cited papers on the "incredible shrinking pipeline," women have continuously lagged behind men in earning Bachelor of Science degrees in computer science at four-year postsecondary U.S. institutions—despite the fact that the percentage of women earning computer science degrees has kept pace with trends in the total number of computer science degree recipients. This pattern is illustrated in figure 12.1, which is based on data from the National Center for Education Statistics, *Digest of Education Statistics* (2003, table 282). Even though the number of female degree recipients increased considerably during the IT "booms" of the mid 1980s and early 1990s, this figure nonetheless reveals a sizable gender gap in the number of women earning computer science and information science degrees during these periods.

Two main forces contribute to the continuous underrepresentation of female Bachelor of Science in computer science degree recipients: fewer women than men enroll in computer science programs at the undergraduate level and more women than men leave these programs. According to a 1995 report from the Office of Technology Assessment, most women drop out of the computer science pipeline when choosing an undergraduate degree—that is, at the enrollment stage. As Camp (2000) predicted, the problem has continued into the present and will likely persist unless direct action is taken. Enrollment has decreased overall (among men and women) since 2000. The national average for female students in undergraduate computer science programs is only 15 percent, according to the *New York Times*, May 22, 2003. With respect to attrition, Cohoon's (2003) study of 210 medium to large undergraduate institutions in the United States found that the percent of women who left the computer science major from 1994–1995 to 1999–2000 was 45 percent on average, compared with 21 percent for men.

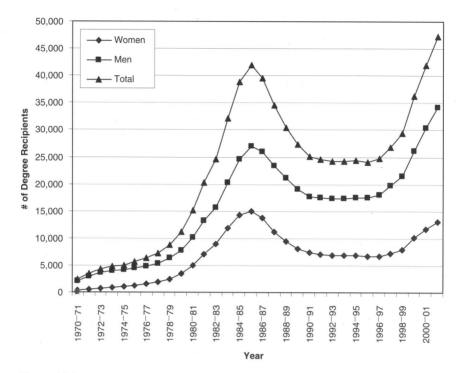

Figure 12.1
Earned degrees in computer and information sciences by gender for selected years, 1970–1971 to 2001–2002
Source: U.S. Department of Education, *Digest of Education Statistics* (Washington, DC: National Center for Education Statistics, 2003).

Although some scholars have reasonably argued that the dearth of women enrolling in computer science programs is the greater of the two forces contributing to the low percentage of female computer science degree recipients (e.g., Scragg and Smith 1998), we focus on attrition in this chapter for several reasons. First, in times like the present, when the United States is experiencing an overall decline in enrollment in undergraduate computer science programs (Zweben and Aspray 2004), it becomes all the more important to retain those students who do plan to major in computer science. Second, and perhaps more critical, loss of women at the undergraduate level perpetuates a societal problem: that fewer women than men are trained to be designers of software, rather than software users. The latter means that women will continue to be denied participation in some of the most challenging

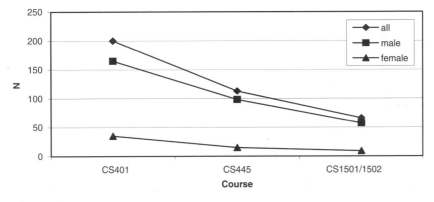

Figure 12.2
Loss of computer science students over time

and financially rewarding jobs in the economy, and correspondingly, that the IT industry will be denied the diverse perspectives and ideas that the participation by both genders can afford.

Our third reason for focusing on attrition in the study reported in this chapter is that recent research indicates that attrition, like enrollment, is a gender issue. This point is graphically demonstrated in the study by Cohoon (2003) cited previously and our prior research (Katz et al. forthcoming). Over the past three years, we have been tracking the progress of a cohort of two hundred prospective computer science majors at the University of Pittsburgh (Katz et al. forthcoming) throughout the sequence of courses that make up the programming core: Introduction to Computer Science Using JAVA (CS401), Data Structures (CS445), and Algorithm Implementation (CS1501). Because students sometimes take another course required for the computer science major (Formal Methods [CS1502]) before taking CS1501, we also tracked student enrollment and performance in this course. These four courses are typically completed within the first two years of the program. As shown in figure 12.2, the retention of students in the program is low overall and the rate of attrition for women is higher than for men. For example, the rate of attrition from CS401 to CS445 is 41 percent for men versus 57 percent for women—a marginally significant difference ($\chi^2 = 3.2$, $p = .07$). Furthermore, as figure 12.3 shows, the program loses many promising students at various points along the way—that is, students who earn a B and above in computer science courses. Reflecting attrition trends for the cohort as a whole (figure 12.2), the sharpest loss of high-achieving students takes

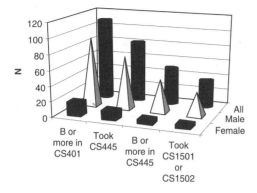

Figure 12.3
Loss of students earning a B or above after two courses in an undergraduate computer science curriculum

place from CS401 to CS445. This pattern continued after CS445. As we will discuss below, achievement was one of the key factors that predicted persistence overall as well as gendered differences in persistence.

These observations from our previous research motivated the more detailed study of achievement described here. Specifically, we asked:

• Are there specific computer science topics that are stumbling blocks to progress as students traverse the undergraduate computer science curriculum? If so, what are these "critical topics"?

• How do men and women compare with respect to this finer-grained analysis of achievement? Does the often-cited finding that women perform as well as or better than men in computer science hold when we look at individual topics as opposed to final grades?

• What student characteristics besides (or in addition to) gender predict performance on critical topics?

To address these questions, we performed a careful analysis of the topics associated with each question on each exam that students in the cohort took during the four courses named previously and used students' scores on these questions as a measure of their grasp of the associated topic(s). Several topics were found to be stumbling blocks to achievement in successive courses and hence barriers to retention. Women significantly outperformed men on several of these topics, especially in the upper-level courses (CS1501 and CS1502). This finding increases our confidence that we identified the right set of critical topics because the few women (seven) who remained in the program after the second course, Data Structures, were apparently those who were able to bypass these stumbling blocks and other obstacles to retention.

After reviewing the relevant research on gendered attrition at the undergraduate level, we describe the critical topics study and its main findings. We then discuss the complex relationship between achievement and retention demonstrated by these quantitative results, and by a qualitative analysis of students' reasons for leaving the computer science program. We conclude with a discussion of issues that this research raises for future research.

Background

Gendered Attrition at the Undergraduate Level

Research conducted mainly in the past decade has shown that gendered attrition is a complex, multifaceted, multilevel problem. Numerous factors contribute to female attrition at the undergraduate level, and the problem percolates upward through various social and organizational structures—from the individual student, through departmental, institutional, and disciplinary levels (e.g., Bunderson and Christensen 1995; Cohoon 2002, 2003; Davies et al. 2000). Below, we briefly summarize the main attrition-causing factors at these levels that have been discussed in the literature. The citations are illustrative rather than exhaustive.

Student Characteristics A complex array of affective, cognitive, and behavioral student characteristics predict female attrition from computer science programs. Affective factors include women's lack of confidence in their ability to succeed (Beyer et al. 2003), which may lead to a lack of interest (Margolis and Fisher 2002); a higher level of computer anxiety than male computer science students, coupled with a lower level of enjoyment or "liking" of computers and programming (Busch 1995; Shashaani 1997); a feeling of disappointment when the actual performance falls short of performance goals and expectations (Jagacinski, LeBold, and Salvendy 1988; Volet and Styles 1992); and a sense of isolation, of not fitting into the "hacker stereotype" (Margolis and Fisher 2002). Cognitive factors include the attribution of poor or suboptimal performance to a lack of ability rather than a lack of effort, as men are more inclined to do (Davies et al. 2000), and the belief that a career in computer science is incompatible with the goal of raising a family

(Scragg and Smith 1998). Behavioral factors include less prior computing experience than men, which contributes to a lack of confidence (Bunderson and Christensen 1995) and strategies for coping with being a minority that can breed isolation from one's peer group; for example, trying to fit the "male hacker" image may alienate female computer science students from other women who refuse to fit this stereotype and instead strive to cultivate diverse interests (Etzkowitz et al. 1994).

Departmental Characteristics The departmental factors that have been cited as contributors to female attrition from computer science programs fall within three categories: a lack of peer support, a lack of faculty support, and problems with the curriculum. A lack of peer support has been observed in the form of male pranks (Didio 1997), harassment, and ignoring female students (Von Hellens and Nielsen 2001). A lack of faculty support also manifests itself in various ways, including classroom behaviors that favor male students, such as asking men more challenging questions than women (Levenson and Klawe 1995); few female role models (Davies et al. 2000; Shelby, Ryba, and Young 1998); insufficient attention to students of both genders, often due to excessive teaching and research requirements that leave little time for mentoring (Binkerd and Moore 2002); and overly stringent grading policies that discourage students (Cohoon and Chen 2003). The criticisms of undergraduate computer science curricula are controversial. For example, some researchers have argued that more mathematics is taught in computer science courses than is necessary and than appeals to women's interests (West and Ross 2002). Others have contended that—to the contrary—mathematics, logic, and problem solving form the core of what draws both genders to computer science, and these foundations are undermined by curricula that emphasize programming languages and hardware (Crews and Butterfield 2003; DePalma 2001).

Institutional Characteristics The institutional characteristics that contribute to female attrition include insufficient financial support for computing facilities, safety, and so on (Binkerd and Moore 2002), and admissions criteria that favor students with a strong precollege background in computer science—for instance, students who took several computer science courses in high school, participated in computer clubs and camps, and so forth. Blum and Frieze (forthcoming) discuss how these admissions policies limited student diversity in the undergraduate computer science program at Carnegie Mellon University, and how a radical change in admissions policies increased diversity in the mid- to late-1990s and consequently eliminated many of the problems that Margolis and Fisher (2002) identified as causes of female attrition from this program.

Disciplinary Characteristics   Several educators have suggested recently that making computer science more interesting would go a long way toward encouraging all students (men and women) to persist in the computer science major, despite the difficulty (and often dryness) of the subject matter, lower-than-desired grades, an over-abundance of "geeks," and so on. According to Peter Lee, the associate dean of the undergraduate computer science program at Carnegie Mellon University, increasing students' interest in computer science needs to take place at the disciplinary level, via the pursuit of ambitious goals that can compete with those of other sciences: "It's hard for voice over Internet Protocol or e-commerce to compete with finding the age of the universe" (quoted in Frauenheim 2004, 2).

Achievement and Persistence

One would expect that achievement predicts persistence—that is, weak students will tend to leave a computer science program, while strong students will tend to stay. We found empirical support for this intuitive relation in the longitudinal study of performance referenced above (Katz et al. forthcoming). Performance was measured on a scale of 1 to 13 (F to A+); persistence was measured on a scale of 1 to 3, where 3 means "3 or more courses" (i.e., students who took CS1501, CS1502, or both all received a persistence rating of 3). Students' persistence rating correlated strongly with their grades in CS401 and CS445 ($r = .61$ and $r = .64$, respectively).

As summarized in the introduction, when we looked at persistence over time—the transition from CS401 to CS445, and then from CS445 to CS1501—we found significant differences in persistence by gender. Sixty percent of men who completed CS401 versus 43 percent of women continued to CS445, a marginally significant difference ($\chi^2 = 3.2$, $p < .07$) (see figure 12.2). When we examined this difference further, we found that the nexus of the gender difference was at the B performance level. Comparing students who earned a C or above with students who earned less than a C in CS401, a chi-square test revealed no significant gender differences in persistence to CS445. Indeed, few students of either sex who earned less than a C in CS401 continued to CS445 (8 percent overall, or 10 percent of men who earned a C or less and 0 percent of women). When we performed the same test using a B as the performance cutoff, however, we found that men who earned less than a B were significantly more likely to continue to CS445 than were women who earned less than a B ($\chi^2 = 3.9$, $p = .05$). Although not statistically significant, a similar pattern held for the transition from CS445 to CS1501: more men who earned less than a B in CS445 (37 percent, or twenty out of fifty-four) continued to CS1501 and/or CS1502 than did women (33 percent, or two out of six) (see figure 12.3). The reasons for this gender difference are unclear and warrant further investigation. This difference could reflect less confidence on women's part to earn better grades in subsequent courses, better judgment on the part of women that allows them to determine early on that they might not be well suited for computer science, or a combination of the two.

Methods

Goals of the Follow-up Study

As discussed in the previous section, we found that achievement is a strong force in determining who will stay and who will leave a computer science program. Apparently, even strong students leave computer science at the undergraduate level when their grades do not match their goals and expectations, and women's performance standard for persisting in the major appears to be higher than that of men. Given the impact of performance goals on persistence, we decided to examine achievement at a finer-grained level than overall course grade. We therefore tracked students' performance on individual test items that were classified as indicators of student ability on specific computer science topics, and we did this throughout the four-course sequence used in our initial study (Katz et al. forthcoming).

Participants

Two hundred students at the University of Pittsburgh voluntarily participated in the study—the same cohort used in the longitudinal analysis of achievement reported on in Katz et al. (forthcoming). Recruitment took place on the first day of the first course taken by all prospective computer science majors: Introduction to Computer Science Using JAVA (CS401). Students were paid a nominal amount for consenting to participate. In order to optimize the number of women in our sample, we recruited from five sections of the course, spanning three academic semesters during 2001–2002.

As shown in figure 12.1, the enrollment of women was significantly lower than that of men. Indeed, even after recruiting participants from CS401 across three aca-

Table 12.1
Ethnic classification of participants

Classification	Males	Females	Total
Caucasian	130 (79%)	26 (74%)	156 (78%)
African American	21 (13%)	5 (14%)	26 (13%)
Asian or Asian American	8 (5%)	2 (6%)	10 (5%)
Other (Hispanic American, American Indian, etc.)	6 (4%)	2 (6%)	8 (4%)

demic semesters, we obtained a sample of only 35 women, compared with 165 men. These samples represent approximately 28 percent of the men in the population of students who were enrolled in CS401 during the recruitment period (165 men out of 590) and approximately 27 percent of the women in this population (35 women out of 130).[1]

Originally, 236 students signed up for the study. We eliminated 36 students because their planned major was not computer science, and they were therefore not required to complete the programming core, they withdrew from CS401, or they did not have SAT scores. Included within the sample of 200 were 9 engineering students, 1 student from the Scientific Computing program, and 9 students who stated that they were "undecided" about majoring in computer science. We included the engineering students because they are required to complete the programming core and several of these students planned a concentration in computer engineering.

As table 12.1 shows, the majority of participants (78 percent) are Caucasian. Thirteen percent are African American, 5 percent are Asian or Asian American, and 4 percent belong to another ethnic group. Because of the small sample of students who could be considered a "minority" in computer science (i.e., students who are not Caucasian, Asian, or Asian American), our analyses do not differentiate students based on race or ethnicity. We differentiate students only according to gender. The mean age of participants is twenty years.

Materials

Students' exams were the primary form of data used in this analysis. We classified the questions on each exam in each of the four computer science courses (CS401, CS445, CS1501, and CS1502) using the descriptors shown in appendix 12.1. From this listing, we selected twenty topics to focus on in our analysis—five topics per course. These topics are shown in table 12.2. Because different instructors taught different sections of these courses, the test questions used to measure students' ability on the selected topics varied. And because each topic could be mapped to more than one test question, we selected one question on the exams from each section of the courses that represented the selected topics. Table 12.3 illustrates the mapping of topics onto test questions.

Six of the topics were scored by instructors as correct or incorrect, 0 or 1: CS401 data types, CS401 recursion, CS445 inheritance, CS1502 first-order logic, CS1502 tautology, and CS1502 proof (complete or justify a given proof). The remaining topics were scored on a scale of 0 to 1.

We used students' SAT scores and their responses to questions on a background survey to identify characteristics that predict performance on the topics shown in table 12.2, as we did for our coarser-grained analysis of the factors that predict course grade (Katz et al. forthcoming).

Results

Identification of Critical Topics

We did not consider whether a particular topic predicted performance in its associated course because students' aggregate grade for a course is determined by their performance on its individual topics. Instead we asked, Does performance topic X predict achievement in subsequent courses—that is, is it a critical topic? We asked this question only of the CS401 and CS445 topics—for example, Does "linked lists" predict achievement in CS445, CS1501, and CS1502? Because data collection for courses past CS1501 and CS1502 is in progress, we did not investigate the relationship between students' scores on these topics and subsequent course performance.

To identify critical topics, we performed two types of tests. First, we ran t-tests to compare the mean score of students who earned a B or above in successive courses of the curriculum with those who earned less than a B. Second, we used chi-square to identify significant differences between high- and low-achieving students (a B or above versus less than a B), with scores for each topic similarly defined as "high" versus "low"—that is, completely correct (1) versus partially correct or incorrect (0). As noted previously, six topics were already scored in this way.

Four CS401 topics predicted achievement in CS445 by distinguishing students who performed above and below the B cutoff: data types ($\chi^2 = 8.4$, $p < .01$), class constructs ($\chi^2 = 6.0$, $p < .01$; also $t(108) = 2.3$), data structures ($\chi^2 = 4.5$,

Table 12.2
Gender differences in performance on selected topics

Topics	N (M, F)	Men		Women	
		Mean	SD	Mean	SD
CS401 topics					
Data types	129, 29	.67	.47	.79	.41
Control constructs	163, 34	.90	.19	.83	.33
Data structures*	155, 29	.48	.48	.66	.46
Recursion	154, 32	.77	.42	.69	.47
Classes	153, 32	.67	.39	.64	.43
CS445 topics					
Linked lists	80, 12	.76	.34	.78	.33
Recursion	79, 12	.62	.40	.69	.42
Sorting algorithm*	78, 12	.63	.37	.82	.31
Inheritance***	91, 14	.81	.39	1	0
Nonlinear data structures	42, 5	.51	.48	.43	.52
CS1501 topics					
Recursion	48, 7	.62	.28	.75	.25
Huffman compression	48, 8	.65	.44	.68	.39
Graphs**	47, 8	.49	.35	.79	.25
String-matching algorithm	48, 7	.77	.26	.77	.31
RSA encryption	47, 8	.60	.38	.76	.32
CS1502 topics					
First-order logic	46, 9	.77	.38	.44	.53
Tautology***	49, 9	.86	.21	1	0
Proof—complete or justify	48, 9	.86	.24	.82	.37
Proof—construct one	45, 9	.85	.22	.83	.18
State machines***	47, 9	.78	.30	.97	.07

Notes:
* Marginally significant difference, $p < .10$
** Significant difference, $p < .05$
*** Significant, $p < .01$

Table 12.3
Examples of coded test questions

Question	Topic

Given the method definition:
    public static int foo(int n) {
      if (n==0)
        return 0;
      else if (is_even(n))
        return (n + foo(n−1));
      else
        return (−n + foo(n−1));
    }
where is_even(n) returns true if n is an even number and false if it is not, what does the statement foo(5) return?
	CS401—recursion

Consider the **Boyer Moore string-matching** algorithm to find a pattern of length M within a text string of length N. a) Considering only the mismatched character (MC) heuristic that we discussed in lecture, state the **best case** and **worst case** number of comparisons to complete a search for a pattern. **For each case, give a pattern string and a text string that will produce that case.** b) Give the **skip array** for the following string: RADIOHEAD	CS1501—string-matching algorithm

$p < .05$; also $t(111) = 2.1$), and classes ($\chi^2 = 5.4$, $p < .05$; also $t(108) = 3.7$). Data structures also predicted CS1502 performance ($\chi^2 = 4.5$, $p < .05$; also $t(52) = 3.7$). To our surprise, recursion did not predict performance in subsequent performance, despite the great deal of difficulty that many students have with this topic.

Two CS445 topics predicted achievement in CS1501 and CS1502. The sorting algorithm distinguished between CS1501 students who earned above and below a B ($\chi^2 = 3.4$, $p < .07$; also $t(49) = 2.0$) while inheritance did the same with respect to CS1502 ($\chi^2 = 4.1$, $p < .05$).

Gender Differences in Critical Topics

Table 12.2 presents means and standard deviations for the selected topics by gender. $N(M, F)$ means the number of men and women, respectively.

Women outperformed men on several critical topics: CS401 data structures ($t(182) = 1.8$, $p < .10$), CS445 inheritance ($t(90) = 4.5$), CS445 sorting ($t(16) = 2.0$), CS1501 graphs ($t(53) = 2.3$), CS1502 tautology ($t(48) = 4.6$), and C1502 state machines $(t(52) = 3.7)$. Rather than viewing these findings as an indication that women are more adept at computer science than men, we see them as an indication that we have identified a valid set of critical topics. Few women remained in the program after CS445; indeed, there were only seven women who went on to take CS1501 or CS1502. Hence, the superior performance of women on this set of topics suggests that only women who could break through these performance barriers persisted in the program. As we saw in our previous work, women who perform below a B tend to leave the program, while men are more likely to persist.

Student Characteristics That Predict Performance on Critical Topics

We identified several factors that predicted students' performance on several of the CS401 topics. Not surprisingly, several of these factors also correlated with overall performance, as measured by course grade (Katz et al. forthcoming). Math SAT score predicted performance on CS401 data types $(r = .22)$, control constructs $(r = .22)$, and classes $(r = .27)$. Verbal SAT score predicted performance on these same topics $(r = .19, r = .26,$ and $r = .19$, respectively). Calculus predicted performance on CS401 control constructs $(r = .17)$ and classes $(r = .17)$. Home access to a computer during high school predicted performance on CS401 data types $(rho = .25)$ and CS401 classes $(rho = .17)$. Finally, having a mentor or role model during high school predicted performance on CS401 data structures $(tau\text{-}b = .24;$ also $\chi^2 = 8.5)$. We did not find any student characteristics that had the long-term effect of predicting performance in subsequent courses (CS445, etc.).

Discussion: Why Do Successful Students Leave Computer Science?

Forty-four students (22 percent of the cohort) left the computer science program unexpectedly, after CS401 or CS445 (figure 12.3); that is, they had earned a B or above in these courses, but did not continue to CS1501 or CS1502. Thirty-eight of these students were men; six were women. The majority (thirty-six) left after CS401—all but eight students, who left after CS445. Why did these academically successful students leave?

As a step toward answering this question, we turned to students' responses on the surveys that we administered at the start of CS401 and near the end of each of the four courses (Katz et al. forthcoming). The end-of-course surveys were designed to identify students who no longer planned to major in computer science and to gather students' self-reported reasons for this decision. Toward this end, the surveys asked questions aimed at gauging students' confidence in their ability to succeed, interest in computer science, attitude toward the computer science department, and so on. The analysis summarized below stems mainly from students' answers to the open-ended question, Why do you plan to leave/continue with a computer science major? (paraphrased), on each end-of-course survey. We were also interested in determining whether some successful students left because even a B did not satisfy their performance goals and expectations. Hence, we considered their responses to background survey questions that asked them to specify the grade they hoped to achieve in CS401 (e.g., earn a C or above, a B or above, an A). We did not issue surveys that asked this question at the start of subsequent courses; however, each end-of-course survey asked students to rate their confidence in earning at least a C, a B, or an A.

Unfortunately, end-of-course survey response rates were low overall and decreased across the four courses. Only twenty-four of the thirty-six successful students who left after CS401 completed the survey; only five of the eight successful students who left after CS445 did the same. Nonetheless, students' answers to the open-ended reasons for staying/leaving question provide a window into the factors that drive good students to leave computer science. Given that so few women are represented in this sample, we did not differentiate reasons for leaving according to gender. We summarize our qualitative analysis of survey responses in the hope that it will guide future inquiry rather than be taken as conclusive.[2]

Among the forty-four successful (B or above) students, we were able to derive possible explanations for why twenty-two of them (50 percent) left, either from their response to the survey question that targeted this issue, from a comparison between their desired and achieved grades, or a combination of the two. Attrition for the remaining 50 percent of the students was inexplicable, either because these students were high achievers (having earned an A−, A, or A+ in CS401 and/or CS445 yet still left the program and did not indicate why on their surveys (or did not complete the surveys), stated that they planned to continue with computer science (but apparently did not), or both. It is possible that some of these students transferred to another university. We were unable to determine this.

Among the twenty-two successful students who we had sufficient survey data for, the most common potential explanations for attrition were a loss of interest, a gap between performance goals and achieved performance (Volet and Styles 1992)—for example, earning a B when an A was desired—or both. Eight students earned a B in the course that preceded their withdrawal from the program (CS401 or CS445), but they did not complete the end-of-course surveys or indicate any loss of interest in computer science in their survey responses. Perhaps these students left because they were disappointed in their performance. Three A students stated that they were leaving because they no longer found computer science interesting or found a different discipline more interesting; for example, as one student remarked, "I found JAVA to be easy to learn as long as I paid attention and attended, yet not interesting at all. So I'm not sure I have a lot of interest, but will probably stick with Compsci." Apparently, this student did not "stick with" computer science. The following examples of loss of interest represent the five students who decided to switch to information science. One of these students explained, "I'm now leaning toward information science as a major. It seems that the field is more general and more free, whereas computer science seems to be more hard-core computing and dealing with 'bits and bytes.'" Another student commented, "I feel confident in my programming ability and have an A in the class. However, I do not believe that I would be able to program all of my life in front of a computer. I switched to information science, which is still related to programming, just not as intense."

We note that in personal communications, students often refer to the switch as "dropping down to information science," suggesting that they perceive this field to be less challenging than computer science and easier to earn good grades in. Hence, this could have been another reason why the students quoted above and their peers switched to information science. These comments also illustrate another apparent reason for the loss of "good" students: disillusionment with what they perceive the discipline entails, whether or not their perceptions are entirely accurate. (For example, many computer scientists spend little time programming.) Another student noted that he planned to leave the major because he did not want to take higher-level math courses.

These remarks suggest that it is important to sustain students' interest in the program, and provide them with an accurate portrait of what the discipline entails and can offer with respect to career opportunities. The reasons that the handful of women who persisted through all three courses gave for staying underscore the importance of interest and an awareness of career opportunities. Four of these women talked about using their degree in computer science to complement or serve another career interest, such as biological research, computational physics, or neuroscience. This interest was sparked during high school or early in college, suggesting the significance of developing students' awareness of computer science applications in high school and postsecondary computer science courses. As one student put it, "I am interested in technology in biological research, and while working in the research setting, I found a great need for computer knowledge and programming skills. Also, I enjoy programming and solving problems."

Women tend to have an applied interest in computer science, while men tend to like computers and programming for their own sake (Margolis and Fisher 2002). The only applied interest we found expressed among the B-and-above male students was video game programming.

Student characteristics can interact in complex ways to cause attrition. For example, as Margolis and Fisher (2002) observed and demonstrated, reduced confidence can lead to reduced interest. We found some instances of this in our cohort. One woman entered CS401 with the goal of earning a B or above, yet she got a seventy-five on the course's second exam, which might have lessened her confidence. On the end-of-course survey for this class, this woman showed that she was like those in Margolis and Fisher's study who compared their required effort with that of their peers (mostly males) and concluded that computer science was not right for them: "I don't think I have the skills to go on as a CS major. The programs that are assigned are incredibly difficult for me, while for others, they are very simple." Similarly, another student described the "vicious chain reaction" involving low motivation and poor performance that he was caught in: "Well, the short and long of it is, I just don't like it, which causes me to not care, and that causes me to not learn the material, and that causes me to not be any good at it. It's a vicious chain reaction."

Conclusion and Future Directions

The study discussed here, when coupled with our previous research (Katz et al. forthcoming), demonstrates the strong impact that performance can have on both student persistence in an undergraduate program and the gender gap in persistence. Performance alone does not explain this gap; rather, it is performance at an expected level that is the important factor, and women appear to be more negatively affected than men when their achieved grades do not measure up to their desired grades. These observations motivated us to investigate achievement more closely in order to determine if there are certain critical topics that predict performance in subsequent courses and hence persistence. We found that students tend to lose their foothold at various points on the climb toward an undergraduate computer science degree. For example, if they don't succeed on data types, control constructs, data structures, and classes in the first course for computer science majors (introduction to computer science using JAVA), they are likely to earn less than a B in the next course (data structures). And if they do poorly on sorting algorithms and inheritance in the data structures class, they are likely to earn less than a B in upper-level courses (e.g., Algorithm Implementation and Formal Methods). We also found that women outperformed men on several critical topics, especially in CS445, most likely because the few women who persisted to this stage were among the strongest students in the program. We discovered that several student characteristics predict performance on critical topics as they do for letter grades as a whole—namely, math and verbal SAT score, number of calculus courses taken before the first course for computer science majors, having sufficient access to a computer at home during high school, and the influence of a mentor or role model. Finally, we found that although successful performance is important for persistence, it is insufficient; a sustained interest in computer science is also critical.

Given the small sample size used in this study (especially of women) and the fact that it was conducted at only one institution, there is a need for further research to determine the extent to which these findings can be generalized. For example, although the University of Pittsburgh's computer science program is influenced by the model curricula suggested by the Association for Computing Machinery, it does not follow these curricula as closely as some other institutions. Hence, it is possible that other critical topics could be identified at institutions that adhere strictly to the association's guidelines. It is also possible that other factors interact with subject matter (topics) to determine student success in subsequent courses, such as the demographic characteristics of students and the quality of the faculty who teach these courses. In addition to validating and extending the set of critical topics identified in this study, several other lines of inquiry are suggested by this research. We describe three goals for further inquiry below.

Determine what it is that makes certain topics difficult for students in order to develop and evaluate instructional interventions Why are some topics like data types, recursion, classes, and inheritance difficult for many students? Are there gender differences in the nature of student difficulty with these topics? Interviews with students, combined with observations of them working through problems that exercise this knowledge, would help to address these questions. This work needs to be done in order to develop interventions that could help struggling students. We suspect that many students run into trouble with some critical topics not because these topics are conceptually difficult, but because students are unsystematic when implementing them. Consequently, we expect that hands-on exercises that guide students in tracing through the execution of sorting algorithms, recursive functions, and so on, would prove helpful, especially if these exercises prompt students to predict the outcome of subsequent steps, explain steps, and carry out other reflective activities that instructional research has found to be beneficial (e.g., Bielaczyc, Pirolli, and Brown 1995). What approach that the instructional interventions to promote understanding of critical topics should take, when and how they should be administered, and how they should be evaluated are all open areas for research.

Increase understanding of the complex relationship between achievement and persistence   Our observation that a gap between students' earned grades and their performance goals can determine their decision to persist in a major is certainly not new (Jagacinski, LeBold, and Salvendy 1988; Volet and Styles 1992). Nonetheless, we know little more about this relationship than that it exists. Does the gender difference that we observed—whereby women who earned less than a B were less likely to continue to subsequent courses than men—generalize to other institutions? Is this gender difference a reflection of less confidence on women's part, better judgment, or both? At what point, and under what circumstances, should academic advisors suggest that students pursue a different major that they are more likely to excel in, as opposed to repeating computer science courses? What, if anything, can be done to sustain the confidence and interest of promising students whose grades do not rise up to their performance goals and expectations?

Research on fundamental issues concerning performance will need to be addressed before we can approach these practical issues. For example, how do students conceptualize academic success, and what role does GPA play in this conceptualization? Why is it that some students appear to be more bothered by low grades, even suboptimal grades (a B or B+), than others—for instance, are grades a large part of these students' identity? Are there social forces that determine early on how one conceptualizes and responds to grades?

Increase understanding of both the role of interest in persistence and how to sustain student interest   We are concerned by our observation that several high-achieving students left the computer science program because they lost interest. How can we sustain the interest of all students through the early stages of computer science instruction, when a large body of rudimentary skills and concepts that are often not inherently interesting must be covered? Several educators have suggested various ways of bolstering student interest, such as discussing the "real-world" applications of computer science concepts and skills in the curriculum early on, inviting professionals who can serve as role models to talk about their work to students in a classroom or informal setting, setting up internship programs with local companies, and so forth (e.g., Blum and Frieze forthcoming; Cohoon 2002). Evaluations of these practices are needed to guide reform.

As noted previously, Lee (quoted in Frauenheim 2004) argued that computer science will fail to compete with other scientific disciplines for students until change occurs at the disciplinary level—in particular, that more "big issues" are addressed. It would be interesting and informative to determine whether other scientific disciplines such as physics—which are addressing big issues like "finding the age of the universe," to quote Lee—have less difficulty retaining students than computer science, despite being challenging.

We expect that investigation into these issues will lead to a deeper understanding of why many students of both sexes, even some of the most promising students, leave the computer science pipeline at the undergraduate level, and what can be done to reverse this trend.

Acknowledgments

This research was supported by a grant from the National Science Foundation (EIA 0089963). The data presented and views expressed here are not necessarily endorsed by this agency. The authors appreciate the helpful comments of the editors and anonymous reviewers.

Appendix 12.1: Topics Used to Classify Test Questions

algorithms-general

algorithms-Boyer Moore

algorithms-compression-Huffman

algorithms-compression-Lossy

algorithms-compression-LZW

algorithms-Divide and Conquer

algorithms-GCD

algorithms-search-BFS

algorithms-search-Binary Search

algorithms-search-DFS

algorithms-search-PFS

algorithms-sort-Bubble Sort

algorithms-sort-Insertion Sort

algorithms-sort-Merge Sort

algorithms-sort-Quick Sort

algorithms-sort-Selection Sort

algorithms-sort-Shell Sort

algorithms-string-Rabin Karp

big O

classes

classes-members

classes-protection

compiler/compilation

control constructs-general

control constructs-do while

control constructs-if/else

control constructs-for loop

control constructs-switch/case

control constructs-while

control flow

data structures-general

data structures-array; can be multidimensional, matrix, etc.

data structures-dictionary

data structures-hash table

data structures-heap

data structures-linked list; single or double

data structures-list

data structures-queue

data structures-stack

data structures-tree

data structures-vector

data structures-other

datatypes-general; byte, int, float, string, etc.

datatypes-assignment

datatypes-casting

datatypes-conversion

encryption-general

encryption-RSA

encryption

errors

exceptions

expressions-create

expressions-evaluate

functions/methods-general

functions/methods-call

functions/methods-creation

functions/methods-return value

garbage collection

grammars (context-free grammars)

graphs

gui; panels, frames, etc.

hashing

hash value

hash function

heuristics; local search

inheritance

input/output

instantiation

interpreter

iteration

iteration → recursion

keywords

listeners

mathematical concept

memory/cpu; memory usage, cpu time, specs, etc.

models; producer/consumer, dining philosophers, traveling salesmen, etc.

operators-bitwise

operators-boolean

operators-comparison

operators-decrement/increment

operators-mathematical

operators-unary

parameters

pattern matching

precedence; operator precedence

programming techniques/practices

recursion

recursion-tail

recursion → iteration

references/pointers

runtime

scope

string manipulation-general

string manipulation-concatenation

string manipulation-parsing

syntax

threads

variables

variables-assignment

Notes

1. The population includes students who were not prospective computer science majors but were enrolled in CS401 during the recruitment period. The frequencies for men and women in the population are approximate. They were derived from direct observation (a count of men and women who attended CS401 examinations) since we were unable to obtain demographic information for students who did not consent to participate in the study.

2. This qualitative discussion is an updated version of the one presented in Katz et al. (forthcoming); it represents recently collected and analyzed survey data.

References

Beyer, S., K. Rynes, J. Perrault, K. Hay, and S. Haller. 2003. Gender differences in computer science students. In *ACM SIGSCE Bulletin* 35, no. 1:49–53.

Bielaczyc, K., P. L. Pirolli, and A. L. Brown. 1995. Training in self-explanation and self-regulation strategies: Investigating the effects of knowledge acquisition activities on problem solving. *Cognition and Instruction* 13, no. 2:221–252.

Binkerd, C. L., and M. D. Moore. 2002. Women/minorities in computer science: Where are they? No attention No retention. *The Journal of Computing Sciences in Colleges* 17, no. 5:8–12.

Blum, L., and C. Frieze. 2005. As the culture of computing evolves, similarity can be the difference. *Fronters* 26, no. 1.

Bunderson, E. D., and M. E. Christensen. 1995. An analysis of retention problems for female students in university computer science programs. *Journal of Research on Computing in Education* 28, no. 1:1–18.

Busch, T. 1995. Gender differences in self-efficacy and attitudes toward computers. *Journal of Educational Computing Research* 12, no. 2:147–158.

Camp, T. 1997. The incredible shrinking pipeline. *Communications of the ACM* 40, no. 10:103–110.

Camp, T. 2000. *The incredible shrinking pipeline unlikely to reverse.* ⟨http://ww.mines.edu/fs_home/tcamp/new-study/new-study.html⟩.

Cohoon, J. M. 2002. Recruiting and retaining women in undergraduate computing majors. *SIGSCE Bulletin* 34, no. 2:48–52.

Cohoon, J. M. 2003. Must there be so few? Including women in CS. In *Proceedings of the twenty-fifth international conference on software engineering*, 668–674.

Cohoon, J. M., and L. Chen. 2003. Migrating out of computer science. *Computing Research News* 15, no. 2:2–3.

Crews, T., and J. Butterfield. 2003. Gender differences in beginning programming: An empirical study on improving performance parity. *Campus-wide Information Systems* 20, no. 5:186–192.

Davies, A. R., M. Klawe, M. Ng, C. Nyhus, and H. Sullivan. 2000. *Gender issues in computer science education.* In *Proceedings of the National Institute for Science Education Forum, Detroit Michigan.* ⟨http://www.wcer.wisc.edu/nise/News_Activities/Forums/Klawepaper .htm⟩.

DePalma, P. 2001. Why women avoid computer science. *Communications of the ACM* 44, no. 6:27–29.

Didio, L. 1997. Boys' club on campus. *Computerworld*, July 28, 64.

Etzkowitz, H., C. Kemelgor, M. Neuschatz, and B. Uzzi. 1994. Barriers to women in academic science and engineering. In *Who will do science? Educating the next generation*, ed. W. Pearson Jr. and I. Fecher. Baltimore: Johns Hopkins University Press.

Frauenheim, E. 2004. Students saying no to computer science. *CNET News.com.* ⟨http://news.zdnet.com/2100–3513_22–5313_22–5306096.html⟩.

Jagacinski, C. M., W. K. LeBold, and G. Salvendy. 1988. Gender differences in persistence in computer-related fields. *Journal of Educational Computing Research* 4, no. 2:185–202.

Katz, S., D. Allbritton, J. Aronis, C. Wilson, and M. L. Soffa. forthcoming. Gender, achievement, and persistence in an undergraduate computer science program. *DATA BASE: Special Section on IT Personnel Research*.

Levenson, N., and M. Klawe. 1995. Women in computing: Where are we now? *Communications of the ACM* 38, no. 1:29–35.

Margolis, J., and A. Fisher. 2002. *Unlocking the clubhouse: Women in computing.* Cambridge, MA: MIT Press.

Scragg, G., and J. Smith. 1998. A study of barriers to women in undergraduate computer science. In *Proceedings of SIGSCE 1998*, Atlanta, GA, 82–86. New York: ACM Press.

Shashaani, L. 1997. Gender differences in computer attitudes and use among college students. *Journal of Educational Computing Research* 16, no. 1:37–51.

Shelby, L., K. Ryba, and A. Young. 1998. Women in computing: What does the data show? *ACM SIGSCE Bulletin* 30, no. 4:62a–67a.

Volet, S. E., and I. M. Styles. 1992. Predictors of study management and performance on a first-year computer course: The significance of students' study goals and perceptions. *Journal of Educational Computing Research* 8, no. 4:423–449.

Von Hellens, L., and S. Nielsen. 2001. Australian women in IT. *Communications of the ACM* 44, no. 7:46–52.

West, M., and S. Ross. 2002. Retaining females in computer science: A new look at a persistent problem. *Journal of Computing in Small Colleges* 17, no. 5:1–7.

Zweben, S., and W. Aspray. 2004. 2002–2003 Taulbee survey. *Computing Research News.* ⟨http://www.cra.org/statistics/survey/03/03.pdf⟩.

III

Pathways into the Workforce

13

The Transition of Women from the Academic World to the IT Workplace: A Review of the Relevant Research

Kathryn M. Bartol and William Aspray

In 2001, women received over 57 percent of the bachelor's degrees conferred in the United States across all disciplines. At the same time, women were granted less than 28 percent of the bachelor's degrees in computer-related disciplines (National Center for Education Statistics 2004). Women comprise only 29 percent of the workers in the U.S. IT job market, compared with 47 percent of the larger U.S. workforce (White House Council of Economic Advisors 2000). Similar patterns occur in Europe. For example, in 1998, only 11 percent of the IT workers in the Netherlands were female, 9 percent of system analysts were female, and 13 percent of programmers were women (Brekel, Klaveren, and Tijdens 1999). It is apparent that women are choosing not to major in IT-related fields and not to enter the IT workplace in representative numbers.

What are the reasons for this underrepresentation of women in the IT workforce? This chapter provides a partial answer to this question by reviewing the (scant) literature that reports research results on the transition of women from the academic world into the IT workforce. Because research in this area is so limited, we draw on related literature to offer a sense of the landscape, point to major gaps in our knowledge, acknowledge the ongoing research of which we are aware, and suggest directions for future research. This chapter also tries to broaden the discussion of women in the IT workforce by setting the issue in larger contexts, such as the search for innovative environments, national economic welfare, and homeland defense. Accordingly, this chapter is divided into two parts. Part 1 reviews the relevant research and discusses future research needs, while part 2 considers the larger context of policy relevance.

Part 1: Review of Research

In proceeding, we note that there are many reasons why so few women are found in IT work. Some are more general factors that apply at various stages of a woman's career and may help to explain, for example, why there are so few women enrolled in high school or college computing courses, such as the lack of female role models and the perception of computers as a male-oriented field. The studies on IT gender issues in K–12 and higher education have been covered in two detailed literature surveys in this volume (Barker and Aspray; Cohoon and Aspray) and generally are not repeated here. We do consider some aspects of academic preparation within higher education as they relate to career choice and transition to the workplace. We also review literature on the IT workplace from the same point of view. Part 1 consists of three sections: academic preparation and career choice, working as an IT professional, and IT career attachment and progression.

In seeking relevant literature, we consulted major electronic databases, such as ABI/Inform and EBSCO (including Academic Premier, Business Premier, Computer Index, and PsychInfo). We also enlisted the help of an experienced librarian, consulted the reference sections of works that we obtained, and enlisted suggestions from colleagues researching in this domain. In this review, we focus mainly on materials that provide empirical evidence with gender comparisons subjected to statistical testing, and also include findings from qualitative studies that approach reasonable standards for the conduct and analysis of qualitative data. In the course of our work, we tap relevant research from countries outside the United States that was available in English through the databases that we searched. To fill in some gaps and point to trends in current research, we mention some preliminary findings and ongoing research from studies funded by the Information Technology Workforce and Information Technology Research/Engineering Workforce programs of the NSF (Trauth 2004). In the end, we have made choices, albeit carefully, in our efforts to provide an overview of a research domain in much need of additional research.

Academic Preparation and Career Choice

In this section, we first consider some issues with the pipeline as a metaphor as well as program and degree alternatives. We then turn to several issues that have been identified by a number of researchers as important to IT academic preparation and career choice—namely, perceptions of IT careers, confidence and self-efficacy, mentors and role models, and career advice.

The Myth of the Pipeline

The literature on the underrepresentation of women in computer science includes many references to the metaphor of a pipeline. A girl enters the pipeline on commencing school, preparing for an undergraduate college major in computer science by taking the right set of preparatory courses and becoming experienced in the use of computers. Further along the pipeline, the young woman enters college and majors in computer science (or perhaps in some other IT-related discipline). College is possibly followed by graduate education in a computing discipline. At the end of the formal education, whether a bachelor's, master's, or doctoral degree, the woman enters the workforce and works through a new part of the pipeline, advancing from entry-level positions through more senior technical or management positions with ever greater responsibility. The pipeline is perceived to be leaky, with some women exiting at each stage, so that the flow through the pipeline becomes smaller and smaller over time (Camp 1997).

There are problems with this metaphor, which implies a linear path in which the first part of one's career is devoted to education while the later part is devoted to work. This metaphor does not square well with the widely held belief that we live in a knowledge economy, and that IT work is emblematic of the knowledge job, in which the worker's ability to perform adequately depends on having a foundational knowledge that requires constant refreshment. This renewal comes, of course, through training and education; and much of the education requires either working and going to school simultaneously, or leaving the workforce temporarily for some specific course of study, such as a master's degree in computer science. In one current study, for example, by Wardell, Rogers, and Sawyer (2004), nearly one-third of the men and one-quarter of the women had enrolled in an educational experience after graduation, based on a survey of 2,823 graduates (20 percent women) of four-year colleges with IT degrees.

Another weakness of the metaphor is that it does not square with actual employment patterns. From 1996 to 1997, for example, according to the Bureau of Labor Statistics, the number of IT jobs in the United States increased by 200,000—from about 1.9 to 2.1 million jobs. Yet according to National Center for Education Statistics (2004), the number of bachelor's degrees awarded in the IT disciplines (computer science, computer engineering, and management and business information systems) totaled only in the 30,000 range. There were slightly under 15,000 master's and doctoral degrees awarded in this area. So these educational programs could only account for 45,000 of the 200,000 new IT jobs created in the United States in

1996. (In fact, there are even more jobs to account for because this analysis does not take into consideration people who leave the field for death, retirement, and change of occupation and have to be replaced.)

Where do the rest of these 200,000 people come from? Some of them hold bachelor's degrees in other closely related disciplines, such as the mathematics, business and management, engineering, or science disciplines. Some take a number of computing courses while in college even though majoring in something far removed from computer science. Others learn through courses at work or school that do not lead to a degree. Still others learn on the job. The point is that there are many different paths to an IT career, and it is not true of even the majority of IT workers, male or female, that they enter IT jobs through this pipeline as it is typically conceived.

Just as there are many different career paths in IT, there are many different roles for education and training to play in this career preparation. Many of these paths are roundabout. Some involve routes that move back and forth between the academy and the workplace. Many people only get started on their IT careers later in life, and are not dependent on having entered the pipeline in junior high school and then managing to stay on track as others veer out (for a more extended analysis of this point, see chapter 5 in Freeman and Aspray 1999). There are many different reasons to pursue a nontraditional education in the IT fields, such as returning to get an IT degree later in life or taking courses in a nondegree program. Some of these are listed in table 13.1.

Table 13.1
Typical reasons for a nontraditional IT education

Training for a specific career	Computer operator
Career advancement	Computer operator training to be a network administrator
Movement toward a professional career	Computer operator seeking a job that normally requires a degree
Continuing education to maintain technical skills	An engineer seeking to learn about a new technology
Career shift	Mechanical engineer retraining to be a software engineer
Specific product information or usage skills	How to use a specific software package

Source: William Aspray, "Educational Pathways to IT Work" (keynote presentation at the AAAS conference on Bringing Women and Minorities into the IT Workforce: The Role of Nontraditional Educational Pathways, Washington, DC, July 21, 2004).

Several studies have examined the nontraditional paths by which women have entered IT careers. These paths do not necessarily involve any formal education. In a telephone survey of 47 women in the U.S. IT industry, Bush and colleagues (2002) found that many of the respondents entered the IT field via "nontraditional pathways." These women did not have formal training in a computer-related field but instead started their careers in nontechnical jobs. The respondents generally segued into more technical jobs after having some job-related experience working with computers. The researchers also found that the most common entry points for women without extensive education or training in computing are jobs as a help-desk support staff or personal computer technician. Turner, Bernt, and Pecora (2002) conducted an online survey of women involved in IT at a multinational company. The instrument consisted of both short-answer and open-ended questions. A total of 275 respondents were surveyed (with an 11 percent response rate). This survey found that almost half of the older respondents first used a computer at work, while 57 percent of the younger women first used computers in school. An Australian survey conducted by Von Hellens and colleagues (2000) found that 9 of the 10 women in this small sample had not entered the IT field as a primary choice but had switched over early in their careers after exposure to computing when they realized that they enjoyed working with computers. According to the SIGIS study in the United Kingdom (Faulkner 2002), 62 percent of all graduates in IT jobs graduated in subjects other than IT.

In a U.S. survey of 186 Northwestern University Master of Science in Information Systems graduates and 249 IT professionals, plus 44 interviews (29 women), Leventman and colleagues (2004) found that 31 percent of the respondents had a traditional pathway, having attained a technical undergraduate degree. Another 38 percent were classified as transitional, having had nontechnical jobs but coming back to school and receiving an IT degree. Finally, 31 percent were classified as self-directed, having received no formal technical bachelor's degree but with a career path that included both IT and non-IT work. People in technical jobs (developers, analysts, and consultants) were more likely to have taken a traditional pathway, whereas corporate managers were more likely to have come from transitional pathways. Women in the traditional pathway are more likely to spend 20 percent or more of their time doing programming, networking, and Web design. Women in the self-directed pathway are more likely to spend 20 percent or more of their time doing customer service, documentation, teaching, training, and technical support. There was also a significant difference in the early educational backgrounds between the respondents on the traditional, transitional, and self-directed pathways in terms of high school courses taken, age when they first started using computers, and computer experience.

Jesse's chapter in this volume examines one important nontraditional pathway for women and minorities entering the IT workforce: the for-profit colleges such as DeVry and the University of Phoenix. Chapple's chapter, also in this volume, considers another nontraditional path, the entry-level training programs associated with regional development activities. Many traditional postsecondary educators are skeptical about programs such as these, which they regard (rightly or wrongly) as focused on training rather than education because they believe a strong foundational knowledge is necessary in order to cope with the rapid changes in the content of IT work. More study of the preparatory value of different kinds of IT education (and the gender context for them) is needed.

Which Program and Degree?

Most of the social science literature on academic preparation for IT jobs and underrepresented groups focuses on the undergraduate computer science degree. Furthermore, the literature concentrates on traditional colleges and universities that tend to serve full-time students who attend college immediately following high school. Is this justified? In three ways, the literature seems too narrowly focused by not considering: degrees other than the baccalaureate, nontraditional universities, and IT disciplines other than computer science.

The literature does not give full consideration to degrees other than the baccalaureate. In 2001 approximately forty-five thousand bachelor's, seventeen thousand master's, and one thousand doctoral degrees were awarded in the computing disciplines in the nation as a whole (National Center for Education Statistics 2004; see the useful presentation of these data at ⟨http://www.cra.org/info/education/us/index.html⟩). The literature on associate and graduate degrees is thin as pertains to women preparing for IT work through these degrees. One study is currently underway looking at the recruitment and retention of graduate student women in computer science and computer engineering at fifty universities in the United States by Janice Cuny, Jolene Kay Jesse, J. McGrath Cohoon, and William Aspray, but no results have been published yet.

The literature does not give full consideration to nontraditional schools. If one considers the schools that produce large numbers of computer science undergraduate degrees, one finds a number of nontraditional suppliers such as Strayer Univer-

Table 13.2
IT-related academic disciplines in the United States

1. Computer Science	11. performance analysis (capacity planning)
2. Information Science	12. scientific computing
3. Information systems	13. computational science
4. Management information systems	14. artificial intelligence
5. Software architecture	15. graphics
6. Software engineering	16. HCI (human-computer interaction)
7. Network engineering	17. web service design
8. Knowledge engineering	18. multimedia design
9. Database engineering	19. system administration
10. System security and privacy	20. digital library service

Source: Peter Denning, "Information Technology: Developing the Profession" (discussion document, ACM Education Committee, December 4, 1998). As quoted in Freeman and Aspray (1999, 28).

sity and the University of Phoenix high on the list. It also turns out that these schools are among the largest producers of degrees for women and minorities in the IT fields (Babco and Jesse 2001). The American Association for the Advancement of Science, together with the Commission for Professionals in Science and Technology, have just completed a two-year study of women and minorities who are choosing nontraditional routes to obtain education in computer science and enter the IT workforce. The study surveys May 2000 graduates from twenty-six colleges and universities in the Maryland, Virginia, and Washington, DC, area as well as the faculty at these institutions plus area employers. A chapter presenting some of these findings is included in this volume (Jesse). In addition to the for-profit universities, there are specialized corporate universities (Meister 1998) and other for-profit training organizations that are more focused on specialized courses and certificates than on degrees. The literature also does not give full consideration to the IT disciplines other than computer science. As table 13.2 indicates, computing educator Peter Denning has identified twenty different IT disciplines that award college degrees.

Some of these degrees (such as software architecture or network engineering) involve material similar to that taught in computer science, but others impinge on other disciplines such as business (management information systems), science (scientific computing), philosophy (artificial intelligence), art (graphics), or psychology (human-computer interaction). The demographics, computer experience, and attitudes toward computing may differ greatly from one of these disciplines to the next.

Two chapters in this volume compare the experiences of women in two or more of these IT-related academic disciplines. Beyer and DeKeuster compare gender issues in undergraduate computer science and management information science degree programs at a small public university. Ogan et al. examine gender issues in computer science and four other applied IT disciplines at several major research universities.

Several other studies are currently underway. O'Donnell and colleagues (2004) have surveyed more than 1,200 students at Rutgers University (412 IT majors and 795 nonmajors), and spoken to 43 majors in computer science, computer engineering, IT, and informatics through focus groups. One of the goals of this study is to consider how gender, attitudes, perceptions, work experiences, and competencies influence the choice by students of different IT-related majors, and how technology-related work experience influences attitudes and perceptions of the IT workforce, interest in IT careers, and persistence in IT jobs. The results are too preliminary to report. A study by Lawley and Henderson (2004) is aimed at identifying factors influencing the choices and retention of females in undergraduate IT programs, and comparing these factors for women in computer science programs. So far, more than two dozen interviews have been conducted with entering first-year students in IT and computer science programs at the University of Rochester in preparation for surveys that will be conducted there and at a number of other higher education institutions.

In addition to the issue of majors, unfortunately, there do not yet exist studies covering each of the many different entry points along the spectrum of training and education for an IT career, ranging from associate degrees that prepare people for careers as computer technicians or Webmasters, to doctoral degrees that prepare people for faculty positions or work as research scientists in industrial laboratories. (Exceptions are the assessment studies of the Distributed Mentor Program and the Computing Research Experience for Women Program that are organized by the Computing Research Association Committee on the Status of Women in Computing Research. These programs are devoted to giving research experiences to undergraduate women during the summer and the school year, respectively, with the aim of increasing their persistence through the doctoral degree and into a computing research career. These programs are discussed in a forthcoming article by Aspray and Cohoon.) There does exist, however, a scattered literature that mainly takes its cues from the undergraduate computer science experience, but talks more generally about various gendered aspects of academic preparation for the IT workplace. Accordingly, much of the literature we will be reviewing in the next four sections will mainly be in that vein.

Perceptions of Careers in IT

One set of factors that drives women away from choosing IT-related occupations seems to be perceptions that most students have about what a career in the IT industry is really like. These perceptions seem to have a disproportionately negative effect on women. They include an expectation of highly technical work, carried out in isolation from other people and with little social relevance. Several studies of university students (described in the next paragraph) attest to this fact, but the American Association of University Women (2000) have reported that these findings apply much earlier as well: at the middle and senior high school levels, girls are often ignorant of IT career options, and are "only vaguely aware of the social, interactive, and creative applications of computers." The SIGIS study in Norway (Berg et al. 2002) points to a body of literature that argues that the notions girls and young women in school have about the IT profession and IT professionals stand in the way of them choosing an information and communication technology education later (Gansmo 1998; Nordli 1998; Kvaløy 1999; Hapnes and Rasmussen 1998).

Several studies suggest that many female university students believe in the stereotype of the "solitary nerd pounding away at the keyboard all day" as representative of most jobs in the IT field. Von Hellens and colleagues (2000) in the WinIT project interviewed ten Australian women within the IT field. These women were primarily senior managers involved in activities promoting opportunities for women in IT. The researchers found that the women in the study believe that other women who were not formally trained in IT do not have an appreciation of the diversity of jobs in the industry, and that this stereotype of lonely, "nerdy" work as the representation of the industry tends to turn women off from seeking IT jobs. A telephone survey of women in the U.S. IT industry by Bush and colleagues (2002) also found evidence supporting this trend. Craig, Paradis, and Turner (2002) conducted a survey of 190 first-year students (64 women) enrolled in computing-related degree programs at four universities in China, the United States, Australia, and the United Kingdom. They found that the women had a higher expectation than the men of computing careers being less social and more isolating. Further research from the Australian WinIT project involved interviews with first-year female students in the undergraduate IT degree program at Griffith University. The twenty-two interviewees expressed uncertainty about the specific skills required in the IT industry and what job opportunities were available to them on graduation (Nielsen, Von Hellens, and Wong 2000). The SIGIS study in Norway (Berg et al. 2002) found that many would-be women computer specialists opt out of doing computer science at the university level because they are put off by the nerd image of the men who do. The image is off-putting because of the single-minded devotion to computers at the expense of interacting with other people. Berg and colleagues cite an earlier study by Rasmussen and Hapnes (1991). They also found that the nerd hacker image of singular technical focus, work addiction, and total absorption in computing makes computer science a difficult subject to study for women, citing studies by Rasmussen and Hapnes (1991), Stuedahl (1997), Berg (2000), and Langsether (2001).

The SIGIS Norway study (Berg et al. 2002) found that young females perceive the IT profession as involving predominantly technical jobs in which IT specialists mainly manage the technical aspects of computers. Thus, IT professionals are expected to be interested in and have a great deal of knowledge about computer engineering, as understood in a narrow fashion. IT professionals, these females believe, sit behind a computer all day and talk through the keyboard more than they talk to other people. The main activity of the job is programming, and the jobs are lonely and stressful because of the singular focus on the machines. The women who Berg and colleagues studied preferred to work with sociology or medicine, in the police force, or as psychologists because they believed those professions are more compatible with their interest in relating to people and their commitment to social issues. The SIGIS Norway study (Berg et al. 2002) cites Hapnes and Rasmussen (1998) on this point. Bartol, Venkatesh, and Williamson (2004) have a study underway among several cohorts of graduating business students that attempts to understand the extent to which gender differences in desired job attributes exist among MIS undergraduate students, particularly as compared to other business majors, but the results are not yet available.

Another body of literature discusses the view that women have of IT as not socially meaningful. In a 2000 report of the American Association of University Women, a large survey of middle and high school women found that the respondents perceived a career in IT as a "waste of intelligence," and that they wanted careers where they could "make a difference," while they felt that boys were just interested in making money. Weinberger (2003) found that 30 percent of college women in female-dominated fields believe that an IT career would not lead to meaningful or socially useful work. Bush and colleagues (2002) also found that women are more interested in the uses and benefits of technology to society rather than the technology itself. Based on e-mail interviews with fifteen female computing professionals mainly from the United States and working in a range of careers, Teague (2002) concluded that exposure to practical applications of computing in the workplace would be helpful in attracting women to IT at the high school and university stages, and even after women have begun careers in other disciplines. One reason is that such exposure provides women making career decisions at various stages with better information about the fairly broad range of options actually open to them within the IT field. This is in line with the Australian WinIT project research (Von Hellens et al. 2000) mentioned above that concluded that more women would likely be attracted to the IT field if they understood more clearly the range of skills, aptitudes, and career paths that are possible. Unfortunately, little research to date has addressed this type of approach in a needed longitudinal way. Perceptions of careers in IT are only one part of the picture, however. Issues of confidence and self-efficacy are another.

Confidence and Self-Efficacy

Throughout the literature on gender and IT, there are widespread findings that even when there is no difference in technical competence, women are less self-confident of their technical abilities. If a woman is not confident of her ability in a given field, she is less likely to select that field as her career choice. This crisis in confidence begins well before the college years. Young (2000) conducted a survey on attitudes toward computing with 220 girls and 242 boys. Among these respondents, 83 percent were in middle school, while the remaining 17 percent were in high school. Approximately 95 percent of the respondents planned to attend college. She found no significant difference between boy's and girl's self-ratings of computer competence. Nevertheless, females were more likely to consider themselves "not the type to do well with computers." Eccles (1994) found clear evidence of gender differences in personal efficacy for various occupations among high school students. The males were more confident in their success in science-related professions and male-typed skilled labor roles, while females were more confident in their abilities with regard to health-related occupations and female-typed skilled labor occupations.

The self-confidence issue continues in college. Weinberger (2003) found that 50 to 70 percent of women surveyed believed that the course work required for an IT career is too hard. More results from the WinIT project in Australia showed that female students considered themselves less competent than did their male counterparts, even though academic results did not bear out this difference (Von Hellens and Nielsen 2001). Similarly, Hingorani and Sankar (1995) found that among the forty-six MIS graduating seniors in two classes at a major southeastern U.S. university, the twenty-four female students reported lower perceptions of their computer skills as well as information science concepts and process skills—despite their higher GPAs. Yet there were no differences between the female and male students on their ratings of their business skills.

Margolis and Fisher (2002) found that the women in the computer science program at Carnegie Mellon University expressed much more self-doubt about their programming abilities than did their male counterparts. Self-evaluations placed the women's average score more than 20 percent below that of the males. Beyer et al. (2003) found that among fifty-six students (twenty-four of them female) enrolled in two sections of a computer science course, women reported lower confidence than did men. Wilson (2003) surveyed fifty-two students (fourteen of them female) enrolled in a first-semester, first-year computer science module at the University of Glasgow. While twenty-six of the males strongly agreed or agreed that they were "good with computers," only two of the females held these views (see also Cohoon and Aspray, this volume).

More broadly, a meta-analysis of eighteen computer anxiety studies conducted among university undergraduates between 1990 and 1996 (Chua, Chen, and Wong 1999) concluded that females were generally more anxious. There was also evidence that computer anxiety is inversely related to computer experience. Thus, computer experience may be a factor in explaining some of the results related to gender across studies. A number of studies have shown differences in the computer usage and experience among male and female students at the K–12 levels, although these differences seem to be lessening over time (see Barker and Aspray, this volume). This is also true at the postsecondary level. For example, a study (Craig and Stein 2000) of 529 entering business undergraduate students at Victoria University in Australia and 345 entering students taking their first computer course at Lincoln University in New Zealand (44 percent of them female) showed that female students were more likely to consider themselves as having average knowledge. The study also found that male students used the computer for longer periods of time compared with female students.

Perhaps because of the experience factor, results are more mixed when considering working adults. In a study of 114 male and 52 female managers from a variety of organizations, Parasuraman and Igbaria (1990) found no gender differences in computer anxiety and attitudes toward microcomputers. Pearson et al. (2002–

2003) found that the computer self-efficacy of the 176 female knowledge workers across twenty companies was lower than the computer self-efficacy of the 176 male knowledge workers. In a study of 735 employees at a large university, Harrison, Rainer, and Hochwarter (1997) found that compared to female faculty, male faculty were older, had more education, and reported greater computer experience, greater use of microcomputers and software, less computer anxiety, and higher computer self-efficacy. Among clerical workers, however, it was the females who had less computer anxiety and higher computer self-efficacy, particularly with respect to word-processing software. The researchers suggested that computer usage for clerical functions may be more basic and repetitive, but they also argued that the sex typing of jobs may also influence sex differences in computer self-efficacy and usage.

Bozionelos (2001) took a different approach to the question of computer anxiety by surveying individuals from three groups with differing computer/work experience: individuals (mainly managers and professionals) in advanced management courses in the British Management School (36 women and 192 men), students in a graduate management course at the same school (51 women and 16 men), and undergraduates in a range of courses at the same university (148 women and 72 men). He expected that the undergraduates would show the least computer anxiety, reasoning that they would have grown up largely since computers have been commonplace and should have been more comfortable with them. Controlling for gender, the individuals in the advanced management course showed less computer anxiety compared to the undergraduate group, suggesting that a combination of work and computer experience may reduce computer anxiety. The fact that the undergraduates came from a variety of majors may have affected the results, but the students in the advanced management courses likely represented a variety of undergraduate majors as well. Additional analyses indicated that roughly double the percentage of women than men scored above the mean on the computer anxiety measure used, with no significant differences in percentages across the gender groups (38.9 percent of the advanced management group, 45.1 percent of the students in graduate courses, and 56.8 percent of the undergraduates for females; 17.7 percent, 25 percent, and 25 percent, respectively, for males), but with the direction supporting the trend toward less anxiety in the advanced management group.

Related research has considered gender issues in the user acceptance of new IT in the workplace. The initial findings (e.g., Venkatesh and Morris 2000; Venkatesh, Morris, and Ackerman 2000) suggested that women may be more concerned with the ease of use, and more motivated by social factors and the view of others, than are males. Yet a more recent and comprehensive longitudinal study conducted at four organizations (Venkatesh et al. 2003) indicates that age and computer experience may moderate gender influences, such that effects are more likely to be found for older workers (with apparently limited computer experience), and particularly during the early stages of experience and adoption. The researchers concluded that: "We interpret our findings to suggest that as the younger cohort of employees in the workforce mature, gender differences in how each perceives information technology may disappear" (469).

None of these studies focuses strictly on IT professionals, but they do suggest that confidence and self-efficacy with respect to computer-related work may be heavily influenced by experience and context, including work context. Interestingly, a recent report by two economists from the U.S. Bureau of Labor Statistics (Hipple and Kosanovich 2003) indicated that women are more likely than men to use a computer or the Internet at work. Computer use for women was 59.9 percent, compared with 47.9 percent for men, while the Internet use rate was 41.2 percent for women and 36 percent for men. The economists observed that the higher rate for women was based on their holding jobs in occupations in which computer use is most common, including managerial, professional, and administrative support occupations. The long-term impact of such trends remains to be seen. Still, more research is needed that addresses the types of experiences that raise the computer self-efficacy of females, not only while obtaining their basic education, but as they enter and progress in the workforce. It would also be useful to track the confidence and self-efficacy of women and men in IT, particularly with respect to specific job functions, to help determine the extent to which this factor may influence women to leave the IT profession.

Mentors and Role Models

Many researchers on gender and IT have noted the importance of mentoring to all students, but particularly to women. The critical need for role models has also been raised.

Within the IT profession, mentors are individuals with advanced knowledge and experience who provide significant guidance and support to aid the success and upward mobility of IT career aspirants. Mentors may be in a position to correct some misperceptions of women students about the nature of the IT workplace. They may also be able to help the students overcome a lack of confidence and thereby increase persistence in the field. Mentors may be high school teachers or college faculty members. They might be school counselors or parents. They might be established members of the profession who come into contact with the student only online, through an operation such as MentorNet (a mentoring network for the STEM disciplines in which over ten thousand students have been matched with mentors since 1997). Eccles (1994) observed that parents, teachers, and school counselors are all in a position to influence individual perceptions of career options through the information and experiences they provide. Turner, Bernt, and Pecora (2002) found that the most important influence on a woman's choice to enter a career in IT was her father. In most cases, the father was portrayed as being able to create an opportunity for his daughter to learn about computing. The fathers described tended to have technical occupations—27 percent had a job title containing the word "engineer." This figure is over five times the national average of 5.1 percent of all jobs classified as technical in nature. In the Leventman et al. (2004) study mentioned above, women reported a greater degree of positive influence than did men about entering an IT career through the guidance of science and math teachers, other teachers, relatives, guidance counselors, high school friends, a spouse/partner, STEM college professors, and college/postcollege friends. After analyzing interviews with twenty-two Australian women in IT, including practitioners and academics, Von Hellens, Nielsen, and Trauth (2001) recommended mentoring programs that would expose high school students to a variety of IT career options and the positive aspects of the IT industry. They argued that through such steps, it might be possible to encourage more women to choose IT-related majors.

Even role models, who typically are successful and reasonably visible women IT professionals with whom young women might be able to identify, can help. A young person is not likely to give consideration to a career in which there is little or no indication that they could participate. The person has to see the career as something they could occupy eventually—a so-called possible self. If female students do not see women in professional positions in IT, they are less likely to see this as a possible occupation for themselves. Ahuja (2002) proposes a model of the factors that influence career choice. She posits, among other factors, that the lack of role models will also negatively influence women's decisions about career options in IT. Women earned less than 18 percent of the doctoral degrees conferred in 2001 (National Center for Education Statistics 2004). This points to the fact that female role models in computer-related academia who could inspire women college students are greatly lacking. At the same time, women comprise less than 11 percent of high-level managerial positions within the IT industry (White House Council of

Economic Advisors 2000), further limiting access to successful female role models for aspiring students. There is a body of literature that supports this position. Eccles (1994) posits that role models may have the effect of legitimizing novel or gender-role deviant options. Bush et al. (2002) reported finding evidence that among women, the lack of peers or role models with similar backgrounds discourages them from entering IT careers.

Further research is needed on the impact of role models and mentors on career choice in IT, particularly over time. In conjunction with their study of academic cultures in eighteen IT-related higher education programs, Robinson et al. (2004) are investigating the impact of the availability of mentorship and role models, among other resources, on the recruitment and retention of female students.

Career Advice

One might speculate that there is differential access by gender to IT career advice, especially if some of this advice is provided through informal "old boy" networks. It might also be that there is a difference in the advice that is given to men and women about IT careers. There has been little, if any, research on these topics to date. More generally, one study argues that educational and career encouragement has been found to be more important for women than for men (Tharenou and Conroy 1994). Other studies consider the gendered effects of informal networks, especially for job recruiting (Ragins and Cotton 1991) and compensation (Ragins and Cotton 1999). In a literature review, Ahuja confirms the lack of research in this area and contends that "career choices in college are often made in consultation with faculty members. If female students lack female role models with whom they can discuss career choices with relationship to lifestyle implications, they may not feel they have complete information to evaluate their options in IT careers. Under such circumstances, female students may, by default, self-select themselves toward careers in which they observe other women, thus further intensifying the gender-based stereotyping of professions" (2002, 26).

There are several studies under way. Kohler and Applegate (2004) are examining the factors that influence enrollment, completion, and employment in more vocationally oriented IT work. Their study is based on data about students enrolled in career and technical education–IT programs, as collected by the Illinois State Board of Education between 1996 and 2004. The results are not yet available. Another study that is currently under way, by the economists Rosenbloom and Ash (2004), considers family background, educational decisions, and career experiences in influencing choices between IT and non-IT career paths as well as retention in the IT workforce. Rosenbloom and Ash are conducting an Internet-based survey that has been completed by more than seven hundred individuals, but the survey is not yet complete and the data remain to be analyzed. Llewellyn and Usselman (2004), based on their ongoing Georgia Tech study, indicate that men tended to choose their vocation in college or later, while women tended to choose a career while still in high school.

What we do know is that today, there are a few online sites that provide career advice and job-searching tools directed at women. Women in Technology International offers career-advice articles and articles on job searches (⟨http://www .witi4hire.com/candidates/search_frm.phtml⟩). Webgrrls also offers career advice and provides a female-only job search bank (⟨http://www.webgrrls.com/⟩). In addition, the site offers tech tools, tutorials and briefings on technology, and online discussion forums to its members. The ACM Web site has a special section for careers (⟨http://campus.acm.org/crc/index-hme1-crc.cfm⟩). There is also a section on women in IT (⟨http://campus.acm.org/crc/cri/categorylist-cri24-crc.cfm?cat_id= 7&CFID=29282093&CFTOKEN=67511951⟩), where it lists articles about many of the topics discussed above, such as mentoring and the nerd image. We have found no research on gender issues related to career advice or job-searching tools, however.

Yet in a qualitative survey of female students and graduates in computer science at Victoria University in Australia, Miliszewska and Horwood found that "the transition from higher education to work environment was an issue of vital concern to all respondents" (2000, 56). Although not a formal study, Teague (1992) reports some success with a one-day seminar aimed at helping female computer science students in their final undergraduate year prepare to seek employment. Sessions were geared to boosting the confidence of the female students in handling the job interview process. Surprisingly little research has addressed how female IT students seek and obtain job offers, assess options, and make choices. Similarly, few studies have explored the early work experiences of female IT graduates (for an exception, see Bartol, Williamson, and Langa, this volume), the socialization processes in organizations, and the factors that facilitate or inhibit initial early success in IT.

Working as an IT Professional
Given the general void of research on actual transitions of female IT students to the workplace, we next turn to some of the available research on women actually in the

IT workplace. Our aim is to enhance our understanding of some of the workplace factors that might facilitate or inhibit the career success and upward mobility of female IT graduates who reach this point. We address five concerns: typical female IT positions, male-dominated culture, pay issues, satisfaction and commitment in IT, and conflicts with family responsibilities.

Typical Female IT Positions   Several studies point to a disparity in the types of positions that tend to be held by women compared to men in IT. For example, Von Hellens et al. (2000) found that women are underrepresented in management, technical and network support, and the areas involving systems operations. Women are disproportionately highly represented in data entry, systems and analysis-programming work, and help-desk work.

Similarly, Igbaria and Chidambaram (1997) surveyed 348 information systems managers and professionals from seven mid-Atlantic chapters of the Data Processing Management Association, of which approximately 20 percent were women. They found that women generally occupy lower-level positions within the typical IT organization. Even among a population that is highly trained technically, such as the membership of the Association for Computing Machinery (ACM), this pattern exists. Igbaria and Parasuraman (1997) conducted a survey of 464 ACM members (91 of them women) located in Pennsylvania, Delaware, and southern New Jersey. The survey yielded the results that the women were more likely to hold less technical, nonmanagerial jobs than the men. Typical female job roles included systems programmers, application programmers, and systems analysts, while male roles generally included project leader, information systems managers, and consultants. They also found that women who had attained high-level management positions in IT were likely to have had formal business training and emphasized their business expertise over technical skills.

When Sumner and Niederman (2003–2004) studied MIS alumni from Saint Louis University and Southern Illinois University at Edwardsville, they found no statistically significant differences in the percentages of time that males and females reported spending on twelve different fairly global job tasks, such as programming, end-user support, and systems analysis. The researchers, however, commented that female respondents seemed to spend a somewhat larger proportion of their time with programming tasks and less time on the "high-end" tasks, such as working with end users. In the Wardell, Rogers, and Sawyer (2004) study mentioned above, men were somewhat more likely to report that their current work involved supervisory roles, while women were slightly more likely to report that their work was controlled by supervisors. Based on a study of 175 software professionals from German and Swiss software development projects, Sonnentag (1994) found that women were reasonably represented as subteam leaders, but not as the higher-level team leaders. It also appeared that less complex work was being done by the teams led by women. The author pointed to the likely detrimental impact on being able to keep up technically in the field.

One possible explanation for these patterns is the limited research on career orientation. An Igbaria, Greenhaus, and Parasuraman (1991) study of ACM members in three mid-Atlantic states found that a higher percentage of men (24.7 percent) than women (14.3 percent) had their strongest career orientation toward the technical aspects of the work, whereas a higher percentage of women (20.8 percent) than men (8.1 percent) were oriented toward lifestyle integration that encompasses concerns for family, career, and self-development. An Igbaria and McCloskey (1996) study of the average scores of forty-two male and forty-eight female IT employees from three companies in Taiwan on a number of career dimensions also showed that women scored higher on lifestyle orientation. Additionally, women gave higher ratings to job security, while men scored higher on managerial and geographic security dimensions. There were no gender differences on the technical dimension, however, or on the autonomy, service, pure challenge, and entrepreneurship dimensions. In the ACM study, similar percentages of women (22 percent) as men (27.1 percent) expressed a dominant orientation toward managerial competence, suggesting that a lack of orientation toward managerial activities may not account for the pattern of differences in managerial jobs held by women versus men.

Another explanation for the mix of females and males in various jobs in IT has been offered by Wright and Jacobs (1994). After analyzing three sets of data from the Bureau of Labor Statistics, the NSF's Survey of Natural and Social Scientists and Engineers, and the U.S. Bureau of the Census, Wright and Jacobs concluded that sex segregation across computer specialties had either not changed or had declined slightly during the period 1971 to 1991, suggesting that the sex segregation of the IT field was not increasing as might be expected if women were being increasingly channeled to the lowest-status computer specialties. They rejected a ghettoization explanation that would posit that lower-status, lower-paying jobs in IT are being increasingly filled by women, leading to the "feminization" of some specialties, but not others. They also questioned a resegregation thesis (e.g., Reskin and Roos 1990), which argues that a shortage of male employees, due to accelerated growth or a decline in the status of an occupation, leads employers to recruit women. This, in turn, leads to male flight from the occupation. Instead, Wright and Jacobs found that after taking into consideration characteristics such as age, experience, and education, women are leaving computer work more often than men. Recent research by Rosenbloom and Ash (2004), based on the Merged Outgoing Rotation Group of the Current Population Survey for 1983 through 2002, also supports this view, showing a "precipitous" decline in the participation rates of women in the IT workforce, with declines "less pronounced" (117) in core IT occupations that include computer systems analysts and computer programmers, but more prominent in areas that include computer operations in which women have tended to be well represented.

In explaining the disproportional attrition of women in IT, Wright (1996, 1997) contends that women are constantly given lifelong social control messages about male-dominated professions. These messages tell women that they do not belong in such occupations and they should not be in them. Consequently, women decline to enter male-dominated fields and often choose to leave such occupations. In the case of IT, she asserts that because of its roots in the field of electrical engineering, the field has an engineering-like culture that operates as the mechanism of social control.

Male-Dominated Culture   Several studies indicate that women perceive the IT work environment as male-dominated and not welcoming to women. Weinberger (2003) conducted a survey of randomly chosen students, 275 of whom were female, at a large public university. About one-third of the female respondents indicated that they would not expect a welcoming atmosphere in the IT careers. None of the male respondents had this same concern. Close to 20 percent of the female respondents also believed that they would not fit in with their coworkers if they pursued an IT career. More than 80 percent of the women in the survey felt that they would not enjoy a career in IT. In her model of factors that influence career choice, Ahuja (2002) also posits that perceptions of the occupational culture will negatively influence women's choice of and persistence in IT as a career.

Taking a slightly different point of view, the SIGIS final report (Faulkner et al. 2004), based on studies of gender and IT in five European countries, argues that this problem of image has more to do with the low relative numbers of women in the field than with a presumed symbolic association of IT and masculinity. According to the SIGIS study in the United Kingdom (Faulkner 2002), managers in the IT field tend to recruit in their own image—that is, young men with a willingness to devote long and often antisocial hours to the job.

This pattern was confirmed by Miller and Jagger (2001) in a comparison of IT jobs in the United States, the United Kingdom, Spain, Taiwan, Canada, and Ireland. In the SIGIS study in Norway, Berg and colleagues (2002) found that the male hacker culture was in sharp contrast with what female computing students desired to do. These females wanted to use computers as tools to solve practical problems in society, and to be occupied with a broader range of social and human aspects of computing. The Norwegian study cited articles by Rasmussen and Hapnes (1991) and Berg (2000); the Berg article pointed out that young women in IT fields had trouble getting integrated into a community dominated by men. The Dutch SIGIS study (Oost 2002), citing Zoonen (2001), identified masculine values and practices as an important reason for the lack of women in both computing education and computing professions.

Wright (1996, 1997; Wright and Jacobs 1994) called for further research on the perceptions of females and males regarding occupational barriers, changes in status, and views of organization culture over time. Stanton, Eischen, and Guzman (2004) are currently conducting a longitudinal study of students in information studies and engineering at Syracuse University and students in computer engineering technology at Onondaga Community College. They are trying to learn about expectations, beliefs, and experiences related to occupational cultures in the IT field along with how these are formed and how they change over time. The results are not yet available. Major and colleagues (2004) are investigating the extent to which organizations that have a strong climate for opportunity and inclusion are able to better attract and retain women in IT positions. So far, they have surveyed more than nine hundred IT employees (39 percent of them women) from eleven companies. The preliminary results suggest that company support for family life, affective support, a positive supervisor-employee relationship, and relative contribution to the work group add to perceptions of a positive climate for opportunity and inclusion. Further work will attempt to link the climate, in turn, to important outcomes, such as lower turnover intentions and higher career success.

In support of the male-oriented culture notion, Grundy's (1994) participant observer study (on temporary assignment from her university) of a U.K. information and computing department at a district health authority described a status hierarchy in which men seem to gravitate toward the more stimulating "pure" computer science research and women were left with the more "messy" jobs, such as correcting data records or writing report programs. Similar conclusions were reached by Woodfield (2000, 2002) based on more than fifty interviews in the U.K. research and development units of two global computer companies, and an ethnographic study at one of them. Among other things, she investigated the possibility that a shift in the computer industry in the early 1990s toward commercialization and away from an almost exclusive concern for technical inventiveness would potentially create improved opportunities for women. The shift was expected to create the need for "hybrid" workers with not only technical skills but also social skills. The hybrid IT professionals were expected to help in better understanding the needs of users for the software development process and in providing improved subsequent support. Because women are often perceived as possessing strong social skills due to their upbringing and socialization, some observers had argued that the need for hybrid workers would help boost the participation of women in the IT field.

Woodfield (2000, 2002) found that although there was strong recognition of the need for hybrid workers, the possession of the requisite skills by women tended to be relatively underrecognized and underrewarded. Instead, identification and recognition of such skills tended to operate within the existing social status structure, which continued to marginalize the contributions of women. Although the organization attempted to put in place official pronouncements regarding the need for hybrid skills and equality, the simultaneous attempt to downplay hierarchical approaches, the assumption of meritocracy, and an interlinking of assessment systems with informal peer review systems allowed the operation of powerful informal social hierarchies in which women were generally not included.

One manifestation of a male-oriented culture may be continuing issues of gender equity in pay.

Pay Issues A number of studies have pointed to gender differences in pay in IT. This perhaps is not surprising, given that pay differences related to gender are quite pervasive not only in the United States but in a number of other countries (e.g., Gender Pay Gap 2002). Such differentials seem to be characteristic of most, if not all, occupations (e.g., Roos and Gatta 1999). In IT, Truman and Baroudi (1994) found that among IT executives surveyed by the Society for Information Management during a three-year period, men and women with the same human capital characteristics—such as age, education, and work experience—tended to be at equivalent levels in the organization. Yet their salaries were significantly lower than males at the same level. In a survey of 4,362 IT professionals (42.7 percent of them female) in Singapore, Tan and Igbaria (1994) found that on average, female IT professionals made less than their male counterparts, but this varied by IT speciality. Ang, Slaughter, and Ng (2002) generally did not find salary differences for females among 1,576 IT professionals from thirty-nine institutions in Singapore who participated in the 1997 Information Technology Management Association's salary survey. These latter results may have been influenced by the severe IT labor shortage in Singapore during the period of this study.

U.S. evidence compiled by Wright and Jacobs (1994) indicated that female computer workers earn 88 percent of the salaries of their male counterparts, and that the gap narrowed slightly during the 1980s (rising from 84 percent in 1982), not only across the board, but in each of seven different specializations within the computer field. They concluded that the increased numbers of women working in the computer field had not had a detrimental impact on salaries in the computer field (contrary to some predictions, such as Strober 1984) and viewed the slight drop in the earnings gap as an improvement. Recent data from *InformationWeek* salary surveys suggest that a relative status quo continues, with women estimated to have earned about 90 percent of their male counterparts in 2000 (Wilde 2000) and varying around that figure, with the salary gap being narrower for female IT managers/executives (Garvey 2004; Goodridge 2002).

Despite chronic wage differences between males and females in IT and most other fields, female entry professionals may fair better in an absolute sense in the IT field. Based on an analysis of two waves of data from the Survey of Income and Program, Brown and Corcoran (1997) found that during the mid-1980s at least, there was a wage premium for females majoring in engineering or computer science (but not math/science majors), compared with what they might have made by majoring in business, a relatively high-paying major used as the comparative standard in the study. The researchers noted that a number of the majors traditionally chosen by women "prepare one for relatively low-wage work" (456). In a further assessment of wage differences in IT, Weinberger and Kuhn (2004) analyzed NSF SESTAT data on bachelor's degree–level college graduates who participated in the 1993 Survey of College Graduates and were resurveyed through 1999. They found that during the 1990s, the earnings of women in computer science grew faster than the earnings of women in any other field and faster than the earnings of men in any field other than computer science.

Thus, the pay situation in IT presents somewhat of a dilemma for women. While there is evidence of continuing inequities in pay within IT, in an absolute sense, the pay tends to be better than women are likely to make in many other occupations, including those more traditionally open to women. There is also evidence that women tend to attribute less importance to pay. For example, Konrad and colleagues (2000) conducted a meta-analysis of job attribute studies and found that among business managers, men deem earnings and responsibility more significant in a job than women do, while women rate challenge, work environment, good social relationships, and good hours as more crucial. Still, mixed feelings among women in IT about the pay issue are reflected in some of the data regarding satisfaction and commitment in IT that we cover below.

Satisfaction and Commitment in IT

The few studies that have directly addressed the job and career satisfaction of women are perhaps surprisingly positive in view of the protracted underrepresentation of women in the IT field as well as the related issues, such as culture. For example, in a study of seventy-six information center employees (forty of them women) from twenty-eight companies in the state of Ohio (Igbaria and Guimaraes 1993), men and women were similar in terms of their satisfaction with work, supervision, pay, and promotion, and reported similar levels of organizational commitment and intention to leave. They also reported similar degrees of stressors, such as role conflict and role ambiguity. Women, however, were more satisfied with their coworkers than were their male counterparts. The primary duties of these workers were coaching, training, equipment demonstration, and technical support for end users. Extending this work, Baroudi and Igbaria (1994–1995) studied 354 members of seven mid-Atlantic chapters of the Data Processing Management Association. After controlling for demographics—such as age, organizational tenure, job tenure, number of years in the information systems field, and education—the analysis showed that females ($n = 86$) and males rated their job satisfaction and organizational commitment equivalently, but females were more likely to be at lower levels, make less money, and have higher intentions to leave.

Similar findings emerged from a Sumner and Niederman (2003–2004) study of MIS alumni from Saint Louis University and Southern Illinois University at Edwardsville. The results showed no gender differences in satisfaction with various aspects of the job, including supervisors, career progress, and coworkers. Females were significantly more satisfied with their financial rewards even though there was no evidence that they were earning higher pay than their male counterparts. Further support of this trend comes from a survey by Jiang and Klein (1999–2000) of 101 entry-level IT personnel (64 men and 37 women) from three large software development organizations in a major metropolitan area of the southern United States. The respondents included systems analysts, programmers, and technical support analysts. The results showed no differences related to gender for career satisfaction or perceptions of supervisor support.

Teague's (2002) qualitative study of fifteen female IT professionals mainly in the United States indicated that the aspects that they have most enjoyed about their jobs tended to be solving problems; the diversity, variety, and challenge of the work; the alternative job opportunities; money and travel; the interactions with various colleagues within and outside their work unit; the flexibility of the hours; and the respect one could earn for doing a good job. Among their dislikes were the paucity of female colleagues, the tendency toward male-oriented environments, and discriminatory practices—particularly with respect to salaries. Teague thus noted, "In summary, it can be said that the issues that deter many girls from computing as a career are not supported by the experiences of women working in the industry. Most women have been able to find niches which they enjoy. They have few dislikes about the work they do" (156). After analyzing interviews with twenty-two Australian women in IT, including practitioners and academics, Von Hellens, Nielsen, and Trauth also concluded that these women "have satisfying careers in the IT industry" (2001, 119).

While some of the studies point to a fair amount of job satisfaction among females in IT and provide some cause for optimism, they may be capturing mainly the views of women who have remained in the IT field. Studies are sorely needed that track the attitudes and concerns of men and women in IT over time, especially during the transition from their university or other educational venue into the workplace. Other transitions, such as job and assignment changes, may be important too. It may be through such transition points that at least some women are lost to the profession. We also need to learn more about the factors that lead women in IT not only to leave their organizations but to transfer to non-IT work as well.

One recurring career issue is conflicts with family responsibilities. We turn next to this concern.

Conflicts with Family Responsibilities

One factor in women's choice of career path is that of striking a balance between work responsibilities and family life. If a woman perceives a particular career as difficult or incompatible with family opportunities and responsibilities, such as long or unpredictable hours, she might either choose a different career or make personal choices such as not marrying, not having children, or not taking responsibility for caring for aging parents so as to make time available for her career. Weinberger's (2003) survey found that 30 to 40 percent of college women felt that careers in IT fields would be incompatible with raising children. The SIGIS report for the Netherlands (Oost 2002) revealed similar results for Dutch women. The report cited the expectation of long work hours, the overtime required, and the difficulty of reconciling work and private life as factors making an IT career less viable (Brekel, Klaveren, and Tijdens 1999). It also pointed to another study (Keuzenkamp and Hooghiemstra 2000) showing that only 9 percent of men change working hours when their child is born. Based on this statistic, the SIGIS report argues that the Dutch ideology of the male as the breadwinner and female as both the homemaker and the mother leaves Dutch men and women with the perception of an incompatibility between career and motherhood in general.

In the United States, the results are similar. In the Wardell, Rogers, and Sawyer (2004) study mentioned above, women were likely to think that their work environments do not allow them to put family matters ahead of their work, and to feel that they have to choose between a career at work or at home. Women were five times more likely to have taken unpaid leave, and they averaged 4.25 months of unpaid leave, compared to 2.25 months for men. In the Llewellyn and Usselman (2004) study, men were significantly more likely to have their children cared for by a spouse during working hours and women were significantly more dissatisfied with the adequacy of benefits on the job.

Igbaria and Parasuraman (1997) found in their survey of ACM members that the women in the sample were much more likely to be single than the men, and if married, the women were less likely to have children. The researchers concluded that women in the IT industry anticipate problems balancing their career and familial responsibilities, and this anticipation leads them in some cases to remain unmarried or childless as a coping mechanism. In a survey of sixty women in IT, Lemons and Parzinger (2001) identified a group who were raised with the belief that they could have a career in the predominantly male IT world, chose not to have children, and instead focused on the pursuit of career goals. Later in their careers, most of these women began to question their choice not to have children.

Bartol, Williamson, and Venkatesh (2004), in a study of IT professionals in a major U.S. company, discovered that perceptions of company support for work-family balance issues were important to both male and female IT professionals. This tracks with a study of ninety-six information systems professionals in a southwestern city in which Holmes (1998) found that men and women both rated challenging tasks as well as sufficient time for personal and family life the highest when asked to indicate the importance of a list of work goals. Other data more generally point to a growing concern among younger workers, male and female, with work-life balance issues (Nord et al. 2002). Whether these trends help to assuage the career issues of women in IT remains to be seen.

IT Career Attachment and Progression

A number of studies do point to evidence of discrimination toward women in the IT workplace in ways that are likely to be detrimental to their careers. For example, in a telephone survey by Llewellyn and Usselman (2004) of 254 Georgia Tech alumni, all of whom had taken at least one programming course, women were significantly more likely to report having been discriminated against in their current jobs. Along these lines, Allen, Reid, and Riemenschneider (2004) held focus groups involving thirty-nine female IT employees from a Fortune 500 manufacturing organization who volunteered to participate. Among the most commonly mentioned barriers and challenges were issues related to promotions, family responsibilities, politics, discrimination, upper management's problematic attitudes, and problems with respect. To a lesser degree, comments were also made about departmental barriers, fear of how others see you or will act, age, policy problems, supervisors' attitudes, limited access to decision makers, lack of consistency at the organizational level and from supervisors, and men taking control.

Some of the difficulties women in IT confront may stem from hiring practices. For example, Ranson and Reeves (1996) studied pay and promotion patterns among 451 IT professionals from fourteen different organizations in a western Canadian city. Although an initial analysis suggested that generally women were less likely than men to become highly paid IT managers and that the lesser experience of the women was a potential explanation, further analysis indicated a more complex and discriminatory set of patterns. The researchers uncovered major differences in conditions within organizations with less than 35 percent women as compared to those with more than 35 percent women. In the organizations with proportionately fewer women, the women seemed to be paid and promoted on a par with men. In the organizations with proportionately more women IT professionals, the women tended to earn less, have less experience, and be slightly less well educated. The researchers speculated that each type of organization showed a hiring pattern that disadvantaged women—in the former case, hiring few women, and in the latter case, hiring women who are "clearly junior to men by all the human capital criteria" (179).

Research has also identified promotion issues that work to the detriment of the career progress of women in IT. Based on a study of 109 information systems employee-supervisor pairs in a large utility company in the eastern United States, Igbaria and Baroudi (1995) found that the performance evaluations received by women and men were similar. Yet the women were viewed by supervisors as less promotable than the men because the performance of the women was less likely to be attributed to ability and effort, and more likely to be viewed as emanating from help and luck—a common problem with performance evaluation situations (Bartol 1999).

When she interviewed eleven men and eleven women IT managers from two companies in the United Kingdom about their career progression, Shapiro (1994) discovered that informal processes were also at work. The evidence indicated that a technical career path was not necessarily a prerequisite for managerial positions in IT. Even when they had a technical background, women had a tendency to be channeled into analyst pathways, rather than more technical ones, suggesting that the lack of technical training did not account for the relatively low numbers of women in IT management in these two companies. Rather, Shapiro found that adhering to the promotion criteria perceived to be considered important by top management (i.e., "fitting in") and operating within the informal promotion procedures (such as networking, becoming known and perceived positively by senior management, and being in the right place at the right time) were important for upward mobility. The study identified differences in the means of attaining knowledge of informal career processes, with female managers often acquiring such knowledge though guidance from a senior male manager and male managers acquiring tacit knowledge through their interactions within the organization. While the men all accepted and complied with the informal career process, women exhibited a range of reactions, with some accepting the informal career process and attempting to adjust to it. Others compromised, particularly with respect to work and family issues, and sometimes were able to influence an adjustment in the process and stay on track. Others rejected the informal career process norms, usually slowing their upward mobility. Shapiro argues that more research is needed into the development of informal career processes in organizations and ways to influence them to aid the upward mobility of women. We also note the need for additional work that addresses the specific career issues for women of color.

In the end, organizations likely pay a price for the career difficulties of women in IT. In the Igbaria and Chidambaram (1997) study of Data Processing Management Association members, women were less likely than men to perceive opportunities for intangible rewards and activities, such as interesting, challenging, and important assignments, but these intangibles were more strongly associated with organizational commitment and an intention to stay for women.

Unfortunately, the IT profession is also likely to pay a price. Closely related to perceptions of careers in IT, and cutting across many of the issues discussed below, is the question of professional identification. Do women identify with professional work in IT in ways different from men? O'Leary-Kelly and colleagues (2004) have investigated a number of factors that might affect professional identification. These include the motivations for entering the field, the fit between family and work identities as well as schedules, self-efficacy, the degree of socialization, and workplace experiences. O'Leary-Kelly's group has surveyed 720 IT workers online (270 of them women). The researchers have found that women are more motivated to have IT careers for extrinsic reasons such as money, advancement, and flexible work hours; felt less well socialized than men in the discipline; have lower levels of technical self-efficacy; report greater career support from their supervisors than men; and have less congruence than men between their work and family identities. For men, there is a positive correlation between professional identification and having received both good mentoring and strong career-related support. Neither was true for women. The study has also shown that women who have overcome obstacles in order to be in the IT profession have a strong attachment to the profession.

There may be steps that organizations can take to help boost the professional commitment of female newcomers to the IT workforce, through factors such as organizational support and job satisfaction. This is a finding of the Bartol, Williamson, and Langa chapter in this volume.

Aside from the benefits to women themselves and their immediate employing organizations, there are number of broader reasons why increasing the representation of women in the IT workforce is vitally important. We address these reasons briefly in part 2.

In closing this review, we point to the continuing need to upgrade the research being done in this area (see Bartol and Martin [1982]), recognize many efforts in this direction, and believe that further longitudinal work would be particularly helpful.

Part 2: A More Encompassing Vision of Why Full Representation of Women in the IT Workforce Is Important

Up to now, we have not addressed directly the issue of why it is important to have full representation of women in the IT workforce. The argument that is at least implicitly made in most of the literature on women and IT is that this underrepresentation is an issue of either gender equity or fairness. Jobs in IT involve interesting work, typically pay well above the median wage, have favorable conditions of employment (no dangerous or hard physical labor involved), and have been readily available and probably will continue to be so (Horrigan 2003–2004). Moreover, having IT skills prepares one for a much larger number of jobs that are IT enabled. Thus, it is only fair to give women equal access to these desirable jobs.

The discussion about the underrepresentation of women in IT can profitably be expanded beyond fairness and equity issues. In this second section, we review some of the other contexts for understanding the underrepresentation of women in IT. These contexts include meeting the workforce needs of U.S. employers, providing a stronger workforce that can reduce the need for temporary foreign workers or outsourcing, improving the innovativeness of the United States so as to enhance national competitiveness and increase the standard of living for all Americans, improving cybersecurity and homeland defense, and offering opportunities for developing alternative and better products through the inclusion of women in product design.

A major reason for eliminating the underrepresentation of women in the IT workforce is to provide an adequate supply of workers to U.S. employers. At the height of the dot-com boom, around the year 1999, U.S. employers were having great difficulty finding enough qualified IT workers. Faced with a shortage of qualified workers, employers had to take a number of unpalatable steps. They had to spend more money on recruiting, overtime, training, working conditions, wages, benefits, and bonuses. They had to reduce the minimum qualifications for the job, and sometimes restructure work or substitute machinery for labor. Also, they had to contract out and sometimes turn down work (Barnow, Trutko, and Lerman 1998).

Employers would not have had to resort to these actions had the nation done a better job of including women and ethnic minorities in the IT workforce. As one major workforce study from the time remarked, "If the number of women in the IT workforce were increased to equal the number of men, even the tremendous shortages of IT workers noted [at the time] could be filled" (Freeman and Aspray

1999, 111). Nevertheless, as mentioned in the introduction, the representation of women in the IT workforce has been much lower than that of men. Even when faced with a severe shortage, companies did not adopt new strategies that moved women toward parity in the IT workforce or increased minority participation to a representative level. Industry's response instead was to import temporary foreign workers—mostly males from India—to fill the open positions.

In the effort to import enough IT workers, there was considerable political wrangling over raising the annual caps on the number of H1–B temporary visas. While industry was generally in favor of higher caps, high-tech guilds of minority workers, such as the Coalition for Fair Employment in Silicon Valley (which has a sizable African American membership), protested against the increase in the number of foreign workers. A similar stance was taken by the Rainbow/PUSH Silicon Valley Project associated with the Reverend Jesse Jackson. This project believed that the ready availability of foreign workers would remove pressure from employers to increase the hiring of U.S. minority and female workers.

There was not much heard specifically from organized women workers at the time of the H1–B debates, perhaps because women were doing somewhat better than ethnic and racial minorities at making inroads into the major centers of IT work such as Silicon Valley. For example, African Americans were almost entirely locked out of the Silicon Valley workforce despite there being large African American populations in nearby communities such as Oakland. This is not to say that women were doing all that well in Silicon Valley. In a survey conducted in 2001 by Women of Silicon Valley, there were many troubling statistics: only 28 percent of the computer engineers were women, only 17 percent of the managers were women, and only 31 percent of the programmers were women; 28 percent of the women reported gender as a significant barrier to advancement, 60 percent of college-educated women said that advancement opportunities were better for men, and 43 percent thought that opportunities for women were equal or better for women outside Silicon Valley (Commission on Professionals in Science and Technology 2001).

But the call for action by women has been heard more clearly in recent times. See, for example, the one by Marcia Stein of Stein Consulting (Cupertino, California), representing Silicon Valley Women in Human Resources (⟨http://www.ourhrsite .com⟩). This political action has partly to do with the wages and working conditions of women, especially immigrant women in the low-wage manufacturing sector of IT (see, for example, the academic accounts by Matthews [2003] and Hossfeld [forthcoming]). There has also been a serious increase in unemployment and underemployment in Silicon Valley since the dot-com bubble burst, and anecdotal reports indicate that this may have disproportionately hit women and minorities. The Sphere Institute reports that the majority of people working at technology companies in California in early 2000 had either left the field or the state by the end of 2003, and more than 40 percent saw their incomes decline. Lower-level workers who shifted from semiconductor manufacturing to health care, for instance, suffered a 31 percent loss in income from 2000 to 2003, adjusting for inflation (see ⟨http:// www.itfacts.biz⟩).

The Silicon Valley Women in Human Resources has specifically objected to the importation of foreign workers through the H1–B and L–1 visa programs. It is likely that these concerns will continue. As recently as November 2004, Congress passed legislation increasing the H1–B cap by twenty thousand for foreigners who earn advanced degrees in the United States.

Much of the concern these days in the U.S. IT workforce is the offshoring of jobs to India, China, and other countries. There is a certain kind of fatalistic view in the IT workforce that all IT jobs are vulnerable in the United States because of the five- or ten-to-one difference in wages between U.S. and these foreign workers, and there are anecdotal reports that women and minorities feel themselves to be among the most vulnerable. When all of the associated costs for evaluating vendors, managing contracts, improving security, extra travel, and severance for laying off employees are taken into consideration, the value advantage of offshoring is lessened. There are also downsides to offshoring, such as the loss of control over the work process; the loss of in-house expertise; the need for additional bureaucracy such as explicit authority relations, operating procedures, and incentive systems; and the risks to data privacy, security, and intellectual property. Many companies say that a major reason why they outsource is to gain access to a labor pool that has adequate numbers of people with the currently needed skills. An increase in the domestic IT labor pool by representative participation by women and minorities would go a long way toward meeting that need. These workers would not face the same cultural problems as foreign workers—ones involving social behavior, attitudes toward authority, and language issues (see Aspray 2004). Much more needs to be studied about the perceived and real threats of offshoring to U.S. IT workers, and in particular, the differential effect these real and perceived threats may have on women and minorities.

One argument that has been made is that the United States can deflect the harmful effects of offshoring through enhanced education and innovation (e.g., Atkinson

2004; Frauenheim and Yamamoto 2004; Koehler and Hagigh 2004). Yet the current underutilization of women in IT represents a major loss toward efforts aimed at IT innovation. This happens for three major reasons.

First, as has already been pointed out, the degree attainment patterns of women represent a significant detriment to the potential numbers of highly educated professionals working in IT. Not only are there relatively few females earning undergraduate degrees in computer science and closely related areas but the proportion of master's degrees and doctorates going to women is even smaller (National Center for Education Statistics 2004). In the context of acute global competitiveness, the loss is enormous.

Second, even when women have the credentials, as we discussed earlier, there is a tendency to channel them to lower-level, less challenging work. This, of course, represents a serious underutilization of available human capital. Although the cumulative effects on organizational and national competitiveness are unknown, they are likely to be enormous.

Third, there is considerable evidence that diversity in teams can be helpful when creativity and innovation are needed (Barkema, Baum, and Mannix 2002). For example, computer scientist Lucinda Sanders of Bell Labs has argued that software development teams made up of both men and women are more innovative than those comprising only males, but says that there have not been enough women to go around (Bhattacharjee 2004). Along with diversity, however, there is a need to attend carefully to the means used by teams to manage and leverage the diversity, including participation in decision making, on behalf of innovation (De Dreu and West 2001; Jackson, Joshi, and Erhardt 2003).

The underrepresentation of women in the workforce can also be considered in light of cybersecurity and homeland defense. At the moment, there is a grave shortage of security workers at all levels in the United States. As of 2001, there were only a few dozen faculty in the United States with significant background in security research, and all of them together were on average graduating only seven PhDs in this area each year (Spafford 2001). Thus, there is not the base of faculty to provide adequate training to people of many different levels to work in the security field.

There have been a few pioneering women in leadership positions in the security field, including Dorothy Denning, Susan Landua, and Jean Camp. This may be an excellent field for women to make their mark in IT. One National Research Council report indicated that 85 percent of all security problems are not purely technical but are instead either social or sociotechnical (Schneider 1999). Given the large number of women trained in the social sciences, there may be excellent opportunities for gender balance in this research and education field.

There is a study currently under way by Rao, Bagchi-Sen, and Upadhyay (2004) to analyze women's entry, retention, and advancement in the cybersecurity field, in connection with the national strategy to address the shortfalls in the number of trained and certified security personnel. The study is surveying and interviewing undergraduate men and women who are recipients of Department of Defense Information Assurance Scholarship Program awards in fifty Centers of Excellence for Information Assurance. The study is also interviewing cybersecurity professionals and women who are chief information or chief security officers in U.S. companies. The results are not yet available.

Our final context for understanding the underrepresentation of women in IT has to do with opportunities for developing alternative and better products through the inclusion of women in product design. Certainly a recurring theme in the literature on computing is the tendency to orient product development toward male users. For example, Rommes (2000) asserts that the first digital city software in the Netherlands, a locally bound information and communication system for the Internet, attracted relatively few female users because the policymaker and designer groups were mainly male, and ultimately developed a user interface with more male connotations. Similar scenarios can be found elsewhere. A report by the American Association of University Women (2000) has cited the relative lack of appropriate computer content for girls as one reason why girls often have less computer experience than their male counterparts. Others have criticized the often narrow technical orientation of development teams, arguing that they have insufficient member diversity and/or make inadequate efforts to obtain the input/involvement of representative potential users (e.g., Grundy 1994; Karasti 1994; Woodfield 2000). Still others have pointed to the common problems of women holding lower-level and less sophisticated technical positions as another manifestation of product development concerns (e.g., McDonald and Spencer 2000; Panteli, Ramsay, and Beirne 1997).

Solutions to the issue of the type of software that should be developed to make computers more interesting and acceptable to girls and women continue to be controversial. For example, Lynn and colleagues (2003) note at least three different views of what to do to make software and Web sites more attractive to girls. One approach is to design software and Web sites to appeal to more traditional gender interests in collaboration, relationships, negotiation, glamour, and creative design. Another approach is to attempt to mimic aggressive game software for boys in versions showing female assertive heroines. A third approach advocates creating gender-neutral content oriented to the common nonviolent interests of both boys and girls. The Lynn group shows evidence for the success of a fourth approach aimed at integrating traditional and nontraditional content along with an emphasis on learning about computer design itself. While resolving these issues is beyond the scope of this chapter, we would argue that broadened involvement in product development is critical to enabling women to take on roles "not simply as consumers and end users of technology, but as designers, leaders, and shapers of the computer culture" (American Association of University Women 2000, 4).

Acknowledgments

This material is based on work supported by the National Science Foundation under grant number EIA–0244604. Any opinions, findings, and conclusions or recommendations expressed in this material are those of the authors, and do not necessarily reflect the views of the National Science Foundation.

We wish to thank Indiana University graduate students Alla Genkina and Troy Campbell for helping to review and summarize articles, librarian Melanie Groth for extensive library and database searches in connection with this chapter, and especially instructor Matthew Hottell for assisting with data collection and outlining material that was used to write several sections of this chapter.

References

Ahuja, M. K. 2002. Women in the information technology profession: A literature review, synthesis, and research agenda. *European Journal of Information Systems* 11:20–34.

Allen, M. W., M. Reid, and C. Riemenschneider. 2004. The role of laughter when discussing workplace barriers: Women in information technology jobs. *Sex Roles* 50:177–189.

American Association of University Women Educational Foundation Commission on Technology, Gender, and Teacher Education. 2000. *Tech-savvy: Educating girls in the new computer age*. Washington, DC: American Association of University Women Educational Foundation.

Ang, S., S. Slaughter, and K. Y. Ng. 2002. Human capital and institutional determinants of information technology compensation: Modeling multilevel and cross-level interactions. *Management Science* 48:1427–1445.

Aspray, W. 2004. Offshore outsourcing review. Paper presented to the ACM Job Migration Task Force, October 8, Chicago.

Atkinson, R. 2004. Meeting the offshoring challenge. Policy report, Progressive Policy Institute, July.

Babco, E., and J. Jesse. 2001. AAAS/CPST studies nontraditional pathways into the IT/CS workforce. *Computing Research News* 3 (May): 7.

Barkema, H. G., J. A. C. Baum, and E. A. Mannix. 2002. Management challenges in a new time. *Academy of Management Journal* 45:916–930.

Barnow, B. S., J. Trutko, and R. Lerman. 1998. *Skill mismatches and worker shortages: The problem and appropriate responses.* Draft final report, submitted by the Urban Institute to the Office of the Assistant Secretary for Policy, U.S. Department of Labor, February 25, 22–31.

Baroudi, J. J., and M. Igbaria. 1994–1995. An examination of gender effects on career success of information systems employees. *Journal of Management Information Systems* 11:181–201.

Bartol, K. M. 1999. Gender influences on performance evaluations. In *Handbook of gender in organizations*, ed. G. N. Powell, 165–178. Thousand Oaks, CA: Sage.

Bartol, K. M., and D. C. Martin. 1982. Managing information systems personnel: A review of the literature and managerial implications. *MIS Quarterly* (special issue): 49–70.

Bartol, K. M., I. O. Williamson, and V. Venkatesh. 2004. Understanding female and minority retention and success in the IT workplace: Total rewards and social networks perspectives. In *Proceedings of the National Science Foundation's ITWF and ITR/EWF principal investigator conference*, ed. E. Trauth, 155–161. Philadelphia: NSF.

Berg, V. A. L. 2000. *Firkanter og rundinger. Kjoonskonstruksjoner blant kvinnelige datainge-niorstudenter ved NTNU.* SKF report 3/2000. Trondheim, Norway: Centre for Feminist and Gender Research.

Berg, V. A. L., H. J. Gansmo, K. Hestflått, M. Lie, H. Nordli, K. H. Sørensen. 2002. Gender and ICTs in Norway: An overview of Norwegian research and some relevant statistical information. In *Digital divide and inclusion measures: A review of literature and statistical trends on gender and ICT*, ed. K. H. Sørensen and J. Stewart. Senter for teknologi og samfunn, report 2002–59, NTNU, Trondheim. ⟨http://www.rcss.ed.ac.uk/sigis/public/displaydoc/full/D02_Part4⟩.

Beyer, S., K. Rynes, J. Perrault, K. Hay, and S. Haller. 2003. Gender differences in computer science students. *ACM SIGCSE Bulletin* 35, no. 1:49–53.

Bhattacharjee, Y. 2004. Random sample: People. *Science* 306, no. 5698 (November 5): 973.

Bozionelos, N. 2001. Computer anxiety: Relationship with computer experience and prevalence. *Computers in Human Behavior* 17:213–224.

Brekel, C. van den, M. van Klaveren, and K. Tijdens. 1999. *The absence of women in the ICT sector.* AIAS–University of Amsterdam/FNV Bondgenoten report. ⟨http://www.union-network.org/uniibits.nsf/0/0e6f44788232efd7c1256bd70040f070?OpenDocument⟩.

Brown, C., and M. Corcoran. 1997. Sex-based differences in school content and the male-female wage gap. *Journal of Labor Economics* 15:431–466.

Bush, S., T. Henle, S. Cohen, D. Jenkins, and J. Kossy. 2002. *Recruiting lower-income women into information technology careers: Building a foundation for action.* Chicago: Women Employed Institute.

Camp, T. 1997. The incredible shrinking pipeline. *Communications of the ACM* 40, no. 10 (October): 103–110.

Chua, S. L., D. Chen, and A. F. L. Wong. 1999. Computer anxiety and its correlates: A meta-analysis. *Computers in Human Behavior* 15:609–623.

Commission on Professionals in Science and Technology. 2001. *Comment* (May 25).

Craig, A., R. Paradis, and E. Turner. 2002. A gendered view of computer professionals: Preliminary results of a survey. *ACM SIGCSE Bulletin* 34, no. 2:101–104.

Craig, A., and A. Stein. 2000. Where are they at with IT? In *Women, work, and computerization: Charting a course to the future*, ed. E. Balka and R. Smith, 86–93. Boston: Kluwer Academic Publishers.

De Dreu, C. K. W., and M. A. West. 2001. Minority dissent and team innovation: The importance of participation in decision making. *Journal of Applied Psychology* 86:1191–1201.

Eccles, J. S. 1994. Understanding women's educational and occupational choices: Apply the Eccles et al. model of achievement-related choices. *Psychology of Women Quarterly* 18:585–609.

Faulkner, W. 2002. Women, gender in/and ICT: Evidence and reflections from the UK. In *Digital divide and inclusion measures: A review of literature and statistical trends on gender and ICT*, ed. K. H. Sørensen and J. Stewart. Senter for teknologi og samfunn, report 2002–59, NTNU, Trondheim. ⟨http://www.rcss.ed.ac.uk/sigis/public/displaydoc/full/D02_Part3⟩.

Faulkner, W., K. Sørensen, H. Gansmø, E. Rommes, L. Pitt, V. L. Berg, C. McKeogh, P. Preston, R. Williams, and J. Stewart. 2004. *Strategies of inclusion: Gender and the information society*. Final report (public version). SIGIS project funded by the European Commission IST Programme. ⟨http://www.rcss.ed.ac.uk/sigis/⟩.

Frauenheim, E., and M. Yamamoto. 2004. Reforms, not rhetoric, needed to keep jobs on U.S. soil. Cnetnews.com, May 4. Available at ⟨www.cnet.com⟩.

Freeman, P., and W. Aspray. 1999. *The supply of information technology workers in the United States*. Washington, DC: Computing Research Association.

Gansmo, H. J. 1998. *Det forvrengte dataspeilet. En kvalitativ studie av hvordan ungdomsskolejenter forstår datateknologiens muligheter I dag og I fremtiden*. STS report 36. Trondheim, Norway: Centre for Technology and Society.

Garvey, M. J. 2004. Is an MBA worth it? *InformationWeek* (November 1). ⟨http://www.informationweek.com/story/showArticle.jhtml?articleID=51201467⟩.

Gender Pay Gap Is Europe-Wide. 2002. *Personnel Today* (July 9): 51.

Goodridge, E. 2002. Salary gap still exists for women in IT. *InformationWeek* (April 29). ⟨http://www.informationweek.com/story/showArticle.jhtml?articleID=6501879⟩.

Grundy, F. 1994. Women in the computing workplace: Some impressions. In *Women, work, and computerization: Breaking old boundaries, building new forms*, ed. A. Adam, J. Emms, E. Green, and J. Owen, 349–364. Amsterdam: Elsevier.

Hapnes, T., and B. Rasmussen. 1998. Internet and multimedia: Demasculinisation of IT? *Kvinder, Køn, and Forskning*, no. 1.

Harrison, A. W., R. K. Rainer Jr., and W. A. Hochwarter. 1997. Gender differences in computing activities. *Journal of Social Behavior and Personality* 12:849–868.

Hingorani, K. K., and C. S. Sankar. 1995. Entry-level MIS jobs: Industry expectations versus academic preparation. *Journal of Computer Information Systems* 35, no. 4 (Summer): 18–23.

Hipple, S., and K. Kosanovich. 2003. Computer and Internet use at work in 2001. *Monthly Labor Review* (February): 26–35.

Holmes, M. C. 1998. Comparison of gender differences among information systems professionals: A cultural perspective. *Journal of Computer Information Systems* 38:78–86.

Horrigan, M. W. 2003–2004. Charting the projections. *Occupational Outlook Quarterly* 47 (Winter): 1–48.

Hossfeld, K. forthcoming. *Small, foreign, and female.*

Igbaria, M., and J. Baroudi. 1995. The impact of job performance evaluations on career advancement prospects: An examination of gender differences in the IS workplace. *MIS Quarterly* 19:107–123.

Igbaria, M., and L. Chidambaram. 1997. The impact of gender on career success of information systems professionals. *Information Technology and People* 10:63–87.

Igbaria, M., J. H. Greenhaus, and S. Parasuraman. 1991. Career orientations of MIS employees: An empirical investigation. *MIS Quarterly* 15:151–169.

Igbaria, M., and T. Guimaraes. 1993. Antecedents and consequences of job satisfaction among information center employees. *Journal of Management Information Systems* 9:145–174.

Igbaria, M., and D. W. McCloskey. 1996. Career orientation of MIS employees in Taiwan. *Computer Personnel* 17, no. 2:3–24.

Igbaria, M., and S. Parasuraman. 1997. Status report on women and men in the IT workplace. *Information Systems Management* 14:44–53.

Jackson, S. E., A. Joshi, and N. L. Erhardt. 2003. Recent research on team and organizational diversity: SWOT analysis and implications. *Journal of Management* 29:801–830.

Jiang, J. J., and G. Klein. 1999–2000. Supervisor support and career anchor impact on the career satisfaction of the entry-level information systems professional. *Journal of Management Information Systems* 16:219–240.

Karasti, H. 1994. What's different in gender oriented ISD? Identifying gender-oriented information systems development approach. In *Women, work, and computerization: Breaking old boundaries, building new forms,* ed. A. Adam, J. Emms, E. Green, and J. Owen, 45–58. Amsterdam: Elsevier.

Keuzenkamp, S., and E. r. Hooghiemstra. 2000. *De kunst van het combineren: Taakverdeling onder partners.* The Hague: Sociaal Cultureel Planbureau.

Koehler, E., and S. Hagigh. 2004. Offshore outsourcing and America's competitive edge: Losing out in the high technology R&D and services sectors. Office of Senator Joseph Lieberman, U.S. Senate, May 11, Washington, DC.

Kohler, P. D., and E. B. Applegate. 2004. Creating pathways to information technology careers through high school career and technical education programs. In *Proceedings of the*

National Science Foundation's ITWF and ITR/EWF principal investigator conference, ed. E. Trauth, 225–229. Philadelphia: NSF.

Konrad, A. M., E. Corrigall, P. Lieb, and J. E. Ritchie Jr. 2000. Sex differences in job attribute preferences among managers and business students. *Group and Organization Management* 25:108–131.

Kvaløy, K. 1999. *Fortellinger om—moderne—flinke—lekne. Unge jenters forhold til datateknologi. En kvalitativ studie av datateknologiens rolle I unge jenters dannelse av kjønnsidentitet.* SKF reprot 3/2000. Trondheim, Norway: Centre for Feminist and Gender Research.

Langsether, H. 2001. *Behov og barrierer for jenter på informatikkstudiet.* SKF report 3/2001. Trondheim, Norway: Centre for Feminist and Gender Research.

Lawley, E. L., and T. Henderson. 2004. Understanding gendered attrition in departments of information technology. In *Proceedings of the National Science Foundation's ITWF and ITR/EWF principal investigator conference*, ed. E. Trauth, 163–167. Philadelphia: NSF.

Lemons, M. A., and M. J. Parzinger. 2001. Designing women: A qualitative study of the glass ceiling for women in technology. *SAM Advanced Management Journal* 66, no. 2:4–12.

Leventman, P. G., P. B. Campbell, T. P. Cullinane, and R. F. Perry. 2004. Multiple pathways toward gender equity in the IT workforce. In *Proceedings of the National Science Foundation's ITWF and ITR/EWF principal investigator conference*, ed. E. Trauth, 143–148. Philadelphia: NSF.

Llewellyn, D., and M. Usselman. 2004. Alternative pathways to success in information technology. In *Proceedings of the National Science Foundation's ITWF and ITR/EWF principal investigator conference*, ed. E. Trauth, 217–223. Philadelphia: NSF.

Lynn, K.-M., C. Raphael, K. Olefsky, and C. M. Bachen. 2003. Bridging the gender gap in computing: An integrative approach to content design for girls. *Journal of Educational Computing Research* 28:143–162.

Major, D. A., D. D. Davis, J. Sanchez-Hucles, and J. Mann. 2004. Climate for opportunity and inclusion: Improving the recruitment, retention, and advancement of women and minorities in IT. In *Proceedings of the National Science Foundation's ITWF and ITR/EWF principal investigator conference*, ed. E. Trauth, 167–171. Philadelphia: NSF.

Margolis, J., and A. Fisher. 2002. *Unlocking the clubhouse: Women in computing.* Cambridge, MA: MIT Press.

Matthews, G. 2003. *Silicon Valley, women, and the California dream.* Palo Alto, CA: Stanford University Press.

McDonald, S., and L. Spencer. 2000. Gender differences in Web navigation. In *Women, work, and computerization: Charting a course to the future*, ed. E. Balka and R. Smith, 174–181. Boston: Kluwer Academic Publishers.

Meister, J. C. 1998. Corporate universities: Lessons in building a world-class workforce. 2nd ed. New York: McGraw-Hill.

Miliszewska, I., and J. Horwood. 2000. Women in computer science: Experiences from Victoria University. In *Women, work, and computerization: Charting a course to the future*, ed. E. Balka and R. Smith, 50–57. Boston: Kluwer Academic Publishers.

Miller, J., and N. Jagger. 2001. Women in ITEC courses and careers, report R1553. Bradford, U.K.: U.K. Resource Centre for Women in Science, Engineering and Technology. See ⟨http://www.womenandequalityunit.gov.uk/publications/women_itec_report.pdf⟩.

National Center for Education Statistics. 2004. ⟨http://www.nsf.gov/sbe/srs/wmpd/pdf/tabc–13.pdf⟩.

Nielsen, S., L. Von Hellens, and S. Wong. 2000. "The game of social constructs: We're going to WinIT." Panel presentation at the meeting of the International Conference on Information Systems, Brisbane, Australia, December 11–13. See ⟨http://www.cit.gu.edu.au/~lhellens/docs/icispane10612.pdf⟩.

Nord, W. R., S. Fox, A. Phoenix, and K. Viano. 2002. Real-world reactions to work-life balance programs: Lesson for effective implementation. *Organizational Dynamics* 30:223–238.

Nordli, H. 1998. *Fra Sprice Girls til Cyber Girls? En kvalitativ studie av datafascinerte jenter I ungdomsskole.* STS report 35. Trondheim, Norway: Centre for Technology and Society.

O'Donnell, A. M., S. Armstrong-West, C. McInerney, S. Dunn, and C. Van Horn. 2004. The influence of gender, university major, and work experience on the perceptions and choice of IT careers. In *Proceedings of the National Science Foundation's ITWF and ITR/EWF principal investigator conference*, ed. E. Trauth, 168–173. Philadelphia: NSF.

O'Leary-Kelly, A., B. Hardgrave, V. McKinney, and D. Wilson. 2004. The influence of professional identification on the retention of women and racial minorities in the IT workforce. In *Proceedings of the National Science Foundation's ITWF and ITR/EWF principal investigator conference*, ed. E. Trauth, 65–68. Philadelphia: NSF.

Oost, E. van. 2002. Gender and ICT in the Netherlands. In *Digital divide and inclusion measures: A review of literature and statistical trends on gender and ICT*, ed. K. H. Sørensen and J. Stewart. Senter for teknologi og samfunn, report 2002–59, NTNU, Trondheim. ⟨http://www.rcss.ed.ac.uk/sigis/public/displaydoc/full/D02_Part7⟩.

Panteli, A., H. Ramsay, and M. Beirne. 1997. Engendered systems development: Ghettoization and agency. In *Women, work, and computerization: Spinning a web from past to future*, ed. A. F. Grunday, D. Kohlere, V. Oechtering, and U. Petersen, 305–315. Berlin: Springer.

Parasuraman, S., and M. Igbaria. 1990. An examination of gender differences in the determinants of computer anxiety and attitudes toward microcomputers among managers. *International Journal of Man-Machine Studies* 32:327–340.

Pearson, J. M., L. Crosby, T. Bahmanziari, and E. Conrad. 2002–2003. An empirical investigation into the relationship between organizational culture and computer self-efficacy as moderated by age and gender. *Journal of Computer Information Systems* 43:58–70.

Ragins, B. R., and J. L. Cotton. 1991. Easier said than done: Gender differences in perceived barriers to gaining a mentor. *Academy of Management Journal* 34:939–951.

Ragins, B. R., and J. I. Cotton. 1999. Mentor functions and outcomes: A comparison of men and women in formal and informal mentoring relationships. *Journal of Applied Psychology* 84:529–550.

Ranson, G., and W. J. Reeves. 1996. Gender, earnings, and proportions of women: Lessons from a high-tech occupation. *Gender and Society* 10:168–184.

Rao, H. R., S. Bagchi-Sen, and S. Upadhyaya. 2004. Women and cybersecurity: Gendered tasks and (in)equitable outcomes. In *Proceedings of the National Science Foundation's ITWF and ITR/EWF principal investigator conference*, ed. E. Trauth, 82–83. Philadelphia: NSF.

Rasmussen, B., and T. Hapnes. 1991. Excluding women from the technologies of the future? A case study of the culture of computer science. *Futures* 23, no. 10:1107–1120.

Reskin, B. F., and P. A. Roos. 1990. *Job queues, gender queues: Explaining women's inroads into male occupations*. Philadelphia: Temple University Press.

Robinson, J. C., M. Ahuja, S. Herring, and C. Ogan. 2004. Toward gender-equitable outcomes in higher education: Beyond computer science. In *Proceedings of the National Science Foundation's ITWF and ITR/EWF principal investigator conference*, ed. E. Trauth, 174–177. Philadelphia: NSF.

Rommes, E. 2000. Gendered user-representation: Design of a digital city. In *Women, work, and computerization: Charting a course to the future*, ed. E. Balka and R. Smith, 137–145. Boston: Kluwer Academic Publishers.

Roos, P. A., and M. L. Gatta. 1999. The gender gap in earnings: Trends, explanations, and prospects. In *Handbook of Gender and Work*, ed. G. N. Powell, 125–141.

Rosenbloom, J. L., and R. A. Ash. 2004. Characteristics and career paths of IT workers. In *Proceedings of the National Science Foundation's ITWF and ITR/EWF principal investigator conference*, ed. E. Trauth, 114–119. Philadelphia: NSF.

Schneider, F. B., ed. 1999. *Trust in cyberspace*. Committee on Information Systems Trustworthiness, National Research Council. Washington, DC: National Academy Press. ⟨http://bob.nap.edu/html/trust/⟩.

Shapiro, G. 1994. Informal processes and women's careers in information technology management. In *Women, work, and computerization: Breaking old boundaries, building new forms*, ed. A. Adam, J. Emms, E. Green, and J. Owen, 423–437. Amsterdam: Elsevier.

Sonnentag, S. 1994. Team leading in software development: A comparison between women and men. In *Women, work, and computerization: Breaking old boundaries, building new forms*, ed. A. Adam, J. Emms, E. Green, and J. Owen, 423–437. Amsterdam: Elsevier.

Spafford, E. 2001. How can we protect our computing networks from attack? Testimony to the Committee on Science, House of Representatives, 107th Congress of the United States, October 10, Washington, DC.

Stanton, J., D. Eischen, and I. Guzman. 2004. Culture clash! The adverse effects of IT occupational subculture on formative work experiences of IT students. In *Proceedings of the National Science Foundation's ITWF and ITR/EWF principal investigator conference*, ed. E. Trauth, 84–88. Philadelphia: NSF.

Strober, M. H. 1984. Toward a general theory of occupational sex segregation: The case of public school teaching. In *Sex segregation in the workplace: Trends, explanations, remedies*, ed. B. Reskin, 144–156. Washington, DC: National Academy.

Stuedahl, D. 1997. *Jenter og informatikkstudiet—en rapport om jenters studiesituasjon ved Institutt for Informatikk*. Oslo: Ministry of Church, Research, and Education.

Sumner, M., and F. Niederman. 2003–2004. The impact of gender differences on job satisfaction, job turnover, and career experiences of information systems professionals. *Journal of Computer Information Systems* 94, no. 2:29–39.

Tan, M., and M. Igbaria. 1994. Turnover and remuneration of information technology professionals in Singapore. *Information and Management* 26:219–229.

Teague, J. 1992. Raising the self-confidence and self-esteem of final-year female students prior to job interviews. In *Proceedings of the twenty-third SIGCSE technical symposium on computer science education*, ed. N. B. Dale, 67–71. New York: ACM Press.

Teague, J. 2002. Women in computing: What brings them to it, what keeps them in it? *SIGCSE Bulletin* 34:147–158.

Tharenou, P., and D. Conroy. 1994. Men and women managers' advancement: Personal or situational determinants? *Applied Psychology: An International Review* 43:5–31.

Trauth, E., ed. 2004. In *Proceedings of the National Science Foundation's ITWF and ITR/EWF principal investigator conference*. Philadelphia: NSF.

Truman, G. E., and J. J. Baroudi. 1994. Gender differences in the information systems managerial ranks: An assessment of potential discriminatory practices. *MIS Quarterly* 20:129–141.

Turner, S. V., P. W. Bernt, and N. Pecora. 2002. Why women choose information technology careers: Educational, social, and familial influences. Paper presented at the annual meeting of the American Educational Research Association, New Orleans.

Venkatesh, V., and M. G. Morris. 2000. Why don't men ever stop to ask for directions? Gender, social influence, and their role in technology acceptance and usage behavior. *MIS Quarterly* 24:115–139.

Venkatesh, V., M. G. Morris, and P. L. Ackerman. 2000. A longitudinal field investigation of gender differences in individual technology adoption decision-making processes. *Organizational Behavior and Human Decision Processes* 83:33–60.

Venkatesh, V., M. G. Morris, G. B. Davis, and F. D. Davis. 2003. User acceptance of information technology: Toward a unified view. *MIS Quarterly* 27:425–478.

Von Hellens, L. A., and S. Nielsen. 2001. Australian women in IT. *Communications of the ACM* 44, no. 7 (July): 46–52.

Von Hellens, L. A., S. H. Nielsen, and E. M. Trauth. 2001. Breaking and entering the male domain: Women in the IT industry. In *Proceedings of the 2001 ACM SIGCPR Conference on Computer Personnel Research*, ed. M. Serwa, 116–120. New York: Association for Computing Machinery.

Von Hellens, L. A., R. Pringle, S. H. Nielsen, and A. Greenhill. 2000. People, business, and IT skills: The perspective of women in the IT industry. In *Proceedings of the 2000 ACM SIGCPR Conference on Personnel Research*, ed. J. Prasad and W. Nance, 152–157. New York: Association for Computing Machinery.

Wardell, M., J. Rogers, and S. Sawyer. 2004. Women in the IT workforce: How level the playing field? In *Proceedings of the National Science Foundation's ITWF and ITR/EWF principal investigator conference*, ed. E. Trauth, 120–126. Philadelphia: NSF.

Weinberger, C. J. 2003. In *Proceedings of the National Science Foundation's ITWF and ITR/EWF principal investigator conference*, ed. R. Varma. Albuquerque: University of New Mexico.

Weinberger, C. J., and P. Kuhn. 2004. Entry, earnings growth, and retention in IT careers: An economic study. In *Proceedings of the National Science Foundation's ITWF and ITR/EWF principal investigator conference*, ed. E. Trauth, 149–154. Philadelphia: NSF.

White House Council of Economic Advisors. 2000. Opportunities and gender pay equity in new economy occupations. Available in the National Archives.

Wilde, C. 2000. Women in IT strive for equal job compensation. *InformationWeek* (June 12). ⟨http://www.informationweek.com/790/gender.htm⟩.

Wilson, F. 2003. Can compute, won't compute: Women's participation in the culture of computing. *New Technology, Work and Employment* 18:127–142.

Woodfield, R. 2000. *Women, work, and computing*. Cambridge: Cambridge University Press.

Woodfield, R. 2002. Woman and information systems development: Not just a pretty (inter)face? *Information Technology and People* 15:119–138.

Wright, R. 1996. Women in computer work: Controlled progress in a technical occupation. In *Women and minorities in American professions*, ed. J. Tang and E. Smith, 43–64. Albany: State University of New York Press.

Wright, R. 1997. *Women computer professionals: Progress and resistance*. Lewiston, NY: Edwin Mellon Press.

Wright, R., and J. A. Jacobs. 1994. Male flight from computer work: A new look at occupational resegregation and ghettoization. *American Sociological Review* 59:511–536.

Young, B. J. 2000. Gender differences in student attitudes toward computers. *Journal of Research on Computing in Education* 33:204–217.

Zoonen, L. v. 2001. *Gender en ICT: Literatuuronderzoek ten behoove van Infodrome*. Amsterdam: Infodrome.

14

Gender and Professional Commitment among IT Professionals: The Special Case of Female Newcomers to Organizations

Kathryn M. Bartol, Ian O. Williamson, and Gosia A. Langa

As noted in a recent President's Information Technology Advisory Committee report (1999), the need for a "continuous supply of well-trained, high-quality professionals" (58) in IT is critical to the maintenance of U.S. global competitiveness. As discussed in the report and elsewhere, chronic shortfalls in the supply of excellent IT professionals have been commonplace for more than two decades, particularly in cutting-edge areas (Council on Competitiveness 1998). Even with the recent slowing in the demand for IT professionals and the increasing globalization, the accelerating pace of technological innovation is making it more imperative than ever to attract strong talent to the IT field. Moreover, five of the U.S. Department of Labor's twenty projected fastest-growing occupations for the next decade are IT related (Horrigan 2003–2004). Yet the continuing underrepresentation of women in IT constitutes a serious loss to the IT field and is widely recognized as an issue of continuing importance (Wardle and Burton 2002). A report produced by the Computer Research Association (Freeman and Aspray 1999) on the supply of IT workers in the United States suggested that increasing the number of women in the IT workforce would be helpful in relieving even the most dire estimates of the IT workforce shortage while more effectively utilizing the potential talent pool. Others have pointed to the inherent competitive disadvantage in failing to tap the intellectual capacity of women, who constitute a sizable portion of the population (see, for example, McDonald 2004). Thus, increasing the participation of women would be a crucial step in both easing market issues and expanding access to a major growth area of the economy and some of the best-paying jobs in the United States.

Evidence indicates that as early as K–12, there are major differences in the interest in computers among female and male students in the educational system. Such differences appear to carry over into secondary and higher education. For example,

Cohoon (2002) has argued that because computing tends to be viewed as a male activity, proactive efforts are necessary to encourage female students to consider IT-related majors. While issues relating to the number of women obtaining IT-relevant formal education are clearly in need of research, a number of sources have pointed to the requirements for more research on workplace issues that appear to impede the participation of women in the IT workforce (see, for instance, Tapia and Kvasny 2004; see also Bartol and Aspray, this volume). Workplace-related research is needed because even if efforts at the elementary, secondary, and postsecondary levels are successful in increasing the number of women with IT training entering the workforce, such efforts will be ineffective if transitions to the workplace undermine the commitment of women to the IT field.

Therefore, the specific focus of our research is professional commitment. Professional commitment refers to the psychological connection between a person and their profession that represents the degree to which one has positive feelings about, is dedicated to, and feels attachment to that profession (Blau 1985; Wallace 1995). Commitment to one's profession has been linked to whether individuals remain in the IT profession or not (Vandenberg and Scarpello 1994). Yet this variable has not been assessed as an aid in tracing reasons why a smaller proportion of women than men remains in the IT profession after receiving undergraduate degrees (Wright 1996). In the course of our inquiry, we consider differences in professional commitment among relative newcomers compared with a set of IT professionals who have been on the job somewhat longer (a group that we label "veterans"). We are also interested in two affective factors related to organizational conditions that might influence professional commitment.

The purposes of this research, then, are threefold. First, we consider the extent to which gender differences in professional commitment exist among IT students preparing to leave their undergraduate programs and enter the workforce. Second, we explore potential differences in professional commitment related to gender and experience (newcomers versus veterans). The newcomer data have been collected by following up with the students a year after their undergraduate graduation. This inquiry can also inform the extent to which professional commitment is aided or harmed in the transition to the workplace among entry-level IT professionals. Finally, we assess the extent to which perceived organizational support and job satisfaction are related to professional commitment, particularly among newcomer women.

Professional Experience and Professional Commitment

One important question with respect to IT professionals is the extent to which there might be gender differences in professional commitment. Research related to other fields shows that gender differences in professional commitment may be minimal (e.g., Aranya, Kushnir, and Valency 1986), but other studies have found significant differences (e.g., Blau and Lunz 1998). Of particular interest here is a study among students in science and technology doctoral programs, in which males reported a greater commitment to their intended research career than did females (Bauer and Green 1994). Given the many difficulties that women experience in IT-related educational programs (Cohoon 2002), the persistent image of IT as mainly a male domain (e.g., Morell 1996; Selby, Ryba, and Young 1998), and some evidence that females hold a lower self-efficacy for IT work than males do (Beyer et al. 2003), it appears likely that women preparing to leave postsecondary IT-related programs will experience a lower commitment to the IT profession than their male counterparts. Therefore we hypothesize that:

Hypothesis 1   Female IT student graduates have a lower professional commitment than do male IT student graduates.

At the same time, there is evidence that younger, newer workers may have a lower professional commitment than individuals with more tenure in the same profession (Blau and Lunz 1998). Little research has addressed this question with respect to newcomers in the IT field, however. This question is important because understanding the patterns of professional commitment may make it easier to design interventions that would increase the retention of females in the IT profession. If, as some researchers have argued, female entry-level IT professionals are likely to face more difficulty in entering the work world due to hostile conditions (e.g., Ahuja 1995; Roldan, Soe, and Yakura 2004), then one might expect the commitment to the profession among female newcomers to be lower than the commitment of their male newcomer counterparts by the end of their first year, a common benchmark in newcomer research. On the other hand, since a lower professional commitment is associated with leaving one's profession, it is likely that longer-term or veteran IT professionals, including female veterans, will have a higher professional commitment than at least the female newcomers. We thus hypothesize:

Hypothesis 2   Gender and professional experience interact to influence professional commitment, such that professional commitment is lowest among female newcomer IT professionals.

Organizational Conditions and Professional Commitment

Because of the possibility that organizational conditions might influence professional commitment, we investigated two important affective factors associated with organizational conditions, perceived organizational support (Eisenberger et al. 1986), and job satisfaction (Brief 1998).

Perceived Organizational Support

According to organizational support theory (Eisenberger et al. 1986; Rhoades and Eisenberger 2002; Shore and Shore 1995), employees develop higher levels of perceived organizational support (POS) when the organization cares about their well-being and values their contributions. Based on the norm of reciprocity (Gouldner 1960), POS is theorized to indirectly impact employee attitudes and behaviors by creating a sense of obligation within individuals that results in reciprocation (Eisenberger et al. 1986; Eisenberger et al. 2001). To date, organizational support theory has received considerable support and appears to be a useful theoretical framework for helping to understand employment relationships in organizations.

Organizational support theory posits that if employees perceive higher support from the organization, they are likely to put forth additional efforts, which in turn lead to greater job involvement and, ultimately, better performance (Eisenberger et al. 1986). Research has generally supported the notion that POS will contribute to employee in-role performance (Armeli et al. 1998; Eisenberger, Fasolo, and Davis-LaMastro 1990) and organizational citizenship behaviors, including helpful behaviors toward peers (Eisenberger, Fasolo, and Davis-LaMastro 1990; Settoon, Bennett, and Liden 1996; Shore and Wayne 1993; Wayne, Shore, and Liden 1997).

To the extent that female IT newcomers enter into the workforce with lower levels of professional commitment then men, it is possible that perceived support from the organization can play a major factor in diminishing this difference. Several scholars have argued that women may leave the IT profession because they perceive the IT workplace as particularly unwelcoming (e.g., Ahuja 1995; Roldan, Soe, and Yakura 2004). Because high levels of POS tend to engender positive work attitudes, encourage job involvement, and aid successful performance, it is logical to suspect that high levels of POS may make IT employees in general, and female newcomer IT professionals in particular, form positive attributions about the IT profession. As a result, female newcomer IT workers who perceive high levels of support from their employer may develop similar levels of commitment to the IT profession as newcomer men and veteran IT workers. Accordingly, we hypothesize:

Hypothesis 3   Perceived organizational support, gender, and professional experience interact to influence professional commitment, such that the positive impact of POS on professional commitment is greatest among female newcomer IT professionals.

Job Satisfaction

Considerable evidence suggests that job satisfaction is especially important for professional workers, and IT professionals in particular. Job satisfaction has been linked to a higher organizational commitment and lower intentions to leave the organization (Bartol and Martin 1982). Considerable evidence also indicates that job satisfaction is associated with professional commitment (e.g., Aranya, Kushnir, and Valency 1986; Blau 2003), although this particular connection has not generally been investigated within the IT profession. A link between job satisfaction and professional commitment is logical in that job satisfaction involves an affective state related to an appraisal of engaging in one's job (Locke 1976).

Related research suggests that job satisfaction is crucial to both female and male IT professionals (Bartol and Martin 1982; Igbaria and Baroudi 1995; Vandenberg and Scarpello 1994). Craig, Paradis, and Turner (2002) found evidence that female undergraduate IT students had higher expectations of job satisfaction than male students. Moreover, a number of researchers have theorized that negative aspects of the work itself—including unfavorable work assignments, insufficient on-the-job training, and inadequate feedback—might undermine the job satisfaction of female IT professionals (e.g., Ahuja 1995; Bartol and Martin 1982), particularly newcomers, thereby leading to decrements in professional commitment. Thus, to the extent that IT professionals experience high levels of job satisfaction, it is likely that this will enhance their IT professional commitment. Furthermore, given prior research findings that suggest that job satisfaction is especially important to female IT students, it is likely that the positive effects of job satisfaction on professional commitment will be particularly strong for female IT newcomers. We therefore hypothesize:

Hypothesis 4 Job satisfaction, gender, and professional experience interact to influence professional commitment, such that the positive impact of job satisfaction on professional commitment is likely to be greatest among female newcomer IT professionals.

Combined Impact of Perceived Organizational Support and Job Satisfaction

Because POS is associated with the degree to which the organization values one's contributions and cares about one's well-being, it represents perceptions of the organization. In contrast, job satisfaction is conceptualized here as affective reactions associated with the job itself. Considered in this way, it is conceivable that the professional commitment of female IT professionals will be affected most when there is both POS and job satisfaction. Hence, we hypothesize:

Hypothesis 5 Perceived organizational support, job satisfaction, gender, and professional experience interact to influence professional commitment, such that the positive impact on professional commitment is likely to be greatest among female newcomer IT professionals.

Method

Overview and Sample

Analysis was conducted using the responses of 628 IT professionals. In order to have representation of both newcomers and veteran IT workers in our study, the data were collected from two different sources. Data on IT newcomers were gathered in two stages. First, we surveyed 393 senior IT students from four different U.S. universities in their last semester of college, prior to them starting their first postcollege full-time job. Two of the colleges were located in the mid-Atlantic and two were located in the South. Students were in programs that can best be characterized as focusing on information systems management. The students were enrolled in senior-level required management courses, mainly covering strategy issues. Access was gained by contacting class instructors. More than 90 percent of the students who were provided surveys completed them. In this initial survey, we measured students' preemployment professional commitment. We then followed up with these individuals after graduation via a mail and/or electronic survey to measure their professional commitment, job satisfaction, and POS. A total of 183 individuals responded to our second survey producing a response rate of 47 percent. Only 117 of these respondents reported being employed, however. As such, all newcomer analysis was conducted using the responses of these 117 individuals. The newcomers in our sample had an average age of twenty-two, 56 percent were male, 3 percent were married, and the average tenure at their current employment was twelve months.

Data on veteran IT workers were collected via a Web-based survey conducted among IT professionals who were members of a large IT association. The association drew a random sample of 3,500 U.S. members, and also sent out an e-mail endorsing the study and encouraging participation. Because of the sensitivity of members to receiving multiple e-mails, the association would not allow us to send reminder e-mails to aid the response rate. There were 634 responses, for a return rate of 18.1 percent. After eliminating incomplete surveys, the responses of individuals who indicated that they were retired or otherwise not in the workforce, and the responses of individuals who indicated they were not working in IT, we conducted analyses on 511 responses. The veteran IT professionals in our sample had an average age of forty-two, 85 percent were male, and 70 percent were married; they had an average of sixteen years experience in the IT profession and seven years experience in their current organization. A majority (95 percent) of these employees had at least an undergraduate degree.

Measures

Professional Commitment   Professional commitment was measured with three items adapted from Blau (1985). A sample item is "If I could do it all over again, I would choose to work in the IT profession." Study participants responded to the professional commitment items using a 7-point Likert-type scale (1 = strongly disagree, and 7 = strongly agree). The Cronbach's alpha for this scale was .79

POS   Following recent research on POS (e.g., Eisenberger et al. 2001; Lynch, Eisenberger, and Armeli 1999; Rhoades and Eisenberger 2001), the three highest-loading items from the Survey of Perceived Organizational Support (Eisenberger et al. 1986) were used to measure employees' POS. The validity and unidimensionality of this scale has been substantiated by previous research (e.g., Eisenberger, Fasolo, and Davis-LaMastro 1990; Shore and Wayne 1993). Because of the scale's unidimensionality, Rhoades and Eisenberger (2002) suggested that many studies have used shortened versions of the original Survey of Perceived Organizational Support for practical reasons scale, and this practice has not been problematic. A sample item is "My organization really cares about my well-being." Study participants responded to the POS items using a 7-point Likert-type scale (1 = strongly disagree, and 7 = strongly agree). The Cronbach's alpha for this scale was .91

Job Satisfaction   Three items adapted from Bretz, Boudreau, and Judge (1994) were used to measure job satisfaction. First, participants were asked to answer yes or no to whether they were "satisfied with their jobs in general." Next, they were asked to indicate on a 5-point Likert scale (1 = very dissatisfied, and 5 = very satisfied) the "level of satisfaction with their jobs in general." Finally, respondents were asked to write the "percentage of time they felt satisfied in their jobs." The scores on these three items were standardized and averaged to form the job satisfaction scale. The Cronbach's alpha for the job satisfaction measure was .90.

Professional Experience   Respondents were categorized as newcomer or veteran IT workers depending on which data source they represented. Specifically, respondents who were students transitioning into their first postcollege IT position were categorized as newcomers, while professionals who were members of the IT professional association sampled were categorized as veterans. A dummy variable was used to represent these two groups, with veterans coded as 1 and newcomers coded as 0.

Gender   The gender of all respondents was measured via a self-report item in the survey. Respondent gender was represented using a dummy variable where 1 = female and 0 = male.

Results

Table 14.1 contains both the means, standard deviations, and correlations between the variables examined in this study. Hypothesis 1 predicts that prior to starting an IT position, female students will have a lower professional commitment than male students. To test this hypothesis, we conducted a simple analysis of variance with gender as the one-way factor. As expected, the results indicated that female students scored lower than males on professional commitment ($F = 7.64$, $df = 114$, $p < .051$; $X = 3.59$ and $X = 4.84$, respectively for females and males).

Hypothesis 2 predicted that there would be a significant interaction between gender and professional experience on professional commitment. To test this hypothesis, we conducted moderated regression analysis. As shown in step 2 of table 14.2,

Table 14.1
Means, standard deviations, and correlations between variables

Variables	Mean	Std. Dev.	1	2	3	4
1. Gender (1 = female)	0.21	0.41				
2. Professional experience (1 = veteran)	0.81	0.39	−.27*			
3. Job satisfaction	0.01	0.91	−.03	.01		
4. POS	4.41	1.45	.05	−.14*	.60*	
5. Professional commitment	5.54	1.24	−.15*	.10	.15*	.14*

Note: N = 628
* $p < .05$

Table 14.2
Results of regression analyses predicting professional commitment

	Step 1	Step 2	Step 3	Step 4	Step 5	Step 6
Constant	5.41*	5.71*	5.72*	5.71*	5.70*	5.69*
Gender	−0.39*	−1.07*	−1.04*	−1.04*	−1.12*	−1.11*
Professional experience	0.26*	−0.08	−0.09	−0.09	−0.08	−0.07
Job satisfaction	0.09*	0.10*	0.09*	0.08	0.12	0.13
POS	0.12	0.10	0.05	0.14	0.10	0.10
Gender × experience	—	0.98*	0.94*	0.94*	1.04*	1.03*
Gender × job satisfaction	—	—	0.37*	0.20	—	—
Experience × job satisfaction	—	—	−0.02	−0.12	—	—
Gender × POS	—	—	—	—	0.09	0.07
Experience × POS	—	—	—	—	−0.06	−0.07
Gender × experience × job satisfaction	—	—	—	0.25	—	—
Gender × experience × POS	—	—	—	—	—	0.03
Change in R^2	—	.02*	.02*	.00	.01	.00
Total R^2	.05*	.07*	.09*	.09*	.08*	.08*

Note: N = 628
* $p < .05$

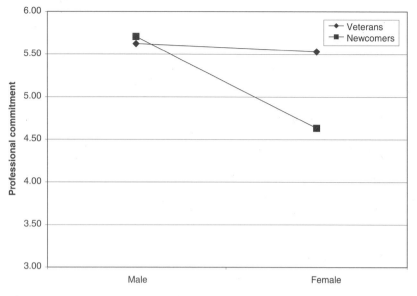

Figure 14.1
Gender × professional experience interaction on professional commitment

the gender × professional experience interaction explained a significant amount of variance in professional commitment over and above the main effects of gender, professional experience, POS, and job satisfaction ($\Delta R^2 = .02$, $p < .05$). To better interpret the meaning of the significant interaction, we plotted the two-way interaction of gender × professional experience on professional commitment in figure 14.1. Following the directions of Aiken and West (1991), the mean values were used for the continuous variables, while the corresponding 1/0 values were used for the gender and professional experience dummy variables. As illustrated in figure 14.1, consistent with the predictions, women newcomers had the lowest professional commitment scores compared to male newcomers, women veterans, and male veterans. Thus, hypothesis 2 was supported.

Hypothesis 3 predicted that there would be a three-way interaction between gender, professional experience, and job satisfaction on professional commitment. As shown in step 4 of table 14.2, however, the gender × professional experience × job satisfaction interaction was not significant. Hypothesis 3 was therefore not supported. Hypothesis 4 predicted a three-way interaction between gender, professional experience, and POS. Yet as shown in step 6 of table 14.2, this interaction did not

Table 14.3

Results of regression analysis predicting newcomer and veteran IT workers' professional commitment

	Newcomer IT workers[a]			Veteran IT workers[b]		
	Step 1a	Step 2a	Step 3a	Step 1b	Step 2b	Step 3b
Constant	5.69*	5.58*	5.82*	5.62*	5.64*	5.63*
Gender	−1.06*	−1.06*	−1.60*	−0.09	−0.11*	−0.07
Job satisfaction	0.19*	0.09	0.04	0.08*	−0.01	0.00
POS	0.12*	0.13*	0.15*	0.09*	0.10*	0.10*
Gender × job satisfaction	—	0.20	0.23	—	0.70*	0.64*
Gender × POS	—	0.02	0.08	—	−0.22*	−0.22*
Job satisfaction × POS	—	0.12*	−0.14*	—	−0.02	−0.01
Gender × job satisfaction × POS	—	—	0.54*	—	—	−0.04
Change in R^2	—	.02*	.05*	—	.02*	.00
Total R^2	.17*	.19*	.24*	.02*	.04*	.04*

Notes: $* p < .05$

[a] Sample size for this analysis was 117

[b] Sample size for this analysis was 51

explain a significant amount of variance in professional commitment. As such, hypothesis 4 was not supported.

Hypothesis 5 predicted an interaction between gender, professional experience, job satisfaction, and POS on professional commitment. To test this hypothesis, we split the study sample along professional experience categories, and then tested the effects of the three-way interaction gender × job satisfaction × POS on professional commitment for both the newcomer and veteran subsamples. The results of these analyses are provided in table 14.3. For the newcomer sample, as illustrated in step 3a, the gender × job satisfaction × POS interaction term explained a significant amount of variance in professional commitment ($\Delta R^2 = .05$, $p < .05$). As shown in step 3b of table 14.3, though, the three-way interaction was not significant for the veteran sample. To better interpret the meaning of the significant finding for the newcomer sample, we plotted the three-way interaction of gender, job satisfaction, and POS on newcomers' professional commitment in figure 14.2. As illustrated in figure 14.2, there was a sizable increase in the professional commitment of newcomer women who experienced high levels of job satisfaction and POS compared to women with low levels of job satisfaction and POS. Conversely, there was a

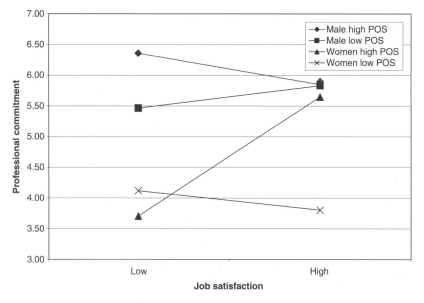

Figure 14.2
Newcomer IT professionals

smaller increase between male newcomers who experienced high levels of job satisfaction and POS compared to males who experienced low job satisfaction and POS. These findings are consistent with the predictions of hypothesis 5 that the positive impact of job satisfaction and POS on professional commitment would be greatest among female newcomer IT professionals.

Because we also had a measure of professional commitment for these newcomers as they were preparing to graduate from their programs (discussed in conjunction with hypothesis 1), we conducted a supplementary analysis using a 2 (gender) × 2 (status) repeated-measures analysis of variance to test whether there was a significant change in participants' reported professional commitment from when they were students to when their professional commitment was measured as newcomers. The results support a significant difference for the within-subjects repeated-measure factor ($F = 21.87$, $p < .000$) and a significant difference for the between-subjects factor ($F = 17.26$, $p < .000$). A test of the interaction of the within-subjects factor (professional commitment) and the between-subjects factor (gender) was not significant. These results indicate that professional commitment increased significantly for both females and males after they entered the workplace, despite the fact that gender differences remained.

Discussion

Overall, our findings extend previous research on gender and attachment to the IT profession in a number of ways. First, we examined the extent to which gender differences in professional commitment exist among IT students preparing to leave their undergraduate programs and enter the world of work. We found that as expected, female IT students reported a lower professional commitment than their male counterparts. We thus contribute to knowledge about professional commitment among students about to graduate from IT-related programs and offer professional commitment as a useful conceptual frame with which to study the transition of women from their undergraduate training to the IT workplace.

Another addition to the literature stems from our investigation of possible differences in professional commitment related to gender and experience. As expected, gender and professional experience did interact, with the lowest professional commitment being reported by the female newcomer IT professionals. Our finding therefore helps identify an important point in the workplace transition at which the retention of women newcomers might be particularly fragile.

We also add to knowledge about the retention of women in the IT profession through our investigation of the impacts of POS and job satisfaction on professional commitment. Interestingly, we did not find support for a role for POS or job satisfaction in boosting professional commitment when these variables were considered separately. Our argument for a joint role for job satisfaction and POS was true for the female newcomer sample. This finding is important because it provides clues as to what steps organizations might take to increase the commitment of newcomer females to the IT field. For female newcomers, who tend to face relatively hostile climates, perceptions that the organization values their contributions and cares about their welfare appears to be a potential plus. But this factor is not enough. Instead, satisfaction with the job itself is also critical. Useful future research might focus on the types of jobs held by female versus male newcomers in order to determine the extent to which desirable jobs are equally distributed. Some evidence suggests that women may be channeled into less interesting and challenging jobs than those allocated to men at a similar experience level (Sumner and Niederman 2003–2004; Von

Hellens et al. 2000), or may otherwise be disproportionately mismatched with their interests within IT (Igbaria, Greenhaus, and Parasuraman 1991).

Of particular interest is the supplementary analysis indicating that although the lagging professional commitment among female IT newcomers was already present as these students were preparing to graduate, professional commitment had improved at a similar rate for females and males as they traversed through their initial workplace experiences. Importantly, it appears that a combination of promoting job satisfaction and perceptions of organizational support has the potential to foster professional commitment in female newcomers and help them achieve a similar level of commitment as their male counterparts.

Future research might explore further the factors that lead to perceptions of organizational support and job satisfaction among IT newcomers. For further research issues relating to the transition of women from the academic world to the IT workplace, see also the review by Bartol and Aspray (this volume).

Of course, like all studies, this study has limitations. The students were from programs that can best be characterized as focusing on information systems management and therefore may not be representative of students in other types of IT-related programs. Our veterans were also from a professional association and hence might be more committed to the IT profession than many IT professionals. Nevertheless, our data do suggest that it is possible for students/newcomers to be as committed to the profession as these association members, in that the professional commitment of male students/newcomers was similar to that of the veterans.

A major implication of these findings is that organizations have much to gain by making sure to convey to female newcomers in particular that their contributions are valued and that the organization cares about their well-being, as well as by attending to their job satisfaction. One reason is that professional commitment has been positively linked to performance (Jauch, Glueck, and Osborn 1978). Along these lines, some researchers have argued that employees who are strongly committed to their profession are more likely to set higher performance standards and be willing to work hard to achieve goals (Wallace 1995).

Another reason is that professional commitment is not only a strong predictor of retention in the profession but also has been found to be associated with a higher commitment to the employing organization and a lower intention to leave that organization (Aranya and Ferris 1983; Aranya and Jacobson 1975; Bartol 1979; Lachman and Aranya 1986). Lachman and Aranya (1986) tested the two competing models on the compatibility of organizational commitment and professional commitment, and their findings suggested that these two types of commitment are congruent with each other. Bartol's (1979) research also supported challenged to the notion that there is an inherent conflict between professionals and their employing organizations. Part of the reason for perceptions of a conflict may be that when individuals decide to switch occupations, they often move to a new organization as well. Aside from their positive effects on the professional commitment of female newcomers, POS and job satisfaction are important predictors of the intention to remain (Allen, Shore, and Griffeth 2003; Vandenberg and Scarpello 1994).

Our research also indicates that colleges and universities may be able to do more to increase the professional commitment of women while they are in IT-related programs. Some suggestions for interventions are contained in earlier chapters in this volume (see, for example, Cohoon and Aspray).

Acknowledgments

This material is based on work supported by the National Science Foundation under grant number EIA–0089941. Any opinions, findings, and conclusions or recommendations expressed in this material are those of the authors, and do not necessarily reflect the views of the National Science Foundation.

References

Ahuja, M. K. 1995. Information technology and the gender factor. In *SIGCPR'95*, ed. L. Olfman, 156–166. New York: Association for Computing Machinery.

Aiken, L. S., and S. G. West. 1991. *Multiple regression: Testing and interpreting interactions.* Thousand Oaks, CA: Sage Publications.

Allen, D. G., L. M. Shore, and R. W. Griffeth. 2003. The role of perceived organizational support and supportive human resources practices in the turnover process. *Journal of Management* 29:99–118.

Aranya, N., and K. R. Ferris. 1983. Organizational-professional conflict among U.S. and Israeli professional accountants. *Journal of Social Psychology* 119:153–161.

Aranya, N., and D. Jacobson. 1975. An empirical study of theories of organizational and occupational commitment. *Journal of Social Psychology* 97:15–23.

Aranya, N., T. Kushnir, and A. Valency. 1986. Organizational commitment in a male-dominated profession. *Human Relations* 39:433–448.

Armeli, S., R. Eisenberger, P. Fasolo, and P. Lynch. 1998. Perceived organizational support and police performance: The moderating influence of socioemotional needs. *Journal of Applied Psychology* 83:288–297.

Bartol, K. M. 1979. Professionalism as a predictor of organizational commitment, role stress, and turnover: A multidimensional approach. *Academy of Management Journal* 22:815–822.

Bartol, K. M., and D. C. Martin. 1982. Managing information systems personnel: A review of the literature and managerial implications. *MIS Quarterly* (special issue): 49–70.

Bauer, T. N., and S. G. Green. 1994. Effect of newcomer involvement in work-related activities: A longitudinal study of socialization. *Journal of Applied Psychology* 79:211–223.

Beyer, S., K. Rynes, J. Perrault, K. Hay, and S. Haller. 2003. Gender differences in computer science students. In *SIGCSE Bulletin 35*, no. 1:49–53. New York: Association for Computing Machinery.

Blau, G. 1985. The measurement and prediction of career commitment. *Journal of Occupational Psychology* 58:277–288.

Blau, G. 1985. The measurement and prediction of career commitment. *Journal of Occupational Psychology* 74:85–93.

Blau, G. 2003. Testing for a four-dimensional structure of occupational commitment. *Journal of Occupational and Organizational Psychology* 76:469–488.

Blau, G., and M. Lunz. 1998. Testing the incremental effect of professional commitment on intent to leave one's profession beyond the effects of external, personal, and work-related variables. *Journal of Vocational Behavior* 52:260–269.

Bretz, R. D., J. W. Boudreau, and T. A. Judge. 1994. Job search behavior of employed managers. *Personnel Psychology* 47:275–301.

Brief, A. P. 1998. *Attitudes in and around organizations*. Thousand Oaks, CA: Sage Publications.

Cohoon, J. M. 2002. Recruiting and retaining women in undergraduate computing majors. *SIGCSE Bulletin* 34, no. 2:48–52.

Council on Competitiveness. 1998. *Competing through innovation: A report of the national innovation summit*. Washington, DC: Council on Competitiveness.

Craig, A., R. Paradis, E. Turner. 2002. A gendered view of computer professionals: Preliminary results of a survey. *ACM SIGCSE Bulletin* 34, no. 2:101–104.

Eisenberger, R., S. Armeli, B. Rexwinkel, P. D. Lynch, and L. Rhoades. 2001. Reciprocation of perceived organizational support. *Journal of Applied Psychology* 86:42–51.

Eisenberger, R., P. Fasolo, and V. Davis-LaMastro. 1990. Perceived organizational support and employee diligence, commitment, and innovation. *Journal of Applied Psychology* 75:51–59.

Eisenberger, R., R. Huntington, S. Hutchison, and D. Sowa. 1986. Perceived organizational support. *Journal of Applied Psychology* 71:500–507.

Freeman, P., and W. Aspray. 1999. *The supply of information technology workers in the United States*. Washington, DC: Computing Research Association.

Gouldner, A. W. 1960. The norm of reciprocity: A preliminary statement. *American Sociological Review* 25:161–178.

Horrigan, M. W. 2003–2004. Charting the projections. *Occupational Outlook Quarterly* 47 (Winter): 1–48.

Igbaria, M., and J. Baroudi. 1995. The impact of job performance evaluations on career advancement prospects: An examination of gender differences in the IS workplace. *MIS Quarterly* 19:107–123.

Igbaria, M., J. H. Greenhaus, and S. Parasuraman. 1991. Career orientations of MIS employees: An empirical investigation. *MIS Quarterly* 15:151–169.

Jauch, L. R., W. F. Glueck, and R. N. Osborn. 1978. Organizational loyalty, professional commitment, and academic research productivity. *Academy of Management Journal* 21:84–92.

Lachman, R., and N. Aranya. 1986. Evaluation of alternative models of commitments and job attitudes of professionals. *Journal of Occupational Behavior* 7:227–243.

Locke, E. A. 1976. The nature and causes of job satisfaction. In *Handbook of industrial and organizational psychology*, ed. M. D. Dunnette, 1297–1343. Chicago: Rand McNally.

Lynch, P. D., R. Eisenberger, and S. Armeli. 1999. Perceived organizational support: Inferior versus superior performance by wary employees. *Journal of Applied Psychology* 84:467–483.

McDonald, M. 2004. A few good women. *U.S. News and World Report* 137, no. 5 (August 16): EE2.

Morell, V. 1996. Computer culture deflects women and minorities. *Science* 271:1915–1916.

President's Information Technology Advisory Committee (PITAC). 1999. *Information technology research: Investing in our future.* Arlington, VA: National Coordination Office for Computing, Information, and Communications.

Rhoades, L., and R. Eisenberger. 2001. Affective commitment to the organization: The contribution of perceived organizational support. *Journal of Applied Psychology* 86:825–836.

Rhoades, L., and R. Eisenberger. 2002. Perceived organizational support: A review of the literature. *Journal of Applied Psychology* 87:698–714.

Roldan, M., L. Soe, and E. K. Yakura. 2004. Perceptions of chilly IT organizational contexts and their effect on the retention and promotion of women in IT. In *SIGMIS'04*, ed. S. Weisband, 108–113. New York: Association for Computing Machinery.

Selby, L., K. Ryba, and A. Young. 1998. Women in computing: What does the data show? *SIGSCE Bulletin* 30, no. 4:62a–67a.

Settoon, R. P., N. Bennett, and R. C. Liden. 1996. Social exchange in organizations: Perceived organizational support, leader-member exchange, and employee reciprocity. *Journal of Applied Psychology* 81:219–228.

Shore, L. M., and T. H. Shore. 1995. Perceived organizational support and organizational justice. In *Organizational politics, justice, and support: Managing social climate at work*, ed. R. Cropanzano and K. M. Kacmar, 149–164. Westport, CT: Quorum Press.

Shore, L. M., and S. J. Wayne. 1993. Commitment and employee behavior: Comparison of affective commitment and continuance commitment with perceived organizational support. *Journal of Applied Psychology* 78:774–780.

Sumner, M., and F. Niederman. 2003–2004. The impact of gender differences on job satisfaction, job turnover, and career experiences of information systems professionals. *Journal of Computer Information Systems*, 29–39.

Tapia, A. H., and L. Kvasny. 2004. Retention is never enough: Retention of women and minorities in the IT workplace. In *SIGMIS'04*, ed. S. Weisband, 84–91. New York: Association for Computing Machinery.

Vandenberg, R. J., and V. Scarpello. 1994. A longitudinal assessment of the determinant relationship between employee commitments to the occupation and organization. *Journal of Organizational Behavior* 15:535–547.

Von Hellens, L. A., R. Pringle, S. H. Nielsen, and A. Greenhill. 2000. People, business, and IT skills: The perspective of women in the IT industry. *SIGCPR*, ed. J. Prasad and W. Nance, 152–157. New York: Association for Computing Machinery.

Wallace, J. E. 1995. Organizational and professional commitment in professional and nonprofessional organizations. *Administrative Science Quarterly* 40:228–255.

Wardle, C., and L. Burton. 2002. Programmatic efforts to encourage women to enter the information technology workforce. *SIGCSE Bulletin* 34, no. 2:27–31.

Wayne, S. J., L. M. Shore, and R. C. Liden. 1997. Perceived organizational support and leader-member exchange: A social exchange perspective. *Academy of Management Journal* 40:82–112.

Wright, R. 1996. Women in computer work: Controlled progress in a technical occupation. In *Women and minorities in American Professions*, ed. J. Tang and E. Smith, 43–64. Albany: State University of New York Press.

15

Foot in the Door, Mouse in Hand: Low-Income Women, Short-Term Job Training Programs, and IT Careers

Karen Chapple

Introduction

Declines in both the production of female computer science degree program graduates and the share of women in the IT workforce have raised alarms about the underrepresentation of women in the IT workforce (Garcia and Giles 1999).[1] Yet from 1990 to 2000, women filled almost 440,000 new IT jobs, while computer science departments produced only 100,000 female graduates with bachelor's or master's degrees.[2] Where did the other workers come from?

One possible explanation is that women are increasingly able to enter IT without a technical degree (Vaas 2000). Another is that the nontraditional educational pathways that Jesse describes (this volume) give the new IT workforce degrees through programs such as Internetworking and database technology, instead of computer science. This chapter adds another explanation, focusing on low-income women: short-term job training programs at nonprofit organizations are offering a new nontraditional path into IT. The number of women who enter IT occupations after graduating from short-term training programs is not large: estimates range up to a few thousand each year (Chapple and Zook 2002). Yet the short-term, nonprofit pathway is of particular interest because of the concentration of both women and minorities in these labor market intermediaries.

Social theorists such as Castells (1996) argue that the spread of IT allows the global economy to use networks that effectively select only certain places and people to participate in the new economy; the existence of networks thus creates a duality, of the "switched-on" and "switched-off," deliberately and selectively including some groups and excluding others, such as women. This chapter, however, shows how it is possible for previously underrepresented workers to get a foot in the door and advance in IT, becoming valued contributors to the new economy. Rather than exacerbating social exclusion, the spread of IT has made upward mobility possible through the changing role of intermediaries, the new emphasis on soft over technical skills, and the growing maturity of workplace culture and career pathways.

This chapter begins by explaining how the down skilling of IT occupations and the rising importance of soft skills have created an opportunity for short-term training programs to prepare less-educated students for IT jobs. It then looks at outcomes for ninety-three graduates from six different nonprofit training programs in the New York metropolitan region, the San Francisco Bay Area, and the Washington, DC, region. Repeated interviews with this sample over the course of three years suggest that most graduates of short-term training programs experience some success in IT. Nevertheless, particularly for those women with little or no college education, upward mobility in IT remains out of reach. The last section of the chapter explores some policy implications to address these nontraditional educational and career pathways in IT.

The Rise of Entry-Level IT Occupations: The Roles of the Skills Training Life Cycle and Soft Skills

Researchers have long argued that the advent of IT increases the cognitive complexity of work and creates a new class of symbolic analysts requiring high levels of education (Reich 1991). Yet while many jobs in the IT sector demand high skill levels, IT occupations are not necessarily inaccessible to workers with low skill levels because of the rise of entry-level IT jobs. Entry-level IT occupations, including computer support specialists, computer and ATM repairers, broadcast technicians, and network and computer systems administrators, accounted in 2003 for about 33 percent of all computer-related jobs, or 1.2 million jobs (a decline from the peak of 1.4 million in 2000).[3]

Some of these are new occupations based on the appearance of new technology—for example, there was little demand for Web developers before the Internet became widely adopted. But others have emerged as appropriate for entry-level personnel because of the evolution of job requirements over time. The computer support specialist occupation provides an illustration. As computers began to become commonplace throughout all economic sectors, computer support specialists were needed to provide technical assistance for users of hardware, software, and systems. At first, the new support tasks were incorporated into existing computer programming jobs, in a process of "job enlarging," but gradually the technical support duties shifted to others, such as clerical workers seeking a promotion who could be trained easily on the job or four-year college graduates with some computer training. Over time, the training for these occupations has evolved from computer science degrees at four-year colleges to short-term training often done at community colleges.[4]

This transfer has been described as a "skill-training life cycle" (Flynn 1988). Skill training first occurs on the job or in special training sessions provided by the producer (e.g., training in networking by Novell). In this initial phase, job enlarging, or increasing the job duties of relatively high-level employees, serves to meet the emerging needs. Over time, as more firms adopt the technology, these new skills evolve from firm specific to general, and are more readily transferable to other companies. Employee turnover increases as a marketplace for the skills emerges. At this stage, employers can find qualified employees by recruiting from other firms. Firms increasingly expect training to be provided by specialized external programs, funded by government or the employees themselves. The case of data processing, which emerged in the 1960s and 1970s, is illustrative. Employers initially hired four-year college graduates with some computer training. As training programs in the field developed, employers turned to community colleges and proprietary vocational schools as well as nonprofit training programs to fill the gap (Useem 1986).

Another factor in the rise of entry-level occupations is the increasing emphasis on soft skills, defined as "skills, abilities, and traits that pertain to personality, attitude, and behavior rather than to formal or technical knowledge" (Moss and Tilly 2001, 44). Employers define the core competencies for entry-level IT occupations in terms of motivation, flexibility, and interaction skills rather than just technical proficiency (Chapple and Zook 2002). These skills become increasingly important for new entry-level IT occupations in part because technological advances make technical skills more routinized and in part because the pace of change in technology means that software-specific skills rapidly become obsolete, making the ability to learn quickly very important. With technologies continually in transition, the one constant becomes the new organization of work, which is increasingly project based, leading to a new emphasis on teamwork skills. Finally, entry-level positions—whether in desktop support, Web design, or networking—increasingly involve customer service, so that the ability to communicate effectively becomes an increasing focus of the job.

With IT occupations reaching a mature point in the skill-training life cycle and entry-level occupations more likely to emphasize soft than technical skills, short-term IT job training programs have come of age. This nonprofit or government-based "second-chance employment and training system" (Giloth 2004)—that is, the educational system for those who have failed to benefit from the first-chance K–12 and postsecondary school system—disproportionately attracts nonwhite, low-income, and less-educated job seekers (Pastor et al. 2003). With college-educated workers increasingly reluctant to take the relatively low-wage computer support specialist jobs (which start at $11 to $15 per hour, typically without benefits), these training programs are a growing source for entry-level IT workers. The next section introduces six such training programs, in the New York metropolitan region, the San Francisco Bay Area, and the Washington, DC, region.

The Nonprofit IT Training Programs

The New York area cases include Per Scholas, in the South Bronx, and Training, Inc., in Newark, New Jersey. Per Scholas is a community-based nonprofit organization founded in 1995 with the mission of repairing computers and donating them to schools that could not afford high-cost technology. Within a couple years, it evolved into a fifteen-week personal computer technician training program, targeting extremely disadvantaged groups such as the homeless, welfare-to-work clients, and others with low incomes and education. The curriculum includes some networking, hardware, and software components as well as the A+ certification; it graduates 100–150 students per year, with a placement rate that remains consistently around 80 percent. Per Scholas has a transformative effect on its students, as the gratitude of a graduate like Fernando testifies: "I love Per Scholas. They are a part of my family; they help me. Here it's very hard that you'll find somebody that will help you, no matter what. 'I don't need your money, I want to help you.'"[5]

Training, Inc. (at Essex County College in Newark) is a branch of a national nonprofit job training organization that offers a unique workplace simulation approach to learning. By the late 1990s, it offered two twenty-week computer-based training programs: the personal computer troubleshooter (leading to the A+ certification) and the software applications specialist. It targets a wide array of groups, from welfare-to-work-clients to dislocated workers, and graduates about 100–150 students per year from the two programs, placing about 80 percent. As graduate Troy affirms, "Training, Inc. wants to change you from who you are to what they say corporate America wants you to be. They help you walk the walk, talk the talk through teamwork, peer support."

In San Francisco, the Bay Video Coalition (BAVC) was founded in 1975 to serve the nonprofit sector with low-cost technical assistance, equipment access, and training on the newest communications technologies. During the late 1990s, BAVC began conducting job training in Web design in its MediaLink program. The sixteen-week program includes HTML, Web-based graphics, and project development, targeting disadvantaged groups, the working poor, dislocated workers, and incumbent workers. Graduating 60–100 students per year, its placement rates have varied widely, from 90 percent at the peak of the dot-com boom to 60 percent at its trough. Employers are confident in the BAVC education; as Chandra asserts, "MediaLink gave me legitimacy. Now I could point to technical skills and people would believe that I had them."

Also in the Bay Area, in the impoverished suburb of San Pablo, is Street Tech, which opened its doors in March 2000. A nonprofit computer training center, Street Tech offers a six-month personal computer technician training and A+ certification class for adults from extremely disadvantaged communities. It graduates 30–50 students per year, with placement rates that also have fluctuated with the business cycle, from 50 to 80 percent. As graduate Shandon says, "Street Tech is like a family. They inspire, push, and motivate you. The teachers care; they're there to help you. At college, they don't even care if you show up. Street Tech is one of the greatest things that ever happened to me."

Per Scholas, Training, Inc., BAVC, and Street Tech all emphasize soft skills, with as much as one-third of the curriculum devoted to communication and workplace protocol, with the explicit goal of job placement. In contrast, the two Washington, DC, cases, Byte Back and Alexandria Continuing Education and Workforce Development at Northern Virginia Community College, offer little or no formal soft skills training and job placement.

Since the mid-1990s, Byte Back has provided advanced computer training to low-income adults through a yearlong internship program. While interning at Byte Back's community technology centers, students learn network administration, programming (Visual Basic), database development, Web development, and personal computer hardware. The program graduates 10–20 students per year; although placement is not tracked systematically, roughly half of the students enter computer-related jobs at the conclusion of training. Graduates praise the program's combined education and work experience approach: as Jamain notes, "We were getting a pretty good bargain, because ain't too many other places that you can go to that's gonna pay you, to teach you. It gave us an education and job experience. And it gave me the chance to work under pressure."

Alexandria Continuing Education and Workforce Development at Northern Virginia Community College offers short-term training in hardware (including A+ certification), networking, Web design, and database development. The program started in 1998 and graduates about twelve hundred students per year. Students come from a variety of backgrounds; the availability of scholarships ensures that students from disadvantaged backgrounds can attend. In general, graduates recommend this program's courses as high quality, but otherwise feel little connection to the institution.

Methods

This chapter draws on three different data sources to explore whether it is indeed possible for women to enter and advance in IT through these training programs: interviews with training program graduates, interviews with employers, and a Web-based survey of entry-level IT workers. Interviews were transcribed and coded using QSR NUD*IST software. To code the data, a framework was developed from theoretical and policy issues raised a priori as well as new issues that emerged from the interviews themselves (Ritchie and Spencer 1994).[6] The analysis presented below generally describes the dominant categories that emerged from this coding process. If a point of view is offered by multiple respondents during open-ended interviews, it typically emerges as a dominant category. For example, although the training program graduates that failed in IT blame a variety of personal factors, the dominant narrative was that they were unable to find jobs because of the recession.

Training Program Graduates   In-depth, semistructured interviews with 112 non-profit training program graduates from the 6 training programs explored the job search and career advancement processes in detail for disadvantaged job seekers transitioning into IT. Interview respondents were drawn from a random sample of fifty graduates provided by each program; approximately 25 to 50 percent from each program sample agreed to participate. Of the initial interviewees, nineteen were disqualified from the study because of extenuating factors such as not completing the training program, leaving ninety-three in the sample.[7] Program personnel deemed the samples representative of their program graduates, who represent a broad cross-section of the working poor, but were generally unable to provide data for verification. Some nonrespondent bias may have occurred as the least successful students declined to participate because of their failure and the most successful ones declined because of a lack of time. Thus, these findings are likely more representative of the average training program graduate than the outliers.

Initial interviews took place about a year after the student graduated from the program, and most of the participants were interviewed several times over the course of this three-year study. The first interviews, conducted in person in 2001 and 2002, asked about the students' background in computers, educational history, job and job search history, career goals and plans, and experiences on the job. Almost two-thirds of the sample also participated in multiple follow-up surveys conducted by e-mail and phone, concluding in fall 2004. These follow-ups checked on the students' career and educational trajectories since their initial interviews.

Employers   In-depth, in-person interviews with forty-nine employers examined the trends in entry-level IT hiring and firm location, the connections of employers to training providers, and the current skill requirements for entry-level IT jobs. I selected the sample of private and public sector employers strategically to represent the variety of economic sectors that employ entry-level IT workers, including IT and IT services, finance and insurance, manufacturing and retail, business and communications, temporary agencies, and the institutional sector (government, education, and health). The sample included a mix of city and suburban employers, mostly from the San Francisco Bay Area, but with a special subsample of eight New York employers to explore regional differences.

Web-Based Survey of Job Seekers   A Web-based survey provided an overview of the job search process and the educational background of entry-level IT workers. The survey sample included 298 job seekers with current résumés posted on the Web. The survey sample was drawn from a strategic sample of approximately 4,000 job seekers with current résumés posted on the Web; excluding inaccurate e-mail addresses, the net response rate was approximately 15 percent. To be included, the résumé had to mention keywords associated with entry-level IT occupations, such as technician, help desk, or Web design, as well as one of the regions under study. An e-mail solicited participation in the survey; the respondents received a $10 gift certificate for participating.

Conducted in 2002, the survey asked the respondents to provide information about their first job in IT and up to eight subsequent IT jobs, including the job description, period of employment, and job search method. The survey also obtained information on educational attainment, including IT training, and other demographic characteristics.

From Training to the IT Workforce: A Sample of Program Graduates

"Technology is what makes people stand out, so it doesn't matter if they're from a certain area anymore. It's the way to progress in the world," observes Aaron, a Training, Inc. graduate. IT is "the way to progress in the world" for a variety of disadvantaged workers: not just for Aaron, who is an African American college dropout with no office work experience, but also for Chia, a Laotian high school dropout who wanted "a decent job, where you don't have to get on your knees and scrub the floors," and for Jo, a white woman who says she "struggled all my adult life with what I was going to do," despite a master's degree in environmental policy. The following looks at who attends short-term nonprofit IT training programs—and who succeeds.

Relative to the U.S. IT workforce overall, this sample is disproportionately minority, female, and less educated (see table 15.1); one-third have just a high school diploma, general equivalency diploma, or less. Most are in their late twenties or thirties; the average age is thirty-five. Most (75 percent) came from jobs in low-paying and/or low-skill sectors, such as retail, clerical, or blue-collar work, but most (about 80 percent) are now working in IT after just this one training program. Three to four years after the program, most (77 percent) of the sixty-four graduates who could still be located were still working in IT.

Most important, all of these groups are making substantial wage progress (table 15.2). From their hourly wages in their last job before entering IT (usually in retail, personal services, or construction), these training program graduates generally experience a 55 percent increase in wages—and for women, 75 percent, from about $12 to $21 per hour. Not surprisingly, workers coming from low-paid service, retail, clerical, or "helping" occupations, in which women are concentrated, experience the largest wage increases. Educational attainment also makes a substantial difference, with the less educated benefiting the most in terms of wages: with just a high school or general equivalency diploma (or less), wages increase by 74 percent, and

Table 15.1
Characteristics of the sample (graduates of nonprofit training programs)

Respondent characteristics		Number	Percent
Race/ethnicity	African American	38	41%
	First-generation immigrant	19	20%
	Latino	10	11%
	Other	5	5%
	White	21	23%
Gender	Female	41	44%
	Male	52	56%
Educational attainment	Less than high school	4	4%
	High school/GED	25	27%
	Some two-year college	20	22%
	Associate's degree and/or some four-year college	21	23%
	Bachelor's degree and/or some graduate school	23	25%
Age group	19–29	26	28%
	30–39	40	43%
	40–49	23	25%
	50+	4	4%
Employment status one year after program	Entry-level IT	59	63%
	Entry-level IT related	8	9%
	Midlevel or advanced IT	8	9%
	Non-IT occupation	8	9%
	Unemployed	10	11%
Employment status three to four years after program	Employed in IT or IT related	49	77%
	Employed, not in IT	12	19%
	Unemployed	3	5%
Occupation prior to IT	Blue-collar or military	14	18%
	Clerical	19	25%
	High-end "helping" (e.g., nursing, social work)	7	9%
	High-end office	11	14%
	Low-end service or retail	25	33%
Program	BAVC	19	20%
	Byte Back	17	18%
	Alexandria/NVCC	15	16%
	Per Scholas	20	22%
	Street Tech	11	12%
	Training, Inc.	11	12%
Region	San Francisco Bay Area	30	32%
	New York metropolitan area	31	33%
	Washington, DC	32	34%

Table 15.2
Wage progress, before and after entering IT, by race/ethnicity, gender, and educational level

Respondent characteristics		Hourly wages in last job prior to entering IT (1999–2001)[a]		Hourly wages at time of last interview (2004) (pre-IT wage sample)[b]		Hourly wages at time of last interview (2004) (full final sample)[c]		Wage progress, pre-IT training to last interview[b]	Wage progress, pre-IT training to last interview[c]
		$	Num	$	Num	$	Num		
Race/ethnicity	African American	$11.02	26	$15.57	15	$16.09	18	41.4%	46.0%
	First-generation immigrant	$13.47	16	$22.72	13	$22.76	14	68.7%	69.0%
	Latino or Asian	$11.73	11	$18.67	6	$21.00	7	59.2%	79.1%
	White	$16.11	18	$24.35	10	$22.95	12	51.1%	42.5%
Gender	Female	$11.74	32	$19.89	17	$20.58	21	69.4%	75.3%
	Male	$13.98	39	$20.23	27	$19.95	30	44.7%	42.7%
Educational attainment	High school diploma, GED, or less	$10.65	24	$18.54	16	$18.54	16	74.1%	74.1%
	Some two-year college	$14.53	17	$23.03	10	$23.03	10	58.5%	58.5%
	Associate's degree and/or some four-year college	$13.68	15	$18.33	11	$18.67	16	34.0%	36.4%
	Bachelor's degree and/or some graduate school	$14.20	15	$22.27	7	$22.79	9	56.8%	60.5%
Occupation prior to IT	Blue-collar	$12.71	13	$18.60	7	$18.60	7	46.3%	46.3%
	Clerical	$11.09	16	$20.62	13	$20.14	14	85.9%	81.6%
	High-end "helping"	$14.50	5	$15.00	2	$16.00	3	3.4%	10.3%
	High-end office	$21.25	8	$26.77	6	$27.70	8	26.0%	30.4%
	Low-end service or retail	$12.23	21	$20.21	11	$20.21	11	65.2%	65.2%

Program	BAVC	$18.17	15	$21.00	9	$21.33	12	15.6%	17.4%
	Byte Back	$15.43	8	$20.67	3	$20.05	5	33.9%	30.0%
	Alexandria/NVCC	$13.95	15	$34.65	6	$34.65	6	148.4%	148.4%
	Per Scholas	$9.73	16	$17.73	11	$17.73	11	82.1%	82.1%
	Street Tech	$10.95	11	$16.56	10	$16.56	10	51.2%	51.1%
	Training, Inc.	$6.58	6	$13.00	5	$15.14	7	97.5%	130.0%
Region	New York metropolitan area	$8.88	22	$16.25	16	$16.72	18	83.1%	88.4%
	San Francisco Bay Area	$15.12	26	$18.66	19	$19.16	22	23.5%	26.8%
	Washington, DC	$14.46	23	$29.99	9	$28.01	11	107.3%	93.6%
Total		$12.97	71	$20.10	44	$20.21	51	55.0%	55.8%

Notes:
a. Includes earnings for all respondents in the year prior to the IT training program
b. Includes only the respondents who provided their hourly wages in the last job prior to entering IT
c. Includes all respondents interviewed in 2004 who were working and willing to provide their current wages

with a college degree, wages increase by an average of 60 percent, but with an associate's degree, wages increase only by 36 percent.

Outcomes vary widely among program graduates, but interestingly, people's overall educational background does not necessarily predict success in the IT workforce: those starting with little or no college are just as likely to rise in IT as those with a college degree. The sample is divided into six types along two dimensions: success in IT and educational attainment (table 15.3). Success in IT is defined as a combination of wage progress, career progress (as measured by new work experience and/or the pursuit of further education), and stated ambition to progress in IT or a related field. Those with high success (dubbed herein "the rising stars" and "the second lives") are not only improving their wages but also adding job responsibilities, while planning to advance in IT. Those with low success ("the complacent" and "the creamers") have made little or no wage progress, but are pursuing or have plans to pursue new educational or job goals. Those with no success ("the discouraged" and "the unlucky") either never made it in IT, are unemployed, or are no longer in IT. Educational attainment is high for those having a college degree (associate's or higher) and low for those with at most some college. Overall, almost 40 percent of the sample is highly successful, whether they began with low or high educational attainment (table 15.3). On the other hand, those with low initial educational levels are much more likely to fail (31 percent versus 23 percent of those with a college degree). Yet in total, almost three-quarters of the sample still experiences low or high success in IT.

Relative to the full sample, the forty-one women follow a slightly different distribution (table 15.4). Women in the high educational attainment group are more likely to experience high success in IT, relative to men. While a proportionate share of women in the low educational group also experience high success, they are also more likely to fail. The following discusses the trajectories associated with the six different types and then explores some of the reasons behind the success of some.

Low Educational Attainment, Low Success in IT: The Discouraged

Overall, just eight of the forty-one women (20 percent) came into the IT training program with little education, and then were unsuccessful at entering and/or advancing in the workforce. In general, the programs that target extremely disadvantaged groups—Per Scholas, Street Tech, and Training, Inc.—account for most of this group, which might be called the discouraged.

Table 15.3
Success in IT by educational attainment

Educational attainment	Success in IT									Total
	None			Low			High			
	Num	%	Type	Num	%	Type	Num	%	Type	
Low	15	30.6%	"The discouraged"	15	30.6%	"The complacent"	19	38.8%	"The rising stars"	49
High	10	22.7%	"The unlucky"	17	38.6%	"The creamers"	17	38.6%	"The second lives"	44
Total	25	26.9%		32	34.4%		36	38.7%		93

Table 15.4
Success in IT by educational attainment, women only

Educational attainment	Success in IT									Total
	None			Low			High			
	Num	%	Type	Num	%	Type	Num	%	Type	
Low	8	40.0%	"The discouraged"	5	25.0%	"The complacent"	7	35.0%	"The rising stars"	20
High	5	23.8%	"The unlucky"	5	23.8%	"The creamers"	11	52.4%	"The second lives"	21
Total	13	31.7%		10	24.4%		18	43.9%		41

For the women who fail, the most typical reason is that IT is not a good fit. As one female Per Scholas graduate working in customer service for a computer repair company admitted, "I'd like to get out of computers. This job doesn't stimulate me. I don't get to use my creativity." This contrasts with the men, who usually fail because of a lack of motivation in the job search; some exhibit a sense of entitlement, and thus are unprepared for what it will take to get a foot in the door. Still, some of these discouraged graduates have been able to leverage their work experience in IT to enter other fields.

High Educational Attainment, Low Success in IT: The Unlucky

A smaller group of students (12 percent of the sample), the unlucky, have some college education, but still are not able to make it in IT; most attended BAVC or Byte Back. Like the first group, many of these have simply found that they're not interested in IT, especially since the wage gains offered by the dot-com surge have evaporated. As Naomi, a former Web designer who is now permanently turned off by IT, said about her e-commerce firm, "It combined the worst things about start-ups with the worst things about corporations." Likewise, several respondents lost their jobs during the recession and were unable to compete against college grads with years of IT work experience in a tight labor market.

Low Educational Attainment, Medium Success in IT: The Complacent

The complacent, at 12 percent, typically have entered the IT workforce successfully, but seem to be content with simply keeping their jobs. Most have graduated from programs like Per Scholas, and come from troubled histories such as homelessness or drug addiction. For these workers, becoming fluent in IT is not so much about upward mobility as it is about getting a foot in the door and surviving; bridging the divide is enough.

Some of the women in this group actually are trying to move up, but aren't sure of the right skill sets: Danita, from Per Scholas, is frustrated that her job is part-time, but she can't seem to figure out what skills she needs to gain a permanent position; for instance, she took a Cisco course at a time when the market was deluged with Cisco trainees, and she has never found a way to use the skills. Likewise, in her 2004 follow-up interview, Shari from Per Scholas said, "It's time to move on. It'll be five years in January. I have learned everything that I needed to learn for me to do my own thing." Nevertheless, she has yet to get the N+ certification that she first mentioned getting in 2001.

High Educational Attainment, Medium Success in IT: The Creamers

Another 12 percent of graduates might be called the creamers, after the practice of creaming, in which programs select those students who are the most likely to succeed and the least in need. These are the students who need some additional training in order to enter IT, but don't really need to attend a free job training program instead of taking out a loan for a college course. These creamers, who mostly attend BAVC, Alexandria, and Byte Back, have no real barriers to entering the workforce. For instance, Cynthia, who graduated from a state university, dismisses the training she got from Training, Inc.: "In the PC field, they want to know you're not off the street, so the degree is what helps." Because these graduates are not particularly wedded to IT, they tend not to advance very far. Instead, they look for the next opportunity, wherever it strikes—or as Cynthia remarked in her 2004 follow-up interview, "I'll probably stay as long as they let me."

Low Educational Attainment, High Success in IT: The Poster Children

About 17 percent of the sample might be described as poster children, rising from very disadvantaged backgrounds to be stars in the IT workforce. Graduates like Cheryl, a twenty-three-year-old African American woman, have their lives transformed by the training program:

I went to Street Tech for basic computer training, but then I was told about A+ and all the other programs. I didn't know what it was. I just knew I had to have it. At eighteen, I didn't care much about college, but since I was twenty-one at the time, I was thinking about school more seriously. And it was because of Street Tech that I was hired at XXX Bank. The bank pays for my school now. They trained me to be certified in Dell and Dell server, and they pay for my school at Phoenix, so Street Tech really opened up one door after the other.

High Educational Attainment, High Success in IT: Formerly Lost Souls

The final category (at 27 percent) might be called the second lives, for those people who have substantial education, but were unable to fit satisfactorily into the workplace prior to entering IT. For men, the problem is generally that they were educated in another country; women more often have found themselves in an inappropriate field, perhaps because of occupational segregation. Marianne, who came to Alexandria from a background in nursing, comments,

Well, you need some extra training or a refresher course or something. And that's when I decided, I enjoyed nursing, but it's hard work, the scheduling is terrible, and I thought here I am, trying to raise three children. I love computers. This is really my chance to try something different. And I just happened to be reading a flyer ... and saw this program, and I said that's the way to get into it.

Unlike the creamers, the second lives are deeply grateful to the training program, which literally changed the direction of their lives. Says BAVC grad Brenda, "It helped to kick us back into professional mode. The training gave us an opportunity to make a living." Further, the second lives have strong ambitions in IT, with clearly articulated job goals and plans for how to reach them.

Overall, about 68 percent of female program graduates—and 60 percent of those with no college degree—are somewhat or highly successful in IT, even a few years after finishing the program. For some, IT is not the right field, and they fail. But what explains the success of the others, which is so surprising given the underrepresentation of women in IT and the exclusivity of the class of symbolic analysts described by theorists? Both the organization of the IT workplace and the preparation by training programs play a role in getting workers from disadvantaged backgrounds to bridge the divide. The following looks at the factors explaining this success, including the acquisition of soft and technical skills, the workplace attitudes toward women, and the availability of career ladders.

Making It in IT: The Role of Qualifications

The following looks at the types of skills in the entry-level workforce, including soft skills, technical skills, and college degrees, from the perspective given by both employers and training program graduates in interviews. Researchers coming from computer science backgrounds tend to emphasize the importance of technical skills in the IT workforce (e.g., Lee, Trauth, and Farwell 1995). Yet sociologists have increasingly found that soft skills, particularly personal motivation and social interaction, are critical to finding and keeping jobs (Moss and Tilly 2001; Holzer 1996).

The employers interviewed for this study are emphasizing soft skills in their entry-level workers, whether they come from traditional or nontraditional pathways, due to several factors, such as bad hiring decisions made during the cycle's peak; the offshoring of more routine work, leading to more emphasis on company culture; and the abundant labor pool of workers with similar technical skills, which makes soft skills more important at the margin. Reflecting the growing maturity of entry-level IT occupations, companies are also relying less on formal credentials. These factors add up to the continued opportunity for female workers from disadvantaged backgrounds to enter IT.

Soft Skills

Asked what are the most important skills they look for in an entry-level employee, almost all the companies interviewed mentioned soft skills first, or both technical and soft skills equally. About one-third of the companies added that experience was the most important way to ascertain an applicant's skill levels, both technical and soft. The new emphasis on soft skills creates a particular advantage for women, who often come into IT with experience in the so-called helping professions (such as nursing).

The companies placing soft skills first came from many different sectors, including IT services, but not hardware or software firms. These pure IT companies were more likely to value technical and soft skills equally, perhaps because their entry-level workforce is performing more complex tasks than the help-desk workers at other firms.

Although firms mention both communication skills and motivation as important, they tend to emphasize personality and fit with the company. In particular, financial and business services companies, as well as temporary agencies, spoke about the significance of attitude and ability to work with others. Some look for compatibility: "I would rather hire someone with a great personality—someone I get along with—over a C++ nerd any day." Other companies stress the importance of presentation: "It is not exactly what you know, it's how you impress people. . . . It's not what you say, it's how you say it." For some, this skill may come from personality, but others acquire it from training programs like Training, Inc. that teach how to "walk the walk" of corporate America.

Communication skills, as well as customer service, remain a strong concern. Because in IT, "you are dealing with people that are already frustrated and upset," tech support workers in particular need strong communication skills. It's also a matter of business value: as an IT service company told us, "It's how you communicate to the end user what you did and how you did it. It goes back to perceived value by the client." Gail, a BAVC graduate, clearly understands: "I like to work with clients. The intonation is subtle, and you need to be face-to-face for a couple hours to pick up what they really want."

Some argue that communication skills can't be taught, that working in help-desk support requires innate patience as well as humility: one IT firm contended that employees who admit that they don't know everything have a better "bandwidth" for learning the technology in the future. Yet one former welfare recipient from Training, Inc. claims that she learned her phone help-desk techniques from raising her five children: "I have the same technique for dealing with people—I put them on hold for a minute and they always calm down."

Companies look for self-starters with a high level of enthusiasm for learning, the "sponges" who love to solve problems, who will read a book to figure out what to do. Said a manager at a financial services firm, "I look for someone who is hungry—hungry to do the work. It's so great to see when the lights come on during the training process—not someone who just wants to fill the chair." Cheryl clearly fits the bill: "I love my job. Everything. It's challenging every day. Everything I do is different. Every year there are different challenges, new responsibilities, the experience continues to grow. I get more to do based on experience and trust."

Technical Skills

The few firms that emphasized the importance of technical skills were quite small, with only a few entry-level positions. This does not mean that technical skills are unimportant but rather that beyond a certain basic level of technical proficiency, entry-level IT workers are expected to learn on the job. Skill sets change so quickly that depth of knowledge loses its value. As BAVC grad Jo says, she no longer had to worry about her skills: "It was new for everyone, so it leveled the playing field."

For entry-level work in computer repair, help desk, networking, or Web design, the essential technical skills can easily be obtained in a short-term training program. No more than an eighth-grade level of math is required, and only rarely do workers have any college-level course work in computer science. In fact, performance in math seems to be a poor predictor of success in getting an entry-level IT job. Asked what their worst class in high school was, half of the sample (mostly women) said math; just one-quarter of the sample claimed math as their best class. With confidence, successful graduates like Carmen can make up for dropping out of high school in tenth grade to have children: "So I was the type of person that when something messed up like my phone or my radio, I would open it up and look and see if anything was wrong, anything was loose. And when I see that paper say computer repair and I love computers, and I said, 'I think I could do this, I would be good at it,' and I gave it a shot. It worked out."

Short-term technical training is not enough for everybody, as the discouraged and unlucky point out. Says Sarah: "I learned a tremendous amount at BAVC. It just wasn't enough once I started working." Likewise, Meredith asserts that "Training, Inc. doesn't prepare you for a career in technology, just a job. I'd like to know what education it would take to get into a technology career. That's not what they do."

The College Degree

Only one-third of the firms interviewed—generally large institutional or IT sector employers—described the college degree as necessary. Employers who avoid workers with degrees cited several reasons: the inability to deal with real-world technical problems, the signal that the degree sends about a person's willingness to work at the entry level, and the relative importance of work experience.

Most prominent is employer concern about the attitude of college graduates. They "aren't willing to get their hands dirty" but still need to be trained for the job—and they often want too much money. Working with users is difficult: "You can't blow up or speak over the top of the head with technical gobbley-gook. I need you to be able to talk with everyone."

The degree may also send the wrong signal to some firms: one manufacturer/retailer commented that if a worker takes the time to go to college, it is a "red flag." Do they really want to be working in computer support? Others complained about the problems of insubordination: "Those with a college degree are more of a management headache than not."

Some firms place such an emphasis on experience that, as a manager at a temporary agency remarked, "I almost forget to look at their résumé to see if they graduated from college." Temporary agencies are particularly likely to overlook the degree because rarely does the employer require degrees for contract workers.

For companies stressing the degree, it signals that the applicant understands the big picture and has the drive to succeed. The ability to think holistically comes not only from technical knowledge but also the very process of getting a degree—the experience of using computers, dealing with complexity, multitasking, conducting research, and asking questions. One institutional employer gave the example of a guy without a college education who kept trying to buy a new server every time they had a new application. He was making the decision based on his knowledge, not the big picture; it was the safe—if inefficient—approach because using separate servers, unexpected snags wouldn't occur.

A college education also signals motivation and ambition. As an IT firm employer put it, "Life is not easy, work is not easy, and they're not going to know that if they didn't go through some tough schooling." The companies that believe in hiring college grads referred repeatedly to these workers' work ethic, "voracious appetite for knowledge," "can-do attitude," and honesty when they can't solve a problem.

Recent experience during the dot-com era with hiring workers without degrees has shown managers that the degree is no longer necessary, creating more opportunities for those without them. For instance, one manufacturer/retailer conducts systematic evaluations of its employee career paths and performance; after discovering that some of its most competent and ambitious employees lacked degrees, the firm changed its hiring requirements.

Ultimately, most IT workers will attend some college. This Web-based survey of IT workers showed that by midcareer, most will have acquired several years of college education; for help-desk/technician, networking/systems, and Web-related jobs, the average is four years of college or more, and for programming, database administration, or management, five years or more. Only in computer programming and database administrator occupations, however, do the majority (78 percent) of workers have a degree in IT. Overall, 54 percent of the Web-based survey sample has a technology-related degree, but only 31 percent of women do; it seems that many women make it in IT with a liberal arts background. Although this survey represented all job seekers, rather than the more disadvantaged ones who graduate from short-term training programs, this discrepancy may also occur among the training program graduates. In the sample interviewed for this study, one-third want to go on to get a degree; for most of the men, the degree will be in a computer-related field, but only half of the women want to do college course work in IT.

Making It in IT: Workplace Issues

In addition to a worker's qualifications, the workplace culture—including the division of labor, the extent of support, the attitude toward promotion, and the level of autonomy—shapes the success of women who come from short-term training programs. The employer interviews yielded a clear sense of a division of labor between men and women within IT. Several companies described concentrations of women in customer service, Web development, and business analyst positions, and a lack of women in the areas of networking and engineering. Some companies even seem uncomfortable with women working in hardware. This gives women the responsibility for changing colleagues' attitudes, as Monica from Alexandria describes:

I can't tell you how much it drove me crazy when I first got hired there, that nobody would let me carry a computer. All these men—and the attorneys—oh, my god—if you crawled under their desk to fix a cable or something, it would just panic them. They wouldn't know what to do. There's this woman crawling around on their floor. And they would say, "No, let me call

Jeff, let me call Jeff, Jeff can do that." . . . I've definitely had to train people to accept me in a role that would allow me to do things like move hardware, move computers, move heavy equipment. But I've definitely broken that barrier.

Just as Monica gained confidence by breaking the barriers, Cheryl boosted her self-esteem simply by being a troubleshooter: "Before, it felt kind of weird, but I totally like it now. It was just that when you come into a branch to service the equipment, they expect to see a man. But I got over it. Because people think it is incredible when you fix something. You're their hero. They really respect you."

One trend among many different companies is to place women in management positions—a surprising finding given the lack of women in management (Marenghi 1992; Johnson 1990; Igbaria and Baroudi 1995). For instance, a manager at one large IT company noted that only 6 percent of her support staff are women, while 62 percent of the managers are. Women end up in management because of their strong communication skills, their ability to manage conflict, and the way they handle feedback from their supervisors. One financial company even said that women are simply more marketable than men: "The most attractive candidate for any upper-level IT job will be a forty-five-year-old woman with the technical back-ground and the business/communication skills." Just two women in the nonprofit training program sample, both from Alexandria, have moved into management, but they both spoke of their employer's proactive attitude toward promotion.

While a growing number of companies seem to desire more women in management, they often experience difficulty in recruiting enough of them. "I've tried to hire women, but if they are sharp, they're gone," according to an institutional employer. Several mentioned that women simply did not see the career track, either because of family responsibilities or a perception based on previous battles in the IT culture that it would be difficult to advance further. Part of the problem seems to be company expectations of women who advance: for example, Chandra wants to advance into a more technical and creative role, but she feels like her bosses want to "turn me into an admin person." Likewise, BAVC grad Lola wanted to move into Oracle, but her boss said, "I don't really see Oracle on your career track."

The transformation of IT—in particular, the advent of the Web and the down skilling of IT occupations—may gradually be changing the relationship between women and the workplace. Web design has attracted women into the profession and, in turn, feminized the work approach. According to BAVC grad Marianne, "The hardest part of my job is psychological, coaxing the customer to make a decision while making them feel like they made the decision themselves." As many of the female BAVC grads work for themselves, they speak glowingly of their new autonomy: "Having 150 dumb clients is better than one dumb boss."

Advancing in the IT Workforce

"I'm a first-generation woman of color, and I'm in technology!" asserted Brenda, a BAVC graduate. "But I haven't made a lot of progress like you're supposed to. I don't have a house, a family, or a full-time job. We're indoctrinated in these stages of life, and I feel like I'm behind and can't catch up.... You know what my job goal is? I want to go to the doctor and the dentist. I want new glasses and a pap smear."

Career progression in IT is rarely a simple linear movement from technical support to management. Most companies offer limited opportunities for advancement within IT, so career progression most typically occurs not through career ladders but lattices, in which workers advance through moving laterally to other divisions within and outside IT. As a recent U.S. Department of Commerce report notes,

Rather than moving step-by-step up a career ladder, IT workers often manage a portfolio of skills ("the skill set").... Individual technical skills in the portfolio may increase or decrease in value, depending on the skill currency or size of demand in the market. There is no common path to building the skill portfolio. In addition, frequent changes in technology and difficulties in forecasting future skill needs mean that IT workers are often left with little guidance on what training to acquire for long-term success in the IT field. (2003, 15)

This lack of clarity about advancement has led firms to become more proactive about defining career paths. In turn, this has helped some graduates of nonprofit training programs move up. Yet others have not; altogether, only half of the sample has expressed interest in moving up within IT, whether because these individuals haven't yet figured out the system or because they are content simply to have crossed the digital divide into a livable wage job.

Career Ladders

Almost all of the employers interviewed, with the exception of those in small firms and small IT divisions in the institutional sector, claimed that there are opportunities to grow within their firms. The following describes company efforts at career development, typical career ladders, and strategies for advancement.

Most of the larger companies with mature human resources departments conduct career development of some kind. This varies from the uniform career paths at large

IT service firms ("We need one model of people for one model of services") to the more flexible, jointly negotiated plans found at mature firms in other sectors. For many companies, career development makes sense from a managerial standpoint since it helps to both conduct strategic planning and reduce turnover: "From a management perspective, you need to create jobs to keep people excited and growing." In anticipation of future skill needs, one IT firm looks for workers with broad skill sets to save training costs: "We can buy it cheaper than we can build it." On the other hand, supervisors spoke of a disincentive to do career development: after providing extensive on-the-job training in IT, they were reluctant to let employees move on.

Asked to describe typical career ladders, employers usually mentioned advancement within a track. Starting from tech support or customer service, workers may move into either support coordinator positions or desktop, applications, or Web support. From there, if they acquire further outside training, they may move into network administration, systems analyst, or other infrastructure positions. Large, centralized firms also suggest moves (with further training) into programming, database administration, applications development, or engineering. As one financial employer said, "The help desk has been a feeder for other groups."

But many companies caution that the rapid advancement of the dot-com period is over: "People come in and expect to advance in two years, but the progression isn't as quick right now." Particularly for workers without a college education, career ladders take time to construct; as an IT employer put it, "The college-educated employees tend to have a little better understanding of what it takes to move up."

Data from the Web-based survey of IT workers suggest that most technical support workers do move up into other areas, but women are less likely to either shift out of support or move into technical fields. Asked what their next job will be, just 17 percent of male support or help-desk workers say they will remain in support, but 27 percent of female workers plan to stay. Indeed, looking at the career trajectories of the workers who started in technical support, just 14 percent of the men, compared with 33 percent of the women, have remained there over the course of their IT careers; the largest share of workers has moved into networking, while others with more college and technical (computer-related) degrees have moved into programming or management (figure 15.1). The main difference between those who remain in support (mostly women) and those who move into programming (mostly men) is where they first obtained IT training: half of those who remain in support

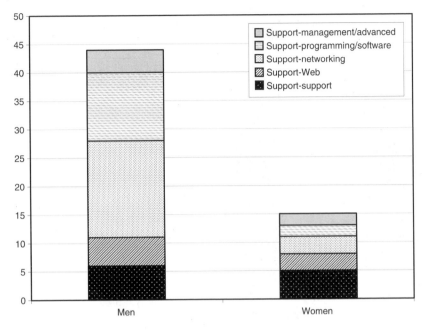

Figure 15.1
Career trajectories of workers starting in help-desk/support occupations

attended technical school, while half of the workers who advance were first exposed to IT in high school.

In contrast, workers in Web-related occupations generally continue working in Web design or applications. Figure 15.2 shows the career trajectories of Web-related workers: overall, 63 percent of the men and 82 percent of the women who started in Web design have remained in the field. Interestingly, the men who moved laterally into other IT-related fields typically hold computer-related degrees.

Thus, for reasons of cost and corporate culture, many firms are interested in re-creating the internal career ladders lost in the reorganization of the IT sector. The Web-based survey suggests that workers starting in relatively low-skill IT occupations, such as help desk, are able to move up. But are IT workers, particularly those from disadvantaged backgrounds, able to take advantage of this opportunity? Even if half of the sample is interested in upward mobility, only one-quarter has a clear plan for moving up. The following looks at the sample's successes and failures in advancing up the career ladder.

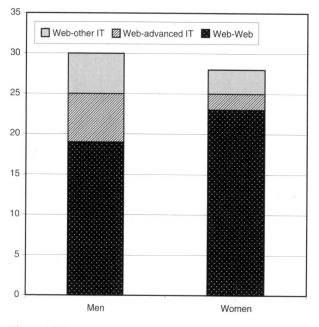

Figure 15.2
Career trajectories of workers starting in Web-related occupations

Advancing through Education and Training

Companies described three paths to advancement: certifications and training, college education, and soft skills. For most, college education is the surest route, which helps to explain why the women in the training program graduate sample are most successful when they have a college degree. Although employees may advance into supervisory positions based on on-the-job training, they typically need some college education to move into either management or other IT divisions. Going back to college shows an employee's interest in moving beyond narrow problem solving—an interest that entry-level technicians or Web developers are not able to demonstrate.

Nevertheless, it takes tremendous initiative for workers to complete a degree while working full-time, and only a few of the training program graduates in the sample are attempting it, despite the aspirations of many. Factors that seem critical to inducing program graduates to go back for the degree are the accumulation of some previous college credit (e.g., through training programs that offer credit, like Street Tech) and financial support (especially from large employers like Cheryl's that help pay for schooling).

The training program graduates who want a college degree are most likely to come from Alexandria, Training, Inc., and Street Tech. These three programs are all connected with a community college—directly in the case of the former two and indirectly for Street Tech—thereby offering students the chance to take classes for college credit. This suggests that the relationship between training programs and community colleges helps graduates think in terms of matriculating and thus becoming more upwardly mobile.

The program graduates who want a degree see it as critical to advancement. As Charlene from Alexandria—who makes $56,000 per year as a Web designer, with just a high school diploma—says:

> I know at some point, I will have to go back to get that—at least a four-year degree.... Because I have friends who have taken a lot of courses, they've gone the course route as opposed to the computer science route—one gentleman is a network person, and he makes good money with EDS, but he will plateau soon because after a while, without the certification of the diploma, you won't go any further. Your salary will stagnate. Then people won't want to hire you because you have too much experience.

A few are pursuing a degree because their company provides financial support and offers them stability if they obtain the degree: as Cheryl says, "I'm staying as long as they keep me. It's hard for me to believe. It's not a choice for me. It's a once-in-a-lifetime opportunity. It's a now-or-never thing. I have to live in the present. I'll do it as long as I have the opportunity and as long as they'll pay."

Not all graduates are as ambitious: over 40 percent have no intention of pursuing a degree, although they might take more classes. For many of these, it is not for lack of interest but due to the constraints of job and family.

Large companies with formal career ladders may also promote workers based on a new certification earned through training, often provided by the company. While work experience is the key to proving one's value to the company, the certification shows a worker's motivation to move up. Cynthia, from Training, Inc., has followed this path: her employer, a large insurance company, has supported her A+ certification and Microsoft Certified Systems Engineer class at local training schools through New Jersey incumbent worker training funds.

Failing to Move Up

One-half of the sample of training program graduates, some of whom have been relatively successful in IT, are not planning to move up further within the field. Many never made it into IT and have given up; others, the "unlucky" ones caught in the dot-com craze and subsequent crash, have already moved out of IT. For instance, Maggie turned down a job paying $55,000 for one paying $45,000 with prospects for advancement, only to get caught in a wave of downsizing. Frustrated with the lack of creative challenge in her job, she went back to her career as an art teacher.

Yet another reason for this lack of ambition in IT emerged from the interviews with women: the critical issue is how to balance an IT job with creative talents or family life. Most of these women simply lack an appetite for the high-pressure IT environment. Michelle hopes to move out of the technology field someday, perhaps when she finishes her bachelor's degree:

Technology is great at the moment. It pays well; it allows me to be financially stable to do the things I want to do and to be financially flexible. As far as making it a long-term thing—not really. If you want to move to higher levels as a female [in the tech field], you have to be willing to devote much of your time because every few months there's something new that you have to learn to stay on top of it. Am I gonna devote that kind of time to a job? No. You want to have time for the other parts of life, like a family—the quality of life things.

Conclusion

Short-term nonprofit IT training programs do help many women get their foot in the door in IT because of the down skilling of IT occupations and the programs' focus on soft skills training. Still, few women advance beyond their entry-level positions in help desk or Web design, at least within the first four years of their careers, and the ones with the most spectacular success come to the field with a college degree, albeit nontechnical. Many formerly low-income workers are content with using the move into IT to acquire their first livable wage jobs and have little ambition to move up. Others would like to advance, but lack the support to obtain the college education typically required to move laterally in IT, which is a common career path. Thus, these programs are necessary, but not sufficient for upward mobility in IT.

The standard workforce preparation model for IT workers is high school and college graduation, followed by an entry-level job. The case of nonprofit training program graduates shows the potential of a new, nonlinear pathway into IT that seems to work particularly for low-income women: women gain familiarity with IT through short training programs, return to college after obtaining substantial work experience, and then move into more technical positions or management. How might women working in IT obtain more support for such nontraditional patterns of advancement?

One opportunity is federal job training monies provided through the 1998 Workforce Investment Act (WIA). The intent of the WIA was to create a new, comprehensive workforce development system, encompassing both job training and employment services for three groups: adults, dislocated workers, and youth. Although the WIA is the major potential funding source for short-term job training programs, there are three major obstacles to using it to help women enter and move up in IT careers: its uneven implementation, its reliance on a school-based voucher system rather than employer-based training, and the barriers it presents to participation by community-based organizations and community colleges.

Because the WIA offers states considerable flexibility in how they implement the changes, resources for job training have varied considerably between regions. For instance, just 26 percent of the WIA participants in California receive job training, while 83 percent of New Jersey participants do.[8] This unevenness means a lack of opportunity for women in certain regions, even if they have high levels of IT demand as in California.

Second, most of the WIA training currently takes place through vouchers, which students use for training at their program of choice. Funding for employer-based training, which mostly occurs through incumbent worker training, is extremely limited and restrictive for employers who wish to participate. Yet incumbent worker training—for example, through short IT certification courses—is one way that women can advance in the workforce.

Finally, restrictive WIA guidelines for eligible training providers make it difficult for community colleges and nonprofits to participate. Requirements for tracking placement and retention for all students in a class (not just the WIA students) are impossible for most community colleges to comply with, so most have opted out of the system. Likewise, eligibility procedures were designed for large for-profit proprietary trade schools, creating a disadvantage for small nonprofits. Thus, just half of the training programs described in this chapter are eligible to participate, and those that are eligible have funded only a couple of students through the WIA because of the extensive red tape.[9]

Trends in the IT workforce suggest that the window of opportunity for workers of disadvantaged origins to advance in IT may be closing. Growth in IT employment is concentrated in advanced-level occupations, such as computer programming and systems analyst positions, rather than entry-level occupations, such as computer repair and support; from 1990 to 2000, the number of advanced-level occupations almost doubled, while entry-level occupations increased just 15 percent.[10] Underlying this shift is another key trend: women working in advanced occupations comprised just 49 percent of the female IT workforce in 1990, but increased their share to 69 percent by 2000.[11] Therefore, it continues to be important to help college computer science departments attract and graduate women. Yet the Bureau of Labor Statistics projects some fifty thousand entry-level IT job openings per year for the next ten years, and short-term job training programs successfully attract women, particularly minority women, to IT. This suggests that supporting this nontraditional pathway into IT may be one way to increase the representation of women in IT professions.

Notes

1. According to the NSF Division of Science Resources Statistics, the number of computer science bachelor's degrees awarded to women decreased from a high of fifteen thousand in 1986 to seven thousand in 1993, before rising to ten thousand in 2000, while the number of degrees awarded to men stayed stable at twenty-seven thousand. The female share of the IT workforce declined from 33 to 29 percent from 1990 to 2000, according to the U.S. Bureau of the Census, Public Use Microdata Sample (calculations by the author).

2. Calculations based on U.S. Bureau of the Census, Public Use Microdata Sample, 1990 and 2000.

3. There are also 5.3 million IT user occupations, such as computer operators and customer service representatives. Advanced IT occupations, which totaled 2.2 million in 2003, include computer and information science managers, computer hardware engineers, computer programmers, computer scientists and systems analysts, computer software engineers, database administrators, network systems and data communications analysts, and technical writers. For a description of trends in IT occupations, see Chapple (2005). From 1999 to 2002, high-skill IT jobs experienced net gains of 2.8 percent, while moderate-skill jobs (requiring long-term on-the-job training or postsecondary vocational education) have lost 15.2 percent and low-skill jobs have dropped 10.8 percent (U.S. Department of Commerce 2003).

4. In the mid-1990s, the Bureau of Labor Statistics assigned the computer support specialist occupation a training level of a bachelor's degree; by 1998, the bureau had revised the training requirements to an associate's degree.

5. All names have been changed herein.

6. This type of "framework analysis" is often used in the context of applied policy research, as compared to the purely inductive "grounded theory," in which theory emerges from the data through a process of rigorous and structured analysis.

7. There were several reasons for disqualification. Several of the graduates from the Alexandria program had been in IT for years, with computer science degrees, and were simply brushing up on skills; because there were no real upward mobility issues for them, they were

eliminated. Several of the Byte Back graduates interviewed never finished the program. Finally, a small program in Silicon Valley was initially included in the study, but then eliminated because only a few of its graduates could be located.

8. Calculated from the WIA Standardized Record Data, available at ⟨http://www.spra.com/wisrd⟩. For more discussion, see Chapple (2005).

9. The problems in using the WIA for short-term IT training programs are described in detail in Chapple (2005).

10. Calculations based on U.S. Bureau of the Census, *Public Use Microdata Sample*, 1990 and 2000.

11. While women have gained almost 440,000 advanced-level IT jobs in that time frame, they have lost almost 60,000 entry-level jobs.

References

Castells, M. 1996. *The power of identity*. Malden, MA: Blackwell Publishers.

Chapple, K. 2005. *Promising futures: Workforce development and upward mobility in information technology*. Berkeley, CA: Institute of Urban and Regional Development.

Chapple, K., and M. Zook. 2002. Why some IT jobs stay: The rise of job training in information technology. *Journal of Urban Technology* 9, no. 1:57–83.

Flynn, P. M. 1988. *Facilitating technological change: The human resource challenge*. Cambridge, MA: Ballinger Publishing Company.

Garcia, O. N., and R. Giles. 1999. *Research Foundations on Successful Participation of Underrepresented Minorities in Information Technology*. Washington, DC: National Science Foundation.

Giloth, R., ed. 2004. *Workforce intermediaries for the twenty-first century*. Philadelphia: Temple University Press.

Holzer, H. J. 1996. *What employers want: Job prospects for less-educated workers*. New York: Russell Sage Foundation.

Igbaria, M., and J. J. Baroudi. 1995. The impact of job performance evaluations on career advancement prospects: An examination of gender differences in the IS workplace. *MIS Quarterly* 19, no. 1 (March): 107–124.

Johnson, M. 1990. Women under the glass. *Computerworld*, December 3, 93–95.

Lee, D. M. S., E. M. Trauth, and D. Farwell. 1995. Critical skills and knowledge requirements of IS professionals: A joint academic/industry investigation. *MIS Quarterly* 19, no. 3:313–341.

Marenghi, C. 1992. There are cracks, but the glass ceiling is still mostly intact. *Computerworld*, February 5, 85.

Moss, P., and C. Tilly. 2001. *Stories employers tell: Race, skill, and hiring in America*. New York: Russell Sage Foundation.

Pastor, M., L. Leete, L. Dresser, C. Benner, A. Bernhardt, B. Brownstein, and S. Zimmermann. 2003. *Economic opportunity in a volatile economy: Understanding the role of labor market intermediaries in two regions.* ⟨http://www.willamette.edu/publicpolicy/lmi/lmi/LMI%20Final-May%202003.pdf⟩.

Reich, R. B. 1991. *The work of nations: Preparing ourselves for twenty-first-century capitalism.* New York: Alfred A. Knopf.

Ritchie, J., and L. Spencer. 1994. Qualitative data analysis for applied policy research. In *Analysing qualitative data,* ed. A. Bryman and R. Burgess, 173–194. London: Routledge.

U. S. Department of Commerce. 2003. *Education and training for the information technology workforce: Report to Congress from the secretary of Commerce.* Washington, DC: U.S. Department of Commerce.

Useem, L. 1986. *Low-tech education in a high-tech world: Corporations and classrooms in the new information society.* New York: Free Press.

Vaas, L. 2000. How to beat the odds: Net economy opens frontiers for women unafraid of risks. *eWeek,* September 11, 61.

Conclusion

Engineering Gender Balance in Computing

High-quality research into women's underrepresentation in computing is becoming available thanks to the support of funding agencies such as the National Science Foundation and the Alfred P. Sloan Foundation. The fruits of NSF support are evident in this book.

Even as these research results are disseminated, it is clear that we still have much to learn. Each chapter in this book raises many questions and calls for more research. We are far from understanding the relationship between gender and participation in IT.

Despite clear gaps in our understanding of the situation, the strong motivation to increase the representation of women and minorities has led to a change in priorities. Rather than focusing on fundamental research, the emphasis is now on action. NSF programs such as the ITWF, the new Broadening Participation in Computing, and Gender and Science and Engineering all seek to foster the wide adoption of practices that attract and retain more underrepresented groups. Nationwide movements, such as the National Center for Women in IT, seek to identify, pilot, and spread promising and effective practices. This new approach asks what works, rather than why it works. Mirroring the distinction between scientific efforts to know or understand, and engineering efforts to make or do, we see a shift away from the science and toward the engineering of computing's gender balance.

The engineering approach to creating gender balance in computing has promise. Just as engineering has produced many benefits in the absence of complete scientific understanding (e.g., SSRI drugs, telescopes, and steam engines), the hope is that it will allow us to move toward parity in computing before we fully understand why women are underrepresented in this and other technology fields. Instead of waiting for full knowledge of a highly complex situation, the plan is to move forward by applying what we know, experimenting, and building on success.

The shift toward a pragmatic what-works approach brings an added need for high-quality evaluation. Evaluation enables us to know whether an intervention works. It sets specific criteria for measuring whether a program achieved its goals and provides evidence about whether the program satisfied those criteria. In this way, evaluation tempers enthusiastic and committed activists who claim that their practices are effective, but have no evidence to support their claims.

This heavy reliance on evaluation raises some concerns. Necessary as it is to provide evidence about the effectiveness of an intervention, evaluation in the absence of fundamental understanding can lead to negative consequences. Most seriously, it can prematurely narrow our focus so that we work at changing the immediate conditions while ignoring their underlying causes; it can undercut support for efforts that would produce long-term yet not quickly measurable results; and it can produce unintended side effects.

A narrow focus on the immediate conditions is like sticking your finger in a hole in a dike, washing floors on a rainy day, drinking diet soda with your cheeseburger and french fries, or saving money in a bank account with 1 percent interest when you carry a credit card balance charging 20 percent. It expends effort to create short-term or local improvement, but does not address the root problem. After twenty years, women's representation in computing could reach parity in the organizations that adopted effective practices, but if the root causes have not changed, the results could remain localized or the trends could reverse when efforts are discontinued.

The value in evaluation depends on how well it is done. Inappropriate comparisons, selection bias, wrong or poorly constructed questions, and sloppy data collection or analysis are only some of the problems that can lead to misleading results. Less well-recognized is how evaluation favors short-term, countable, anticipated outcomes. For example, we can measure whether women in a peer-support program persist in their computing major at higher rates than women who are not in the program, but we seldom think to measure whether participants enroll in computing graduate programs after raising their families. If we did, we might find that the support program had no immediate effect on undergraduate persistence, although it did result in more returning women graduate students. Similarly, we might miss the success of interventions with high school teachers of AP computer science if we look only for greater gender balance in their high school classes, and ignore the more positive image of computing those teachers communicate and the subsequent higher rates of students from their school declaring a computer science major in college. If evaluation finds no immediate positive results for such programs, the programs would likely be labeled as ineffective and discontinued, despite the fact that they actually produced longer-term or unanticipated positive results. The practical constraints that focus evaluation on immediate and recognizable results raise the chances that these types of mistakes will occur.

Other unintended side effects of the heavy reliance on evaluation can result from acting in the absence of understanding the interrelated factors that produce a situation. Funding only interventions that have been proven effective can lead to a small range of cookie-cutter programs even though one size might not fit all. For example, it is possible that private or selective institutions might have success with methods to attract, retain, and advance women in computing that would not be practical or effective in public or less selective institutions. Failing to recognize the role that institutional control plays in the success of a program could lead to misplaced efforts or the discontinuation of support for programs that work only in particular settings. Even more problematic is the potential for an incomplete understanding to result in our working against true gender equity—for instance, by drawing women into mostly dead-end IT jobs—or harming the discipline—say, by emphasizing aspects of the field with little potential for significant advancement or impact.

The bottom line is that both the scientific and engineering approaches to improving the gender balance in computing are valuable, and each has its strengths and weaknesses. The three literature reviews in this book show the many gaps in our knowledge, and they lead us to call for more research on the root causes of the underrepresentation of women in computing. We believe that many of the chapters in this volume provide examples of how to do this research. But we cannot afford to wait to act until we have a perfect understanding of the issues; we are wasting too many resources by having so few women involved in computing—a waste for their own careers and for the nation as a whole. We can learn while we act, so long as we are careful about the way we conduct and assess our interventions.

Contributors

Manju Ahuja Ahuja is an assistant professor of information systems at Indiana University, and previously taught at Florida State University and Pennsylvania State University. She obtained her PhD in MIS from the University of Pittsburgh. Prior to starting a PhD program, Ahuja worked as a systems analyst designing online database systems for six years. She is co–principal investigator of "Toward Gender Equitable Outcomes in IT Higher Education: Beyond Computer Science," funded by the National Science Foundation. Her articles can be found in *Management Science, MIS Quarterly, Organization Science, Communications of the ACM*, the *European Journal of Information Systems*, the *Journal of Management, Decision Support Systems*, the *Database for Advances in Information Systems*, and the *Journal of Computer-Mediated Communications*. Ahuja's research interests include virtual teams and organizations, social networks, human resources issues in IT, and gender in IT.

David Allbritton Allbritton received his PhD in cognitive psychology from Yale University in 1992 and is currently an associate professor of psychology at DePaul University. His published work includes research on language comprehension, memory, instructional technology, tutoring, and intelligent tutoring systems.

John Aronis Aronis received his BA in mathematics from the State College of New York at New Paltz in 1979 and his MS in mathematics from Syracuse University in 1981. After working several years as a research programmer at Carnegie Mellon University, he entered the Intelligent Systems Program at the University of Pittsburgh and earned his PhD in 1993. He was a research associate in the Department of Computer Science at the University of Pittsburgh until being appointed as a lecturer in 1999.

William Aspray Aspray is a Rudy Professor of Informatics at Indiana University in Bloomington. He has prepared several reports on IT workforce issues, including ones on the IT workforce in the United States (with Peter Freeman), women graduate students (with Janice Cuny), minority graduate students (with Andrew Bernat), and computer science faculty (with John Stankovic). His current studies include one organized by ACM on offshore outsourcing (Moshe Vardi, chair), and a Computing Research Association study on recruiting and retaining women graduate students (J. McGrath Cohoon, principal investigator). Aspray is cochair of the Social Science Network of the National Center for Women in Information Technology. His other research includes various studies on the policy and history of IT.

Lecia J. Barker Barker directs the ATLAS Evaluation and Research Group at the University of Colorado, Boulder. She conducts research on increasing the participation of underrepresented groups in computing. Her current research explores messages and media that could affectively persuade middle school girls to enter a high school computer magnet (with Kathy Garvin-Doxas). In their research on the undergraduate level, Barker and Garvin-Doxas identified the concrete communicative behaviors in computer science classrooms that lead to a defensive climate where women feel they do not belong, in contrast with the climate of an IT certificate program where knowledge sharing and mutual support are the norm. Barker evaluated the Richard Tapia Celebration of Diversity in Computing Conference in both 2001 and 2003, and is currently evaluating the 2004 Grace Hopper Conference. She is also a senior research scientist for the National Center for Women and Information Technology.

Kathryn M. Bartol   Bartol is a Robert H. Smith Professor of Management and Organizations at the Robert H. Smith School of Business, University of Maryland, College Park. She has conducted research on IT workforce and gender issues that has appeared in leading journals, such as the *Academy of Management Journal,* the *Journal of Applied Psychology,* the *Academy of Management Review, Personnel Psychology, MIS Quarterly,* and the *Industrial and Labor Relations Review.* Her current work focuses on understanding factors that lead to the workplace retention and career success of IT professionals, particularly women and minorities. She is a fellow at the Academy of Management, the Society for Industrial/Organizational Psychology, and the American Psychological Society. Bartol is also the current dean of the fellows at the Academy of Management, as well as a past president of the Academy of Management.

Sylvia Beyer   Beyer is an associate professor of psychology at the University of Wisconsin, Parkside. She has conducted research on first-year undergraduates' perceptions of computer science. Her work has also examined factors that play a role in the entry and retention of female and male computer science and MIS students. Beyer is a member of the Social Science Network of the National Center for Women in Information Technology. She has also conducted experimental research on the accuracy of women's and men's self-perceptions as well as the accuracy of gender stereotypes.

Karen Bradley   Bradley is an associate professor of sociology at Western Washington University. Her research centers on women's representation in higher education within a cross-national focus. She and Maria Charles have been awarded a National Science Foundation grant (HRD–0332852) to examine sex segregation in engineering and math/computer science fields of study. Her recent articles, coauthored with Maria Charles, include "Uneven Inroads: Understanding Women's Status in Higher Education" (*Research in Sociology of Education* 14:247–274). "Equal but Separate? A Cross-National Study of Sex Segregation in Higher Education" (*American Sociological Review* 67, no. 4 [2002]: 573–599).

Karen Chapple   Chapple is an assistant professor of city and regional planning at the University of California, Berkeley, where she teaches courses on poverty, local economic development, and regional economic analysis. She is author of several works on high-tech occupations and workforce development in IT (with AnnaLee Saxenian and Ann Markusen). Her current research focuses on the relationship between metropolitan occupational structure and offshore outsourcing in IT occupations.

Maria Charles   Charles is a professor of sociology at the University of California, San Diego. Her research explores the patterns and processes of social inequality. Her recent work has focused on understanding the international similarities and differences in women's role in the labor market and higher education. Charles is coauthor (with David Grusky) of *Occupational Ghettos: The Worldwide Segregation of Women and Men* (Stanford University Press, 2004), and (with Karen Bradley) "Equal but Separate? A Cross-National Study of Sex Segregation in Higher Education" (*American Sociological Review* 67, no. 4 [2002]: 573–599).

J. McGrath Cohoon   Cohoon is an assistant professor in the Department of Science, Technology, and Society at the University of Virginia. Cohoon is also a senior research scientist for the National Center for Women in Information Technology. She employs perspectives and methods from sociology to study the interplay of gender, technology, and education. Cohoon received her BA in philosophy from Ramapo College of New Jersey, her MA in student personnel administration in higher education from Columbia University, Teachers College, and her PhD in sociology from the University of Virginia. She conducted the first nationwide studies of recruitment and retention in computer science departments at the undergraduate and graduate levels. Her current studies include one organized by the Computing Research Association and funded by the National Science Foundation to investigate the outcomes of participation in the Grad Cohort Program for Women.

Pamela E. Davis-Kean   Davis-Kean is an assistant research scientist at the Institute for Social Research and the Institute for Research on Women and Gender at the University of Michigan. She is the co–principal investigator, with Jacquelynne Eccles, of a National Science Foundation grant to study the participation of women and minorities in math, science, and engineering fields. Davis-Kean's research includes studies on gender differences in math and science achievement, and contextual influences in the pursuit of math and science careers for women and minorities.

Michelle DeKeuster   DeKeuster is a recent graduate of the University of Wisconsin, Parkside, with a BS degree in psychology. During the completion of her course work, she worked full-time for Sylvia Beyer as the project coordinator for research funded by the National Science Foundation. This research focused on gender differences in computer science and MIS students. Currently, DeKeuster is working as an employment support specialist in the human services field for Goodwill Industries of Southeastern Wisconsin, helping individuals with barriers to employment find secure work. She plans to attend graduate school in 2006 in the area of industrial/organizational psychology.

Jacquelynne S. Eccles   Eccles, a McKeachie Collegiate Professor of Psychology at University of Michigan, received her PhD from the University of California, Los Angeles, in 1974, and has served on the faculty at Smith College, the University of Colorado, and the University of Michigan. In 1998–99, she was the interim chair of psychology at the University of Michigan. She is a past president of the Society for Research on Adolescence, and the current editor of both the *Journal of Research on Adolescence* and *Research on Human Development*. Her research focuses on topics ranging from gender-role socialization, to classroom influences on motivation, to social development in the family, at school, among peers, and within wider cultural contexts. Much of this work centers on the socialization of self-beliefs and the impact of self-beliefs on many other aspects of social development.

Rachel Estrella   Estrella is a PhD candidate at the Graduate School of Education and Information Studies at the University of California, Los Angeles. Her research interests center around the use of the arts as an educative tool as well as a vehicle for social and political empowerment. Estrella's dissertation, "Lessons from the Wall: Muralism and the Art of

Empowerment," focuses on the experiences of students who worked on *The Great Wall of Los Angeles*, a historic mural that highlights the contributions of people of color to the history of California and this nation. For four years, Estrella served as a researcher for the NSF-funded "Out of the Loop" and "Constructing the Pipeline" studies. She also served as a consultant to the Digital Coast Roundtable. Estrella was recently awarded grants from the Corinne A. Seeds CONNECT foundation and the University of California, Los Angeles, Community Partnerships Office to create a mural-making curriculum for grades K–6. She is also a Ford Fellow.

Kathy Garvin-Doxas   Garvin-Doxas is a research associate with the ATLAS Institute's Evaluation and Research Group at the University of Colorado, Boulder. She conducts research on increasing the participation of underrepresented groups in the development, use, and understanding of IT and computational sciences (research conducted with Lecia J. Barker). Her other research focuses on the development of a biology concept inventory as well as on student misconceptions about classroom collaboration and cooperative learning in an effort to provide concrete guidance for educators. Garvin-Doxas works with professors and technology developers to ensure that educational technologies help to enhance student learning experiences in the sciences, particularly in physics, space science, astronomy, and biology.

Joanna Goode   Goode is a postdoctoral fellow at the Institute for Democracy, Education, and Access at the University of California, Los Angeles, and the Center for Diversity in Mathematics Education. She recently completed her dissertation, which examined the technology identities of university students and the influence of computer knowledge on undergraduate's academic pathways. As a former high school mathematics and computer science teacher in an urban high school, Goode's general research interests focus on issues of access and equity for underrepresented minorities and women around technology. For four years, she has examined the computer science pipeline in urban high schools as a member of the NSF-funded "Out of the Loop" and "Constructing the Pipeline" studies. Goode serves as the director for the AP Computer Science Institute at the University of California, Los Angeles, a joint enterprise of the university's School of Education, School of Engineering, and a large urban school district. She is also involved in a longitudinal research study on urban teacher retention.

Susan C. Herring   Herring is a professor of information science at Indiana University in Bloomington. One of the world's foremost experts on gender and computer-mediated communication, a field she helped to define in the early 1990s, Herring is the editor of five collections on computer-mediated communication, and the author of numerous articles on gender and the Internet; she also edits the *Journal of Computer-Mediated Communication*. Currently, she is studying the representation of women and men in multimedia computer interfaces (with Anna Martinson), girls' and boys' engagement in educational multiuser virtual environments (Sasha Barab, principal investigator), and the experiences of women in applied IT programs in U.S. universities (with Jean C. Robinson, Christine Ogan, and Manju Ahuja). Her other research includes discourse and content analysis of emergent computer-mediated communication technologies such as Weblogs.

Jolene Kay Jesse   Jesse is a program director for cross-directorate activities in the Directorate for Social, Behavioral, and Economic (SBE) Sciences at the National Science Foundation, where she oversees programs to promote education issues, and to increase the numbers of women and minorities in the SBE fields. Previously, she was a senior program associate in the American Association for the Advancement of Science's Directorate for Education and Human Resources Programs, where she conducted research on science, technology, engineering, and math education and policy issues, with special emphasis on the representation of women and underrepresented minorities in those fields. She received her MA from the American University in Washington, DC, and her PhD in political science from the University of Wisconsin, Milwaukee.

Sandra Katz   Katz received her MS in information science from the University of Pittsburgh in 1989, and her Doctor of Arts degree in English from Carnegie Mellon University in 1985. She is currently a research associate at the University of Pittsburgh's Learning Research and Development Center. Her published work includes research on instructional dialogue, the underrepresentation of women and minorities in computer science, and intelligent tutoring systems.

Deepak Kapur   Kapur is a professor in and chair of the Department of Computer Science at the University of New Mexico. Even though his main research interests are automated reasoning, symbolic computation, and formal methods, he has also been interested in the representation of women and minorities in computer science education. Kapur is a co–principal investigator with Roli Varma on the NSF grants "Why So Few Women in Information Technology?" and "Cross-Ethnic Differences in Undergraduate Women's Preference for Information Technology."

Gosia A. Langa   Langa is a fourth-year PhD student at the Robert H. Smith School of Business, University of Maryland, College Park. In addition to IT and gender issues, she also focuses on the factors predicting employee turnover and a variety of individual-level characteristics influencing employee behavior. Langa has presented papers at the national meetings of the Academy of Management and the Society for Industrial and Organizational Psychology.

Oksana Malanchuk   Malanchuk is a senior research associate at the Institute for Research on Women and Gender at the University of Michigan. Her research interests include gender identity, gender differences in math and science among youth and college students, and most recently, both the quantitative and qualitative investigation of factors influencing women and minority interest in IT fields. Malanchuk's other interests include the study of occupational aspirations and how their attainment or loss impacts on mental health.

Jane Margolis   Margolis is a reseach educationist at the Graduate School of Education and Information Studies at the University of California, Los Angeles. She is coauthor, along with Allan Fisher, of *Unlocking the Clubhouse: Women in Computing* (MIT Press, 2002), and the principal investigator on two NSF-funded research projects investigating why so few African American, Latino/a, and female students are learning computer science at the high school level. Margolis is also a member of the Social Science Network of the National Center for Women and IT, and serves as an advisory board member for multiple projects investigating the gender gap in computing and the sciences.

Christine Ogan   Ogan is a professor of informatics and journalism at Indiana University. She is co–principal investigator of "Toward Gender Equitable Outcomes in IT Higher Education: Beyond Computer Science," funded by the National Science Foundation. She has also conducted a national study of journalism educators in higher education on the relationship between gender and stress, including the stress derived from the use of technology in the classroom and research. Earlier in her career, her research focused on equity issues for women in newspaper management. Ogan also studies issues of communication technology and culture in Europe and the Middle East.

Amit Prasad Prasad completed his PhD, which is a cross-cultural study of magnetic resonance imaging research and development in the United States and India, in the sociology department at the University of Illinois, Urbana-Champaign, in April 2004. Since September 2004, he has been working as a postdoctoral fellow at the School of Public Administration at the University of New Mexico on an NSF-funded project to investigate gender and cross-ethnic issues in computer science and computer engineering undergraduate education in the United States.

Jean C. Robinson Robinson is a professor of political science and gender studies at Indiana University in Bloomington. She is the project director for "Toward Gender Equitable Outcomes in IT Higher Education: Beyond Computer Science," funded by the National Science Foundation, and also developed an NSF-funded program for retaining undergraduate women in the natural and mathematical sciences. Robinson's other research focuses on gender and social policy, including education equity.

Eric Snow Snow is a doctoral candidate in the Research and Evaluation Methodology Program at the School of Education at the University of Colorado, Boulder. His research centers on underrepresented groups in IT, information and communications technology literacy, and using Web-based applications and relational databases to support mixed-methods research. He is currently serving as a lead evaluator for the Colorado Undergraduate Education for Women in Information Technology Program, which aims to develop focused strategies for increasing women's awareness of IT, the need to pursue a four-year IT degree program, and IT career paths.

Mary Lou Soffa Soffa is the Owen R. Cheatham Professor in and chair of the Department of Computer Science at the University of Virginia. She moved from the University of Pittsburgh to Virginia in September 2004. Soffa received her PhD in computer science from the University of Pittsburgh in 1977. Her research interests include optimizing and parallelizing compilers, program analysis, and software tools for debugging and testing programs.

Roli Varma Varma is a Regents' Lecturer and an associate professor at the School of Public Administration at the University of New Mexico. She has served as a guest editor of a special issue of *IEEE Technology and Society* on women and minorities in IT. Varma has published several articles on women and minorities in IT education at the undergraduate level, funded by both the National Science and the Sloan Foundations. She has also organized the NSF's ITWF conference and produced the proceedings. Her current studies include Native Americans in IT (funded by the Sloan Foundation), and new immigrants in science and engineering (funded by the NSF).

Ian O. Williamson Williamson is an assistant professor of management and organizations at the Robert H. Smith School of Business, University of Maryland, College Park. He has conducted several studies on the IT workforce in the United States. In particular, his research draws on the organizational behavior concepts of person-organization fit, embeddedness, and perceived organizational support to examine the job attitudes and career commitment of

IT workers. Williamson has presented his research at the Academy of Management National Conference, the International Conference on Information Systems, and the Society for Industrial and Organizational Psychology Conference.

Tim Weston Weston, who earned his PhD at the University of Colorado School of Education in Research and Evaluation Methodology, is a research associate for the Alliance for Technology, Learning, and Society Evaluation and Research Group at the University of Colorado. His specialty is the evaluation of education technology and the systematic reform of undergraduate instruction. Weston's research has examined the use of Web modules for university teaching, the design and implementation of biomedical software for the Visible Human Project, and the use of the Web to conduct formative course evaluation. As an evaluator, he has conducted a number of quantitative and qualitative studies of novel technology and technology curriculum. Currently, Weston is evaluating the Science Education for New Civic Engagements and Responsibilities project.

Christine Wilson Wilson received her BS degree in computer science and MS degree in education from the University of Pittsburgh. She is presently employed as a computer programmer at the University of Pittsburgh's Learning Research and Development Center. Wilson contributes to research on the underrepresentation of women and minorities in computer science and natural-language tutorial dialogue systems.

Nicole Zarrett Zarrett, who holds an MS degree from University of Michigan, is a doctoral student of developmental psychology at Ann Arbor and a research assistant in the Gender and Achievement Research Program (under the mentorship of Jacquelynne Eccles). The other research she has conducted regarding the underrepresentation of women and blacks in the IT workforce includes a paper (with Oksana Malanchuk) titled "Who's Computing? Gender and Race Differences in Young Adults' Decisions to Pursue an IT Career," to be published in Reed Larson and Lene Jensen (series ed.) and J. Jacobs and S. Simpkins (vol. eds.), *New Directions for Child and Adolescent Development* (Wiley, forthcoming). Zarrett's research primarily focuses on gender and race differences in the initial engagement, persistence, and achievement in academic and extracurricular activities, with special emphasis on the impact of stereotypes, discrimination, and other contextual factors that influence an individual's interests and motivation.

Index